INTERMEDIATE PROGRAMMING PRINCIPLES AND TECHNIQUES USING PASCAL

INTERMEDIATE PROGRAMMING PRINCIPLES AND TECHNIQUES USING PASCAL

T. M. SMITH
Northeastern University

West Publishing Company
St. Paul New York Los Angeles San Francisco

PRODUCTION CREDITS

Cover Image *Turner Whitten, Bell Laboratories, "Spheres" (1980). Courtesy of AT&T Archives.*
Cover Design *Paula Schlosser Design*
Text Design *David Farr, ImageSmythe, Inc.*
Copyeditor *Linda Thompson Copyediting Services*
Artwork and Composition *G & S Typesetters, Inc.*

Printed in the United States of America

98 97 96 95 94 93 92 91 8 7 6 5 4 3 2 1 0

Library of Congress Cataloging-in-Publication Data

Smith, T. M. (Terry M.)
Intermediate programming principles and techniques using Pascal / T. M. Smith.
p. cm.
Includes index.
ISBN 0-314-66314-2 (hard)
1. Pascal (Computer program language) I. Title.
QA76.73.P2S63 1991
005.13'3—dc20 90.46011
CIP

To my late father,
Marvin Harris Smith,
who still inspires me

CONTENTS

Chapter 10 ADVANCED SEARCHING ALGORITHMS 471

Chapter 11 SORTING ALGORITHMS 523

Appendixes

PREFACE

Intermediate Programming Principles and Techniques Using Pascal is designed for use in a second college level computer science course. The coverage of topics is comprehensive and the examples sufficiently diverse enough to make it an appropriate text for a variety of courses that may differ in focus.

A first course in computer science typically introduces most of the standard syntax and data types of a programming language and emphasizes modular program design via programmer-defined procedures and functions. A second course in computer science not only presents advanced features of the programming language, such as the variant record and Pascal pointer type but, more importantly, hones the students' problem-solving capabilities and organizational skills. Here, the student is taught to think more abstractly about data types and their accompanying operations and to use sophisticated algorithmic techniques, such as recursion. Students learn that selection of data structures precedes and drives development of the algorithms that manipulate this data; therefore, the organization of the course is usually based on the successive presentation of different, programmer-defined data structures.

As each second-course homework project becomes more complex, students must take a systematic approach to program development, devising and hand-testing a program design of pseudocode algorithms (*modules*) on paper and then converting this outline to a working Pascal program (if written properly, modules convert neatly to procedures and functions). Students are encouraged to design algorithms that are reasonably efficient in their execution and employ a clear and consistent programming style to conserve *programmer-time;* i.e., to minimize the time needed to produce a working program, or the time needed by another programmer to modify it later. Students must also use careful and thorough verification and debugging techniques when testing program code since, in the words of Niklaus Wirth, co-inventor of the Pascal language, "the devil hides in the details." In summary, a second course in computer science begins to train the student to be a programming professional who takes a thoughtful, systematic approach to problem-solving.

This text plays a crucial role in that training because many of the topics presented in a second course in computer science are highly conceptual. Having taught freshman computer science courses for a number of years, the author came to recognize areas in which students typically have the most difficulty and, in preparing this text, geared the depth and pace of the discussions accordingly. Particular attention was paid to the selection and presentation of examples which may range from a brief Pascal code segment to one of its twenty-four applications. The text explains how to approach each problem via a careful selection of the appropriate data types and then devise and refine the necessary algorithms. Often, a pseudocode version (part English, part Pascal) precedes the complete Pascal version of an algorithm and a module tree diagram is given before each full Pascal program, showing the order in which routines are called. Some of the applications presented are such classics as the Eight Queens Problem and Towers of Hanoi. Other applications are unique, such as the backtracking problem, In Search of the Golden Floppy, based on the popular "Indiana Jones" movies. All applications were chosen to bring a particular topic to life.

It is also important that students in a second course in computer science (and in courses to follow) develop the ability to examine and understand programming code written by *another* programmer, a common task when working with a team of programmers on a large project. Hundreds of lines of *working* Pascal code are therefore included: code segments, declaration sections, procedures, functions, and whole programs. These sections provide the added benefit that students can see the final Pascal representation of an algorithm or program that has been discussed. The Pascal code that appears in the text is the actual code which the author has tested.

Objectives and Features

In writing *Intermediate Programming Principles and Techniques Using Pascal,* the author strove to produce a quality text that satisfied three fundamental objectives:

1. **Completeness:** To cover all important topics for a second course in computer science, based on the nationally recognized guidelines established by the Curriculum Committee of the Association of Computing Machinery (ACM). These guidelines are described in *Recommended Curricula for CS2* by David Stemple, Caroline Wardle, and Elliot Koffman (*Communications of the ACM,* August 1985). This text describes all the essential data types in detail:

○ Integer	○ Set	○ Stack	○ Graph
○ Real	○ Array	○ FIFO queue	○ Spanning tree
○ Character	○ Character string	○ Binary search tree	○ 2-3 tree
○ Boolean	○ Record	○ Priority queue/heap	○ Hash table
○ Enumerated	○ Linked list	○ Game tree	○ B-tree

This text also reviews sound program development principles, debugging techniques, mathematical tools for analyzing the relative efficiencies of algorithms, and an in-depth presentation of recursion.

2. **Clarity:** To present clear discussions of all topics, based on classroom-proven lectures. This text is truly written for new programmers, carefully explaining potentially troublesome subjects, such as recursion and the Pascal pointer type, by using straightforward language and starting with simple examples before evolving into more complex applications. The accompanying figures and tables are especially helpful.
3. **Consistency:** To offer a systematic, comprehensible writing style that introduces each data type as an ADT, and then describes how it may be represented in Pascal. High-level discussion is followed by concrete examples in Pascal, often including descriptions of computer memory representations.

In short, the author's intent is to make learning interesting and fun for the student while freeing the instructor to offer additional discussion and examples in class. To this end, the following features have been incorporated:

- A list of chapter contents previews the topics of that chapter.
- Data types introduced using a succinct ADT description, followed by discussions of how the types may be represented using Pascal language.
- Strict adherence to standard Pascal throughout plus the use of the common, nonstandard String type.
- 24 complete applications and many shorter examples.
- Over 250 detailed figures and tables.
- To help students review and practice what they have learned in each chapter:
    - Concise chapter summary
    - Alphabetized list of key terms
    - Comprehensive review questions
    - Challenging exercises and programming projects.
- Primitive routines for data structures—working Pascal code—in the appendixes. This placement unclutters the chapters, provides quick reference, and facilitates visual comparisons of similar routines; typically, both sequential storage and linked list versions of these routines are given.

Prerequisites

It is generally assumed that the student in a second Pascal programming course is familiar with the topics covered in the first course, including basic program structure; variables and constants; the assignment, arithmetic, relational, and logical operators; the `IF`, `FOR`, `WHILE`, `REPEAT`, and `CASE` statements; `BEGIN/END` blocks; the `Read`, `Readln`, `Write`, and `Writeln` procedures; standard arithmetic functions; the syntax of programmer-defined procedures and functions with parameter passing; `CONST`, `TYPE`, and `VAR` declarations; the standard data types integer, real, character (`char`), Boolean, set, array, and (nonvariant) record, as well as the common, nonstandard String data type; and comments.

Many of these topics are presented in this text, but formally and in great detail. Chapter 1 and Appendixes L and M review the principles of sound program design, including programming style and debugging. Chapters 2 and 3 describe all data types typically covered in the first programming course but with a rigorous, ADT approach which presents advanced features of these types; e.g., the variant record and bitwise operations on integer values. This overlap insures that *all* students begin their second programming course with the same fundamental knowledge about program design and data types before going on to more advanced topics. For example, the data types reviewed in Chapters 2 and 3 are the building blocks of more complex data structures presented later. This strict ADT approach with familiar data types also acclimates the student toward thinking systematically about all data types. Basic high school algebra including logarithms is a sufficient background in mathematics for the use of this text.

Organization

Chapter 1 focuses on the principles of constructing, verifying, and debugging computer programs, emphasizing top-down and bottom-up design and sound programming style. It begins by posing three logic puzzles which exemplify difficulties that programmers frequently encounter when designing and debugging programs. The first section of the chapter explores the characteristics of any well-written program, including program *structure* (modularity, parameter passing, and programming style), *functionality* (reliability, versatility, and portability), and *performance* (user-friendliness, efficiency, and robustness). The next section goes into greater detail, dividing the entire process of developing any computer program into seven stages, and focuses on the construction of the program design. As an illustration in the use of these stages, an interactive program for the blackjack card game is designed from beginning to end in Appendix M. The final section discusses common syntax and logic errors and presents concrete strategies for locating and fixing them.

Chapter 2 describes the standard, simple data types integer, real, character (`char`), Boolean, and enumerated. The chapter begins with a discussion of the different ways of classifying data used in programming, including the fundamental definition of *data type* (domain of values plus set of possible operations) and the concepts of ordinality and divisibility (simple versus structured type). Also presented are the three levels of representation of any data type: ADT, programming language, and physical memory. The remaining chapter sections describe the five simple types at each of the three levels of representation.

Chapter 3 describes the standard structured data types (*data structures*) set, array, character string, and record. The chapter begins by explaining two different methods of storing items: (1) based on the key value of each item (key-value storage method), or (2) based solely on when the item is stored (the time-of-arrival method). The resulting types of structure (set, linear list, hierarchy, and network) are then described. This section also reiterates the pivotal message of Chapter 1 that the choice of data structure and its accompanying fundamental operations drives the development of algorithms. The next sections describe the four structured data types at the ADT, Pascal, and physical memory levels, including discussion of the **`WITH`** statement and the variant record. The classic Game of Life program is given in Application 3.1 within the section on arrays. Next, the ADT table is described as a generic time-of-arrival data type, and the chapter concludes with an introduction to the mathematical analyses of algorithms.

Chapter 4 describes the use of memory external to a program's executable image space. The chapter begins by distinguishing internal, external, and secondary memory and presents the concept of a file. Next, the binary file is described as an ADT, followed by its use with Pascal programs (opening and closing files, reading and writing file elements) along with its physical memory representation (file window, file pointer, file buffer variable) and a comparison between files and arrays. Application 4.1 illustrates the use of binary files and discusses many interesting design issues in the development of an electronic menu program for Captain Nemo's Seafood Emporium. The next section presents the text file as an ADT, followed by a discussion of its use with Pascal programs and details of its physical memory representation. Operations germane to text files, such as automatic type conversion and standard end-of-line (`Eoln`) and end-of-file (`Eof`) functions, are described using examples. The final section introduces the dynamic allocation of activation records and program variables in heapspace memory. A detailed discussion of the Pascal pointer type is presented, along with the use of the standard Pascal procedures `New` and `Dispose`.

Chapter 5 focuses on the linked list data structure and its variations. The general concept of a linked list is introduced and contrasted with the use of a single array using the example of a list of participants for a progressive dinner. The linked list is then formally introduced as an ADT, followed by numerous discussions and applications using the dynamic allocation representation. Application 5.1 demonstrates how one data type, such as a linked list, may be used to represent another data type (here, ADT character string), and explains the general process of building a linked list using Pascal. In Application 5.2, linked list primitives for searching, insertion, deletion, and traversal are developed in the course of designing a program for an interactive telephone-address directory; also discussed is saving a linked list to a file. In Application 5.3, an array of linked lists is used in two distinct ways to implement an interactive dictionary program. Application 5.4 illustrates the use of a nonlinear linked list to represent a sparse matrix. Linked list enhancements are presented next: circular and doubly-linked lists, and interesting techniques for indexing into a linked list (Application 5.5). The next section describes the sequential storage (array) representation of a linked list, and the chapter concludes with helpful advice about debugging linked list algorithms.

Chapter 6 describes two time-of-arrival data structures, the stack and the FIFO queue. Each is formally introduced as an ADT followed by a description of the Pascal representation, using both linked list and sequential storage representations. The program in Application 6.1 reverses a character string to illustrate that stacks are generally useful for processing any collection of data in the *reverse order* in which the data items are stored (whereas a FIFO queue is useful for processing any collection of data in the *same order*). This concept is exemplified further with the program developed in Application 6.2 which evaluates infix arithmetic expressions. The application illustrates the use of a flowchart and demonstrates how a fully-functional program can be built by starting with a simple version and then adding Pascal code in stages, allowing the program to handle increasingly complex input.

Chapter 7 presents the fascinating and powerful technique of recursion. The chapter begins gently with simple examples of how the looping effect of self-reference is useful in defining a set of objects or the steps for solving a problem. Application 7.1 contrasts the nonrecursive and recursive approaches to computing a factorial. The next section demystifies recursion by using heapspace diagrams to illustrate how activation records stack up to preserve the values of local variables. As an example, Application 7.2 presents a recursive version of the stack-based procedure in Application 6.1 that reverses a string. The next three sections discuss terminating recursion, parameter passing, and guidelines for designing recursive algorithms. Six more applications of increasing complexity follow, demonstrating such concepts as preorder versus postorder recursion, binary searching, and backtracking. The succeeding section summarizes the differences and conversion between recursive and nonrecursive algorithms, and then explains when recursion is and is *not* appropriate; as examples, Application 7.9 calculates the *N*th value of the Fibonacci series and Application 7.10 presents the Towers of Hanoi problem. The chapter concludes with helpful advice about debugging recursive algorithms.

Chapter 8 describes several tree data structures, beginning with general concepts and definitions. The binary search tree is introduced as an ADT, followed by discussion of its linked list Pascal representation and all fundamental operations. A mathematical analysis of tree searching and its dependency on tree shape is also described, along with steps for saving a tree to a file. Application 8.1 describes the development of a program that builds an alphabetical identifier index for any source computer program. The next section describes the sequential storage representation of a binary search tree. The chapter then introduces the priority queue and describes several representations, focusing on the heap data structure. It concludes with an introduction to game trees, the MiniMax method, and Application 8.2 (an interactive tic-tac-toe game).

Chapter 9 focuses on graph data structures, starting with general concepts and definitions. The graph is formally introduced as an ADT, and both the adjacency matrix and adjacency list Pascal representations are described. Fundamental graph operations are discussed using the adjacency list representation, including traversals, finding a path via a depth-first search, finding a shortest path via a breadth-first search, and saving a graph to a file. Advanced operations include finding minimal cost paths (Dijkstra's algorithm), building a minimal cost spanning tree (Prim's and Kruskal's algorithms), and maximizing network flow (the Ford–Fulkerson algorithm). As a hypothetical example of the last topic, Application 9.1 develops a program to maximize the rate of water flow through a network of pipes and pumping stations from Lake Yahoo to the town of Lost Wages, Nevada.

Chapter 10 introduces several data structures and techniques for searching a collection of items. The chapter begins with the 2-3 tree, introduced as an ADT and represented in Pascal using a binary search tree approach. Next, a survey of indirect and direct searching techniques leads to hashing as a technique for surpassing the log *N* efficiency limit of search algorithms presented thus far. The hash table is presented as an ADT and different hash functions and collision-resolution strategies (chaining versus open addressing) are described. Next, the subject of searching for items in external memory (files) is introduced with a description of magnetic disks and key tables. The B-tree is then presented as an ADT, followed by discussion of its fundamental operations and the primary and secondary index versions. The chapter concludes with a brief discussion of external hash addressing.

Chapter 11 surveys ten popular sorting algorithms; for each algorithm, the chapter provides a Pascal routine and mathematical analysis of its relative efficiency. For many of these algorithms, the discussion explores enhancements as well. Algorithms for sorting arrays include bubble sort, straight selection sort, straight insertion sort, the recursive merge sort and quicksort, and the binary search tree and heap sorts. Next, algorithms are described for sorting linked lists: the straight insertion sort and the natural merge sort. Another type of merge sort algorithm is then presented for sorting a file. The final algorithm is a topological sort for arranging the nodes of a PERT graph based on functional dependency. Application 11.1 demonstrates this algorithm by developing a program that produces a list of university course numbers in order of their prerequisites.

The **appendixes** offer a variety of useful information and quick references. Appendix A lists all standard Pascal identifiers, operator symbols, procedures, and functions. Appendix B compares the binary, octal, decimal, and hexadecimal number systems, and describes typical memory representations of negative integer values. Appendix C provides the ASCII character set. Appendixes D through I contain Pascal routines for the fundamental operations of linked lists, stacks, FIFO queues, binary search trees, priority queues/heaps, and graphs; both linked list and sequential storage representations are included. Appendix J contains Pascal routines for the sorting algorithms of Chapter 11 plus several searching routines. Appendix K contains a variety of primitive Pascal routines, such as a random number generator and a string-to-integer conversion routine. Appendix L describes popular conventions of programming style. In Appendix M, a program is developed for the card game blackjack in which the user plays against the computer. Many interesting design issues are discussed and the complete Pascal program is included as well.

Suggestions for Pedagogy

While it is generally recommended that the text chapters be used in numerical order, instructors may choose to cover certain topics in a slightly different order. Please note the following:

- It is recommended that Chapters 1, 2, 3, and Section 4.1 (files) of Chapter 4 be covered at the start of the course and in that order. Also, Appendixes L and M provide excellent reviews of programming style and the general process of program development in conjunction with Chapter 1.
- Discussion of the ADT characteristics and sequential storage representation of stacks and FIFO queues (Chapter 6) may be covered anytime after Section 4.1. The sections describing linked list representations should follow Section 4.2 (heapspace and dynamic allocation) and Chapter 5 (Linked Lists).
- Most of Chapter 7 (Recursion) involves Pascal syntax learned in a first course in programming, and therefore may be covered at any time after Chapter 3; a few examples involve dynamically allocated linked lists.

- The algorithms of Chapter 11 may be covered in groups once the requisite topic for that group has been discussed: The nonrecursive array-sorting algorithms (Sections 11.2 and 11.3) and the file sorting algorithm (Section 11.7) may be covered anytime after Section 4.1. The recursive array-sorting algorithms (Section 11.4) may be covered anytime after Chapter 7. The binary tree sorts (Section 11.5) may be covered anytime after Chapter 8. The linked list algorithms (Section 11.6) may be covered anytime after Chapter 5, and the topological sort algorithm (Section 11.8) may be covered anytime after Chapter 9.

The author sincerely hopes that students and instructors alike enjoy using this text as much as he enjoyed writing it. Happy programming!

T. M. Smith

ACKNOWLEDGMENTS

I would like to extend my deep gratitude toward the West Publishing Company, with particular thanks to the following people for their unwavering enthusiasm and professional support throughout the entire project: Jay Ricci (Editor), Mary Garvey Verrill (Production Editor), Sharon Adams (Developmental Editor), and Stephanie Johnson (Product Manager).

I owe special thanks to the following people who provided plenty of personal support and understanding along the way, especially on those many evenings and weekends when I was so busy working on "that book": my mother, Rae Smith; Nance and Michael Newbold; Marcie Ravech-Williams; Rebecca, Lindsay, and Whitney Drake; Katherine and James McClure; Tim King; Beth Thomas; and Jennie Colangelo.

Several others in particular contributed their unique technical expertise and I extend my appreciation to them for their valuable assistance: Carol Schaal (Associate Editor of Notre Dame Magazine, Notre Dame, Indiana) and Gloria Leblanc (Document Design/Editing Specialist, Information Mapping, Waltham, Massachusetts) provided thorough editing of the early manuscript and offered much advice regarding the structure of chapters; Dr. Alice Fischer (University of New Haven) was a remarkable manuscript reviewer, and offered detailed, helpful comments throughout the manuscript; Dr. Harpal Dhama (Technical Programmer, Mitre Corporation, Burlington, Massachusetts) was an outstanding reviewer, especially regarding various sections on analyses of algorithms, the chapter on graph structures (Chapter 9), and all end-of-chapter review questions and exercises; Richard Rasala (Director of Undergraduate Studies, College of Computer Science, Northeastern University) provided a wealth of insight into the craft of designing algorithms and furnished algorithms on which the `FindMCPaths` (minimal cost paths) and `BuildMCSTree` (minimal cost spanning trees) routines in Section 9.3 and Appendix I were based.

Instructors in the College of Computer Science at Northeastern University who reviewed sections of the manuscript and provided helpful suggestions include: Cynthia Brown, Robert P. Futrelle, John Gauch, Carol Hafner, Luc Longpré, Vierra Proulx, and Betty Salzberg. Students in the College of

Computer Science at Northeastern University who reviewed sections of the manuscript were: Robert Abbott, Beth-Anne Harvey, Vassilios Kliropulos, Sarah Mocas, Brian Perry, and David Shorr.

Many other professionals in the computing field reviewed portions of the manuscript and offered useful feedback, and I extend my appreciation to them:

Ronald E. Bass
Austin Community College

Andrew Bernat
University of Texas at El Paso

Robert P. Burton
Brigham Young University

Helen Casey
Sam Houston State University

Joyce Jenkins
U.S. Air Force Academy

Anselmo A. Lastra
Duke University

A. Z. Leibowitz
Central Connecticut State University

Phil Novinger
Florida State University

J. M. Purser
Millsaps College

A. Quesada
University of Akron

Anita Read
Salem State College

Ingrid Russell
University of Hartford

Ellen Skeels
Rochester Institute Of Technology

Stephen F. Weiss
University of North Carolina at Chapel Hill

Laurie A. White
University of Florida at Gainesville

Anna Peng Ziermann
College of St. Francis

T. M. Smith

CHAPTER ONE

DEVELOPING COMPUTER PROGRAMS

This chapter focuses on the principles of constructing, verifying, and debugging computer programs. It begins with three interesting logic puzzles that relate to difficulties programmers commonly encounter when designing and debugging computer programs. Section 1.2 explores the qualities of any well-written program and desirable program characteristics beyond merely generating correct results. Section 1.3 goes into greater detail, dividing the entire process of developing a program into seven stages, with emphasis on construction of program design specifications. (As an exercise in the use of these stages, a program based on the card game blackjack is designed from beginning to end in Appendix M.) The final section describes common syntax and logic errors and strategies for locating and fixing them.

1.1 FOOD FOR THOUGHT

Too often, programmers set up mental roadblocks that impede their creative thinking. To illustrate this phenomenon, Figure 1.1 poses three interesting puzzles for you to solve. The difficulty of each puzzle stems from a particular mental impediment that often arises when designing and debugging programs. Solutions to these puzzles are presented below, and their relevance to designing and debugging programs is discussed in Section 1.4.

Solution to Puzzle 1

People sometimes have trouble solving a simple problem because they automatically assume it is very difficult or they are distracted by some irrelevant aspect of the problem. The problem posed in Puzzle 1 is greatly simplified with the recognition that the ratio of gray socks to black socks is irrelevant: Regardless of the ratio, you must pull out *three socks* to guarantee a matching pair, although a match may occur after pulling out only two. What immediately appears to be an exercise in probability theory is just an exercise in common sense.

Solution to Puzzle 2

Puzzle 2 requires *sideways logic;* when careful, systematic, and traditional steps fail to render a solution, you must be creative enough to consider a somewhat *unusual* solution. Many people fail to solve this puzzle because they do not think to extend the lines beyond the matrix of circles or simply *assume* that such an extension is not allowed. Figure 1.2 depicts two solutions.

Solution to Puzzle 3

Puzzle 3 illustrates an inexplicable consequence stemming from an erroneous initial assumption (see Figure 1.3). The puzzle asserts that the mirror is reversing the image in a horizontal direction—if this is true, then the absence of any vertical reversal is perplexing indeed! Actually, the mirror is not reversing anything—*the act of turning the book to face the mirror* produces the horizontal reversal. A mirror merely shows the front of the book, whose image is reversed by virtue of turning it toward the mirror.

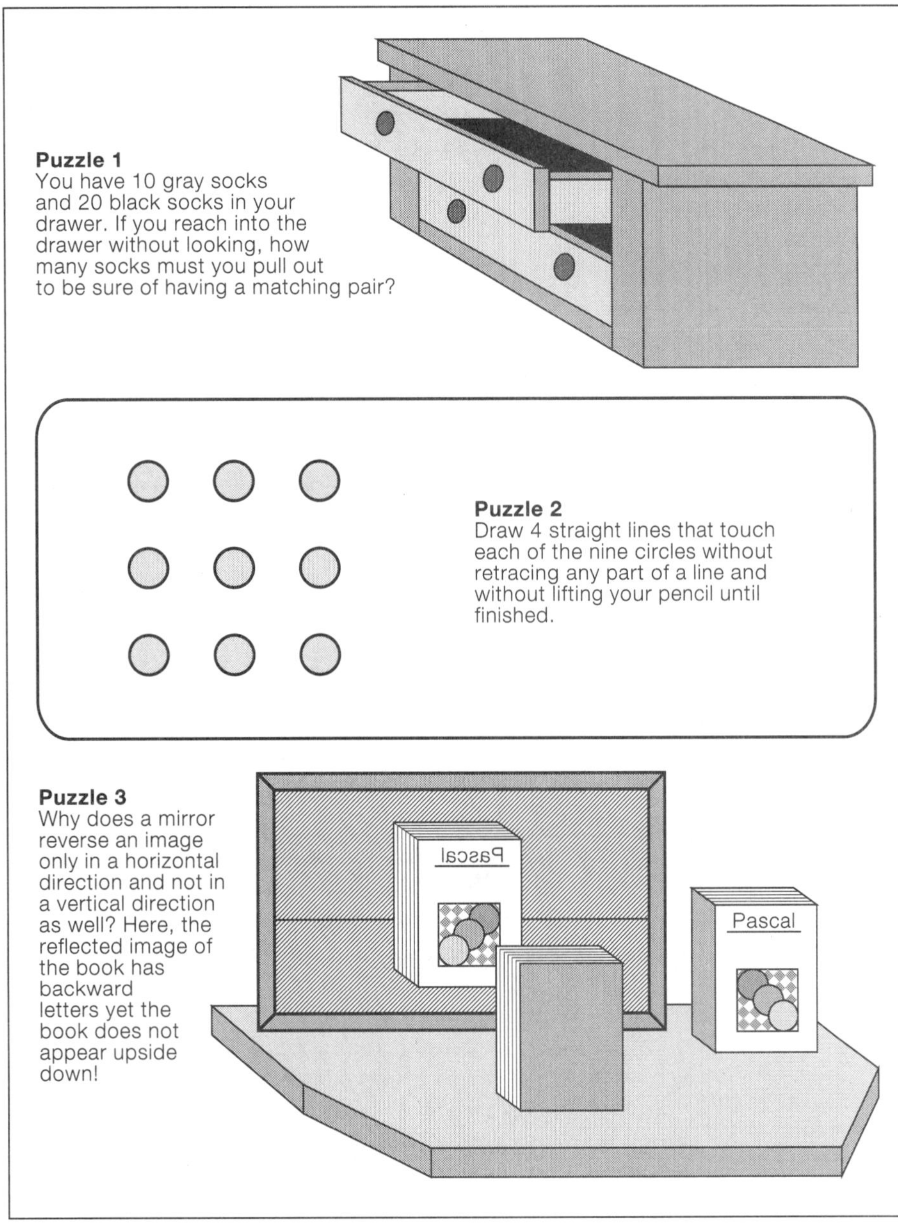

FIGURE 1.1 **Three Puzzles**

Since the book itself is not inverted vertically, its reflected image should not (and does not) appear inverted.

1.2 QUALITIES OF A WELL-WRITTEN PROGRAM

Preliminaries

In your first programming course, the early assignments were probably quite simple. Perhaps you had to write a program to print a bill or to perform some mathematical calculations on a list of company sales figures. These programs were probably rather short and logically straightforward,

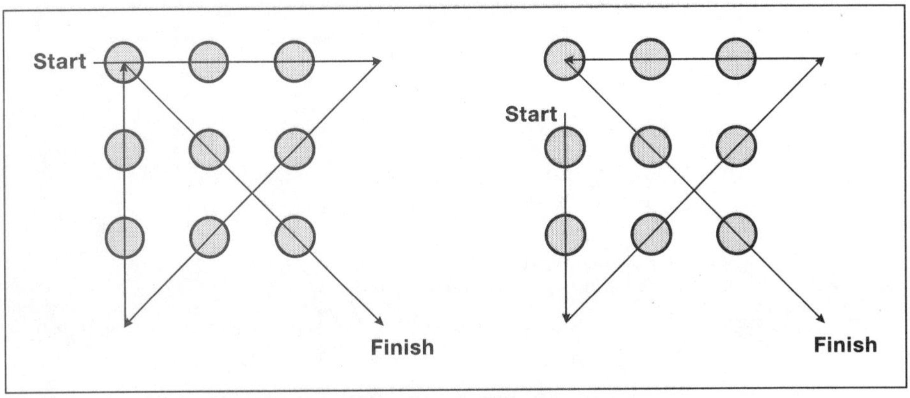

FIGURE 1.2 Two of Several Solutions to Puzzle 2

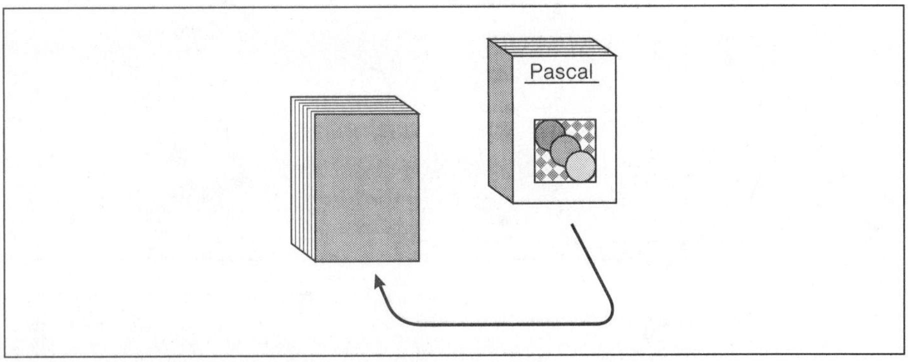

FIGURE 1.3 Turning the Book to Face the Mirror

miniprojects intended to acquaint you with the syntax of the programming language, the mechanics of compiling a program, and with the computer itself.

Later programs no doubt took a bit more thought and planning. Maybe you had to write a program to simulate the play of a slot machine or the screen interaction of a bank-teller machine, complete with a set of basic transactions on customer accounts. These programs simply did more, and writing the code involved real problem solving. Learning to manage your time and effort can be as challenging as learning the programming concepts themselves.

How do students tackle programming assignments? There are several common approaches:

- *Sheer terror:* These students panic, then freeze, avoiding even thinking about the assignment until the last minute, when they resort to "hacking away" or plagiarizing other students' codes (both of these approaches are discussed later). After several assignments, these students often drop the course altogether.
- *Delayed mania:* These students also wait until the last minute from simple procrastination rather than fear. They can be found living in the computer laboratory during the three days before an assignment is due; they survive on vending machine food and a few hours of sleep and can often be found mumbling or cursing aloud to their computers!

- *Theft:* These students simply steal assignment code from other classmates, but, because they do not learn the programming concepts by writing their own codes, they usually fail course examinations and quizzes. After several assignments, these students also typically drop the course.
- *Hacking away: Hackers* are programmers who throw together chunks of code hoping that, somehow, the program will work. These students tend to know much about basic Pascal syntax, a little about advanced features of the language, and almost nothing about programming style. They rush to the computer and type away as soon as an assignment is issued, without planning and hand-testing the entire program on paper first. As a result, their programs are usually sloppy patchworks of code—difficult to read, debug, and modify and often longer and less efficient than is necessary.
- *Sound understanding and planning:* These students take the time to understand thoroughly what the assignment is asking for and what their program is supposed to produce. They break the assignment into many subassignments and describe steps to complete each of these; i.e., they write a *program design* (the program design is the focal topic of Section 1.3). These students write the entire Pascal program on paper, hand-test this version and *then* type in the code at a computer (at this point, most of the errors will have already been found and fixed). They carefully test and debug the entire program until it is complete.

A primary purpose of this chapter is to teach you that taking a careful, consistent, divide-and-conquer approach to writing programs truly pays off; this approach helps you produce a working program in a minimum amount of time. Most students find it hard to believe that devising a program design on paper, and then writing and hand-testing the entire Pascal program on paper—before even sitting down at a computer—can possibly save any time, especially when they see other classmates in the laboratory already working at computers. If you are diligent enough to follow the steps described in this chapter, you may see those same students still working on their programs as you leave the laboratory with a finished program in your hand. *Become a master programmer: Learn and employ sound design skills.*

In Section 1.3 we examine the general stages of sound program development and then put these ideas into practice by developing a program to play the card game blackjack (in Appendix M). Our program will perform a simulation of the game, pitting the human user against the computer. This program must not only display cards and messages correctly and neatly and provide a pleasant, easy-to-use interface, it must also make intelligent decisions during play—i.e., decisions that help the dealer win while conforming to the rules of blackjack (these rules will be summarized for you in Appendix M). You may sense already that this is not a trivial program to write! Surely, dashing off to the nearest computer to type in Pascal code fast and furious is not a useful approach. Careful planning will be important to produce, in a minumum amount of time, a correct program whose code and logic are readily understandable by another programmer.

Since our goal is to produce a program that works correctly within a reasonable amount of time and with a reasonable amount of effort, we will examine the general quality of any well-written computer program first.

Program Correctness and Other Qualities

In your first programming course, you and your instructor were probably satisfied if the early programs merely produced the correct results and output. Programs should certainly run correctly, but this is not enough. The programs you develop in the future will become increasingly more complex, perhaps spanning many thousands of lines and involving a team of other programmers. You must learn to manage your resources: As a student you must budget the time and energy you spend on a project to leave time and energy for other responsibilities. As a professional programmer, you may be budgeting the time and energy of other programmers, too, as well as budgeting financial expenses associated with a project. And the computer itself may have its own limited resources when the program is run, such as the amount of available memory and the speed with which it can execute instructions.

Therefore, many issues beyond the basic correctness of the output must be considered when designing and developing computer programs, including the following:

- Can the program code and its underlying logic be understood readily by another programmer?
- Is the code written so it can be modified with a reasonable effort?
- Will the program be easy to use by its intended user?
- Does the program make an acceptable use of available computer memory and perform its operations for the user with reasonable speed?

We can gauge the quality of a computer program as a function of three characteristics, *program structure, functionality, and performance:*

1. **Program structure** refers to how the program code is actually written and arranged within the program. Program structure is largely a product of the following:
   - ***Modularity*** refers to distributing the workload of a program among numerous routines and having a concise main routine.
   - ***Parameter passing*** is using procedure parameters and function arguments in lieu of referring to global variables directly within procedures and functions.
   - ***Programming style*** indicates clarity, conciseness, and consistency in coding. Source code comments are included and a written programming guide is furnished for use by other programmers.
2. **Program Functionality** indicates how correctly the program actually does what it was originally intended to do and how easily the program may be used for other, similar applications and on other computers. Program functionality is largely a measure of the following:
   - ***Reliability*** means the program produces correct results.
   - ***Versatility*** indicates the program is useful for a variety of related applications.
   - ***Portability*** means the program can be run using other compilers or computers.
3. **Program performance** indicates how well the program interacts with its human user or with another device, manages the resources of computer

memory and execution time, and handles unusual circumstances that arise at runtime. Program performance can be gauged by the following:

- ***User-friendliness*** means the program is easy and pleasant for the user. A user manual—both online and written— is often provided.
- ***Efficiency*** means the program makes reasonable use of computer resources, such as memory and execution time.
- ***Robustness*** indicates that the program handles special cases, such as erroneous input or arithmetic overflow.

A computer *program* has these qualities when the programmer is careful enough to design and implement *routines* with these qualities. We now examine each of the nine qualities in detail.

Program Structure

Again, the term *program structure* refers to how the code is actually written and physically structured within a program. It is determined primarily by modularity, parameter passing, and programming style, all of which are described in this section.

Modularity

Modularity is one of the most important qualities of a computer program. A program is said to be *modular* when it is divided logically and physically into

- *Numerous routines* (procedures and functions), each responsible for a particular task or set of tasks, and
- A *concise main routine* that provides central control of the program's execution flow.

As we shall see, for large, complex programs, distributing a program's work load among many independent routines (transferring data via parameters) is far better than writing one large main routine with few or no procedures and functions.

The main routine should be succinct, consisting primarily of calls to other program routines and any necessary looping or conditional structures, such as **IF** and **CASE** statements. As a general rule, keep the main routine free of `Read`, `Write`, and assignment statements as well as other low-level details better deferred to procedures and functions. *A reading of the main routine should provide a concise overview of the logic flow of the entire program.* Look ahead briefly to the main routine of program `ElectronicMenu`, Application 4.1, as an example.

Primitive Operations

Primitive operations are basic, general-purpose operations and routines that serve as building blocks to support more complex, **high-level operations** in a program. For example, in a bank-teller machine program, determining if passwords entered are legitimate and transferring money from users' savings accounts to their checking accounts are both high-level operations. The routines for these high-level operations must rely upon many primitive operations; these may include displaying user prompts, reading such information as the password, and adding and subtracting numbers. Everything in daily life, in fact, involves this high-level, low-level dichotomy. If you own an automobile, for instance, you rely upon the primitive operations performed by the pistons, distributor, water pump, and many other parts to support your high-level operations, such as driving the car to work or pulling a trailer. Your very ability to think and move depends upon the primitive activity of organs that, in turn, rely upon the even more primitive activity of constituent cells, and so forth.

The original authors of Pascal believed some operations were so fundamental to most programming applications that they should be built into (**native** to) the language directly or provided as library routines. Appendix A describes all standard Pascal symbols, identifiers, and operators. As previously explained, all such native functions and procedures reside in a special **library file,** already compiled and known to the Pascal compiler and linker programs in use. Nonstandard compilers may be designed to recognize additional (nonstandard) syntax, operators, identifiers, and native library routines.

In addition to the predefined procedures and functions provided by standard Pascal, every application requires **programmer-defined primitive routines** to perform operations—primitive and high-level—specific to that application. Such routines must be provided for those operations that are not built into the language or provided by native routines. For example, if a program uses an array to hold a list of items (perhaps records or integers), the following seven programmer-defined primitive operations may prove useful (each is implemented as a procedure or function):

ListInit Initialize the array as "empty" by setting to zero the integer variable used to hold a count of the number of items in the array.
EmptyList Determine if the array is empty.
FullList Determine if the array is full; i.e., there are no available array elements for additional items.
ListSearch Search for a particular item in the array, returning its element index number if found.
ListInsert Add another item to the array, in an unused element.
ListDelete Remove a particular item from the array (perhaps overwriting it with the content of another array element).
ListTraverse Visit each item in a particular order, processing the item (i.e., performing some operation involving the item).

The Boolean functions `EmptyList` and `FullList` and the five procedures `ListInit`, `ListSearch`, `ListInsert`, `ListDelete`, and `ListTraverse` are *not* predefined—the programmer must design and code them. Again, these primitive routines will probably be used frequently within a program that manipulates an array of data items. By designing them early in the program development process, the programmer is free to build more complex, high-level routines that may contain calls to these primitive routines. Identifying and designing primitive routines early means that a programmer does not have to "reinvent the wheel" each time a high-level operation must be performed.

Program routines (and program design modules) must be kept functionally independent of each other, exchanging data through parameters and arguments as necessary. This is a design philosophy called **information hiding:** Implementation details specified within the primitive routines are hidden from the higher level routines. For example, if a high-level procedure in a bank program must locate a customer account, it would call another (primitive) routine to search the list of customer accounts. The high-level procedure does not care how the primitive routine performs its search; the high-level routine merely provides the account number to the primitive routine and awaits the result of the search. As another example, you have probably been using the standard `Writeln` procedure since your very first programming assignment, but do you know how this procedure is actually coded? To use `Writeln` you need know only how to pass parameters to it; its implementation is hidden to simplify its use. Once primitive routines are written, information hiding frees you to focus on details pertinent to a particular (higher) level of the design and is an example of the dichotomy of abstraction and implementation. Abstraction is the separation of the (abstract) logical properties of something from its actual (concrete) implementation.

The Benefits of Modularity

Why the emphasis on keeping procedures and functions independent of each other? Why not design a program as one large main routine? A modular program structure provides several important benefits:

- *A modular program is easier to build and verify.* Each routine can be written and tested independently of the other routines by using a series of temporary versions of the program's main routine (**program stubs**). A stub calls only the single routine being tested, passing parameter values intended to test some functionality of that routine. When each routine works by itself, the stub can be modified to test two routines working together, then three routines, and so forth. The related benefit of information hiding was discussed previously.
- *A modular program structure is easier for another programmer to read and follow.* Just as a textbook is easier to read when it is divided logically into chapters and subchapters, a program is easier for another programmer to read when it is divided logically into a number of procedures and functions, employing full parameter passing. Like a textbook's table of contents, *a program's main routine should offer a succinct overview of the logic flow of the entire program.* A modular program is therefore easier to modify and enhance later, with minimal effects on other routines.
- This gives rise to yet another benefit: *A modular program structure is easier to debug.* Imagine a program that allows an airline pilot to calculate arrival time, total distance, and fuel consumption for a particular flight. If all program output is accurate except for the calculated fuel consumption, the debugging process might begin with an examination of the routine responsible for displaying this information, work backward to the routine responsible for actually calculating the amount, then go backward to the routine that calls this routine, and so on. Unre-

lated routines, such as the one that calculates arrival time, can be initially excluded from suspicion.

The GoTo *Statement*

In a Pascal program, the **GoTo** statement directs the computer to take an unconditional branch to a particular statement within the program, which is labeled.

In the early days of computer programming (pre-1960s), a **GoTo**-like statement was the only way for the programmer to create a loop or an **IF**-like conditional structure. The **GoTo** form of unconditional branching is still necessary for these purposes in a low-level assembly language. Its use is discouraged in a language like Pascal, however, because it is unnecessary and undermines the principles of top-down design. Imagine one **GoTo** causing a branch to a previous statement, another **GoTo** causing a branch to a later statement, a third **GoTo** causing a branch to a still later statement, another **GoTo** causing a branch to a previous statement, and so forth, producing a morass of "spaghetti logic"! (Refer to Figure 1.4).

Instead, program logic should flow in a linear fashion, from the beginning of a routine until its end, including the bodies of loop structures. In almost every application, the standard Pascal **FOR**, **WHILE**, **REPEAT**, **IF**, and **CASE** statements and **BEGIN/END** block structures are sufficient to control execution flow. Even such early high-level languages as FORTRAN and COBOL have had their standards modified to become more like Pascal by including these statements and structures, thereby rendering the **GoTo** unnecessary.

One legitimate use of the **GoTo** is to provide a mechanism whereby execution flow can quickly and easily escape a deeply nested set of conditional structures when some error situation has been detected by the program and further processing must be precluded. Here, the inclusion of a **GoTo** statement may replace many statements that otherwise must be included just to handle one or two special cases. This rare use of the **GoTo** would actually simplify and shorten the code.

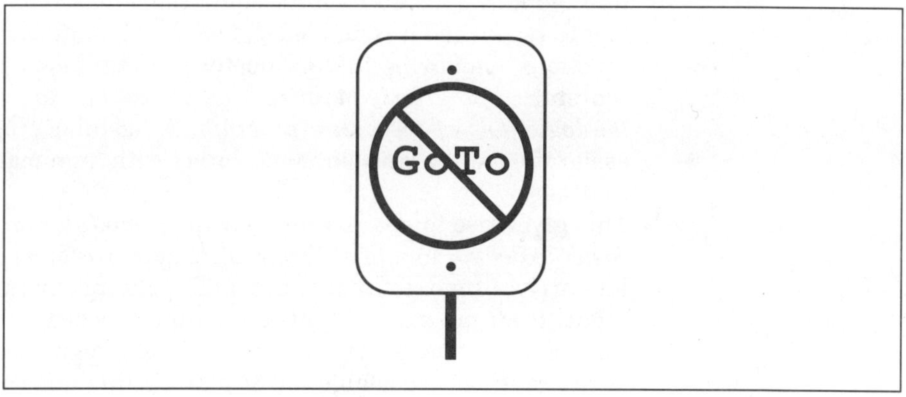

FIGURE 1.4 The International No GoTo Symbol

Parameter Passing

Procedures and functions operate on *information* to complete their tasks. This information may consist of numbers, characters, or some other type of data. We may consider each program routine as having a "contract" with its calling routine. When one routine calls another, the calling routine typically passes certain information that allows the called routine to do its work. Each called routine agrees to perform certain tasks and possibly to pass back to the calling routine certain information as a result.

Figure 1.5 uses the analogy of a pressure cooker to depict the channels by which information flows into and out of procedurs and functions.

No part of Pascal has been a source of more errors than the use and misuse of global variables. In most cases, pass parameters to procedures and functions rather than referencing these variables globally within the procedures and functions. Referencing a global variable within a module rather than passing it as a parameter may undermine modularity by obscuring *how* that procedure has access to the variable.

Parameter passing is important for three reasons:

- *As an aid to the debugging process.* Parameter passing provides clear channels through which data are passed to and from a routine, thereby establishing the execution path along which routines use and modify their values. This simplifies the process of tracking down exactly where a praticular variable may acquire a particular value. During debugging, temporary `Writeln` statements can be inserted at strategic locations in the program to display current parameter values.
- *To reduce the possibility of side effects.* Parameter passing minimizes the danger of changing the value of a global variable inadvertently within a procedure or function.
- *To retain local values.* In recursive routines, non-**VAR** parameters retain local values, as if they were local variables (they are commonly referred

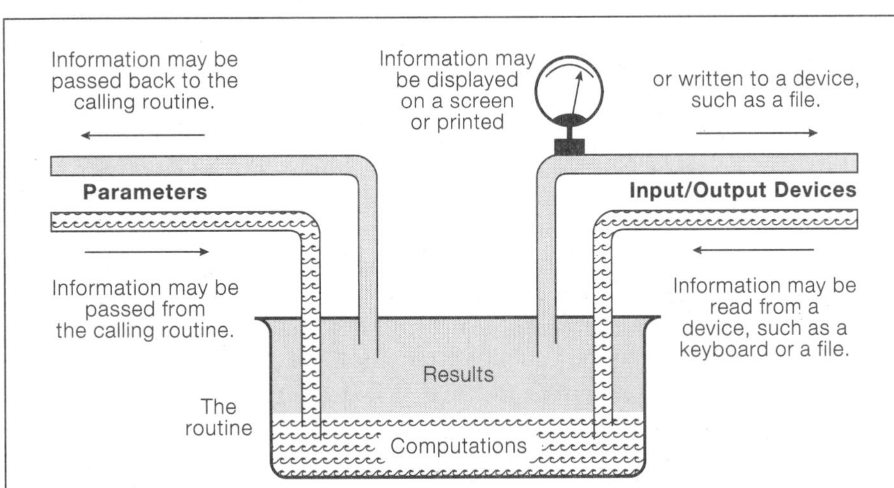

FIGURE 1.5 Information Flow Into and Out of a Routine

to as pseudolocal variables). Many of these routines rely upon this as an integral part of their algorithms, referencing these variables upon return from recursive calls (recursion is the topic of Chapter 7).

As a common exception, any local declaration of a routine is global to the routines nested within it, so parameters are typically not passed to these nested routines unless absolutely necessary.

`VAR` parameters must be used with care:

- A `VAR` parameter is necessary for a return value. (An exception to this is the fact that information can be returned indirectly through a non-`VAR` pointer parameter. Pointer variables and dynamic allocation are discussed in Section 4.2 and throughout Chapter 5.)
- `VAR` parameters are implemented by indirect addressing, which takes slightly more execution time than the direct addressing used for value parameters.
- `VAR` parameters improve efficiency when passing records and arrays that are longer than two words of memory, although the efficiency of access time is reduced. Thus, we have a trade-off: If the parameter is really long, use a `VAR`. If it is short (one or two words of memory), do not use a `VAR`. If the parameter length lies somewhere in between, you must consider the frequency of use.
- `VAR` parameters are like leaky pipes. It may not be obvious that a particular program bug occurs because a calling routine's data are being "polluted" with the data returned from another called routine (a type of side effect). This is why `VAR` parameters should be used *only* if data are intended to be returned and/or if the parameter is a large array or record.

Programming Style

In the 1960s and into the 1970s, computer memory was small and computer execution time was slow by today's standards. Therefore the emphasis was on writing programs that conserved memory and time by whatever means possible. The means sometimes involved obscure programming tricks designed to save a few instructions or a chunk of memory, with the resulting program often unintelligible to any programmer other than its author. This practice was not only acceptable but even regarded with some personal pride because, at that time, programs were often designed, coded, verified, and maintained by the same programmer.

Since that time, a plethora of software has been designed for scientific, educational, industrial, communications, and recreational applications. Over the years, execution speed has become faster and computer memory has become cheaper to manufacture and, therefore, more plentiful. As commercial programs have become larger and more complex, they have evolved from strictly a single-programmer effort to a multiprogrammer team effort. Implementing the design principles espoused in this chapter when developing programs—especially the principles of modularity and programming style—is essential in making the best use of total programmer time.

Programming style is as individualized as English prose and evolves gradually with practice. With programming, however, form must follow function—i.e., the program must be easy to read and maintain—so veteran programmers tend to follow a set of common stylistic guidelines when writing code. These guidelines are enumerated fully in Appendix L, but their common aim may be summarized as follows:

> Programs should be written using accepted stylistic conventions *consistently* to represent algorithms in a manner that uses a minimum number of statements, while still clearly conveying to the human reader the underlying logic of those algorithms.

To this end, *source-code comments* must accompany any code segment for which the underlying logic may not be clear to the reader.

NOTE

> The overriding purpose of employing sound programming style when writing programs is to minimize programmer time and effort—for the benefit of both the original author(s) of the program and for programmers who must deal with the code later.

Sound programming style therefore requires clarity and conciseness in the coding.

Clarity

As a simple example regarding clarity, is the purpose of each of the following three code segments obvious? (Assume that variables `P`, `Q`, and `Temp` are all of the same numeric data type.)

Segment 1	Segment 2	Segment 3
`P := P + Q;`	`P := P * Q;`	`Temp := Q;`
`Q := P - Q;`	`Q := P DIV Q;`	`Q    := P;`
`P := P - Q;`	`P := P DIV Q;`	`P    := Temp;`

Each of these code segments swaps the contents of `P` and `Q`. Segments 1 and 2 do so without the need of a third variable (`Temp`), as required by segment 3, and may seem more attractive for their cleverness. Although segments 1 and 2 are more efficient than segment 3 in terms of computer memory use, examination of other issues reveals that segment 3 is the best choice. Because the logic of segment 3 is most obvious to any programmer looking at the code, it is more efficent in terms of programmer time and convenience. (Beyond the clarity issue, segments 1 and 2 also have the functional limitation that variables `P` and `Q` must both contain positive values or both contain negative values; also, in segment 2, `P` and `Q` must both be of integer data type. Further, segments 1 and 2 are less efficient than 3 in terms of execution time because each involves additional arithmetic operations. Worse yet, these operations may result in *arithmetic overflow* or *underflow*.)

Conciseness

As an example of conciseness, we will devise a Boolean function named `ALeapYear` to determine if a particular year is a leap year. In 1582, the Gregorian calendar replaced the Julian calendar, which had been in use since Julius Caesar ordered its design in 45 B.C. This new calendar was named in honor of Pope Gregory XIII, who refined the formula for calculating leap years as follows:

> Years evenly divisible by 4 are leap years; however, century years are leap years only if they are evenly divisible by 400.

For example, 1992, 1600, and 2000 are leap years, but 1993 and 1900 are not. The skeleton of function `ALeapYear` follows:

```
FUNCTION ALeapYear ( Year : Integer ) : Boolean;

BEGIN
 {function body}
END;
```

Consider the following three function bodies for `ALeapYear`:

Version 1

```
IF Year MOD 4 <> 0 THEN
  ALeapYear := FALSE
ELSE
  IF Year MOD 100 <> 0 THEN
    ALeapYear := TRUE
  ELSE
    IF Year MOD 400 = 0 THEN
      ALeapYear := TRUE
    ELSE
      ALeapYear := FALSE
```

Version 2

```
IF (Year MOD 4 = 0) AND ( Year MOD 100 <> 0 ) THEN
  ALeapYear := TRUE
ELSE
  IF Year MOD 400 = 0 THEN
    ALeapYear := TRUE
  ELSE
    ALeapYear := FALSE
```

Version 3

```
ALeapYear :=( ( Year MOD 4 = 0 ) AND ( Year MOD 100 <> 0 ) ) OR
               ( Year MOD 400 = 0 )
```

Although all three versions work properly, version 3 is best because it is the most concise representation of the original algorithm and still conveys the logic of the algorithm clearly.

In many cases, the most concise form of an expression may be obtained readily from a **truth table.** The truth table in Figure 1.6 was built by carefully extracting the three relevant tests from the written definition of a leap year given earlier and listing all possible permutations of test results. Ex-

Year **MOD** 4 = 0	Year **MOD** 100 = 0	Year **MOD** 400 = 0	ALeapYear
FALSE	FALSE	FALSE	FALSE
FALSE	FALSE	TRUE	FALSE
FALSE	TRUE	FALSE	FALSE
FALSE	TRUE	TRUE	FALSE
TRUE	**FALSE**	FALSE	**TRUE**
TRUE	**FALSE**	**TRUE**	**TRUE**
TRUE	TRUE	FALSE	FALSE
TRUE	TRUE	**TRUE**	**TRUE**

FIGURE 1.6 A Truth Table to Determine If a Year Is a Leap Year

amine the table to determine which values of the three tests `ALeapYear` evaluates to a true value. The boldface Boolean values in columns 1 and 2 point out that `ALeapYear` should be assigned a true value if *a year is evenly divisible by 4 but not evenly divisible by 100,* regardless of whether or not the year is also evenly divisible by 400. The boldface Boolean values in column three indicate that `ALeapYear` should be assigned a true value *anytime a year is found to be evenly divisible by 400.*

Appendix L describes a variety of stylistic conventions in programming and proper techniques for documenting code.

> *At this time, please read Appendix L.*

Program Functionality

Recall that the term *program functionality* refers to how correctly a program actually does what it was intended to do when designed. The term also refers to how easily a program may be adopted for use on different computers and for other similar applications.

Reliability

Certainly a program must be reliable, accurately generating the results it was originally intended to produce, although this feat is not always easy to verify. Consider, for example, a set of complex computer programs used aboard naval combat ships to track the positions of other ships, aircraft, and enemy missiles and to control the deployment of the ship's own weapons. Because an almost infinite variety of circumstances may arise while such programs are actually used, exhaustive testing of the programs in a computer laboratory is simply not possible. Instead, much of the program testing occurs while the ships conduct mock-battle maneuvers at sea.

One aspect of correctness somewhat beyond the control of a programmer is the computer memory representation of some numeric values. Because computer memory involves hardware that is *finite* in size, only *a finite set of values* can be represented internally. This also imposes upper and lower limits on the magnitude of numbers that may be represented. (The maximum integer value for any Pascal system is assigned automatically to the standard named constant, **MAXINT**.) Although very large and very small real numeric values can easily be represented and manipulated in mathematics, they can only be *approximated* inside a computer.

A common side effect of internal approximation is *round-off error,* which may arise from the use of real numbers. For example, a computer evaluating the expression `(22 / 7)` can store the result 3.1428571 if the computer memory representation of real values allows seven places of real precision or 3.14286 if it allows only five places of real precision. Typically, the final representable digit is rounded upward if necessary (in the example, the 5 becomes a 6). Such automatic rounding may accumulate across a series of operations involving real values, producing a result that is slightly higher or lower than the result computed using greater precision. (Section 2.3 discusses the memory representation of real values in much greater detail.)

Versatility

A program is versatile if it can be used in a variety of situations. Versatility applies to program declarations and routines as well. Making functions, procedures, and global declarations as versatile as possible allows them to be used with little or no modifications. In addition, making functions and procedures versatile often minimizes the total number of functions and procedures, thereby minimizing total size of the program and, consequently, total programming time and effort. In later chapters we develop a wide variety of versatile primitive routines and their necessary global declarations (the actual Pascal code for most of these are contained in the appendices).

Portability

When compiling a source program, a compiler generates instructions that include both native machine code and many calls to procedures within the computer's operating system program. Therefore, every Pascal compiler is designed to produce object code to run under a particular operating system and on a particular computer. Pascal and other high-level languages free the programmer from being too concerned with the mechanics of very low level operations, which are the responsibilities of the operating system; an example is how electronic signals are actually transferred from a keyboard into a special memory device called the input buffer. Very low level operations such as these are said to be **transparent** to the programmer, who may instead focus his or her efforts on higher-level operations, such as processing the characters just read from the input buffer via a `Read` statement. This is the same concept as information-hiding, discussed earlier.

Even with this transparency, any high-level program will be tied somewhat to a particular computer because its instructions must be recognized by a compiler; compilers are themselves tied to a particular operating system, which is tied to a particular computer. Portability is a measure of the degree to which a source program is *not* tied to any one computer—i.e., a measure of how readily a program may be run on computers other than the computer used to develop the program. Most Pascal compilers are nonstandard, however, because they recognize special syntax, identifiers, operators, and native procedures and functions in place of or beyond those specified by standard Pascal. Many of these nonstandard extensions are related to file-handling operations and screen display operations. The more a program's code adheres to the Pascal standard, the more compatible it is likely to be with other compilers and computers; i.e., the more portable it is.

Program Performance

The term *program performance* refers to how the program interacts with its human users, how it makes use of computer memory and time resources, and how it deals with unusual circumstances, such as erroneous input.

User-friendliness

To be truly useful, a program must be relatively easy and pleasant to use. The program should be straightforward to run, with a minimum number of special start-up tasks required of the user; these might include loading certain files or performing a particular set of operations first. All program output should be formatted neatly and labeled appropriately, with an overall professional appearance. Just as comments must be included in the source code of a program to aid another programmer reading the code, online and offline documentation should be provided to program users, as necessary.

That portion of a program devoted to the interaction between user and program is called the **human interface,** and two general approaches to it may be taken: With **batch processing,** once the program begins it has virtually no interaction with the user other than some periodic output indicating the program's progress and diagnostic output signaling the end of program execution. With **interactive processing,** the program does interact with the user while the program is running. Typically, this involves the program's reading data from the keyboard and displaying data to the screen.

An example of batch processing is a program run each night by data processors at a bank to update customer accounts, based on the day's transactions (deposits, withdrawals, credit card payments, etc.). Such a program might prompt a data processor for the name of a file containing descriptions of all such transactions for the day and then perform the transactions without the need for further human intervention. An example of interactive processing, on the other hand, is a 24-hour bank-teller machine used by a customer to deposit, withdraw, or transfer funds. Actions performed by this program require some user input periodically, such as a bank card, a password, or an indication of the desired transaction, such as the dollar amount of a deposit or withdrawal. The applications and examples in this textbook employ interactive processing.

Prompting For Input

Four basic techniques programmers employ frequently to interactively obtain input from the keyboard include command-lines, menus and icons, individual prompts, and continuous asynchronous input. A brief discussion of each technique follows.

Command Lines

In the command-line technique, the program displays a particular symbol or set of characters to indicate that it is waiting for the user to type in a **command line.** The syntax for a command line typically includes a *command* *mnemonic* (i.e., an abbreviation of a command name) that may (or may not) be followed by a series of command-line *arguments*. Command-line arguments supply additional, necessary information about the command. Each command line is read and interpreted by the program, then the appropriate routine is called to carry out that command.

For example, IBM's MS-DOS™ operating system displays a > symbol as its request for user input (in this example, the C: indicates that disk drive C is the current drive). If the user wishes to rename the PROJECT1.PAS file to PROJ1.BAK, he or she would type in the following characters and press the RETURN keyboard key

```
C:> RENAME PROG1.PAS PROG1.BAK
```

A program using command-line input can read the entire line into a string variable, then parse the string (i.e., examine it character by character) to extract the mnemonic and, if necessary, its arguments.

Menus

In the menu technique, the program displays a list (**menu**) of possible program commands or choices of response to a program question; then it prompts the user to select one of these commands or choices. An example of this is the menu of Application 5.3, a computerized dictionary program. In this program, the main routine calls procedure `ObtainMenuOption` to display the menu of options as follows:

```
***** Online Dictionary Menu of Options *****

  0. QUIT Program
  1. Check spelling of a word
  2. Add a word interactively
  3. Delete a word
  4. Display dictionary
  5. Save dictionary to a text file
  6. Add words from text file

==> Enter choice ( 0 - 6) :
```

Procedure `ObtainMenuOption` reads the user's choice and returns it to the main routine of the program as a parameter. The main routine then uses a **`CASE`** statement to call the appropriate procedure (`AddWord`, `DeleteWord`, `CheckSpelling`, etc.), based on the choice value returned. A popular variation of this form of menu is the **pull-down menu,** used in conjunction with a computer mouse.

Individual Prompts

Almost every interactive computer program requires some specific prompting of the user for input, even if the program is primarily menu-driven or command-line drive. To minimize user confusion and invalid input, it is important that such **individual prompts** be *very specific* about the type of input expected by the program. This includes the format of the input or the range of legal value ranges; these are typically indicated within parentheses. As an example, examine the following two code segments, both of which prompt for the same information. In the segments, variable `InputLine` is of (nonstandard) String data type. (After the `Readln`, the balance, account plan, and date must be extracted from the string and the opening balance and account plan converted to numeric values.)

```
Writeln ( 'Enter opening balance, account plan, date: ' );
Readln ( InputLine );

Write ( 'Enter <opening balance> <account plan (1-3)> <date (MM-DD-YY)>: $' );
Readln ( InputLine );
```

The second prompt is clearly more informative than the first. Also, notice that a dollar sign (`$`) appears at the end of the prompt to dissuade the user from entering his own dollar sign, and `Write` is used instead of `Writeln` so the user's response is echoed on the same line as the prompt.

The process of entering information can be made more convenient for the user if the program offers a default response. A common convention is to display the default response within `[ ]` symbols, selected by merely pressing the RETURN or ENTER key. In the following sample code segment, which illustrates this technique, variable `FileName` is of String data type:

```
Write ( 'Enter filename of file containing words to be loaded: [Words.TXT]  ' );
Readln ( FileName );
IF Length ( FileName ) = 0 THEN  {IF the user merely pressed RETURN or ENTER}
  FileName := 'Words.TXT';       {  THEN the default response is used}
```

Continuous Asynchronous Input

Some applications are highly interactive and the user—rather than the program—must control when information is supposed to be read. For example, consider a computer video game involving a simulated battle between spacecraft. The user controls his or her own spacecraft and weapons to ward off attacks by the enemy spacecraft, whose actions are determined by the computer program. Anytime during a game, the user can press the keyboard space bar to fire photon torpedoes or press one of the keyboard arrow keys to maneuver a spacecraft around the screen. Because the game is supposed to simulate the fast action of combat, the program cannot stop the action every 2 seconds just to ask the user what to do next!

Instead, the program must allow the user to enter a keystroke or manipulate a joystick at any time to request a particular program operation. This is an example of **continuous asynchronous input**, i.e., input that the user may enter at any time, without program prompting, which is intended to be processed immediately by the program. By contrast, keyboard input prompted for and read at the program's discretion is synchronous with the computer's internal system clock. The system clock regulates when program instructions are executed and therefore regulates when all program instructions are executed, including calls to the standard `Write`, `Writeln`, `Read`, and `Readln` procedures.

Many nonstandard Pascal systems provide a Boolean function that returns a true value if a keyboard key has been pressed since the last time the function was called and a false value otherwise. The combat video game program might contain a main loop consisting of instructions to manipulate the program-controlled spacecraft, with a call to the Boolean keypress-detector function near the bottom of the loop. The skeleton of such a main routine follows (here, the Boolean function is named `KeyWasPressed`):

```
{***  Main routine for program  ***}

BEGIN
{Instructions that call initialization routines}
REPEAT

  {Instructions that control the enemy spacecraft}

  IF KeywasPressed THEN
    {Instructions to analyze the user input and respond accordingly}

UNTIL  {End-of-game condition becomes true}
END.
```

Pressing a key does not cause a true program interrupt, as would pressing the Ctrl and C keys simultaneously to terminate the program (as supported by many operating systems). Here, the system clock still determines when the `KeyWasPressed` function call itself is executed regardless of when the user pressed the key, but the program's rapid execution gives the illusion of a genuine interrupt.

In addition to the basic keyboard keys, a program can use a variety of interesting devices to obtain a user's menu choice, provided the necessary supporting hardware and nonstandard Pascal software are available. These include special keyboard function keys, a joystick, touch screen, and light pen. One of the most popular alternatives to a keyboard is the mouse, by which the user selects which program to run next or selects an option within a program by "clicking" on a small drawing (an icon) that represents that program or program option. This provides a visual alternative to the menu technique.

Program Output

When a program displays information on the screen, it must allow the user enough time to read this output, especially if the display is scrolling the lines rapidly. With most operating systems, the user can press the CTRL and S keys simultaneously to freeze the current screen display, and then press these two keys again, or else press the CTRL and Q keys simultaneously to resume the display process. This technique requires the user to have fairly quick reflexes, however, and may become tedious after many screens of output are displayed.

There are two alternative, programmer-defined techniques that are preferable when large amounts of data are displayed quickly by a program. Both techniques require that a count of the number of lines displayed be accumulated in an integer variable, named `LineCount` in the examples that follow. In the first technique, after one screen of output is displayed, the program starts an **idle loop,** designed merely to expend a fixed amount of time for the user to read the output. For this purpose, many nonstandard versions of Pascal provide a native procedure, typically named `Delay`. As an example of its use, the following code segment would be embedded within a display loop. Here, `MaxScreenLines` is a named constant, perhaps initialized to the value 23, and the argument to `Delay` is the amount of delay, typically specified in milliseconds.

```
IF LineCount MOD MaxScreenLines = 0 THEN
  Delay ( 5000 );   {Nonstandard - this delay is for 5 seconds}
```

In the second technique, after displaying one screen's worth of output, the program halts the display process temporarily and prompts the user to indicate that he or she is finished reading the display. This is illustrated by the following code segment that, again, would be embedded within a display loop:

```
IF LineCount MOD MaxScreenLines = 0 THEN
  BEGIN
  Write ( '>>> Press the RETURN key to continue <<<' );
  Readln
  END
```

If many screens of data are to be displayed, this technique can be enhanced to allow the user to specify whether or not he or she wishes to view any remaining screens (here, `Choice` is of String type):

```
IF LineCount MOD MaxScreenLines = 0 THEN
  BEGIN
  Write ( '>>>  Press C to continue or Q to quit display:  [C]  <<<' );
  Readln ( Choice );
  IF Length ( Choice ) = 0 THEN              {User merely pressed RETURN}
    QuitDisplay := FALSE
  ELSE                                       {The user entered some character}
    QuitDisplay := Choice IN [ 'Q', 'q' ]
  END
```

Appendix K contains two procedures named `Pause` to facilitate this type of freezing.

Many nonstandard versions of Pascal provide native procedures and functions for "fancy" screen management. Common operations include the following:

- Deleting an existing line on the screen or inserting a blank line, or clearing the entire screen.
- Flashing the display or switching between bright and dim display: This is useful for contrasting portions of displayed text, such as error messages, program prompts, and user input.

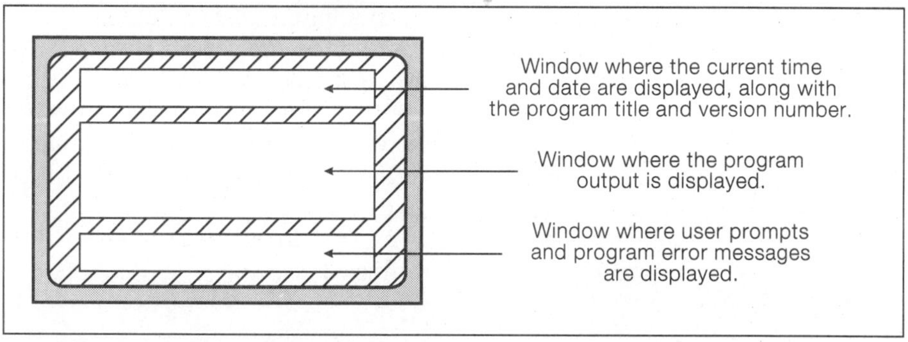

FIGURE 1.7 Example of a Program Partitioning the Screen into 3 Windows

- Positioning the screen cursor explicitly before to a call to `Write` or `Writeln` controls exactly where the next line of output will be displayed; this is done in lieu of having the output lines scroll, as done by default. For example, Borland's Turbo Pascal™ system furnishes the procedure `GoToXY (X,Y)`, in which parameter `X` is the screen column coordinate (typically 1 to 80) and parameter `Y` is the screen row coordinate (typically 1 to 25).
- *Windows* are rectangular portions of the screen to which output may be displayed (by default, the entire screen is the window). Text output displayed within a window scrolls as necessary, and a program may create and switch between different windows to partition the screen logically, as depicted in the simple, generic example of Figure 1.7.

Other interesting output techniques include speech and music synthesis, the output of data to another computer, and the computer control of some mechanical (analog) device. You are encouraged to examine the reference manual of your own compiler to determine if and how any of the features described here are supported.

Efficiency

As previously mentioned, until the mid-1970s, when a computer's internal memory was relatively small and expensive and execution time was relatively slow, saving memory and execution time was the cornerstone of program design. As internal memory became larger and cheaper to manufacture, central processing unit (CPU) execution time became significantly faster, and programs themselves became steadily more complex, the emphasis began to shift from conserving computer resources to conserving human resources—namely, programmer time and energy. Accordingly, modular program design and sound programming style have become crucial, since they result in programs that run correctly and may be modified and enhanced, all in a minimum amount of time.

This does not mean that efficient use of computer resources has become unimportant. The programmer must still be careful when designing routines that process large amounts of data or any routine containing a loop, so that large amounts of computer time and memory are not wasted. The shift merely frees the programmer to write the Pascal code for an algorithm with an eye toward making the code easy for any programmer to read and understand. This makes the entire program easy to debug and modify, even if a less clear version would save a slight amount of execution time or memory. Section 3.7 provides an introduction to the mathematical techniques for measuring the relative efficiencies of algorithms. As we develop algorithms in the remaining chapters of this textbook, we will frequently examine modifications and enhancements to reduce execution time and memory consumption.

A program should be logically clear and reasonably efficient to minimize computer execution time and memory usage. Logical clarity should not be compromised for the purpose of efficiency, however, unless the application dictates that absolute efficiency is critical—for example, in *real-time* applications, such as a telephone directory assistance program or a program used aboard a naval combat ship. Efficiency and clarity are companions, not enemies. Too often, programs are designed poorly or modified and extended repeatedly, so that the final product bears little resemblance to the original program design. Typically, both clarity *and* efficiency can be improved by redesigning the logic of such convoluted programs.

Miscellaneous Efficiency Techniques

At this point, let us consider a variety of general principles that should be applied when designing computer programs. These principles are designed to conserve computer memory and execution time:

- *Minimize shifting or duplicating of data in memory,* since these operations tend to be time-consuming, especially when the data are large records or arrays. Look ahead briefly to Figure 5.14, which depicts an array of records maintained in order of ascending name field value. The figure illustrates the burden of having to shift array records within the array to keep the records ordered whenever a single record is inserted or deleted.
- *Minimize file access,* the number of times data are read from or written to a file stored on a magnetic disk or tape. File accessing involves mechanical actions and may take as much as a thousand times as long to complete than it takes for a purely electronic, internal operation, such as adding two values or assigning a value to a variable.
- *Use a* **VAR** *parameter* before a formal parameter that is a large record or array if this does not create a problem back in the calling routine. By using a **VAR**, only the address of the actual parameter for the procedure or function rather than an entire copy of the actual parameter is stored in the activation record. (Activation records are discussed in Section 4.2.)
- *Remove invariant operations,* those that must be performed regardless of the outcome of some earlier decision and, therefore, should be performed only once. As a simple example, Figure 1.8 contains two versions of the body of procedure `ExtractRoots`. Both versions calculate and return, via parameters `Root1` and `Root2`, the roots of a quadratic expression. (We consider enhancements for error testing when we examine this procedure again in our discussion of logical errors in Section 1.4.)

$$\frac{-b \pm \sqrt{b^2 - 4ac}}{2a}$$

Equation to extract the roots from a quadratic equation

```
PROCEDURE ExtractRoots (a, b, c : Real; VAR Root1, Root2 : Real);

BEGIN
Root1 := ((-b + Sqrt (b * b - 4 * a * c)) / (2 * a);
Root2 := ((-b - Sqrt (b * b - 4 * a * c)) / (2 * a)
END;
```

Invariant — Invariant

```
VAR
  SquareRoot, Divisor : Real;

BEGIN
SquareRoot := Sqrt (b * b - 4 * a * c);
Divisor    := 2 * a;
Root1 := (-b + SquareRoot) / Divisor;
Root2 := (-b - SquareRoot) / Divisor
END;
```

FIGURE 1.8 Two Simple Versions of a Procedure that Extracts the Roots of a Quadratic Equation

These principles of efficiency are applied whenever possible in the programs and code segments presented in this textbook.

Robustness

Robustness is a measure of how well a program handles unusual circumstances, such as illegal user input or attempting to access a nonexistent file. When designing any routine, the programmer must consider all possible special cases that require additional code.

Many **fatal runtime errors,** or errors that cause a program to crash, occur when the program is unsuccessful in its attempt to read data from the keyboard or a file, write data to the screen or a file, or open or close a file. A program can be made more robust if it includes code to detect such an error itself and respond appropriately, rather than having the operating system crash the program when it detects the error. To this end, many nonstandard compilers recognize special compiler directive statements in the source code that temporarily turn off automatic I/O (input/output) checking, thereby allowing the program to deal with a problem, perhaps by displaying an error message. This technique requires a native, nonstandard routine that the program can call immediately after an I/O type operation is attempted to determine if the operation was successful. If the attempt is not successful, this routine would indicate the nature of the problem.

As an example of this error-handling technique, examine the following code segment whose nonstandard syntax is based on Borland's Turbo Pascal™ system. The segment prompts the user for a number repeatedly until a valid number is entered. Here, `Value` is of real data type, `ErrorCode` is of integer data type, and `IOResult` is a Turbo Pascal™ function that returns an integer value indicating the result of the last I/O operation performed (in this case, the `Readln` call). The returned value describes the type of error; for example, 0 represents no error and −130 stands for illegal number syntax. `{$I-}` and `{$I+}` are not comments but, instead, represent the Turbo

Pascal ™ syntax for the compiler directive that turns I/O checking off or on; the pair of characters { $ signals the start of a compiler directive. By default, I/O checking is on.

```
REPEAT
  Write ( 'Enter a real number: ' );
  {$I-}                              {Turn off I/O checking}
  Readln ( Value );                  {Now, nondigit input will not crash program}
  {$I+}                              {Turn on I/O checking again}
UNTIL IOResult = 0;                  {Obtain code from last I/O operation; 0 = okay}
```

Examine the reference manual of your own compiler to determine if it recognizes some type of compiler directive syntax to turn I/O checking on and off as well as providing a native I/O checking function similar to `IOResult`.

A common alternative to turning off I/O checking before reading numeric input is to always read any numeric input as a character string, which the program must then convert to either an integer or to a real value. As with the I/O checking example, invalid input can be detected and handled by the program rather than by the operating system.

1.3 SOFTWARE DEVELOPMENT

Taking a Modular Approach to Designing Programs

Recall from Section 1.2 that a program is modular when it is constructed using (a) numerous routines, each responsible for a particular task or set of tasks, and (b) a concise main routine that provides central control of the program's execution flow. For large, complex programs, distributing a program's workload among many independent routines (and transferring data via parameters) is a far better practice than writing one large main routine and few or no procedures and functions.

The modular approach to program design consists of two strategies: *top-down design* and *bottom-up implementation:*

Top-down design is the "divide-and-conquer" process of redefining a problem as a set of smaller subproblems; by solving each subproblem in turn, the overall problem is solved.

Bottom-up implementation is the process of solving the lowest-level subproblem first, then solving the next higher level of subproblem that relies on a solution from the first subproblem, and so forth, until the original problem is solved.

The concept of modularity through top-down design and bottom-up implementation is not limited to the problem of constructing a computer program but is useful in solving almost any problem or completing any complicated project, such as building a house.

Someone wishing to build a house on an empty lot probably would not perform all the work alone. Instead, the person would hire an architect to design the house and a general contractor to supervise the actual construction. Initially, the architect has the freedom to structure the house in virtually any way the owner desires, without having to worry too much about construction issues (after all, almost anything is possible on paper!). The architect can specify that the master bath should contain a whirlpool bath, for example, without knowing exactly how to install a whirlpool bath.

Of course, the architect cannot become totally divorced from *all* construction issues during the design stage. The floor of the master bathroom must be strong enough to support the full weight of the whirlpool when it is used, which means the bathroom must be adjacent to a supporting wall. Nor is the design phase necessarily complete once construction begins. Unforeseen problems, such as high groundwater or a substantial increase in the cost of building materials, may require the architect to modify the original design or even replace it altogether. The owner, architect, and general contractor must work together closely until the entire house is built. Even with such idyllic cooperation, subtle flaws in initial design and/or construction may become apparent only later, when the owner actually lives in the house.

The general contractor, like the owner, will likely not build the entire house alone but will instead employ a variety of subcontractors who will hire and supervise the actual workers, as indicated in Figure 1.9.

The general contractor calls upon the various subcontractors in particular order because some tasks are *functionally dependent* upon other tasks; i.e., some tasks must be completed before others can begin. For example, the foundation must be poured before carpenters can lay the flooring. With some tasks, however, order is not critical. The inside finishing work could be performed before, after, or simultaneously with the outside finishing work.

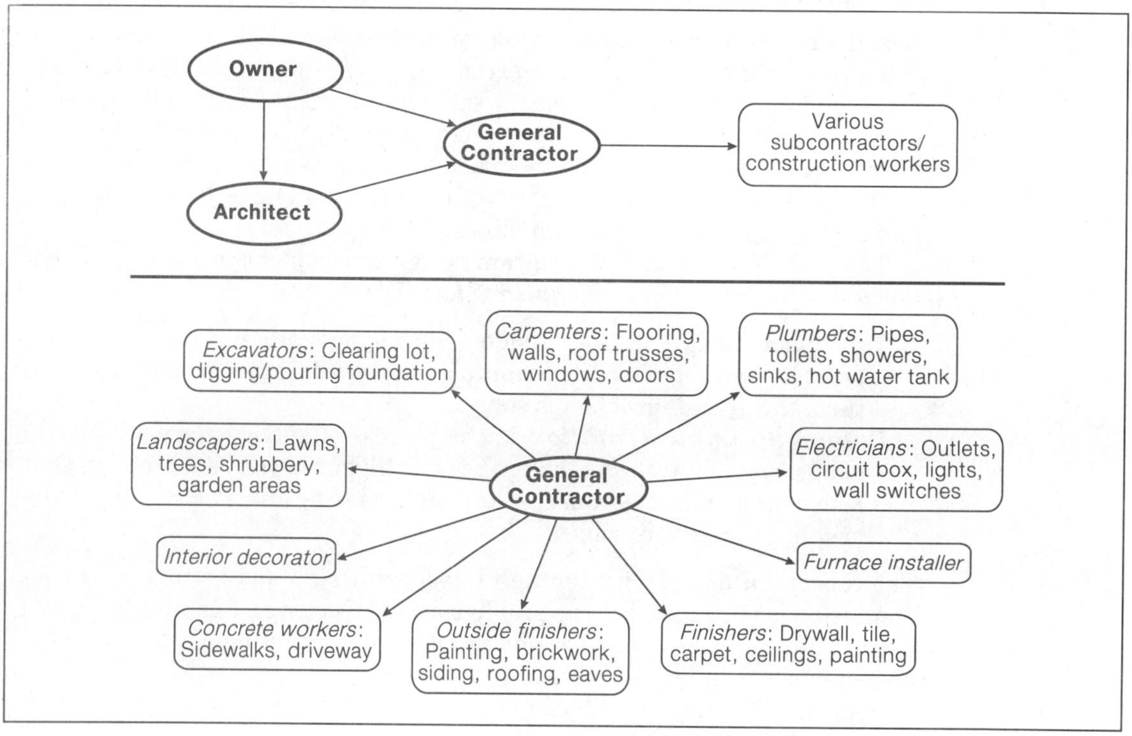

FIGURE 1.9 Division of Labor in the Construction of a House

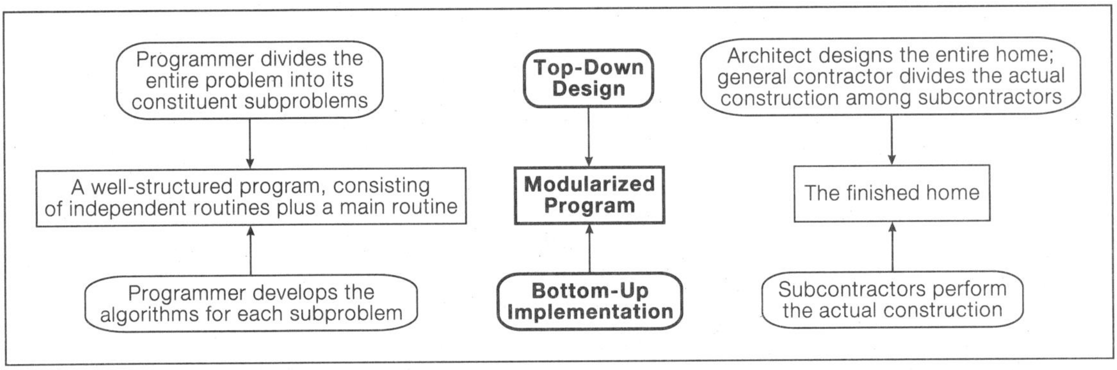

FIGURE 1.10 Top-Down Design Plus Bottom-Up Implementation Produces a Modular Program

The architect and general contractor perform a top-down design of the building process by carefully specifying the individual parts and tasks in advance. The various subcontractors then perform the bottom-up implementation of these plans. The construction of a computer program should proceed in much the same way, divided generally into the planning and actual construction stages. Figure 1.10 provides a comparison between constructing a house and constructing a computer program, illustrating how top-down design and bottom-up implementation produce a well-modularized program.

Once a sound understanding of the program's objectives is achieved, the programmer can devise a **program design**—a concise summary of the program's logic, describing each program **module.** A module is a self-contained algorithm or set of algorithms describing the steps necessary to solve a subproblem. A module for a program design is analogous to a single blueprint used by one of the building subcontractors for a single task, such as installing the kitchen cabinets or building the garage roof. Each such blueprint describes the necessary building materials for that task along with a (diagrammatic) description of how the task is to be accomplished. Just as copies of all blueprints are assembled by the general contractor into a master blueprint binder, a program design is a collection of module descriptions, including a description of the main routine.

As with a recipe for a cake or the instructions for assembling a bicycle, the format of a particular module in a program design may vary widely in terms of specificity and form. The following three general formats are used most commonly by programmers:

Pseudocode The algorithm to solve a subproblem is described using a combination of a programming language, such as Pascal, and a natural language, such as English. The program design of the blackjack program in Appendix M uses pseudocode.

Outline The algorithm to solve a subproblem is described in English (or some other natural language) in *outline* form.

Flow chart The algorithm to solve a subproblem is described as a diagram of geometric shapes (boxes, diamonds, circles, etc.), each representing an operation. Arrows connect the shapes, thereby representing the logical flow from one operation to the next. Application 6.2 uses a flowchart in its design of an infix calculator program.

The outline format is easy to write but is cumbersome for representing loops. The flowchart format provides an excellent visual overview of the logic flow of an algorithm or an entire program but is tedious to draw and modify. Pseudocode is therefore used for most applications in this textbook, but do consider the other formats as well for whatever application you are working on.

Like the architect's blueprints and the general contractor's binder of subcontractor tasks, a useful program design is the product of considerable thought and must be carefully hand-tested before it can be transformed into source code. Even with the most careful planning, **verification** (testing) of the resulting program may reveal flaws in its initial design that warrant some degree of redesign and recoding. Generally, it is far easier to make changes early, on paper, than to make changes at the computer while debugging the program. Here is a simple rule of thumb:

> Every hour spent carefully developing and hand-testing the program design saves at least 3 hours of debugging the coded program.

Just as the general contractor calls upon the various subcontractors to perform the actual construction, a computer program should be designed so its main routine calls upon various functions and procedures to do the work of the program. A computer program is best designed as a collection of independent modules and routines (procedures and functions), each performing a specific set of tasks, as described in the program design. Here is an overview of how the act of building a house mirrors the modular approach to designing a well-structured (modular) program:

Home building		Program designing
Owner, architect	→	Programmer
Collection of blueprints	→	Program design
General contractor	→	Program's main routine
Subcontractors	→	Program's routines (procedures and functions)

Development of the *program design* is therefore the most important step for any application:

> Through the program design, the programmer carefully identifies, isolates, and describes each task as a module. These modules will eventually be implemented as Pascal procedures and functions that are called upon by the main routine and by other routines.

Once written and verified, a set of programmer-defined primitive routines may be useful for other programs as well. To avoid having to retype the same source code instructions of each new program, many nonstandard compilers recognize special syntax that allows a programmer to save library type file(s). Two nonstandard techniques for doing this make use of *source code include files* and *separately compiled, programmer-defined routines:*

Source code include file An include file may contain a set of Pascal procedures, functions, and/or global declarations, just as they would appear in the main program file. At the place in the program where these routines would normally appear, the programmer inserts a nonstandard *compiler directive* that contains the name of the include file. When the compiler encounters this directive during compilation, it opens the include file specified and physically inserts the contents of the include file into the program. It then continues the compilation process, starting with the just-inserted source code.

Separately compiled, programmer-defined routines Whereas an include file contains source code that is compiled along with the rest of the main program, a set of procedures, functions, and/or declarations may be contained in another file and compiled separately. The Pascal linker program must then be called explicitly to physically append these separately compiled routines to the already-compiled main program.

Any procedure, function, or declaration in an include file or separately compiled, programmer-defined routine may be referenced within the program just as it would be if it were entered within the main program. You are encouraged to examine the reference manual of your own compiler and linker programs to determine if and how these techniques are supported.

Stages of Software Development

For large software projects, such as the development of a new operating system by a team of programmers, the concept of modularity extends to the programmers' efforts as well. Once the program design is completed, each programmer in a team is given the responsibility of transforming a particular set of modules into the actual routines. For each module, the program design must be very specific about its purpose, what information is needed from the calling module, and what information is returned to the calling module. This allows each programmer to work on a set of routines, apart from the other programmers on the team. Include files and separately compiled routines are especially helpful for this type of individual development and verification and eventual assimilation of all routines into a complete program.

As we shall see in Chapters 2 and 3, the concept of modularity applies not only to programs but to data types as well. A computer program may be developed in seven stages, as mapped out in Figure 1.11. Notice that the process is conceptual in the beginning and then becomes increasingly concrete.

The operation of Stage 1 is to define and understand the problem. Certainly, you cannot write a program to solve a problem and perform tasks without a sound understanding of the problems and desired tasks. For course projects, do not even begin writing a program design until you can describe aloud, without looking at helpful notes or diagrams, the program's intended functionality and the following:

- What information is provided by the user
- What information is provided by files
- What information (generally) is to be calculated
- What information is to be displayed or written to a file

Scrutinize any and all instructor handouts and textbook sections germane to the programming project.

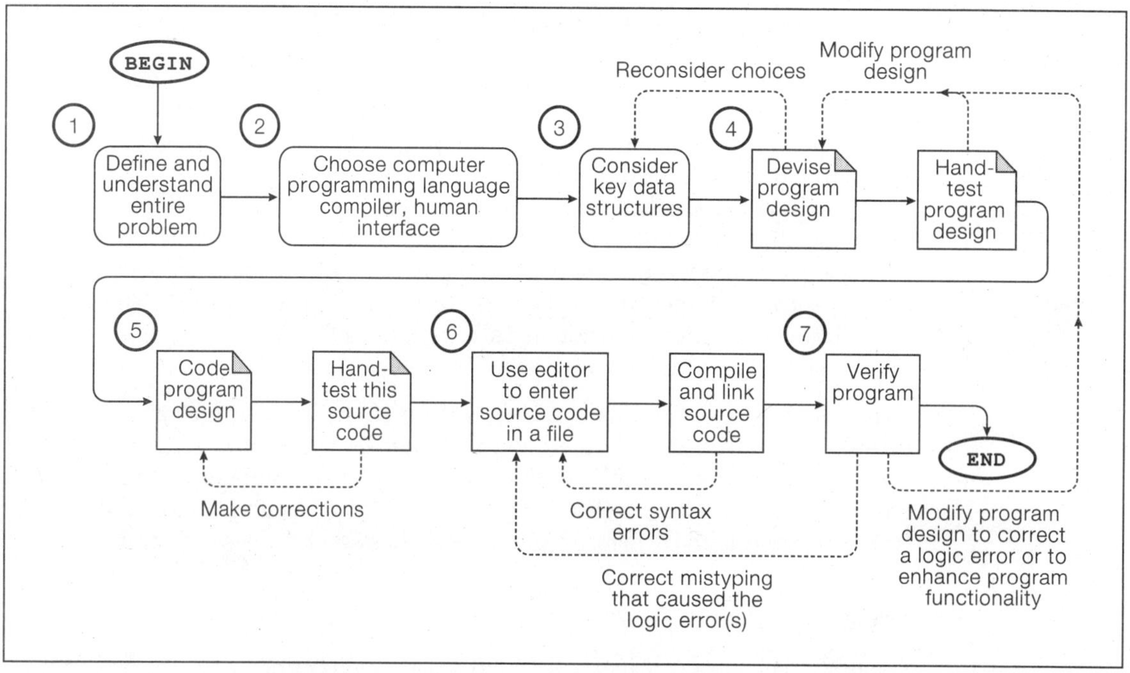

FIGURE 1.11 Stages of Program Development

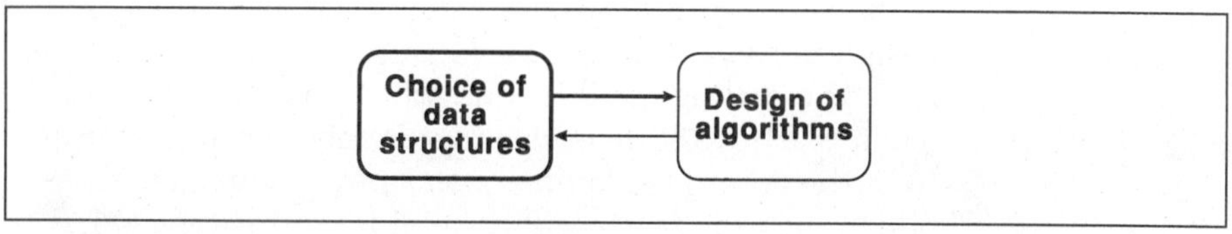

FIGURE 1.12 Interdependence of Choosing Data Structures and Designing Algorithms

After Stage 2—choosing the computer programming language, compiler, and human interface—we must consider the key data structures in Stage 3. Why choose the data structures at this point? Won't the algorithms themselves (yet to be written) drive these choices? Certainly, the *selection of data structures* and the *design of algorithms* that manipulate the data stored in the data structures are *interdependent issues*. Determining which should be considered initially (Figure 1.12) may seem reminiscent of the classic problem of determining which came first, the chicken or the egg!

We do choose key data structures before designing the algorithms (in Stage 4) simply because imagining the types of data necessary for a problem is typically easier and more intuitive than imagining the details of all necessary algorithms. To make meaningful choices about the data structures, however, we must consider, at least in an abstract way, many of the algorithms that will likely be performed on the data. We will simply be careful not to get bogged down in the details of these operations at this point. We may need to reevaluate our choice of data structures when we formally devise the program design and code the algorithms.

At this point, many novice programmers might feel compelled to race to the nearest computer and begin typing in Pascal source code as fast as possible. We are, in fact, a long way from the coding stage (Stage 5)—we must devise and hand-test the program design first, and then code the design in Pascal on paper; this must be hand-tested, as well. Only then should we enter the source code using an editor.

Recall from our discussion of modularity that the program design provides a concise summary of the program's logic, describing the algorithms to solve each subproblem. Each algorithm or set of related algorithms is packaged in a module. We will use the following format for the program design:

{Program name and author, date created and last modified, and summary description of program functionality}

I. Key Variables
{Descriptions of important variables; mainly, data structures}

II. Primitive Modules
{Descriptions of algorithms for primitive operations}

III. High-Level Modules
{Descriptions of algorithms for high-level operations}

IV. Main Module
{Descriptions of the main module operations}

A program design should describe each module using the following format:

{Module name} {Statement of module's purpose}

Needs: {The data needed from the calling module or input device}
Returns: {The data returned to the calling module or output device }

```
BEGIN
  {Pseudocode description of operations}
END;
```

At the actual coding stage (Stage 5), each module is represented as a Pascal procedure or function. The data *needed* from and *returned* to the calling routine will be represented as formal parameters. Appendix M contains a complete program design in its discussion of the development of an interactive blackjack program.

At this time, please read the program design in Stage 5 of Appendix M.

After a program is compiled, it must be verified as completely as possible. Some programs are so large and have so many functions that complete verification is difficult, if not impossible, so **beta-testing** is crucial. A program is beta-tested by giving it to one or more typical users to use extensively for a set period of time. (Programs used aboard naval combat ship computers, mentioned earlier, must be beta-tested during actual maneuvers at sea.) Even if beta-testing is planned, program verification should be systematic and carefully executed, so representative samples of possible program scenarios are generated and tested. Thorough verification may be almost as complex as creating the program design itself and may reveal design flaws not detected earlier.

The verification process should begin with tests of individual routines, one by one:

1. Write a single routine.
2. Write a short, temporary main routine (a *stub*) that calls the routine.
3. Debug the routine or a portion of the routine, as necessary.
4. Go on to the next routine.

With large programming projects involving a team of programmers, verification is a formal process monitored by the team leader, who keeps a verification log. In top-down design fashion, the verification usually begins at a high level and then examines the program at lower and lower levels. This is typically a four-stage process: walkthrough, inspection, complete code testing, and then beta-testing.

1. In the walkthrough, the team meets in a conference room and examines both the program design and the actual coded program. The team simulates execution of the program using test input data and keeping track of program data on paper or a blackboard. The walkthrough is not intended to verify all possible scenarios but rather to stimulate team discussion about how the programmers devised the program design and how they implemented the design in Pascal.
2. In the inspection, the team examines the coded program line by line in search of errors or enhancements. Individual code segments may be executed manually to insure that they handle special cases.
3. With complete testing, the team executes the program and tests the program as thoroughly as possible. Because so many diverse scenarios may arise with a complicated program, a team is often limited to identifying and testing only a representative set of cases.
4. After the complete testing stage is complete, the program is delivered to just one or several customers who agree to beta-test the program before it is released for general sale. That is, these customers agree to use the program extensively over a particular time period and report any errors or make suggestions for improvement promptly; in return, the customers are typically given free copies of the program as it is corrected and enhanced.

Design Principles and Practices

The following list summarizes important strategies when designing and verifying programs:

- *Follow the seven stages that are illustrated in Figure 1.11.*

  1. Define and understand the entire problem.
  2. Choose the computer language and compiler, computer, and the human interface.
  3. Consider key data structures.

4. Devise and hand-test the program design.
5. On paper, code the program from the design; hand-test it thoroughly.
6. Enter the source code at a computer, routine by routine, using an editor program; compile and link the program.
7. Execute and verify each routine and then the entire program.

- *Understand the problem.* Earlier comments about Stage 1 are so important they are worth repeating here. Do not even begin writing the program design until you can *describe aloud,* without looking at helpful notes or diagrams, *the program's intended functionality,* including a general description of program input and output. Scrutinize any and all instructor handouts and textbook sections germane to the programming project.
- *Program design.* Take the time to devise carefully a comprehensive and detailed program design; then hand-test this design thoroughly before writing the program. If you do not know how to begin writing the design, start with *main routine comments* and then group comments as procedure and function comments. Eventually, the form of the program will evolve.

  A statement about this stage made earlier is also worth repeating here:

  > Every hour spent carefully developing and hand-testing the program design saves 3 hours of debugging the finished program.

- *Begin basically.* Always begin with the most basic version of a program, devoid of error-handling code and other enhancements. Once the basic version runs correctly, you can begin extending the functionality of the program, one feature at a time.
- *Programming style.* Employ sound programming style in *every* code segment you write, including temporary verification/debugging statements.
- *Documentation.* Include comments in the program as you write the code; do not wait until the program is entirely written and debugged.

At this time please read Appendix M.

1.4 DEBUGGING STRATEGIES

Although prompt and effective program debugging is a craft acquired over many hours and programs, your own learning curve can be shortened dramatically by following a number of well-proven practices. In this section, we examine general strategies for debugging computer programs.

As we have seen, the form of a particular computer program takes shape over a number of stages, the foremost of which is Stage 4, Devise the Program Design. Obviously, the more error-free this design, the faster an error-free program can be developed. Even so, there are typically one or more issues and details that do not seem to surface until the program is actually coded and verified (Stages 5, 6, and 7). All but the most trivial of programs invariably contain errors initially, so do not be discouraged if yours fails to compile and execute perfectly the first time.

There are two basic types of programming error:

Syntax errors are violations of the Pascal language, usually detected by the compiler during compilation.

Logic errors involve statements that do not necessarily violate the syntax of the Pascal language, yet product incorrect results during execution because one or more instructions are inappropriate for the intended operation(s). Logic errors that cause the program to crash are dubbed *fatal runtime errors*.

We will now examine both types of errors and ways of dealing with them.

Syntax Errors

Typically, a syntax error is easier to locate and correct than a logic error is because, with each syntax error, most compilers will issue an error message indicating

1. Where in the source program a particular error is detected, and
2. A brief guess as to its cause.

The operative word here is *guess,* however, and the novice programmer learns quickly that such error messages should not be read too literally. A compiler error message merely indicates that some kind of syntactical mistake has occurred *at or before* the implicated statement and offers only a (possible) clue as to the nature of the problem. The actual cause of the problem and the location of the errant statement may be quite different.

It is important to figure out and fix the first error first! Errors early in the program can cause the compiler to generate many confusing error messages later in the program. Accordingly, correcting one syntax error can eliminate dozens of spurious compiler error messages that follow. If a compiler error message does not seem to make sense, carefully examine the code starting with the flagged statement and work backward, toward the `PROGRAM` statement.

A common syntax error with far-reaching effects is the *undelimited comment*—i.e., a comment in which the } or *) delimiter characters are missing. Such an omission may cause the compiler to flag a number of otherwise legal Pascal statements as being illegal. The *undelimited literal string* is also typically less destructive because most Pascal compilers do not permit a literal string to extend to a second line. Other common syntax errors include the following:

- Misspelled identifier, including a procedure or function name
- Unbalanced parentheses within an expression
- Incompatible actual and formal parameters or arguments
- Incorrect reference to a record field

- Missing **END**
- Missing semicolon(**;**)
- Missing or misplaced **BEGIN** and **END** pair within an **IF**, **WHILE**, or **FOR** statement
- Missing parentheses around Boolean expressions within an **IF** statement

Logic Errors

Just as a compiler issues an error message during compilation when the source code violates the rules of Pascal syntax, the operating system will terminate the program and issue an error message during runtime anytime the program violates the rules of execution. And just as syntax errors halt the compilation process, fatal runtime errors—as the term implies—cause the execution process to halt. The following common logic errors will typically cause an operating system to crash a program.

- Arithmetic errors
  - Division by zero
  - Passing a negative argument to the standard `Sqrt` function
  - Passing an invalid argument to the standard `Sin`, `Cos`, and `ArcTan` functions
  - Passing an invalid argument to the standard `Ln` function
  - Arithmetic underflow or overflow
- File-handling errors
  - Opening a nonexistent file for reading
  - Opening a nonexistent file for writing when not enough memory is available in the directory or volume for a new file
  - Referencing a file that has not been opened
  - Reading from a file opened for writing, or vice versa
  - Reading past the physical end of a file
  - Reading a nondigit character from a text file into a numeric variable
- Memory reference or usage errors
  - Using an invalid pointer-type address value
  - Illegal use of the **NIL** pointer value
  - Heapspace overflow

Undelimited Comments and Literal Strings

Sometimes the undelimited comment and undelimited literal string will escape detection by the compiler because no rules of syntax are violated, yet either may cause logical errors at runtime. The following enhanced version of the `ExtractRoots` procedure first presented in Section 1.2 will compile cleanly even though it contains serious logic errors. Unlike the initial version of the procedure, this version is intended to perform error handling of the parameter values. As an exercise, find the logic errors and predict the types of incorrect processing that might result if the procedure were executed as is:

```
PROCEDURE  ExtractRoots ( a, b, c : Real;  VAR Root1, Root2 : Real );

VAR
  Square, Divisor,
  SquareRoot       :  Real;

BEGIN
Square   := b * b - 4 * a * c;
Divisor  := 2 * a;

IF Square < 0 THEN                    {Error:  Cannot take Sqrt of a negative number
  Writeln ( 'ERROR:  b*b - 4ac = , Square,  which is negative' )
ELSE                                  {Quantity is positive; can derive the roots}
  SquareRoot := Sqrt ( Square );

  Root1  := (-b + SquareRoot) / Divisor;  {Derive the 1st root}
  Root2  := (-b - SquareRoot) / Divisor   {Derive the 2nd root}
END;
```

The first logic error involves the comment on the same line as the **THEN**: Because the } is missing, the comment is undelimited as a one-line comment. The compiler interprets all characters on subsequent lines as part of the comment until the next } is encountered. This effectively leaves a simple **IF** statement:

```
IF Square < 0 THEN
  SquareRoot := Sqrt ( Square );
```

Consequently, whenever `Square` contains a negative value, `Sqrt` will be called anyway, causing the operating system to crash the program. Equally disastrous, when `Square` contains a positive value, this assignment to `SquareRoot` is bypassed completely, and an undefined `SquareRoot` value is therefore used in the `Root1` and `Root2` assignment statements that follow.

When the first comment is properly delimited and `Square` does contain a negative value, the second logic error is revealed: Two quotation marks are missing in the error message within the `Writeln` statement. With these omissions, the compiler recognizes a single literal string parameter to `Writeln` rather than three parameters. This causes the computer to display the following message, exactly as shown here:

```
ERROR: b*b - 4ac = , Square, which is negative
```

Even if the first two errors are corrected, a third logic error will make its presence known whenever `Square` has a negative value. The `Root1` and `Root2` assignment statements should be executed only if `Square` is found to have a positive value and its square root was derived. Because these two assignment statements are not enclosed within a **BEGIN/END** block following the **ELSE** (along with the `SquareRoot` assignment statement), they will always be executed, regardless of the sign of the `Square` value. Omission of a necessary **BEGIN** and **END** is a very common error, especially when the statements are otherwise properly indented, as with the Root1 and Root2 assignment statements. Here, the indentation is actually misleading to the reader.

Sporadic Off-By-One Errors

Errors that produce incorrect results only sporadically can be particularly frustrating to track down. Among these is the pesky **off-by-one error,** which may or may not result in a runtime error. For example, the following function is intended to read a series of integers until a negative number is read (the *trailer method* of delimiting input), then the function calculates and returns the average of these values. Find the logic error:

```
FUNCTION Mean : Real;

VAR
  Sum, Count, Value : Integer;

BEGIN
Writeln ( 'Enter positive integer values, the last of which is negative:' );
Sum    := 0;
Count  := 0;
REPEAT
  Read ( Value );
  Sum    := Sum + Value;
  Count  := Count + 1
UNTIL Value < 0;
Mean := Sum / Count
END;
```

The off-by-one error here stems from the fact that the negative number read is figured into the calculation of the mean, although it was intended only to flag the end of the input stream. To fix the error, we can rotate the loop body so the value just read is tested immediately. This rotation requires an additional Read statement before the loop to prime the process. We must also replace the **REPEAT** loop with a **WHILE** loop to handle correctly the *special case* that the initial value itself might be negative. The corrected and enhanced portion of function (after the initialization of Count) follows:

```
Sum    := 0;
Count  := 0;
Read ( Value );             {This "primes" the process}
WHILE Value >= 0 DO
  BEGIN
  Sum    := Sum + Value;
  Count  := Count + 1;
  Read ( Value )            {Rotated; Value now tested before added to Sum}
  END;

IF Count > 0 THEN           {Error-testing necessary if first value is negative}
  Mean  := Sum / Count
ELSE
  Mean  := 0                {Flag value indicating first value was negative}
END;
```

Many Pascal compilers require that the source include an explicit compiler directive statement if it is to include machine-code instructions that perform **array-bounds checking.** Array-bounds checking tests the legality of each array reference; an illegal reference found only at runtime causes the program to crash. An explicit compiler directive is required by these compilers because the additional machine-code instructions may significantly increase the size of the compiled program. Programmers typically include such a directive while the program is being developed and verified and then remove the directive to shorten the length of the compiled program.

As another source of off-by-one errors, most Pascal compilers will evaluate all subexpressions within a Boolean expression, even if the falsity of one subexpression should, intuitively, preclude the evaluation of the remaining subexpressions. As an example, assume that Items is an array of 100 elements, each capable of holding an integer value. The following code segment is intended to locate the first element that contains the value **MAXINT** and assign its index number to integer variable Index. Unfortunately, if array-bounds checking is turned on and none of the values in the array contains the value **MAXINT**, execution of this segment will cause the program to crash; do you see why?

```
Index := 1;
WHILE ( Index <= 100 ) AND ( Items [ Index ] <> MAXINT ) DO
  Index := Index + 1;
```

Both subexpressions of the Boolean expression in the **WHILE** statement are always evaluated, even when `Index` contains 101 and the program crashes because the expression `Items [ 101 ]` is illegal. To correct this problem, the tests for end-of-array and a matching element value must be made independently, with the test for end-of-array made first. A corrected version follows:

```
Index := 1;
Done  := FALSE
WHILE ( Index <= 100 ) AND NOT Done DO
  IF Items [ Index ] = MAXINT THEN
    Done := TRUE
  ELSE
    Index := Index + 1
```

This need to break up tests arises often when working with lists, as we shall see in Chapter 5 discussions regarding linked lists.

The absence of array-bounds checking, however, may produce a particularly strange and sporadic off-by-one error. For example, consider the following simple code segment:

```
VAR
  Items      : ARRAY [ 1..100 ] OF Integer;
  Index, K   : Integer;

BEGIN
Index := 0;
FOR K := 1 TO 101 DO
  Items [ K ] := MAXINT;
```

If array-bounds checking is turned off when `K` acquires the value 101, the integer worth of memory following the 100th array element is assigned the value **`MAXINT`**, since the array contains only 100 elements. Because of the ordering of the variable declarations, this is the memory location for the variable `Index`. Therefore, the value of `Index` is changed from zero to **`MAXINT`**, although there is no explicit assignment of this value to `Index` in the code.

Debugging Principles and Practices

Tracking down the source of a logic error is especially challenging if the error is nonfatal and, therefore, no operating system error messages are displayed. In these situations, the programmer must play detective, proposing and testing theories while carefully narrowing the suspected area within the program where the error might have occurred. The hunt may begin with the examination of several procedures and functions, then concentrate on a particular procedure or function, then focus on a particular code segment, and, finally, pinpoint a particular statement. The error may be slight, such as a missing **`BEGIN`** and **`END`**, or the error may reveal a substantive flaw in the program design. Logic errors often involve the program's inability to handle special cases.

Sound Advice

Think back to the three logic puzzles presented at the start of this chapter. The difficulty of each puzzle stems from a particular mental roadblock that can arise when designing and debugging programs. (If necessary, review these puzzles and their solutions at this time.)

- *Consider simple solutions first.* The socks puzzle (Puzzle 1) illustrates that a problem appearing complex at first glance does not necessarily require a complex solution. Seek out and test simple solutions to problems before wasting time devising and testing complex solutions.
- *Consider unusual explanations.* The nine-dot puzzle (2) suggests that, when traditional debugging techniques fail to uncover a logic error, you should consider *unusual* explanations for a program's abnormal behavior. Similarly, if you cannot think of traditional methods when designing an algorithm to solve a problem, consider unusual methods.
- *Make no assumptions.* The mirror puzzle (3) illustrates the fact that programmers often hinder their own efforts at problem solving by making unproven assumptions. They are then at a loss to explain a program's unexpected behavior. Do not assume that a particular programmer-designed procedure, function, main routine, or any code segment works (or does not work) without explicitly testing it. When you find yourself saying, "I don't have to test my routine, I simply know it works," immediately *stop* and test that routine!
  Remember: A Pascal compiler will not compensate for your invalid assumptions.

It is sometimes necessary to make creative leaps in the otherwise sequential investigative process. A novice programmer might spend hours examining and reexamining procedure `X`, swearing aloud that its logic is flawless, and conclude that the compiler is defective. This programmer may not even consider, for example, that a problem *outside* procedure `X` is affecting the activity *within* that procedure. Perhaps invalid data are being passed into procedure `X` when it is called. Perhaps when procedure `Y` is called from within `X`, it is inadvertently returning a contaminating parameter value because **VAR** was accidently inserted in front of one of its formal parameters. When the obvious answers do not pan out, even the improbable and indirect ones must be considered. And when all else fails, test the relevant native Pascal routines—perhaps you misunderstand how they work, or, in very rare cases, one of them may contain a bug.

The following is a potpourri of sound advice regarding the debugging process (many of these items are applicable to the task of devising a program design as well):

- Don't cut corners—become a master programmer
  - *Fully understand your program both as it was intended to be coded and as it has actually been coded.* You cannot track down and correct subtle logic errors in a program you do not understand. One reason a great deal of learning about programming occurs during debugging is that the process forces programmers to understand the rules of Pascal syntax and the logic of their own programs thoroughly.
  - *Accordingly, do not make any code modifications that you do not understand thoroughly.* Avoid making random changes to the program in the hopes that, by luck, you will happen upon the magical solution. This is typically a waste of time and, if at all successful, usually results in only a partial, nonversatile fix that may spawn new logic errors.
- Play it safe
  - *Use only current information.* Always work with a hard copy of the source code that reflects the current state of the source code. Pencil in changes as they are made; then obtain a fresh hard copy after making many such changes.
  - *Retain the last working copy.* As you debug, save a hard copy and a soft copy of the original source code (i.e., as it appeared before the debugging process began), as well as a copy of the last working version before the most recent changes were made. This way you can always return to the last working version if necessary.
  - *Back up, back up, back up!* A task that most novice programmers find difficult to discipline themselves to do (along with typing in source code comments) is to back up their work regularly. Few experiences in life rival the agony of losing hours of work because of a system crash or accidently deleting or overwriting a file. (The latter tends to happen most frequently late at night, after long programming sessions, so be especially careful of this danger when you are tired.)

    Maintain at least two soft copies of important programs. Keep the copies on separate disks and store the disks in different places. Always keep at least one of these disks at home, safely tucked away and protected from extreme heat or cold, magnetic fields, and prying fingers. As you work at the computer, save your editing work to a text file at least once every 20 minutes if the editor does not do this automatically for you. Save your work on a backup disk at least once an hour and at the end of a lengthy session. Use your second disk for less frequent backups.

- Be conservative
  - *Correct any uncovered logic errors immediately.* Whenever any logic error is discovered, correct it and recompile the program immediately, even if the error seems unrelated to the error originally pursued. Often, there is a connection and the correction of one error may automatically remove many others.
  - *Make only marginal modifications.* When you suspect the cause of an error, make only small changes to the program rather than rewriting large portions all at once. Verify these modifications before making further modifications. Be careful that the change itself does not create new logic errors.
  - *If it isn't broken, don't fix it!* Stick to fixing errors and simply getting a basic version of the program running correctly and completely first. Do this before making nonessential changes, such as enhancements that produce slightly neater output or make the program run slightly more efficiently.
  - *Clean up your code.* Programs tend to become messy after several rounds of modifications, and bugs can hide in the mess. Periodically, clean up your code. Simplify logic where you can. Fix any indenting that is wrong. Make sure you are following the instructor's guidelines for style and parameter use. A surprising number of errors are found in this cleanup process.

- Manage your resources wisely
  - *Debug with fresh eyes and an alert mind.* Intense debugging often becomes frustrating and fruitless when you become mentally tired. Choose to debug during that time of day when you are most alert. Although the process of debugging a program often extends far into the night, skipping meals and sleep will only slow you down and cloud your analytical prowess.

    If a prolonged and earnest debugging effort proves fruitless, take a break. Go for a walk, exercise, watch a movie with a friend, or visit your favorite restaurant. Resume debugging only after you feel relaxed, perhaps after a sound night's sleep, and you may be surprised at how quickly and easily the process flows from there. You must learn to recognize when you are becoming ineffective due to fatigue and then suspend your efforts for a time.
  - *Do not skip programming classes to work on a programming project.* Often, your instructor will talk about the project explicitly or lecture on topics germane to the project, and questions by other students often lead to interesting and informative discussions. By attending class regularly, you may also discover that the instructor has modified the project constraints, that the data file everyone in class has been using is faulty, or even that the project deadline has been extended.
  - *Consider all sources of assistance.* Review class notes, peruse textbooks, and discuss the problem with your instructor and classmates as necessary. Be careful to ask your instructor to what extent discussion among classmates is permissible and not considered cheating.

- *Perhaps start over.* If you find yourself making substantive changes to the program repeatedly, perhaps the Pascal implementation of the program design—or the program design itself—is so flawed that the entire coded program, and possibly the program design as well, should be thrown away. After taking a good rest and a deep breath you can make a fresh start. This is not giving in to failure but, instead, reflects the wise reallocation of your time and energy.

The Debugging Process

Tracking down and correcting logic errors involves repeated application of the following two operations:

1. *Theorizing and reconnaissance* involves guessing about the nature of the error and then inserting one or more temporary code segments—perhaps involving `Writeln` statements—to gather information to support or refute the guess.
2. *Coding a tentative solution and verifying the change.*

Some errors may be obvious to you and can therefore be located and corrected immediately. Others are more elusive and require additional information. The `Writeln` statement provides a window into the program during runtime and provides two valuable types of trace information:

- A trace of the *execution flow* throughout the program—i.e., an indication of which instructions in the program the computer actually has executed or where it currently is in the program.
- The *value of a variable* at any point during runtime.

Each `Writeln` should display the word `DEBUG` or some other indication distinguishing temporary output from the regular program output. Also, each temporary `Writeln` line should be ended with `{DEBUG}` or some other kind of comment, such as your initials, so these statements can be quickly located and removed once the logic error is found and corrected.

When you do not know where to start, *start at the beginning*. Trace the execution flow by hand, starting with the very first statment in the program's main routine. *Do not assume that any programmer-defined routine works without explicitly testing it.* Carefully examine and hand-test a hard copy of the program in a quiet surrounding before testing during runtime on a computer. Plod along slowly but systematically. Draw and redraw pictures of data structures and their contents and use the ***inverted-stack technique*** for simple data type variables: Next to each routine, write the name of each parameter and local variable with a pen, underlining each name. The first time a variable acquires a value, write that value beneath the variable's underlined name. Each time a variable acquires a new value as you hand-execute the program, write this new value directly beneath the prior value, which should be crossed out. Drawing pictures and using the inverted-stack technique are also useful during a computer science examination when you must hand-execute a code segment.

To generate a runtime trace of the complete execution flow, insert an informative `Writeln` as the first and last executable statement in each procedure and function. Also insert a `Writeln` in any loop suspected of containing a bug (always display the value of the loop variable). The `Writeln` is especially useful in locating where in the source code a program is crashing mysteriously. Additional information may be displayed within the `Writeln` as well.

Neatly label and align all values displayed by a temporary `Writeln`. The additional time required to do this will be more than compensated for by the time saved in debugging, especially when a variety of values are being displayed. If values are not labeled, you will run a real risk of misinterpreting them as they are displayed.

SUMMARY

Many issues beyond the basic correctness must be considered when designing and developing programs. The quality of a program is a function of its program structure, functionality, and performance. Program structure refers to how the program is actually written and arranged within the program and is largely a product of modularity, programming style, and parameter passing. Program functionality refers to how correctly the program actually does what it was originally intended to do and how easily it may be used for other, similar applications and on other computers. Functionality is gauged by reliability, versatility, and portability. Program performance indicates how well the program (a) interacts with its human user or with another device, (b) manages the resources of computer memory and execution time, and (c) handles unusual circumstances, such as erroneous input, that arise at runtime. Performance is measured by the program's user-friendliness, efficiency, and robustness.

Primitive operations are basic, special-purpose operations that serve as building blocks to support more complex high-level operations in a program. In addition to the predefined primitive procedures and functions provided by a Pascal compiler (i.e., native routines), programs typically require programmer-defined routines—primitive and high-level—specific to the application at hand. Program routines must be kept functionally independent from each other, exchanging data through parameters and arguments as necessary. This design philosophy of information hiding is an example of the dichotomy of abstraction and implementation—i.e., the separation of the (abstract) logical properties of something from its actual (concrete) implementation.

A program is modular when it is designed such that the work load is distributed among numerous routines and the program has a concise main routine that, when read by any programmer, provides an overview of the logic flow of the entire program. Generally, the more modular a program is the easier it is to build and verify, to have another programmer follow the logic flow, and to debug. Use of the Pascal `GoTo` statement should be avoided because it is almost always unnecessary and results in spaghetti logic flow for any programmer reading the code.

Devising a modular program involves top-down design and bottom-up implementation. Top-down design is the divide-and-conquer process of redefining a problem as a set of smaller subproblems; by solving each subproblem in turn, the overall problem is solved. Bottom-up implementation involves solving the lowest-level subproblem first (via a procedure or function), then solving the next higher level of subproblem that relies on a solution from the first subproblem, and so forth until the original problem is solved.

A program should be written using accepted stylistic conventions consistently to represent algorithms in a manner that uses a minimum number of statements while still clearly conveying to the human reader the underlying logic of those algorithms. This minimizes programmer time and effort. Often, the most concise form of an expression may be obtained readily from a truth table.

Program reliability refers to how well the final program actually generates the results it was originally intended to produce. A program or routine is versatile if it can be used in a variety of different situations. Program portability is a measure of how readily a compiled program may be run on computers other than the original computer used to develop that program.

Two forms of interaction between a user and the program (the human interface) are batch and interactive processing, and a program may involve aspects of both. Four basic techniques for a program to obtain input from the keyboard interactively are command lines, menus and icons, individual prompts and continuous asynchronous input.

When designing programs, (a) minimize shifting data about in memory, (b) minimize file accesses, (c) use **VAR** before any large formal parameter, and (d) remove invariant operations.

When a new program is developed, much of the programmer's time should be spent to devise, fine-tune, and hand-test the program design, which is then transformed into a Pascal program (modules become procedures and functions). A program design is written by a programmer to organize and summarize the logic of a program. Through the program design, the programmer carefully identifies, isolates, and describes each task as a module, which will eventually be implemented as Pascal procedures and functions that are called upon by the main routine and other routines. It may be written in the form of pseudocode, an outline, or a flowchart.

Two nonstandard techniques for making code available to other programs involve the use of source code include files and separately compiled, programmer-defined routines.

Stages of program development include (1) understanding the overall problem, (2) choosing the programming language, compiler, and basic human interface, (3) considering key data structures, (4) devising and hand-testing the program design, (5) on paper, coding the program from the design and hand-testing it thoroughly, (6) entering the source code at a computer, (7) executing and verifying each routine, groups of routine, and then the entire program.

Two basic types of programming error are syntax errors (violations of Pascal language) and logic errors (errors that produce incorrect results or crash the program). When debugging, one should consider simple solutions first, consider unusual explanations, and make no assumptions about the correctness of a given procedure or function without actually testing it. (Section 1.4 contains a list of other valuable advice regarding debugging and designing programs.) Tracking down and correcting logic errors involves repeated application of the following: (a) theorizing and reconnaissance (guessing about the nature of the error and inserting temporary statements to gather information) and (b) coding a tentative solution and then verifying the change.

KEY TERMS

Array-bounds checking
Batch processing
Beta-testing
Bottom-up implementation
Command line
Efficiency
Fatal runtime error
Flowchart
High-level operation
Individual prompt
Information hiding
Interactive processing
Invariant operation
Library file of routines
Logic error
Menu
Modularity
Module
Module tree diagram
Native
Nonstandard routine
Off-by-one error
Parameter passing
Portability
Primitive operations
Program design
Program functionality
Program performance
Program structure
Program stub
Programmer-defined routine
Programming style
Pseudocode
Pull-down menu
Reliability
Robustness
Routine
Separately compiled routines
Source code include file
Syntax error
Top-down design
Transparent operation
Truth table
User-friendly
Undelimited comment
Versatility

REVIEW QUESTIONS

1. Describe the qualities of a well-written computer program.
2. A modular program results when the programmer has employed ***top-down design*** and *bottom-up implementation*. Define these two terms and describe how they contribute to a well-structured program.
3. What is a program design and how does it relate to the finished, coded program? Describe the three formats commonly used to represent a program design.
4. Name the channels through which information flows into and out of a routine. In what respects does every module or routine have a contract with every routine that calls it?
5. Distinguish among algorithm, module, and routine. Distinguish among predefined, native, standard, and programmer-defined routines.
6. Contrast high-level and primitive routines.
7. Distinguish between the use of an include file and the use of a separately compiled routine. How and why might such nonstandard practices be helpful, especially with a large, multiprogrammer program?
8. Describe three advantages to taking a modular approach in programming.
9. What is meant by *programming style?*
10. Distinguish between versatility and robustness.
11. Distinguish between batch and interactive processing.
12. Contrast the command-line, menu, and individual prompts as interactive methods of obtaining input. Describe other nonstandard methods of obtaining input and displaying output.
13. Describe the general principles of efficiency given in Section 1.2.
14. State three reasons for employing full parameter passing in programs.
15. Describe the seven stages of program development given in Section 1.3. Why does the choice of data structures drive the choice/development of algorithms rather than the converse?

16. Describe the format of a program design.

17. Distinguish among syntax error, logic error, and fatal runtime error. Could a particular programming error (e.g., an undelimited comment) be classified as being all three types of error? Does a compiler issue a message for all types of syntax errors? Does an operating system issue a message for all types of logic error?

18. Correcting logic errors involves the repeated application of what two operations? Placement of temporary `Writeln` statements provides a window into the program and provides what two types of trace information?

CHAPTER TWO

FUNDAMENTAL SIMPLE DATA TYPES

In the first section of this chpater you will learn about the different ways of classifying information useful to computer programming and about the interdependence of data and operations performed upon the data. Two important products of the discussion will be the *abstract data type (ADT) specification* as a template for accurately describing a particular data type and the importance of *data abstraction* during the design phase of program development. The remaining sections describe five fundamental simple data types.

2.1 DESCRIBING A DATA TYPE

All computer programs direct a computer to manipulate data in order to produce some result(s). Exactly what is meant by the term *data*? Webster's *New Universal Unabridged Dictionary, Second Edition,* by Dorset and Baber, defines the term datum (a singular data item) as follows:

> (2) a real or assumed thing used as a basis for calculations . . . ;
> (3) . . . certain relations or quantities, given or known, from which unknown quantities are determined.

Implicit in these definitions is the notion of usefulness. In designing a computer program (or solving any problem, for that matter), the programmer certainly needs to identify and write instructions to manipulate only that information that is relevant—information that moves the entire problem-solving process closer to a solution.

Some data seem inherently similar in nature, such as numbers or characters. If items all share a common set of characteristics, they are said to belong to the same **data type.** In Pascal, the value of every constant, variable, and function belongs to a particular data type. The type of each variable and function must be explicitly specified in a Pascal **CONST**, **TYPE**, or **VAR** declaration or at the end of a **FUNCTION** header statement. In this section, we will examine the criteria for defining data types that are fundamental to programming.

Basic Definition

The definition of any data type begins with a description of its two fundamental characteristics:

1. **Domain.** The set of all possible values.
2. **Fundamental operations.** The collection of possible operations that may be performed on these values.

For example, the symbol 5 represents the number five, which belongs to a data type in Pascal called integer. In an abstract, mathematical sense the integer data type includes the set of whole numbers whose values range from negative infinity to positive infinity. Within the Pascal language, however, the domain is much narrower, since the computer must ultimately represent integer values using a finite physical memory space. Among the possible integer operations are addition, subtraction, multiplication, and division. Concatenation—the operation of joining two character strings to form a single character string—is *not* an operation applicable to integers. For example, `'15'` concatenated with `'82'` produces the character string `'1582'`, whereas the number 15 cannot be concatenated mathematically with the number 82 to produce 1582! The 15 and 82 may, of course, be combined using a valid mathematical operation such as addition or multiplication.

This level of precision in defining a data type may seem tedious for common types such as integer, real, and char because you probably used them extensively in your first programming course. For many other useful data types such as stacks, queues, trees, and graphs, it is the very act of describing exactly what values and what operations are possible that truly creates the data type.

Recall that a predefined (native) routine is a routine automatically known to the compiler in use, unlike a programmer-defined routine, which must be explicitly coded within the program. Similarly, a predefined (native) data type is a type that a compiler already knows about—i.e., the compiler recognizes the identifier used in a variable declaration (integer, real, etc.) as well as special symbols used as operators for that type (+, /, **DIV**, etc.) and predefined identifier constants (**TRUE**, **MAXINT**, etc.). Each compiler recognizes a set of predefined data types, operators, and predefined constants as well as a set of procedures and functions, such as `Write`, `Readln`, `Trunc`, and `Length`. A **standard data type** is a type that is native to all Pascal compilers, as required by International ANSI Pascal Standard.

Eleven data types are standard for Pascal compilers and involve the following identifiers or notations used in a **TYPE** or **VAR** declaration:

`Integer`	**ARRAY OF**
`Real`	**RECORD**
`Boolean`	**SET OF**
`Char`	**FILE OF**
enumerated type notation	`Text`
^ (Pascal pointer type)	

Pascal compilers also allow a programmer to specify a subrange of integer, char, and enumerated type constant values using `..` syntax.

For each of these types, a Pascal compiler already knows the allowable operations and the domain (all but the first four require that the programmer furnish additional information in the declaration describing the size and/or items in the domain). Some operations on these types are so commonly needed in programs that standard Pascal requires all Pascal compilers to recognize special symbols and identifiers for them. Appendix A lists all standard operator symbols and other standard syntax.

An important feature of Pascal is that it allows a programmer to invent a **programmer-defined data type** and its accompanying set of fundamental operations. The domain of values and fundamental operations will actually be based on native data types and operations used in some restrictive way, as determined by the programmer. In the coming chapters, we examine many of the programmer-defined types that are commonly used in programming, including the following:

Tables	General trees	Graphs
Linked lists	Binary search trees	Spanning trees
Tries	Priority queues	2-3 trees
Stacks	Heaps	Hash tables
FIFO Queues	Game trees	B-trees

As an example of a programmer-defined type, we will create a data type called `Primes`, whose domain consists only of prime numbers. (A prime number is an integer greater than 1 whose only positive integer divisors are itself and 1.) For example, 3, 5, 7, 11, and 53 are prime, whereas −3, 0, 4, and 51 are not. We can represent this data type in Pascal using the standard data type integer, as follows:

```
TYPE
  Primes = Integer;          {Restricted by usage to prime integer values}

VAR
  PrimeVariable : Primes;
```

All integer operations except assignment will be applicable to `Primes` type values and variables. We must restrict assignment to `PrimeVariable` so that only prime numbers are assigned. The standard assignment operator (`:=`) alone is insufficient, since it does not distinguish between the assignment of a *prime integer value* and the assignment of a *nonprime integer value*. Of course, the compiler or operating system would detect the attempted assignment of a noninteger value, but this is not sufficient, since many integer values are not prime. For example, consider the following statements:

```
PrimeVariable  := 3.14;  {Compile-time error: 3.14 is real, not integer}

PrimeVariable  := 6;     {Logic error not detected by compiler: 6 is not prime}
```

The second assignment is not an illegal use of the integer data type, but is an illegal use of the `Primes` data type.

Since `Primes` is a programmer-defined type, the error-checking that must precede an assignment operation must be programmer-defined as well. The following `APrime` Boolean function and `PrimeAssign` procedure have been written for this purpose. Function `APrime` evaluates to a true value if its argument is prime. `PrimeAssign` assigns the value of `NewValue` to `Target` if this value is prime; function `APrime` returns a true value if its argument—`NewValue`—is prime. Therefore, a call to `Primes` is tantamount to an assignment operation on `Target` if `NewValue` contains a prime value. `APrime` repeatedly divides the test value (`NewValue`) by a divisor value (`Divisor`), which is increased by 2 after each division, until the test value is evenly divisible by the divisor (failure) or else the divisor becomes greater than the square root of the test value.

```
FUNCTION APrime ( NewValue : Primes ) : Boolean;

VAR
  Divisor,
  Limit   : Integer;
  Success : Boolean;

BEGIN
IF ( NewValue < 1 ) OR ( NewValue > 3 ) AND ( NewValue MOD 2 = 0 ) THEN
  APrime  := FALSE
ELSE
  BEGIN
  Success := TRUE;
  Limit   := Trunc ( Sqrt ( NewValue ));
  Divisor := 3;
  WHILE Success AND ( Divisor <= Limit ) DO
    IF NewValue MOD Divisor = 0 THEN
      Success := FALSE
    ELSE
      Divisor := Divisor + 2;
  APrime := Success
  END
END;
```

```
PROCEDURE PrimeAssign ( VAR Target : Primes; NewValue : Primes;
                        VAR Success : Boolean );

BEGIN
Success := APrime ( NewValue );
IF Success THEN
  Target := NewValue
END;
```

Divisibility

Every object is really a universe of other objects, and we can describe a particular object directly by name or in terms of its constituent parts. That is, we can *decompose* any object—whether it be an abstract concept or a physical entity—in different ways and to different depths. Conversely, we can *compose* an object by combining objects to form a larger object. Both operations may produce completely different forms of the same information.

For example, consider a library book as a single object. The operation of a student checking the book out from the library involves the book in its entirety. Back in the dormitory, the student reading the book regards it as a logical collection of chapters and subchapters, with comprehension occurring at the chapter, section, paragraph, sentence, and word levels. The typesetter and bookbinder who assembled that book regarded it as a physical collection of pages, ink, and glue. A chemist would view the pages, ink, and glue as collections of molecules, which are themselves collections of atoms. Since the late 1800s, physicists have regarded every atom as, at least, a collection of electrons, protons, and neutrons, and modern research from the perspective of quantum mechanics supports the existence of even smaller objects such as mesons, leptons, and quarks. As scientists continue their quest for the one absolute and nondecomposable particle, the notion of *smallest* is frequently redefined.

On the composing end of the spectrum, books may be grouped in different ways. Books on a given shelf are organized by call numbers. Shelves of books form a single bookcase of books, and each library room may contain many such bookcases. All rooms of bookcases comprise the entire library, which may be one of several libraries on campus. And all the campus libraries may be part of a national association of university libraries, which is a subset of all libraries in the country. And it is unclear just how many libraries of books might exist throughout the universe!

Computer data can be similarly described at different levels of **divisibility** and classified as being either simple or structured:

- **Simple data type.** Each item in the domain of a simple data type is a nondecomposable, *single value.*
- **Structured data type.** Each item in the domain of a structured data type is a decomposable *collection of values,* each of which may be either simple or structured.

The standard data types integer, real, Boolean, and char are *simple* because a variable of any of these types is capable of holding only a *single value.* Such types are said to be nondecomposable, or atomic, because the authors of high-level languages such as Pascal have *chosen* not to break them into smaller entities when defining the language.

For example, the assignment statement `X := 7` stores the integer constant `7` in variable Int. To the Pascal programmer, both the constant `7` and integer variable `X` are nondecomposable. To the programmer at the assembly-language level, on the other hand, `X` is decomposable, since an examination of its physical representation within computer memory reveals that the value `7` is actually represented as a collection of binary bits of information, each thought of as having a value of either 1 or 0. A computer technician would view the same integer information at an even lower level, concerned with the actual voltage levels of each bit (binary 1 is represented as a higher-voltage signal and binary 0 is represented as a lower- or no-voltage signal). And just as the molecules of the ink are of no interest to the reader of the library book, the memory medium and bit-level representation are typically of no interest to the high-level programmer.

```
TYPE
  Phys = RECORD
            Birth  : String [ 6 ];
            Female : Boolean;
            Height,
            Weight : Real;
         END;


  App  = RECORD
            Name      : String [ 20 ];
            Phone     : String [ 10 ];
            PhysData  : Phys;
            Smoker    : Boolean;
            Hobbies   : ARRAY [ 1..5 ]
                        OF String [ 10 ]
         END;


  Apps = RECORD
            List  : ARRAY [ 1..300 ]
                    OF App;
            Count : 0..300
         END;


VAR
   Clients : Apps;
```

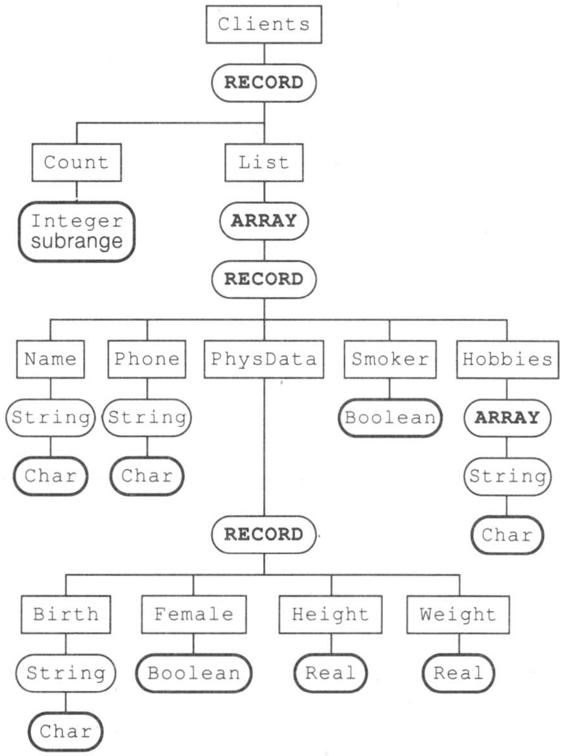

FIGURE 2.1 Nested Pascal Declarations and Corresponding Hierarchy Diagram

The standard array data type is *structured* because a variable of this type is capable of holding a *collection of values*. The entire array is both a single entity and a collection of entities called elements, each of which may be of either simple or structured data type. Any structured data type can be decomposed into simple data types, which are, by programming-language design, nondecomposable. As an example, Figure 2.1 contains a set of declarations and a diagram depicting the hierarchy of variable declarations (in rectangles) and data type definitions (in ovals, with simple data type identifiers in boldface). The `Clients` variable stores information about applicants for a dating service.

Standard Pascal also supports one data type that is neither simple nor structured: the *pointer* type, which has as its domain the address values of a portion of internal memory called heapspace. The pointer type is regarded as a *dynamic data type* and is used to create and reference a *dynamically allocated* variable—a variable whose memory space is allocated at runtime rather than at compile-time. (The pointer type, heapspace, and dynamic allocation are all discussed in detail in Section 4.2.)

We now examine additional characteristics of simple data types. Further discussion about the characteristics of structured data types is presented at the beginning of Chapter 3.

Ordinality (Linearity) and Orderliness of a Simple Data Type

The notions of ordinality and order describe the relationship among items belonging to the same simple data type:

- A simple data type is **ordinal** (**linear**) if its values can be mapped to the numbers 0, 1, 2, 3, . . . , except for the integer data type, which is mapped onto itself. These numbers represent the **ordinal position** of the value within the entire domain. Each value except the first and last has a unique predecessor and unique successor value.
- A simple data type is **ordered** if two values of that type may be compared using relational operators, such as =, <, and >=.

The standard Pascal data types integer, char, Boolean, and enumerated type and a subrange of any of these types are all ordinal (and therefore ordered), whereas the standard real data type is ordered but not ordinal. The compiler knows that 8 follows 7 and that the character *f* precedes character *g* based on the character set in use, such as ASCII. This built-in knowledge allows a Pascal compiler to generate the appropriate machine code for `CASE` statements or to make sense of subrange syntax, such as `'a'..'z'` or `1..MAXINT`. Standard Pascal even provides the functions `Succ` and `Pred` for obtaining successor and predecessor values, respectively, and the `Ord` function for obtaining a value's ordinal position.

The standard Pascal data type real is not ordinal because real values are strictly implementation-dependent and therefore cannot be mapped onto a fixed sequence of ordinal numbers. For example, although 7.5 is greater than 7.1, subrange syntax such as `7.1..7.5` is ambiguous and therefore syntactically illegal. What follows `7.1`? Is it `7.2`, `7.11`, `7.101`, `7.10000001`? From an abstract, mathematical perspective, there are infinitely many real values between any pair of real values.

Because a computer must be able to represent real numbers in memory, there *will* be a particular successor to `7.1`, but its exact value is dictated by the degree of precision employed by the computer in use. As we shall see in Section 2.3, a computer may be limited to representing only an *approximation* of a real value. Pascal compilers will not rely on this approximating process to resolve ambiguities such as `7.1..7.5`, however, and therefore do not permit the use of real values in `CASE` or `FOR` statements, within subrange syntax, or as arguments to the `Ord`, `Succ`, or `Pred` functions. The real data type is ordered because Pascal compilers will allow comparisons between two real values, such as `(Volume >= 7.934)` since a simple subtraction operation is sufficient to obtain the result of the comparison. Because real values are represented in memory as approximations, such comparisons may yield incorrect results.

Levels of Representation of Computer Data

Any entity (an object, idea, item of information, etc.) can be described or represented on three different levels:

1. At the *abstract level,* the entity is a purely imaginative concept, in which anything is possible, with the details of its actual representation suppressed in favor of more important characteristics.

2. At the *symbolic level,* the abstract entity is modeled using symbols (speech, pictures, characters, etc.). This representation allows humans to share ideas and to plan for the physical representation of those ideas. Because of the limits of the symbolic medium used, the symbolic representation may impose restrictions on the original abstract representation.
3. At the *physical level,* the entity is actually represented using physical objects. Again, restrictions may be imposed due to real-life factors, such as physical and technological limitations, financial budgeting, etc.

Everyday examples of this trichotomy are plentiful. A new building is first conceived, then represented by an architect through blueprints, and then actually built. A vacation is imagined wistfully and then simulated by examining maps, making reservations, and packing; finally, this planning is actually carried out (the actual vacation often differs from its original conception). The role of government in dictating and controlling certain social behaviors is frequently debated by members of a legislature. Their conclusions are described on paper in the form of laws, intended to be obeyed by the general population and enforced by police and court systems.

Data types can also be viewed and described at any of three levels:

1. The **abstract** level is an imaginary concept of the domain of values and possible fundamental operations (as well as structure for a data structure). The focus here is on inherent properties and functionality, independent of representation issues.
2. The **programming language representation** level is a symbolic description of the data type within the syntax and limitations of a particular programming language, such as Pascal. Since every programming language is designed for representation on a physical computer, some restrictions on the abstract domain of values and operations are necessarily imposed at this level.
3. The **computer memory representation** level is the way in which a value of a data type is actually stored or represented electronically in a physically memory device.

The diagram in Figure 2.2 describes how a particular data type may be viewed at each of these three levels.

In this textbook, each data type will be introduced as an **abstract data type (ADT),** with a focus on its inherent properties and functionality (ab-

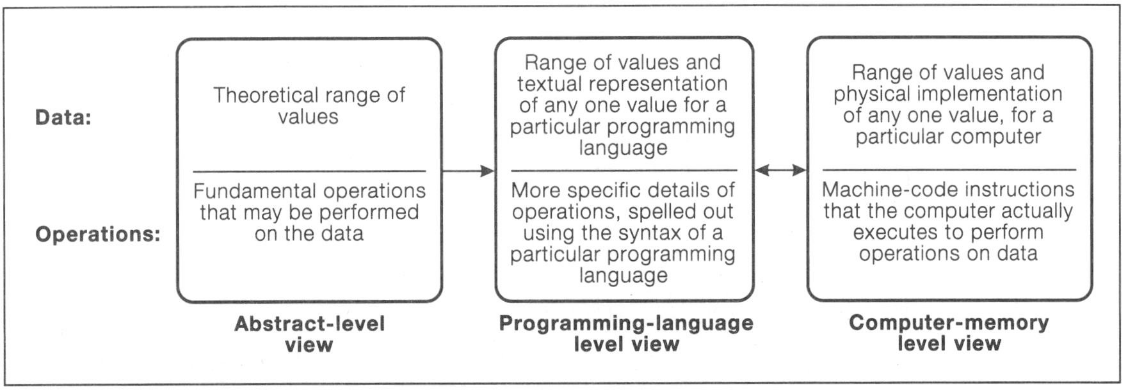

FIGURE 2.2 Three Views of Data and Operations

stract level view). We will describe the data type as it is represented within the Pascal language (programming language view). Finally, we will examine how each fundamental simple and fundamental structured data type is typically represented within computer memory (computer memory level view). Pascal is said to be rich in data typing because of the ease by which a programmer may represent abstract data types, making Pascal an ideal language for learning fundamental programming concepts.

Abstract Data Type (ADT) Specification

Again, the data types presented in this book will be introduced with a concise ADT specification that defines the data type by describing the following:

1. *General description.* Divisibility, order, and either ordinality for simple types or structure for structured types, as well as other relevant information about the type.
2. *Domain.* Range of possible values.
3. *Fundamental Operations.* Collection of basic operations that may be performed on these values or variables containing these values.

An ADT specification therefore describes a data type in terms of its inherent characteristics and how items of that type may be manipulated. The specification does not describe exactly how any one datum is actually represented in physical computer memory, nor does it describe the algorithmic mechanics of each operation. In fact, the primary advantage of designing a computer program using an ADT approach to data and operations is that it simplifies the entire design process by hiding such representation details.

Designing a computer program requires selecting data types and basic operations on the data to accomplish a particular task or set of tasks. Since the choice of data types and operations drives program development, taking an ADT approach to selecting data types and operations (via the program design) allows the programmer to focus on high-level program logic rather than being distracted by (and even bogged down with) lower-level details. The Pascal programmer usually does not have to be concerned with what a given record looks like in computer memory or exactly which machine code instructions are generated by the compiler. After all, the quintessential function of any computer itself is to perform repetitive, mundane tasks, thereby freeing humans for more interesting and creative endeavors.

The ADT approach to designing computer programs provides other advantages as well. As explained in Chapter 1, modularity in program design means assigning the component tasks of a problem to independent procedures and functions (modules), with information flowing in and out via parameters and arguments. Each module has a "contract" with the calling routine, by which it agrees to perform a particular task or set of tasks. An ADT specification is really the result of taking a modular approach to data typing by describing precisely the *functionality* of a particular data type.

Programming Language Representation

A programming language bridges the gap between the abstract concepts of data types and fundamental operations and the physical hardware that actually stores data values and executes instructions to manipulate the data (refer to Figure 2.2). Before the mid-1950s, programmers wrote programs directly in machine code, with each instruction or constant value written as a string of 1s and 0s to represent bit values. The first compilers for the FORTRAN and COBOL languages allowed programmers to write programs that more closely resembled the natural language of English. High-level languages such as these and, later, PL/1, ALGOL, and Pascal, simplified both the design and debugging of computer programs. Thus, a programmer does not need to be too concerned with exactly *how* data and instructions are actually represented on the computer. (Of course, an understanding of such representation may guide the programmer in designing code that maximizes the efficiency of a program in terms of time and memory use, so discussion of memory representations are included in this chapter and in Chapter 3.)

As stated earlier, the value of every constant, variable, and function in Pascal belongs to a particular data type. The compiler recognizes the data type of constants such as `3.4`, `-MAXINT`, or `'Howdy'` by default, whereas the data types of variables must be explicitly declared. By knowing the data type of a variable (or constant), the compiler is able to generate the appropriate machine instructions to represent source-code instructions, to allocate internal memory for global variables, and to flag certain errors involving data manipulation, such as the attempted assignment of a real value to an integer varaible.

At the beginning of any program, procedure, and function, a declaration section may be specified. The **CONST** portion of a declaration section may be used to associate an identifier, such as `PI`, `Radius`, or `TaxRate`, with a constant value. During the compilation process, the compiler will replace a named constant within the scope of such a declaration with its specified value. The **TYPE** portion of a declaration section may be used to define a programmer-defined data type. The **VAR** portion of a declaration section specifies what type of data each program variable can hold. As the compiler passes over the source code, it builds a *symbol table* of information about each variable declared, helping it to remember this and other information about the variables.

Computer Memory Representation

This section provides a very brief overview of the topic of computer memory; more information is presented later in this chapter and in Chapters 3, 4, 5, and 10.

Data and program instructions may be represented both within external memory and internal memory. External memory is used to hold programs, data, or any text between program executions. Examples of external memory media include hard disks, floppy disks, and magnetic tape. (The fundamental unit of external memory—the *file*—is discussed in greater detail in Section 4.1.) Internal memory typically includes the following three hardware devices:

- A *register* is a small memory that the CPU uses to temporarily hold data or the next instruction to be executed.
- A *buffer* is memory used to hold data just acquired from an input device, such as a keyboard, or about to be sent to an output device, such as a screen or printer.

- *Main memory* is the largest internal memory structure, used to hold the computer's operating system program and data structures, the user program being executed, and heapspace memory available for use by both programs.

Six of the most common units of memory are the bit, byte, word, page, file, and directory:

- A **bit** is the smallest (nondecomposable) data value considered in programming, with the possible binary values of 0 or 1, corresponding to a particular voltage or magnetized state within the actual memory device. Bit is the acronym for *b*inary dig*it*.
- A **byte** is a collection of bits (typically 8).
- A **word** is a collection of bytes (e.g., 2 for a 16-bit word computer, 4 for a 32-bit word computer).
- A **block**, or **page**, is a collection of words, typically, 256, 512, or 1024 words (the exact quantity varies among computer manufacturers).
- A **file** is both a *physical unit* (a particular named collection of words, usually in whole blocks) and a *logical unit* (a complete and separate entity such as a entire Pascal source program file or an entire data file).
- A **directory** (or *volume* or *folder*) is a collection of files.

Every data type and program instruction can be decomposed ultimately into a pattern of *bit* values; in low-level assembly language programming, the bit is the simplest data type. Since the computer represents information electronically, a bit may have only two values: higher voltage or lower or no voltage. As depicted in Figure 2.3, a bit may be likened to a switch that is either on or off. For programming purposes, bit values may be thought of as binary numbers: 1 for higher voltage and 0 for lower voltage. The 8-bit byte depicted in Figure 2.3 represents the binary value 01001110_2, which is 78 in the decimal system. (If you are unfamiliar with the binary system of numbers, Section 2.3 and Appendix B provides an introduction.)

Figure 2.4 shows a simplified model layout of main memory after a Pascal program has been compiled and is awaiting execution. This is a greatly simplified, generic model; typically, actual memory layouts are more complex and vary among computers. Main memory may be thought of as one large one-dimensional array of integer values in which each word has a unique numeric address, which is analogous to the index value of an array element.

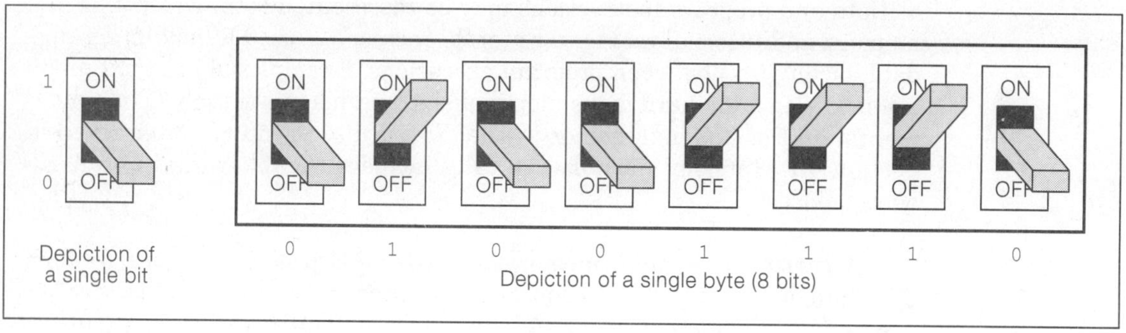

FIGURE 2.3 Depiction of a Single Bit as a Switch and a Byte as Eight Switches

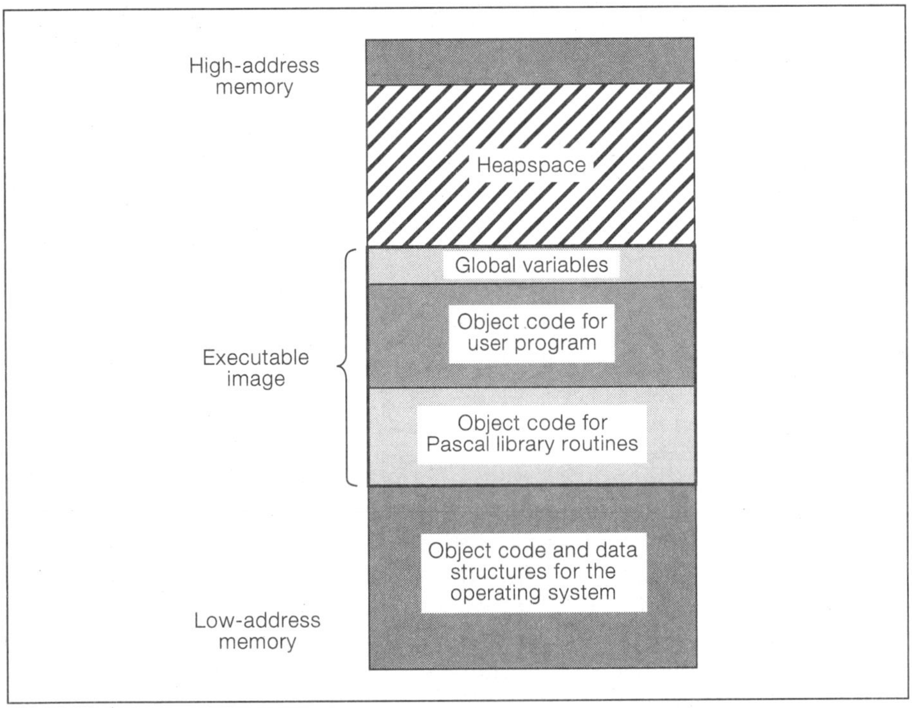

FIGURE 2.4 A Simplified Model Layout of Main Memory

In any kind of computer memory, data and instructions are represented as groups of bits, regardless of how the original source program and data were represented (whether in a high-level language, such as Pascal or LISP, or in a low-level assembly language). For example, the 8-bit pattern depicted in Figure 2.3 may represent the decimal number 78 or the character N (based on the ASCII character set) or may be part of some instruction.

2.2 INTEGER DATA TYPE

Specifications for the ADT Integer

The **ADT integer** is a simple, ordinal data type whose items are ordered $-\infty, \ldots, -1, 0, +1, \ldots, +\infty$.

Domain

The domain is the negative and positive whole numbers ranging from $-\infty$ to $+\infty$, including 0.

Fundamental Operations

1. *Assignment to integer variable:* Assigning an integer value to a variable or function identifier.
2. *Arithmetic operations:* Mathematical operations, such as addition, subtraction, multiplication, and division, that combine two values to produce an integer result.

3. *Scalar operations:* Operations involving the integer's ordinal position within the domain of integers, such as relational (comparison) operations.

Pascal Representation of the ADT Integer

An integer expression is an expression that evaluates to an integer value. Such an expression may be specified in source code by any of the following:

- An integer constant
- An integer variable, array element, or record field
- An integer function call
- The combination of an integer operator and one or two integer operands (as appropriate)

Figure 2.5 contains the syntax diagram for an integer constant, which may be signed or unsigned. In Pascal, the absence of a sign implies a positive value and embedded commas are not allowed.

As indicated in the syntax diagram, the standard Pascal notation for an integer constant is base 10 (**decimal notation**). Some nonstandard compilers recognize special syntax for other numeric bases as well. For example, the dollar sign character (`$`) is often used to indicate a hexadecimal (base 16) value; e.g., `$7A52` would be the hexadecimal representation of the decimal value 31,314. Appendix B provides a comparison of the binary, octal (base 8), decimal, and hexadecimal number systems.

In the declaration of a variable, record field, file type, or array, all Pascal compilers recognize the identifier `Integer` as specifying a subset of the ADT integer. **`MAXINT`** is a predefined constant that all Pascal compilers recognize as being equivalent to the largest integer that may be represented *using that particular computer.*

Standard Pascal syntax related to the ADT integer follows, and descriptions of all standard operators and special symbols are given in Appendix A. The `Trunc` and `Round` functions are described in Section 2.3.

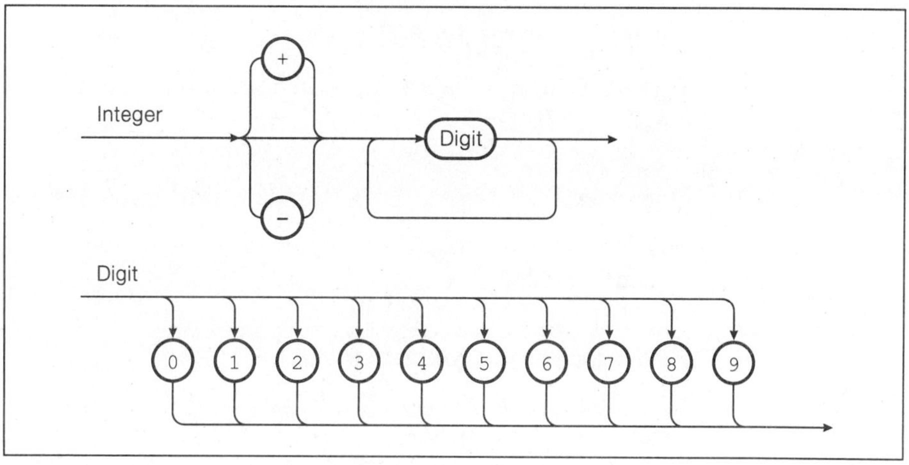

FIGURE 2.5 **Syntax Diagram for a Signed Integer Constant**

Declaration of an integer variable

```
VAR {variable identifier} : Integer;
```

Predefined integer constant

Greatest integer value	**MAXINT**

Standard operators

Assignment	:=		
Addition	+	Multiplication	*
Subtraction, negation	–	Integer division	**DIV**
		Remainder after integer division	**MOD**

Standard functions

Absolute value	`Abs`	Convert real to integer by simple truncation	`Trunc`
Square	`Sqr`		
Successor	`Succ`	Convert real to integer by rounding	`Round`
Predecessor	`Pred`		
Ordinal position	`Ord`	Determine if integer argument is odd	`Odd`
Convert integer to char	`Chr`		

Standard data-transfer procedures and techniques

Read integer from keyboard or text file	`Read, Readln`
Write integer to screen or text file	`Write, Writeln`
Read from binary file of integer	`Get, Read`
Write to binary file of integer	`Put, Write`
Parameter passing	
Return an integer function value	

The techniques of converting an integer value to a real value and vice versa are discussed in detail in Section 2.3.

Computer Memory Representation of the ADT Integer

Although the types represented in a computer language are not necessarily determined by or limited to those supported by a computer's hardware, the domain of possible integer values is tied to the computer's word size. Typically, an entire word of memory is used to represent an integer value. Recall that a word of memory comprises bit values, the exact number of which depends on the computer in use (16 and 32 bits are typical). Recall also that, because each bit may have only the value 1 or 0 (corresponding to high voltage or low voltage), the one-word representation is really a binary-based representation, as opposed to the decimal-based representation of an integer value commonly used in Pascal source code and in daily life. Whereas each digit of a decimal number is really that digit times a power of 10, each digit of a binary number is really that digit times a power of 2. Appendix B provides a brief comparison of the decimal and binary numbering systems.

Only 1 bit is needed to represent the decimal number 0 or 1, whereas 4 bits are needed to represent the range of numbers from 0 to 15, and 7 bits are needed to represent the range 0 to 127. Since an integer expression is typically limited to a single word of memory, the value of **MAXINT** is therefore based on the computer's word size in bits:

$$\textbf{MAXINT} = 2^{(\text{word size} - 1)} - 1$$

The 1 is subtracted from the exponent because the most significant bit in each word is used in the representation of the sign of the value (0 for positive, 1 for negative). The value of **MAXINT** for a 16-bit computer is, therefore, 32,767; it is 2,147,483,647 for a 32-bit computer.

Bitwise Integer Operations

Many nonstandard Pascal compilers permit an expression consisting of a logical operator and two *integer* operands, in which case a **bitwise operation** is performed, resulting in an integer value. At the bit level, `0 AND 0` yields `0`, `0 AND 1` yields `0`, and `1 AND 1` yields `1`. The **AND** operator can be used in this way to isolate the value of a particular bit or byte, which is referred to as **masking** the unwanted bits. For example, if we wanted to know if bit 7 was set in the value 1776, we could mask all other bits by **AND**ing 1776 with 128, as follows (a 16-bit word size is assumed):

$$\begin{aligned} 1776_{10} &= 0000\ 0110\ 1111\ 0000_2 \\ 128_{10} &= \underline{0000\ 0000\ 1000\ 0000_2} \\ 1776_{10}\ \textbf{AND}\ 128_{10} &= 0000\ 0000\ 1000\ 0000_2 = 128_{10} \end{aligned}$$

The expression (`1776 AND 128`) evaluates to the integer value 128, which means that only bit 7 is turned on (i.e., set to 1).

To obtain the numeric value formed by a group of adjacent bits within a word, we would again use **AND** to mask off the unwanted bits and then **DIV** by an appropriate power of 2 to shift the nonzero bits into the rightmost byte. As an example that again assumes a 16-bit integer representation, the following code segment displays the decimal value of the third byte (bits 8 through 15) of whatever value is currently contained in integer variable `Value`:

```
Value := Value AND 3840;  {3840₁₀ = 0000 1111 0000 0000₂}
Value := Value DIV  256;  {Right-shift result by 8 bits}
Writeln ( 'The decimal value contained in the 3rd byte is ', Value );
```

For example, if `Value` originally contains the value 10,714 ($0010\ 1001\ 1101\ 1010_2$, the resulting integer value displayed is 9).

2.3 REAL DATA TYPE

In mathematics, no distinction is made between the numbers 5 and 5.0 or −127 and −127.0 in terms of data type and allowable operations; they are all numbers to which arithmetic operations may be applied. In a programming language, however, there is a difference in terms of the allowable operations and the computer memory representation: 5 and −127 are integer constants, whereas 5.0 and −127.0 are real constants. The ADT specification for the real data type follows.

Specifications for the ADT Real

The **ADT real** is a simple data type that is nonordinal although its items are ordered.

Domain

The domain is negative and positive numbers ranging in value from $-\infty$ to $+\infty$, including 0. Each number contains an integer portion (the *integral*) and a fractional portion following the decimal point (the *fraction*).

Fundamental Operations

1. *Assignment to real variable:* Assigning a real value to a variable or function identifier.
2. *Arithmetic operations:* Operations such as addition, subtraction, multiplication, and division, which combine two numbers into a real result.
3. *Relational operations:* Comparing two real numbers using a relational operator.

Pascal Representation of the ADT Real

A real expression is an expression that evaluates to a real value. Such an expression may be specified in source code by any of the following:

- A real constant
- A real variable, array element, or record field.
- A real function call
- Any arithmetic expression involving the real division operator and/or a real value

In the declaration of a variable, record field, file type, or array, all Pascal compilers recognize the identifier `Real` as implying a subset of the ADT real. In either the decimal or exponential notation (both described shortly), the total number of significant digits (the **precision** of the number) will vary among computers, with seven digits being a typical maximum. No real type equivalent of **MAXINT** is defined in standard Pascal; the typical domain for real values with a 16-bit computer is −1.7E+38 to 1.7E+38 (such exponential notation is discussed shortly.) Standard Pascal syntax related to the

ADT Real follows, and descriptions of all standard operators and special symbols are given in Appendix A.

Declaration of a real variable

```
VAR {variable identifier} : Real;
```

Standard operators

Assignment	:=		
Addition	+	Multiplication	*
Subtraction, negation	–	Real division	/

Standard functions

Absolute value	`Abs`	Sine	`Sin`
Square	`Sqr`	Cosine	`Cos`
Square root	`Sqrt`	Arctangent	`Arctan`
Convert real to integer by simple truncation	`Trunc`	Natural log (base e)	`Ln`
		Exponent (base e)	`Exp`
Convert real to integer by rounding	`Round`		

Standard data-transfer procedures and syntax

Read from keyboard or text file	`Read, Readln`
Write to screen or text file	`Write, Writeln`
Read from binary file of real	`Get, Read`
Write to binary file of real	`Put, Write`
Parameter passing	
Return a real function value	

Exponential and Nonexponential Notation

Although nonexponential notation is probably sufficient to represent most real numbers in everyday life, it is cumbersome for representing very large or very small values. For example, the distance in miles that a beam of light would travel continuously for one year (a light year) can be approximated as follows:

$$186{,}000 \text{ miles per second} \times (60 \times 60 \times 24 \times 365) = 5{,}865{,}696{,}000{,}000 \text{ miles}$$

This value may be represented instead using the following **exponential notation:**

`5.865696E+12` which means 5.865696×10^{12}

With exponential notation, the combination of integral and fraction is called the **mantissa** and the number following the *E* is called the **exponent.** Exponential notation indicates that the mantissa is multiplied by the quantity 10 raised to the power given by the exponent. In other words, *the*

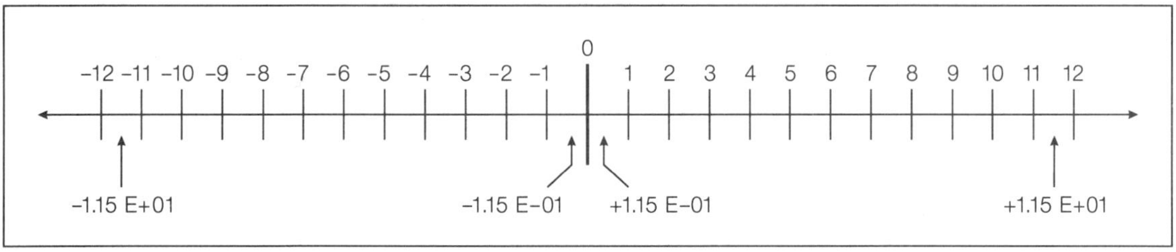

FIGURE 2.6 A Number Line Contrasting the Possible Signs of the Mantissa and Exponent for ±1.15E±01

value of the exponent is the number of places that the decimal point is shifted. If the resulting number is greater than zero, the sign of the exponent is positive; otherwise, it is negative. Both the mantissa and exponent may be signed, as indicated in the four sign variations of ±1.15E±01 along the number line depicted in Figure 2.6.

In standard Pascal, a real constant may be written in either decimal or exponential notation. Figure 2.7 shows the syntax diagrams for a real constant using either notation. As with the integer data type, the standard base for a real constant is base 10 (decimal), the absence of a leading sign implies a positive value, and embedded commas are not allowed. (The term *digit* was defined in Figure 2.5.)

Whenever standard procedures `Write` or `Writeln` are called to output a real value, that value is typically written in exponential notation by default. A field-width descriptor may be used to output the real value in decimal notation instead as well as specifying the degree of precision—i.e., the number of digits following the decimal point. For example, examine the following statement and the output it produces:

```
Write (22/7,'    ', (22/7):6:4,'    , (22/7):1:0 );
```

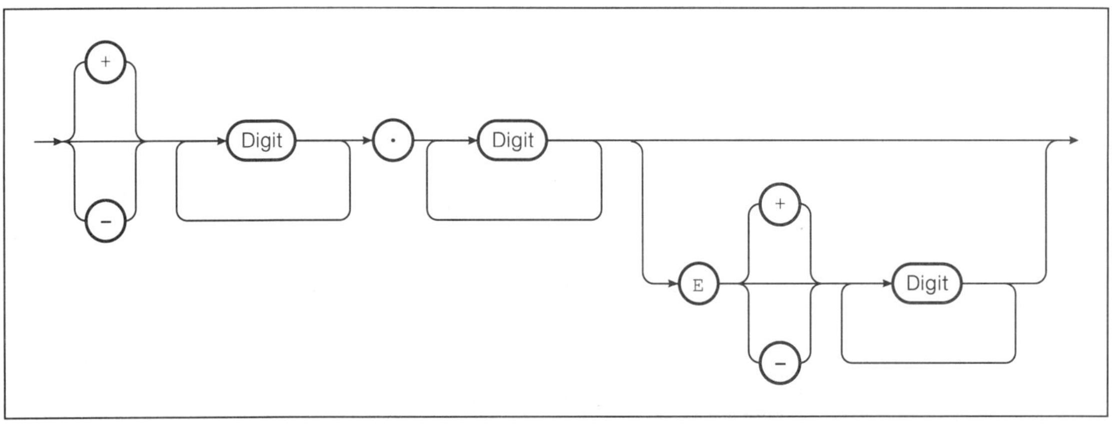

FIGURE 2.7 Syntax Diagram for a Signed Real Constant (Decimal and Exponential Notation)

The output (with seven places of precision) is:

```
3.1428571 3.1429 3
```

Converting Between Real and Integer

Frequently, an application needs to convert a real value to an integer value, and standard Pascal provides two functions for this: `Trunc` and `Round`. The `Trunc` function simply eliminates the fractional part of the real number. The `Round` function first rounds the value away from zero by adding 0.5 if the number is positive or −0.5 if the number is negative; then it performs a `Trunc` operation.

An integer value may be *automatically* converted to a real value in either of the two ways:

- *Automatic conversion.* Whenever an integer value is assigned to a real variable via an assignment statement, a `Read` or `Readln` statement, or other parameter-passing, the compiler will automatically include machine-code instructions during compilation, which converts the integer value to a real value before it is assigned.
- *Real division.* Whenever an arithmetic expression includes the real division operator (`/`) and/or a real value, any integer operand(s) will first be converted to real.

Computer Memory Representation of the ADT Real

In mathematics, the integer numbers are merely a subset of real numbers. In computer memory, however, the two data types are represented quite differently. And while every Pascal compiler represents the real data type, some computers have special hardware for real operations, whereas others use a software-based representation and set of operations.

The integral portion of a real value is represented in the decimal system using positive powers of 10 and the fractional portion represented using negative powers of 10. In the binary system, the integral portion is represented using *positive* powers of 2 and the fractional portion is represented using *negative* powers of 2. Figure 2.8 contrasts the decimal and binary systems for representing real values.

As an example, the decimal fraction 1.6875 may be expressed and decomposed as follows, using both the decimal system (a) and the binary system (b), with four places of precision:

$$\text{(a) } 1.6875_{10} = (1 \times 10^{0}) + (6 \times 10^{-1}) + (8 \times 10^{-2}) + (7 \times 10^{-3}) + (5 \times 10^{-4})$$

$$\begin{aligned}\text{(b) } 1.1011_{2} &= (1 \times 2^{0}) + (1 \times 2^{-1}) + (0 \times 2^{-2}) + (1 \times 2^{-3}) + (1 \times 2^{-4}) \\ &= 1_{10} + 0.5_{10} + 0.00_{10} + 0.125_{10} + 0.0625_{10} \\ &= 1.6875_{10}\end{aligned}$$

The preceding example illustrates that the decimal number 1.6875 can be represented exactly using the binary number system, with only four places of precision. The representation of most real values, however, can only be *approximated* by the binary system. For example, the decimal number 0.3

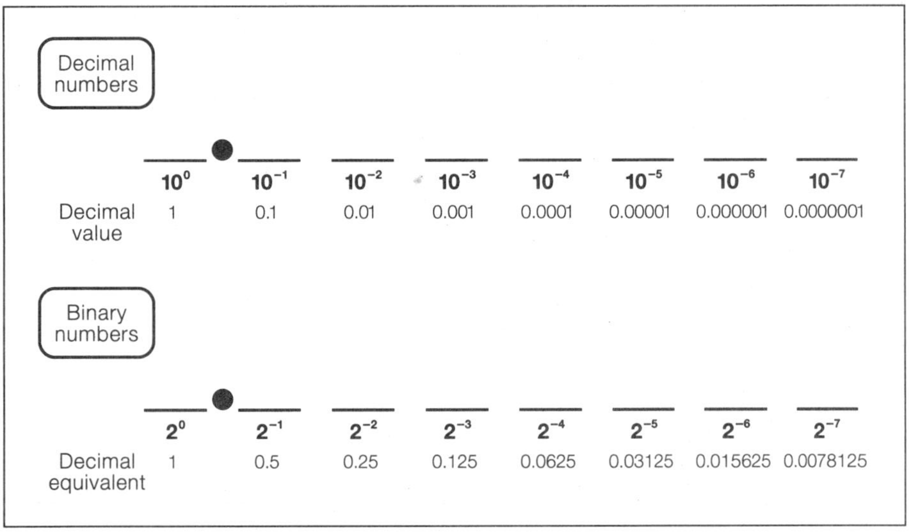

FIGURE 2.8 Representations of Fractions in Decimal and Binary Systems

cannot be represented exactly in the binary number system, regardless of the number of places of precision. This value can only be approximated, by adding very small quantities to 0.01_2 (which is 0.25_{10}) until the result approaches 0.3 with some acceptable degree of precision, as follows:

$$
\begin{aligned}
&0.01_2 && && && = 0.25_{10}\\
&0.01_2 &&+ 0.00001_2 && &&= 0.01001_2 = 0.28125_{10}\\
&0.01_2 &&+ 0.00001_2 &&+ 0.000001_2 &&= 0.010011_2 = 0.296875_{10}
\end{aligned}
$$

The binary-based computer memory representation of a real number is, in fact, limited in three ways:

1. *The memory size is limited.* As with the representation of integers, the boundaries of the domain of real values are constrained by the fact that there are only a finite number of bits with which to represent any real number.
2. *The domain of real values is nonlinear.* Between any two real values lies an infinite number of real values; again, a computer has just a finite number of bits with which to represent the entire domain of reals. A computer can therefore represent only an approximation of any real value, which may be satisfactory for many applications; however, a cumulative round-off error may prove critical for others.
3. *There is an uneven distribution of representable numbers.* Those numbers that cannot be represented exactly and must, instead, be approximated are not evenly distributed across the domain of reals. In fact, the closer to zero a real number is, the smaller the difference between it and the next real that may be represented.

As proof of the third limitation, examine the real number line depicted in Figure 2.9. The number line is divided into four different regions based on

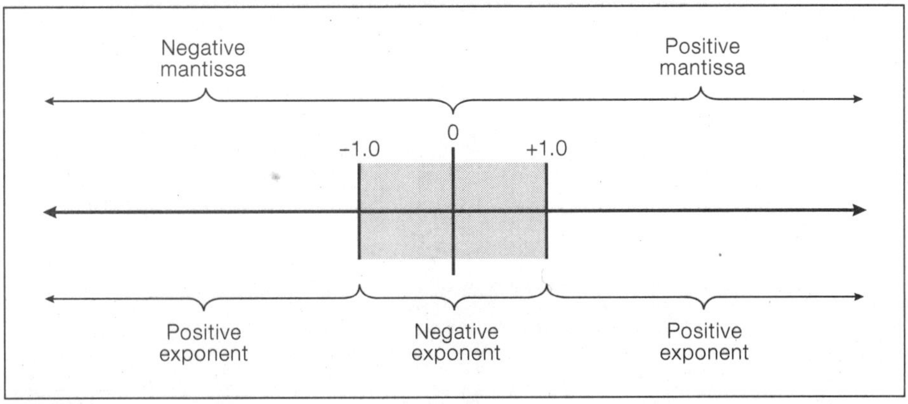

FIGURE 2.9 A Number Line Showing Regions Based on the Sign of the Mantissa and Exponent

the sign of the mantissa and exponent. In the exponential notation of a real number, if the positive and negative magnitudes of the exponent are equal, one-half of all the real numbers that may be represented lie between −1.0 and +1.0—i.e., within the shaded region in Figure 2.9, in which the exponent is negative.

Let us assume that the exponent values for a particular version of Pascal values range from −38 to +38, with seven places of precision. Figure 2.10 shows the number line of Figure 2.9 and indicates the general locations of some sample values.

All values with negative exponents lie between −1.0 and +1.0. Since the magnitude of the positive exponent (+38) is equal to the magnitude of the negative exponent (−38), there are as many values for positive exponents as there are values for negative exponents, and these values are either greater than +1.0 or less than −1.0 (see Figure 2.9). Since the region for negative exponents is much smaller than the region for positive exponents, while containing the same quantity of real numbers, it must contain a *denser* collection of representable values. In fact, as numbers become very large or very small, the quantity of significant digits becomes less useful in accurately representing the number, leaving gaps of unrepresentable values.

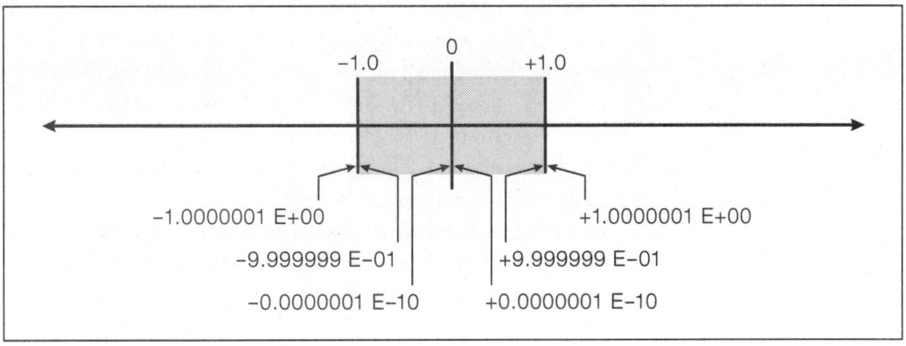

FIGURE 2.10 Key Representable Values Along a Number Line, for a Precision of Seven Digits

Decimal:	1	7	2	3	.	5	4	6	1	0	8	9
Binary:	0001	0111	0010	0011		0101	0100	0110	0001	0000	1000	1001

FIGURE 2.11 BCD Representation of 1723.5461089_{10}

Two common techniques for representing real values in computer memory are the *binary coded decimal (BCD)* representation and the *floating-point* representation. A discussion of both schemes follows.

Binary Coded Decimal (BCD) Representation

A **binary coded decimal (BCD)** represents a real value by using 4 bits to represent each digit, always resulting in an exact representation of the original value. The number of 4-bit quantities varies among Pascal systems that support BCD, but the first 4-bit group is typically to represent the sign. As an example, the representation of the decimal number 1723.5461089 is depicted in Figure 2.11.

Floating-Point Representation

BCD can represent any real value exactly within a particular range, unlike the **floating-point** representation, which can approximate only certain real values. Even so, the floating-point representation is more commonly used because the BCD representation requires more bytes of memory, the range of representable values is much narrower, and, most importantly, the floating-point representation employs a format that is easier for a computer to use in performing arithmetic computations (especially for multiplication and division).

Floating-point is actually a modified exponential notation representation. Figure 2.12 depicts a typical memory-allocation scheme for a 16-bit or

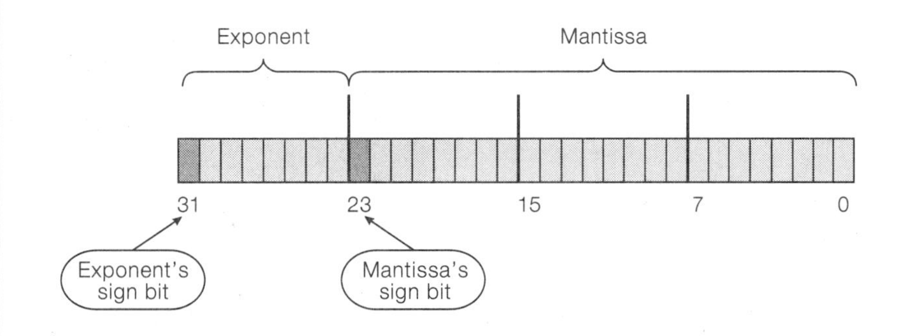

FIGURE 2.12 A Typical Memory Allocation Scheme for a Floating-Point Representation

32-bit computer involving four 8-bit bytes (for a 16-bit computer, two words are regarded as a single 32-bit quantity).

The exponent is stored as a signed-magnitude, 8-bit integer in bits 24 through 31. The most significant bit of the exponent serves as the exponent's sign bit. The mantissa is stored as a normalized number in bits 0 through 23 and its most significant bit (bit 23) serves as the sign bit. A negative real number is represented by assigning a one to the sign bit of the mantissa, similar to the signed-magnitude technique for integers.

2.4 CHARACTER DATA TYPE

Specifications for the ADT Character

The **ADT character** is a simple, ordinal data type whose items are ordered, based on a particular character set.

Domain

The domain includes any single character.

Fundamental Operations

1. *Assignment to character variable:* Assigning a character value to a variable or function identifier.
2. *Scalar operations:* Operations involving the character's ordinal position within the domain specified by the character set in use, such as a relational (comparison) operation.

Pascal Representation of the ADT Character

A character expression is an expression that evaluates to a character value. Such an expression may be specified in source code by any of the following:

- A character constant
- A character variable, array element, or record field
- A character function call

Appendix C describes the basic ASCII character set, which is used most often with microcomputers.

Most characters in a character set are printable and may be displayed on a screen or printed, whereas other characters are nonprintable. Printable characters include the decimal digits, uppercase and lowercase letters, arithmetic and relational symbols, and a variety of grammatical symbols. (Many nonstandard Pascal compilers recognize an extended ASCII character set containing other printable characters as well.) Some nonprintable characters provide directives for hardware devices, such as the line-feed and carriage-return characters that indicate the end of a line in a text file and cause a screen cursor or a printer print head to be moved to the next screen or print line.

Certain pairs of characters, such as the escape character (the 27th ASCII character) plus another printable character (forming an *escape sequence*) are often used for a variety of purposes—e.g., indicating the end of a file or turning screen underlining on or off. When a keyboard key is pressed, the integer character set value associated with it is read by the operating system. For some keys that do not correspond to a single character, such as the arrow, Tab, Backspace, and Return keys, two integer character set codes are read (usually an escape sequence).

In standard Pascal, the notation for a character constant is the character immediately preceded and followed by a single apostrophe, as indicated in the following 11 examples. (In the fifth example, note that the apostrophe character itself is indicated by two adjacent apostrophes enclosed within two apostrophes.)

```
'A' 'x' ' ' '2' '''' '?' ',' '~' '.' '-' '_'
```

A nonprintable character (and any printable character) may be specified using the standard `Chr` function, as indicated in the following examples, which are based on the ASCII character set:

`Chr ( 27 )` refers to the 27th character of the ASCII character set, the Escape character
`Write ( Chr ( 7 ) )` will output the 7th ASCII character, sounding a beep
`Chr ( 97 )` and `'a'` both specify the same character

In the declaration of a variable, record field, file type, or array, all Pascal compilers recognize the identifier `Char` as implying a subset of the ADT character, based on the character set currently in use. Standard Pascal syntax related to the ADT character follows, and descriptions of all standard operators and special symbols are given in Appendix A.

Declaration of a character variable

```
VAR {variable identifier} : Char;
```

Standard operator

Assignment :=

Standard functions

Successor	`Succ`	Ordinal position	`Ord`
Predecessor	`Pred`	Convert position to character	`Chr`

Standard data-transfer procedures and syntax

Read character(s) from keyboard or text file	`Read, Readln`
Write character(s) to screen or text file	`Write, Writeln`
Parameter-passing	
Return a character function value	

A collection of characters enclosed within single apostrophes is a character string constant, or *literal string*—e.g., `'hello'`, `'Enter choice:'`, or `'123'`. Five data structures that may be used to hold character strings are discussed later in this textbook:

1. Simple arrays of char:	Section 3.4
2. Packed arrays of char:	Section 3.4
3. Nonstandard String type:	Section 3.4
4. Linear linked list	Application 5.1 (Implementing ADT String)
5. Trie structures	Application 5.3 (Computerized Dictionaries, A Nonlinear Trie-based Dictionary)

Computer Memory Representation of the ADT Character

In a character set such as ASCII, each character is associated with a unique integer value. A char value is represented in memory as the bit pattern that is the binary equivalent of this integer. For example, an 8-bit byte may be used to represent up to 2^8, or 256, different characters (the basic ASCII character set lists 128 characters and is described in Appendix C). This numeric memory scheme not only defines how a character value may be represented internally but also facilitates the quick comparison of two character values, since their corresponding integer values are actually compared. For example, when a Pascal compiler encounters the source code expression `'a' >= 'A'`, it generates appropriate machine-code instructions for the test `97 >= 65` (here, based on the ASCII character set).

In standard Pascal, each character integer value occupies an entire word of memory (as with an integer), but most compilers operate more efficiently by packing together the bytes that contain information and eliminating the unused bytes. This involves storing two or more numeric values per word (depending on the word and byte size). Figure 2.13 shows the characters `'c'`, `'a'`, and `'t'` as they would be represented unpacked across three words, and then packed into two words.

```
VAR
  Ch1, Ch2, Ch3 : Char;

BEGIN
Ch1 := 'c';
Ch2 := 'a';
Ch3 := 't';
```

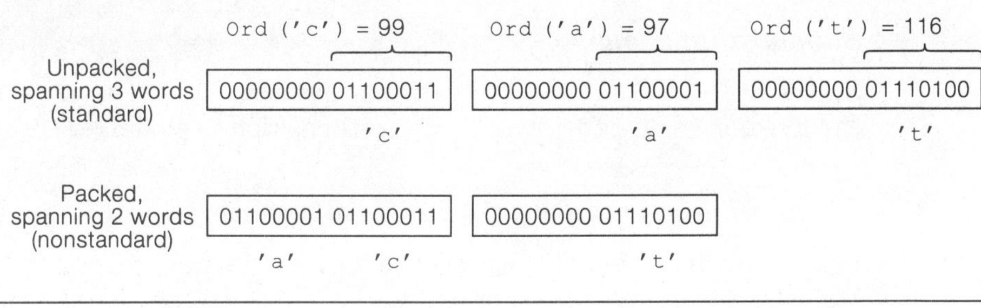

FIGURE 2.13 The Characters `'c'`, `'a'`, `'t'` Unpacked (Standard Pascal) and Packed

2.5 BOOLEAN DATA TYPE

Specifications for the ADT Boolean

The **ADT Boolean** is a simple, ordinal data type whose items are ordered `FALSE`, then `TRUE`.

Domain

The domain consists of only two possible values: `FALSE` and `TRUE`.

Fundamental Operations

1. *Assignment to Boolean variable:* Assigning a Boolean value to a variable, array element, record field, or function identifier.
2. *Scaler operations:* Operations involving a Boolean value's ordinal position within the two-value domain, such as relational (comparison) operations.
3. *Logical operations:* Combining two Boolean expressions or reversing the value of a Boolean expression, using a logical operator. Logical operators include logical equivalence, exclusive-OR (XOR), logical implication (→), logical conjunction (AND), logical disjunction (inclusive-OR, IOR), and logical negation (NOT).

Figure 2.14 contains two truth tables that summarize fundamental logical operations (arrows represent the implication operation).

A	B	A = B	A AND B	A IOR B	A XOR B	NOT A	A → B
FALSE	FALSE	**TRUE**	FALSE	FALSE	FALSE	**TRUE**	**TRUE**
FALSE	**TRUE**	FALSE	FALSE	**TRUE**	**TRUE**	**TRUE**	**TRUE**
TRUE	FALSE	FALSE	FALSE	**TRUE**	**TRUE**	FALSE	FALSE
TRUE	**TRUE**	**TRUE**	**TRUE**	**TRUE**	FALSE	FALSE	**TRUE**

Algebraic Property	Sample Expression	Equivalent Expression
Commutative Property	A **AND** B A **OR** B	B **AND** A B **OR** A
Associative Property	A **AND** (B **AND** C) A **OR** (B **OR** C)	(A **AND** B) **AND** C (A **OR** B) **OR** C
Distributive Property	A **AND** (B **OR** C) A **OR** (B **AND** C)	(A **AND** B) **OR** (A **AND** C) (A **OR** B) **AND** (A **OR** C)
Identity	A **AND** A A **OR** A A **AND FALSE** A **AND TRUE** A **OR FALSE** A **OR TRUE**	A A **FALSE** A A **TRUE**
Complement	A **AND NOT** A A **OR NOT** A **NOT NOT** A	**FALSE** **TRUE** A
DeMorgan's laws	**NOT** (A **AND** B) **NOT** (A **OR** B)	**NOT** A **OR NOT** B **NOT** A **AND NOT** B

FIGURE 2.14 Truth Tables for Boolean Operations

Pascal Representation of the ADT Boolean

A Boolean expression is an expression that evaluates to a Boolean value. Such an expression in source code may comprise any of the following:

1. A Boolean constant
2. A Boolean variable, array element, or record field
3. A Boolean function call
4. Two or more Boolean expressions combined using a logical operator
5. Any pair of numeric values, character values, Boolean values, or enumerated type values that are compared using a relational operator

In the declaration of a variable, record field, file type, or array, all Pascal compilers recognize the identifier `Boolean` as specifying a subset of the ADT Boolean. Standard Pascal syntax related to the ADT Boolean follows, and descriptions of all standard operators and special symbols are given in Appendix A.

Declaration of a Boolean variable

```
VAR {variable identifier} : Boolean;
```

Predefined Boolean constants

FALSE **TRUE**

Standard operators

Assignment	:=		
Equal	=	Greater than or equal	>=
Not equal	<>	Less than	<
Greater than	>	Less than or equal	<=
Logical equivalence	=	Logical disjunction	**OR**
Logical conjunction	**AND**	Exclusive-OR	<>
Logical negation	**NOT**	Logical implication	<=

Standard functions

Predecessor	`Pred`	Test for end of text file line	`Eoln`
Successor	`Succ`	Test for end of file	`Eof`
Ordinal position	`Ord`		

Standard data-transfer procedures and syntax

Write a Boolean value to screen or text file	`Write, Writeln`
Read a Boolean value from binary file of Boolean	`Get, Read`
Write to binary file of Boolean	`Put, Write`
Parameter passing	
Return a Boolean function value	

In standard Pascal, reading a Boolean value using the Read or Readln procedures is not permitted. Writing these values using the Write or Writeln procedures is permitted, however, outputting the string **'TRUE'** or the string **'FALSE'**.

In the following examples of Boolean expressions, HasVoted, X, and Y are Boolean variables and Age is an integer variable:

```
FALSE                             {Boolean constant}
AbleToVote                        {Boolean variable}
Age >= 18
(Age >= 18) AND HasVoted
(Age >= 18) AND NOT HasVoted
X OR Y                            {Inclusive-OR}
X <> Y                            {Exclusive-OR}
NOT X AND NOT Y                   {NAND -- true if X and Y are both false}
```

Although the following pairs of code segments are equivalent, the form on the left is the simplest and most preferred:

`IF HasVoted THEN`	is equivalent to	`IF HasVoted = TRUE THEN`
`IF NOT HasVoted THEN`	is equivalent to	`IF HasVoted = FALSE THEN`

A single assignment statement can often replace an entire **IF** statement. Another example of this follows (here, AbleToVote is a Boolean variable):

```
AbleToVote := Age >= 18 ;     is equivalent to     IF Age >= 18 THEN
                                                     AbleToVote := TRUE
                                                   ELSE
                                                     AbleToVote := FALSE;
```

Computer Memory Representation of the ADT Boolean

Boolean algebra is the mathematical foundation in the design of all electronic computer architectures and, accordingly, for the (binary) representation of all data in computer memory. The properties of this algebra were first described in 1847 by an English logician named George Boole in *The Mathematical Analysis of Logic*. Boolean algebra is useful in the design of computer circuitry, since any electrical wire or memory device may have only two states—on or off, or high-voltage or low-voltage signals. Computer circuits contain semiconductor devices that behave as Boolean operators, taking electrical input (each line of which is a high-voltage or low-voltage signal) and producing a single electrical voltage signal as a result.

A Boolean Pascal value is typically represented in memory by a single byte: A byte of all zeros represents a **FALSE** value, whereas any other collection of bit values within the byte represents **TRUE**. An entire byte is usually allocated even though a single bit might seem sufficient because most computers can address only whole words and bytes and not individual bits.

2.6 ENUMERATED DATA TYPE

Specifications for the ADT Enumerated Type

The **ADT enumerated type** is a simple, ordinal data type for which the programmer specifies (1) all the constants for the type (a list of unique identifiers) and (2) the ordering of these constants (based on order in which these identifiers are listed in the type declaration). Enumerated type constants map to the numbers 0, 1, 2, . . . (number of constants − 1).

Domain

The domain is a collection of unique *identifiers,* specified in the declaration.

Fundamental Operations

1. *Assignment to enumerated type variable:* Assigning an enumerated value to a variable, array element, record field, or function identifier.
2. *Scalar operations:* Operations involving an enumerated value's ordinal position within the domain specified by the declaration of the enumerated type, such as a relational (comparison) operation.

Pascal Representation of the ADT Enumerated Type

The simple data types discussed thus far have had domains of values that are either predefined by standard Pascal (as with integer, real, Boolean) or are dependent upon the particular computer or character set in use (as with character). With the enumerated data type, the domain and ordering of values within the domain are programmer-defined. An enumerated type expression is an expression that evaluates to an enumerated type value. An enumerated type expression may be specified in a source code by any of the following:

- An enumerated type constant
- An enumerated type variable, array element, or record field
- An enumerated type function call

Standard Pascal syntax related to the ADT enumerated type follows and descriptions of all standard operators and special symbols are given in Appendix A.

Declaration of an enumerated variable

```
VAR  {variable identifier} : {description of domain, as given in Figure 2.15};
```

Standard operator

Assignment :=

Standard functions

Predecessor	`Pred`	Ordinal position	`Ord`
Successor	`Succ`		

Standard data-transfer procedures and syntax

Read from a binary file of enumerated type	`Get, Read`
Write to a binary file of enumerated type	`Put, Write`
Parameter passing	
Return an enumerated type function value	

In standard Pascal, reading or writing an enumerated value from the keyboard or a text file using the procedures `Read`, `Readln`, `Write`, or `Writeln` is not permitted.

Figure 2.15 shows the syntax diagram for the declaration of the domain of an enumerated data type. The syntax diagram for an identifier describes any identifier used in a Pascal program to name a program, procedure, function, enumerated type constant, variable, or a named constant. Each identi-

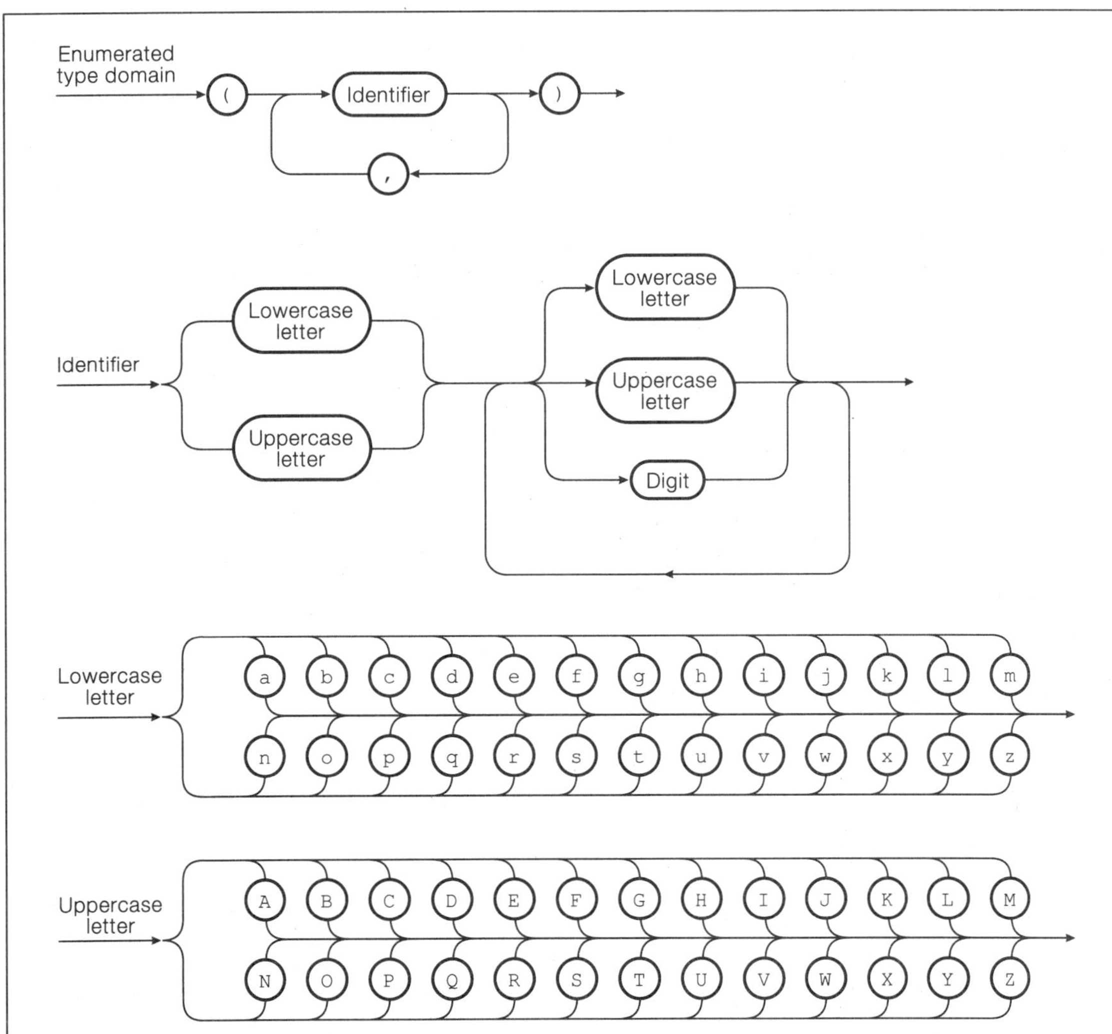

FIGURE 2.15 Syntax for the Declaration of the Domain of an Enumerated Data Type

fier is a constant of that enumerated type. (The term *digit* was defined in Figure 2.5.)

Examples of enumerated type declarations follow:

```
TYPE
  Months     = ( January, February, March, April, May, June, July, August,
                 September, October, November, December );

  Calendar   = ARRAY [ January..December ] OF Real;

  Sunny      = June..August;

VAR
  AnyMonth        : Months;       {Any of the months}
  Temperatures    : Calendar;     {List of average monthly temperatures}
  SpringMonth     : March..May;   {A month in spring}
  WarmMonth       : Sunny;        {A month with a high average temperature}
```

Given these sample declarations, the following Pascal code segment is legal:

```
AnyMonth      := November;
SpringMonth   := April;
WarmMonth     := July;

FOR AnyMonth := January TO December DO
  Temperatures [ AnyMonth ] := 0.0;
```

The identifier constants used in an enumerated type declaration *must be unique* within the scope of that declaration. An enumerated constant cannot be a Pascal reserved word or predefined constant or a constant in the domain of some other data type that is either standard or programmer-defined. For example, including the following declarations as a continuation of the previous **TYPE** declarations would be illegal, because these constants belong to a data type that already has been declared previously:

```
MonthAbbreviations  = ( 'Jan', 'Feb', 'Mar', 'Apr', 'May', 'Jun',        {ILLEGAL}
                        'Jul', 'Aug', 'Sep', 'Oct', 'Nov', 'Dec' );     {ILLEGAL}

AutumnMonthNumbers  = ( 9, 10, 11 );                                     {ILLEGAL}

SnowMonths          = ( December, January, February, March );           {ILLEGAL}

ReservedIdentifiers = ( PROCEDURE, BEGIN, OF, END );                     {ILLEGAL}
```

Note that the previous declaration for data type `Sunny` is legal because it specifies a collection of identifier constants that span a subrange of an existing data type (`AllMonths`). The `SnowMonths` declaration is illegal, however, because it attempts to reuse the four constants already used in the declaration of `AnyMonth` to establish a new data type with its own domain of values. (Even if the `SnowMonths` identifiers were kept in the same relative `AnyMonth` order, this declaration would be still be illegal.) Because an enumerated type declaration establishes the inherent ordering of the constants, reusing constants would create ambiguities for scalar operations.

For example, the Boolean expression in the following **IF** statement evaluates to a true value based on the `Months` declaration (since `February` occurs in the declaration before `December`).

```
AnyMonth := February;
IF AnyMonth < December THEN
```

If the compiler failed to flag the `SnowMonths` declarations as illegal, would the enumerated constant December be greater than or less than the enumerated constant February? The same ambiguity occurs with the following expressions, both of which evaluate to February based on the `Months` ordering.

```
Pred ( March )
Succ ( January )
```

Because standard Pascal does not permit the reading of an enumerated type value from the keyboard or text file using `Read` or `Readln`, or the writing to the screen or a text file using `Write` or `Writeln`, enumerated types are useful only within the source code of a Pascal program, *to make the code more meaningful for a programmer who reads it.* As an example, the error codes specified in the enumerated data type called `ErrorType` in the following code segment represent some of the possible human errors that might occur while interacting with a 24-hour bank-teller program. When such errors occur, appropriate error messages are displayed to the user. Since a program cannot directly write an enumerated type constant, a **CASE** statement must be used to determine which message to display; i.e., it effectively converts an enumerated value to a literal string value, which is displayed:

```
{Global declaration}

TYPE
  ErrorType = ( IllegalInput, AccountNotFound, BadPassword,
                UnauthorizedTransaction, ExpiredCard, InsufficientFunds );
```

```
PROCEDURE DisplayErrorMessage ( ErrorCode : ErrorType );

BEGIN
Write ( 'ERROR:  ' );
CASE ErrorCode OF
  IllegalInput             : Writeln ( 'Illegal input' );
  AccountNotFound          : Writeln ( 'No such account number' );
  BadPassword              : Writeln ( 'Wrong password for this account' );
  UnauthorizedTransaction  : Writeln ( 'Unauthorized transaction' );
  ExpiredCard              : Writeln ( 'Your card has expired' );
  InsufficientFunds        : Writeln ( 'Balance insufficient for transaction')
END;
Write ( '===>  Press RETURN to continue ...' );
Readln
END;
```

For example, if a bank customer attempts to withdraw $100 from an account whose balance is only $73.17, the program would make the following call to display the sixth error message:

```
DisplayErrorMessage ( InsufficientFunds );
```

(A **VAR** placed before the ErrorCode formal parameter would be illegal, of course, since the actual parameter, InsufficientFunds, is a constant.)

Perhaps it has occurred to you that the Boolean data type is really a predefined enumerated type:

```
TYPE
  Boolean = ( FALSE, TRUE );  {Predefined declaration}
```

The domain of Boolean—**FALSE** and **TRUE**—is already known to any Pascal compiler and therefore does not actually have to be declared in a program.

Computer Memory Representation of the ADT Enumerated Type

While the concepts of numbers and characters are familiar enough, by now you may be wondering exactly what enumerated values such as February or BadPassword really mean. In memory, an enumerated type constant is represented as a 1-byte unsigned integer in the following range:

0 . . (the number of constants for the type) − 1

This integer reflects the ordinal position of that constant relative to the other constants in the declaration, starting with position zero. The standard Ord function can be used to determine the ordinal position of an enumerated type constant. For example, the expression Ord (July) evaluates to 6 based on the declarations given earlier. Once a source program is compiled, any enumerated type constant identifiers are not retained after compilation; this is why a standard Pascal program cannot read or write such identifiers.

SUMMARY

A programmer must identify and write instructions to manipulate only relevant information—data—that moves the entire problem-solving process closer to a solution. Data that are inherently similar in nature, such as characters or whole numbers, are said to belong to the same data type. A basic definition of any data type describes its domain (possible values) and fundamental operations (basic operations that may be performed on these values). Pascal compilers recognize special identifiers and operators for predefined or native data types (refer to Appendix A). Pascal allows programmers to invent programmer-defined data types along with accompanying sets of fundamental operations; typically, this involves designing programmer-defined routines that manipulate a native data type in some special way.

Computer data can be further described at different levels of divisibility. Each item in the domain of a simple data type is a nondecomposable, single value. Each item in the domain of a structured data type is a decomposable collection of values, each of which may be either simple or structured. A third data type—the dynamic or pointer type—is introduced in Section 4.2.

Ordinality and order describe the relationship among items belonging to the same simple data type. A simple data type is ordinal if each value except the first and last has a unique predecessor and unique successor value. A simple type is ordered if two values of that type may be compared using relational operators.

Data types can be described or represented on three different levels: The abstract data type (ADT) level is an imaginary concept of the domain and fundamental operations (as well as structure for a data structure), with a focus on inherent properties only. The programming language representation level is a symbolic representation of the data type within the syntax and limitations of a particular programming language, such as Pascal. The computer memory representation level is the way in which a value of a data type is actually stored/represented in a physical memory device. The choice of data types and operations drives the development of any program. Taking an ADT approach to selecting data types and operations allows the programmer to focus on high-level program logic rather than being distracted by lower-level details.

The ADT integer is a simple, ordinal data type whose items are ordered $-\infty, \ldots, -1, 0, +1, \ldots, +\infty$. Its domain is negative and positive whole numbers ranging from $-\infty$ to $+\infty$, including 0. Fundamental operations include assignment of an integer value to a variable, arithmetic operations that produce an integer result, and scalar operations. Integers are represented in memory as a collection of bits, so the representation is really a binary number representation.

The ADT real is a simple data type that is ordered but is nonordinal. Its domain includes all negative and positive numbers, including 0. Each number contains an integer and a fractional portion, such as 3.7, −3.7, and 3.0. Fundamental operations include assignment of a real value to a variable, arithmetic operations that produce a real result, and scalar operations. Real values may be represented in a Pascal program using either nonexponential or exponential notation, and may be represented in computer memory using either floating-point or binary coded decimal (BCD) schemes. Any binary-based representation of a real number, such as floating-point, is only an approximation due to finite memory size, the fact that the domain of real values is nonlinear, and an uneven distribution of representable numbers across the domain.

The ADT character is a simple, ordinal data type whose items are ordered based on a particular character set, such as ASCII (refer to Appendix C). Its domain is a collection of single characters, based on a particular character set in use. Fundamental operations include assignment of a character to a variable and scalar operations. A character value is represented in computer memory as the integer value of its ordinal position within the character set currently in use.

The ADT Boolean is a simple, ordinal data type whose items are ordered `FALSE`, `TRUE`. Fundamental operations include assigning a Boolean value to a variable, scalar operations, and logical operations. A Boolean value is represented in computer memory using a single bit.

The ADT enumerated type is a simple, ordinal data type for which the programmer specifies both the constants (identifiers) and the ordering of these constants via a type declaration; its domain is the collection of these identifiers. Fundamental operations include assignment of an enumerated type value to a variable and scalar operations. Since standard Pascal does not permit the reading an enumerated type value from the keyboard or text file or writing such a value to the screen or a text file, such values are useful only within a source code program, to make the code more meaningful for a programmer who reads it (they may be thought of as named constants).

KEY TERMS

Abstract data type (ADT)
ADT Boolean
ADT character
ADT enumerated type
ADT integer
ADT real
Binary coded decimal (BCD)
Bit
Bitwise operation
Block
Byte
Computer memory representation
Data type
Directory
Divisibility
Domain
Exponent
Exponential notation
File
Floating-Point
Fundamental operation
Linearity of a simple data type
Mantissa
Masking bits
Orderliness of a simple type
Ordinal position
Ordinality of a simple data type
Page
Programmer-defined data type
Precision
Program language representation
Simple data type
Standard data type
Structured data type
Word

REVIEW QUESTIONS

1. What are the two components of a basic definition of any data type? State other ways in which a data type may be described.
2. Name all standard Pascal data types and operators. What is the difference between a standard data type and a programmer-defined data type?
3. Distinguish between a simple data type and a structured data type, and give examples of both.
4. Define ordinality and orderliness. Why is the Pascal real data type not ordinal?
5. What are three levels at which any entity may be described? What are three levels at which computer data may be represented? Describe the data-type integer at each of these levels.
6. What are the three parts of an ADT specification? Give the ADT specifications for the ADT integer.
7. Distinguish bit, byte, word, page, and file. Why are instructions and data stored in computer memory as binary numbers? Describe a general model layout of internal memory.
8. Describe how integer data are typically represented in memory. What limitations are imposed when this data type is represented in a programming language such as Pascal?
9. Describe three methods of representing negative integers in memory. Give a formula for calculating the value of `MAXINT` for an N-bit computer.
10. Describe ADT real, including the domain and fundamental operations. Describe all standard Pascal operators, functions, and procedures for this data type. What limitations are imposed when this data type is represented in a programming language such as Pascal?

11. If the domain of representable real numbers by a programming language is $-X^Y$ to $+X^Y$, explain why one-half of all these numbers lie between −1.0 and +1.0, regardless of the values of `X` and `Y` or the degree of precision.

12. Describe two methods of representing real data in memory. Describe why many real values can only be approximated in memory.

13. Describe the ADT character, including the domain and fundamental operations. Describe all standard Pascal operators, functions, and procedures for this data type. Describe how character data are typically represented in memory; distinguish between packed and unpacked character data.

14. Describe the ADT Boolean, including the domain and fundamental operations. Describe all the standard Pascal operators, functions, procedures, and constants for this data type. Describe how Boolean data are typically represented in memory.

15. Describe the ADT enumerated type, including the domain and fundamental operations. Describe all standard Pascal operators, functions, and procedures for this data type. How is this data type markedly different from all other simple standard Pascal types? What is the benefit in using an enumerated type? Describe how enumerated type data are typically represented in memory.

EXERCISES

1. State the values of $2^0, 2^1, 2^2, \ldots, 2^{12}$.

2. Write the following six numbers using Pascal exponential notation with only one digit to the left of the decimal point:

   1000.0   15.0   −3467   123,456,789   0.001234   −0.0009010

3. a. Write each of the following 15 decimal numbers as an equivalent binary number (assume seven places of precision):

3	7	8	10	16	31	100	128
550	1024	21,973	1.5	0.3	0.02	0.01560	

   b. Convert each of the following 10 binary numbers to its decimal number equivalent:

111	1101	11111	10101010	111111111111111
1.1	1.01	1.00101	1.111	1.00001

4. Assuming that your computer uses one word of memory to represent a single integer value, complete function `ExtractByte`, which should return the integer value of the byte of argument `N` specified by argument `WhichByte`:

```
FUNCTION Extract Byte ( N, WhichByte : Integer ) : Integer;
```

   For example, if your computer uses two bytes to represent an integer, the bit pattern of value `1774` is shown below:

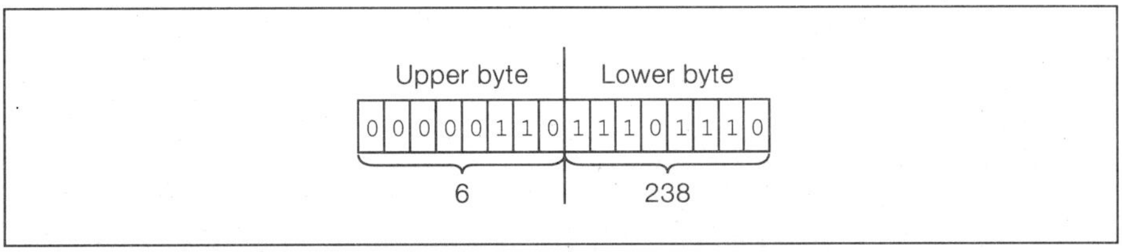

The call `ExtractByte ( 1774, 2 )` would therefore return the value 6, and the call `ExtractByte ( 1774, 1 )` would return the value 238.

5. Complete function `BitOn`, which should return a true value if the bit specified by parameter `Bit` in parameter `N` is on (a binary 1 value) and false otherwise:

```
FUNCTION BitOn ( N, Bit : Integer ) : Boolean;
```

The least significant bit in a word is bit zero. Thus, the call `BitOn ( 1774, 11 )` returns a false value, whereas the call `BitOn ( 1774, 7 )` returns a true value (refer to the diagram in Exercise 6). `BitOn` should also return a false value if the value of either parameter is invalid—i.e., too small or too large.

6. Section 1.2 described bitwise **AND**, **OR** (inclusive-OR), and XOR (exclusive-OR) operations on integer values. **AND** and **OR** are standard operators. Complete function `XOR`, which should perform a bitwise exclusive-OR operation on the two parameters:

```
FUNCTION XOR ( N1, N2 : Integer ) : Integer;
```

7. Complete procedure `NewBase`, which should display the value of parameter `N` as a binary, octal, or hexadecimal number, depending on the value of parameter `Base`:

```
{Global TYPE declaration}
BaseType = ( Binary, Octal, Hexadecimal );

PROCEDURE NewBase ( N : Integer; Base : BaseType );
```

CHAPTER THREE

FUNDAMENTAL STRUCTURED DATA TYPES

In this chapter you will learn how to describe a data structure in terms of the ordering of constituent items and the structure that results. Also, sections 3.2 through 3.5 review the structured data types set, array, character string, and record. The chapter concludes with an examination of the generic table data type and an introduction to analyzing the efficiency of algorithms mathematically.

3.1 DESCRIBING A STRUCTURED DATA TYPE

Preliminaries

Although the specification of the domain and possible operations provides a sufficient description of a simple data type, it is insufficient for a structured data type (also commonly referred to as a *data structure*). Because a data structure contains a collection of items, its specification must also describe the *relationships* among the items in its domain. A structured data type is typically used to represent a sorted *table* of information; therefore, its fundamental operations are oriented toward the storage, access, and traversal of items. As we shall see, particular relationships among the stored items will strongly influence how these operations are implemented.

While it may be clear to you that integer, real, character, and Boolean are data types, it may seem odd that record and array also may be considered as data types; perhaps they seem more like mere containers of data rather than types of data. Record and array are data types, however, because each has a *domain* of "items"; e.g., array items are called *elements* and record items are called *fields*. Also, both the record and the array support a limited number of fundamental operations. For example, the record and the array support two fundamental operations: referencing a particular field or element and assigning the contents of an entire record or array to another identically declared variable.

If we have an array of integer elements, arithmetic operations such as addition and subtraction are also array operations as well. Do not confuse the collection of possible operations of a structured data type with the collection of possible operations for its constituent items. Although addition and multiplication are fundamental operations for any of the array's integer elements, adding and multiplying arrays are not among the fundamental operations for arrays themselves. A programmer may, of course, devise a function that performs matrix addition or multiplication, but such operations are not considered fundamental to all arrays.

Four of the most commonly used data structures are the array, character string, record, and linked list (the focus of Chapter 5). Each of these data structures may be used in two ways:

1. *Simply as they are,* by adhering to the fundamental set of operations for these data structures.
2. *To represent other structured data types,* by imposing additional restrictions on how the structures may be used. For example, while elements may be inserted or deleted anywhere within an array, when an array is used to represent a data type called a *stack,* elements may be added or deleted only at one particular end of the array (ADT stack is discussed in Section 6.1).

Structured data types may be described in terms of their *ordering* and *structure:*

- The **ordering of a data structure** is the general strategy that dictates how items are *stored.*
- The **structure of a data structure** is the resulting arrangement of items, which dictates how items are *retrieved* from the data structure.

The methodologies of information *storage* and subsequent *retrieval* are complementary. Items are stored in a particular manner in order to later access them efficiently in a particular manner. (The term *retrieve* means to remove an item from a data structure; the term *access* means merely to reference the item or make a copy of it. Of course, the ability to retrieve implies the ability to access.)

Ordering

A program that maintains a collection of information must be able to store and retrieve information efficiently. While different programming applications call for different data storage-retrieval strategies, all such strategies are typically variations of the following:

- **Time-of-arrival method:** An item is positioned within the data structure, when it is stored, solely on the basis of when that item is stored, relative to other items already stored.

- **Key-value method:** An item is positioned within the data structure, when stored, on the basis of a special (key) value contained in the item, such as a name or Social Security number.

Some programming applications require that an item be processed purely on the basis of *when* that item was stored (relative to the other items stored) rather than by searching for a particular unit of information within the structure; this is the time-or-arrival scheme. For example, imagine a group of students going to their favorite restaurant for lunch. By the time they arrive, the restaurant is so busy that their names are put on a waiting list. Presumably, customers are seated on a first-come, first-served basis as tables become available. It would make little sense (and would certainly infuriate anyone waiting) if customers were seated by order of Social Security number, alphabetically by last name, or by names randomly selected from the list!

By contrast, the key-value method *processes data based on key value of each item*—i.e., the value in the item used to distinguish it from all other items (often, the item is a record with a field named `Key`). With this method, accessing an item requires a *search* of the structure, looking for a match on the key value of the item sought. Exactly when the item was stored plays no role in determining where it is positioned within the structure or determining which item is available for retrieval next. For instance, each student in the restaurant example also has an academic record that is kept by the university's registrar among a collection of all student records. If student records are to be accessed in a university data base by using student Social Security number as the key value, all records should somehow be stored in order of these numbers to minimize the average access time.

Structure

The structure of a data structure is the resulting arrangement of the items that reflects the relationships among items; these relationships are imposed by the ordering scheme used to store the items. There are four types of structure, for which descriptions follow. The differences in these structures are best understood in terms of a retrieval operation in which an algorithm advances from one item to the next within the data structure.

1. In a **set structure,** there is no relationship among the elements. For this structure, the concept of linearity does not apply, since the items have neither predecessors nor successors. The algorithm must access each item directly.
2. In a **linear list structure,** there is a one-to-one relationship among the items. The structure is linear because each item may have, at most, one predecessor and/or one successor. An important list structure—the linked list—is discussed in Chapter 5.
3. In a **hierarchy (tree) structure,** there is a one-to-many relationship among the items. The structure is nonlinear because each item may have, at most, one predecessor but may have many successors. One of the items (the *root*) has no predecessors. Trees are discussed in chapter 8.
4. In a **network (graph) structure,** there is a many-to-many relationship among the items. The structure is nonlinear and nonhierarchical because

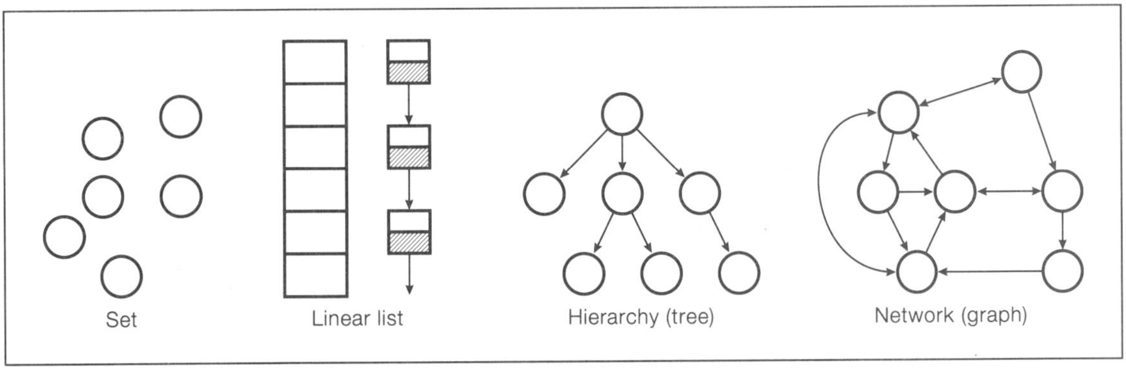

FIGURE 3.1 Depictions of the Four Types of Structure

each item may have many predecessors and many successors. Graphs are discussed in Chapter 9.

Figure 3.1 provides a diagrammatic depiction of each of these relationships (each white-filled circle or rectangle represents a data item).

A set imposes no relationship among its items, although the items themselves may belong to an ordered data type. An item merely belongs to the set or it does not, and the notion of linearity (predecessors and successors) does not apply. A linear list is any sequence of items aligned as a single row or column. Each item has a particular predecessor and successor, except for the first and last items.

The items in a hierarchy (tree) form tiers called *levels*. To store or access a particular item in a hierarchy, an algorithm must start with the single item at the "top" of the structure (the root item) and descend into the structure via other items. The ability to advance from a particular item to, perhaps, several other items facilitates searching schemes that are typically faster than a linear search on a linear list. A network (graph) is also a nonlinear collection of items, but—unlike the case of a hierarchy—each item may have no, one, or many predecessors and successors. In fact, each item may have as its predecessor and its successor any other item in the network.

Figure 3.2 lists all simple and structured data types presented in this book.

3.2 SET DATA TYPE

The mathematical term *set* refers to any collection of items that all share a similar property or properties. Items either belong to the set or they do not, based on their having or not having this same property. The notion of a set also implies that there is no linearity about the collection; each item (or element) of the set is completely independent and unrelated to the other elements of the set. This is an important characteristic: A set of numbers can be likened to a collection of separate islands of information, whereas a linear list of numbers (e.g., a one-dimensional array of numbers) can be likened to a row of islands, with some form of access from one island to the next.

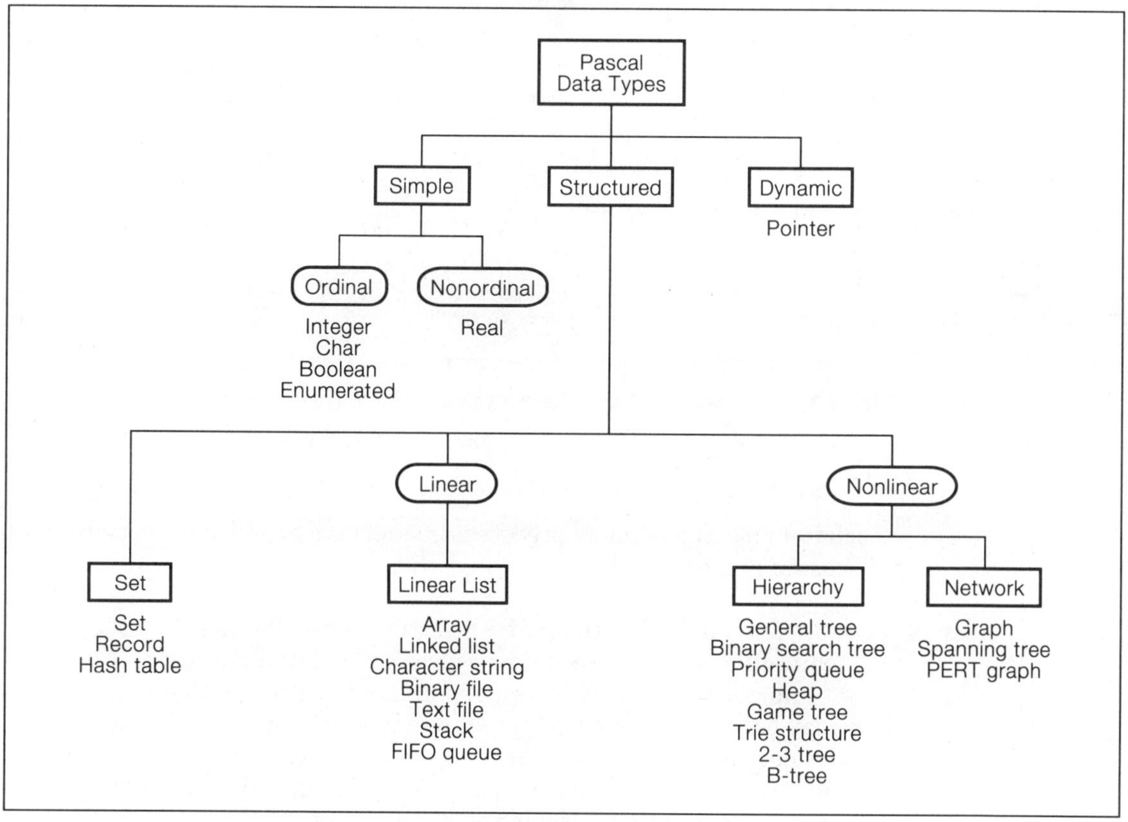

FIGURE 3.2 Data Types Presented in This Text

Specifications for the ADT Set

The **ADT set** is a structured data type whose elements belong to the same type, yet no ordering is imposed by the structure. Each item is completely independent of other items, so the concept of linearity does not apply.

Domain

The domain is elements of the same data type.

Fundamental Set Operations

1. *Assignment to set variable:* Assign the entire contents of one set to another set.
2. Test for **membership:** Determine whether or not an item is a member of a particular set.
3. Test for *equality:* Determine if two sets have exactly the same elements.

4. *Reference element:* Reference a particular element of a set; once an element is referenced, any operation appropriate for an item of that element's data type may be performed on the field as well.
5. *Form* **union** *of two sets:* Form a set that holds all elements of two sets, with no duplicate members.
6. *Form* **intersection** *of two sets:* Form a set of those elements common to two sets.
7. *Form* **difference** *of two sets:* Form a set of those elements that are not common to two sets (the corollary of intersection).
8. Form **subset:** Determine if one set is contained within another set.

Pascal Representation of the ADT Set

There are two levels of divisibility at which the ADT set may be represented as a data structure within Pascal:

- The set comprises members of the same *simple, ordinal* data type.
- The set comprises members of the same *structured* data type.

For the first level of divisibility, standard Pascal provides a predefined data type named `set` to represent a finite number of members (often 128 or 256) of the same simple, ordinal data type (character, Boolean, enumerated, or else a subrange of these types or of integer type). Pascal compilers also recognize the constant set notation depicted in Figure 3.3, as well as various standard set operators.

For the second level of divisibility, each element is a structured data type (typically a record), and most fundamental operations are completely programmer-defined. Two common representations are an array of records and a linked list of records (linked lists are discussed in Chapter 5). At the abstract level, because there are no relationships among members of a set, a particular set member cannot be accessed using an element-by-element search, such as a linear search. Instead, a *direct access scheme* must be employed, in which a key field value is transformed into a value indicating the location of the member within the structure. Direct-access schemes, such as *hashing,* are discussed in Section 10.2.

A primitive routine is free to represent a set using any data structure and to employ any type of searching algorithm to store and subsequently retrieve elements. This does not violate the fact that linearity does not apply to sets—it merely reflects the mechanical requirements imposed by the physical memory representation. To the higher-level routine that calls this set-management primitive, the data structure is still a set for which element-by-element accessing is not allowed. The remainder of this section on sets focuses on the standard data type called set, and any reference to a set data structure is a reference to this type.

In a Pascal program, a set structure may be specified using any of the following:

1. Constant set notation (as described in Figure 3.3)
2. A variable of type set
3. Either of the preceding along with a set operator, as appropriate

Standard Pascal syntax related to ADT set follows, and descriptions of all standard operators and special symbols are given in Appendix A.

Declaration of a set variable

```
VAR
  {variable identifier} : SET OF {base type identifier}
```

Standard operators

Assignment :=

Membership	IN	Equality	=
Union	=	Inequality	<>
Intersection	*	Proper subset	<= >=
Difference	–		

Standard data-transfer procedures and techniques

Read from binary file of set	Get, Read
Write to binary file of set	Put, Write
Parameter passing	

An entire set may be referenced using either an explicit specification or declaring a variable to be a set of some ordinal type and then assigning the actual members to this set via an explicit specification. Figure 3.3 shows the syntax diagram for a set constant.

Examples of the use of set constants and variables follow:

```
TYPE
  Months     =  ( January, February, March, April, May, June, July, August,
                  September, October, November, December );

  MonthSet   =  SET OF Months;

  CharSet    =  SET OF Char;

VAR
  AnyMonth              :  Months;       {All Months values}
  SpringMonth           :  March..May;   {Subrange of Months types}
  MonthsInSpring,
  SecondQuarter,
  SomeMonths            :  MonthSet;       {Set of zero or more Months type constants}
  AllChars,    LowerCase,
  Digits,      LowerDigits,
  Vowels,      LowerVowels,
  Consonants            :  CharSet;        {Set of zero or more Char characters}
```

Compare the declaration of `Months`, `AnyMonth`, `SpringMonth`, and `MonthsInSpring`. `AnyMonth` is capable of containing one of the values of the enumerated data type `Months`. `SpringMonth` is also capable of con-

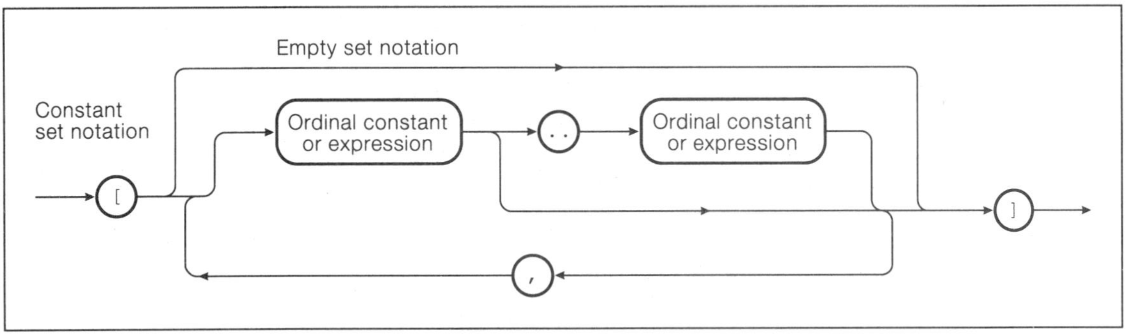

FIGURE 3.3 Syntax for Constant Set Notation

taining a single value of the enumerated data type `Months`, but only those values between `March` and `May`, inclusive. `MonthsInSpring` is capable of holding a structured data type value; i.e., an entire set of `Months` values. (All ordinal constants or variables within the same specification must be of the same data type.)

Given these sample declarations, the following Pascal code segment contains legal syntax:

```
AnyMonth        := July;
MonthsInSpring := [ March, April, May ] ;
IF (AnyMonth IN MonthsInSpring)  OR (AnyMonth IN [ June..August ]) THEN
   Writeln ( 'These are warm, sunny months' );
SecondQuarter  := MonthsInSpring;                        {Duplicate set}
SomeMonths     := [ ] ;                                  {Empty set}
```

In the third statement, constant set notation is used to assign a set of `Months` values to the set variable, `MonthsInSpring`. Because members of a set are unordered, any of the following notations could have been used:

```
[ March, April, May ]   [ May, April, March ]   [ April, May, March ]
```

In the data type `Months`, `April` immediately follows `March` and `May` immediately follows `April`, so the following two notations in an assignment statement are equivalent:

```
[ March, April, May ]   [ March..May ]
```

The **IF** statement just given tests `AnyMonth` for membership in either of two sets. The set in the first Boolean expression is specified by the identifier `MonthsInSpring`, whereas the set in the second Boolean expression is specified by explicit set notation. Here, the subrange notation is used, so `July` is included in the set of all `Months` between `June` and `August`, inclusive. After the third assignment statement is executed, `SecondQuarter` contains a set that is identical to the set in MonthsInSpring, so the expression (SecondQuarter = MonthsInSpring) would subsequently evaluate to a true value if tested. The fourth assignment statement stores an empty set (i.e., a set containing no members) in variable SomeMonths, which may be assigned a nonempty set of elements at a later time.

CharSet, defined earlier, is a set data type capable of containing members that are char characters. Examine the following Pascal instructions, (based on the ASCII character set—Appendix C) the first of which is *illegal:*

```
Digits        := '0'..'9';                {ILLEGAL}
Digits        := [ '0'..'9' ];            {LEGAL}

LowerCase     := [ 'a'..'y', '?' ];
LowerCase     := LowerCase + [ 'z' ];     {Adding member    (union)}
LowerCase     := LowerCase - [ '?' ];     {Deleting member  (difference)}

AllChars      := Digits + LowerCase +
                 [ ''..'/', ':'..'@', 'A'..'Z', '{'..'~' ];  {Union}
Vowels        := [ 'A', 'a', 'E', 'e', 'I', 'i', 'O', 'o', 'U', 'u'];

Consonants    := AllChars  -  Vowels;  {Difference; set of non-vowel letters}
LowerVowels   := LowerCase *  Vowels;  {Intersection; set of lowercase vowels}
LowerDigits   := LowerCase *  Digits;  {Intersection; an empty set}
```

If these assignment statements are executed, each of the following Boolean expressions would evaluate to a true value. These expressions involve the six *containment relations* operators related to equality and subsets:

```
Digits   =   [ '0'..'9' ];      {Equality}
Vowels   <>  AllChars;          {Inequality}
Vowels   <=  AllChars;          {Subset; members of Vowels are members of
                                 AllChars}
```

The use of a set can simplify a Pascal code segment that performs the testing of some condition. For example, without set notation, the Boolean expression in the following **IF** statement would be have to be replaced with a far more complex Boolean expression, the first part of which is also shown:

```
IF AptNumber IN [ 9..13, 15, 17, 19, 27..32, 39..54, 67..85, 87, 88, 93, 94 ] THEN

IF ((AptNumber >= 9) AND (AptNumber <= 13))  OR  (AptNumber = 15) OR
   (AptNumber = 17) OR  (AptNumber = 19) OR
                                                          ... etc., etc.
```

The **IN** operator behaves like a multiple equality (=) operator, and the commas separating set members behave like inclusive-OR (**OR**) operators.

Computer Memory Representation of the ADT Set

A variable declared to be of standard Pascal set type is represented in memory as a **bit map.** Enough words of memory are allocated for a set variable

```
VAR
  SomeMonths : SET OF Months;

  SomeMonths := [ July ];
```

0	0	0	0	0	0	0	0	0	1	0	0	0	0	0	0
15	14	13	12	11	10	9	8	7	6	5	4	3	2	1	0

```
  SomeMonths := [ March, April, May ];
```

0	0	0	0	0	0	0	0	0	0	0	1	1	1	0	0
15	14	13	12	11	10	9	8	7	6	5	4	3	2	1	0

```
  SomeMonths := [ January, February, March, April, May, June, July, August,
                  September, October, November, December ];
```

0	0	0	0	1	1	1	1	1	1	1	1	1	1	1	1
15	14	13	12	11	10	9	8	7	6	5	4	3	2	1	0

```
  SomeMonths := [ ];
```

0	0	0	0	0	0	0	0	0	0	0	0	0	0	0	0
15	14	13	12	11	10	9	8	7	6	5	4	3	2	1	0

FIGURE 3.4 Bit Maps of Set Variable `SomeMonths` upon Assignments to It

such that there is at least one bit for every potential element in the set. Recall that all elements of a particular simple set have the same simple, ordinal data type. Therefore, each bit in the bit map corresponds to the ordinal position of a potential set element within the domain of its data type (a set containing a subrange of integer values is mapped onto the bit numbers 0, 1, 2, etc.). For example, to indicate that a set of characters contained `'a'` as a member, the 65th bit of the set's bit map would be turned on in memory (a 1, or high-voltage signal).

Shown in Figure 3.4 are four assignment statements involving set variable `SomeMonths` of enumerated type `Months` whose declaration was given earlier. Following each statement is the bit-map representation of `SomeMonths` as it would appear *after* the statement is executed. Since the maximum size of a `Months` set is 12 elements, a single 16-bit word is large enough to hold a single bit map and is so depicted in the figure.

3.3 ARRAY DATA TYPE

Although the ADT set described in Section 3.2 does facilitate the storage of a collection of data, it has three major drawbacks that ADT array overcomes:

- *Set elements must be simple constants.* A variable of standard Pascal set data type can store only constants of the same simple data type. The elements of an array variable also must be of the same data type, but they behave as variables, which may be of either simple or structured type.

- *No sequential access of set elements.* A particular element of a set must be accessed directly because the concept of linearity does not apply to a set; therefore, set elements cannot be accessed sequentially. An array variable supports direct access via indexing and, as a linear structure, supports sequential access of elements as well.
- *Relatively limited number of set elements.* Because the standard Pascal set type is represented using a bit map, a relatively small upper limit on the number of elements (typically, 256) will be imposed by the Pascal compiler in use. The number of possible elements of an array is typically much larger, limited only by the amount of internal memory available for the program's executable image.

Specifications for the ADT Array

The **ADT array** is a structured data type whose items form a linear list.

Domain

The domain is elements that are variables of the same simple or structured data type.

Fundamental Array Operations

1. *Assignment to array variable:* Assign the entire contents of one array to another identically-declared array or assignment to one array element.
2. *Reference element:* Reference an element using the array name plus the index value, which indicates the relative position of the element within the structure. Once an element is referenced, any operation appropriate for an item of that element's data type may be performed on the element.

Arrays may be one-dimensional, with elements accessed via a single index value, or they may be multidimensional, with elements accessed via several index values, one per dimension. For example, a two-dimensional array (commonly called a *matrix*) requires two indices: one for rows and the other for columns.

Pascal Representation of the ADT Array

Standard Pascal syntax related to the **ADT array** follows, and descriptions of all standard operators, special symbols are given in Appendix A.

Declaration of an array variable

```
VAR
  {variable identifier} : {array type identifier or description}
```

Standard operator, syntax

Assignment	:=
Element reference	`[ {index value} ]`

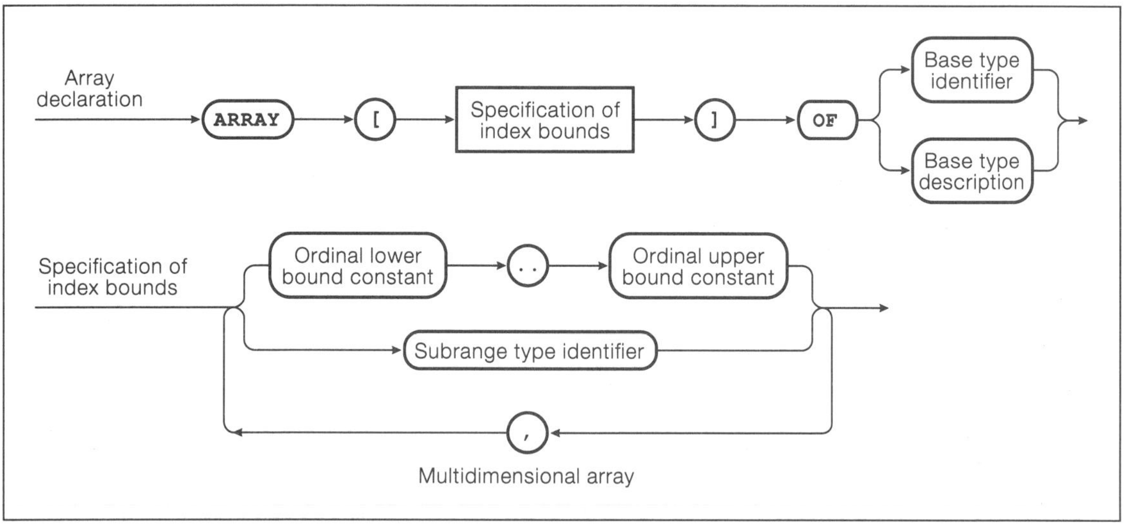

FIGURE 3.5 Pascal Syntax for an Array Declaration

Standard data-transfer procedures and syntax

Read from binary file of array	`Read, Get`
Write to binary file of array	`Write, Put`
Parameter passing	

All Pascal compilers recognize the reserved identifier **ARRAY** as referring to the ADT array data type. An array declaration specifies four items of information:

1. Base type (i.e., the data type of all elements)
2. Size of the array (i.e., how many elements)
3. Data type of the index or indices
4. Upper and lower bounds of each index (i.e., the maximum and minimum index values allowed), specified using a subrange

Figure 3.5 depicts the syntax used in the specification of the indices in an array declaration.

An array declaration specifies the subrange of lower- and upper-bound index values for each array dimension. The type of the index or indices must be simple and ordinal. The total number of elements in an array may be calculated from its declaration, as follows:

$$\text{Size of a dimension} = (\text{upper bound}) - (\text{lower bound}) + 1$$

$$\text{Total array size} = (\text{size of 1st dimension}) \times (\text{size of 2nd dimension}) \times \ldots (\text{size of last dimension})$$

The base data type of each array element may be any simple or structured data type other than a file. If the base type is not a standard type, its declaration must precede the declaration of the array.

Examine the following sample declarations, comparing these to the set declarations given in Section 3.2:

```
TYPE
  Months          =  ( January, February, March, April, May, June, July,
                       August, September, October, November, December );

  MonthSet        =  SET OF Months;

  MonthArray      =  ARRAY [ 1..12 ] OF Months;

  DaysArray       =  ARRAY [ January..December ] OF 28..31;
    {equivalent to   ARRAY [ Months ]  OF  28..31;}

VAR
  SomeMonths  :  MonthSet;       {Set of up to 12 enumerated values}
  AllMonths   :  MonthArray;     {Array of 12 enumerated values}
  Days        :  DaysArray;      {Array of 12 integers}
  AnyMonth    :  Months;         {Enumerated type; 12 possible values}
```

As with a set, an entire array may be referenced by using the identifier of the array. Whereas an element of a *set* must be referenced by using the element's value or name, any element of an *array* may be referenced by using the array name plus an index value. The syntax diagram for an element reference is given in Figure 3.6.

The set identifier `SomeMonths` references the entire set of `Months` values it contains, whereas the identifier `AllMonths` references an entire array of enumerated values, and the identifier `Days` references an entire array of integer values. The fifth element of `AllMonths`, for example, is referenced by the syntax, `AllMonths [ 5 ]`. A variable may be used to hold the index value (rather than using a constant value) and varied within a loop, thereby allowing an algorithm to reference elements *sequentially*.

In most applications, the index data type is integer, and its lower bound is 1. In other applications, the index value itself may play an important role beyond merely referencing an array element. As an example, procedure `DistributionOfTemperatures`, which follows, prompts the program's user to enter the average daily temperature for a 365-day period, builds a frequency distribution of average daily temperatures, and then displays the distribution both as a tabular list and as a bar graph.

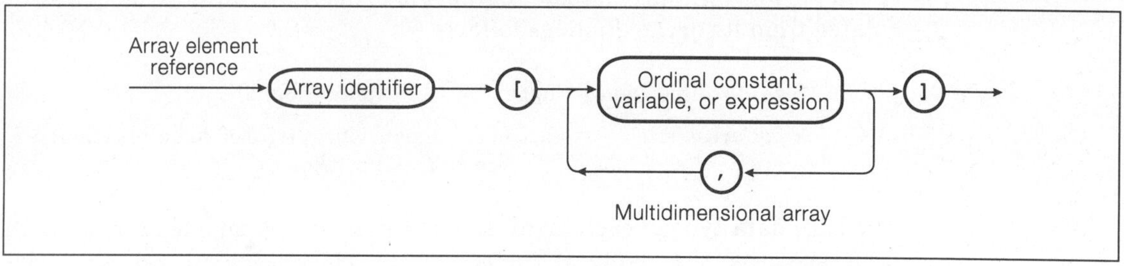

FIGURE 3.6 Pascal Syntax for an Array Element Reference

```
{The following procedure is given in Appendix K}

PROCEDURE Pause;
```

```
PROCEDURE DistributionOfTemperatures;

CONST
  MinTemp = -40;                                  {Minimum temperature}
  MaxTemp = 110;                                  {Maximum temperature}

TYPE
  AllTemperatures  =  ARRAY [ MinTemp..MaxTemp ] OF Integer;

VAR
  Temperatures : AllTemperatures;                 {Holds day-count for each temperature}
  Day, Count   : Integer;
  OneTemp      : MinTemp..MaxTemp;

BEGIN
FOR OneTemp := MinTemp TO MaxTemp DO
  Temperatures [ OneTemp ] := 0;                  {Initialize distribution to all zeros}

{Build distribution by counting the number of days for each temperature}

FOR Day := 1 TO 365 DO
  BEGIN
  Write ( 'Enter temperature (', MinTemp, '..', MaxTemp, ') for day #', Day, ':  ' );
  Readln ( OneTemp );
  Temperatures [ OneTemp ] := Temperatures [ OneTemp ] + 1
  END;

{Display frequency distribution in tabular form}

Writeln; Writeln ( 'Temperature      No. of Days' );
Writeln ( '-----------      -----------' );  Writeln;
Count := 0;
FOR OneTemp := MinTemp TO MaxTemp DO
  BEGIN
  Writeln ( OneTemp:7, Temperatures [ OneTemp ]:24 );
  Count := Count + 1;
  IF Count MOD 23 = 0 THEN
    Pause                                         {Pause screen scrolling if necessary}
  END;
Pause;                                            {Pause screen scrolling if necessary}

{Display frequency distribution as a horizontal bar graph}

Count := 0;
FOR OneTemp := MinTemp TO MaxTemp DO
  BEGIN
  Write ( OneTemp:3, ' | ' );
  FOR Day := 1 TO Temperatures [ OneTemp ] DO
    Write ( '*' );
  Writeln;
  Count := Count + 1;
  IF Count MOD 23 = 0 THEN
    Pause                                         {Pause screen scrolling if necessary}
  END
END;
```

Computer Memory Representation of the ADT Array

The notion of multidimensional arrays having rows and columns is an illusion that allows the programmer to design routines to manipulate arrays in an intuitive way. All memory—whether internal or external—is conceptually linear (i.e., "flat") and may be more accurately envisioned as one long row of memory units called words. This is why an array representation of another data structure, such as a stack, queue, or tree, is referred to throughout this textbook as a **sequential storage** representation. Array elements occupy adjacent memory locations, and, during compilation, the array name is associated with the internal memory address of the first array element (the *base address* of the array).

When a compiler encounters syntax, such as `Temperatures [ OneTemp ]` or `Fibonacci [ K - 2 ]` or `Gens [ CurrentGen, 3, 5 ]`, it must generate machine code that directs the computer to perform a **mapping function** that transforms the index value(s) into the actual internal memory address of the indicated element. This transformation consists of translating the index value(s) into a single *offset value,* which can then be added to the base address to obtain the word address of the element or find where the element begins if it spans more than one word. (For simplicity, we will assume that *whole-word addressing* is being used by the computer, although *byte addressing* is used by many computers as well.)

As examples, assume that a program has assigned values to the following two arrays:

```
VAR
  D1 : ARRAY [ 1..4 ]        OF Integer;
  D2 : ARRAY [ 1..3, 1..4 ] OF Integer;
```

Figure 3.7 depicts the programmer's conception and the corresponding memory configuration of memory for `D1` and `D2` along with some sample ele-

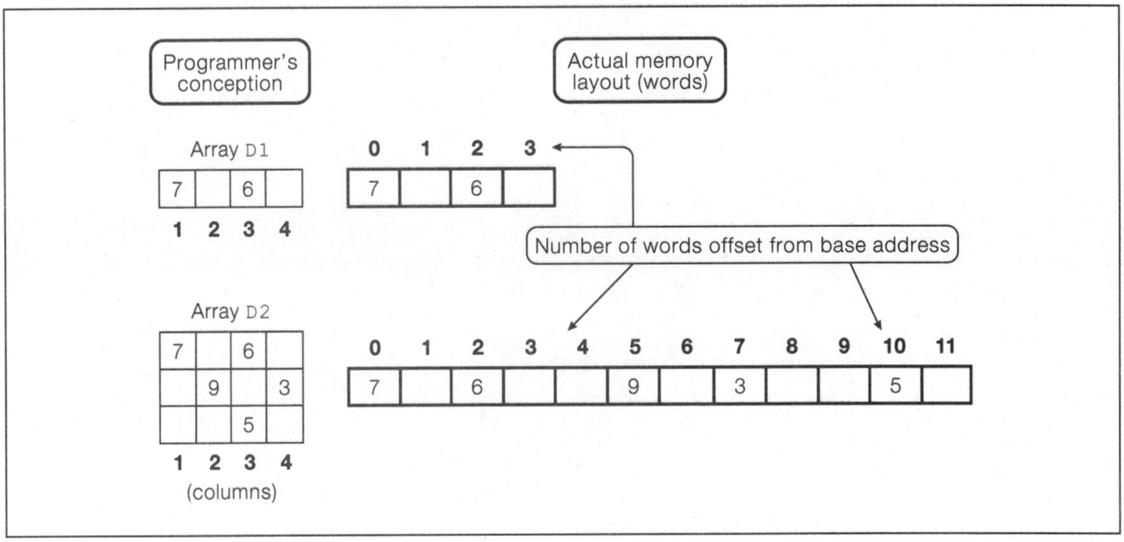

FIGURE 3.7 Conceptual and Actual (Row Order) Memory Representation of Two Integer Arrays

ment values, assuming that one word of memory is being used to store each integer value (zero values are not shown). Compilers vary as to whether they generate the machine code to store and reference array elements in *row order* or *column order;* row order is depicted in Figure 3.7.

As a compiler transforms source code into object code, it must retain information about the variables it encounters, such as data type (as specified in declarations) and memory address. For arrays, compilers must retain a variety of information, including the following:

- Source code name (typically only the first eight characters are retained)
- Base type (i.e., element data type)
- Element length (typically in bytes)
- Base address of the array
- Number of dimensions
- Array bounds (a list of the valid index values for each dimension)

This information is typically packaged in a single record called an *array descriptor.*

APPLICATION 3.1 The Game of Life

As an example of the use of a multidimensional array, we examine a famous algorithm devised by mathematician John Horton Conway in 1970. The Game of Life is not really a game at all but rather a simple yet fascinating simulation of the evolution of a bacterial colony. The rules by which bacteria are born, survive, or die are as follows:

1. All bacteria live in a two-dimensional, rectangular area divided into square cells: A cell may house a single bacterium or may be empty. No bacteria of the colony live beyond the borders of the colony. Each cell (empty or not) has, at most, eight neighboring cells (see Figure 3.8).
2. If a particular cell has *exactly two bacteria* among its neighboring cells, *that cell remains as is into the next generation.* (If the cell is currently occupied, that bacterium survives to the next generation.)
3. If a particular cell has *exactly three bacteria* among its neighboring cells, there will be *a bacterium in that cell in the next generation.* (If the cell is currently empty, a bacterium will be born in the next generation.)
4. If a particular cell has *fewer than two or more than three bacteria* among its neighboring cells, there will be *no bacterium in that cell in the next generation.* (If zero or one, an existing bacterium dies of loneliness; if four or more, an existing bacterium dies of overcrowding.)

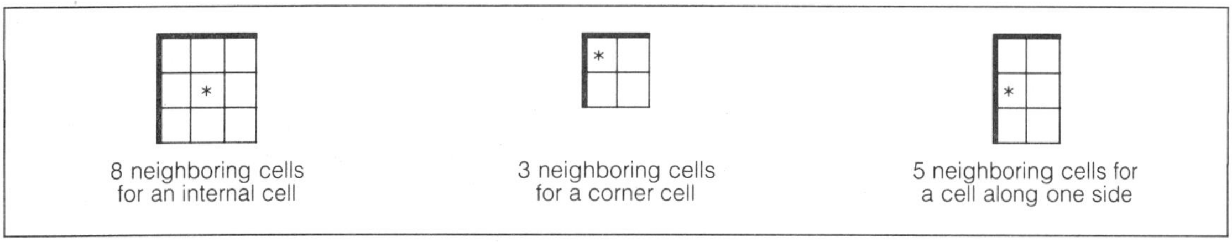

FIGURE 3.8 Neighboring Cells

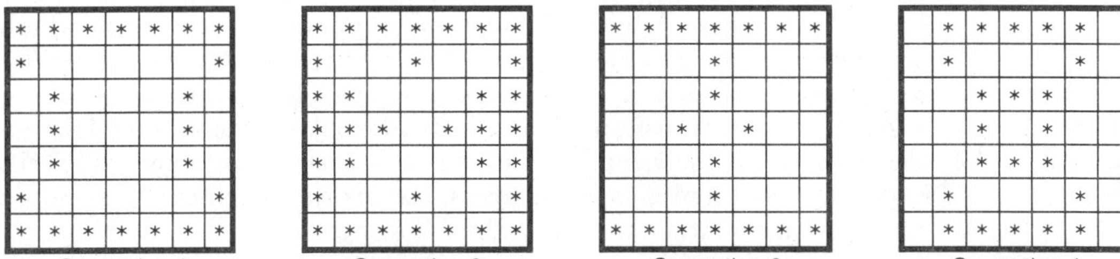

FIGURE 3.9 Sample Game of Life Display over Four Generations

5. All births and deaths occur simultaneously, so that the birth or death of a bacterium in the current generation does not affect the neighbor-counting for an adjacent cell.

Bacteria in the initial generation may be arranged randomly or in any pattern you choose—a symmetrical mosaic, a picture, or even a face! By following these rules and displaying each generation, the original pattern evolves like a kaleidoscope display. Figure 3.9 shows a small sample colony as it develops over four generations.

Consider how you would design a Pascal program to implement the Game of Life using a two-dimensional array to represent the current generation. A one-cell border of empty cells around the colony simplifies the algorithm that counts neighbors; with this lifeless border, counting the neighbors of edge cells is no longer a special case. Of course, the savings in execution time is somewhat offset by the additional memory required, an example of the *execution time/memory space trade-off,* which arises frequently in the design of algorithms; this phenomenon is discussed at length in Section 3.7. The following version of the program was used to generate the display in Figure 3.9. It packages into a three-dimensional array a pair of two-dimensional arrays—one for the current generation and the other for the next generation.

```
PROGRAM GameOfLife ( INPUT, OUTPUT );

CONST
  MaxRow    = 8;                            {Colony itself is 7 rows of cells}
  MaxColumn = 8;                            {  by 7 columns of cells,}
  MaxGens   = 4;                            {Evolving over 4 generations here}

TYPE
  DualGens  = ( CurrentGen, NextGen );
  GenType   = ARRAY [ DualGens, 0..MaxRow, 0..MaxColumn ] OF Char;

VAR
  Gens      : GenType;                      {Holds current and next generation}
  GenCount  : Integer;                      {Generation count}
```

```
{The following procedure is defined in Appendix K}

PROCEDURE Pause;
```

```
PROCEDURE InitializeCurrentGeneration ( VAR Gens : GenType );

VAR
  N  : Integer;

BEGIN
FOR N := 0 TO MaxColumn DO                      {Initialize empty borders}
  BEGIN
  Gens [ CurrentGen, 0, N ]           := ' ';  {Initialize top border}
  Gens [ CurrentGen, MaxRow, N ]      := ' ';  {Initialize bottom border}
  Gens [ CurrentGen, N, 0 ]           := ' ';  {Initialize left border}
  Gens [ CurrentGen, N, MaxColumn ]   := ' '   {Initialize right border}
  END;

{Insert code storing * in Gens [ CurrentGen, 1..MaxRow-1, 1..MaxColumn-1]}
END;
```

```
PROCEDURE DisplayCurrentGeneration ( VAR Gens : GenType );

VAR
  Row, Column : Integer;

BEGIN
Writeln;
FOR Row := 1 TO MaxRow - 1 DO
  BEGIN
  FOR Column := 1 TO MaxColumn - 1 DO
    Write ( Gens [ CurrentGen, Row, Column ] );
  Writeln
  END
END;
```

```
PROCEDURE UpdateCurrentGeneration ( VAR Gens : GenType );

VAR
  Row, Column : Integer;
  NewChar     : Char;
```

```
  FUNCTION CountNeighbors ( Row, Column : Integer ) : Integer;

  VAR
    R, C, Count : Integer;

  BEGIN
  Count := 0;
  FOR R := Row - 1 TO Row + 1 DO
    FOR C := Column - 1 TO Column + 1 DO
      IF Gens [ CurrentGen, R, C ] <> '^' THEN
        Count := Count + 1;
  IF Gens [ CurrentGen, Row, Column ] <> '^'THEN
    Count := Count - 1;
  CountNeighbors := Count
  END;
```

```
{*** Main routine for UpdateCurrentGeneration ***}

BEGIN
FOR Row := 1 TO MaxRow - 1 DO
  FOR Column := 1 TO MaxColumn - 1 DO
    BEGIN
    CASE CountNeighbors ( Row, Column ) OF
      0, 1, 4..8 : NewChar := ' ';
               2 : NewChar := Gens [ CurrentGen, Row, Column ];
               3 : NewChar := '*'
    END;
    Gens [ NextGen, Row, Column ] := NewChar
    END;
FOR Row := 1 TO MaxRow - 1 DO
  FOR Column := 1 TO MaxColumn - 1 DO
    Gens [ CurrentGen, Row, Column ] := Gens [ NextGen, Row, Column ]
END;
```

```
{***  Main  Routine  ***}

BEGIN
InitializeCurrentGeneration ( Gens );
DisplayCurrentGeneration ( Gens );
Pause;
FOR GenCount := 1 TO MaxGens DO
  BEGIN
  UpdateCurrentGeneration ( Gens );
  DisplayCurrentGeneration ( Gens );
  Pause
  END
END.
```

For an in-depth study of this simulation and its implications, you are encouraged to read *The Recursive Universe* by William Poundstone (New York, N.Y.: William Morrow & Company, Inc., 1989). In his book, Poundstone discusses a variety of interesting patterns that may be regarded as unique "creatures," evolving in a predictable manner, seemingly with personalities of their own. Twelve of these creatures are shown in Figure 3.10. Some creatures like the Block and Tub are stable, whereas others—such as the Blinker, Beacon, and Beehive—*oscillate* between two particular shapes indefinitely. The T Tetromino evolves into nine geometric shapes before becoming a four-part Blinker, which Poundstone calls a Traffic Light.

Some creatures, such as the Glider and the Eater, move across the colony, changing their shapes along the way but always returning to their original forms. The Eater can actually "devour" certain creatures as it moves (e.g., it can eat a Glider in four generations!). Two Eaters can even attack each other: They will devour parts of each other, repair themselves, and then continue on their separate ways!

The R Pentamino is especially interesting because, over many generations, it produces a wide assortment of familiar patterns. After 1103 generations, a colony that begins with a single R Pentamino stabilizes; i.e., no two patterns interact again, and the entire colony's behavior becomes completely predictable. At this point, the colony consists of eight Blocks, six Gliders, four Beehives, four Blinkers, a Boat, a Loaf, and a Ship. Like a DNA molecule, the original R Pentamino contains all the "genetic data"

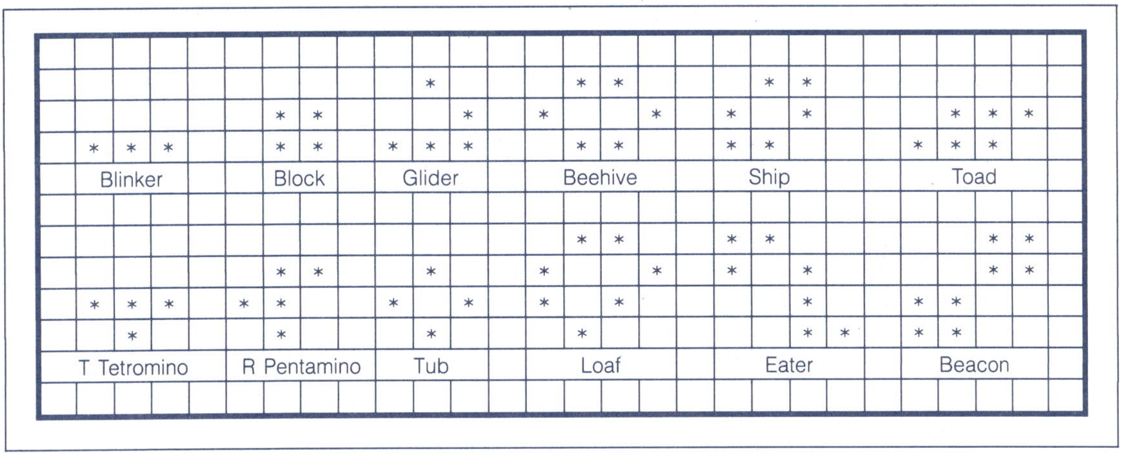

FIGURE 3.10 Some Patterns that Display Interesting Behavior (from *The Recursive Universe* by William Poundstone. Copyright © 1989 by William Poundstone. By permission of William Morrow & Co., Inc.)

necessary to spawn a variety of other "creatures" (an entire colony of them, in fact).

3.4 CHARACTER STRING DATA TYPE

Many applications involve the manipulation of strings of characters rather than single characters. Character strings were probably discussed in your first computer science course in the context of labeling output—e.g., `Writeln ( 'The average is', average );`. Here, `'The average is'` is a **literal string,** as mentioned in Section 2.4. The value of this constant is fixed at compile-time and the actual characters are included by the compiler in the machine code generated to output them.

Because a literal string is a constant, it may be given a name (i.e., associated with an identifier via a **CONST** declaration) as in the following example:

```
CONST
  CompanyName = 'Hardly-Able Construction Company, Inc.';
  .
  .
Writeln ( 'Make the amount of $', AcctReceivbl:6:2, ' payable to ', CompanyName );
```

In this way, the constant `CompanyName` may be used anywhere within the scope of **CONST** declaration without having to reenter the full company name in the source code. This does not result in any savings of memory in the resulting machine code, however, since the compiler will merely replace the constant identifier `CompanyName` with the characters representing the name of the company. Named constants are provided in standard Pascal merely as a convenience to the programmer: If the program is to be used by another company, the programmer need change only the value of `CompanyName` in the declaration (and recompile) to change its value throughout the program.

A literal string is limited in its usefulness because its value is fixed. It is typically more useful to assign to a character string variable the entire string of characters at once or to combine two or more strings into one string (**concatenation**), to access a particular group of characters within the character string (**substring**), or to perform a variety of other text-oriented operations. We can describe the ADT for a data structure especially suitable for holding a character string and for string operations—the ADT character string—whose specifications follow.

Specifications for the ADT Character String

The **ADT character string** is a linear list of single characters, typically used to represent textual data.

Domain

The domain is single characters.

Fundamental Operations

1. *Nullify string:* Initialize the string as a **null string**—i.e., a string containing no characters.
2. *Assignment to string variable:* Assign an entire character string to a string variable.
3. *Test for emptiness:* Test a character string to determine if it is null.
4. *Obtain current length:* Obtain the current length of the string.
5. *Form concatenation of strings:* Combine two character strings to form a third string.
6. Form *substring:* Extract part of a character string.
7. *Search for a particular pattern:* Return the ordinal position where the desired pattern begins if found, or zero if not found.
8. *Insert string pattern:* Insert a character string within another character string.
9. *Delete string pattern:* Delete a string of characters from a character string.

Pascal Representations of the ADT Character String

Data structures commonly employed to represent the ADT character string include the following:

1. Simple (unpacked) array of char data type (introduced in this section)
2. Packed array of char data type (introduced in this section)
3. String data type (nonstandard Pascal type, introduced in this section)
4. Linked list (Application 5.1)
5. Trie structure (Application 5.3)

Simple (Unpacked) Array of Char Data Type

A basic way to store a character string is within a variable declared as an *array of char*. The entire character string may be referenced merely by using the variable identifier, and individual characters may be referenced using the indexing syntax common to all arrays. Such an array is an **unpacked array of char;** i.e., an *entire word* will be allocated to store a single character, even though only a *single byte* is really all that is needed. And just as we cannot read or write an integer array in its entirety, we cannot read or write an unpacked character array in its entirety (the exception in both cases is with binary files, discussed in Section 4.1). Nor can we assign a literal string to the array using a single assignment statement or use a relational operator to compare two character arrays or compare one character array and a literal string.

Packed Array of Char Data Type

Standard Pascal provides a special data type called the **packed array of char,** which overcomes many of the shortcomings of the unpacked array. The array is said to be *packed* because only a single byte is allocated for each character, allowing the computer to "pack" two characters into a single 16-bit word or four characters into a 32-bit word. The syntax for declaring a variable to be a packed array of char follows:

```
VAR
  {variable identifier} = PACKED ARRAY [ 1..{upper bound} ] OF Char;
```

Since a variable declared to be a packed array of char is an array variable, all rules regarding simple array usage apply to packed arrays of char as well, with these additional rules:

1. The lower subscript value in the subrange declaration must be 1 and the array must be one-dimensional, with the base type as char.
2. Unlike other arrays, most compilers permit all array elements to be initialized or written in their entirety using only the array identifier in the `Read`, `Readln`, `Write`, or `Writeln` statements. Typically, a single character value cannot be assigned to a single element via a `Read` or `Readln` statement.
3. A packed array of char variable may be assigned a literal string value, but the length of the literal string must equal the declared size of the packed array.
4. A packed array of char variable may be compared to a literal string using a relational operator but, again, the length of the literal string must equal the declared size of the packed array.

When a program reads characters into a packed array of char from the keyboard or a text file, the characters are stored starting in element 1 of the array; i.e., they are **left-justified** within the array. If there are more characters available in the input stream than can fit in the array, the excess characters are simply ignored. If there are fewer characters, then each of the remaining elements is assigned a blank character; i.e., the array is padded with trailing blanks. When writing the contents of a packed array of char variable to which a field width specification is appended, if the specified width is greater than the size of the array, *leading blanks* will be automatically written. Figure 3.11 gives an example of the padding and justification

```
VAR
  Response : PACKED ARRAY [ 1..8 ] OF Char;

BEGIN
Write ( 'Enter some text and press [RETURN]: ');
Readln ( Response );
```

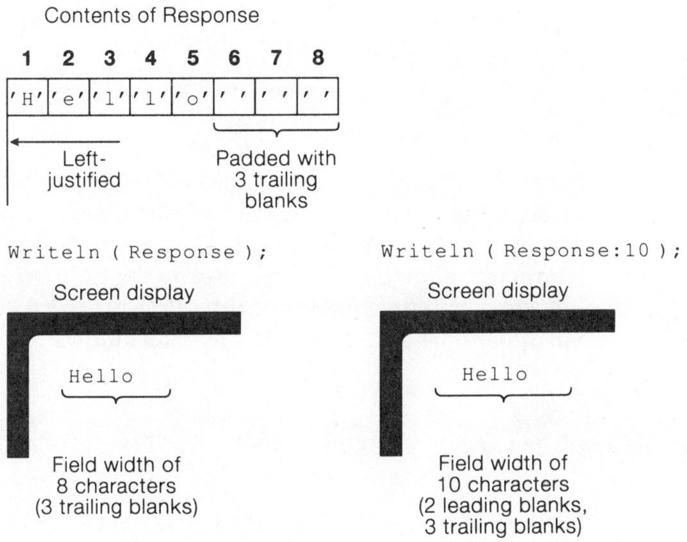

FIGURE 3.11 Sample Input and Output Using a Packed Array of Char

in which the user enters the string `'Hello'`. Both the input and output are padded with three spaces and the total field width of the output is eight characters, the first three of which are spaces.

To genuinely represent the ADT character string accurately with all its fundamental operations, a *count of the characters stored* must also be maintained—i.e., the current **string length.** Such a count would not include any leading blanks that are automatically stored. Sample declarations for this follow:

```
CONST
  MaxLength   = ??;                        {Application-dependent; 256 is typical}

TYPE
  StringType = RECORD
                 Chars  : PACKED ARRAY [ 1..MaxLength ] OF Char;
                 Length : 0..MaxLength
               END;

VAR
  Str : StringType;
```

Programmer-defined procedures and functions could be devised for all the fundamental operations to manipulate a `StringType` string.

String (Nonstandard) Data Type

Because of the importance of string operations, most nonstandard Pascal compilers recognize a data type called String. (In this text, the capitalized word String refers to this data type and the lowercase word, string, refers to character strings in general.) The syntax for declaring a variable of String type follows:

```
VAR
  {variable identifier} : String [ {maximum number of characters} ] ;
```

The following sample declarations are given to contrast a simple array of char, a packed array of char, and a String, all capable of holding up to 40 characters:

```
TYPE
  SimpleArray        = ARRAY [ 1..40 ] OF Char;
  PackedArray        = PACKED ARRAY [ 1..40 ] OF Char;
  NonstandardString = String [ 40 ];        {Nonstandard}

VAR
  Str1 : SimpleArray;
  Str2 : PackedArray;
  Str3 : NonstandardString;
```

The following is a summary of the characteristics of the String data type typical nonstandard. This type is generally more flexible and useful than either of the string representations discussed thus far:

1. As with the packed array of char, all array operations and element referencing syntax apply to a variable of type String. The String array is one-dimensional, and the lowest subscript value is 1.
2. As with the packed array of char, most compilers will allow the array to be assigned or written in its entirety, using the String identifier in an assignment, `Read`, `Readln`, `Write`, or `Writeln` statement. Typically, a character value cannot be assigned to a single element via a `Read` or `Readln` statement.
3. String variables have a *current length* between zero and the maximum length, as specified in its declaration. The value of the current length is maintained in a single byte (the **length,** or **zeroth, byte**) that immediately precedes the String array in memory. The length byte may be set to zero length by assigning a *null literal string* value to the String variable. A null literal string is indicated by two adjacent, single apostrophes (`''`).
4. A String variable may be assigned a literal string value of any length, up to the declared maximum length. Extra characters are ignored and no blank-padding occurs if fewer characters are read. The value of the length byte is automatically updated upon assignment to the entire variable, but not upon assignment to a single element.
5. The contents of a packed array of char may be transferred to a String variable (or vice versa) *only* element by element, i.e., character by character.

6. A String variable may be compared to a literal string of *any* length or to another String variable of *any* length. The computer will equalize the length for comparison purposes using space characters prior to the comparison. A String variable cannot be compared with a variable declared to be a packed array of char, however.

Another benefit of the nonstandard String type is that a Pascal system equipped with a compiler recognizing this type will typically also contain a variety of string-handling routines (for fundamental operations) in its library of predefined routines.

Computer Memory Representation of the ADT Character String

The computer memory representation of an unpacked array of char has already been described in Section 3.3, and the representation of a packed array of char was described earlier in this section on character strings. The String data type is actually a packed array of char with an additional preceding byte (the length byte) to hold a binary value representing the current length of the string. For example, a 16-bit computer has 8 bits per byte, and a single byte is allocated to hold the length; the maximum length of any String variable is, therefore, $2^8 - 1$, or 255, characters. String variables grow and shrink in length only conceptually; enough memory is *always* allocated at compile-time to hold the maximum declared number of characters. A string-type variable therefore does not save memory over a packed array of char variable. On the contrary, it requires one more byte—the length byte. Nonetheless, the convenience of the String type and its predefined routines makes it the most convenient type for representing the ADT string.

3.5 RECORD DATA TYPE

Basic Record Data Type

We have seen that, as a linear structure, ADT array has an advantage over ADT set in that any element or sequence of elements may be accessed using an array index, whereas only individual elements of a set may be accessed using the element's value directly. A characteristic of both arrays and sets is that their constituent items are *homogeneous data;* i.e., all elements of a particular array and all members of a particular set must be of the same data type. This is a drawback for many applications in which the programmer would like to package together data of different data types within the same structure.

For example, imagine a program used by a bank to store and access a variety of information about each customer. This information might include character string data (e.g., name, address, account password), enumerated data (e.g., type of account), Boolean data (e.g., 24-hour bank teller machine privileges), integer data (e.g., account number), and real data (e.g., current balance). In the **parallel arrays technique**, one array is allocated for each datum. All data across the parallel arrays is associated with a particular customer by using the same index value for each array. Figure 3.12 depicts such an arrangement.

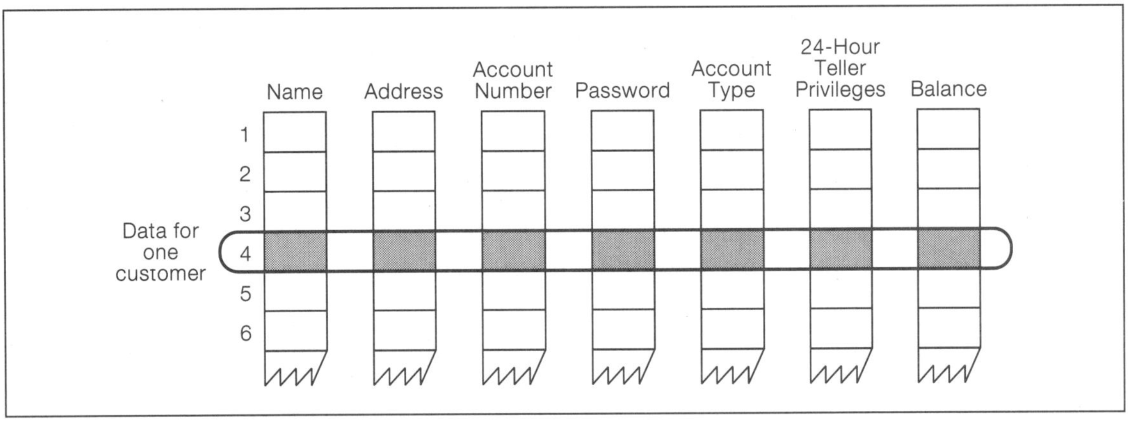

FIGURE 3.12 Example of the Parallel Arrays Technique for Associating Data of Different Types

This approach is rather cumbersome and really does not package together data about a particular customer in a way that is convenient for the programmer. To pass information about one customer to a procedure within the program, the calling statement must pass all arrays (or, at least, their addresses if **VAR** parameters are used) plus the common index value identifying that customer. Fortunately, standard Pascal provides a data structure whose items may be of different data types: the *record*.

Specifications for the ADT Record

The **ADT record** is a structured data type in which (like ADT set) no ordering of the items (fields) is imposed by the structure. Each field is completely independent of other fields, so the concept of linearity does not apply.

Domain

The domain consists of items (*fields*), each of which may be of a simple or structured data type. The fields within a record may be of different data types (excluding file type), and each behaves like a variable of that data type.

Fundamental Operations

1. *Assignment to record variable:* Assigning the entire contents of one record variable to another, identically typed record variable.
2. *Reference field:* Referencing a particular field using the record variable name plus the field identifier. Once a field is referenced, any operation appropriate for an item of that field's data type may be performed on the field.

Pascal Representation of the ADT Record

The standard syntax related to the ADT record follows, and descriptions of all standard operators and special symbols are given in Appendix A.

Declaration of a record variable

```
VAR
  {variable identifier} = RECORD
                            {field descriptor(s)} (see bottom of Figure 3.14)
                          END;
```

Standard syntax, operators

Field access .
Assignment :=

Standard data-transfer procedures and techniques

Read from binary file of record	`Get, Read`
Write to binary file of record	`Put, Write`
Parameter-passing	

Field identifiers must be unique from all other identifiers within the scope of its declaration. A sample set of declarations for the previous banking example follows.

```
CONST
  MaxAccts   = 100;                                {Sample value}
  MaxName    =  25;                                {Sample value}
  MaxAddr    =  33;                                {Sample value}

TYPE
  AcctKinds  = ( Personal, Commercial, EquityLine );
  AcctInfo   = RECORD
                 AcctType           : AcctKinds;
                 Priveleges24Teller : Boolean;
                 CheckBalance,
                 SavingsBalance     : Real
               END;

  OneAcct    = RECORD
                 AcctNo   : Integer;
                 AcctData : AcctInfo;
                 Name     : String [ MaxName ];
                 Address  : String [ MaxAddr ]
               END;

  AllAccts   = ARRAY [ 1..MaxAccts ] OF OneAcct;

VAR
  OneCustomer, Temp1  : OneAcct;
  AllCustomers, Temp2 : AllAccts;
```

Arrays and records have similarities and dissimilarities. Both hold a collection of component data items stored contiguously in memory, and their entire collections may be referenced using a single identifier. Both data structures may be written to or read from a binary file in their entirety but not written to a screen, printer, or text file or read from a keyboard or text file in their entirety (a common exception to this for arrays is the nonstandard String type or packed array of char, described in Section 3.4). Each array element or record field may be used in any operation that is legal for a variable of that data type. As illustrated in the previous set of declarations, arrays and records may be *nested*—i.e., another record or array within a record and an array of arrays or records. And for both data structures, all elements or fields may be assigned values in their entirety via a single assignment statement, as indicated in the following statements:

```
OneCustomer  := Temp1;        {All field values transferred}
AllCustomers := Temp2;        {All field values for each element transferred}
```

As previously mentioned, an important difference between arrays and records is that records may contain component items of different data types, whereas all elements of an array must be of the same data type. This rule is not violated in the declaration of `AllAccts`, even though `OneAcct` is a record type with fields of different data types, because all elements of `AllAccts` are of the same data type: `OneAcct`. Unfortunately, this advantage is somewhat counterbalanced by the difference in the way constituent items are referenced. An *array element* is referenced using an index value, which may be a constant, a variable, or some arithmetic expression. This direct access scheme allows a program to reference a sequence of elements or to determine at runtime which element(s) to access. As previously indicated, to reference a *record field,* a constant—the field name—must be used, as with the elements of the standard Pascal set type. Therefore, record fields cannot be accessed sequentially within a loop by varying an index variable.

The following code segment illustrates this difference between array element and record field references (`K` is an integer variable):

```
FOR K := 1 TO MaxAccts DO    {Initialize all checking and savings balances}
  BEGIN
  AllCustomers [ K ].AcctData.CheckBalance   := 0.0;
  AllCustomers [ K ].AcctData.SavingsBalance := 0.0
  END;
```

Since the third and fourth fields of the record (`CheckBalance` and `SavingsBalance`) are both of real data type, it would seem logical that they could be accessed sequentially. This is not allowed, however, so the following code segment could not be substituted for the entire **BEGIN/END** block above (`J` and `K` are integer variables):

```
FOR J := 3 TO 4 DO      {Initialize the 3rd and 4th OneAccount fields}
 AllCustomers [ K ].AcctData [ J ] := 0.0    {ILLEGAL}
```

For the basic, nonvariant record discussed thus far, the relative positioning of fields within a record is irrelevant, playing no role in how a particular field is accessed. As we shall see in the next section, however, positioning of fields is important within a *variant record.*

Computer Memory Representation of the ADT Record

Record fields are represented in memory as if they were separate variables. As with array elements, the fields are stored contiguously, occupying adjacent bytes. During compilation, the compiler builds a symbol table to "remember" the memory address where a particular record begins as well as the data types of each field.

Chapters 4 and 5 discuss techniques for creating and storing large lists of data in a portion of internal memory outside the program's executable image called *heapspace,* which is typically much larger than the entire executable image itself. Section 4.1 introduces the *ADT file* as a portion of external memory, typically much larger than heapspace, to preserve data between program runs as well as to store a collection of data too large to fit entirely within internal memory.

The WITH Statement

Because record field references include the names of fields, the resulting syntax may be quite long. Also, if several fields within the same record are referenced within the same loop structure (as in the previous example), much of the syntax is duplicated. Standard Pascal provides the **WITH** statement, to establish a scope within which fields may be referenced using only the field identifiers. Figure 3.13 shows the syntax diagram for the **WITH** statement. The phrase *complete record reference* refers to syntax that identifies a particular record and the term *statement* refers to either a simple or compound statement.

As an example, the following two versions of **FOR** statements are equivalent (K is an integer variable). In the second loop, **BEGIN** and **END** delimit the scope of the **WITH** statement in which the compiler will couple a field identifier with the specified record reference:

```
FOR K := 1 TO MaxAccts DO
   BEGIN
   AllCustomers [ K ].AcctData.CheckBalance    := 0.0;
   AllCustomers [ K ].AcctData.SavingsBalance := 0.0
  END;


FOR K := 1 TO MaxAccts DO
   WITH AllCustomers [ K ].AcctData DO
      BEGIN
      CheckBalance   := 0.0;
      SavingsBalance := 0.0
      END;
```

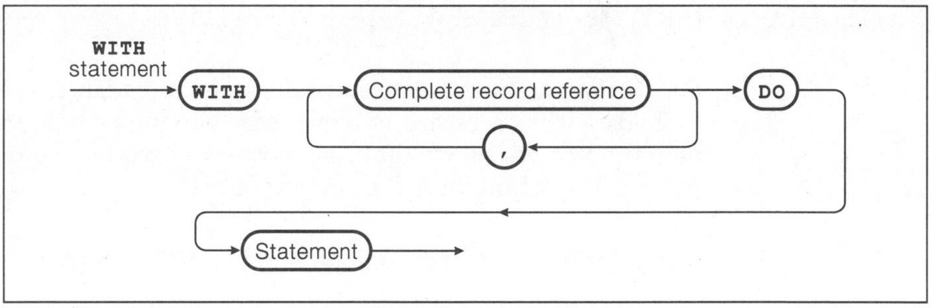

FIGURE 3.13 Syntax Diagram for the WITH Statement

More than one complete record reference may be specified if the **WITH** statement includes references to fields in different records. The following **WITH** statement expands the functionality of the previous **WITH** statement, initializing the AcctNo field as well as the two balance fields:

```
FOR K := 1 TO MaxAccts DO
  WITH AllCustomers [ K ].AcctData,   AllCustomers [ K ] DO
    BEGIN
    CheckBalance   := 0.0;
    SavingsBalance := 0.0;
    AcctNo         := 0
    END;
```

Use of the **WITH** statement shortens both the *source* code and the *compiled* code because it permits the compiler to compute an array's base address once and then use it many times. Its use may lead to some confusion on the part of another programmer reading the code, however, if the **WITH** statement itself is a very long compound statement and he must frequently stop to ponder whether an identifier, such as CheckBalance, is a record field reference or simply a local variable.

Variant Records

The basic (nonvariant) record described in the previous section has fields that are fixed at compile-time and runtime. That is, at runtime the data content of the record may be interpreted only one way, using the field identifier associated with a particular datum in the record. A **variant record,** on the other hand, contains a portion of data called the **variant part**, the content of which may be interpreted in *different* ways (i.e., **recast**) during runtime. A basic record permits data of different types within the same structure; a variant record goes one step further by permitting different interpretations of data within the same record. Thus, a variant record provides the ability to evade type checking at compile-time when the application simply cannot otherwise be programmed in a reasonable way. Whereas any of the fields in the fixed part fields may be accessed anytime, the current value of a particular field of the fixed part—the **tag field**—determines which fields of the variant part may be accessed.

All fields within the **fixed part,** including the tag field, may be referenced the same way that fields are referenced in a basic, nonvariant record. A variant record may contain one or no fixed part, followed by a single variant part. The variant part consists of an unusual version of the **CASE** statement, and the entire record concludes with a single **END** statement (variant part fields are grouped within matching parentheses). The tag field following the identifier **CASE** may be referenced just as any fixed part field, but it serves a very special purpose:

> The current value of the tag field dictates which fields in the variant part may be accessed—that group of variant fields is associated with the constant value, which matches the current value of the tag field.

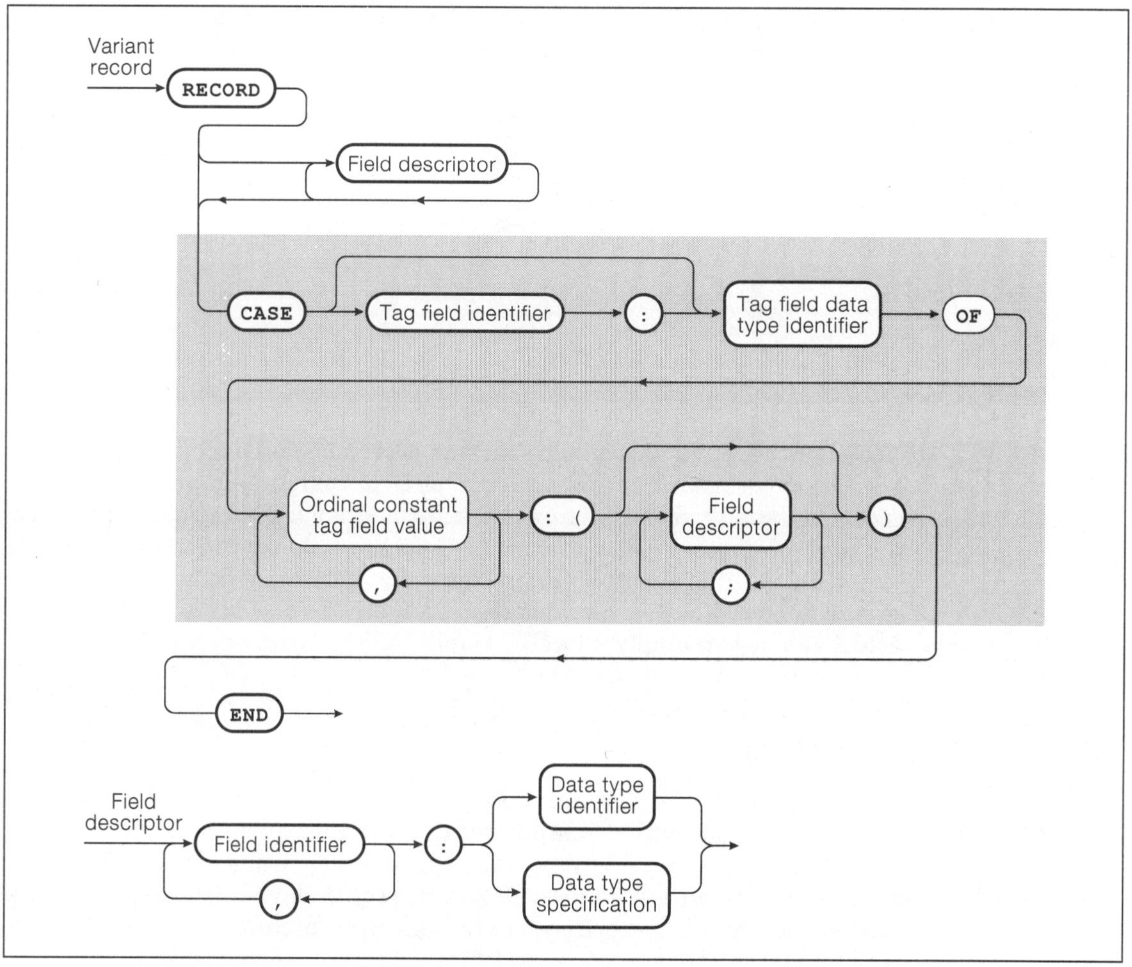

FIGURE 3.14 Syntax Diagrams for a Variant Record Declaration

As with any record, all field identifiers must be unique from any other identifier within the scope of the declaration.

Figure 3.14 shows the syntax diagram for a variant record data type description. In the figure, the shaded portion is the variant part. Nested variants are also allowed, although—for simplicity—the syntax diagram does not show this.

As an example, the following declarations specify a variant record that might be used to maintain an internal data base of clients for an insurance company. Each `ClientRec` record stores information for a single insurance policy. For example, if a particular customer has a life insurance policy and an auto insurance policy, two `ClientRec` records are necessary to store the information.

```
CONST
  MaxClients   =  100;
  MaxName      =   23;
  MaxAddr      =   33;
  MaxID        =   13;

TYPE
  NameType     =  String [ MaxName ] ;
  AddressType  =  String [ MaxAddr ] ;
  PolicyKind   =  ( Property, Vehicle, Life );
  YearRange    =  1850..2050;

  ClientRec    =  RECORD
                    {***  Fixed part follows (through PolicyType)  ***}

                    LastFirstName : NameType;
                    PolicyNumber  : Integer;
                    HomeAddress   : AddressType;
                    Premium       : Real;
                    StartDate,
                    StopDate      : PACKED ARRAY [ 1..6 ] OF Char;

                    CASE PolicyType : PolicyKind OF        {PolicyType is the tag field}

                      {*** Variant part follows:  ***}

                      Property  :  ( PropType       : ( Home, Commercial, Apts );
                                     Coverage       : ( Regular, Replacement );
                                     PropAddress    : AddressType;
                                     YearBuilt      : YearRange;
                                     Reimbursement,
                                     PDeductible    : Real );

                      Life      :  ( Payoff         : Real;
                                     Benefactor     : NameType;
                                     BenAddress     : AddressType );

                      Vehicle   :  ( IDNo           : String [ MaxID ] ;
                                     Collision,
                                     Comprehensive,
                                     Medical,
                                     VDeductible    : Real;
                                     YearMake       : NameType )
                  END;

  AllClients   =  RECORD
                    Data  : ARRAY [ 1..MaxClients ] OF ClientRec;
                    Count : Integer
                  END;

VAR
  Client   : ClientRec;
  ClientDB : AllClients;
```

The following procedure, `InitializePolicy`, interactively initializes fields for a single insurance policy. This procedure might be part of a program that maintains a data base of client records in the `ClientDB.Data` array, declared earlier. Here, the fixed-part fields are assigned values that are read from the keyboard. (Normally, all code would be enclosed within a **WITH** statement—**WITH** Client **DO BEGIN/END**—but this is omitted here to make the record field references easier to read.)

```
PROCEDURE InitializePolicy ( VAR Client : ClientRec );

VAR
  WhichPolicy : Char;

BEGIN
Write ( 'Enter Last name, First Name, Middle initial:  ' );
Readln ( Client.LastFirstName );
Write ( 'Enter policy number:  ' );
Readln ( Client.PolicyNumber );

    { ... etc. for fields HomeAddress, Premium, StartDate, and StopDate}
```

Before initializing any variant fields, this procedure must determine which kind of policy the record is supposed to represent. The tag field in our example is of enumerated type, which cannot be assigned directly from the keyboard and, instead, must be assigned in a roundabout manner. Only after the tag field is assigned can the appropriate group of variant fields be assigned, as illustrated in the following abbreviated remainder of the procedure.

```
Write ( 'Enter kind of policy (P=property, L=Life, V=Vehicle):  ' );
Readln ( WhichPolicy );
CASE WhichPolicy OF            {CASE on char input to determine policy type}

  'L','l'  :  BEGIN            {Life}
              Client.PolicyType := Life;
              Write ( 'Enter total payoff amount:     $' );
              Readln ( Client.Payoff );
              Write ( 'Enter full name of benefactor:  ' );
              Readln ( Client.Benefactor );
              Write ( 'Enter address of benefactor:    ' );
              Readln ( Client.BenAddress )
              END;

  'P','p'  :  BEGIN            {Property}
              Client.PolicyType := Property;

                {... etc. for PropType, Coverage, PropAddress,
                 YearBuilt, Reimbursement, PDeductible fields}

              END;

  'V','v'  :  BEGIN            {Vehicle}
              Client.PolicyType := Vehicle;

                {... etc. for IDNo, Collision, Comprehensive, Medical,
                 VDeductible, YearMake fields}

              END
END  {CASE}
END;
```

Notice that the syntax does not "go through" the tag field, `PolicyType`, to reference a particular variant field. For example, the syntax to reference the `Benefactor` field is the following:

```
Client.Benefactor
```

It is *not* the following:

```
Client.PolicyType.Benefactor    {ILLEGAL}
```

The latter syntax is illegal because `PolicyType` is not a record containing a field called `Benefactor`.

If the `PolicyType` tag field has the value `Vehicle`, for example, the procedure should not reference the `Client.PropType` field, or the `Client.BenAddress` field, or any other variant field other than those associated with the `Vehicle` group of variant fields. Examine the following code segment, which displays the comprehensive deductible amounts of vehicle policies and the deductible amounts of all home property policies. You may assume that the first `ClientDB.Count` records of the `ClientDB.Data` array have already been initialized for a variety of policy types and that `K` has been declared as an integer variable:

```
FOR K := 1 TO ClientDB.Count DO
  WITH ClientDB.Data [ K ] DO
    IF PolicyType = Vehicle THEN
      Write ( 'Vehicle policy deductible:  $', VDeductible:6:2 )
    ELSE
      IF PolicyType = Property THEN
        IF PropType = Home THEN
          Write ( 'Home policy deductible:  $', PDeductible:6:2 );
```

Notice that, following the **ELSE** statement, the tests of `PolicyType` and `PropType` are divided into two **IF** statements. This separation avoids a possible invalid reference to the `PropType` field when `PolicyType` does not have the value `Home`:

```
IF ( PolicyType = Property ) AND ( PropType = Home ) THEN   {Potentially INVALID}
```

Changing the value of the tag field allows the program to use another group of variant fields for that record. For example, the insurance agent entering data in response to the prompts of procedure `InitializePolicy` might decide later to change a particular vehicle insurance policy to a life insurance policy. Another procedure in the program can be written so the agent can access the errant record and then call `InitializePolicy` to assign the value `Life` to the `PolicyType` tag field; the agent can then enter data for the `Payoff`, `Benefactor`, and `BenAddress` fields of that record. The new input will *overwrite* the existing contents of that record's variant part.

A **CASE** constant in the variant part may be followed by an empty set of variant fields—i.e., matching parentheses with no variant fields in between. An example of this follows:

```
TYPE
  NameType       =  String [ 20 ] ;
  ObjectType     =  ( Star, Planet, Comet, Unidentified );
  Body           =  RECORD
                      Name,
                      Constellation  : NameType;
                      MeanDistance   : Real;
                      DateDiscoverd  : String [ 6 ] ;
                      Discoverer     : NameType;

                      CASE Object : ObjectType OF
                        Star         : ( Magnitude   : Real;
                                         Fixed       : Boolean );
                        Planet       : ( Diameter    : Real;
                                         Composition : NameType;
                                         Moons       : Integer );
                        Comet        : ( StarFoci    : NameType );
                        Unidentified : ( )
                    END;
```

When the tag field `Object` has the value `Unidentified`, there are no variant fields to access, since the fixed part fields hold all data necessary to describe unidentified celestial bodies.

Computer Memory Representation of the Variant Record

The fixed part of a variant record is represented in exactly the same manner as that of a nonvariant record. Because standard Pascal supports only fixed-length records and not variable-length records, the compiler will automatically allocate enough space for the variant part to hold the largest variant group of fields. If a particular record variable is used to hold variant data that requires less than the total space allotted to the variant part, this excess if simply not used when the program is executed. Memory waste can be minimized if the variant portions used most frequently are the largest portions (ideally, all variant portions would be equal in size).

Figure 3.15 shows a possible general memory layout of a `ClientRec` record (from the previous example). Unused memory within each variant group is indicated with stripes. In the figure, two memory words are allocated for each field of real data type, commensurate with the model memory representations presented in Section 2.2.

Using a group of variant fields, such as those associated with the tag field value `Property` or `Life`, is like laying a *template* over the variant part, specifying how to interpret correctly the raw data in that portion of the record. The tag field value indicates which template to use. If the `PolicyType` tag field has the value `Vehicle` from a prior use of the record, this means that the data in the variant part were stored in the order `IDNo` (packed array of 14 character bytes), followed by `Collision` (a two-word real value), etc. Upon accessing this record, the program could ignore

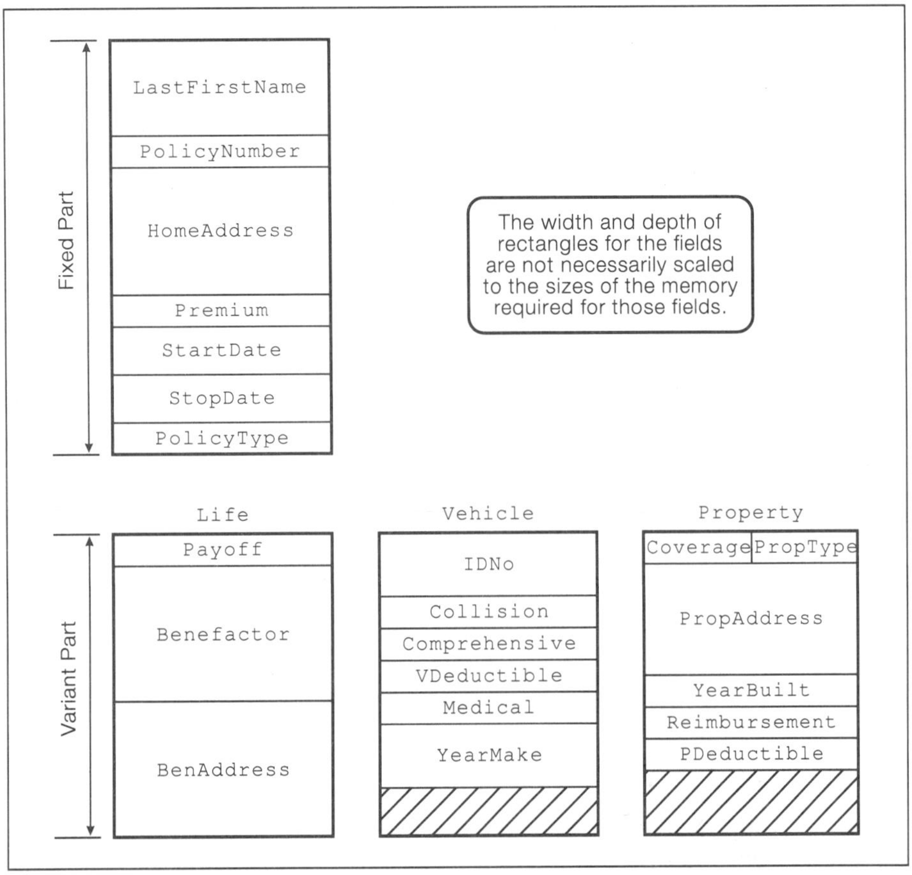

FIGURE 3.15 Model Memory Layouts of a `ClientRec` Variant Record

the tag field value and reference the `Payoff` field anyway, but this would result in the program's misinterpreting the first four bytes of the `IDNo` data as a two-word real value (since `Payoff` is of real type).

3.6 TABLES

At the start of this chapter, two approaches to the storage and subsequent retrieval of data items were described:

- *Time-of-arrival method:* An item is positioned within the data structure solely on the basis of when that item is stored, relative to other items already stored.
- *Key-value method:* An item is positioned within the data structure, when stored, on the basis of a key value contained in the item, such as a name or Social Security number.

Any data structure whose constituent items are organized by key value is referred to as a *table*.

Specifications for the ADT Table

The **ADT table** is a structured data type whose items are ordered, by some key value within each item (the item itself may be a single key value).

Domain

The domain is items (typically records).

Fundamental Operations

1. *Initialize as empty.*
2. *Test for emptiness.*
3. *Test for fullness.*
4. *Search for a particular item.*
5. *Insert an item:* Insert an item into the appropriate location in the table, keeping the table ordered by key value.
6. *Delete an item.*
7. *Traverse table:* Visit and process every item in the table, in some particular, meaningful order.

Pascal Representations of the ADT Table

In this textbook, the following representations of the ADT table are presented:

Representation of the ADT Table	Introduction	Access Algorithm
1. ADT array (when ordered)	Section 3.3	Binary search
2. ADT linked list (when ordered)	Chapter 5	Linear search
3. ADT binary search tree	Section 8.2	Binary tree search
4. ADT 2-3 tree	Section 10.1	Binary tree search
5. ADT hash table	Section 10.2	Hashing
6. ADT B-tree	Section 10.3	Tree search

These representations vary in terms of the way in which items are arranged within the structure upon storage and subsequent retrieval. For example, items within an array are physically adjacent in memory, whereas items within a linked list may not be adjacent. With all representations, items are sought by comparing the key value of the desired item with the key values of items within the collection of items that are encountered during the search. (Items in a hash table are sought by first transforming the key value sought itself into a value representing a location of the desired item.)

These representations also differ in terms of how efficiently they support each of the fundamental operations. For example, an item in an ordered array may be sought using a *binary search* (presented in Application 7.4), which provides the fastest average search time for a linear list. Unfortunately, the operations of insertion and deletion of an array item are relatively slow because other array items must be shifted. Choosing the appropriate representation for a particular table involves the following:

- ***Key operation(s).*** Identifying those fundamental operations that will be performed most frequently.

- ***Efficiency*** *of key operation(s).* How fast the key operation(s) may be performed, in the average and worst cases, using each of the possible list representations.
- ***Ordering of the data.*** Identifying in what order the data are needed for processing—i.e., in what order data items must be stored and/or retrieved to support the various fundamental operations.

The next section provides an introduction to the mathematical techniques used to measure the relative efficiency of an algorithm.

3.7 INTRODUCTION TO THE ANALYSIS OF ALGORITHMS

The phrase **analysis of algorithms** refers to the area of computer science that employs mathematical techniques for comparing the efficiencies of algorithms. Such calculations are commonly worked out for algorithms that perform similar operations, such as a set of searching algorithms or a set of sorting algorithms. For example, knowing the relative efficiencies of quicksort and bubble sort is helpful in choosing one over the other for a particular application (both of these particular algorithms are described in Chapter 11).

Measuring Efficiency

Recall from Section 1.2 that the term efficiency denotes two issues:

- *Human expenditure* of time and energy to design, code, verify, and maintain software.
- *Computer expenditure* of execution time and memory (variable storage space) in the execution of software.

Techniques for analyzing algorithms measure significant differences in the computer expenditure of execution time. The expenditure of computer memory and all human expenditures, although important, are typically left as separate issues.

Perhaps the intuitive approach to measuring the efficiency of a particular algorithm is simply to implement the algorithm in Pascal or another language and then execute it, measuring both the execution and variable storage space expended. This approach is a poor one, however, since the measuring process may be contaminated by the following:

- *Choice of representation.* The same algorithm may be actually coded in a language in several different ways, based largely on the data structures and the programming style employed. Mathematical analyses should measure the inherent efficiencies of the fundamental algorithms themselves and not the efficiencies of particular representations of the same algorithm.
- *Choice of data.* The same algorithm may exhibit a radically different efficiency depending on the particular data chosen to test the algorithm. The greatest danger is choosing data that cause the algorithm to run uncharacteristically fast or slow, leading to incorrect conclusions about that algorithm's average efficiency.

- *Choice of computer.* Different computers may require different amounts of time to execute the same program based purely on hardware constraints, such as CPU design and clock speed.

As an alternate approach, the mathematical analysis of an algorithm should be independent of a particular programming language representation, test data set, or computer. To this end, a **growth-rate function** for the execution-time requirements of an algorithm is derived (again, variable storage space requirements and human expenditures are left as separate issues). A growth-rate function is a formula that predicts relative efficiency as a function of problem size (the number of items that the algorithm must process). Calculating problem size is a prerequisite task that varies from algorithm to algorithm. For example, problem size for an algorithm designed to sort a list is the number of items in the list, and problem size for an algorithm designed to search a table is the total number of items in the table.

An algorithm's growth-rate function does not predict the exact amount of computer time required to execute an implementation of that algorithm. Instead, it states how quickly the algorithm's execution time requirement grows as a function of problem size; i.e., it is only a *relative measure* of efficiency. A growth-rate function for some algorithm Z is expressed as follows ($f(N)$ is the growth-rate function):

Algorithm Z requires time proportional to $f(N)$

where N is the problem size. The efficiency of Z may alternately be stated using **big O notation,** as follows:

Algorithm Z is $O(f(N))$

This is read as "Z is order $f(N)$."

In Chapter 11, we calculate that the bubble sort algorithm requires time proportional to N^2, whereas the quicksort algorithm requires time proportional only to log N. (Mathematicians usually omit the base number of the log, but you may find it helpful to consider the base 2; e.g. $\log_2 N$.) Actual timings of a particular implementation of the quick sort algorithm executed on a particular computer using a particular data set may reveal that the growth rate for quick sort is actually $4 \times \log N$ seconds or, perhaps, $3/5 \times \log N$ seconds. The three "contaminating issues" account for such coefficients, and the fundamental growth-rate function as a measure of the algorithm's inherent efficiency remains $\log_2 N$.

Growth-rate functions provide a numerical basis for comparing the inherent efficiencies of two or more algorithms that perform the same operation. Suppose Z and Y are two sorting algorithms and the growth-rate function for Z is less than the function for Y. Although the functions do not predict actual execution times for Z and Y, they do predict that Z will require significantly less time than Y *for large problem sizes*. That is, the execution time requirement for Z increases at a slower rate than for Y when many items are sorted. Even if Z actually requires $8 \times N$ seconds and Y actually requires $1/5 \times N^2$ seconds, as N increases the time required by Y becomes significantly greater than the time required by Z. For large problem

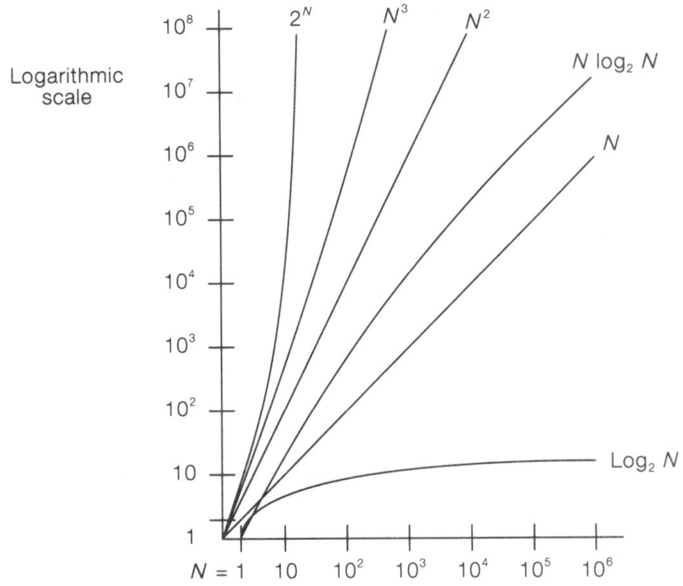

***f*(*N*) seconds**	Problem Size: ***N*** 10	100	1000	10,000	100,000	1,000,000
$\text{Log}_2 N$	3.32 seconds	6.64 seconds	9.96 seconds	13.28 seconds	16.60 seconds	19.93 seconds
N	**10.00 seconds**	**1.67 minutes**	**16.67 minutes**	**2.78 hours**	**27.78 hours**	**11.57 days**
$N \text{ Log}_2 N$	33.20 seconds	11.07 minutes	2.77 hours	36.89 hours	19.21 days	230.67 days
N^2	1.67 minutes	2.78 hours	11.57 days	3.17 years	317.10 years	317.10 centuries
N^3	16.67 minutes	11.57 days	31.71 years	317.10 centuries	317,097.92 centuries	$10^{8.50}$ centuries
2^N	17.07 minutes	$10^{20.60}$ centuries	10^{293} centuries	$10^{3,000}$ centuries	$10^{30,092}$ centuries	$10^{301,020}$ centuries

FIGURE 3.16 Comparisons of Six Common Growth-Rate Functions

sizes, the growth-rate will dominate all other factors affecting an algorithm's efficiency.

Figure 3.16 provides two comparisons of the six common growth-rate functions. All values are approximations (for simplicity, consider the values to be seconds) and, in the chart, growth-rate functions ($f(N)$) are listed in order of decreasing function value rates of growth.

Notice the drastic differences in the various rates of growth, many of which are commonly referred to by name. For example, doubling the number of items, N, leads to the following increases in time (as predicted by the growth-rate function):

• **Linear time:**	Time directly proportional to N	Doubling $N \rightarrow$ twice as long
• **Logarithmic time:**	Algorithm is O (log N)	Doubling log $N \rightarrow$ slightly longer
• **Quadratic time:**	Algorithm is O (N^2)	Doubling $N^2 \rightarrow$ four times as long
• **Cubic time:**	Algorithm is O (N^3)	Doubling $N^3 \rightarrow$ eight times as long
• **Exponential time:**	Algorithm is O (2^N)	Doubling $2^N \rightarrow$ N^2 times as long

Let us elaborate on the meaning of big O notation, O ($f(N)$), and the statement "Algorithm Z requires time proportional to $f(N)$." They mean that given any (reasonable) implementation of algorithm Z executed on any (reasonable) computer, there is some constant c such that Z requires no more than the following amount of time to solve a problem involving N items (with, perhaps, a finite number of exceptional N values):

$$c \times f(N) \qquad \text{\{time units, such as seconds\}}$$

The constant c is referred to as the **constant of proportionality,** and its value is independent of the value of N. Certain N values are discounted when they lead to a nonsensical function value. For example, if algorithm Z is O(log N) and $N = 1$, then the value of the function is 0, regardless of the value of c:

$$c \times \log 1 = 0$$

Presumably all algorithms require more than 0 time units, even to solve a problem involving only 1 item.

One interesting property of big O notation is that low-order terms may be dropped without invalidating the function. For example, if algorithm Z is O ($N^3 + 5N^2 - \frac{3}{4}N$), then it is also O ($N^3$) because this term dominates the other terms when N is large.

As one of the contaminating issues described earlier, an algorithm may require varying amounts of time to solve different problems of the same size, depending on the particular data used. For example, a searching algorithm might find a particular item immediately because it happened to be the first item examined (the **best case**), whereas the search for another item may take much longer. The best case of any algorithm is therefore O (1).

The **worst-case** analysis of an algorithm produces a growth-rate function for the maximum amount of time required to solve a problem of size N. For example, if an algorithm searches for an item in a list by performing item-by-item examinations (i.e., a *linear search*), the worst case arises when the algorithm must examine every item in the list.

An **average-case** analysis produces a growth-rate function for the average amount of time required to solve a problem of size N. Typically, an average-case analysis is more difficult to perform than is a worst-case analysis because the relative probabilities of certain events encountered by the algorithm on an average data set must be determined.

Exactly which operation(s) should be measured to derive a growth-rate function for an algorithm? The answer varies depending on the application. Just as the high-order terms dominate the value of a growth-rate function, certain operations require more cumulative execution time than all other operations. Three issues guide the selection of the key operation(s):

1. A single instance of the operation itself is very time-consuming.
2. The operation is performed repeatedly by the algorithm—i.e., within a loop.
3. The operation is common to all algorithms within the class of algorithms being analyzed.

For sorting algorithms, the key operation is typically the swapping of two items, whereas for searching algorithms, the key operation is typically the comparison between the item sought and an item within the entire collection of items. Now we can truly appreciate the meaning of the value obtained from an algorithm's growth-rate function:

> A growth-rate function predicts the number of times the key operation(s) will be performed by an algorithm as a function of problem size when problem size is large.

Execution Time/Memory Space Trade-off

Often, a routine or data structure can be modified slightly to save execution time. For example, recall that in the `GameOfLife` program of Application 3.1, a two-dimensional array is used to represent a colony of bacteria (the data structure actually consists of two two-dimensional arrays—for current and next generations—packaged into a single three-dimensional array). The colony itself is seven rows by seven columns of cells, but the program automatically initializes an outer layer of cells (rows 0 and 8 and columns 0 and 8) as empty. This was done so that `CountNeighbors`, the function that counts the surrounding neighbors of each cell in the colony, does not have to treat cells along the true colony border (rows 1 and 7, columns 1 and 7) as special cases. That is, Boolean tests do not have to be added to `CountNeighbors` to determine if the current cell is a border cell and, if so, branch off to execute instructions just for border cells.

By adding an empty border and omitting these additional tests, an appreciable amount of execution time is saved, since `CountNeighbors` must be called once for each cell in the colony, for each generation. This savings in execution time comes at the expense of memory space, however; namely, the memory required for the empty border (a slight amount of execution time must be expended to initialize this border, but only at the start of the program). Very often, to save execution time we must expend more memory; conversely, we can frequently conserve memory space by expending more execution time. This phenomenon is commonly referred to as the **execution time/memory space trade-off.**

In the Game of Life application, the expenditure of 32 more character elements is a small price to pay for saving time in the execution of function

`CountNeighbors`. In other applications, however, the trade-off may not be so clear cut. You must carefully analyze the time and memory requirements of each application to determine if time or memory can be saved by a slight redesign of a data structure or the routines that manipulate it, and whether or not the benefits of your redesign outweigh the ultimate costs.

Efficiency of Linear Searching

A **linear search** (or **sequential search**) involves searching for a particular item within a linear list, item by item, until either the sought item or else the end of the list is encountered. A pseudocode algorithm for a versatile version of this simple searching technique follows:

```
{Values passed in:     List:   The list to search
                       Key:    Key value of item sought
                       Low:    Location of item where search begins
                       High:   Location of item where search stops, if not found

 Values passed back:   Found:  TRUE if sought item is found; FALSE otherwise
                       Index:  Location of sought item if Found = TRUE}


ALGORITHM LinearArraySearch ( VAR List : ListType; Low, High : IndexType;
                              VAR Key : KeyType; VAR Index : IndexType;
                              VAR Found : Boolean );
BEGIN
Index  :=  Low;
Found  :=  FALSE;
WHILE  ( Index <= High ) AND NOT Found DO
  IF Key = Item in position Index THEN
    Found  := TRUE
  ELSE
    Index  := Next location of an item
END;
```

We will assume that the list searched is in an array named `List`, containing N elements, although our analysis generalizes to any type of linear list, such as a linked list (the topic of Chapter 5).

As stated earlier, the worst case of linear search arises when the algorithm must examine every item in the list, so the following is true:

$$f(N) = N + 1$$

In the worst case, linear search is therefore O (N)

The average-case analysis involves two types of estimates:

P_K = probability that the item sought occupies `List [ K ]`

Q = probability that the item sought is not in `List` at all

For simplicity, we will make the following assumptions:

- There is a high probability that an item sought is actually in the list; i.e., $Q \approx 0$.

- Each item may occupy any position within the list with equal probability; i.e.,

$$P_K = \frac{1}{N}$$

With these simplistic assumptions, we can simply average the number of comparisons necessary for a successful search:

1. Add the number of comparisons needed for a successful search of each item in the list.
2. Divide this sum by N, the number of items in the list.

The calculations are as follows:

$$1 + 2 + 3 + \cdots + (N - 1) + N = \frac{N(N + 1)}{2}$$

$$\frac{1 + 2 + 3 + \cdots + (N - 1) + N}{N} = \frac{N(N + 1)}{2N}$$

$$= \frac{N + 1}{2}$$

$$\approx \frac{1}{2}N = \mathrm{O}\,(N)$$

For this special case of linear search (i.e., the simplified case based on the two assumptions we made), linear search is also O (N) in the average case.

SUMMARY

The array, character string, record, and linked list are data structures commonly used simply as they are, such as an array of integer numbers, or used to represent another structured type, such as a stack tree. Do not confuse the list of possible operations of a structured data type with the list of possible operations of its constituent items.

Because a structured data type is a collection of items, its ADT specification must also describe the relationships among the items; i.e., the ordering and resulting structure. The ordering of a data structure is the general scheme that dictates how items are stored. The mechanics of storage and retrieval are complementary. In the time-of-arrival scheme, an item is positioned with the data structure when it is stored, solely on the basis of when that item is stored. In the key-value method, an item is positioned within the data structure, when stored, on the basis of a special key value contained in the item, such as a name or Social Security number, and requires a search algorithm to store and later retrieve a particular item.

The structure of a data structure is the resulting arrangement of items. The different structures include the set (no relationship among items), linear list (one-to-one relationship), hierarchy or tree (one-to-many), and network or graph (many-to-many).

The ADT set is a structured data type whose elements are completely independent—i.e., no ordering is imposed by the structure. Its domain consists of the members of the set, all of the same data type. Fundamental operations include assignment of the entire contents of one set to another set, testing for set membership or equality between two sets, referencing a particular element, and obtaining the union, intersection, difference, or subset. Within Pascal, the ADT set may be implemented as a simple set using the syntax **SET OF** if all members are of the same simple data type. A variable declared to be of standard Pascal set type is represented in computer memory as a bit map. If, instead, the members are all of the same structured data type (e.g., a structured set of records), the set data structure and its fundamental operations must be programmer-defined.

The ADT array is a structured data type whose items form a linear list. Its domain is the collection of elements that are all variables of the same simple, structured, or pointer type. Fundamental operations include assignment of the entire contents of one array to another array and referencing a single element by using the array name plus an index value. Arrays may have a single or multiple dimensions. A Pascal array declaration, using **ARRAY OF** syntax, specifies the array's base type, size, data type of the index or indices, and the upper and lower bounds of each index. Advantages of a Pascal array over a standard Pascal set are that elements need not be of simple data type, elements may be accessed sequentially, and that, typically, a greater number of array elements than set elements may be stored. All elements of an array, regardless of the number of array dimensions, occupy adjacent memory locations; the array-based representation of another data type, such as a stack or tree, is commonly referred to as a sequential storage representation of that data type.

The ADT character string is a linear list of single characters, used typically to represent textual data. Its domain is the collection of all single characters. Fundamental operations include nullifying the string, obtaining a string's current length, assignment of an entire string to a variable, concatenation, searching for a pattern of characters within a string, substringing, and insertion or deletion of a pattern. Pascal representations include a simple array of char data type, packed array of char data type, nonstandard native String data types, linked list, and tries.

The ADT record is a structured data type in which no ordering of the items (fields) is imposed by the structure. Each field is completely independent of other fields, so the concept of linearity does not apply. Its domain consists of fields, each of which may be of simple, structured, or pointer data type. The fields within a record may be of different data types and each behaves like a variable of that type. Fundamental operations include assignment of the entire contents of one record to another, identically typed record, and referencing a particular field. A Pascal record declaration uses **RECORD** syntax.

A variant record contains a variant section in addition to a fixed portion. The content of the variable section of a variant record may be recast (reinterpreted) during runtime, thereby permitting a program to store and retrieve data of different types within the same record at different times. In a variant record, the current value of the tag field is used to indicate which group of fields in the variant section may be accessed. A Pascal variant record declaration uses **CASE OF** syntax.

Both nonvariant and variant records are represented in computer memory with fields occupying sequential locations. During compilation, enough memory is allocated to accommodate the largest variant section of a variant record. The standard Pascal **WITH** statement may be used to simplify the syntax of any record's field reference.

The data structures array, linked list, binary search tree, 2-3 tree, hash table, and B-tree are commonly used to implement the generic data type, table. The ADT table is a structured data type whose items are ordered by some key value within each item (the item itself may be a single key value). Its domain is the collection of items, typically records. Fundamental operations include initializing the table as empty, testing the table for emptiness or fullness, searching for a particular item, inserting or deleting an item and, for most tables, traversing the table in a particular order. Common searching algorithms include linear, binary, and binary tree searches, and hashing.

The phrase analysis of algorithms refers to the application of mathematical techniques to compare relative efficiencies of similar-purposed algorithms. An analysis should be independent of a particular programming language, test data set, or computer. A growth-rate function provides a numerical basis for comparing the inherent efficiencies of two or more algorithms as a function of problem size (i.e., the number of items that the algorithm must process). Efficiency usually refers to execution time, although memory use is often considered as well.

A growth-rate function for some algorithm Z of large problem size N is expressed as *Algorithm Z requires time proportional to* $c \times f(N)$, with c as the constant of proportionality. Such an expression is commonly abbreviated using big O notation as $O(f(N))$. Common growth-rate functions are linear time ($O(N)$), logarithmic time ($O(\log N)$), quadratic time ($O(\log N^2)$), cubic time ($O(\log N^3)$), and exponential time ($O(\log 2^N)$). Algorithms are typically analyzed in terms of the best-, average-, and worst-case performances.

Often, to save execution time we must expend more memory and, conversely, we can frequently conserve memory space by expending more execution time; a phenomenon commonly referred to as the execution time/memory space trade-off.

KEY TERMS

ADT array
ADT character string
ADT record
ADT set
ADT table
Analysis of algorithms
Average case
Best case
Big O notation
Bit map
Concatenation
Constant of proportionality
Cubic time
Difference (of two sets)
Efficiency
Execution time/memory trade-off
Exponential time
Fixed part of record
Growth-rate function
Hierarchy (tree) structure
Intersection (of two sets)
Key operation
Key-value method
Left-justified
Length, or zeroth, byte
Linear list structure
Linear, or sequential, search
Linear time
Literal string
Logarithmic time
Mapping function
Membership (of a set)
Network (graph) structure
Null string
Ordering of a data structure
Packed array of char
Parallel arrays technique
Quadratic time
Recast
RECORD
Sequential storage
SET OF
Set structure
String length
String type
Structure of a data structure
Subset

Substring	Union (of two sets)	Variant record
Tag field	Unpacked array of char	**WITH DO**
Time-of-arrival method	Variant part	Worst case

REVIEW QUESTIONS

1. What additional information must be stated when describing a structured data type that is not stated when describing a simple data type?
2. Name the four commonly used data structures. Name two general ways in which each may be used.
3. Distinguish between ordering and structure regarding structured data types. Describe the relationship between the operations of data storage and data retrieval. Distinguish between the time-of-arrival and key-value storage-retrieval methods.
4. Distinguish among the set, linear list, hierarchy, and network types of structure. State everyday examples of organizations and objects that are structured as either a set, linear list, hierarchy, or network.
5. In standard Pascal, what special limitation is imposed on functions regarding simple, structured, and dynamic data types? Does this limitation extend to procedures as well?
6. Distinguish between simple and structured data types. Explain why set, array, record, character string are indeed data types and not merely containers of data.
7. Describe the ADT set, including the domain, fundamental operations, and structure. Describe all operators, functions, and procedures for the standard Pascal version of the set data type. What limitation is imposed on the ADT set by its standard Pascal representation? What benefit may be derived by using standard Pascal sets?
8. Standard Pascal supports both set constants and set variables; describe the syntax of both. Describe how a variable of standard Pascal set type is typically represented in memory.
9. Describe the ADT array, including the domain, fundamental operations, and structure. In what way is an array more useful than a set? Describe the standard Pascal operators for an array. What operator symbols are shared by both an array and a set? Are these symbols used exactly the same way for both data types?
10. What four points of information are given by the **TYPE** declaration of an array type?
11. Describe how an array variable is typically represented in memory for both one- and multidimensional arrays. How does the computer transform the indices of a two-dimensional array into the memory address of the indicated element?
12. Describe the ADT record, including the domain, fundamental operations, and structure. Compare the advantages and disadvantages offered by the set, array, and record data types.
13. Describe the ADT character string, including the domain, fundamental operations, and structure. What data structures are commonly used to hold a character string? Compare and contrast (unpacked) array of char, packed array of char, and String type: For each, what can and cannot be compared or assigned using a relational or assignment operator?

14. Distinguish between the operations of concatenation and substringing. If a String–type variable is never assigned a value, does it have a null length?

15. Describe how a variable of type array of char, a variable of type packed array of char, and a variable of nonstandard type String are typically represented in memory.

16. Describe the ADT record, including the domain, fundamental operations, and structure.

17. How does use of the **WITH** statement shorten both the source code and the compiled code?

18. Compare the advantages and disadvantages offered by variant and nonvariant records. What is the role of a tag field? Describe how a variant record can be declared and used without a variant section for a particular tag field value.

19. Describe how variant and nonvariant record variables are typically represented in memory. What determines the actual memory size allocated for a variant record?

20. Why do computer scientists analyze the efficiency of algorithms? What two main factors are considered?

21. Perhaps the intuitive approach to measuring algorithm efficiency is actually to code the algorithm in Pascal, execute it on a computer, and measure the execution time. What three issues contaminate this approach, rendering it inaccurate?

22. What is a growth-rate function and what does it represent? Distinguish between a growth-rate function and its big O notation. What happens to the low-order terms of a growth-rate function for its corresponding big O notation? Why are growth-rate functions useful only for large problem sizes?

23. Rearrange the following growth-rate functions in ascending order:

$$N^3, \quad \log N, \quad N^2, \quad 2^N, \quad N, \quad N \log N$$

Similarly, arrange the following in ascending order:

Quadratic time, linear time, logarithmic time, cubic time, exponential time

What is the effect of doubling the problem size (N) for each of these?

24. What is the typical key operation for sorting algorithms? For searching algorithms? What is the role of the constant of proportionality?

25. Explain why there is often a trade-off between time and memory space requirements in programming. Give several examples.

26. State the big O notation for the worst and average cases of linear searching (as presented in this chapter).

EXERCISES

1. Variables Q, X, Y, and Z each have been declared as a **SET OF** Char and initialized as follows:

```
X := [ 'a'..'d' ]; Y := [ 'b','c' ]; Z := [ 'd','e' ];
```

State the value of Q after each of the following assignments to it (hand-execute the assignment Q := [ ] before hand-executing each of these assignment statements). Indicate whether or not any of the statements are syntactically illegal.

a. `Q := X + Y;` d. `Q := X * Y;` g. `Q := Z <= X;` j. `Q := X - [ ];`
b. `Q := X + Z;` e. `Q := Y * Z;` h. `Q := X + ['Y'];` k. `Q := [Chr (64)];`
c. `Q := X - Y;` f. `Q := Y <= X;` i. `Q := [ ] + 'a';` l. `Q := [X];`

2. In one computerized tic-tac-toe game, the user selects a particular board position by entering a single digit corresponding to one of the nine board positions, as indicated in the following game screen display. The board is represented in memory using a two-dimensional array with three rows and three columns. Complete procedure `MapCoords`, which should map the user's choice to the appropriate array row and column coordinates; assume the calling routine will pass only valid `Row` and `Column` values. For example, if `UserChoice` is 6, `MapCoords` should return a `Row` value of 2 and a `Column` value of 3. `MapCoords` must not use **CASE** or **IF** statements.

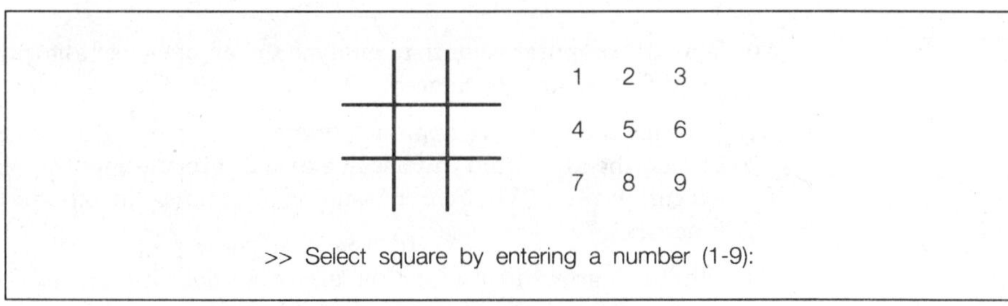


```
PROCEDURE MapCoords ( UserChoice : Integer; VAR Row, Column : Integer );
```

3. Write three functions that calculate and return the mean, median, and mode of an array of integer values; the mode function should return a **-MAXINT** value if no mode is found.

4. Assume that a one-dimensional array named `Poly` is being used to represent a polynomial in one variable, `X`, based on the following global declarations:

```
CONST
  MaxExpo   = ??;  {Maximum exponent of X; i.e., maximum number of terms}

TYPE
  PolyType = RECORD
               Coeffs : ARRAY [ 1..MaxExpo ] OF Integer;   {Coefficients}
               Terms  : Integer                            {Number of terms}
             END;

VAR
  Poly : PolyType;
```

For example, the polynomial $2X^4 + 7X^3 - X + 9$ would be represented in the `Poly.Coeffs` array as follows:

0	0	0	0	0	0	2	7	0	-1	9	← Coefficient values
10	9	8	7	6	5	4	3	2	1	0	← Exponent values

a. Complete function `EvaluatePoly`, which should return the value of the polynomial represented by `Poly` and `X`:

```
FUNCTION EvaluatePoly ( Poly : PolyType; X : Real ) : Real;
```

b. Redeclare `Poly` as a three-dimensional array to represent a polynomial in three variables, then modify `EvaluatePoly` to evaluate and return the value of the polynomial.

5. Assume that a program contains the following global **TYPE** declaration (`MaxItems` is a named constant whose value is application dependent):

```
ListType  =  RECORD
               Items : ARRAY [ 1..MaxItems ] OF InfoType;
               Count : Integer          {Count of items in Items array}
             END;
```

Complete procedures `ListInsert` and `ListDelete`. `ListInsert` should insert `Item` into the `Items` array in the element `Current`, shifting other elements within the array as necessary. `ListDelete` should delete `Item` from the `Current` element within the array, shifting other elements within the array as necessary. The procedures should have no effect on the `Item` arrays if `Current` is invalid or if the array is full (for insertion) or empty (for deletion).

```
PROCEDURE ListInsert ( VAR List : ListType; VAR Item :
                       InfoType; Current : Integer );

PROCEDURE ListDelete ( VAR List : ListType; VAR Item :
                       InfoType; Current : Integer );
```

6. A *complex number* consists of two parts: a real part and an imaginary part, both of which are of real data type. The addition, subtraction, and multiplication operations between two complex numbers may be summarized as follows:

C1 is a complex number with real part R1 and imaginary part I1.
C2 is a complex number with real part R2 and imaginary part I2.
(C1 + C2) has real part (R1 + R2) and imaginary part (I1 + I2).
(C1 − C2) has real part (R1 − R2) and imaginary part (I1 − I2).
(C1 × C2) has real part (R1 × R2 − I1 × I2) and
imaginary part (R1 × I2 + R2 × I1).

a. Give the declaration for a record that can be used to represent a complex number.

b. Write three procedures, `ComplexAdd`, `ComplexSub`, and `ComplexMult`, to perform addition, subtraction, and multiplication, respectively, on two complex number records passed as parameters. Each function should return the result as a complex number record.

7. Complete procedure `MatrixOp`, which either adds, subtracts, or multiplies two matrices (based on the value of parameter `OpType`), and returns the result in a third matrix. Parameters `RowSize` and `ColSize` indicate the number of rows and columns of all three matrices for the current call, thus allowing the same three array data structures to be used for matrices of different sizes (`MaxRows` and `MaxCols` are named constants whose values you may choose).

```
TYPE
  MatrixType  =  ARRAY [ 1..MaxRows, 1..MaxCols ] OF Integer;
  OpType      =  ( Add, Subtract, Multiply );

PROCEDURE MatrixOp ( VAR Matrix1, Matrix2, Matrix3 : MatrixType;
                     RowSize, ColSize : Integer; Op : OpType );
```

8. Use the insurance policy variant record declaration given in Section 3.5 to do the following:

a. Write a code segment that displays the policy number and the policyholder's name for all life insurance policies.
b. Write a function named `MeanPremium`, which should return the average premium of all insurance policies for homes built between 1930 and 1960. The function should have three arguments: the `ClientDB` record and both year bounds.
c. Write a code segment that uses a one-dimensional array of three elements to count the number of home, commercial, and apartment policies (i.e., build a frequency distribution in the array), and display the count when tabulated.

9. The Looney-Tunes Music Shop uses a data-base program to manage its inventory of phonograph recordings, cassette tapes, and compact discs. In the program, `Inventory` is a record variable containing an array of `OneItem` variant records. Each `OneItem` record describes one phonograph recording, cassette tape, or compact disc. Regardless of the type of item, each record stores the item price, title, manufacturer's name and address, and the quantity in stock. For a phonograph recording, the record also stores the quantity per package and an indication of whether it is an album or a 45 RPM disk. For a cassette tape, the record also stores the playing time (30, 60, or 90 minutes) and an indication of whether the tape is blank or is prerecorded. For a compact disc, the record also indicates whether the disc is video (a movie) or audio (strictly music).

a. Given the following global declarations, add a declaration for the variant record `OneItem`:

```
TYPE
  OneItem   =  ??        {Variant record describing one item}

  ListType =  RECORD
                Items : ARRAY [ 1..500 ] OF OneItem;
                Count : Integer
              END;

VAR
  Inventory, OnSale : ListType;
```

b. Write a procedure named `MarkDown`, which should examine each record in `Inventory` and sequentially store in a second array named `OnSale` all records for video compact discs and 30-minute prerecorded cassette tapes. `MarkDown` should reduce the price of each item by 30 percent before storing a record in the second array.

10. In Section 3.3, a formula is given to map a pair of coordinates for a two-dimensional array to a single value, which is then added to the array's base address to derive the corresponding memory address. Give a more general formula to map *N* coordinates to the corresponding memory address for any array of *N* dimensions.

11. Complete procedures `Encode` and `Decode`. `Encode` should return in `EString` an encoded version of the contents of `InString`, and `Decode` should perform the converse operation:

```
TYPE
  BuffType = String [ 80 ];

PROCEDURE Encode ( VAR InString, EString : BuffType );

PROCEDURE Decode ( VAR InString, EString : BuffType );
```

A simple technique for encoding is to shift characters upward in the ASCII character set by some constant number of characters, wrapping around to the start of the printable characters if necessary. For example, by shifting the characters in `'Hello'` by 20 characters upward and wrapping around for the `e`, `l`, and `o` characters, `'\y!!$'` is produced. Think of other nonlinear and more complex techniques.

CHAPTER FOUR

FILES AND HEAPSPACE

In this chapter, you will learn about creating and accessing data structures that are stored in memory external to a program's executable image. This includes binary and text files and heapspace memory (dynamic allocation).

4.1 BINARY FILES AND TEXT FILES

Preliminaries

Imagine that you are in the school library in the evening, writing an extensive term paper entitled "The History of Computer Science" for one of your classes. The desk at which you are working is small but sufficient, with a single shelf mounted above to hold your reference books and notebooks. On the desktop is your handwritten outline, a blank tablet of paper, some pencils, and a cup of hot coffee (it is going to be a long night!). You will be referring to your books and notebooks often, and it will prove helpful at times to have several books and notebooks open before you on the table. As you compose the paper, you may need to modify or add to the notes in the notebooks. Since the desktop cannot accommodate every book and notebook being open at once, you will need to bring just a few at a time down from the shelf, open them for reading and/or writing, and then replace them on the shelf when finished.

As we shall see, this scenario is analogous to how a computer may use both internal and external memory in its execution of a program. Three types of memory for storing program data and instructions are available:

- Internal **(main) memory**
- External online memory
- Secondary (external offline) memory

Internal (main) memory is one of the four fundamental components of a computer, along with the CPU and input and output devices, and is used and reused like a scratch pad while a program is running. The information contained in internal memory typically includes a user program, the operating system program and related buffer space, and a large portion of available memory called the *heapspace* (this is discussed in Section 4.2). It may include one or more executable images as well. Internal memory also includes a computer's registers and its input and output buffers (these are discussed later in this section). Internal memory is **volatile;** i.e., data contained within it are lost when the power is removed.

Online **external memory** is additional memory that is accessible while a program is running; i.e., the memory is **online.** Examples of online external memory include a mounted floppy diskette, a mounted hard disk, and a mounted magnetic tape. (A mounted diskette is a diskette that is physically enclosed in the diskette drive and the operating system has electronic access to it.) **Secondary memory** is external memory that is *not* accessible by an operating system while a program is running; i.e., it is **offline.** Examples of secondary memory include an unmounted floppy diskette (perhaps lying in a plastic box on the table), an unmounted hard disk, an unmounted magnetic tape, or a stack of punched cards.

Unlike internal memory, external memory (whether online or offline) is **nonvolatile,** so it may be used to hold program instructions and data when the computer is powered down or when the program that manipulates the memory is not in use. Although the CPU of a computer can access internal memory much faster, external memory is typically much larger and less expensive to manufacture. And because such media are typically capable of holding far more information than internal memory can, they may be used by a program as an extension of internal memory (a larger scratch pad) to hold data temporarily while a program is running.

Let us return to writing the term paper. The entire desktop, including the tablet of paper, is analogous to a computer's internal memory: limited in size but providing fast access to information stored within it. The shelf above the desk is analogous to an online external memory, holding a variety of information that is not stored on the desktop (due to either size limitations or the lack of immediate need). However, being directly accessible, it may be **downloaded** to the desktop as necessary, just as a program might be downloaded from a magnetic disk into internal memory. All information on the shelf is divided into separate books and notebooks, similar to the notion of separate *files* of information. Whereas the desktop is used and reused and is eventually cleared by the library's night custodian (i.e., the desktop is a volatile holder of information), information in the books and notebooks themselves is preserved when they are not in use (i.e., they are nonvolatile). Finally, the library may have books and other material useful to the paper but not directly accessible as you sit at the desk. Instead, they lie on the many library shelves (just as files reside quietly in offline external memory), waiting to be placed on your desk shelf (i.e., placed online), later to be downloaded to the desktop for use at some point.

Files

A **file** is a named collection of data in external memory. (An operating system also may create temporary *internal files* within internal memory for "scratch pad" type use while a particular program is running, but we will focus on external files in this chapter.) Files may be used to hold anything from a letter to your parents composed using a word processor program to the source code for a program that controls a robot in an automobile factory. In many applications, one program may read the contents of one file and produce another. For example, a Pascal compiler program transforms a file of source code into a file of object code file (the machine code version of the source code). The object code file is then read by a linker program to build the final executable image file, which may then be executed directly. A **directory,** sometimes called a **volume,** or **folder,** is a named collection of zero or more files in external memory.

Each operating system establishes its own naming conventions for files and directories. For example, the IBM MS-DOS™ operating system permits file names to be one to eight characters in length (letters, digits, and some grammatical symbols), which may be followed by a period plus an extension of between zero and three characters. A file name extension is often used to convey the purpose or format of the file.

The file is one of the most fundamental units of memory in programming, fulfilling a diversity of needs:

- *Storing programs.* Files hold the instructions of a program between executions of that program.
- *Storing data.* Files can be used to preserve program-generated data between program executions.
- *Sharing data.* Files allow two or more programs to share information; one program can write to a data file, whereas another program may read from the same file at a different time.
- *Providing input.* Information can be read from a file rather than from the keyboard interactively, allowing the program user to rerun the program without having manually to reenter the same information; this is especially useful when verifying and debugging a program.
- *Capturing output.* Information can be written to a file rather than to the screen, thereby "capturing" calculated data.

The ability to use files effectively in programming requires some understanding of their actual physical memory representation. A file is similar to a one-dimensional array in that it consists of a linear list of items called elements, all of the same data type. A file may be a collection of integers, records, arrays, or any data type—simple or structured—except another file. Unlike an array, however, the length of a file is not specified in a declaration. Instead, its length may grow and shrink and is limited only by the size of medium on which the file is stored. As we will see, another important difference between files and arrays is the way in which individual elements are accessed.

There are two basic types of files:

- **ADT binary file.** Sometimes referred to as a *structured,* or *formatted, file,* a binary file stores data in the same format as that data would be represented within internal memory.
- **ADT text file.** A text file is used to store all information as a long list of characters. Unlike binary files, text files may be manipulated directly using a text I/O (input/output) device, such as a screen or printer, as well as a text-oriented program, such as a word processor. Text files are sometimes referred to as **ASCII files** when the character set used to store and interpret the file is ASCII.

We begin with the ADT specifications and general discussion for a binary file.

Binary Files

Specifications for the ADT Binary File

A binary file is a structured data type consisting of a linear list of elements that are stored and accessed using a first-in, first-out (FIFO) time-of-arrival method.

Domain

The domain consists of items called **file elements,** all of the same data type, which may be simple or structured.

Fundamental Operations

1. *Open the file for reading or writing.*
2. *Read an element.*
3. *Write an element.*
4. *Close the file.*

These operations are common to both binary and text files, although the syntax required for their representation in a program may differ. Other operations, such as deleting a file element and traversing the entire file, are not fundamental operations and must be performed using a series of read and write operations; these operations are discussed later in this section.

Pascal/Computer Memory Representation of the ADT Binary File

This section discusses binary file operations based on the syntax and operations specified by standard Pascal.

Note: File handling (often referred to simply as **file I/O**) is the area of greatest variation among nonstandard Pascal compilers. Before writing Pascal programs using a particular compiler, carefully examine the accompanying programmer's manual to uncover any possible variations from the syntax of standard Pascal presented in this textbook.

Typically, the syntactical differences among compilers are relatively minor, and a program written for one compiler can easily be modified for compilation using another compiler. A description of standard syntax related to binary files follows, and descriptions of all standard operators and special symbols are given in Appendix A.

Declaration of a file variable (File variables are discussed shortly.)

```
VAR
  {file variable} : FILE OF {data type identifier or description};
```

Standard syntax

Reference a file buffer variable	`{file variable}^`

Standard function

Detect end of file	`Eof`

Standard data-transfer procedures and syntax

Open binary file for reading	`Reset`
Open binary file for writing	`Rewrite`
Read from binary file	`Get, Read`
Write to binary file	`Put, Write`

Passing the file variable as a **VAR** parameter

Each of the four fundamental file operations is now discussed in turn.

The File Variable

A file is known to an operating system by its file name, which is stored in external memory in a directory table. This table is created and maintained by the operating system and contains information describing each file in a particular directory—e.g., name, type, size, and starting address in external memory. A file in external online memory may be accessed by a Pascal program (which is itself stored in internal memory) by using a special variable called a **file variable.** As with any program variable, a file variable must be declared in a declaration section and follows the normal scoping rules for declarations. This declaration uses the **FILE OF** syntax just described. The following sample declarations of file variables are referenced in our discussion of each of the four basic file operations.

```
TYPE
  NameType          = String [ 25 ] ;
  OneStudent        = RECORD
                        LastFirstName : NameType;
                        SSN           : PACKED ARRAY [ 1..9 ] OF Char;
                        Programs,
                        Exams         : ARRAY [ 1..4 ] OF Integer;
                        FinalGrade    : PACKED ARRAY [ 1..2 ] OF Char
                      END;

  FileOfStudents     = FILE OF OneStudent;
  FileOfInstructors  = FILE OF NameType;
  FileOfGrades       = FILE OF Integer;

VAR
  StudentFile    : FileOfStudents;    {File variable for student records file}
  InstructorFile : FileOfInstructors; {File variable for instructor names file}
  NumbersFile    : FileOfGrades;      {File variable for temporary storage}
```

In these declarations, `StudentFile` is the file variable for a binary file in which each file element is a `OneStudent` record. Accordingly, each file element in an `InstructorFile` file is a `NameType` packed array, and each element in a `NumbersFile` file is an integer. The declarations do not yet specify exactly with which file in external memory the program should work—this is specified when the file is actually opened (the next file I/O operation to be discussed).

When a file is opened and a program wishes to read a single file element, the operating system (which performs the actual acquisition of data from the file) must know how big of a "chunk" of memory to copy from the file as well as know how to interpret that memory. A file variable declaration specifies the data type of every element in a file. In this context, a file variable serves the same purpose for a file that a tag field serves for a variant record: *A file variable declaration tells the compiler how each element's worth of data in the file is to be interpreted when read (or structured when written),* just as a tag field value determines which variant portion fields are to be used when interpreting (or assigning) the contents of a variant record.

As with any program variable, a file variable may be declared either globally or else locally within a procedure or function. A file variable may be passed to a procedure or function but only a call-by-reference (**VAR**) parameter. As a point of programming style, if a file is used exclusively within a single procedure or function (and possibly within subordinate procedures/functions), its file variable should be declared locally and the file opened and closed within that procedure.

Opening A File

A file must be opened for reading or for writing before any file elements can be accessed, and several files may be open at the same time. For each open file, the operating system maintains a **file pointer**, which holds the external memory address of the currently accessible file element. The file pointer controls a **file window** that is the size of one file element, and a program can access the file only through this window, one file element at a time. As file elements are read or written, the file pointer and file window advance away from the head of the file.

Standard Pascal dictates that a file may be open for reading or writing but not for both purposes simultaneously. A file is opened for reading or for writing by calling the standard procedures `Reset` or `Rewrite`, as follows:

```
Reset   ( {file variable} );    {Opens the file for reading}
Rewrite ( {file variable} );    {Opens the file for writing}
```

As examples, the following call statements open the three files whose file identifiers were declared previously:

```
Reset ( StudentFile );       {Open for reading OneStudent records}
Reset ( InstructorFile );    {Open for reading NameType strings}

Rewrite ( NumbersFile );     {Open for writing integers}
```

Files must be opened before they are used for two basic reasons:

- *Association.* To associate the (internal) file variable with the actual (external) file name.
- *Positioning file pointer.* To position the file pointer (and thereby the file window) to the beginning of the file.

In addition, when a file is opened for writing and that file does not already exist, the file is *created* by the operating system. (Attempting to open a nonexistent file for reading typically results in a fatal runtime error.) Within the same program run, a program may open a file for writing, close the file, and then reopen it for reading later; the opposite series of events is also permissible. A program may also open a file for reading, perform read operations, and then make another call to `Reset` merely to reposition the file pointer at the start of the file.

Continuing with our sample files, let us assume that before they are opened, the `FileOfStudents` file already contains 23 records, the `FileOfInstructors` contains 15 strings, and the `FileOfNumbers` file

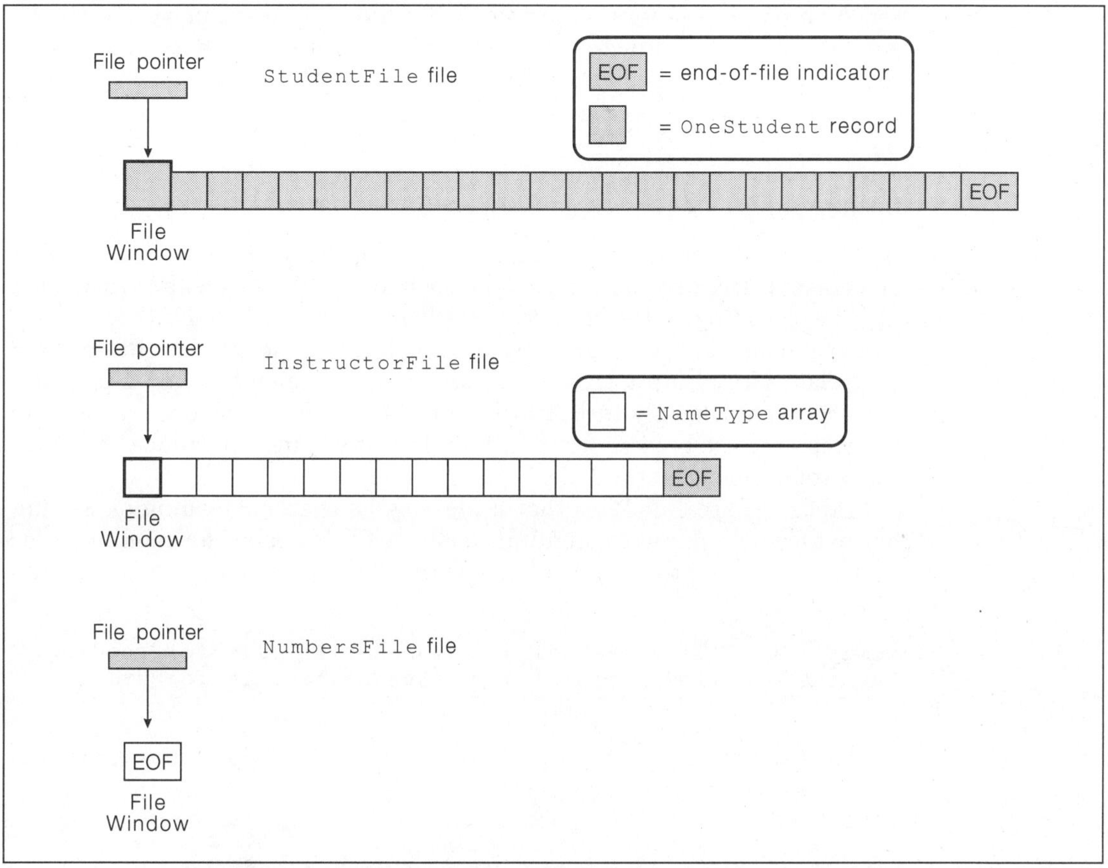

FIGURE 4.1 Depictions of the Three Sample Files after They Are Opened

does not exist at all. Figure 4.1 depicts all three files immediately after they have been opened.

A file opened for reading is said to be in a **state of inspection**; the previous contents are unchanged and the file window is positioned over the very first element. A file opened for writing is said to be in a **state of generation**; the previous contents (if any) are lost, the file pointer points to the beginning of the now-empty file, and the file window is positioned to receive the first element. In the figure, EOF represents a special value, the **end-of-file indicator**, stored to flag the physical end of the file; an important marker for the operating system actually performing the reading and writing of file elements.

As stated earlier, one of the purposes of opening a file was to associate the file variable with the directory file name (as it is known to the operating system). How is this association actually made? In standard Pascal, all file variables must be listed as **program parameters**, within the parentheses in the **PROGRAM** statement. Each of these program parameters must be declared in the global **VAR** declaration section, as previously discussed, except for the standard identifiers **INPUT** and **OUTPUT**, which refer to the keyboard and screen, respectively. (An operating system regards the keyboard as a read-only text file and the screen as a write-only text file. These two identifiers need to be included only if the program reads from the keyboard and writes to the screen. Further discussion of this topic is deferred to the following section on text files.)

Standard Pascal compilers assume that the operating system command which starts the execution of a program will include a list of directory file-names of all external files to be referenced within that program. When the program is executed, the operating system reads the list and associates the next directory file name with the next file variable in the **PROGRAM** statement, just as actual and formal parameters are associated when a procedure is called.

The **PROGRAM** statement for a program manipulating the three sample files, in compliance with standard Pascal and involving keyboard input and screen output, follows:

```
PROGRAM Roster ( INPUT, OUTPUT, StudentFile, InstructorFile, NumbersFile );
```

Many nonstandard Pascal compilers recognize special syntax that allows the programmer to specify the directory file name during compile-time or runtime. For example, UCSD Pascal ™ compilers use a modified form of the `Reset` and `Rewrite` statements:

```
Reset ( StudentFile, 'Students.DAT' );      {Opens file Students.DAT for reading}
Rewrite ( NumbersFile, 'Numbers.DAT' );     {Opens file Numbers.DAT for writing}
```

As another example, Borland's Turbo Pascal ™ uses the standard Pascal `Reset` and `Rewrite` syntax, but this must be preceded by a call to Turbo's own `Assign` procedure:

```
Assign ( StudentFile, 'Students.DAT' );
Reset  ( StudentFile );
```

By using a literal string in the two previous examples, the selection of a file to open is fixed at compile-time. By reading a file name into a (nonstandard) String type variable instead, this selection can be deferred until runtime. In the following example, `FileName` is a String type variable, and the `Write` and `Readln` statement may be followed by either the UCSD Pascal™ version of the `Reset` call statement or else the Turbo Pascal™ `Assign` and `Reset` call statements:

```
Write  ( 'Enter filename of student data file: [.DAT]  ' );
Readln ( FileName );

Reset  ( StudentFile, FileName );  {UCSD Pascal™ syntax}
```

or

```
Assign ( StudentFile, FileName );  {Turbo Pascal™ syntax}
Reset  ( StudentFile );
```

The prompt directs the user to enter a filename with a `.DAT` extension.

In source code appearing in this textbook, we will open a file via a call to the standard `Reset` or `Rewrite` procedures, and the call statement will be preceded by an appropriate comment, as shown in the following example. The comment before the call to `Reset` serves only as a reminder to include whatever code is necessary for the Pascal system you are using to associate the file variable with its directory name (including replacing the `Reset` or `Rewrite` statement itself if necessary).

```
Write  ( 'Enter filename of student data file: [.DAT]  ' );
Readln ( FileName );

{Include code to associate file 'Students.DAT' with file variable StudentFile}
Reset  ( StudentFile );
```

Closing a File

When all file manipulations are completed, that file must be closed. Any file may be closed by calling a predefined but nonstandard procedure typically named `Close`, as specified in the following generic call statement:

```
Close ( {file variable} );
```

(Examine the system you are using to determine if its version differs from this version, which will be used throughout this textbook.)

A file must be closed to free it for access by another program or to switch its mode of access—i.e., reading to writing or vice versa. Some operating systems create an additional temporary external file when a file is opened for writing and, if the `Close` statement is omitted or the program crashes before the `Close` statement is executed, this temporary file may be left in the local directory. In many nonstandard systems, a file open for reading will be closed automatically by the operating system when the program terminates.

Reading from and Writing to a Binary File

A **file buffer variable** is the "container" used to hold a single datum that has just been read from a file or is about to be written to a file. Unlike all other program variables, a file buffer variable is not declared explicitly in a program declaration section. Instead, it is created automatically when a file is opened. The data type of a file buffer variable is the same data type of a file element, which is specified in the declaration of the file variable. The syntax to reference the contents of any file buffer variable is as follows:

```
{file variable}^
```

The ^ character is called a caret and, in some systems, an up-arrow or at-symbol (@) may be used instead. The three file buffer variables for the files in the previous student database example are:

```
StudentFile^       {File buffer variable for StudentFile file}
InstructorFile^    {File buffer variable for InstructorFile file}
NumbersFile^       {File buffer variable for NumbersFile file}
```

A file buffer variable (not to be confused with a *file variable*) is manipulated by a program that uses the standard `Get` and `Put` procedures to read elements from or write elements to a binary file; these procedures are discussed shortly.

As previously mentioned, a file is the external counterpart of an array in many respects. Both contain a linear list of elements, all of the same data type. The entire collection may be referenced with a single identifier, the file variable, or individual elements may be accessed via the file buffer variable. One important difference, however, is the following:

> Standard Pascal permits the **direct access** of array elements while permitting only **sequential access** of file elements.

That is, array elements can be accessed in any order, whereas file elements can be accessed only element by element, starting at the beginning of the file. Every time a file element is read, the file pointer (and file window) *automatically* advances to the next element. To read the seventeenth file element, for example, all 16 preceding elements must be read first; if the eleventh element were read last, 6 more file elements must be read just to advance the file pointer to the seventeenth element. The file pointer always *advances* away from the head of the file as elements are read or written; it cannot be backed up to a previous file element. If the program has just read the seventeenth file element and now needs to reread the eleventh element, another call to `Reset` must be made, repositioning the file pointer to the first file element, and then the program must successively read 11 elements from the file.

The two standard Pascal procedures used to read from a binary file are `Get` and `Read`. The two standard Pascal procedures used to write to a binary file are `Put` and `Write`. (The standard procedures `Readln` and `Writeln` may be used only with text files and not with binary files.) We examine the `Get` and `Put` procedures first; then we examine the `Read` and `Write` procedures.

The syntax of call statements for `Get` and `Put` follow:

```
Get ( {file variable} );
Put ( {file variable} );
```

Functional descriptions of both procedures follow:

`Get` copies the contents of the file element from the current file window (i.e., the element currently pointed to by the file pointer) into the file buffer variable.

`Put` copies the current contents of the file buffer variable to the file window.

For example, the following call statement loads the file element pointed to by the file pointer into file buffer variable `StudentFile^` and then advances the file pointer to the next file element:

```
Get ( StudentFile );
```

Recall that a file buffer variable has the same data type as an element of its associated file, so `StudentFile^` is a `OneStudent` record. After the call to `Get`, the program could display the program grades just read in either of two ways:

- Assign the contents of the file buffer variable to a variable of the same data type, or
- Use the file buffer variable *directly*.

The following two sample code segments are functionally equivalent, showing both uses of the file buffer variable. In both segments, the next student record is read from the file and four `Programs` scores are displayed (necessary global declarations are given first).

```
VAR
 OneRec : OneStudent; {Record type describing one student}
 K      : Integer;
```

Assignment to another variable first:

```
Get ( StudentFile );
OneRec := StudentFile^;
FOR K := 1 TO 4 DO
  Writeln ( OneRec.Programs [ K ] );
```

Use of the file buffer variable directly:

```
Get ( StudentFile );
FOR K := 1 TO 4 DO
  Writeln ( StudentFile^.Programs [ K ] );
```

Note that the use of `Writeln` is legal in both code segments because it displays data to the screen, which is regarded by the operating system as a text file.

What if we wished to display information for every student record in the file? If the program knew how many records there were, a **FOR** loop could be employed to make a number of calls to `Get` and `Writeln`. (Some nonstandard Pascal systems include a predefined integer function named `FileSize`, which returns a count of the file elements currently contained in a particular file.) If the program does not know how large the file is, a **WHILE** or **REPEAT** loop must be used instead. Because a file always contains a special end-of-file indicator flagging the file's physical end, we could design a code segment that reads from the file until this indicator is encountered by the operating system. Standard Pascal furnishes a Boolean function for this very purpose, named `Eof`. `Eof` evaluates to a true value if the file pointer is currently pointing to the end-of-file indicator and a false value otherwise. The generic syntax of a call to `Eof` is as follows:

```
Eof ( {file variable} )
```

The loop body should continue to call `Get` as long as `Eof` does not return a true value.

One more important point must be made before the code segment can be written:

> When a file is opened for reading, its file buffer variable is automatically loaded with the contents of the first file element. This is an important issue only when using `Get`, not when using `Read`.

A procedure to open the `StudentFile` file and read and display all information in each record follows. Refer to Figure 4.1 as you examine the code.

```
PROCEDURE DisplayAllStudentData ( VAR StudentFile : FileOfStudents );

VAR
  K : Integer;

BEGIN
{Include code to associate file 'Students.DAT' with file variable StudentFile}
Reset ( StudentFile );

WHILE NOT Eof ( StudentFile ) DO  {WHILE end-of-file not reached, display}
  BEGIN                           {  data in each record}
  Writeln;  Writeln;
  Write ( StudentFile^.LastFirstName, StudentFile^.SSN:20 );  {Display name, SSN}

  Write ( 'Program Scores:  ' );
  FOR K := 1 TO 4 DO                                          {Display program scores}
    Write ( StudentFile^.Programs [ K ]:7 );

  Write ( 'Exam Scores:     ' );
  FOR K := 1 TO 4 DO                                          {Display exam scores}
    Write ( StudentFile^.Exams [ K ]:7 );
  Writeln;

  Get ( StudentFile )             {Copy file window record into StudentFile^}
  END;
Close ( StudentFile )
END;
```

Writing data to a file via `Put` works in a converse way. For example, the following segment stores the integers 10 through 100 in file `NumbersFile`, one integer per file element (again, `K` is an integer variable). Refer to Figure 4.1 before examining this code segment and refer to Figure 4.2 when you are finished:

```
{Include code to associate file 'Numbers.DAT' with file variable StudentFile}
Rewrite ( NumbersFile );

FOR K := 1 TO 10 DO
  BEGIN
  NumbersFile^ := K * 10;  {Load the integer into the file buffer variable}
  Put ( NumbersFile )      {Output the file buffer variable to file window}
  END;
Close ( NumbersFile );
```

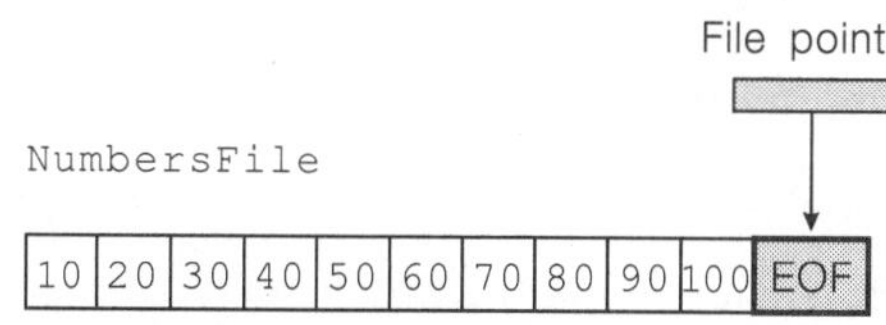

FIGURE 4.2 Depiction of the `NumbersFile` File after Ten Integers Are Written to It

When a file is opened for writing, the element written last is always stored at the end of the file. Since the file pointer for such a file always points to the memory space where the next element will be stored, the function call `Eof ( {output file variable} )` always evaluates to a true value for a file open for writing. That is, the file pointer for a file open for writing always points to the end-of-file indicator; when an element is written to the file, this indicator is effectively "shifted over" in memory to make room for the just-added element. Figure 4.2 depicts the `NumbersFile` file after the preceding code segment is executed.

Because algorithms commonly need to read or write several file elements at a time rather than only one, standard Pascal provides two more procedures for accessing binary files: `Read` and `Write`. (These procedures are also used to access text files, but in a different way, as is explained in Section 4.1.) The syntax for calls to these procedures is

```
Read ( {file variable}, {variable 1}, {variable 2}, {etc.} );
Write ( {file variable}, {expression 1}, {expression 2}, {etc.} );
```

Functional descriptions of both procedures are

`Read` Copies the next file element(s) from the file window into each of the variables in its parameter list and then advances the file pointer to the next element in the file. Each variable in the parameter list must be of the same data type as a file element.

`Write` copies the value or content of each expression in the parameter list to the file window; the file pointer advances after each writing. Each expression in the parameter list must be of the same data type as a file element.

Many programmers prefer using the `Read` and `Write` procedures rather than the `Get` and `Put` procedures to avoid having to manipulate the file buffer variable in the source code and because the resulting program requires fewer statements to access files. A pair of equivalent code segments involving `Read`, `Get`, `Write`, and `Put` follows, preceded by declarations of variables used in the code segments:

```
TYPE
  InfoType = ??;                 {Any type, for this example}

VAR
  FileVar : FILE OF InfoType;
  A, B, C : InfoType;

BEGIN
Reset ( FileVar );

Read ( FileVar, A, B, C );   is equivalent to  A  :=  FileVar^;
                                               Get ( FileVar );
                                               B  :=  FileVar^;
                                               Get ( FileVar );
                                               C  :=  FileVar^;
```

APPLICATION 4.1

AN ELECTRONIC MENU FOR CAPTAIN NEMO'S SEAFOOD EMPORIUM

The manager of Captain Nemo's Seafood Emporium wishes to computerize the process of tallying a customer's check. We will therefore devise an interactive program that does the following:

- Obtains from a menu database the price of any food item. The program will prompt for a series of food names and then tally the total bill and display a receipt.
- Allows the manager to change a price.
- Allows the manager to add or delete a food item to or from the menu database.
- Displays descriptions of all items in the menu database.

Since the program will be used each day, the description of food items should be saved in an external file so the manager does not have to reenter the descriptions each time the program is started. A food item name will be represented as a collection of characters, and its price will be represented as a real number. The program will allow a user to specify a food name by entering its four-character abbreviation. All three data will be packaged together in a single record of three fields: `Name` (full name), `Abbrev` (abbreviated name), and `Price`. The file storing food item descriptions will therefore be a file of record.

The price lookup process could be designed as a function that reads file records repeatedly until the `Abbrev` field of the record read matches the food item name entered by the cashier and then returns the `Price` field value. Looking up a price is probably the most frequently used program operation, however, and accessing external memory takes significantly more time than accessing internal memory. Therefore, the program will begin by reading all records into an internal structure, such as an array. This way, subsequent price lookups will be performed on the array rather than on the file directly. At the conclusion of the program, all array records will be written back to the file if changes are made to one or more of them.

Accessing any *external* device (e.g., a disk, screen, printer, or keyboard) is a significantly slower process for a computer than is accessing any

> *internal* memory structure. Design your programs to minimize the frequency of such external accesses.

(In later chapters we examine a variety of internal structures, such as search trees, which are specifically designed to provide fast lookups of items. Searching external memory efficiently is the topic of Section 10.3.)

By using an array we have merely substituted an internal array structure for the external, array-like file structure for the sake of saving access time. This illustrates another important distinction between arrays and files (in addition to different access techniques previously mentioned):

- *Arrays have a static (fixed) length,* which is specified and established at compile-time.
- *Files have a dynamic (variable) length,* which is determined by the number of element values (as well as the size of each element) written to a file while the file is open for writing at runtime.

Since our menu program will begin by copying records from the file to an array, we must specify the size of the array within the source code; i.e., at compile-time, we must *estimate* the maximum number of food items in the menu. If the estimate is too low, the program will be unable to read in and store all file records; if the estimate is too high, array space (within internal memory) will be wasted. We could avoid the use of an array by having the program access the file directly; however, this approach was dismissed earlier as being unacceptably slow, requiring too many file accesses. (Other data structures, such as the linked list and search tree, may be preferable but we will use an array here and defer discussion of these structures to later chapters.)

As mentioned in Section 3.7, when attempting to improve the efficiency of a program's performance (especially in the realm of search operations), we are often faced with a trade-off between *saving execution time* and *saving memory space*. In some applications, making such decisions requires a careful mathematical analysis of the average requirement of memory and time for opposing strategies and an introduction to such formal analyses was presented in Section 3.7. Here, we can take an intuitive, less formal approach.

In the present application, using an array instead of performing lookups directly on the file is the better choice for three reasons: First, the array clearly saves execution time over the repeated file access approach, but it does not pose a serious danger of wasting internal memory. Each array element is fairly small, and the entire list of food item descriptions is probably not very large, so the necessary size of the array probably can be estimated with an acceptable degree of precision. Second, because standard Pascal does not permit a file to be open for both reading and writing at the same time, it is not possible to read a record, modify it (e.g., change the price), and then immediately write it back to the file. This form of immediate updating is possible, however, with an array.

The third reason for using an array is that a record cannot be deleted from a file by having all following records "shift back" by one record to fill the vacancy. How can our program delete a record from the file? Remember that the list of records will exist in two places while the program is running. One copy—the *active data base*—will exist within the array in internal memory, reflecting the current restaurant menu and all changes made since the program began running. The other copy—the *inactive data base*—lies dormant in the file; its purpose is merely to preserve the active data base when the program is not running. To delete a food item description, the program can therefore be designed to do either of the following:

- *Remove by overwriting.* Actually remove a record from the array, shifting all following records down one element to fill in the vacancy.
- *Mark for deletion.* Rather than actually deleting the record from the array, simply mark it for deletion by using an additional Boolean field called `Deleted` or, to save memory in each record, by using a special value of an existing field (e.g., a negative price).

Immediately before the program terminates, it will either write *all array records* to the file if the first deletion strategy is used or output *all records not marked for deletion* if the second strategy is used. As designers we again are faced with a trade-off between saving execution time and saving memory space: Shifting array elements is a relatively expensive operation timewise but will conserve array space that might otherwise get cluttered with records marked for deletion. This time, we will choose to expend time over memory space because our estimate of the necessary array size must reflect an estimation of the greatest number of food items in the menu, even with deletions and additions. Allowing unused records to remain in the array, marked for deletion, complicates this estimation process and requires an array to be larger than is necessary. Also, both deletion and addition of records are probably infrequent operations, so little time will be wasted.

Each record in the array must contain a key field, whose value distinguishes that record from all other records. The most natural choice for each food item is the name of that item; however, our program should be user-friendly enough to require only the first four letters. This convenience does require that the character pattern entered uniquely identify a particular food. For example, the string `'fren'` could serve as an abbreviation for `'French fries'`, but `'milk'` is ambiguous; it is a viable abbreviation as is or may instead be an abbreviation for `'milkshake'`. For this reason, a separate String `Abbrev` record field must be used as the key field for searching rather than using a substring of the `Name` field, which contains a complete string name.

At this point we also should consider the security of the data base. The program should allow only the restaurant manager to modify food item prices or to add and delete items to and from the menu. To control this, we will designate the first file record as a **header record** whose sole purpose is to store a *password* in its `Name` field. When the file is opened and records are read into the array, the `Name` field of the first array element will contain this password, a value that the program will prompt when the user selects the modify, add, or delete food item options. (The file could, instead, be declared to contain variant records with two variant groups—one for a password and the other for food item data—but our present approach is sufficient.)

Why bother to store the password in the file rather than simply "hard-code" it into the source code as a named constant? By storing a variable password value in the file, the manager can change the password from time to time, as one of the interactive features of the program. We could, however, include a second master password as a hard-coded named constant in the code, known only to the programmer. It would grant the programmer access to all functionality of the program. This might prove useful if the manager forgets the current password or an unauthorized person changes the current password without the manager's knowledge. If either of these events occurs, the programmer could gain full access to all program operations using the master password and then store a new variable password of the manager's choosing. As a named constant, the master password will be compiled along with the rest of the program and cannot be changed unless the source code is changed and recompiled. Programmers often write programs with a master password (sometimes called a **back door**) that allows them to circumvent regular security measures for rescue or debugging purposes.

The entire electronic menu program follows. Only the procedures and functions that pertain to our discussion of file operations are shown, with the other routines left as exercises. Notice that the program obtains the user's choice of commands via a menu of displayed options. Also, the array of food item records is kept ordered by ascending `Abbrev` field value, and subsequently written back to the binary file in this order. A particular food item record is sought using a simple sequential search algorithm (element-by-element) although a binary search algorithm could be used instead; this algorithm is presented in Application 7.5. Figure 4.3 contains a module diagram for the program.

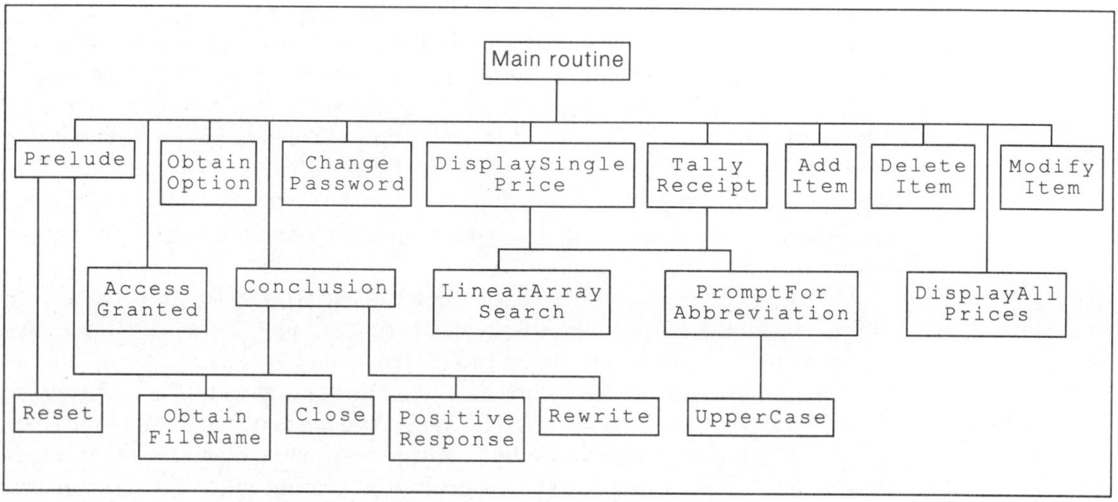

FIGURE 4.3 Module Tree Diagram for the `ElectronicMenu` Program

```
PROGRAM  ElectronicMenu ( INPUT, OUTPUT );

CONST
  MasterPassword  =  'Back Door';  {Allows programmer access}
  MaxIndex        =  100;          {Maximum number of food/beverage items}
  MaxName         =   15;          {Maximum number of name characters}
  MaxAbbrev       =    4;          {Maximum number of abbreviation characters}
  TaxRate         =    0.05;       {Tax %}

TYPE
  KeyType       =  String [ MaxAbbrev ];
  NameType      =  String [ MaxName ];
  OneItem       =  RECORD
                     Key       :  KeyType;        {Unique name abbreviation}
                     FullName  :  NameType;       {Full name of food or drink}
                     Price     :  Real            {Price of this item}
                   END;

  FileOfitems   =  FILE OF OneItem;
  ListType      =  ARRAY [ 1..MaxIndex ] OF OneItem;

  MenuOfItems   =  RECORD
                     Items     :  ListType;       {Name/price pairs}
                     Count     :  Integer;        {Number of items stored}
                     Password  :  NameType        {Security for altering database}
                   END;

VAR
  ItemFile      :  FileOfItems;     {File variable for file of food item records}
  Menu          :  MenuOfItems;     {Record containing array of food item descr.}
  Option        :  Char;            {The option selected}
  ChangesMade   :  Boolean;         {Flag indicating change to data base made}
```

```
{The following function is defined in Appendix J}

PROCEDURE LinearArraySearch ( VAR List : ListType; Low, High : Integer;
                              VAR Key : KeyType; VAR Index: integer;
                              VAR Found : Boolean);
```

```
{The following functions are defined in Appendix K}

FUNCTION PositiveResponse ( Ch : Char ) : Boolean;

FUNCTION  UpperCase ( Ch: Char ) : Char;
```

```
PROCEDURE ObtainFileName ( VAR FileName: NameType );

BEGIN
Write ( 'Enter data file name: [MenuFile.DAT]  ' );
Readln ( FileName );
IF Length ( FileName ) = 0 THEN                  {User merely pressed RETURN}
  FileName := 'MenuFile.DAT'
END;
```

```
PROCEDURE PromptForAbbreviation ( VAR Abbrev : KeyType );

VAR
  K  : Integer;

BEGIN
Write( 'Enter abbreviation or ''Q''  : ' );
Readln(Abbrev);
FOR K := 1 TO Length ( Abbrev ) DO              {Capitalize letters as necessary}
  IF Abbrev [ K ] IN [ 'a'..'z' ] THEN
     Abbrev [ K ] := UpperCase ( Abbrev [ K ] )
END;
```

```
PROCEDURE Prelude (  VAR Menu : MenuOfItems; VAR ChangesMade : Boolean );

VAR
  FileName  : NameType;
  ItemRec   : OneItem;

BEGIN
Writeln ( '*****  Electronic  Menu  Program  *****' );
Writeln; Writeln;
ObtainFileName ( FileName );

{Include code to associate directory filename with file variable ItemFile}
Reset ( ItemFile );                                   {Open file of records}

WITH Menu DO
  BEGIN
  Read ( ItemFile, ItemRec );                         {Read header node}
  Password := ItemRec.FullName;                       {Obtain password from 1st record}
  Writeln;  Writeln;  Write ( 'Loading food item records from disk ...' );
  Count := 0;
  WHILE NOT Eof ( ItemFile ) AND ( Count <= MaxIndex ) DO
    BEGIN
    Read ( ItemFile, ItemRec );                       {Read record from file}
    Count := Count + 1;
    Items [ Count ] := ItemRec                        {Store record in array element}
    END;
  Writeln ( 'DONE -- ', Count, ' items in the menu database.' )
  END;
Close ( ItemFile );
ChangesMade := FALSE                                  {Initialize flag}
END;
```

```
PROCEDURE ObtainOption ( VAR Option : Char );

BEGIN
REPEAT
  Writeln; Writeln;
  Writeln ( '*****  Electronic  Menu  Options  *****' );  Writeln;
  Writeln ( '0.  Quit program' );
  Writeln ( '1.  Display single price' );
  Writeln ( '2.  Tally receipt' );
  Writeln ( '3.  Display all prices' );
  Writeln ( '4.  Modify item name or price' );
  Writeln ( '5.  Add item' );
  Writeln ( '6.  Delete item' );
  Writeln ( '7.  Change password' );  Writeln;
  Write ( 'Enter option number:  ( 1 - 7):  ' );
  Readln ( Option )
UNTIL Option IN [ '0'..'7' ]
END;
```

```
PROCEDURE DisplaySinglePrice ( VAR Menu : MenuOfItems );

VAR
  Abbrev  :  KeyType;
  Index   :  Integer;
  Found   :  Boolean;

BEGIN
WITH Menu DO
  BEGIN
  PromptForAbbreviation ( Abbrev );
  LinearArraySearch ( Items, 1, Count, Abbrev, Index, Found);
  IF NOT found THEN
    Writeln ( '!!! ERROR:  ', Abbrev, ' not found !!!' )
  ELSE
    WITH Items [ Index ] DO        {Display abbreviation, full name, price}
      Writeln ( Key:9, FullName:20, '$', Price:5:2 )
  END
END;
```

```
PROCEDURE TallyReceipt ( VAR Menu : MenuOfItems );

VAR
  Total, Tax  :  Real;
  Index       :  Integer;
  Abbrev      :  String [ MaxAbbrev ];
  Found       :  Boolean;

BEGIN
Total := 0.0;
Writeln ( '>>>  Tallying Receipt  <<<' ); Writeln;
REPEAT
  PromptForAbbreviation ( Abbrev );
  IF Abbrev <> 'Q' THEN
    WITH Menu DO
      BEGIN
      LinearArraySearch ( Items, 1, Count, Abbrev, Index, Found );
      IF NOT found THEN
        Writeln ( '!!! ERROR:  ', Abbrev, ' not found !!!' )
      ELSE
        WITH Items [ Index ] DO
          BEGIN
          Writeln ( Key:9, FullName:20, '$', Price:5:2 );
          Total := Total + Price
          END
      END
UNTIL Abbrev = 'Q';

Writeln ( 'Subtotal:   $   ', Total:6:2 );
Tax := TaxRate * Total;
Writeln ( 'Tax:            ', Tax:6:2 );
Writeln ( 'TOTAL       $   ', (Total + Tax):6:2 )
END;
```

```
PROCEDURE Conclusion ( VAR Menu : MenuOfItems;  ChangesMade : Boolean );

VAR
  Index     :  Integer;
  Reply     :  Char;
  Rec       :  OneItem;
  FileName  :  NameType;

BEGIN
IF ChangesMade THEN       {IF options 4, 5, 6, and/or 7 selected at some time ...}
  BEGIN
  Writeln;  Write ( 'Save changes?  (N/Y):  ' );
  Readln ( Reply );
  IF PositiveResponse ( Reply ) THEN
    BEGIN
    ObtainFileName(FileName);      {Obtain name of output file}
    {Include code to associate directory filename with file variable ItemFile}
    Rewrite ( ItemFile );

    WITH Menu DO
      BEGIN
      Rec.FullName := Password;     {Store password in header file record}
      Write ( ItemFile, Rec );      {Write header record to file}
      Write ( 'Saving records to disk ... ' );
      FOR Index := 1 TO Count DO    {Write remaining records}
        Write ( ItemFile,  Items [ Index ] );
      Writeln ( 'done:  ', Index, ' records saved.' )
      END;
    Close ( ItemFile )
    END
  END;
Writeln ( '****  Electronic  Menu  Program  terminated  ****' )
END;
```

```
{The following procedures are left as exercises:}

PROCEDURE DisplayAllPrices ( VAR Menu : MenuOfItems );

PROCEDURE ChangePassword ( VAR Password : NameType );

PROCEDURE ModifyItem ( VAR Menu : MenuOfItems );

PROCEDURE AddItem ( VAR Menu : MenuOfItems );

PROCEDURE DeleteItem ( VAR Menu : MenuOfItems );
```

```
FUNCTION AccessGranted ( VAR Menu : MenuOfItems ) : Boolean;

VAR
  Response : NameType;

BEGIN
Write ( 'Enter password:  ' );
Readln ( Response );
AccessGranted := ( Response = Menu.Password ) OR ( Response = MasterPassword )
END;
```

```
{ ***  Main routine for ElectronicMenu  *** }

BEGIN
Prelude ( Menu, ChangesMade );      {Build Menu from file, initialize ChangesMade}
REPEAT

  ObtainOption ( Option );          {Display list of user options, query user}
  CASE Option OF

    '0'  :  Conclusion ( Menu, ChangesMade );  {Save database to file}

    '1'  :  DisplaySinglePrice ( Menu );

    '2'  :  TallyReceipt ( Menu );

    '3'  :  DisplayAllPrices ( Menu );

    '4','5','6','7'  :  IF AccessGranted ( Menu ) THEN
                          BEGIN
                          ChangesMade := TRUE;
                          CASE Option OF
                            '4' : ModifyItem ( Menu );
                            '5' : AddItem (Menu );
                            '6' : DeleteItem ( Menu );
                            '7' : ChangePassword ( Menu.Password )
                          END
                          END
  END {CASE}

UNTIL Option = '0'
END.
```

Text Files

Text files are important because many hardware devices such as keyboards, screens, and printers as well as many utility programs, such as word processors, require that the data they manipulate be in character format. The ADT specifications for a text file follow.

Specifications for the ADT Text File

A test file is a linear list of characters organized into units called **lines.** This list is stored and accessed using a FIFO scheme.

Domain

The domain is a sequence of single characters, divided into *lines*.

Fundamental Operations

1. *Open the file for reading or writing.*
2. *Read character(s):* Read a single character, a sequence of characters, or an entire line.

3. *Write character(s):* Write a single character, a sequence of characters, or an entire line.
4. *Close the file.*

Computer Memory Representation of the ADT Text File

As in the case of the binary file, you must have some understanding of the physical memory representation of a text file to program with it effectively. When a word processor editor program is used to edit *text* (long strings of characters), the characters are displayed as rows of *lines*. The screen cursor drops to the next line whenever the RETURN or ENTER key is pressed (in this discussion, we will ignore the phenomenon of line *wraparound*). At the end of an editing session the text must be "saved" to a text file for printing, later editing, and/or compilation if the file contains a source program. Figure 4.4 depicts four lines of sample text as they are (1) displayed on the screen by the word processor and (2) actually represented within a text file upon being saved to the file. Notice that a text file, as with a nontext, binary file, is delimited by an *end-of-file indicator* (represented by EOF in Figure 4.4).

Each line is delimited by a special character or pair of characters commonly referred to as the **end-of-line indicator**. When the ASCII character set is used, the end-of-line indicator is typically represented by a **line-feed character** (the tenth ASCII character) followed by a **carriage-return character** (the thirteenth ASCII character). When the word processor is run again to edit this text, it will read the contents of the text file (or parts of the file if the file is very large) into an internal memory data structure. As the word processor program displays the text and an end-of-line indicator is encountered by the operating system's screen-handling routine, the program responds by advancing the screen cursor to the first column on the next screen line. The screen appearance of a text file is therefore merely an illusion provided as a convenience, allowing the human user to view the text in a natural format. On some systems, special character sequences are also

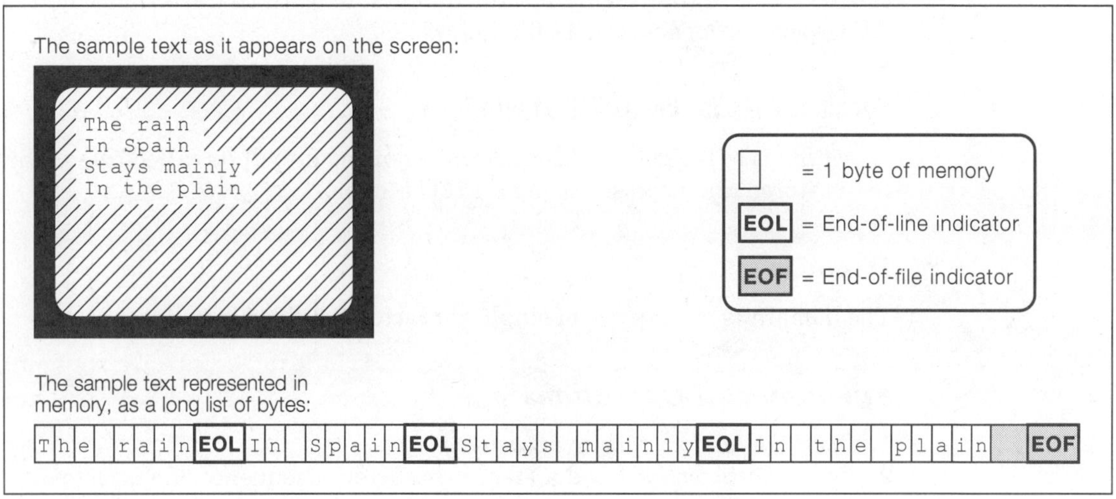

FIGURE 4.4 Sample Text Displayed on a Screen and Stored in Memory

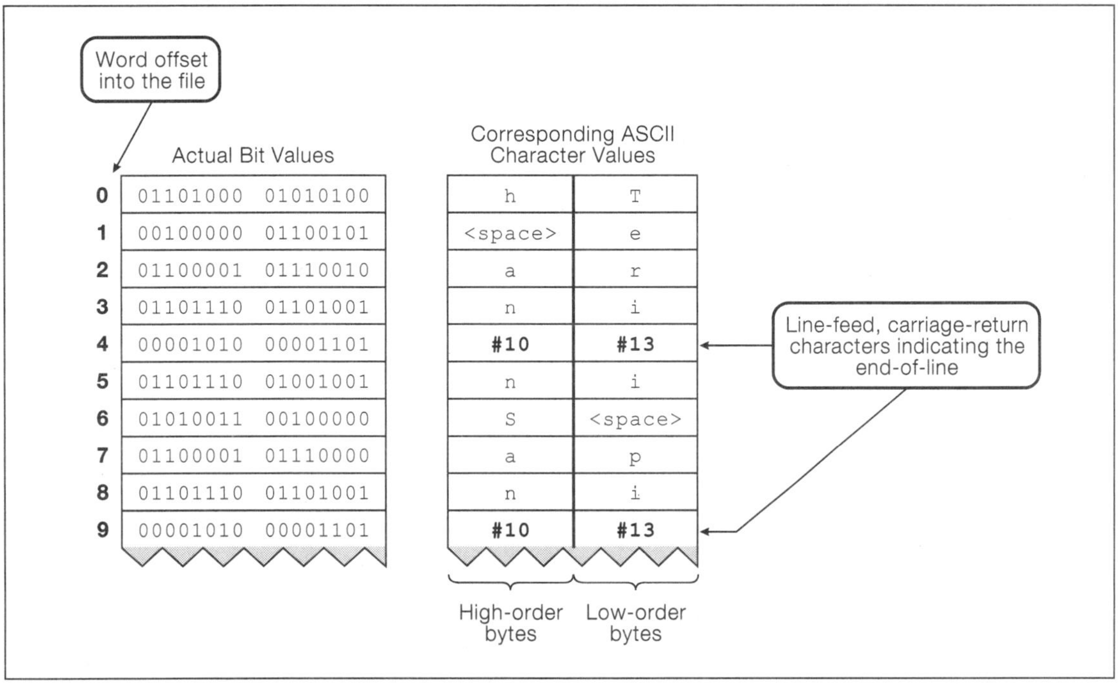

FIGURE 4.5 ASCII-based Bit Patterns for the First Two Lines of the File of Figure 4.4

used for special effects such as underlining and "compressing" the text to avoid having to store strings of blank characters.

Recall that a character is a simple data type that is represented in memory as a number based on the character set in use, such as ASCII. The character set dictates which numeric value is to be used to store a particular character in memory and, conversely, how a particular byte value may be properly interpreted as a character. A text file is a linear list of characters, typically one character per byte. Whereas Figure 4.4 shows the screen appearance and somewhat more accurate memory depiction of four lines of text, Figure 4.5 shows the actual text file representation of the first two lines of this text (based on the ASCII character set and a 16-bit word size). In Figure 4.5, each word is shown as being divided into the **low-order byte** (right byte, bits 0–7) and the **high-order byte** (left byte, bits 8–15).

As previously stated, many utility programs and hardware devices are designed to deal exclusively with data as a stream of characters. Most editors and word processors, for example, can operate only on text files. Keyboards, screens and printers, and **modems** (devices that send and receive data via telephone lines) are all text devices in which the basic unit of information read or written is a single character. All characters entered at a keyboard are stored in a special internal memory structure called an **input buffer**, from which data may be read by a user program, usually via calls to the operating system. Conversely, a program displays data by sending it to an **output buffer**, again via calls to the operating system.

Any time the output buffer is not empty, the operating system program interrupts the user program, extracts the buffer characters, displays on the screen symbols that correspond to these characters, and then allows the user program to resume execution. Printers and modems often have buffers of their own. For example, to print a text file a program may send characters to the computer's output buffer, which the operating system then empties, sending the characters to the printer's input buffer. Detecting that its input buffer is suddenly not empty, the printer then extracts and prints the contents until it becomes empty.

Buffering input and output is done to make better use of a computer's CPU time. Printing characters, for example, is a mechanical process requiring a significantly long period of time compared to internal operations performed by a computer's CPU, such as adding the contents of two memory registers. In the time it takes even a high-speed printer to print a single character, an average CPU might execute up to a thousand non-I/O-related instructions. By sending text to the printer's input buffer, the CPU can continue to execute the program instructions rather than wait for each character to be printed. Of course, if the printer's buffer is not large enough to hold all the text to be printed, the operating system will have to interrupt the program periodically to send out another bufferful of text.

Although input and output buffers are regarded as text files by the computer's operating system and by any Pascal program, an important difference exists between these buffers and bona fide text files in external memory: When a character is read from an input or output buffer, the character is actually removed; when a character is read from a text file only a copy of the character is made, leaving the text file as it was prior to the read operation.

Pascal Representation of the ADT Text File

Descriptions of Pascal syntax pertaining to text files follow, and all standard operators and special symbols are defined in Appendix A.

Predefined constants

Keyboard file variable:	**INPUT**
Screen file variable:	**OUTPUT**

Declaration of a file variable

```
VAR
  {File variable} : Text;
```

Standard function

Detect end of file	`Eof`
Detect end of line	`Eoln`

Standard data-transfer procedures and syntax

Open text file for reading	`Reset`
Open text file for writing	`Rewrite`
Read from text file	`Read, Readln`
Write to text file	`Write, Writeln`

Passing the file variable as a **VAR** parameter

The Text File Variable

A file variable for a text file must be declared using the standard identifier `Text`. To a compiler, the identifier `Text` is not exactly equivalent to the declaration **`FILE OF`** `Char`. A file of char is simply a contiguous collection of bytes; the content of each is interpreted as a char character. The identifier `Text`, on the other hand, indicates to the compiler that the file is divided into sequences of lines, each delimited by a special pair of characters serving as end-of-line indicators.

Opening and Closing a Text File

The syntax for opening and closing text files is identical to the syntax for binary files. The nonstandard variations of the `Reset` and `Rewrite` call statements to open binary files apply to text files as well. As with a binary file, a text file is closed via a call to the standard `Close` procedure.

Reading From and Writing to a Text File

Whereas the standard procedures `Get` and `Put` or `Read` and `Write` are used to read and write data with a binary file, the standard procedures `Read`, `Readln`, `Write`, and `Writeln` are used to read and write data with a text file, including reading from the keyboard's input buffer and writing to the screen's output buffer. The generic syntax for call statements to these routines follows:

```
Readln  ( {file variable}  );     {Merely advances the file pointer to the next line}
Readln  ( {file variable}, {variable 1}, {variable 2}, ..., {variable N}  );
Read    ( {file variable}, {variable 1}, {variable 2}, ..., {variable N}  );

Writeln ( {file variable}  );     {Merely writes an end-of-line indicator}
Writeln ( {file variable}, {expression 1}, {expression 2}, ..., {expression N}  );
Write   ( {file variable}, {expression 1}, {expression 2}, ..., {expression N}  );
```

The items within each of these parameter lists, other than the file variable, are *data descriptors*. The rules regarding data descriptors are identical to the syntax these procedures use to read from a keyboard or write to a screen, which you no doubt learned in your first programming course. A data descriptor in a `Read` or `Readln` call statement must be a variable identifier, whereas a data descriptor in a `Write` or `Writeln` call statement may be a constant, variable, function call returning a simple data type value, or any other expression that can be fully evaluated. A field-width specifier may be appended to any data descriptor being written, specifying total horizontal spacing and, for real data, the number of digits following the decimal point in a non–scientific notation format as well. Standard Pascal dictates that a data descriptor may not be of the following data types:

enumerated type, Boolean (for reading), pointer, and any structured data types (except for the packed array of char and the nonstandard String).

When executing the Read and Readln procedures, a computer reads just enough data to satisfy the list of data descriptors, advancing the file pointer by one character past each data descriptor item in the file or keyboard input buffer. For Readln, the computer then performs an additional operation: It advances the file pointer to the first character beyond the next end-of-line indicator in the file—i.e., the file pointer is automatically repositioned so the next reading operation starts on the next line in the file. Accordingly, Readln can be called without any parentheses and data descriptors to simply advance the file pointer to the start of the next line, effectively bypassing any remaining data on the current line. If a file variable is omitted from the list of data descriptors, the identifier **INPUT** is implied; i.e., the computer will read from the keyboard input buffer rather than from a text file.

Both the Write and Writeln procedures direct the computer to write the values of each data descriptor as the file pointer in the text file or screen output buffer advances. For Writeln, the computer performs an additional operation: Writeln writes an end-of-line indicator value and advances the file pointer to the memory location just beyond it; i.e., the file pointer is automatically repositioned so the next writing starts on a new line in the file. Accordingly, Writeln can be called without any parentheses and data descriptors to simply write an end-of-line indicator. When Writeln is called in this way to write data to the screen, the cursor is simply moved to the leftmost column on the next screen line. If a file variable is omitted from the list of data descriptors, the identifier **OUTPUT** is implied, i.e., data will be written to the screen rather than to a file.

Automatic Type Conversions

If a text file contains only characters, how can a program read or write numeric values? The reading and writing of noncharacter values is facilitated by **automatic type conversion** code inserted in the program by the compiler during compilation: When a Pascal compiler encounters a Read, Readln, Write, or Writeln procedure call, it generates the additional machine-code instructions to convert characters strings to numbers and vice versa as necessary. That is, a text file effectively stores numbers in binary coded decimal format, as explained in Section 2.3 for real numbers, one character per digit or other symbol (e.g., −, +, ., or E).

For the upcoming example, assume that the following declarations are used in a program:

```
VAR
  SSN               : String [ 9 ];  {Social Security number}
  EmplNo            : Integer;       {Employee number}
  Blank             : Char;          {Space character}
  Overtime          : Boolean;       {Overtime flag}
  Rate, Gross       : Real;          {7 places of precision are assumed}
  InFile, OutFile   : Text;
.
```

Figure 4.6 depicts how a Readln statement results in the conversion of file characters to numeric values (EOL represents the end-of-line indicator).

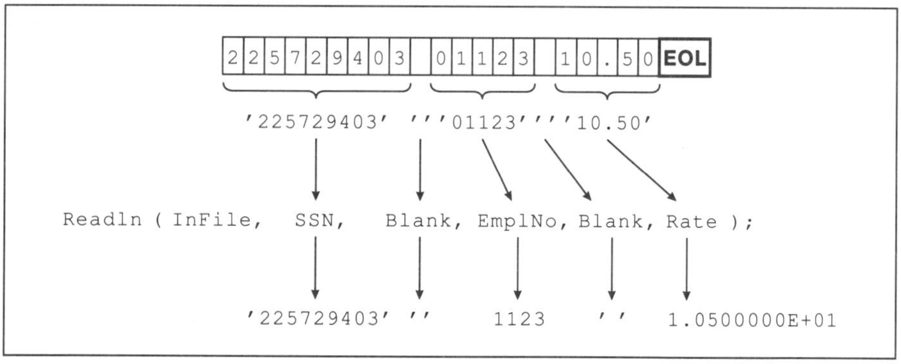

FIGURE 4.6 Example of Automatic Conversion when Reading from a Text File

Figure 4.7 depicts how a `Writeln` writes data to a text file, assuming that real variable `GrossPay` contains the value 982.2 and Boolean variable `Overtime` is set to a true value.

This text conversion may have a significant impact on the size of a text file. For example, a text file containing the representations of the 21 integer values −10, −9, . . . , 0, . . . , 9, 10, one value represented per file line with no spaces, will span 75 bytes (33 bytes for the character digits plus 42 bytes for the end-of-line indicators), whereas a file declared as a file of integer containing the same values requires only 42 bytes (2 bytes per integer). Even if the same values were all stored on a single text file line with a single space between each pair of values, 55 bytes of memory would still be required (33 bytes for the character digits plus 20 bytes for the space characters, plus the 2-byte end-of-line indicator).

This difference becomes much greater as the numbers stored involve a greater amount of digits. The text file representation of the integer value −32767 on one line requires 8 bytes ('-', '3', '2', '7', '6', '7', plus the end-of-line indicator), whereas only 2 bytes are required in a file of integer values (again assuming one integer per 2-byte word). Fourteen bytes are required to represent the real value −3.1428571E+12 in a text file line, but only 4 bytes are needed if stored in a 4-byte floating-point format (based on the computer memory representation of real values described in Section 2.3).

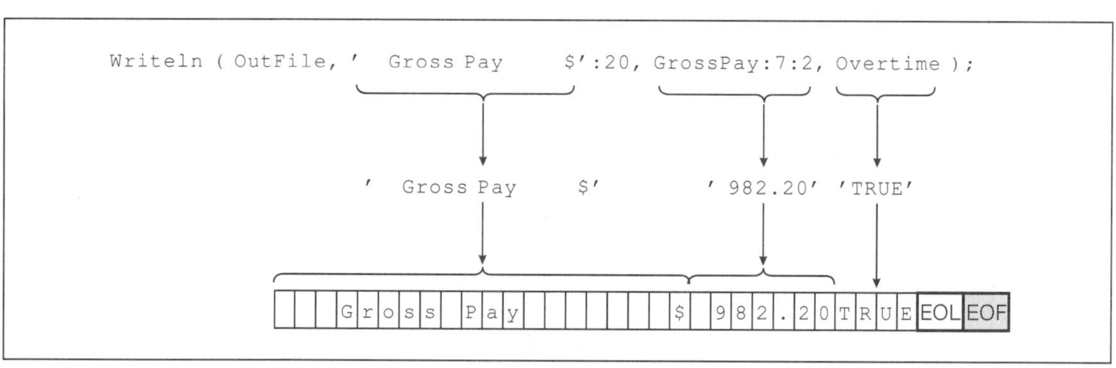

FIGURE 4.7 Example of Automatic Conversion when Writing to a Text File

Programmers often use programs and temporary data files just to create a final data file or to test a large program during development. A common practice is to store data in a text file, using a regular text editor, and then to write and execute a program that reads this text file and stores the information in a binary file. Many commercial data-base programs exist that allow the user to build a data base of records interactively; however, these files can typically be read later only by that particular data-base program. A programmer developing a program that involves data files—whatever the application might be—must be able to build those files quickly and accurately, if only for development and testing purposes.

For example, assume that we are designing a data-base program for a company that wishes to computerize its payroll operations, so all employee records must be stored in a binary file. Because we need the file first, to develop our program, and because there are so many employee records, we need a mechanism for building the file easily and quickly. (Of course, the finished program will allow users to add, delete, and modify records, but the program is not finished yet and adding so many records one by one would be tedious.) We could write a temporary program that prompts for employee information and then stores these data in records of a binary file immediately. Instead, using an editor program to enter the information in a text file and then to execute a program that reads lines of text and writes records of information to the binary file offers three advantages:

1. It is easier to enter and modify input. Using an editor program to enter information about each employee allows us to make corrections or changes to these data as they are being entered or even after they are entered but prior to running the final binary file.
2. It provides versatility because the data are available to be read by other programs. The text file can be modified and reused to create other binary files for development and testing purposes.
3. It preserves the input for debugging purposes. The text file provides a printable, raw data description of the information that the binary file is *supposed* to contain after its creation. If the results from the payroll calculations seem incorrect, looking at the raw data will quickly indicate whether the mistakes reflect true logic errors or merely typographical errors made when the data were entered initially.

Of course, not all types of data can be represented in a text file as they can be in a binary file. Enumerated and Boolean values and sets cannot be represented directly, so the programmer must represent them *indirectly*. For example, the character `T` could be stored to represent a Boolean **`TRUE`**value, or the constants of an enumerated type could be chosen such that each begins with a unique letter of the alphabet and one of these letters could be stored to represent a particular constant. One of the exercises at the end of this chapter provides practice in building a binary file from a text file.

4.2 HEAPSPACE AND DYNAMIC ALLOCATION

Figure 4.8 contains the generic depiction of internal memory that appeared in Figure 2.4. An enlarged depiction of the heapspace portion of memory also is shown. **Heapspace** is that portion of internal memory that is avail-

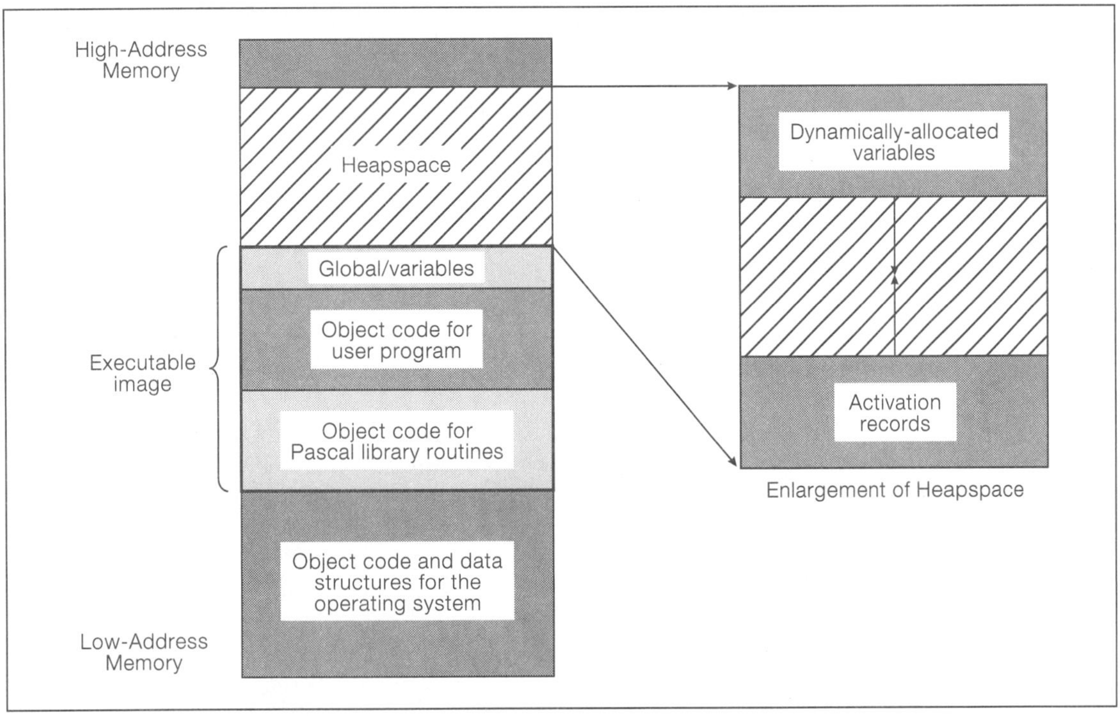

FIGURE 4.8 Simplified Model Layout of Internal Memory with an Enlargement of the Heapspace

able for use and reuse (*allocation* and *deallocation*) by a user program. (This textbook uses the term *heapspace* instead of the more common term *heap* to avoid confusion with an unrelated data structure named heap, which is presented in Section 8.3.)

As the figure indicates, heapspace is used to store *activation records* and *dynamically allocated variables*. The act of allocating memory space for these two types of structures during runtime is called **dynamic allocation,** as opposed to the **static allocation** of memory space for global variables performed by the compiler. Typically, when a user program begins execution, the heapspace is empty. The topic of activation records is presented next and the topic of dynamically allocated variables is presented later in this chapter.

Activation Records

Each time a procedure or function is called during the execution of a user program, the operating system allocates a record of information necessary for the computer to execute that routine's code. Such a record is called an **activation record**, or **frame**, and is represented in memory just as a Pascal record data type is represented. Activation records contain memory space for the following:

- Each local variable.
- Each call-by-value (non-**VAR**) parameter.
- The address of each call-by-reference (**VAR**) parameter.

- The return address; i.e., the memory location of the instruction following the call statement (this is where execution flow continues when the routine is exited).
- For functions, the current value of the function (in some computers this is kept in a register rather than in an activation record).

Activation records may hold additional information that is not relevant to our discussion here. As with any record, the actual size of an activation record will vary depending upon the quantity and data type of the information stored.

The compiled instructions for all procedures and functions lie entirely within the executable image of the program, whereas the (local) variables to hold data for a given procedure or function are stored in an activation record (for that procedure or function). Each call to a procedure or function results in a new activation record being allocated in heapspace, stacked one after the other. (When the compiler encounters a call statement in the source code, it generates the necessary machine-code instructions for this allocation.) If the main routine calls procedure `X` and `X` calls function `Y`, which then calls procedure `Z`, three activation records will have been stacked up after `Z` is called. Figure 4.9 depicts the activation record activity that results from the calling and exiting of sample routines `X`, `Y`, `Z`, and `W`.

The activation record allocated last is the *current activation record* (for the currently executing procedure or function), and the computer maintains the address (a **frame pointer**) to the start of this record. When a procedure or function is exited, its activation record is **deallocated** (i.e., made available for overwriting later, if necessary) and the frame pointer is changed to hold the address of the *previously allocated* activation record, which then becomes the current activation record.

Let us return for a moment to the `X`, `Y`, `Z` example: When procedure `Z` is exited, execution flow returns to the statement in procedure `Y` following the call statement to `Z` (remember that the return address was stored in `Z`'s activation record), and execution flow continues from there. Procedure `Y`'s activation record stores still contains variable values and other data for procedure `Y`. When function `Y` calls procedure `W`, a new activation record for `W` is

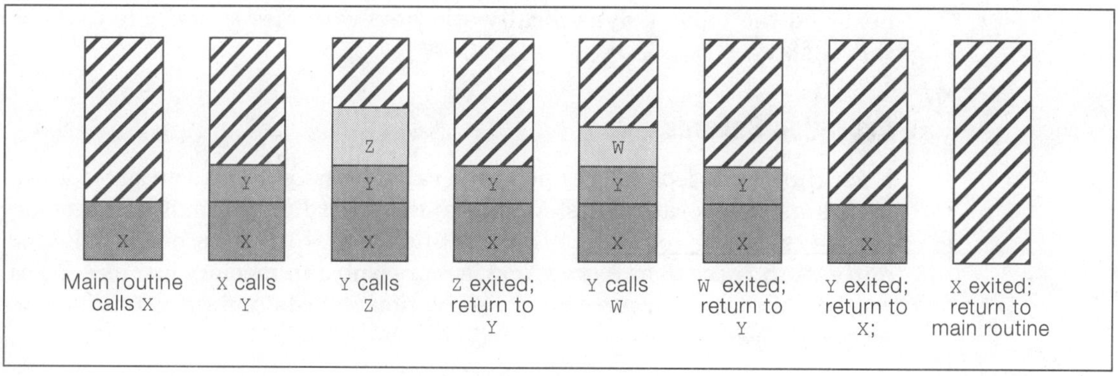

FIGURE 4.9 Depiction of Activation Record Allocation and Deallocation for Sample Routines X, Y, and Z

allocated, overwriting part or all of the memory previously allocated for `Z`. One by one, activation records are deallocated in the *reverse order* of their allocation and stacking so that execution flow exits procedure `W` and returns to function `Y`, then exits `Y` and returns to `X`, and then exits `X` and returns to the main routine. Because activation records are deallocated (and later possibly overwritten by other activation records of activation records) and the value of the frame pointer changes, a routine's local variables are not accessible after that routine is exited.

Dynamically Allocated Variables

Although the allocation and deallocation of activation records is automatically performed by the computer, the other end of the heapspace may be allocated and deallocated by including in the source code explicit instructions for doing so. Heapspace may be used in this way by a program directly to create variables during runtime. This explicit allocation and deallocation of heapspace memory allows a program to make better use of internal memory space in three ways:

1. *Flexible length.* Dynamically allocated variables may be linked together to form a *linked list* data structure, which literally grows and shrinks during runtime, with insertions and deletions of constituent variables.
2. *Temporary storage.* A variable can be allocated that, like a local variable and *unlike* a global variable, is needed only temporarily in the program.
3. *Large amount of memory available.* Often, a data structure can be allocated in heapspace that otherwise would otherwise be too large to fit within the executable image as a global variable.

(Although activation records certainly involve dynamic allocation, the phrase *dynamically allocated variable* refers to a variable that the program has created explicitly and not to the automatic allocation of activation records by the operating system.)

In many applications a program needs to store a varying quantity of data. For example, a dry cleaning company may wish to maintain a data base of customer records in which each record stores a customer name, telephone number, laundry identification number, description of garments and services requested, date dropped off, and so on. The quantity of laundry currently being cleaned by the laundry will vary widely, requiring the frequent insertion and deletion of records. Also, the total quantity of laundry being held by the cleaners is probably quite large and limited only by the amount of storage space within the building. (Even with this limitation, the owner will no doubt find additional space before turning away a customer.) Although an array representation of the customer data base would support the relatively fast binary search algorithm, insertion and deletion operations would prove costly timewise, and the total size would be fixed.

A better strategy would be for the program to construct and maintain a chain, or linked list, of records that can grow as customers drop off their laundry or shrink when customers pick up their laundry; the ADT linked list is the focal topic of Chapter 5. Dynamic allocation of this and other structures allows a program to allocate only as large a portion of memory as is needed and then returns to the heapspace for later reallocation of any memory not currently needed.

As indicated in Figures 4.8 and 4.9, when new variables are dynamically allocated, the collection of all such variables grows from the opposite end of heapspace, toward the stack of activation records. The total memory available for creation of dynamic variables is the total heapspace size *less* the memory required for all activation records currently allocated. In most computers, this is probably sufficient for a great many applications; however, a program could conceivably run out of heapspace—e.g., if it executes an executes an "infinite" loop that contains instructions to dynamically allocate large record variables. If the attempted dynamic allocation of another variable results in the entire stack of dynamic variables *colliding* with the stack of activation records or the edge of the heapspace, the operating system will typically abort the execution of the user program and display a message to indicate this **heapspace overflow** condition.

Before discussing the exact Pascal syntax for dynamic allocation, we will review how and where memory for program variables may be allocated:

- *Globally (static allocation).* The compiler reserves enough memory within the executable image to contain all variables declared in the program's global declaration section. Each **global variable** has a fixed length and, since many computers impose an upper limit on the total size of the executable image (32,767 or 65,534 words is typical), as the global section increases, less memory remains for program instructions and vice versa. Global variables may be referenced anywhere within the program.
- *Local to a procedure or function (static allocation).* When a Pascal compiler encounters a procedure or function call, it generates and inserts machine-code instructions to allocate an activation record of *fixed* size. Each activation record itself is dynamically allocated as necessary, but the memory size for each **local variable** within the record is fixed at compile-time. Machine-code instructions are also inserted automatically by the compiler at the end of each procedure and function to deallocate the associated activation record when that routine is exited during runtime. Variables local to a routine may only be referenced within that routine.
- *Dynamically allocated in heapspace (dynamic allocation).* When a Pascal compiler encounters source instructions to dynamically allocate a variable, it generates and inserts the machine-code instructions to allocate enough memory in heapspace to contain the newly created variable. When a compiler encounters source-code instructions to deallocate the space for a dynamically allocated variable, it generates the machine-code instructions to free up the memory. Dynamically allocated space remains allocated for the duration of the program or until instructions are executed that explicitly deallocate the space. Dynamically allocated variables may be referenced anywhere within the program.

If a variable is created during runtime it must certainly be accessible to the program to be of any use. In a program's source code, global and local variables may be referenced using their identifiers (names) as one of the many conveniences afforded to programmers using a high-level language. During compilation, the compiler maintains a special symbol table of variable identifiers and their memory addresses within the program (as well as other information about the variable) so that, in generating the corresponding machine-code instructions, it can substitute a memory address for each identifier. The address for a local variable includes the frame pointer address value plus an offset into that activation record.

A dynamically allocated variable, on the other hand, could reside anywhere in heapspace during runtime, long after the compiler has generated the machine-code version of the source code.

> Whereas a statically allocated variable is referenced in the source code using its *identifier,* a dynamically allocated variable is referenced by using its heapspace *memory address.*

Such an address is termed a **pointer value** (or, simply, a **pointer**), and standard Pascal provides a special *pointer data type* whose domain of values includes all viable heapspace addresses. The ADT specifications for the pointer type follow.

Specifications for the ADT Pointer Type

The **ADT pointer type** is a dynamic data type whose values (viable heapspace memory addresses) are ordered.

Domain

Each value is a heapspace memory address; the domain includes all viable heapspace addresses.

Fundamental Operations

1. *Dynamic allocation of heapspace memory:* Dynamically allocating a variable.
2. *Dynamic deallocation of heapspace memory:* Deallocating space for a dynamically allocated variable.
3. *Referencing a dynamically allocated variable.*
4. *Assignment to a pointer variable:* Assigning a heapspace address or `NIL` to a pointer variable.
5. *Test for equality, inequality:* Comparing two pointer values for equality or inequality.

Pascal Representation of the ADT Pointer Type

In a Pascal program, to allocate heapspace memory for a dynamic variable, to reference that variable, and later to deallocate the memory for that variable, the following must be done:

1. Declare a pointer data type, which involves describing the data type of the variable to be dynamically allocated.
2. Declare a **pointer variable** of that pointer data type—i.e., a variable capable of holding a heapspace address (a pointer value).
3. Call standard procedure `New` to actually allocate heapspace memory for the new variable and return its heapspace address in the pointer variable parameter.
4. Reference the variable using special pointer notation.
5. Call standard procedure `Dispose` to deallocate the heapspace memory for the variable when it is no longer needed—i.e., make its heapspace available for reallocation.

Standard Pascal syntax related to pointer values follows, and all standard operators and special symbols are given in Appendix A.

Declaration of a pointer variable

```
TYPE
  {pointer type identifier}  = ^{TYPE identifier of variable to be created};

  {TYPE identifier of variable to be created} = {data type description};

VAR
  {pointer variable} : {pointer type identifier};
```

Standard pointer constant (**`NIL`** is discussed in detail later in this section.)

Pointer value indicating "points to nothing"	**`NIL`**

Standard syntax

Reference a dynamically allocated variable	`{pointer variable}^`

Dynamic allocation and deallocation of heapspace

Allocate memory for a variable	`New`
Deallocate a dynamically allocated variable	`Dispose`

Standard data-transfer procedures and syntax

Parameter passing
Return a pointer type function value

A variety of sample declarations of pointer variables follow.

```
TYPE
  IntPtr      =  ^Integer;        {Pointer type for an integer variable}
  APosVal     =  ^PosVals;        {Pointer type for integer subrange}
  PosVals     =  0..MAXINT;       {Integer subrange}
  RealPtr     =  ^Real;           {Pointer type for a real variable}
  BoolPtr     =  ^Boolean;        {Pointer type for a Boolean variable}

  OneCourt    =  ^CourtType;      {Pointer type for enumerated type variable}
  CourtType   =  ( Racquetball, squash, handball, tennis, basketball );
  NameType    =  String [ 25 ];
  Res         =  ^OneRes;         {Pointer type for a record variable}
  OneRes      =  RECORD
                   Name              :  NameType;
                   CourtKind         :  CourtType;
                   CourtNumber,
                   NumberOfPlayers   :  Integer;
                   DateToPlay,
                   DateReserved      :  PACKED ARRAY [ 1..6 ] OF Char;
                   Balance           :  Real
                 END;

  StaffPtr    =  ^Staff;              {Pointer type for an array variable}
  Staff       =  ARRAY [ 1..40 ] OF NameType;

  Status          =  ^MachineStatus; {Pointer type for a set variable}
  MachineStatus   =  SET OF Char;

VAR                           {Variable capable of holding the address of ...}
  OneInt   :  IntPtr;         {  an integer variable}
  PosInt   :  APosVal;        {  a PosVals integer subrange variable}
  OneReal  :  RealPtr;        {  a real variable}
  OneBool  :  BoolPtr;        {  a Boolean variable}
  Court    :  OneCourt;       {  a CourtType variable}
  P        :  Res;            {  a OneRes record variable}
  Faculty  :  StaffPtr;       {  a Staff array variable}
  MStatus  :  Status;         {  a MachineStatus set variable}
```

Unlike other declarations, a Pascal pointer type declaration references another data type *prior to* the declaration of that data type. As we have just seen, the **TYPE** declaration of Res states that Res is the identifier for a pointer type that is the heapspace address for a variable of record type OneRes; the declaration for OneRes appears *after* the Res declaration. (Pointer variable P can hold the address of a single Res type record. Establishing a list of Res type records, requires creating a structure such as an array to hold the list, which is not done here.)

Simply declaring a pointer variable does not automatically allocate any heapspace memory—standard procedure New must be called to do this. This procedure takes a single pointer variable identifier as a parameter:

```
New ( {pointer variable} );
```

New performs two operations:

1. *Allocation.* Procedure New allocates enough heapspace for one variable of the data type associated with its pointer variable parameter.

2. *Assignment.* Procedure New returns via its pointer variable parameter the heapspace address of the variable just allocated.

When a pointer variable contains the heapspace address of a dynamically allocated variable, we say that it *points to* the just-allocated variable. Four sample calls to New, using the pointer variables declared earlier, follow:

```
New ( OneReal );  {OneReal now points to a real type variable in heapspace}
New ( P );        {P now points to a Res type record variable in heapspace}
New ( MStatus );  {MStatus now points to a Status type set variable in heapspace}
New ( OneInt );   {OneInt now points to an integer variable in heapspace}
```

The pointer variables OneReal, P, MStatus, and OneInt each contain the heapspace address of a variable, the data type of which was specified previously in the **TYPE** and **VAR** declarations. Each of these pointer variables may now be used to reference the dynamic heapspace variable to which it points.

Pointer Variables and Values, Dynamically Allocated Variables

Dynamically allocated variables are referenced using a caret (^), or ↑, or @ symbol:

```
{pointer variable}^
```

Examples using previously declared pointer variables include OneInt^, Posint^, Court^, Faculty^, and P^. To use dynamic allocation effectively in programming, you must clearly understand the difference between the following:

- *Pointer variable.* Capable of holding a heapspace address.
- *Pointer value.* Heapspace address contained in the pointer variable.
- *Dynamically allocated variable.* The heapspace variable itself.

In particular, do not confuse a pointer value (an address) with the actual dynamically allocated variable being pointed to. This distinction is described in the following simple example (you may assume that New (P) has already been called):

Syntax	Example	Meaning
{pointer variable}	P	Refers to the address of the dynamically allocated variable; P contains this address.
{pointer variable}^	P^	Refers to the dynamically allocated variable itself; P^ is the variable that was dynamically allocated.

Perhaps the difference between P and P^ is best illustrated by the following analogy: Imagine someone in your classroom pointing to a window. The

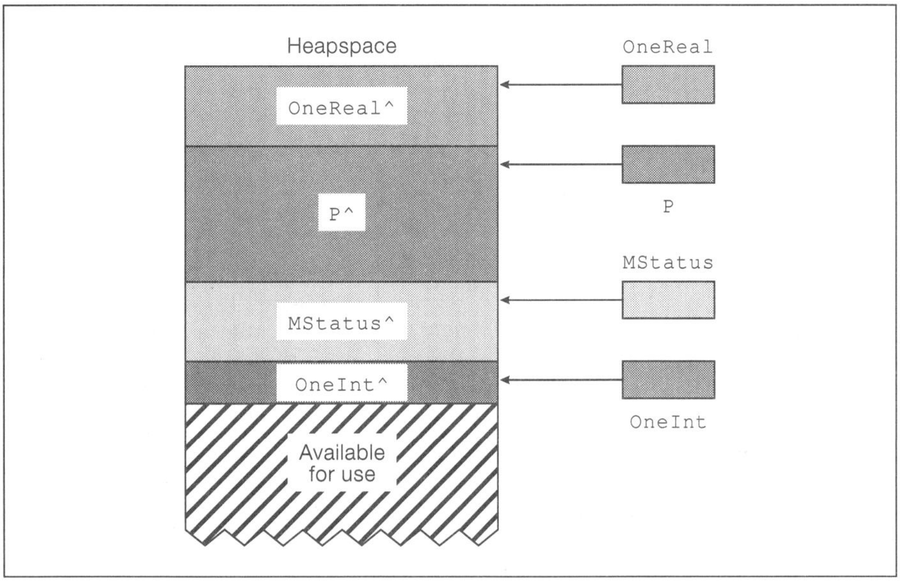

FIGURE 4.10 Depiction of Four Pointer Variables Pointing to Heapspace Variables

finger is the *pointer,* whereas the window is the *object being pointed to,* and there is certainly a clear difference between a finger and a window. Figure 4.10 depicts how the pointer variables point to the various dynamically allocated variables after the calls to `New`. (In the figure, the size of each rectangle in the heapspace is not intended to reflect accurately the relative size of the variable it represents.)

A dynamically allocated variable behaves like any variable of its data type. Examine the following three (unrelated) code segments; comments are included to remind you of the **TYPE** declarations given earlier. Although dynamic allocation and pointer values are typically used with linked list, tree, and graph structures (the topics of Chapter 5, 8, and 9, respectively), the following examples are given to extend your understanding of pointers:

```
OneInt^  := -1234;                         {VAR OneInt    : ^Integer}
OneReal^ := Sqrt ( Abs (OneInt^) );        {VAR OneReal   : ^Real}
```

```
                                           {TYPE Status   = ^MachineStatus;
                                            VAR MStatus   :  Status;  }
MStatus^ := [ 'A'..'D', 'G', 'S'..'V' ];   {MachineStatus  = SET OF Char}
```

```
                                           {TYPE OneRes = RECORD...}
WITH P^ DO                                 {VAR P        : ^OneRes;    }
  BEGIN
  OneBool^ := Balance > 50.0;              {VAR OneBool : ^Boolean}
  IF OneBool^ THEN
    Balance := Balance * 1.05;
  Writeln ( 'New balance for ', Name, ' is $', Balance:6:2 )
  END;
```

```
Write ( 'Enter the court number:  ' );        {TYPE PosVals =  0..MAXINT }
Readln ( PosInt^ );                            {VAR PosInt   :  ^PosVals; }

IF ( PosInt^ <= 18 ) AND ( PosInt^ >= 1 ) THEN
  CASE PosInt^ OF
     1..10 : P^.CourtKind := Racquetball;
    11..15 : P^.CourtKind := Squash;
    16..18 : P^.CourtKind := Handball
  END;
```

In the set of declarations given earlier, variable `Faculty^` is declared as an array of fixed length, containing memory for 40 elements, each of which is a 20-character string. Assume that the following call has been made:

```
New ( Faculty );
```

Further assume that while reading a source code program you encountered the expression, `Faculty^ [ 17 ] [ 5 ]`. How would you make sense of this syntax?

> Whenever writing or visually examining any "complicated" Pascal syntax, always progress from left to right, from the general to the specific.

This approach may be applied to `Faculty^ [ 17 ] [ 5 ]` as follows:

Pascal syntax	What the syntax references
`Faculty`	The pointer or heapspace address of the entire array
`Faculty^`	The array itself
`Faculty^ [ 17 ]`	The seventeenth element of the array (itself, an array)
`Faculty^ [ 17 ] [ 5 ]`	The fifth letter of the name contained in the seventeenth element

Pascal is very consistent in its rules of syntax. Adhering to the left-to-right rule simplifies the process of devising or visually comprehending any Pascal expression, no matter how complicated.

As we have seen, a pointer variable acquires a pointer value when standard procedure `New` is called, passing the variable as a parameter. Another way a pointer variable may acquire a pointer value is via an explicit assignment statement. When a pointer variable is assigned the value of another pointer variable, both variables then point to the same dynamically allocated variable. Examine the declaration and assignment statements that follow:

```
VAR
  Ptr1, Ptr2  :  IntPtr;  {Capable of pointing to an integer variable}

BEGIN
New ( Ptr1 );              {Ptr1 points to an integer variable in heapspace}
Ptr2 := Ptr1;              {Ptr2 now points to the same integer variable}
New ( Ptr2 );              {Ptr2 now points to a new integer variable in heapspace}
Ptr1 := Ptr2;              {Ptr1 now points to this new integer variable as well}
```

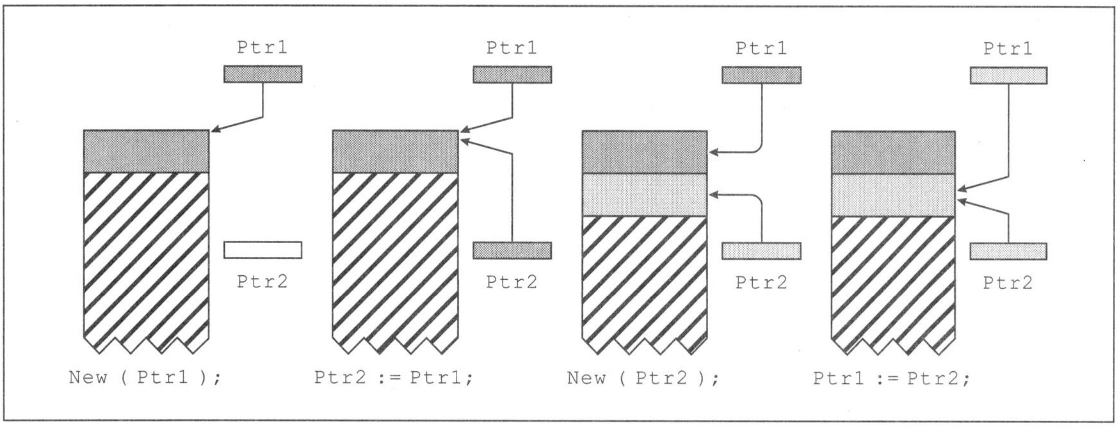

FIGURE 4.11 Heapspace and Pointer Variable Activity after Several Assignments

Figure 4.11 depicts heapspace and pointer variable activity resulting from these assignments. For simplicity, you may assume that the heapspace is empty before the assignments are made.

Note that after the fourth assignment statement, the first dynamically allocated integer variable is *no longer accessible* because its address was not retained in a pointer variable. Such inaccessible variables are commonly called **dead space,** or simply **garbage.** Leaving garbage behind instead of properly deallocating the memory via a call to standard procedure `Dispose` (to be discussed shortly) clutters up the heapspace and may result in the program's running out of needed heapspace.

The `NIL` Pointer Type Constant

Standard Pascal furnishes a pointer type constant called **`NIL`**, which may be assigned to any pointer variable. A **`NIL`** pointer value is used universally among Pascal programmers to mean "points to nothing." As an example, the following two assignment statements are a continuation of the previous four assignment statements:

```
Ptr3 := NIL;     {Ptr3 points to nothing}
Ptr1 := Ptr3;    {Now, Ptr1 points to nothing as well}
```

Note that `Ptr2` still points to the dynamically allocated integer (from the assignment statements given previously).

Pointer variables may be compared for equality (=) or inequality (< >) with each other or with **`NIL`**:

```
IF ( Ptr1 = Ptr3 ) AND ( Ptr1 = NIL ) AND ( Ptr1 <> Ptr2 ) THEN
  Writeln ( 'The pointer variables Ptr1 and Ptr3 point to nothing!' );
```

Standard Pascal does not permit any arithmetic operators or any relational operator other than = and < > to be used.

A pointer variable must be assigned a valid heapspace address value (either through an explicit assignment statement or a call to `New`) before it can be used to reference heapspace memory. As a simple example, consider the following declaration and call to `Writeln`:

```
VAR
  Ptr : ^Integer;

BEGIN
   .
   .
Writeln ( Ptr^ );  {Display value of the integer variable pointed to by Ptr}
```

If `Ptr` contains either a **NIL** value or an undefined value rather than a valid heapspace address via an explicit assignment or a call to **New**, the execution of this call to `Writeln` will probably result in a fatal runtime error; *typically this error crashes both the user program and the operating system.*

What use is a pointer variable with a **NIL** value? In Chapter 5 you will learn about an important data structure called a *linked list,* consisting of a collection of records, each of which is dynamically allocated. Each record in the list not only stores information relevant to the application at hand but also contains a record field of Pascal pointer type, commonly referred to as a *link field.* As the program allocates heapspace memory for each record, it assigns the address of the just-allocated record to the link field of the *previous* record, resulting in a linked list in which each record is said to point to the next record in the list.

To mark the end of the linked list, the program must be designed to assign a **NIL** value to the link field of the final record. Briefly look ahead to Figure 5.17, which depicts a linked list of five nodes. In the figure, each shaded area of each rectangular node represents that node's link field, each arrow depicts the pointing-ahead of the link field to the next node, and the stripe-filled area represents a **NIL** link field value. (As explained at the end of Chapter 5, a linked list also may be constructed without dynamic allocation within an array of records, in which array indices are used as addresses in place of Pascal pointer type values.)

Scope of Pointer Variables and Dynamically Allocated Variables

When a variable is dynamically allocated within a procedure or function, the variable still *exists* in heapspace even after the routine is exited, unlike a local variable that is deallocated automatically upon exiting. To illustrate this distinction, in the following simple code segment, parameter variable `Num1` may be referenced only within procedure `X` and pointer variable `Num2` may be referenced only within procedure `Y`; both are local to the procedures in which they are declared. However, the dynamic integer variable allocated by the call to `New` in procedure `X` may be referenced in either procedure via `Num2^` (in procedure `Y`) or `Num1^` (in procedure `X`).

```
TYPE
  IntPtr  =  ^Integer;     {Pointer type for an integer variable}
```

```
PROCEDURE Y ( Num2 : IntPtr );

BEGIN
  {Num2 contains the address of the dynamic integer variable allocated by the call to
   New in procedure X; Num2 may be used to reference this dynamic variable even though
   Num1 is local to procedure X}
END;
```

```
PROCEDURE X;

VAR
  Num1 : IntPtr;

BEGIN
New ( Num1 );
Y ( Num1 )
END;
```

Deallocating and Reusing Heapspace Memory

If a dynamically allocated variable is no longer needed by the program, its memory space should be explicitly deallocated by the program—i.e., made available to be overwritten later in the program if necessary. Recall from Figure 4.9 that all dynamically allocated variables must share the heapspace with activation records and that an inefficient use of this memory may cause the program to "run out" of heapspace. Simply abandoning unwanted heapspace variables by no longer using a particular pointer variable or perhaps by reusing a pointer variable in later calls to `New` results in garbage memory strewn about the heapspace.

Standard Pascal provides a procedure named **`Dispose`**, which makes allocated memory space available for subsequent reallocation via another call to `New`. The generic syntax for a call to `dispose` is

```
Dispose ( {pointer variable} );
```

Calling `Dispose` with a pointer variable that does not contain a legal pointer value or whose current value is **`NIL`** typically results in a fatal runtime error. When such a call to `Dispose` is made, the variable formerly pointed to by `P` becomes inaccessible to the program; however, that memory space may be reused via another call to `New`. For example, if `P` is a pointer variable and heapspace is allocated via the call `New ( P )` and then later deallocated via the call `Dispose ( P )`, the program cannot use the reference `P^` until `P` is reassigned a valid pointer value.

Unfortunately, standard Pascal does not dictate exactly *how* or *how efficiently* disposed heapspace memory is reallocated upon subsequent calls to `New`. This task is left to the designers of each Pascal compiler, who also design all predefined functions and procedures in the library of compiled predefined routines that accompanies a compiler. A `Dispose` procedure cannot merely shift all heapspace variables toward the beginning of the heapspace, since this would render all current pointer variable values invalid.

In one memory management strategy called the **first-fit method**, the `New` procedure starts at the beginning of the heapspace and searches for the first chunk of available memory into which the new variable may fit. The **best-fit method** makes even better reuse of heapspace by searching for the smallest chunk of available memory into which the new variable will fit. This improvement reduces the amount of garbage left but does so at the cost of the additional search time—yet another example of the trade-off between saving execution time and saving memory. Many Pascal systems include nonstandard predefined routines that allow the user program itself to manage the use and reuse of heapspace directly. You are encouraged to investigate these resources on the particular system you are using.

Computer Memory Representation of the Pascal Pointer Type

A pointer value itself is typically represented in memory as a positive "long integer"—e.g., double the size of a standard integer for the computer in use. The value of a pointer value cannot be displayed directly using `Write` or `Writeln`, as attempted in the following example:

```
New ( P );
Writeln ( 'P contains the address value', P );    {ILLEGAL}
```

Accordingly, a pointer value cannot be read from the keyboard via a `Read` or `Readln` statement. When designing and debugging source code, the programmer must be especially careful when the code involves pointer values. Drawing pictures on paper to represent heapspace structures, such as the diagrams in Figures 5.17, 5.20, and 5.23, often prove helpful while debugging programs that allocate and deallocate heapspace memory. Pointer values are runtime-dependent, so they should not be saved to a file.

SUMMARY

Three types of computer memory available for storing program data and instructions are internal (main), external online, and secondary (external offline) memory. Internal memory is volatile, whereas both types of secondary memory are nonvolatile.

A file is a named collection of data in memory; a directory, volume, or folder, are named collections of files. Files are used for program and data storage, to share data among programs, to provide input to a program, and to capture output from a program. Files have a dynamic (variable) length, whereas arrays have a static (fixed) length. The two basic types of file are (1) the binary file, in which data are stored in the same format as that data would be represented within internal memory and (2) the text file, in which data are stored as a long list of characters. Both may be regarded as abstract data types themselves.

The ADT binary file is a structured data type consisting of a linear list of elements that are stored and accessed using a first-in, first-out (FIFO) time-of-arrival scheme. Its domain consists of file elements, all of the same data type, which may be simple or structured. Fundamental operations include opening the file for reading or writing, reading or writing a single element, and closing the file. In a Pascal program, a file variable must be declared using **FILE OF** syntax. The standard `Eof` function is used to detect the end of a file and the standard procedures `Get` and `Read` are used to read from a binary file, whereas `Put` and `Write` are used to write to a binary file. For each open file, the operating system maintains a file pointer, which holds the external memory address of the currently accessible file element and is reset to the first element when a file is opened.

In standard Pascal, binary file elements are read or written one at a time, sequentially, from the start of the file. Each element is accessed via a file buffer variable; its data type is the same data type for a single file element. The contents of a file buffer variable are referenced in a Pascal program using the syntax `{file variable}^` and the file pointer advances to the next file element each time an element is read or written. When a file is opened for reading, its file buffer variable is loaded automatically with the contents of the first file element.

The ADT text file is a linear list of characters that is stored and accessed using a FIFO scheme. Its domain is a sequence of single characters, grouped into lines. Fundamental operations include opening the file for reading or writing, reading or writing a string of characters, and closing the file. A line is delimited by a special end-of-line indicator, which may be detected by the standard Pascal `Eoln` function. In a Pascal program, the file variable is declared to be of type `Text`. The `Eof` function and activity of the file pointer are the same as with binary files although, with text files, a file element is always a single character. When data of a type other than character are written to a text file via the standard procedures `Write` or `Writeln`, the data are automatically converted to character strings by the operating system before they are written. The converse is true upon reading via the standard procedures `Read` or `Readln`.

Heapspace is that portion of internal memory in which variables can be created or returned (allocation and deallocation) at runtime. Each time a procedure or function is called at runtime, the operating system automatically allocates an activation record in heapspace to hold such information as each local variable, each non-**VAR** parameter, the address of each **VAR** parameter, the return address, and, for functions, the current value of the function.

A program variable may be (1) a global variable within the program's executable image at compile-time, (2) a local variable for a procedure or function within an activation record in heapspace, or (3) a dynamically allocated variable created during runtime in heapspace. Dynamically allocated variables provide the advantages of flexible size, temporary storage, and having a greater amount of memory than is typically available within an executable image.

Whereas a statically allocated variable is referenced in the source code using its identifier, a dynamically allocated variable is referenced using its heapspace memory address. Such an address is referred to as a pointer value, or simply "pointer." In standard Pascal, the domain of the pointer type includes all heapspace memory addresses which are viable during that runtime. Fundamental operations include dynamic allocation and deallocation, accessing a variable, assignment of the contents of one pointer variable to another pointer variable, and the scalar operations of comparing two pointer values for equality or inequality. A pointer type is typically represented in computer memory as a long (multi-word) integer.

Both the pointer data type and its corresponding pointer variable must be declared. Standard procedure `New` allocates the heapspace memory for a variable whereas `Dispose` deallocates it. If `P` is a pointer variable, the identifier `P` represents the address of the dynamic variable, whereas `P^` refers to the dynamic variable to which `P` "points." A dynamically allocated variable behaves like any variable of its data type. The standard Pascal identifier **NIL** is a universal pointer address value commonly assigned by programmers to a pointer variable to indicate "points to nothing." Two schemes for deallocation are the first-fit and best-fit methods.

KEY TERMS

Activation record
ADT binary file
ADT pointer type
ADT text file
ASCII file
Automatic type conversion
Back door
Best-fit method
Carriage-return character
`Close`
Deallocate
Dead space
Direct access
Directory
`Dispose`
Download
Dynamic allocation
End-of-file indicator
End-of-line indicator
`Eof`
`Eoln`
External memory
File
File buffer variable
File element
File I/O
FILE OF
File pointer
File variable
File window
First-fit method
Folder
Frame
Frame pointer
Garbage
Global variable
`Get`
Header record
Heapspace
Heapspace overflow
High-order byte
INPUT
Input buffer
Internal memory
Key field
Line
Line-feed character
Local variable
Low-order byte
Main memory
Modem
`New`
Nonvolatile memory
NIL
Offline
Online
OUTPUT
Output buffer
Pointer, or pointer value
Pointer variable
Program parameters
`Put`
`Read`
`Readln`
`Reset`
`Rewrite`
Secondary memory
Sequential access
State of generation
State of inspection
Static allocation
Volatile memory
Volume
`Write`
`Writeln`

REVIEW QUESTIONS

1. Describe the ADT binary file, including the domain, fundamental operations, and structure. Describe related standard Pascal functions and procedures. Compare and contrast this data type with ADT array.
2. What is an area of great variation among nonstandard Pascal compilers?
3. Distinguish among the following in terms of concept and usage: file, file variable, file buffer variable, file pointer, file window, and actual file name.
4. Name five uses of files. Describe the two basic types of files.
5. What is the data type of a file buffer variable in terms of its associated file? Does a file buffer variable have to be declared explicitly in the source code of a program? What is the naming convention for a file buffer variable, and why must the ^ (or @ or ↑) symbol be used?

6. What is the role of a file pointer, and how is initialized? Can a file pointer be repositioned without closing its associated file?

7. State two reasons why a file must be opened and closed explicitly. In standard Pascal, can the same file be open for reading and writing simultaneously? In standard Pascal, can a file open for reading be closed and reopened for writing, all within the same program execution? Does the operation of opening a file have any effect on its contents? What effect does opening a file for reading have on its associated file buffer variable?

8. What may happen if a program attempts to open a nonexistent file for reading or a nonexistent file for writing? If a program opens an existing file for writing and writes to one file element's worth of data, where in the file will this data be written?

9. Distinguish between standard Pascal arrays and files, regarding the accessing of their respective elements. What type of file-related operation may a nonstandard Pascal compiler support that a standard Pascal compiler would definitely not support?

10. In the `Electronic Menu` application, the entire contents of a file of record are read into an array at the start of the program and then are written back to the file (if there are any changes) at the end of the program. If the program needs to access a particular record, it linearly searches through the array for a matching food-item abbreviation. An alternative approach would be for the program not to use an array and merely read records from the file until either the desired record is found or else the end of the file is reached. Describe the advantages and disadvantages of both strategies and why the former approach was chosen.

11. In the `Electronic Menu` application, what were the two deletion strategies presented? Which strategy was actually chosen for the program and why?

12. Describe the ADT text file, including the domain, fundamental operations, and structure. Describe the standard Pascal identifiers, function, and procedures. Compare this data type with the ADT binary file: Is the standard identifier `Text` equivalent to the declaration segment **FILE OF** `Char`?

13. Distinguish between the standard Pascal mechanisms of reading from and writing to binary files and text files. Distinguish between the actions of the `Read` and `Readln` and the `Write` and `Writeln` procedures as they pertain to text files.

14. What are input and output buffers? How do the standard identifiers **INPUT** and **OUTPUT** relate to text files?

15. How does the display of a text file by an editor compare to the actual representation of that file in memory?

16. Describe the process of automatic type conversion for text files.

17. Describe how a text file may be used to store values in a binary file. Values of what data types cannot be stored in a text file, displayed on a screen, or read from a keyboard? Describe strategies for representing a Boolean value, an enumerated type value, and a standard Pascal set structure each on a single line of a text file.

18. What are the logical and syntactical differences between storing information in heapspace and storing information in a file?

19. Distinguish between static and dynamic memory allocation and global and local memory space. Is a global or local named constant stored in memory in

the same way that a global or local variable might be stored? What are the parts of an executable image, as described in one of the figures in this chapter?

20. What data might an activation record store? When and how are activation records allocated and deallocated? What is stored in an activation record for a **VAR** parameter as opposed to a non-**VAR** parameter?

21. Distinguish between the syntax used to reference a statically allocated variable and the syntax used to reference a dynamically allocated variable within source code.

22. Describe the Pascal pointer, including the domain, fundamental operations, standard operator, identifier, and procedures. Is the pointer type a simple or structured type?

23. Dynamic allocation allows a program to make better use of internal memory in what three ways?

24. Distinguish among the following: Pointer, pointer value, pointer type, pointer variable. If `P` is a variable of pointer type, what is the logical difference between `P` and `P^`?

25. Distinguish between the first-fit and best-fit methods, regarding managing heapspace memory.

26. What advantage might an array of pointers to records provide over an array of records, assuming the same record declaration in both cases?

EXERCISES

1. In the following code segment, `Sum`, `Count`, and `Val` are integer variables, `Mean` is a real variable, and `InFile` is declared as a **FILE OF** `Integer`. You may assume that a statement has already been executed to associate the actual file name with the file variable, `InFile`, and that this file contains at least one integer file element. The code segment is intended to average the integer values read from the file. Is the segment syntactically correct? If so, is it logically correct as well? If each statement within a comment is substituted for the statement on the same line, would the segment be syntactically correct? If so, would it also be logically correct?

```
Sum   := 0;
Count := 0;
Reset ( InFile );
WHILE NOT Eof ( InFile ) DO
  BEGIN
  Get ( InFile );            {Read ( InFile, Val )}
  Sum   := Sum + InFile^;    {Sum := Sum + Val}
  Count := Count + 1
  END;
Mean := Sum / Count;
Close ( InFile );
```

2. State whether or not each of the following ten declaration segments is syntactically legal:

```
FILE OF Integer                          FILE OF Char
FILE OF Boolean                          FILE OF Text
FILE OF ARRAY [ 1..10 ] OF Integer       FILE OF Set OF Char
FILE OF RECORD                           FILE OF (Up, Down, Sideways)
FILE OF FILE OF Real                     FILE OF 'a'..'z'
```

3. Answer Exercise 9 at the end of Chapter 3 again, but this time replace the arrays `Inventry.Items` and `OnSale.Items` with the two binary files,

Inventry.DAT and OnSale.DAT; i.e., each file record is a variant record describing one item—a phonograph recording, a cassette tape, or a compact disc. Rewrite the global declarations given, and rewrite procedure MarkDown without referring back to your solution for Exercise 10.

4. Complete procedure FileAppend, which should append the contents of binary file File2 to the contents of binary file File1 (File1 and File2 are file variables). The procedure should open and close both files.

```
PROCEDURE FileAppend ( VAR File1, File2 : FileType );
```

5. Complete procedure MergeFiles, which should merge the contents of the File1 and File2 files, producing a third file, whose file variable is File3. FileType is **FILE OF** Integer. Assume that the File1 and File2 files have their elements ordered by ascending integer value, as should the File3 file. MergeFiles should open and close the File1 and File2 files and leave them unchanged when finished.

```
PROCEDURE MergeFiles ( VAR File1, File2, File3 : FileType );
```

6. Binary file AllMail.DAT contains electronic mail for many computer users and was created using the following global declarations:

```
TYPE
  Info       = String [ 80 ];               {One mail message}
  NameType   = String [ 20 ];
  MailBox    = RECORD
                 Owner    : NameType;       {Owner's name}
                 Messages : ARRAY [ 1..10 ] OF Info;
                 Count    : Integer;        {Count of mail messages}
               END;

  EMailFile  = FILE OF MailBox;
```

Complete procedure DisplayMail, which should open AllMail.DAT for reading and begin reading MailBox records in search of the record whose Owner field matches parameter UserName. If no such record is found, DisplayMail should display an error message; otherwise it should display all Count messages contained in the Messages array of the record. DisplayMail should then close the file. You may assume that no more than one MailBox record exists per UserName.

```
PROCEDURE DisplayMail ( VAR UserName : NameType );
```

7. The structure used in Exercise 6 may waste file memory because enough memory is allocated for each record to contain ten InfoType mail messages, even though a given record may have been assigned fewer than ten messages before the record is stored in the file. Although standard Pascal supports only *fixed-length records,* we can use variant records to effectively implement *variable-length records:*

```
TYPE
  Info       =  String [ 80 ];
  NameType   =  String [ 20 ];
  MailBox    =  RECORD
                  CASE MessageRec : Boolean OF
                    TRUE  : ( Message : Info );     {One mail message}
                    FALSE : ( Owner   : NameType;   {Owner's name}
                              Count   : Integer )   {Number of message}
                END;                                { records that follow}

  EMailFile  =  FILE OF MailBox;
```

Using these declarations, the AllMail.DAT file will contain one MailBox record per user, with a false MessageRec tag field value. In this record, the

`Owner` field contains the owner's name and the `Count` field contains a count of the number of message records in the file elements that immediately follow—i.e., records with a true `MessageRec` tag field value—and the `Message` field containing the text of one message. This approach also allows more than ten mail messages per user to be stored.

a. Rewrite procedure `DisplayMail` to again display mail messages for a particular user, this time for a file structured using the variant record declaration.

```
PROCEDURE DisplayMail ( VAR UserName : NameType );
```

b. Write a complete program that not only displays existing mail messages but also allows the user to interactively enter new messages for a particular user.

8. Write a program that generates a *file dump* of the `MenuFile.DAT` binary file used in the `ElectronicMenu` application; i.e., a program that neatly displays the contents of each `OneItem` record, including the password, if one is stored. Label all output and display a count of the records read.

9. Modify your program of Exercise 8 by sending all output to a text file rather than displaying it. Query the user for the names of the input (binary) file and the output (text) file.

10. Hardly Able, a local politician, is running for reelection, but his campaign manager feels that his speeches have been too long and too emphatic. His next speech is stored in a text file named `Humbug.TXT`. Write a program that reads lines of text from the file and does the following:

- Counts and displays the total number of words.
- Counts and displays the total number of sentences.
- Counts and displays the average number of words per sentence.
- Replaces all ! characters with periods (.) in the file.

11. Write a program that reads lines of text from a text file named `RawData.TXT` and builds a binary file of records, named `BinData.TXT`, containing this data. Each record in the binary file should be of type `Empl`, as given in the following declarations. Each line of text should describe one employee of a particular company, including the seven types of data indicated in the `Empl` declaration. You must make up the actual values and must devise a strategy for representing enumerated, Boolean, and set values in the text file.

```
TYPE
  DivType          =  ( Administrative, Clerical, Shop, Maintenance, Other );
  Char9            =  PACKED ARRAY [ 1..9 ] OF Char;
  Char5            =  PACKED ARRAY [ 1..5 ] OF Char;
  RankType         =  '1'..'7';
  PayDeductions    =  ( Fed, State, FICA, Local, Medical, Pension, Illness );
  PaySet           =  SET OF PayDeductions;
  Empl             =  RECORD
                        SSN         :  Char9;       {Social security number}
                        EmplNo      :  Char5;       {ID number}
                        Rate        :  Real;        {Hourly rate of pay}
                        Division    :  DivType;     {Division within company}
                        Rank        :  RankType;    {Rank within given division}
                        FullTime    :  Boolean;     {FALSE = Part-time}
                        Deductions  :  PaySet       {Applicable payroll deductions}
                      END;

  FileOfEmployees  =  FILE OF Empl;

VAR
  EmplFile  :  FileOfEmployees;
  RawData   :  Text;
```

12. Write a program that is capable of doing the following (provide a menu of options for the user):

    - Displays the length of a file—i.e., a count of characters, words, and lines
    - Writes to a text file all the lines that are in one text file but not another
    - Merges two text files into a third, on a line-by-line basis, so that the third file contains all lines "in order" (*Hint:* Regard each file line as one string; then compare strings using the <= operator.)

13. You have been hired by your university to print form letters congratulating each student who has made the dean's list. Rather than type all letters by hand, you do the following:

    - Store in a text file a congratulatory form letter of your design, but with the character # stored in place of a student's full name, @ stored in place of a student's full address, and $ stored in place of the current date.
    - Store on each line of a separate text file the name and address of each student, separated by a / character.

    Write a program that begins by prompting the user for the current date and the names of the name and address and form letter files. After opening both files for reading, the program should write to a third text file a complete letter, produced by reading from the text files and substituting an actual student name, address, and the current date for each #, @, and $ character, respectively. The program should generate a complete form letter for every student in the name-address file, naming each file written to as `DL1.TXT`, `DL2.TXT`, and the like.

14. A program correctly reads the contents of a binary file only if the declarations used to create the file are known to the programmer. In some applications where the original declarations are not known, a word-by-word file dump is useful. A *disassembler program* reads words of an object file program to produce its corresponding assembly language program.

    Write a program that begins by prompting for the name of a binary file; the file variable should be declared as a **FILE OF** `Integer`. The program should open this file for reading and then read each integer (actually a single word of the file) and display the following information:

```
{word}  {upper byte}  {lower byte}  {binary value}
{no.}   {character}   {character}   {of each byte}
```

    If the integer value of the upper and/or lower byte cannot be converted to a character, the program should display a # character followed by the value as a decimal number. Sample output for an imaginary four-word binary file follows (based on the ASCII character set, a two-byte word is assumed):

```
1   h   T      01101000   01010100
2   e   ' '    01100101   00100000
3   @   n      01000000   01000000
4   6   #26    00000110   00011010
```

15. Write a *pretty-printer program* that formats the source code of another Pascal program stored in a text file. Your program should read lines of text and do the following:

    - Store three blank lines before each procedure and function.
    - Store one blank line before and after each declaration section.
    - Indent each line properly and consistently; i.e., store leading blanks at the beginning of each line according to the elements of programming styles described in Appendix L.

    Any leading blanks already included on a source code line should be ignored. Design your program based on the assumption that the source code in the input file is syntactically correct; e.g., assume there is an **END** for each **BEGIN**, semicolons are correctly placed, and so on.

16. Assume that a program contains the following declarations:

```
TYPE
  InfoType   =  Boolean;
  Ptr        =  ^Node;
  Node       =  RECORD
                  Data : InfoType;
                  Next : Ptr
                END;

VAR
  P, Q : Ptr;
```

What are two effects of the call `New ( P )`? Distinguish among the following expressions, stating whether or not a compiler would flag the syntax as illegal: `P, P^, ^P, P^.Data, P^.Next, P^.Next^, P^.Next^.Data`

17. Assume that three different programs contain the global declarations given in Question 16. Assume further that each of the following three code segments represents the start of a program's main routine:

```
BEGIN                      BEGIN                      BEGIN
New ( P );                 New ( P );                 New ( P );
P^.Data := FALSE;          P^.Data := TRUE;           P^.Data := TRUE;
Writeln ( P^.Data );       Q := P;                    P := Q;
                           Writeln ( Q^.Data );       Writeln ( P^.Data );
```

Describe what each code segment does.

18. State whether or not each of the following ten **TYPE** declarations of `PtrType` is syntactically legal. If a particular declaration is not legal, make the least modification necessary to render it legal.

```
Ptr1  =  ^Integer;                          Ptr10  =  ^Char;
Ptr2  =  ^Boolean;                          Ptr11  =  ^Text;
Ptr3  =  ^ARRAY [ 1..10 ] OF Integer;       Ptr12  =  ^( Up, Down, Sideways );
Ptr4  =  ^SET OF Char;                      Ptr13  =  ^^Integer;
Ptr5  =  ^Ptr6;                             Ptr14  =  ^Ptr15;
Ptr6  =  SET OF Char;                       Ptr15  =  'a'..'z';
Ptr7  =  ^RECORD
            X, Y : Integer
          END;
Ptr8  =  ^Ptr9;
Ptr9  =  ^Integer;
```

19. The computer science department at a particular university offers a number of courses and one or more sections of each course. The following global declarations may be used to store information about courses, sections, and students:

```
CONST
  MaxCourses   =  50;
  MaxSections  =  15;
  MaxStudents  =  60;
  MaxProgs     =   6;
  MaxExams     =   4;

TYPE
  Str9         =  String [  9 ];
  NameType     =  String [ 15 ];
  CodeType     =  String [  7 ];

  StudentPtr   =  ^OneStudent;
  OneStudent   =  RECORD
                    ID           :  Str9;          {Identifies each student}
                    Name         :  NameType;      {Student name}
                    Programs     :  ARRAY [ 1..MaxProgs ] OF Real;  {Program scores}
                    Exams        :  ARRAY [ 1..MaxExams ] OF Real;  {Exam scores}
                    Total        :  Real;          {Total points}
                    Final        :  String [ 2 ]   {Final grade}
                  END;

  SectionPtr   =  ^OneSection;
  OneSection   =  RECORD
                    SectionCode  :  CodeType;      {Identifies each section}
                    Instructor   :  NameType;      {Instructor name}
                    AllStudents  :  ARRAY [ 1..MaxStudents ] OF StudentPtr;
                    Count        :  Integer        {Number of students in section}
                  END;

  CoursePtr    =  ^OneCourse;
  OneCourse    =  RECORD
                    CourseCode   :  CodeType;      {Identifies each course}
                    CourseName   :  NameType;      {Course name}
                    AllSections  :  ARRAY [ 1..MaxSections ] OF SectionPtr;
                    Count        :  Integer        {Number of sections this course}
                  END;

  EachCourse   =  RECORD
                    AllCourses   :  ARRAY [ 1..MaxCourses ] OF CoursePtr;
                    Count        :  Integer        {Total number of courses}
                  END;

VAR
  Courses  :  EachCourse;
```

Write a code segment for each of the following tasks:

a. Display the course code of the fifth course
b. Display the names of all instructors of the fifth course
c. Display the name of the sixth student in first section of the twelfth course
d. Display the names of all students who received scores of 90 or above on the first exam in the course whose course code is `'COM1101'`
e. Update the `Total` field (i.e., add all program and exam scores) of all students in the course whose course code is `'COM1101'`

CHAPTER FIVE

LINKED LISTS

In this chapter you will learn about representing a list of information as a chain, or linked list, of *nodes*, each typically of record type. Each node contains both data pertinent to the application and the address of the next node in the list. Several variations of the ADT linked list will be discussed.

5.1 PRELIMINARIES

When Nancy and Mike Newcomer moved into their new home on Belmont Avenue, the Bauers, who lived across the street, wanted to extend a warm welcome from the neighborhood. As a gesture of congeniality and as an opportunity for the Newcomers to meet many of their new neighbors, the Bauers planned a "progressive dinner" in which each household provides a different course of the dinner. The Newcomers would begin with appetizers at the Wilkinson home, then move on to the Bauer home for the first course, followed by the second course at the Harris home. Eventually, the Newcomers would arrive at the Gillespie home for a party attended by all participants. Figure 5.1 shows the schedule for the entire progressive dinner.

To make the evening even more fun and informal, the Bauers did not give a copy of the menu and schedule to the Newcomers. Instead, they merely told Nancy and Mike to begin at 1134 Belmont Avenue (the Wilkinson home) at 6:00 P.M. At 6:44 P.M., the Wilkinsons directed them to 1133 Belmont Avenue (the Bauer home) for the next part of the dinner. At 7:29, the Bauers directed Nancy and Mike to 1136 Belmont Avenue (the Harris home) for the second course. And so the progressive dinner evolved, with the residents of each household knowing the address of the next household that the Newcomers were to visit, until the end of the chain at 1140 Belmont Avenue. Figure 5.2 shows the route taken by the Newcomers over the course of the evening.

Figure 5.3 depicts the entire schedule of events as a *linked list,* with each of the six large rectangles indicating the residence, the serving, and the time of the serving. Each of these rectangles contains a smaller, vertical rectangle bearing the address of the next house to visit for the next serving.

The schedule of events for the entire progressive dinner may therefore be depicted as either of the following:

Address	Family	Approximate arrival time	Mystery serving
1134 Belmont Ave.	Wilkinson	6:00 P.M.	Hors d'oeuvres
1133 Belmont Ave.	Bauer	6:45 P.M.	First course
1136 Belmont Ave.	Harris	7:30 P.M.	Second course
1137 Belmont Ave.	Weldy	8:15 P.M.	Third course
1139 Belmont Ave.	Oren	9:00 P.M.	Dessert
1140 Belmont Ave.	Gillespie	9:45 P.M.	Party with all

FIGURE 5.1 Schedule for the Progressive Dinner

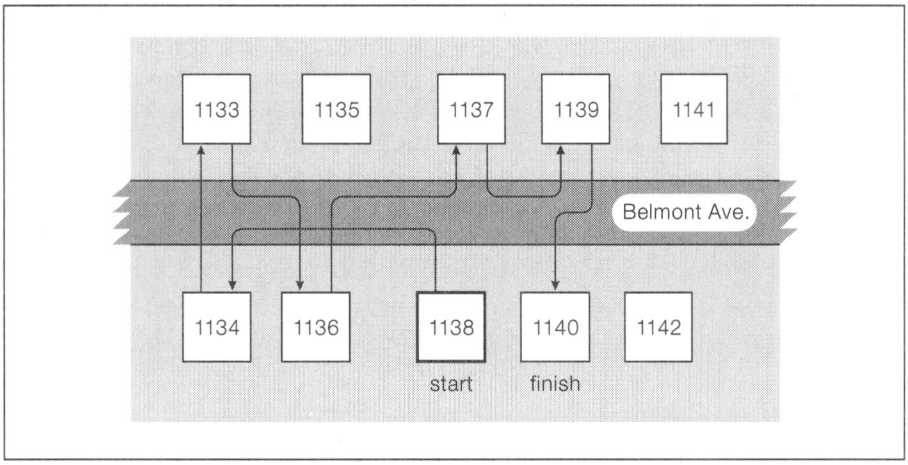

FIGURE 5.2 The Chain of Homes for the Progressive Dinner

- A *simple linear list,* as depicted in Figure 5.1
- A *linear linked list,* as depicted in Figure 5.3

Both versions of the schedule are accurate. If a Pascal program were written to store information about the schedule in computer memory, however, each version would require a fundamentally different storage scheme—i.e., a different physical representation of the same list.

The simple linear list version could be represented in Pascal as an array of records, one record per household event. Since array elements are stored in adjacent memory locations, an array representation of a list is commonly referred to as a **sequential storage representation**. In the linked list representation, records are again used to store information about a household event. These records are dynamically allocated somewhere in heapspace memory; they need not be adjacent in memory, just as houses visited by the Newcomers were not necessarily adjacent on Belmont Avenue. The sequence of records in the list is established instead by linking the records: Each record has a *link field* of pointer type, which contains the heapspace address of the next record in the list. And just as the Newcomers had to visit the

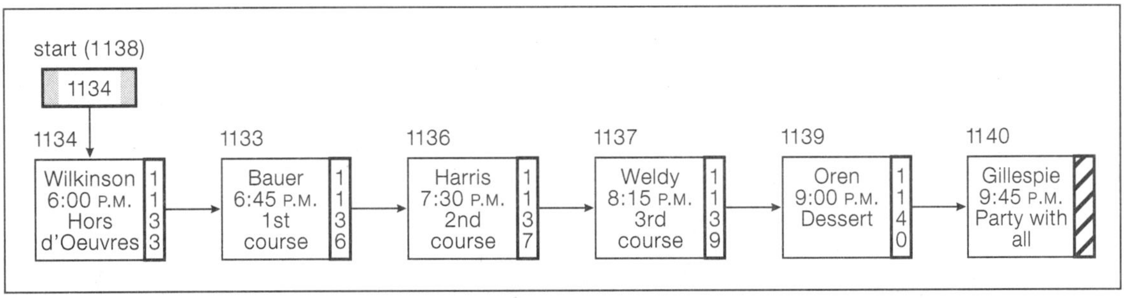

FIGURE 5.3 The Progressive Dinner Represented as a Linked List

Harris' home before they could visit the Weldy home, which is next in the dinner list, the records of a linked list, commonly called **nodes,** typically must be visited only in a linear, node-by-node manner.

Often, the programmer is faced with the choice of using an array or a linked list to represent a list of information. As we shall see, the sequential storage and linked list representations each offer advantages and disadvantages. For example, an array has a fixed length determined at compile-time, whereas a linked list can literally grow and shrink during runtime as nodes are inserted and deleted. An array supports the fast binary search technique (to be presented in Application 7.5), whereas a linked list supports only a linear search, which is typically much slower. We return to this comparison later in the chapter.

Specifications for the ADT Linked List

The **ADT linked list** is a structured data type forming a linear list of items; the list may or may not have its items ordered by key field values, depending on the application.

Domain

The domain consists of items called nodes, typically of record data type. Each node contains two types of field:

- The ***data field*** contains information relevant to the application, possibly including one or more key fields, for the purposes of ordering and searching.
- ***Link field(s)*** contain the address of the next node in the list. A second link field may be used to contain the address of the previous node.

Fundamental Operations

1. *Initialize as empty:* Initialize the linked list as empty; i.e., containing no nodes `[LLInit]`.
2. *Test for emptiness:* Test the list for emptiness `[LLEmpty]`.
3. *Search for a particular item:* Perform a linear search for a particular node `[LLSearch]`.
4. *Insert an item:* Insert a new node in the list `[LLInsert]`.
5. *Delete an item:* Delete an existing node from the list `[LLDelete]`.
6. *Traverse the list:* Visit and "process" each node in the list once, in a particular order `[LLTraverse]`.

Figure 5.4 shows the generic notation used to diagram a **singly linked list**—in this example, a linked list of six nodes. The shaded horizontal rectangle represents the **list head variable**, the variable that contains the address of the very first node in the list. Each arrow represents an access path from the list head variable to the first node or from one node to the next. Each node is represented by a rectangle; the white portion of a rectangle represents the node's data field(s) and the shaded portion represents the

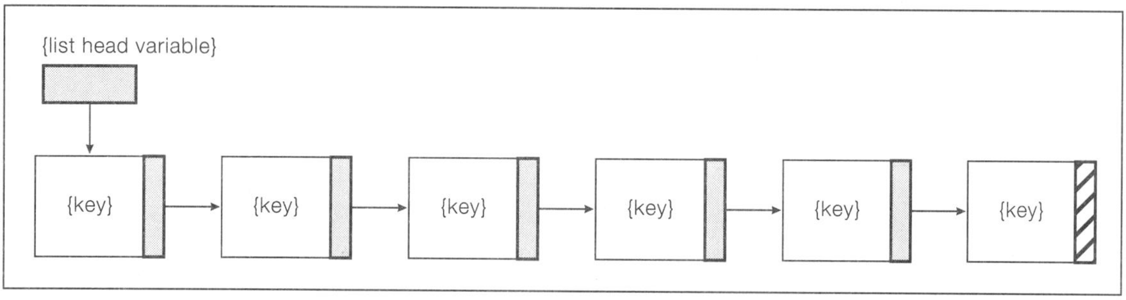

FIGURE 5.4 **Notation used to Represent a Linked List**

node's link field(s). Typically only key values are shown in the data rectangles of node diagrams. In the diagrams in this textbook, a `NIL` value will be indicated by a link field rectangle that is striped rather than shaded.

Pascal Representations of the ADT Linear Linked List (Overview)

Typically, linked lists contain nodes that are dynamically allocated in heapspace, with pointer type link fields. The ADT linked list may actually be represented using either dynamic allocation or sequential storage, however. Figure 5.5 distinguishes these two methods of representing a linked list. Section 5.2 examines the fundamental operations for linked lists using the dynamic allocation representation and Section 5.3 looks at the details of representing a linked list using sequential storage.

5.2 DYNAMIC ALLOCATION REPRESENTATION OF THE ADT LINKED LIST

A set of generic global declarations for any singly linked list follows.

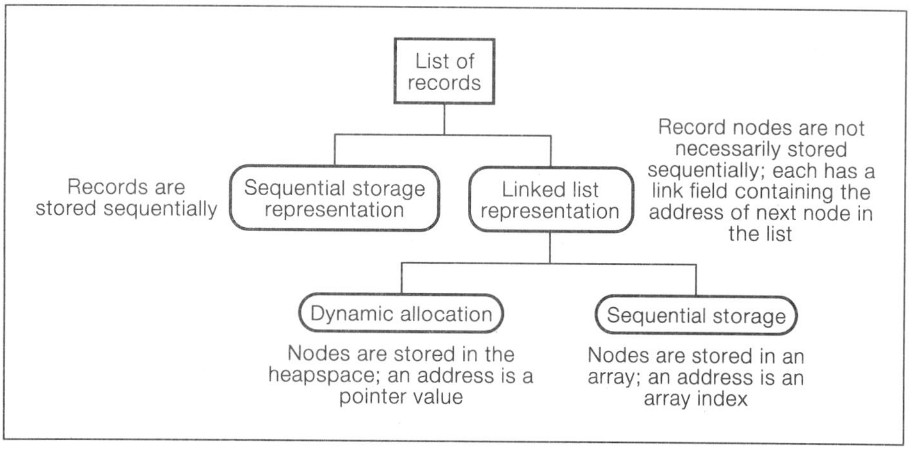

FIGURE 5.5 **List Representations**

```
TYPE
  KeyType    =  ??;                              {Application dependent}
  InfoType   =  RECORD
                  Key   : KeyType;               {Key value}
                  {Other fields, as necessary}
                END;

  NodePtr    =  ^Node;
  Node       =  RECORD
                  Data  : InfoType;              {Data portion of node}
                  Next  : NodePtr                {Link field; address of next node}
                END;

  LListType  =  RECORD
                  Head  : NodePtr;               {Address of 1st node in the list}
                  Count : Integer                {Number of nodes in the list}
                END;

VAR
  LList : LListType;
```

We now examine the fundamental operations of a linked list in the context of two applications. In the first application, we represent the ADT character string using a linked list; in the second application, we construct a telephone/address directory using a linked list ordered by last and first name.

APPLICATION 5.1 Representing the ADT Character String

As an introduction to the creation and use of a linked list, we will represent the ADT character string as a linked list in which the data portion of each node is a single character; i.e., in the declarations just given, `KeyType` is of char data type. We will build a simple three-node list to hold the string `'Joy'`, as shown in Figure 5.6. As we shall see, *the responsibilities of creating and linking the nodes of a linked list properly lie with the program/programmer.* We must be especially careful to assign the heapspace address of the first node to the `LList.Head` field in order to provide access to the list after it is built.

We will now devise a procedure named `BuildStringFromKeyboard`, which builds a linked list to represent a string of characters read from the keyboard. Again, the string is `'Joy'` and the resulting linked list is depicted in Figure 5.6 (the procedure will be capable of representing a much longer string). The procedure will prompt the user for a string that will then

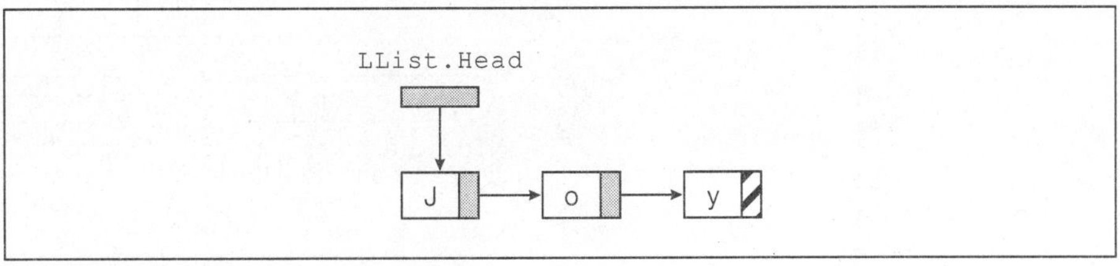

FIGURE 5.6 Sample Linked List to Store the String `'Joy'`

be read character by character. Since the memory for each node will be dynamically allocated in the heapspace and we are building a linked list, a pointer variable named `Current` will be needed to hold the address of the node most recently created. As we shall see, a second pointer variable named `Previous` will also be necessary for the process of linking the previous node to the current node.

`BuildStringFromKeyboard` begins by initializing the linked list as empty—i.e., as a list of zero nodes with the list head variable containing a **NIL** value. The starting portion of this procedure follows (the procedure will be shown in its entirety a bit later):

```
PROCEDURE BuildStringFromKeyboard ( VAR LList : LListType;
                                    MaxNodes : Integer );
VAR
  Current, Previous : NodePtr;  {Temporary node pointer variables}

BEGIN
Writeln ( 'Enter a string of 1 to ', MaxNodes, ' characters:  ' );
```

Recall from Section 4.1 that all characters entered at a keyboard are automatically stored by the operating system in a special internal memory structure known as an *input buffer,* which may be thought of as a text file with the file identifier **INPUT**. `BuildStringFromKeyboard` will read characters from the input buffer via the standard `Read` procedure until the end-of-line indicator is detected. This indicator is stored in the input buffer (and represented as `EOL` in figures) when the user presses the RETURN, or ENTER, keyboard key and may be detected using the standard `Eoln` function.

We will assume that the user has entered the string `'Joy'` and then pressed the RETURN key. The resulting contents of the input buffer are depicted in Figure 5.7. Note that Figure 5.7 portrays a slow motion depiction of input buffer activity. In actual practice, a character would be extracted from the input buffer via a `Read` call immediately after the character is typed and long before the RETURN key is pressed. Probably only a single character would sit in the input buffer—and only for a very brief time in this application. The figures in this application depict the buffer as a text file for visual clarity.

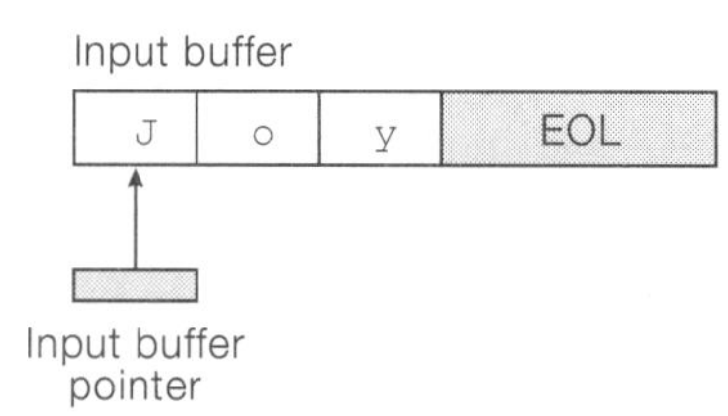

FIGURE 5.7 Keyboard Input Buffer after the User Enters `'Joy'` and Presses RETURN

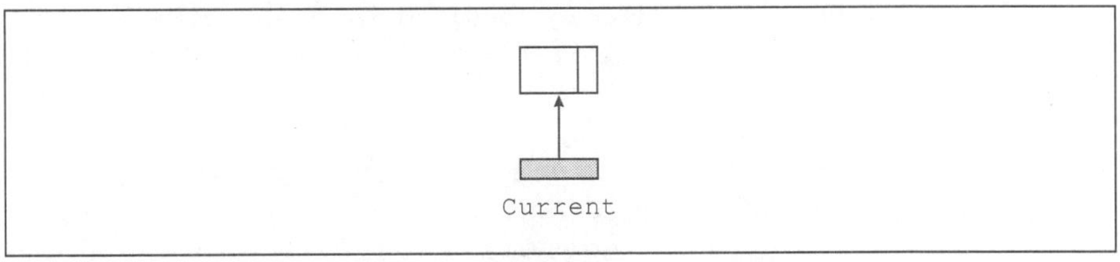

FIGURE 5.8 A Single Empty Node in the List

To insert the first node in the empty list, we must allocate memory in the heapspace for a single Node-type record. The following call to New allocates memory for such a record and returns its heapspace address in parameter Current:

```
New ( Current );
LList.Count := 1;
```

At this point, the list consists of a single empty node, pointed to by Current, as indicated in Figure 5.8.

Now a character must be read into the Data.Key field of this record. (We will use the Key field, although the character is not a true key. In database applications, a node's key value serves to distinguish that node from all other nodes in the database in order to order and search the list.) This reading and assignment may be accomplished by the following two statements, which require the additional local declaration of character variable Ch:

```
Read ( Ch );                    {Read a character}
Current^.Data.Key := Ch;
```

This code segment may be reduced to the following statement, so that a Ch variable is not needed:

```
Read ( Current^.Data.Key );
```

The call to Read assigns to the Key field the character J and advances the input buffer pointer to the o character. Figure 5.9 depicts the input buffer and the list thus far (note that we have not yet assigned a value to the node's link field, Current^.Next).

Before allocating the next node, for character o, we must be careful to save the address of the first node, using the list head field of the LList record. Failure to save the address of the first node will result in the program's having no way to access nodes after the list is completely built.

```
LList.Head := Current;  {Save address of first node}
```

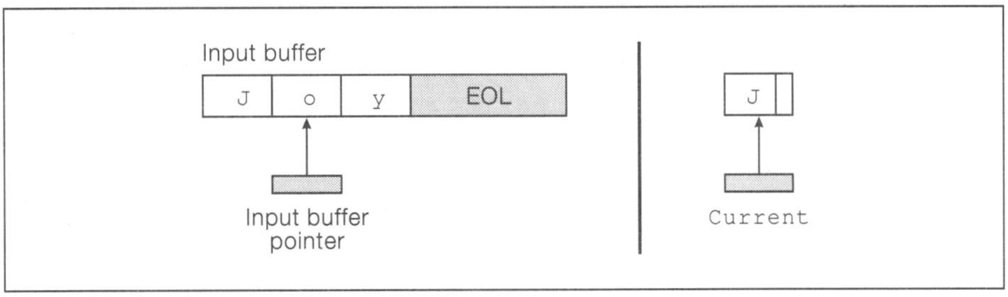

FIGURE 5.9 The List after Reading and Storing the First Character

Now we can allocate memory for the next node record, character o, via another call to procedure New. Before doing this, however, we must save the address of the J node in pointer variable Previous. This is necessary because, after allocating the new node for o, we must *assign the address of the current node (the* o *node) to the link field of the previous node (the* J *node); this way, the link field of the* J *node will point to the* o *node.*

```
Previous     := Current;           {Save address of J node}
New ( Current );                   {Current now points to new node, for o}
LList.Count := LList.Count + 1;    {Increment total node count}
```

Since the input buffer pointer is currently pointing to the o character, another call to Read will transfer the o character into the Key field of the just-allocated node:

```
Read ( Current^.Data.Key );
```

Figure 5.10 depicts the input buffer and linked list thus far.

We can now link up the first and second nodes of the linked list. This is accomplished via a single assignment statement, as follows:

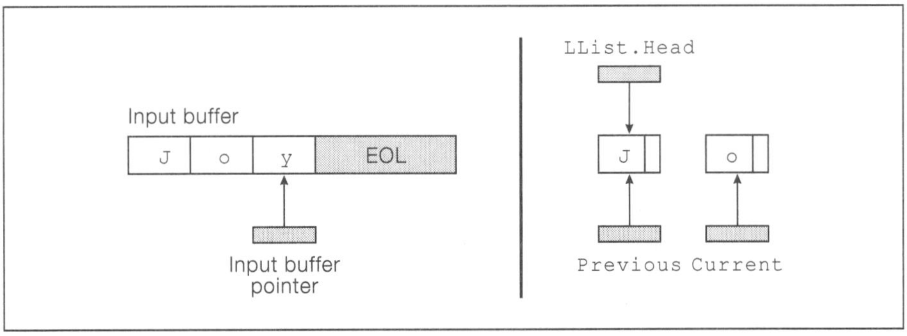

FIGURE 5.10 After Reading the o Character—Two Unlinked Nodes in the List

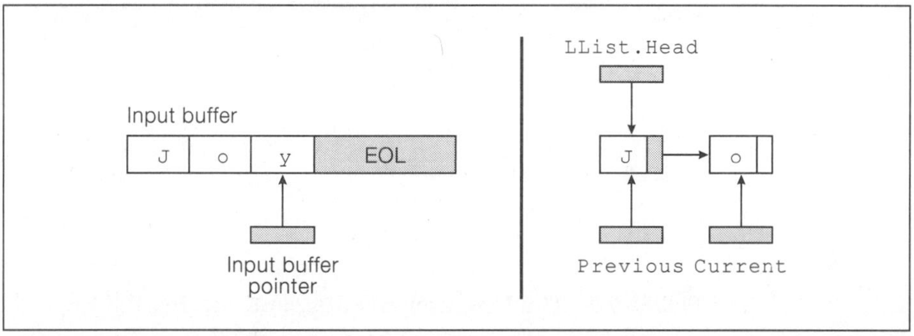

FIGURE 5.11 A Linked List of Two Nodes

```
Previous^.Next := Current;  {1st node now points to 2nd node}
```

The `Current` variable and `Previous^.Next` field both contain the same heapspace address, so they both point to the same heapspace variable—namely, the second node (o node). Figure 5.11 depicts the input buffer and linked list thus far. The `Previous` variable must now "catch up" to the `Current` variable by being assigned the contents of `Current` because the o node will become the "previous" node when the third node (for y) is allocated:

```
Previous := Current;  {Previous "catches up" to Current}
```

Figure 5.12 depicts the input buffer and linked list thus far.

The third (y) node is appended to the list in a similar way. When the list is completed, it is crucial that the `Next` field of the final node be assigned a **NIL** value. Assigning a **NIL** value to a link field is the universal technique among Pascal programmers for marking the end of a linked list. Algorithms that search for a particular node or simply traverse the entire list, processing each node, will compare the link field value of the node currently being examined with **NIL** to determine whether or not there are additional nodes

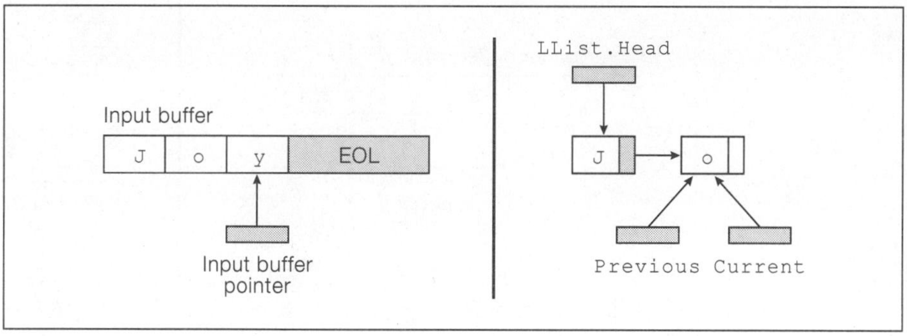

FIGURE 5.12 A Linked List of Two Nodes

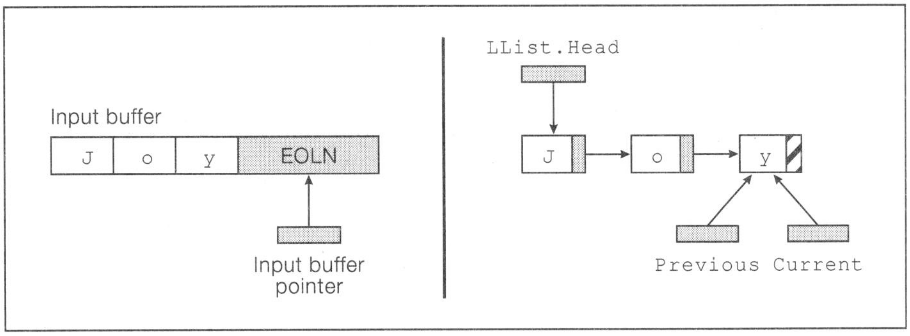

FIGURE 5.13 Final State of the Input Buffer and Complete Linked List

to search or visit. Figure 5.13 depicts the final state of the input buffer and linked list.

Since most of the steps undertaken to build the list are repeated, we can set up a loop to build a linked list of almost any length (limited, of course, by the amount of available heapspace). Procedure `BuildStringFromKeyboard`, which follows, constructs a linked list of char characters until either the end-of-line indicator is encountered or else a `MaxNodes` number of characters has been stored (in `MaxNodes` nodes). Examine the procedure carefully, hand-testing it by drawing a linked list on paper.

```
PROCEDURE BuildStringFromKeyboard ( VAR LList : LListType;
                                        MaxNodes : Integer );

VAR
  Current, Previous : NodePtr;     {Temporary node pointer variables}

BEGIN
WITH LList DO
  BEGIN
  Writeln ( 'Enter a string of 1 to ', MaxNodes, ' characters:  ' );

  New  ( Current );                {Current points to new Node type record}
  Count :=  1;                     {Initialize total node count}
  Read ( Current^.Data.Key );      {Read next character into new node}
  Head  :=  Current;               {Save address in Head field}

  WHILE NOT Eoln ( INPUT ) AND ( Count < MaxNodes ) DO
    BEGIN
    Previous := Current;           {Previous catches up to Current}
    New ( Current );               {Current points to new Node type record}
    Count := Count + 1;            {Increment total node count}
    Read ( Current^.Data.Key );    {Read next character into new node}
    Previous^.Next := Current      {Previous node now points to new node}
    END;

  Current^.Next := NIL             {Final node points to nothing}
  END
END;
```

Once the linked list is built, the program can perform a **traversal**, from the first node to the last, processing each node. Exactly what processing entails is application-dependent. In the present application, we will define processing as *echoing* (redisplaying) each character read. A generic `LLTraverse` procedure and a `Process` procedure for the present application follow. To visit and process every node in the list, the initial call to `LLTraverse` is `LLTraverse ( LList.Head )`.

```
PROCEDURE Process ( Current : NodePtr );

BEGIN
Write ( Current^.Data.Key )
END;
```

```
PROCEDURE LLTraverse ( Current : NodePtr );

BEGIN
WHILE Current <> NIL DO
  BEGIN
  Process ( Current );                         {Process the current node}
  Current := Current^.Next                     {Advance to next node in list}
  END
END;
```

The initial call passes the address of the first node to formal parameter `Current`. Because this value is not **NIL**, the **WHILE** loop is entered and `Process` is called to display the contents of the `Data.Key` field of the first node. `Current` is then assigned the address stored in the first node's link field; i.e., `Current` is assigned the address of the next node in the list. Eventually, `Current` will point to the final node (the y node in our simple example). After `Process` is called to display the y character stored in this node, `Current` is assigned the value of that node's link field, which is **NIL**. The Boolean expression `Current <> NIL` in the **WHILE** statement will then evaluate to a false value, terminating the loop. Reexamine Figure 5.6 as you trace the execution of `LLTraverse` and `Process`.

APPLICATION 5.2 A Telephone-Address Directory Program

In this application, we will devise an interactive program that creates and manipulates a directory of names, telephone numbers, and home addresses. In the course of developing this program, we will devise algorithms for the remaining fundamental linked list operations—`LLSearch`, `LLInsert`, `LLDelete`—as well as discussing how a linked list may be saved in a binary file.

The following information will be stored for each person in the directory:

- Name (last, first)
- Home address (street address, city, state, zip code)
- Home telephone number

Clearly, a Pascal record is the data structure of choice to hold this information. We will keep the entire collection of records ordered by key value (the combination of last and first names). Our program should be able to perform the following basic functions:

- Create an empty directory.
- Search for and display the contents of a particular entry.
- Insert a new entry.
- Delete an existing entry.
- Save the entire directory to a binary file.
- Reconstruct the entire directory by reading records from a binary file.

We must now decide how to represent the directory structure, using either *sequential storage* (i.e., a simple array) or a *linked list.*

Sequential Storage versus Linked List Representations

If we store directory records in a one-dimensional array of records, *how large* should we declare the array to be? We would have to guess the maximum number of entries we might choose to store, but if our guess is too low some entries will be excluded. If our guess is too high, on the other hand, memory is wasted. Even if we are able to estimate the size with an acceptable degree of accuracy, we are faced with another problem. Recall that we want to keep the list of records ordered by last and first name. To insert a new entry somewhere within the directory, the program must shift all existing entries following the point of insertion to make room for the new entry. Conversely, to delete an existing entry, the program must again shift all existing entries following this entry to fill in the gap left by the deletion. With long lists, this shifting of entries may create noticeable time delays while the program is running. Figure 5.14 depicts a portion of an array-based directory structure just prior to the insertion of a new entry and the deletion of an existing entry.

The sequential storage representation therefore has two drawbacks:

- *Length is fixed.* The length is fixed at compile-time (may waste memory).
- *Shifting is required.* Insertions and deletions usually require the shifting of existing entries, expending additional execution time.

As we shall see in the examples throughout this textbook, these two drawbacks arise anytime a data base is represented using a simple array. (We shall also see, in Application 7.5, that a significant advantage is provided by an array-based data base that is sorted: The binary search algorithm may be used, and it is significantly faster in the average case of searching than is the linear search algorithm.)

Unlike the length of arrays, the length of a linked list is not fixed at compile-time and this immediately alleviates the first drawback mentioned. Of course, the size of any dynamically allocated linked list is limited by the amount of available heapspace, but this amount is probably more than sufficient for most applications. Regarding the second drawback mentioned, we will see that insertions and deletions are typically faster for linked lists because no shifting is necessary. A major drawback to the use of a linked list, however, is that it will support only a linear search (node by node) instead of the faster binary search. Figure 5.15 contains a table summarizing the advantages and disadvantages of both representations.

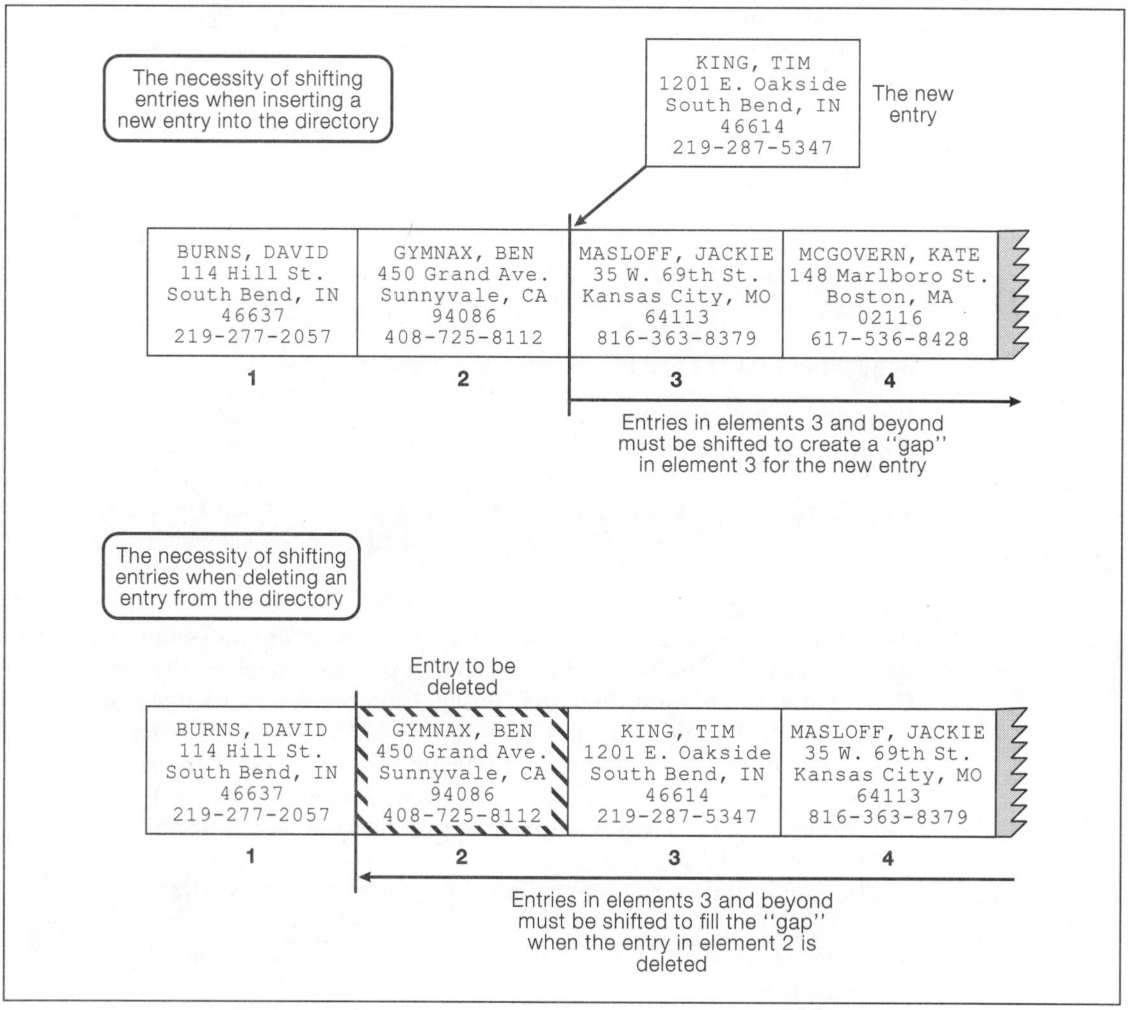

FIGURE 5.14 Array-based Directory Prior to Insertion and Deletion of an Entry

	Sequential storage	Linear linked list
Item storage and access	Elements are physically adjacent in memory and are accessed via index values.	Nodes are linked together and therefore may not be physically adjacent in memory. Nodes are accessed via pointer values.
List length	Fixed during runtime.	Variable during runtime.
Insertion and deletion	Less efficient; usually requires shifting many array elements.	More efficient; nodes are inserted or deleted by changing link field values.
Searching	More efficient; a binary search (Chapter 7) can be used if the list is ordered by key value.	Less efficient; a linear search is required.
Coding and debugging	Somewhat easier, since array elements are accessed directly via index values, which may be displayed via `WriteIn`.	More involved, since link fields must be maintained and Pascal pointer values cannot be displayed directly via `WriteIn`.

FIGURE 5.15 Comparison of the Sequential Storage and Linked List Representations

If the list is ordered by key value, as in the present application, arguments about which representation is more efficient for the operations of inserting and deleting nodes are somewhat circular. The point of insertion or deletion may be found faster in the average case using a binary search; however, once found, other array elements must be shifted. No such shifting is necessary when a node is inserted into or deleted from a linked list; however, the slower linear search must be employed to find the point of insertion or deletion. As we see in Chapter 8, a search tree structure provides the best of both worlds, offering flexible size, relatively easy insertion and deletion operations, and fast searching (if the tree is fairly balanced).

Looking Ahead: Header Nodes

In the present application, we will stay with the dynamically allocated linked list representation. We can use the same set of global declarations given earlier, but with `InfoType` and `KeyType` defined specifically for this application (other declarations will be added in the actual program code).

```
CONST
  MinVal     =  ' ';                      {Header node key value}

TYPE
  Str80      =  String [ 80 ];
  Str25      =  String [ 25 ];

  KeyType    =  Str25;
  InfoType   =  RECORD
                  Key     : KeyType;      {Full name: LAST, FIRST}
                  Address : Str80;        {Full address}
                  Phone   : Str25         {Full telephone number}
                END;

  NodePtr    =  ^Node;
  Node       =  RECORD
                  Data    : InfoType;     {Information about 1 directory entry}
                  Next    : NodePtr       {Link field; address of next node}
                END;

  LListType  =  RECORD
                  Head    : NodePtr;      {Address of header node}
                  Count   : Integer       {Number of nodes in the list}
                END;

  FileType   =  FILE OF InfoType;

VAR
  Directory  :  LListType;                {Record containing list head}
```

In the ADT character string representation example, each new node was simply appended to the end of the list and we did not need to delete or search for any nodes after the list was built. In the present application, however, the program must be able to insert (or delete) a new node *anywhere* within the list while keeping the list ordered by ascending `Key` field (name) value. The program must also be able to search the linked list for a particular node or for the point of insertion for a new node or the point of deletion for an

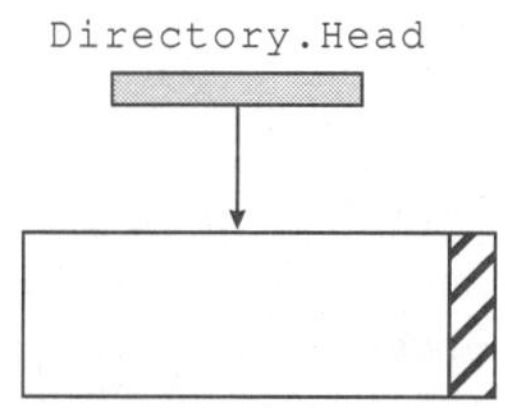

FIGURE 5.16 The Directory List after it is Initialized

existing node. We must therefore design algorithms for the primitive routines `LLSearch`, `LLInsert`, and `LLDelete`.

We begin by initializing the linked list node count (`Directory.Count`) to zero and creating a new node called a **header node**, to which `Directory.Head` will always point, even if the list contains no other nodes. No `Data` field values will be assigned to the header node, so diagrams depicting linked lists will show it as a "blank box." Figure 5.16 depicts the directory list after it is initialized (as in all linked list diagrams, a stripe-filled rectangle represents a **`NIL`** link field value). We have expended a `Node` record's worth of memory for the header node. Again, the header node allows the node insertion and deletion operations to perform more efficiently (i.e., require less execution time), as we shall see shortly. Testing for list emptiness involves comparing `Directory.Count` to zero.

> *At this time, examine the following routines in Appendix D.*

```
PROCEDURE LLInit ( VAR LList : LListType );

FUNCTION LLEmpty ( VAR LList : LListType ) : Boolean;
```

Let us assume that a linked list of `Node`-type records emanating from the header node has already been built, allowing us to focus on the `LLSearch` algorithm next, which must be called as a prerequisite to node insertion and deletion. For simplicity, we will use the four-entry list depicted in Figure 5.17. In the figure, the values of all initialized `Data` fields are shown, although future diagrams for this case study will show only the `Key` field values.

Searching a Linear Linked List

We will now design the `LLSearch` procedure, to which is passed the key value of the desired node and the address of the node where the search begins (typically, the address of the header node). As a convenience for the calling routine, `LLSearch` will pass back a value to indicate success or failure, via Boolean parameter `Found`, which is set to a true value if `LLSearch` encounters a node with a matching key field value and a false

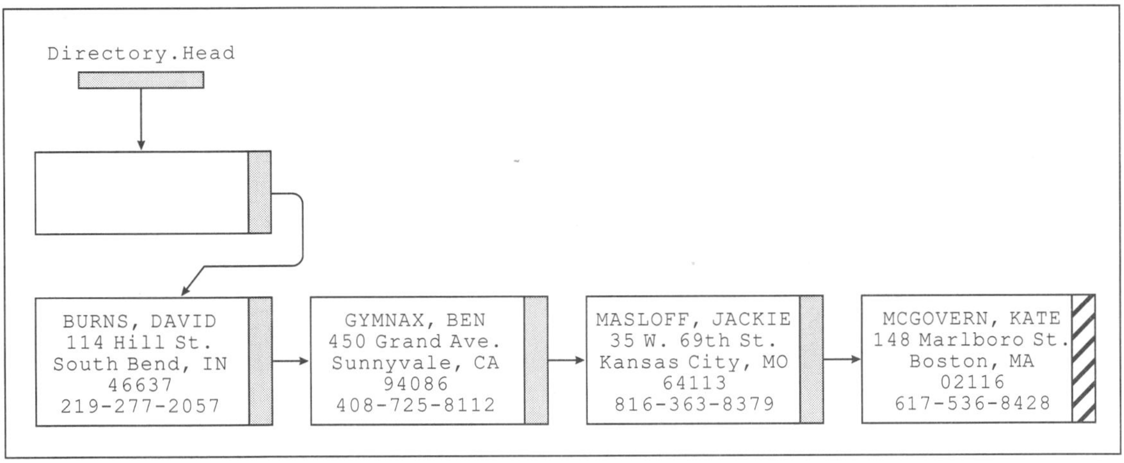

FIGURE 5.17 The Existing Four-entry Directory

value otherwise. If the sought node is actually found, `LLSearch` will also pass back via parameter `Previous` the address of its preceding node or else a **NIL** value if it is the first node in the list. As in the `LLTraverse` routine, `LLSearch` must visit nodes by "following" the links. Searching is necessary in *any* application involving a collection of items ordered by key value for three reasons:

1. To access a particular node via simple searching
2. To find the point of insertion of a new node
3. To find the point of deletion of a node

As in the restaurant menu program of Application 4.1, the directory program must uppercase each name string before storing it in a node and before using a name read from the keyboard to search the list. Again, this is necessary because the computer distinguishes between uppercase and lowercase character values when strings are compared; e.g., `'McGovern, Kate'` is not equivalent to either `'MCGOVERN, KATE'` or `'mcgovern, kate'`.

In the search for any ordered linked list, the searching process is *terminated* when any of the following terminal conditions become true:

- A node's key value matches the desired key value (success).
- A node is encountered with a key value greater than the desired key value (failure).
- The end of the list is reached (failure).

The second terminal condition is useful only if the list is ordered and provides the advantage that the searching routine may terminate (unsuccessfully) without making needless additional key comparisons. For example, if `LLSearch` were called to search for `'LEBONTE, STEVE'` and encountered `'MASLOFF, JACKIE'`, it could conclude that a node with the key value `'LEBONTE, STEVE'` was not in the directory without having to examine the `'MCGOVERN, KATE'` node. (Of course, this savings in search time is offset somewhat by the additional searching necessary to find the point of insertion for each entry inserted to keep the list ordered. Presumably, a database program such as ours spends significantly more time searching than it does inserting or deleting items.) The code for procedure `LLSearch` is as follows.

```
PROCEDURE  LLSearch ( VAR Key : KeyType;  Start : NodePtr;
                      VAR Previous : NodePtr;  VAR Found : Boolean );

VAR
  Done    : Boolean;
  Current : NodePtr;

BEGIN
Previous := NIL;                                  {Initialize Previous}
Current  := Start;                                {Begin with Start node}
Found    := FALSE;                                {Not found yet}
Done     := FALSE;                                {More nodes to examine}
WHILE ( Current <> NIL ) AND NOT Done DO          {WHILE more nodes to examine:}
  IF Current^.Data.Key > Key THEN                 { Failure: This key > key sought}
    Done := TRUE                                  {  No need to search further}
  ELSE
    IF Current^.Data.Key = Key THEN               { Success -- sought key is found:}
      BEGIN
      Done  := TRUE;                              {  No need to search further}
      Found := TRUE                               {  Set success flag to TRUE}
      END
    ELSE
      BEGIN                                       { Otherwise, keep searching:}
      Previous := Current;                        {  Advance Previous}
      Current  := Current^.Next                   {  Advance Current to next node}
      END
END;
```

For example, the call to `LLSearch` to search for `'GYMNAX, BEN'` is as follows:

```
LLSearch ( 'GYMNAX, BEN', Directory.Head, Previous, Found );
```

Upon return from this call, `Previous` contains the address of the node for `'BURNS, DAVID'` node, `Previous^.Next` contains the address of the `'GYMNAX, BEN'` node, and `Found` contains a true value.

As pointed out in Chapter 1, we must consider all cases that may arise during the execution of an algorithm, including special cases, when designing and testing a new algorithm. The following list describes the variety of cases that `LLSearch` must handle:

1. a. The node sought is *not found;* the search fails when the first (non-header) node is examined.
   b. The node sought is *not found;* the search fails somewhere within the list.
   c. The node sought is *not found;* the entire list is searched.
2. a. The node sought is *found;* it is the first node after the header node.
   b. The node sought is *found* somewhere within the list.
   c. The node sought is *found* as the last node in the list.
3. The list is *empty.*

	Key	Found	Previous	Previous^.Next	Implication
1.a	'ABBOT, BUD'	FALSE	Address of header node	Address of BURNS node	Failed at list head
b	'MCCLURE, JIM'	FALSE	Address of MASLOFF node	Address of MCGOVERN node	Failed within list
c	'SCHAAL, CAROL'	FALSE	Address of MCGOVERN node	NIL	Failed at list end
2.a	'BURNS, DAVID'	TRUE	Address of header node	Address of BURNS node	Found at list head
b	'MASLOFF, JACKIE'	TRUE	Address of GYMNAX node	Address of MASLOFF node	Found within list
c	'MCGOVERN, KATE'	TRUE	Address of MASLOFF node	Address of MCGOVERN node	Found at list end
3.	(Any key—list is empty)	FALSE	Address of header node	NIL	List is empty

FIGURE 5.18 Resulting `Found`, `Previous`, and `Previous^.Next` Values upon Return from `LLSearch`

Are any of these special cases? The chart in Figure 5.18 lists the combinations of `Found`, `Previous`, and `Previous^.Next` values resulting from a call to `LLSearch`, given the sample `Key` value passed in (the numbering of each line corresponds to the aforementioned list). Study this table and the code for `LLSearch` to convince yourself that `LLSearch` handles all cases appropriately.

The `LLSearch` algorithm is coded with the assumption that all key values (names, here) in the list are unique. For applications in which duplicate keys are permitted, the search algorithm must be modified to examine both a **primary key** and one or more **secondary keys** as well. Together, the primary and secondary keys for a node must distinguish that node from all others. Consider which field in the `InfoType` record might serve as a good secondary key and how the `LLSearch` procedure must be altered if duplicate primary keys are allowed in the directory.

Insertion into a Linked List

We will now consider the insertion operation to be performed by `LLInsert`. As an example, suppose we wish to insert an entry for `'LEKA, LYNETTE'`. A new node for this person should be inserted between the `'GYMNAX, BEN'` and `'MASLOFF, JACKIE'` nodes, since all nodes are positioned within the list by ascending key value. Obtaining the `InfoType` information is really not the responsibility of `LLInsert` routine, so we shall assume that an entire `InfoType` record has already been initialized (either by prompting the user for keyboard input or by reading from a file) and passed as a parameter. We shall assume again that all key values are unique among list nodes.

`LLInsert` may begin by allocating a new heapspace `Node` variable, storing data in this variable, and incrementing the node-count field:

```
PROCEDURE  LLInsert ( VAR LList: LListType;  VAR Data : InfoType;
                      Previous : NodePtr );
VAR
  P : NodePtr;

BEGIN
WITH LList DO
  BEGIN
  New ( P );                {Allocate a new record in the heap}
  P^.Data := Data;          {Store Data in this new record}
  Count   := Count + 1;     {Increment total node count}
```

Note that the call to `LLSearch` must be made by the calling routine and is not made within `LLInsert` itself. This design decision was made for two reasons:

- *Modularity.* Conceptually, searching and insertion are two distinct fundamental operations.
- *Versatility.* Designing `LLInsert` as a generic routine allows the calling routine to request an insertion anywhere in any linked list—e.g., simply appending a node to the end of a list. Also, because all linked lists are not ordered by some key value, insertion of a new node is not always preceded by a search for its key-based insertion point.

Figure 5.19 shows how the list appears after the statements are executed. Again, only the `Key` and `Next` link fields are depicted in this and future list diagrams for this application.

Unlike the array insertion, in which many array elements had to be physically shifted, `LLInsert` needs to manipulate only a couple of pointer values to insert our new node within the list. The `'GYMNAX, BEN'` node must point to the new node for `'LEKA, LYNETTE'`, and this new node must, in turn, point to the node to which `'GYMNAX, BEN'` *used to* point—namely, the `'MASLOFF, JACKIE'` node. The following two lines of code can now be added to our insertion algorithm:

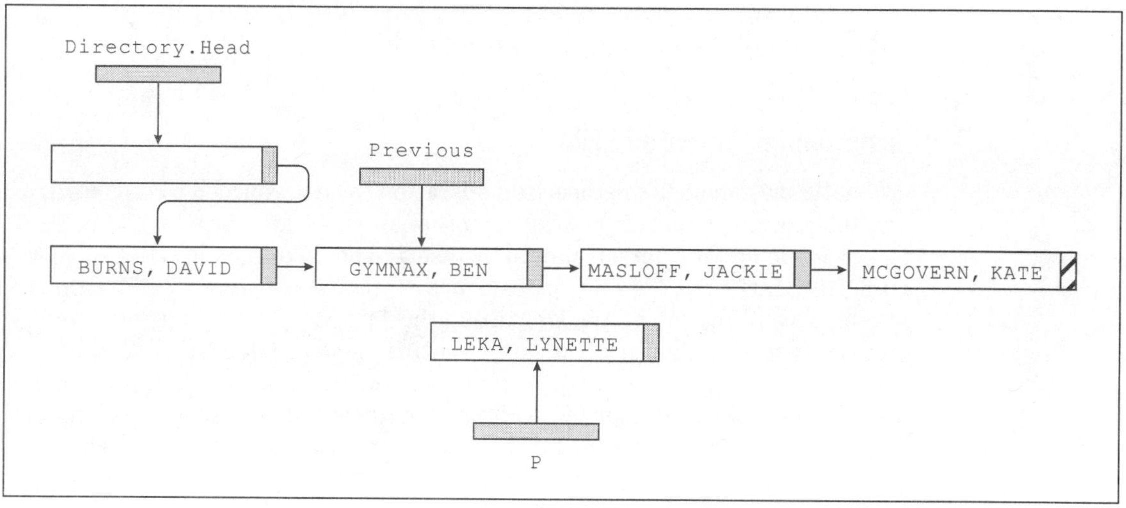

FIGURE 5.19 The List after a New Node is Allocated and Initialized

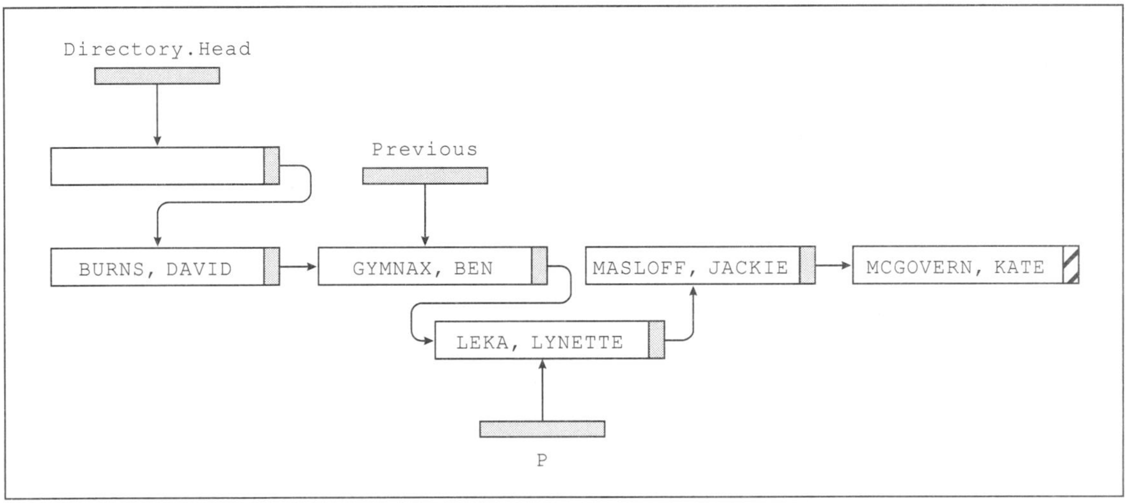

FIGURE 5.20 The List after the `'LEKA, LYNETTE'` Node is Inserted

```
P^.Next := Previous^.Next;    {New node points to where Previous points}
Previous^.Next := P;          {Previous node now points to new node}
```

Figure 5.20 depicts the list after these two instructions are executed.

Our insertion algorithm seems to be working fine for the standard case of insertion (i.e., insertion somewhere within an existing list); however, we must again determine if our algorithm works for *all* cases:

1. A new node is to be inserted at the head of the list (i.e., immediately after the header node).
2. A new node is to be inserted somewhere within the list.
3. A new node is to be inserted at the end of the list (i.e., after the last node).
4. A new node is to be inserted into an empty list (this is really the same as case 1).

The chart in Figure 5.21 lists the combinations of `Found` and `Previous` values resulting from a call to `LLSearch`, given the sample `Key` value passed to it. The numbering of each line corresponds to the aforementioned list of cases and, for the sake of testing insertion into an empty list, line 4 in the chart assumes that the list is empty when the `'BURNS, DAVID'` node is being inserted.

	`Data.Key`	`Previous`	Implication
1.	`'ABBOT, BUD'`	Address of header node	Insert at list head
2.	`'LEKA, LYNETTE'`	Address of `GYMNAX` node	Insert within list
3.	`'SCHAAL, CAROL'`	Address of `MCGOVERN` node	Insert at list end
4.	`'BURNS, DAVID'`	Address of header node	Insert at list head

FIGURE 5.21 Examples of the Cases for `LLInsert`

The existence of a header node allows `LLInsert` to insert a new node for each of these cases without any special handling. Without a header node, cases 1 and 4 are really special cases because the list head variable, `Directory.Head`, would have to be assigned a new value, the address of the new first node:

```
PROCEDURE  LLInsert ( VAR LList : LListType;  VAR Data : InfoType;
                      VAR Previous : NodePtr );
VAR
  P : NodePtr;

BEGIN
WITH LList DO
  BEGIN
  New ( P );                {Allocate a new record in the heap}
  P^.Data := Data;          {Store Data in this new record}
  Count   := Count + 1;     {Increment total node count}
```

```
{With header node}

  P^.Next := Previous^.Next;
  Previous^.Next := P
  END;
Previous := P
END;
```

```
{Without header node}

  IF Previous <> NIL THEN
    BEGIN
    P := Previous^.Next;
    Previous^.Next := P
    END
  ELSE
    BEGIN
    P^.Next := Head;
    Head    := P
    END
  END;
Previous := P
END;
```

In the code segment written for a list without a header node, the code segment following the **ELSE** is necessary to handle both cases of insertion at the head of a list (cases 1 and 4). Regardless of which case `LLInsert` is being called upon to handle, the **IF** statement would be executed. This is another example of choosing between expending extra memory (the header node) and extra execution time (evaluation of the **IF** statement's Boolean expression each time). Since cases 1 and 4 are probably relatively infrequent and the additional memory required for a header node is probably insignificant, the use of a header node is preferable. Also notice that variable `Previous` is assigned to the address of the new node, `P`, and returned. This makes `LLInsert` more versatile: A calling routine can build a linked list by appending nodes to the end of it simply by calling `LLInsert` repeatedly; `Previous` will always contain the address of the last node in the list.

Deletion from a Linked List

For our discussion of deletion we begin once again with the four-node data base depicted in Figure 5.16. As with the `LLInsert` procedure, `LLSearch` must be called first to locate the node to be deleted. If `LLSearch` locates the node to be deleted, it returns the address of its preceding node in parameter `Previous`. The deleted node must then be deallocated from heapspace memory via the standard `Dispose` procedure, its memory space made available for later reallocation.

As an example we will delete the node `'MASLOFF, JACKIE'`. The `LLDelete` procedure begins as follows:

```
PROCEDURE  LLDelete ( VAR LList : LListType;  VAR Previous : NodePtr );

VAR
  P : NodePtr;

BEGIN
WITH LList DO
  BEGIN
  Count := Count - 1;     {Decrement count of nodes in the list}
  P := Previous^.Next;    {Temporarily save pointer to node being deleted}
```

As with the `LLInsert` routine, the call to `LLSearch` is not made within `LLDelete` itself, since not all linked lists are ordered by key value, and programs must be given the flexibility to delete any node in the list. Figure 5.22 shows how the list appears after these two statements are executed.

To the `'MASLOFF, JACKIE'` node, `LLDelete` must assign to the link field of the previous node (the `'GYMNAX, BEN'` node) the address of the node following the `'MASLOFF, JACKIE'` node (the `'MCGOVERN, KATE'` node). This address is readily available in the link field of the node pointed to by `Previous^.Next`. Also, `Dispose` must be called to deallocate the node pointed to by `Current`:

```
Previous^.Next := P^.Next;
Dispose ( P );
```

Figure 5.23 shows how the list appears after the `'MASLOFF, JACKIE'` node is deleted. At this point, the `'MASLOFF, JACKIE'` record is actually still in heapspace memory (although the program has no way to access it),

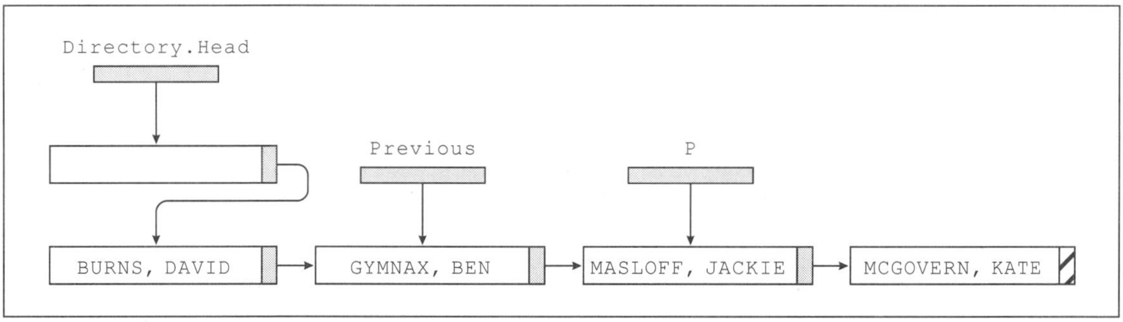

FIGURE 5.22 The List after Searching for 'MASLOFF, JACKIE' Node Prior to Deletion

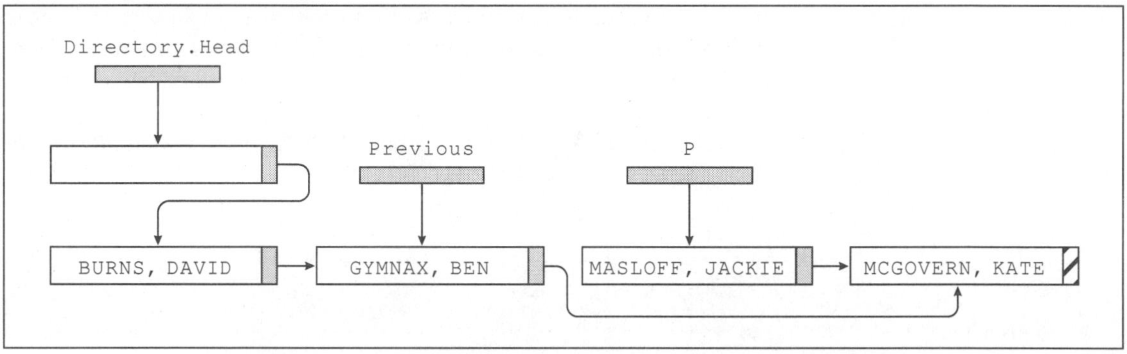

FIGURE 5.23 The List after the `'MASLOFF, JACKIE'` Node is Deleted (but Prior to `Dispose`)

but the memory space they occupy is now available for reallocation via a subsequent call to the `New` procedure.

Our deletion algorithm seems to be working fine for the standard case of deletion (i.e., deletion of a node somewhere within an existing list). However, we must again determine if our algorithm works for *all* cases:

1. The node is deleted from the head of the list (i.e., the first nonheader node).
2. The node is deleted somewhere within the list.
3. The node is deleted from the end of the list (i.e., the last node).
4. The last node in the list is deleted (this is the same as case 1).

The chart in Figure 5.24 lists the returned values of `Previous` resulting from a call to `LLSearch`, prior to calling `LLDelete`, given the sample `Key` value passed in. The numbering of each line in the chart corresponds to the aforementioned list of cases; to test the deletion from a one-node list, line 4 assumes that the `'BURNS, DAVID'` node is the only nonheader node in the linked list.

As with `LLInsert`, the existence of a header node allows `LLDelete` to delete a node for each of these cases without any special handling. Without a header node, cases 1 and 4 are special cases because the list head variable, `Directory.Head`, would have to be assigned a new value; the address of the new first node:

	Key of node to delete	Previous	Implication
1.	`'BURNS, DAVID'`	Address of header node	Delete first (nonheader) node
2.	`'MASLOFF, JACKIE'`	Address of `GYMNAX` node	Delete within list
3.	`'MCGOVERN, KATE'`	Address of `MASLOFF` node	Delete last node
4.	`'BURNS, DAVID'`	Address of header node	Delete only (nonheader) node

FIGURE 5.24 Examples of Cases for `LLDelete`

```
PROCEDURE  LLDelete ( VAR List : LList;  Previous : NodePtr );

VAR
  P : NodePtr;

BEGIN
WITH LList DO
  BEGIN
  Count := Count - 1;  {Decrement count of nodes in the list}
```

```
{With header node}

  P := Previous^.Next;
  Previous^.Next := P^.Next;
  Dispose ( P )
  END
END;
```

```
{Without header node}

  IF Previous <> NIL THEN
    BEGIN
    P := Previous^.Next;
    Previous^.Next := P^.Next;
    END
  ELSE
    BEGIN
    P    := Head;
    Head := Head^.Next
    END;
  Dispose ( P )
  END
END;
```

Without a header node, the code segment following the **ELSE** is necessary to handle both cases of deletion at the head of a list (cases 1 and 4). Regardless of which case `LLDelete` is being called upon to handle, the **IF** statement would be executed. In this choice between expending extra memory (the header node) or extra execution time (evaluation of the **IF** statement's Boolean expression), the use of header node is again justified, since cases 1 and 4 are probably relatively infrequent and the additional memory required for a header node is probably insignificant.

Saving a Linked List in a File and Rebuilding a Linked List

Some applications may require building and using a temporary list of information, which does not need to be saved between program runs. In most applications, however, a list constructed by a program must be saved in external memory and then rebuilt when the program is run again. We will certainly want to preserve our telephone/address directory so that a user would not have to reenter all the data each time the program is executed!

Our directory structure is represented using a linear linked list, with potentially many nodes in internal heapspace memory and with link fields providing an access path from one node to the next. A file is also a linear data structure, consisting of file elements that reside in external memory. To the Pascal programmer, file elements may seem contiguous, as if the file were a large one-dimensional array of file elements, although in reality, portions (*blocks*) of the file are typically scattered throughout external memory. These portions are linked together by the operating system in a manner similar to the way nodes in a linked list are linked together in heapspace. Therefore, the operation of saving a linked list to a file really involves copying one type of linear list onto another and following an important rule: *When a linked list is stored to a file, only the data portions of the nodes—and never the link field values—are saved.*

This makes sense because the file elements do not need any linking by the programmer to form a single list (the file); the operating system will link together all file elements properly. Also link field pointer values are **run-time dependent;** i.e., internal memory addresses are valid *only* during the execution of the program during which those values are obtained via the `New` procedure. When a linked list is rebuilt upon a subsequent program run, the `New` procedure may return different addresses when nodes are dynamically allocated, even if the exact same sequence of data is stored in the list. This happens because the heapspace may be configured slightly differently from the way it was configured during previous program executions due to other dynamic allocation performed by the program and by the operating system.

Figure 5.25 depicts the transfer of data from the original four-node directory data base to a binary file named `Directry.DAT`. In the figure, the shaded rectangle containing EOF represents the end-of-file indicator, and the boldface arrows depict the transfer of data from each linked list node to a file element. Also, to simplify the diagram the file elements are depicted as being contiguous in external memory.

A program must perform three operations to save a linked list in a file:

1. Open the file for writing.
2. Traverse the entire linked list, processing each node (except the header node) by storing just the data portion of the node to the next file element.
3. Close the file.

The `LLTraverse` procedure we have already written is sufficient for traversing the list; we need only to write a different `Process` procedure. Carefully examine procedure `Finale` in the complete `Directory` program,

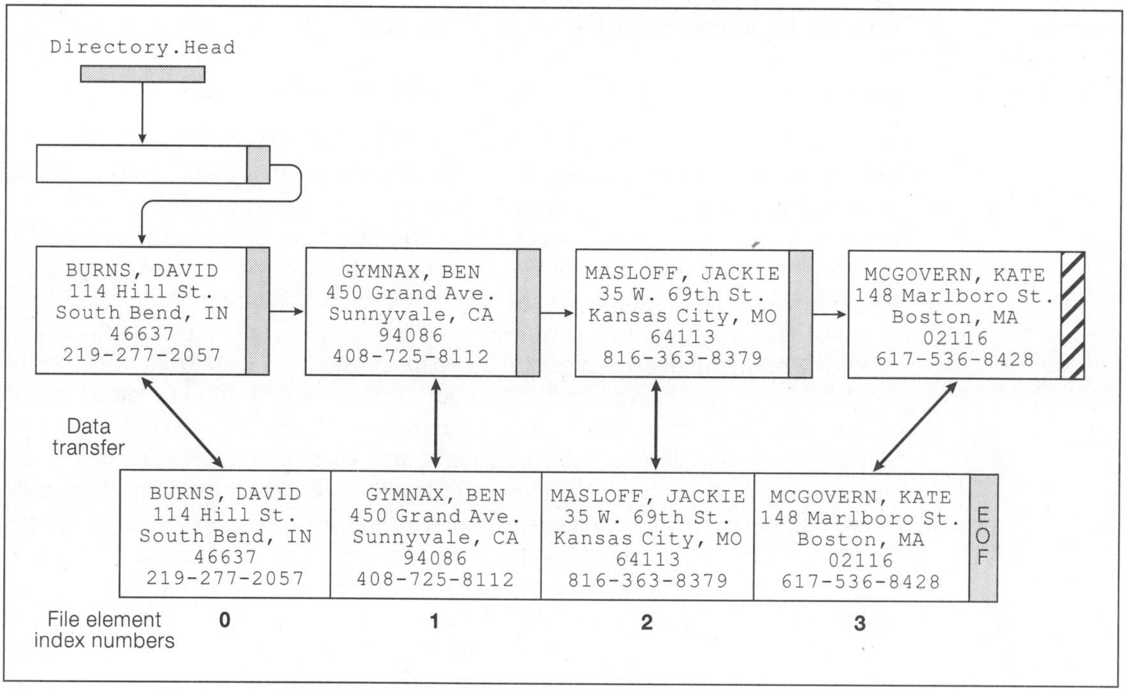

FIGURE 5.25 Depiction of Saving a Linked List to a Binary File

which follows. The main routine calls `Finale` immediately before program execution terminates to perform the three operations just described. Pay particular attention to procedure `Process` in this program; it is called from `LLTraverse` to save the data portion of a single node to the next file element.

A program must perform four steps to rebuild a linked list from a file:

1. Open the file for reading.
2. Initialize the linked list as empty, including creating the header node.
3. Traverse the entire file by sequentially reading file elements; process each file element by allocating a new node, storing the file element contents into the `Data` field of the record, then appending the new node to the end of the list.
4. Close the file.

In Step 3, new nodes are simply appended to the end of the linked list being built, with the assumption that the file elements are ordered by key value; this assumption is valid if the ordered list was saved in the file via the three previous steps. If the file ordering is unknown, then `LLSearch` must be called to find the appropriate point of insertion for each new node.
We have developed primitives for the linear linked list fundamental operations `LLInit`, `LLSearch`, `LLInsert`, `LLDelete`, and `LLTraverse`. With these "building blocks," the entire interactive program to manage the directory data base may now be written; a version of this program follows.

The Basic Directory Program

Figure 5.26 contains a module tree diagram for the `Directory` program. The complete, basic directory program (an enhanced version is presented in the section following the program) is

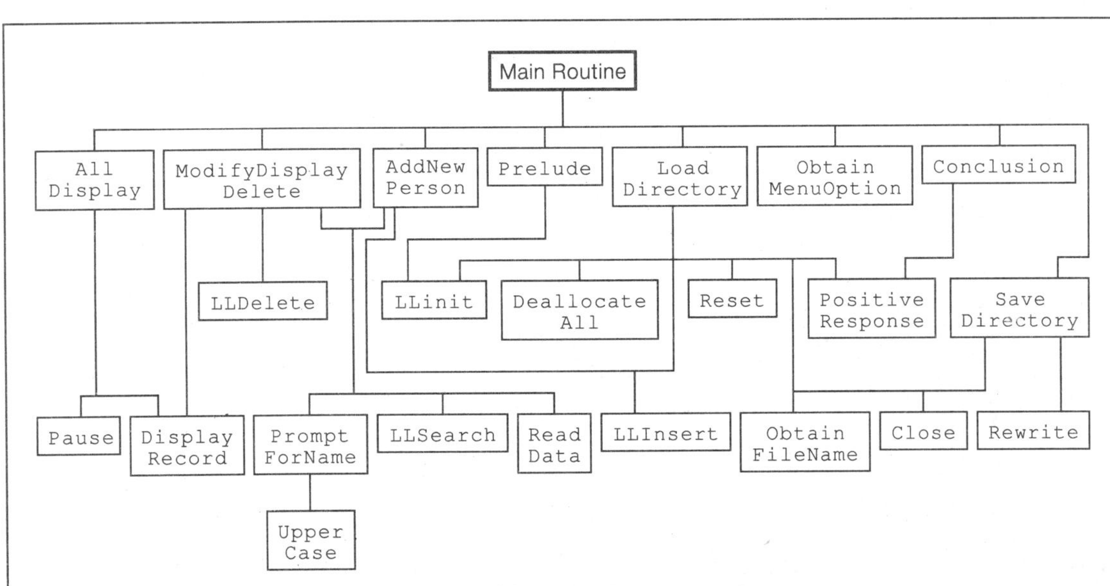

FIGURE 5.26 Module Tree Diagram for the `Directory` Program

```
PROGRAM Directory ( INPUT, OUTPUT);

CONST
  DefFileName  =  'Directry.DAT';          {Default name of binary file}
  MinVal       =  ' ';                     {Header node key value}

TYPE
  Str80        =  String [ 80 ];
  Str25        =  String [ 25 ];

  KeyType      =  Str25;
  InfoType     =  RECORD
                    Key     : KeyType;     {Full name is the key}
                    Address : Str80;       {Full address}
                    Phone   : Str25        {Full telephone number}
                  END;

  NodePtr      =  ^Node;
  Node         =  RECORD
                    Data    : InfoType;    {Data portion}
                    Next    : NodePtr      {Link field; address of next node}
                  END;

  LListType    =  RECORD
                    Head    : NodePtr;     {Address of header node}
                    Count   : Integer      {Number of nodes in the list}
                  END;

  FileType     =  FILE OF InfoType;
  Options      =  ( Quit, DisplayAll, Add, Modify, Display, Delete, Save, Build );

VAR
  Directory    :  LListType;               {Record containing list head}
  ChangesMade,                             {Flag indicates directory changes}
  Found        :  Boolean;                 {Flag for LLInsert, LLDelete}
  Option       :  Options;                 {User's program option}
  Data         :  InfoType;                {Record containing input data}
  Previous     :  NodePtr;                 {Pointers to Node type nodes}
```

```
{The following routines are defined in Appendix D}

PROCEDURE LLInit ( VAR LList : LListType );

PROCEDURE  LLSearch ( VAR Key : KeyType;  Start : NodePtr;
                      VAR Previous : NodePtr; VAR Found : Boolean );

PROCEDURE  LLInsert ( VAR LList: LListType;  VAR Data : InfoType;
                      VAR Previous : NodePtr );

PROCEDURE  LLDelete ( VAR LList: LListType; Previous : NodePtr );

PROCEDURE DeallocateAll ( VAR List : LListType );
```

```
{The following functions are defined in Appendix K}

FUNCTION PositiveResponse ( Ch : Char ) : Boolean;

FUNCTION UpperCase ( Ch : Char ) : Char;

PROCEDURE Pause;
```

```
PROCEDURE Prelude (  VAR Directory : LListType;  VAR ChangesMade : Boolean );

BEGIN
LLInit ( Directory );                {Initialize list as containing 1 header node}
Changesmade := FALSE;                {Initialize flag}
Writeln ( '****  Online Address/Telephone Directory  ****' );
Writeln; Writeln
END;
```

```
PROCEDURE DisplayRecord ( VAR Data : InfoType );

BEGIN
Writeln;  Writeln ( Data.Key );      {Display full name}
Writeln ( '    ', Data.Address );    {Display full address}
Writeln ( '    ', Data.Phone )       {Display full telephone number}
END;
```

```
PROCEDURE  AllDisplay ( Current : NodePtr );

VAR
  Count : Integer;

BEGIN
Count := 0;
WHILE Current <> NIL DO
  BEGIN
  DisplayRecord ( Current^.Data );  {Display the record}
  Count := Count + 4;               {3 lines of data plus 1 blank line}
  IF Count MOD 20 = 0 THEN          {Pause every 20th screen line}
    Pause;
  Current := Current^.Next          {Advance to next node}
  END;
Pause                               {Pause after last display}
END;
```

```
PROCEDURE PromptForName( VAR Name : KeyType );

VAR
  K : Integer;

BEGIN
Writeln ( '>>>  Enter name:  <last>, <first>   ' );
Write ( '    ' );
Readln ( Name );
FOR K := 1 TO Length ( Name ) DO    {Capitalize name letters}
  IF Name [ K ] IN  [ 'a'..'z' ] THEN
    Name [ K ] := UpperCase ( Name [ K ] )
END;
```

```
{ObtainMenuOption displays a menu of options; user enters number, corresponding
 enumerated type is returned:

  0.  QUIT Program          -->   Quit
  1.  Display  all entries  -->   DisplayAll
  2.  Add      entry        -->   Add
  3.  Modify   entry        -->   Modify
  4.  Display  entry        -->   Display
  5.  Delete   entry        -->   Delete
  6.  Save     directory    -->   Save
  7.  Load     directory    -->   Build

Code for this procedure is left as an exercise}

PROCEDURE ObtainMenuOption ( VAR Option : Options );
```

```
PROCEDURE ReadData ( VAR Data : InfoType );

VAR
  Reply : Char;

BEGIN
REPEAT
  Writeln ( '>>>  Enter street address, city, state abbreviation, zip code:' );
  Readln ( Data.Address );
  Writeln ( '>>>  Enter area code and telephone number:  ' );
  Readln ( Data.Phone );
  Write;  Write ( '>>>  Is this information correct? (Y/N):  ' );
  Readln ( Reply )
UNTIL PositiveResponse ( Reply )
END;
```

```
PROCEDURE ObtainFileName ( VAR FileName : Str80 );

BEGIN
Write ( '>>>  Enter filename [', DefFilename, ']:  ' );
Readln ( Filename );
IF Length ( Filename ) = 0 THEN      {User merely pressed RETURN key}
  Filename := DefFilename
END;
```

```
PROCEDURE SaveDirectory ( VAR Directory : LListType;
                          VAR SaveChanges : Boolean );

VAR
  FileName   :  Str80;
  DataFile   :  FileType;
  Current    :  NodePtr;

BEGIN
ObtainFileName ( FileName );
{Insert instructions to associate FileName and DataFile}
Rewrite ( DataFile );                          {Open file}

Current := Directory.Head^.Next;               {Start at list head}
WHILE Current <> NIL DO                        {Visit each node...}
  BEGIN
  Write ( DataFile, Current^.Data );           {  Write node data portion to file}
  Current := Current^.Next                     {  Advance to next node}
  END;
Close ( DataFile );
Writeln ( Directory.Count, ' records saved to ', FileName );
Writeln;
SaveChanges := FALSE                           {Reinitialize flag to FALSE}
END;
```

```
PROCEDURE Conclusion ( VAR Directory : LListType; ChangesMade : Boolean );

VAR
  Reply :  Char;

BEGIN
IF ChangesMade THEN
  BEGIN
  Write ( '>>>  Save changes?  (Y/N):  ' );
  Readln ( Reply );
  IF PositiveResponse ( Reply ) THEN
    SaveDirectory ( Directory, ChangesMade )  {Save database to file}
  END;
Writeln; Writeln ( '***  Online Directory Program Terminated  ****' )
END;
```

```
PROCEDURE LoadDirectory ( VAR Directory : LListType );.

VAR
  Reply     :  Char;
  Filename  :  Str80;
  Data      :  InfoType;
  DataFile  :  FileType;
  Success   :  Boolean;
  Previous  :  NodePtr;

BEGIN
DeallocateAll ( Directory );                  {Dispose of entire list}
Writeln ( '>>>  Current directory just deleted.' );

{The following prompt allows the user to simply delete the directory (just done)
 without having to rebuild another one from file}

Write ( '>>>  Load existing directory from file? (Y/N)  ' );
Readln ( Reply );

IF PositiveResponse ( Reply ) THEN
  BEGIN
  ObtainFilename ( FileName );
  {Insert instructions to associate FileName name and DataFile}
  Reset ( DataFile );

  LLInit ( Directory );         {Initialize list as containing 1 header node}
  Previous := Directory.Head;   {Prepare to insert nodes after header node}

  WHILE NOT Eof ( DataFile ) DO
    BEGIN
    Read ( DataFile, Data );    {Read single record from file}
    LLInsert ( Directory, Data, Previous )    {Add record to database}
    END;

  Writeln ( Directory.Count, ' records read from ', Filename );
  Close ( DataFile )
  END
END;
```

```
PROCEDURE  AddNewPerson ( VAR Directory : LListType );

BEGIN
PromptForName ( Data.Key );
ReadData ( Data );
LLSearch ( Data.Key, Directory.Head, Previous, Found );  {Find insertion point}
IF Found THEN
  Writeln ( '>>> ERROR:  Duplicate Name.' )
ELSE
  LLInsert ( Directory, Data, Previous )
END;
```

```
PROCEDURE ModifyDisplayDelete ( VAR Directory : LListType; Option : Options );

VAR
  Previous  :  NodePtr;
  Found     :  Boolean;

BEGIN
PromptForName ( Data.Key );
LLSearch ( Data.Key, Directory.Head, Previous, Found );  {Find insertion point}
IF NOT Found THEN
  Writeln ( '>>>  ERROR:  Entry Not Found.' )
ELSE
  BEGIN
  DisplayRecord ( Previous^.Next^.Data );      {Display current data values}
  IF Option = Modify THEN
    ReadData ( Previous^.Next^.Data )          {Obtain new values}
  ELSE
    BEGIN
    IF Option = Delete THEN
      LLDelete ( Directory, Previous );        {Delete the record}
    Writeln ( '    -- just deleted' )
    END
  END
END;
```

```
{*** Main  routine for Directory ***}

BEGIN
Prelude ( Directory, ChangesMade );              {Initialize list as empty}
REPEAT
  ObtainMenuOption ( Option );                   {Query user for an option}
  IF ( Option IN [ DisplayAll, Modify, Display, Delete ] ) AND
    ( Directory.Head^.Next = NIL) THEN
    Writeln ( '>>> Directory empty' )
  ELSE
    BEGIN
    IF NOT ChangesMade THEN
      ChangesMade := Option IN [ Add, Modify, Delete, Build ] ;

    CASE Option OF
      Quit         :  Conclusion ( Directory, ChangesMade );
      DisplayAll   :  AllDisplay ( Directory.Head^.Next );
      Add          :  AddNewPerson ( Directory );
      Save         :  SaveDirectory ( Directory, ChangesMade );
      Build        :  LoadDirectory ( Directory );
      Modify,
      Display,
      Delete       :  ModifyDisplayDelete ( Directory, Option )
    END
    END
UNTIL Option = Quit
END.
```

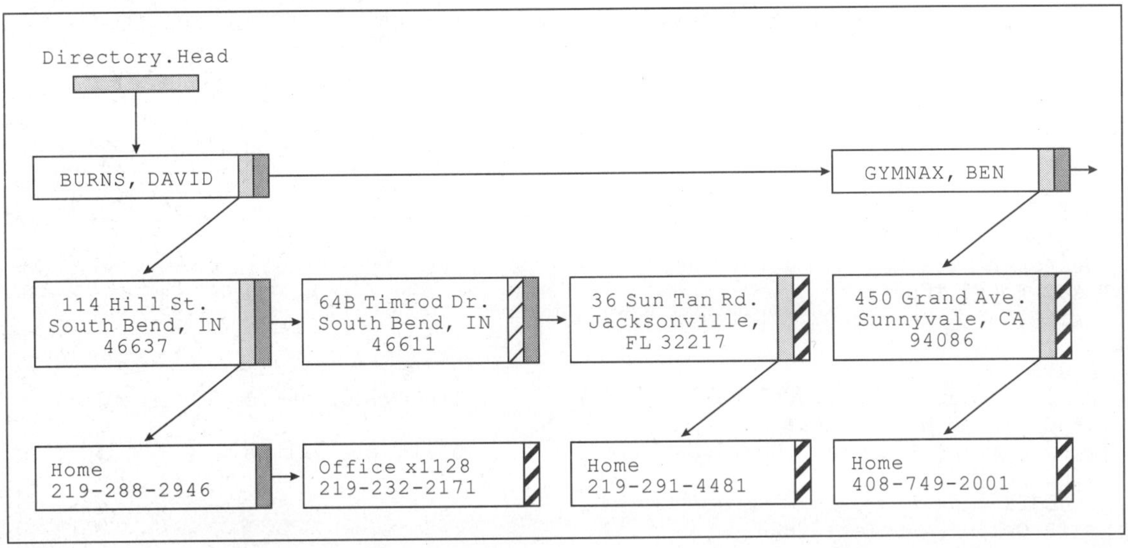

FIGURE 5.27 Beginning Portion of an Enhanced Telephone/Address Directory

A Nonlinear Telephone-Address Directory

The directory program just presented assumes that each person listed in the directory has a single address and a single telephone number. The directory would be more useful if it could store several addresses and telephone numbers for each person—e.g., for the person's residence, office, vacation home, and the like. As an example, Figure 5.27 shows the beginning portion of such a **nonlinear structure**. Notice that the topmost horizontal linked list of names has been stored in ascending alphabetic order. A linked list extends downward from each name node and consists of address and telephone number nodes for a given name. Notice that three addresses are stored for `'BURNS, DAVID'`, with two telephone numbers for the Hill Street address, no telephone for the Timrod Drive address, and one telephone number for the SunTan Road address. `'GYMNAX, BEN'`, on the other hand, has a single address and telephone number stored.

Notice also that the structure contains no header nodes. Because the structure contains so many linear lists—the single list of names and each address and telephone list—it is better to expend slightly more time with the longer versions of the `LLInsert` and `LLDelete` algorithms in order to save memory space, one node per linked list. (The different versions of `LLInsert` and `LLDelete` were discussed in Section 5.2 and appear in Appendix D as well.) Also, the operations of insertion and deletion are probably performed less frequently than is simple searching, so the extra expenditure of execution time is likely to be insignificant.

You are encouraged to design a directory program based on this structure. A set of global declarations for this structure follows.

```
TYPE
  InfoType   =  String [ 60 ] ;
  NodePtr    =  ^Node;
  Node       =  RECORD
                  Data  : InfoType;   {Holds name OR address OR phone}
                  Next,               {Address of next name, address, or phone}
                  Down  : NodePtr     {Address of first address or first phone}
                END;

  LListType  =  RECORD
                  Head  : NodePtr;    {Holds address of first node}
                  Count : Integer     {Total count of names}
                END;

VAR
  Directory  :  LListType;
```

APPLICATION 5.3 Computerized Dictionaries

In this application, we create two data structures to represent a dictionary of English words. The first structure will employ a collection of linear linked lists (as shown in Figure 5.28) and the second structure will employ non-linear *trie* structures (as shown in Figure 5.30).

A Linear Linked List–Based Dictionary

As with any dictionary, the entire list of words in our computerized dictionary will be distributed over 26 sublists based on the first letter of the word. Since each sublist will have a varied number of words, we will implement it as a dynamically allocated linked list; 26 list head variables are therefore required. Because this quantity is fixed, we can use a 26-element array of pointers, each containing either the heapspace address of the first node of a linked list of words or else a **NIL** value indicating that there are no words beginning with that letter. The array may be thought of as containing 26 *list head variables*. Figure 5.28 shows an arrangement for a dictionary of 12

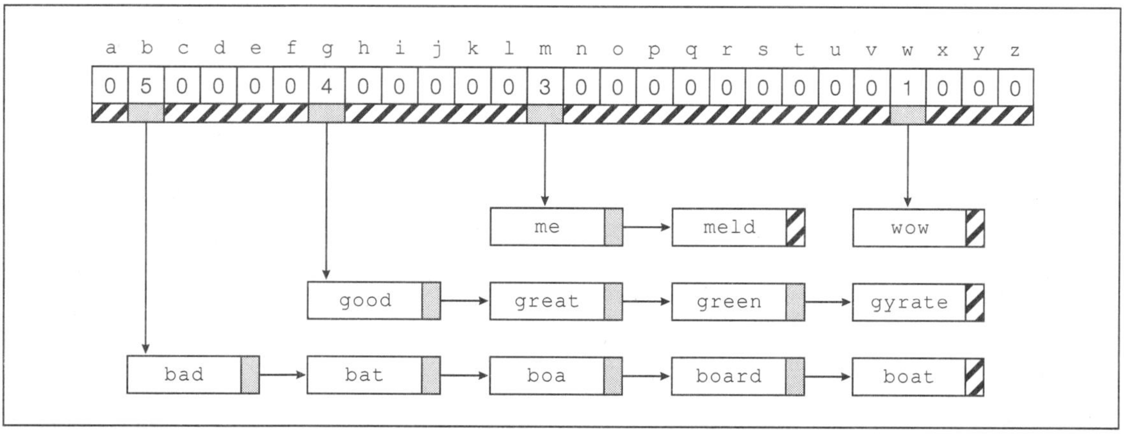

FIGURE 5.28 A Simple Dictionary of Twelve Words

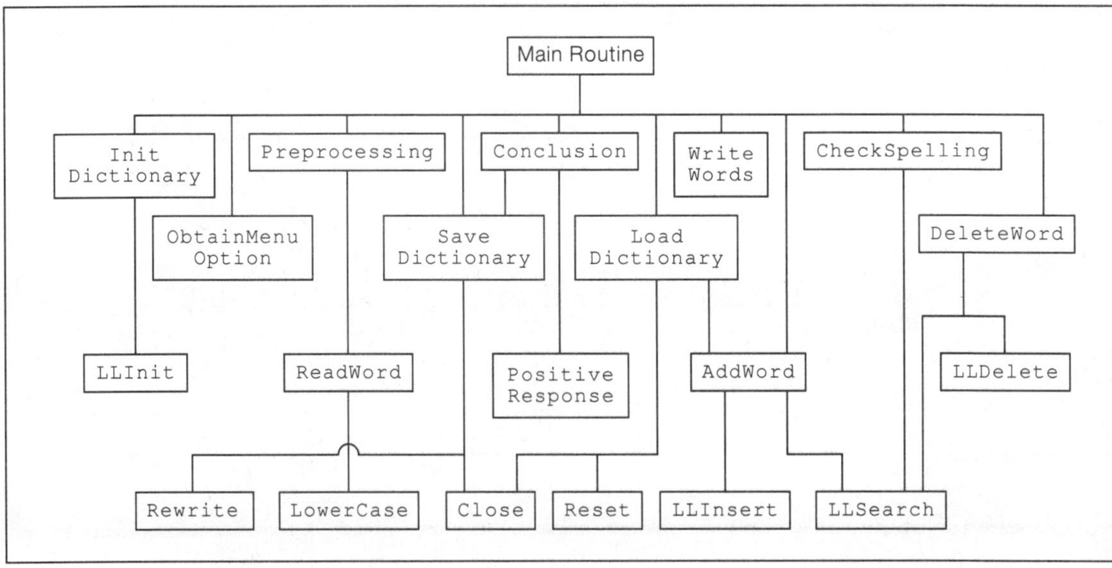

FIGURE 5.29 Module Tree Diagram for `OnLineDictionary` Program

words: `'bad'`, `'bat'`, `'boa'`, `'board'`, `'boat'`, `'good'`, `'great'`, `'green'`, `'gyrate'`, `'me'`, `'meld'`, and `'wow'`. (Header nodes are not used with each linked list of words.)

The program should allow the user to do the following:

- Check the spelling of any word entered interactively
- Add or delete a word
- Load the dictionary from a file
- Save the dictionary to a file

We must write an initialization procedure that calls the `LLInit` procedure 26 times to initialize each of the 26 linked lists. The `LLSearch`, `LLInsert`, and `LLDelete` procedures require only minor modifications. Consider how you would make these modifications before examining the complete program, which follows. The program is written to be commensurate with Figure 5.28—i.e., for a structure without header nodes. (If the program is modified to employ header nodes, parameter `List.Head^.Next` must be passed in each call to `LLSearch` rather than passing `List.Head`.)

Figure 5.29 contains a module tree diagram for the `OnLineDictionary` program.

The complete program is as follows.

```
PROGRAM OnLineDictionary ( INPUT, OUTPUT );

CONST
  MaxChars    = ??;                    {Maximum word length}

TYPE
  Str80       = String [ 80 ];
  KeyType     = String [ MaxChars ] ;

  InfoType    = RECORD
                  Key     :  KeyType    {Single word}
                END;

  NodePtr     = ^Node;
  Node        = RECORD
                  Data    :  InfoType;  {Single word}
                  Next    :  NodePtr    {Address of next node in the list}
                END;

  LListType   = RECORD
                  Head    :  NodePtr;   {Points to list of words with same first letter}
                  Count   :  Integer    {Count of words in this list}
                END;

  DictType    = RECORD
                  Heads        :  ARRAY ['a'..'z'] OF LListType;
                  Count        :  Integer;  {Count of all words}
                  ChangesMade  :  Boolean;  {Flag indicates dictionary changes}
                END;

  Options     = ( Quit, WordChk, Add, Delete, Display, Save, Build, Garbage );

VAR
  Dictionary   :  DictType;                {Array of word lists}
  Key          :  KeyType;                 {1 word}
  FirstLetter  :  Char;                    {First letter of current word}
  Option       :  Options;                 {User's choice of program functions}
```

```
{The following procedures are defined in Appendix D}

PROCEDURE  LLInit ( VAR LList : LListType );

PROCEDURE  LLSearch  ( VAR Key : KeyType;  Start : NodePtr;
                       VAR Previous :  NodePtr;  VAR Found : Boolean );

PROCEDURE  LLInsert   ( VAR List: LListType;  VAR Data : InfoType;
                        Previous : NodePtr );

PROCEDURE  LLDelete   ( VAR List: LListType;  Previous : NodePtr );

PROCEDURE DeallocateAll ( VAR List : LListType );
```

```
{The following routines are defined in Appendix K}

FUNCTION LowerCase ( Ch : Char ) : Char;

FUNCTION PositiveResponse ( Ch : Char ) : Boolean;
```

```
PROCEDURE InitDictionary ( VAR Dictionary : DictType );

VAR
  Ch  :  Char;

BEGIN
Writeln ( '****  Online Dictionary Program  ****' );
Writeln; Writeln;
WITH Dictionary DO
  BEGIN
  FOR Ch := 'a' TO 'z' DO               {Initialize each word list as empty}
    LLInit ( Heads [ Ch ] );
  Count := 0;                           {Initialize each list count to zero}
  ChangesMade := FALSE                  {Initialize flag}
  END
END;
```

```
{Displays a menu of options; user enters number and a corresponding enumerated type
 is returned via Options param. (code for this procedure is left as an exercise):

  0.  QUIT Program             ->  Quit      4.  Display dictionary        ->  Display
  1.  Check spelling of a word ->  WordChk   5.  Save dictionary           ->  Save
  2.  Add word interactively   ->  Add       6.  Add words from text file
  3.  Delete a word            ->  Delete        (1 word per line)         ->  Build   }

PROCEDURE  ObtainMenuOption ( VAR Option : Options );
```

```
PROCEDURE ReadWord ( VAR Key : KeyType; VAR Option : Options );

VAR
  K  :  Integer;

BEGIN
Writeln; Write ( 'Enter word (1-', MaxChars, ' chars.):  ' );
Readln ( Key );
K := 1;
WHILE ( Option <> Garbage ) AND ( K <= Length ( Key )) DO
  IF NOT ( Key [ K ] IN ['A'..'Z','a'..'z','''','-'] ) THEN {IF invalid input THEN}
    Option := Garbage                                       { change Option to Garbage}
  ELSE
    BEGIN
    IF Key [ K ] IN [ 'A'..'Z' ]  THEN                      {Lowercase each letter}
      Key [ K ] := LowerCase ( Key [ K ] );
    K := K + 1
    END
END;
```

```
PROCEDURE Preprocessing ( VAR Key : KeyType;  VAR Option : Options;
                          VAR FirstLetter : Char;
                          VAR ChangesMade : Boolean );

BEGIN
ReadWord ( Key, Option );               {Obtain word from user}
IF Option <> Garbage THEN               {IF it contains letter characters THEN}
  BEGIN
  FirstLetter := Key [ 1 ];             {  Extract 1st letter}
  IF Option <> WordChk THEN             {  IF option is to add, delete, or modify}
    ChangesMade := TRUE                 {      set flag to TRUE}
  END
END;
```

```
PROCEDURE AddWord ( VAR LList : LListType; VAR Key : KeyType );

VAR
  Previous   :  NodePtr;
  Found      :  Boolean;
  Data       :  InfoType;

BEGIN
LLSearch ( Key, LList.Head, Previous, Found );  {See if word is already stored}
IF NOT Found THEN                               {IF it is not THEN}
  BEGIN
  Data.Key := Key;                              {  Store the word}
  LLInsert (  LList, Data, Previous );          {  Insert the new-word node}
  Dictionary.Count := Dictionary.Count + 1;     {  Increment total-word count}
  Writeln ( '>>>  "', Key, '" added to dictionary' )
  END
ELSE
  Writeln ( '>>>  "', Key, '" already in dictionary.' )
END;
```

```
PROCEDURE DeleteWord ( VAR LList : LListType; VAR Key : KeyType );

VAR
  Data       :  InfoType;
  Previous   :  NodePtr;
  Found      :  Boolean;

BEGIN
LLSearch ( Key, LList.Head, Previous, Found );  {Search for the word}
IF Found THEN                                   {IF is in the list THEN}
  BEGIN
  LLDelete ( LList, Previous );                 {  Delete it}
  Dictionary.Count := Dictionary.Count - 1;     {  Decrement total-word count}
  Writeln ( '>>>  "', Key, '" deleted from dictionary' )
  END
ELSE
  Writeln ( '>>>  "', Key, '" not found in dictionary' )
END;
```

```
PROCEDURE WriteWords ( VAR Dictionary : DictType; VAR FileVariable : Text );

VAR
  FirstLetter   : Char;
  Current       : NodePtr;

BEGIN
IF Dictionary.Count = 0 THEN
  Writeln ( '>>>  Dictionary is empty.' )
ELSE
  BEGIN
  FOR FirstLetter := 'a' TO 'z' DO                     {Visit all 26 word lists}
    BEGIN
    Current := Dictionary.Heads [ FirstLetter ].Head;
    WHILE Current <> NIL DO                            {  Traverse each list}
      BEGIN
      Writeln ( FileVariable, Current^.Data.Key );     {    Display each word}
      Current := Current^.Next
      END
    END
  END
END;
```

```
PROCEDURE SaveDictionary ( VAR Dictionary : DictType );

VAR
  Filename  :  Str80 ;
  WordFile  :  Text;

BEGIN
Write ( '>>>  Save to dictionary text file (or only RETURN to cancel):  ' );
Readln ( Filename );

IF Length ( Filename ) = 0 THEN    {User merely pressed RETURN, to abort}
  Writeln ( '>>>  Save cancelled' )
ELSE
  BEGIN
  {Insert instructions to associate contents of Filename with WordFile}
   Rewrite ( WordFile );

  WriteWords ( Dictionary, WordFile );
  Close ( WordFile );
  Writeln; Writeln ( '>>>  ', Dictionary.Count, ' words saved to ', FileName );
  Dictionary.ChangesMade := FALSE
  END
END;
```

```
PROCEDURE LoadDictionary ( VAR Dictionary : DictType );

VAR
  Data          :  InfoType;
  FirstLetter   :  Char;
  WordFile      :  Text;
  Filename      :  Str80;
  Previous      :  NodePtr;
  Found         :  Boolean;

BEGIN
WITH Dictionary DO
  BEGIN
  Write ( '>>>  Load dictionary text file:  ' );
  Readln ( Filename );
  IF Length ( Filename ) = 0 THEN    {User merely pressed RETURN, to abort}
    Writeln ( '>>>  Load dictionary cancelled.' )
  ELSE
    BEGIN
    {Insert instructions to associate contents of Filename with WordFile}
     Reset ( WordFile );

    ChangesMade := NOT Eof ( WordFile );
    WHILE NOT Eof ( WordFile ) DO
      BEGIN
      Readln ( WordFile, Data.Key );                   {Read word from file}
      AddWord ( Heads [ Data.Key [ 1 ]], Data.Key )  {Add it to a list}
      END;

    Writeln ( '>>>  ', Count, ' words added to dictionary' );
    Close ( WordFile )
    END
  END        {WITH Dictionary DO}
END;
```

```
PROCEDURE Conclusion ( VAR Dictionary : DictType );

VAR
  Reply : Char;

BEGIN
WITH Dictionary DO
  IF ChangesMade AND ( Count > 0 ) THEN
    BEGIN
    Write ( '>>>  Save changes?  (Y/N):  ' );
    Readln ( Reply );
    IF PositiveResponse ( Reply ) THEN
      SaveDictionary ( Dictionary )                    {Save database to file}
    END;

Writeln; Writeln ( '***  Online Dictionary Program Terminated  ***' )
END;
```

```
PROCEDURE CheckSpelling ( VAR LList : LListType; VAR Key : KeyType );

VAR
  Found     :  Boolean;
  Previous  :  NodePtr;

BEGIN
LLSearch ( Key, LList.Head, Previous, Found );        {Search for the word}
IF Found THEN
  Writeln ( '>>>  "', Key, '" spelled correctly' )
ELSE
  Writeln ( '!!!  "', Key, '" spelled incorrectly or not in dictionary  !!!' )
END;
```

```
{***  Main  Routine  ***}

BEGIN
InitDictionary ( Dictionary );
WITH Dictionary DO
  REPEAT
    ObtainMenuOption ( Option );
    IF Option IN [ WordChk, Add, Delete ] THEN
      Preprocessing ( Key, Option, FirstLetter, Changesmade );

    CASE Option OF
      Quit     :  Conclusion ( Dictionary );
      Add      :  AddWord ( Heads [ FirstLetter ], Key );
      Delete   :  DeleteWord ( Heads [ FirstLetter ], Key );
      WordChk  :  CheckSpelling ( Heads [ FirstLetter ], Key );
      Display  :  WriteWords ( Dictionary, OUTPUT );
      Save     :  SaveDictionary ( Dictionary );
      Build    :  LoadDictionary ( Dictionary );
      Garbage  :  Writeln ( '>>>  ERROR:  Invalid word syntax.' )  {Preprocessing}
    END
UNTIL Option = Quit
END.
```

A Nonlinear Trie-Based Dictionary (Advanced)

In the previous dictionary structure, linear linked lists were used to store whole words. In this version, each collection of words beginning with the same letter will be represented in a nonlinear linked list structure called a

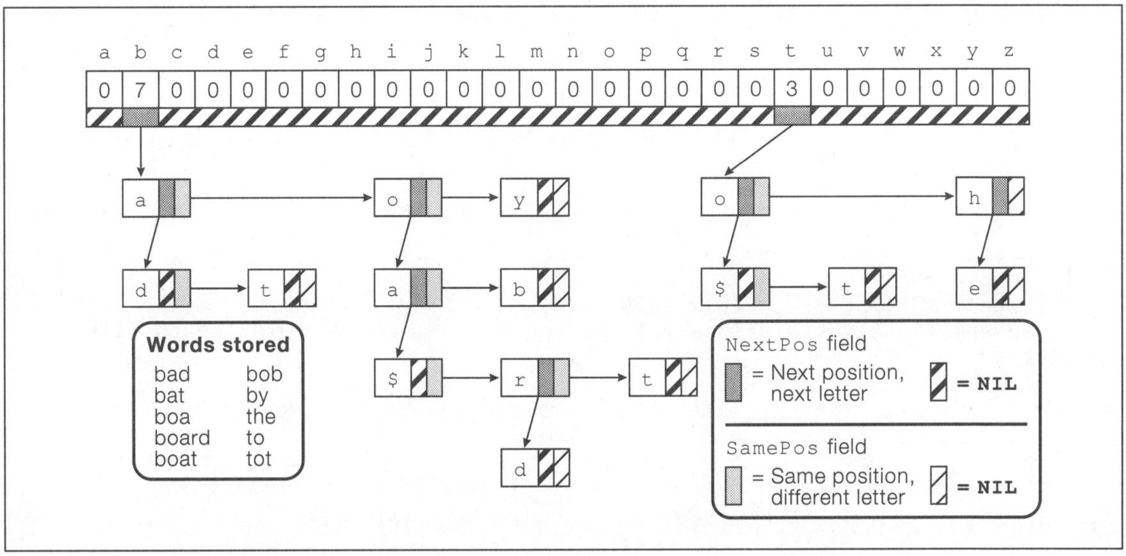

FIGURE 5.30 A Sample Trie-based Dictionary of Ten Words

trie (pronounced "try") **structure.** This new dictionary will again employ an array of 26 elements of pointer type, indexed from character a to character z, corresponding to the first letter of one or more words. In addition to not bothering to store the first letter of a word (after all, the array index indicates this), a trie takes advantage of the fact that many words begin with the same pattern of letters. For example, `'boa'`, `'boat'`, and `'board'` all begin with the substring `'boa'`. If the previous dictionary structure is used to store these three words, the string `'boa'` is stored three times. A trie, on the other hand, would store this pattern only once for all three words.

Figure 5.30 illustrates a sample trie-based dictionary containing ten words. Every array element contains either a **NIL** value or else points into one trie of dynamically allocated nodes. Unlike a node in the previous dictionary, which contained an entire word plus a link field, each trie node contains a single character letter and two link fields. Following a *downward path* in a trie, node by node, corresponds to *moving across a given word* character-by-character, whereas following a *rightward path* in a trie, node by node, corresponds to *substituting different possible characters for the same position* in a given word. With so many linked lists in the complete structure and insertion and deletion being infrequent operations, header nodes are not used.

The trie-based dictionary retains the knowledge that both `'boa'` and `'boat'` are words via the special $ character. A $ character means that the characters accumulated thus far, by following a path from the array, form a complete word and that additional character(s), when appended, form *additional* word(s). For this reason, `'boar'` is not a word in the dictionary because the string `'boar'` must be followed by a d. To add `'boar'` to the dictionary, another node containing the character $ must be added: The node containing r would point down to it, and this new node would point rightward to the node containing d (formerly pointed to in a downward direction by the r node).

Global declarations for this dictionary structure follow:

```
TYPE
  LetterPtr    =  ^OneLetter;
  OneLetter    =  RECORD
                    Letter   : Char;       {The letter stored}
                    SamePos,               {Pointer to substitute letter}
                    NextPos  : LetterPtr   {Pointer to next letter}
                  END;

  LListType    =  RECORD                   {Words which start with same letter}
                    Head  : LetterPtr;     {Address of 1st node of trie}
                    Count : Integer        {Number of words in that trie}
                  END;

  ListType     =  RECORD
                    Heads : ARRAY ['a'..'z']  OF LListType;  {26 tries}
                    Count : Integer                          {Count of all words}
                  END;

VAR
  Dictionary  :  ListType;                {Array of trie list head pointers}
```

An algorithm to determine if a particular word is represented in the dictionary is similar to an algorithm for adding a new word. Both algorithms use the first character to determine with which of the 26 tries to work. Both algorithms must carefully examine each character in the word and advance appropriately in the trie—i.e., follow the appropriate link field of each node visited. One difference, of course, is that the add-word algorithm must insert letter nodes correctly to add the new word.

For example, to add the word `'bye'`, an add-word algorithm would start with the b element of the array, advance to the first a node, and then follow `SamePos` links until encountering the y node. This indicates a b letter followed by a y letter, with no letters following the y, since the `NextPos` field of the y node is **NIL**. The algorithm then allocates a new node and assigns e to its `Letter` field. Next, the algorithm assigns the heapspace address of this node to the `NextPos` field of the y node. In Figure 5.30, the new node for e would be drawn beneath the y node, and a downward arrow would be drawn to the node from the `NextPos` field of the y node. Notice that the nodes along each horizontal or vertical linked list (i.e., using `SamePos` or a `NextPos` link fields, respectively) are kept ordered by alphabetic `Letter` values; this is done to expedite linear searches. A delete-word algorithm is more complex than an add-word algorithm, since a number of words may begin with the same pattern of characters of the word about to be deleted. You are encouraged to implement the `OnLineDictionary` program operations using trie structures in place of linear linked lists.

Perhaps you have already noticed that the enhanced telephone directory also involved trie structures. A trie is really a type of tree data structure, and a variety of tree structures are described through Chapter 8 and in Sections 9.3, 10.1, and 10.3. These structures are *nonlinear* because, from each node, it may be possible to advance to more than one other node.

APPLICATION 5.4 Sparse Matrices

Many applications involve very large matrices in which most of the elements contain null or zero values. Imagine a two-dimensional array representing the floor of an ocean, with each element representing a particular square area and containing a real value reflecting the probability of a subterranean oil deposit. Or imagine a two-dimensional array representing a map of the night sky or a demographic map of the United States. Implementing such a **sparse matrix** using the standard Pascal array data type can waste a prohibitively large amount of memory, even if the entire array itself is dynamically allocated within heapspace.

As an example, Figure 5.31 shows a sparse matrix using standard mathematical matrix notation along with a depiction of its two-dimensional array implementation. (This particular matrix is small enough that a conventional two-dimensional array would suffice.)

We can replace the array structure with a structure containing linked lists of nodes that are linked to form virtual rows and columns, as depicted in Figure 5.32. In the figure, only those nodes superimposed on the large shaded area correspond to elements of the array of Figure 5.31. The horizontal linked list above this shaded area contains header nodes to indicate the start of a particular column, and the *vertical linked list* to the left of this shaded area contains header nodes to indicate the start of a particular row. The node in the upper left corner containing `Data.Key`, `Row`, and `Column` fields of zero serves as a header node for the list of column header nodes and for the list of row header nodes.

Because of the memory "overhead" of the header nodes and two link fields per data node, a linked list implementation of a sparse matrix saves memory over the array implementation *only* if the array is very large and very sparse. The structure of Figure 5.32 requires more memory than does the two-dimensional array of Figure 5.31 because this sample matrix, while very sparse, is also relatively small. The programmer must estimate the total memory requirements of both implementations of a given matrix to determine if the linked list implementation offers a substantial savings of memory.

A set of generic, global declarations for this structure follow:

$$\begin{bmatrix} 8 & 0 & 0 & 0 & 0 & 0 & 0 & 2 \\ 0 & 0 & 1 & 0 & 0 & 0 & 0 & 0 \\ 0 & 0 & 5 & 0 & 0 & 0 & 0 & 3 \\ 0 & 0 & 0 & 0 & 0 & 0 & 0 & 0 \\ 1 & 0 & 0 & 0 & 6 & 3 & 0 & 0 \end{bmatrix}$$

Rows \ Columns	1	2	3	4	5	6	7	8
1	8	0	0	0	0	0	0	2
2	0	0	1	0	0	0	0	0
3	0	0	5	0	0	0	0	3
4	0	0	0	0	0	0	0	0
5	1	0	0	0	6	3	0	0

FIGURE 5.31 A Sample Sparse Matrix and its Array Implementation

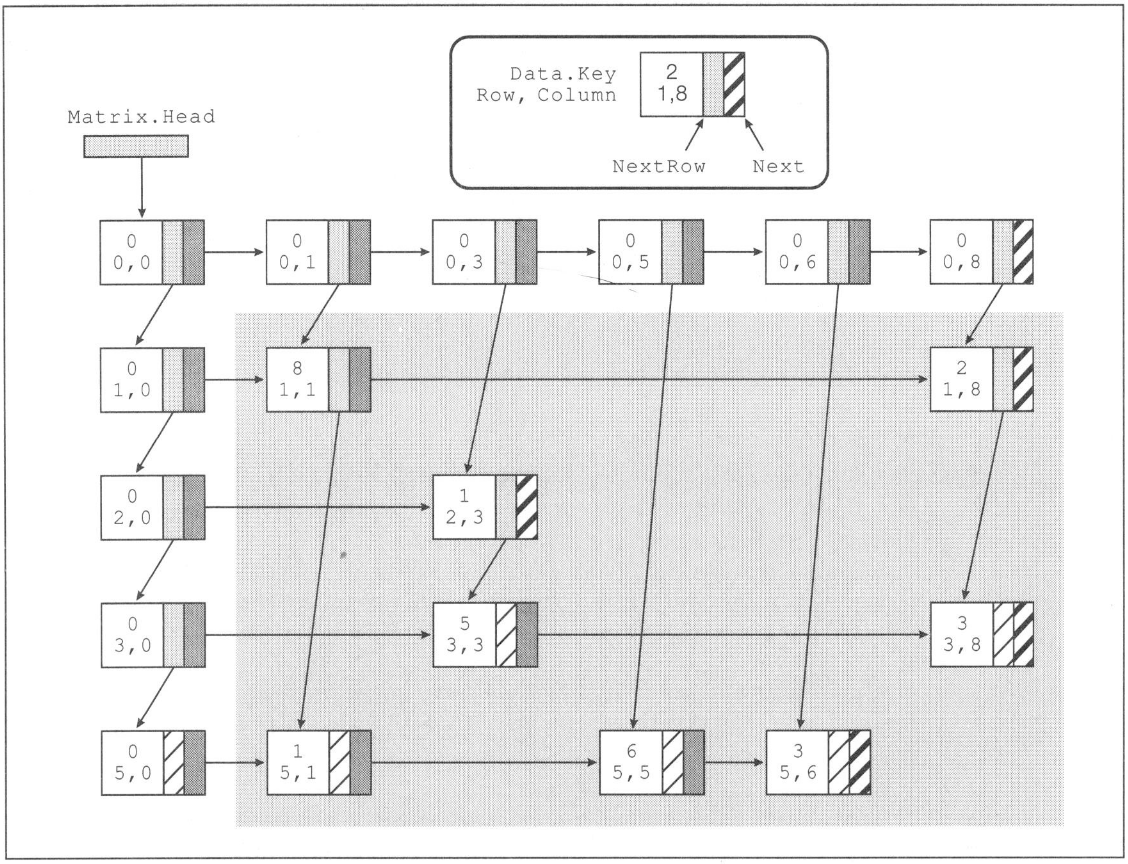

FIGURE 5.32 Linked List Implementation of the Sample Sparse Matrix

```
TYPE
  KeyType     =  Integer;                {Application dependent}
  InfoType    =  RECORD
                   Key      : KeyType;
                   {Other fields, as necessary}
                 END;

  NodePtr     =  ^Node;
  Node        =  RECORD                  {Data node}
                   Data     : InfoType;
                   Row,                  {Row index number}
                   Column   : Integer;   {Column index number}
                   Next,                 {Next column}
                   NextRow  : NodePtr    {Next row}
                 END;

  MatrixType  =  RECORD
                   Head     : NodePtr;   {Address of corner sentinel node}
                   Count    : Integer    {Number of data nodes}
                 END;

VAR
  Matrix  :  MatrixType;
```

Circular Linked Lists

Thus far, our searches and traversals have always begun with the first node in a list (whose address is stored in the list head variable) and terminated with the node whose link field is set to **NIL**. With some special handling, searches and traversals *could* begin with some node other than the first node. In such cases, when the end of the list is encountered, the search or traversal would simply wrap around—i.e., resume at the beginning of the list.

As a programming convenience for some applications, rather than storing a **NIL** value in the final node we can store the address of the *first* node instead, so that searching and traversing can wrap around without special handling (in fact, there would be no final node). Such an arrangement is called a **circular linked list**. Our generic declarations will work as they have been written, and we still need a list head variable to hold the address of one of the nodes. Figure 5.33 depicts a sample circular linked list with a header node. In the figure, the key value of the header node is depicted as $-\infty$, with the value of **-MAXINT** actually stored, since the data type of keys here is integer.

Unfortunately, the convenience of circularity creates some new special cases for the LLTraverse and LLSearch algorithms, since both involve complete or partial traversals of the list and a **NIL** link field is no longer used to flag the end of the list. (The original LLInit and LLEmpty algorithms, on the other hand, work just as they have been written.) LLTraverse can be modified to solve this problem: It should save the address where the traversal begins and then visit and process every node until this start node is revisited.

This simple solution will not work for the LLSearch algorithm if the list is ordered by key values. When a noncircular list is ordered by key value and a node is encountered with a key value greater than the key passed in, the searching algorithm may safely conclude that the key value sought does not exist among the remaining nodes. This assumption cannot be made with the circular list unless the search always begins with the header node, which defeats the purpose of maintaining the list as circular. If the search may begin anywhere, then LLSearch must be modified in order to examine *every* node before safely concluding that a particular node is not in the list. For this reason, circular lists are more frequently employed with unordered lists for applications involving little or no searching, as in the *merge sort* algorithm of Section 11.4.

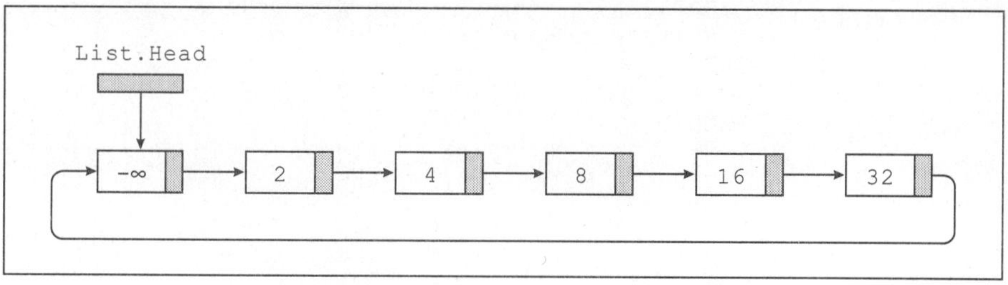

FIGURE 5.33 A Sample Circular Linked List With a Header Node

Doubly Linked Lists

Throughout this chapter, we have been working with singly linked lists—i.e., linked lists in which each node contains a single link field providing the address of the *next* node in the list. In most cases of insertion and deletion, it has been necessary to access the previous node for linking purposes, and this has required that `LLSearch` "drag" a `Previous` pointer behind as it searches and returns its final value. This technique is sufficient for applications in which we need to access the node *immediately* preceding a particular node but obviously will not work if we need to access *any* preceding node. For applications in which this is important, we can use a **doubly linked list** instead —i.e., a linked list in which each node has *two link fields:* `Next` holds the address of the *next* node, and `Prev` holds the address of the *previous node.* In addition to the list head variable, a **list tail variable** is frequently helpful as well.

Figure 5.34 depicts a sample doubly linked list in which the `Key` value of each node is an integer (the list is shown without a header node).

A set of generic global declarations for a doubly linked list of records follows:

```
TYPE
  KeyType     =  ??;                   {Application dependent}
  InfoType    =  RECORD
                   Key   : KeyType;    {Key value}
                   {other fields, as necessary}
                 END;

  DNodePtr    =  ^DNode;
  DNode       =  RECORD
                   Data  : InfoType;   {Data portion of node}
                   Next,               {Address of next node in list}
                   Prev  : DNodePtr    {Address of previous node in list}
                 END;

  DLListType  =  RECORD
                   Head,               {Address of 1st node in list}
                   Tail  : DNodePtr;   {Address of last node in list}
                   Count : Integer     {Total node count}
                 END;

VAR
  DLList  :  DLListType;
```

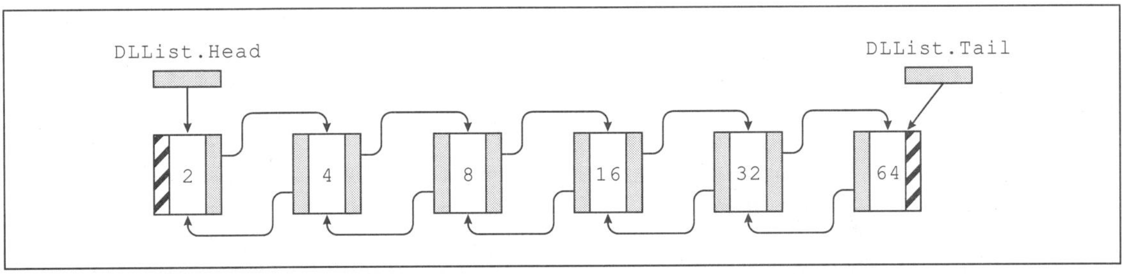

FIGURE 5.34 Sample Doubly Linked List

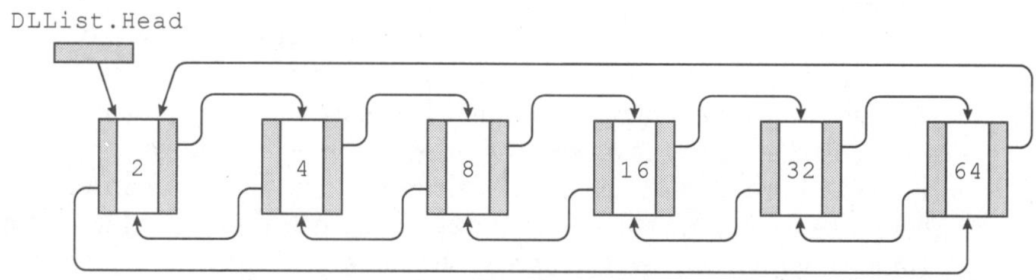

FIGURE 5.35 **The Doubly Linked List of Figure 5.34 as a Circular List**

A doubly linked list can even be made circular, in which case there is no need to maintain a list tail variable, since the `Prev` pointer of the first node holds the address of the last node in the list. Figure 5.35 depicts the sample list of Figure 5.34 as a circular doubly linked list.

The Pascal implementations of all fundamental operations for a doubly linked list are left as exercises.

Indexing into a Linked List

In many applications, it is useful to store the same data in different lists. This allows a traversal algorithm to process the same data in different orders and may provide faster access to portions of the list. Our next application will explain how to store data among different lists without having to duplicate the `Data` portions of nodes. Remember that, at the *abstract level,* a linked list is merely a collection of nodes with properly assigned link fields.

APPLICATION 5.5 Managing Passenger Lists for Sky-High Airlines

Sky-High Airlines has routes connecting many major cities in Europe. For each flight, the airline must maintain a record of general flight information as well as a list of passenger information. In this application, we will design portions of a computer program to manage information about a *single* flight. Although the seating capacity of any airliner has a fixed upper limit, we will represent the list of passenger information using a linked list rather than an array of such records, due to the frequent insertions and deletions. The list of information must be stored in a binary file between program executions.

Whenever a Sky-High Airlines ticketing agent issues a ticket, the agent simultaneously issues a seat assignment. In addition to allowing a ticketing agent to access a particular passenger record by name, the program must display the entire passenger list in any of the following three orders:

- Row number
- Section (first class, coach nonsmoking, coach smoking)
- Last name

One obvious technique for the multidisplay capability would be to keep three separate lists. This would be a poor choice, however, since three copies of the same passenger record not only wastes internal and external memory space but also poses the requirement that any modification to a single copy of the record must be made to *all* copies of that record. Instead, we will employ a technique that does the following:

- Maintains a single copy of each passenger record.
- Maintains different lists only conceptually via different pointer fields in each node, one pointer field per list.

We will begin by building a single linked list of passenger nodes. Each of these nodes is a dynamically allocated record that has as its primary key the row number of the seat (or a zero value if the passenger has reserved a ticket but no seat has been assigned yet); the entire list will be kept ordered by ascending row number. At the head of the list is a globally declared record that contains general flight information as well as a list head variable (`ByRow`) to hold the address of the first passenger node. Unlike the passenger nodes, the single flight information record is allocated statically; i.e., its memory is set aside within the program's executable image at compile-time. Figure 5.36 depicts a sample arrangement of nodes for flight 119 after five passengers have booked passage. For simplicity, all linked lists in this application will be depicted without header nodes; as you read, you may consider whether or not the use of a header node is preferable.

The arrangement depicted in Figure 5.36 is sufficient for a traversal of the entire passenger list in row number order, to display passenger information, for example. To display the entire passenger list in order of section—first class, coach nonsmoking, and coach smoking—the program must maintain three more link fields in the flight information record. Each of these link fields will contain the address of the first node where that section begins. Let us assume that first class always begins in row 1, coach nonsmoking always begins in row 8, and coach smoking always begins in row 25. Fig-

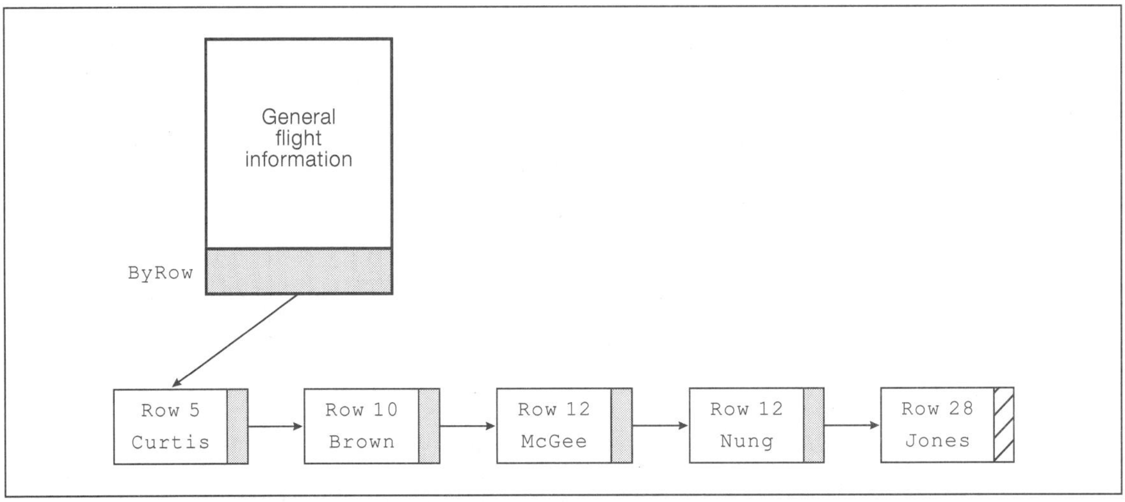

FIGURE 5.36 A Single Linked List, Ordered by Row Number

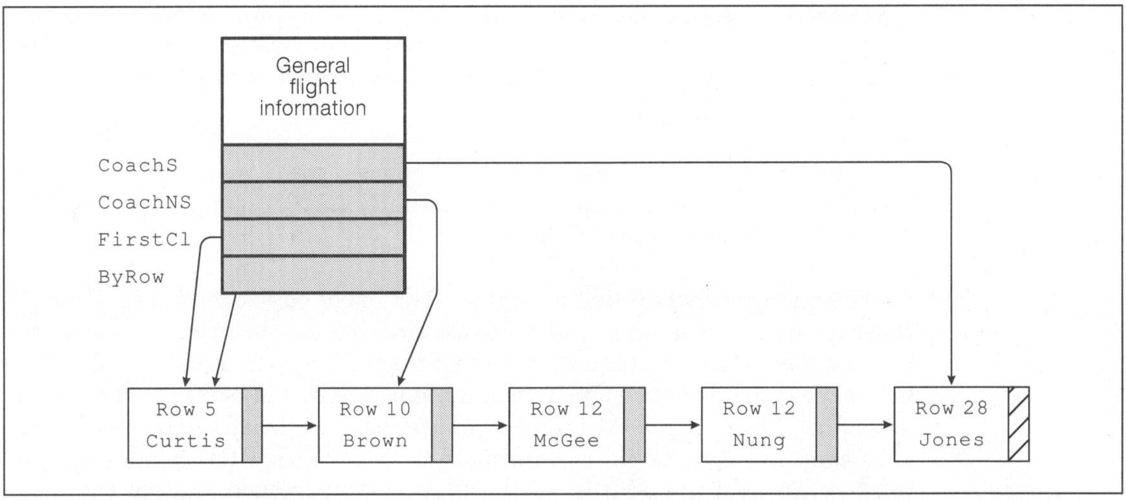

FIGURE 5.37 Two Linked Lists, Ordered by Row Number and by Section

ure 5.37 shows the arrangement of nodes with these link fields included. In the figure, `CoachS` is the link field for the coach smoking section, `CoachNS`, for the coach nonsmoking section, and `FirstCl`, for the first class section.

How may a traversal algorithm display only coach nonsmoking passenger information? If the `CoachNS` field contains a non **NIL** address value, the algorithm can start at that address and traverse the list until one of the following is encountered:

- The end of the entire passenger list (i.e., a **NIL** link field value)
- A node whose address is contained in the flight information record `CoachS` link field—i.e., the start of the coach smoking section

Conceptually, there are now *four linked lists:* the entire passenger list and three section sublists.

> A *linked list* is merely an abstract notion—a collection of nodes and link fields. Several linked lists may share the same physical resources. A particular linked list is defined only in the way an algorithm follows link fields.

Let us expand upon this idea so we can access passenger nodes in order of last name as well. That is, we would like to have *another* linked list, ordered by last name, without having to replicate entire nodes of passenger information. Since a particular linked list is defined by its link fields, we can set up another linked list by doing the following:

- Adding one more link field to the flight information record
- Adding a link field to each dynamically allocated passenger node

Figure 5.38 depicts such an arrangement of links (for clarity the `CoachS`, `CoachNS`, and `FirstCl` link arrows emanating from the flight informa-

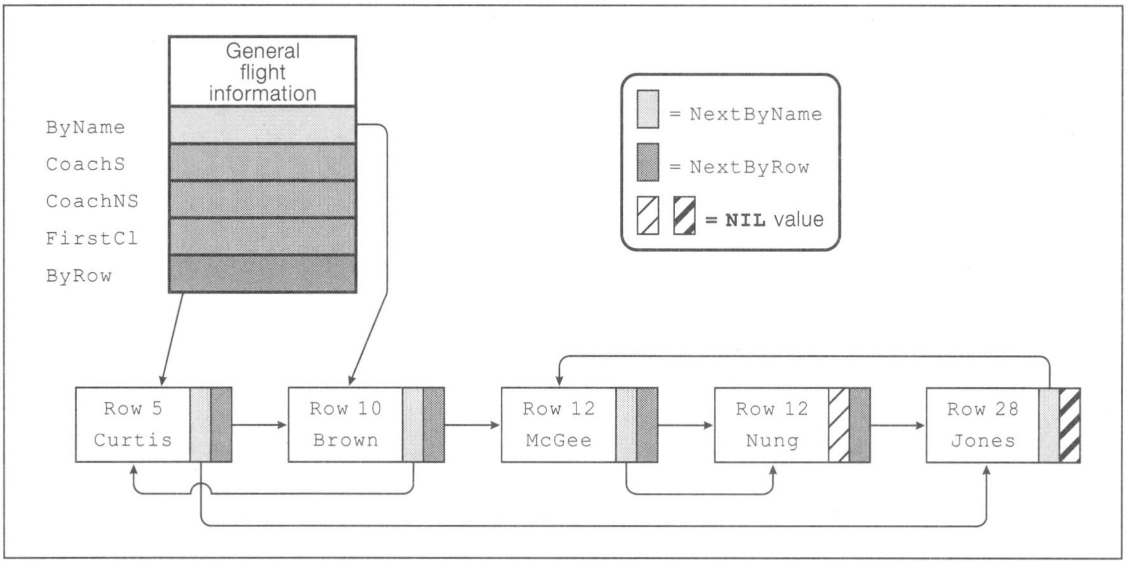

FIGURE 5.38 Multiple Lists by Row Number and Name

tion record are not shown). In addition to displaying passenger information in order of row number or section, the program can also display the same information in order of last name by starting with the address stored in the flight information record's `ByName` field and following all the `ByName` link fields (the lighter-shaded link fields in the figure) among the nodes.

To build this double list, each time a new passenger record is added to the list, the program's insertion algorithm must actually perform two search-and-insert operations:

1. An insertion into the list ordered by row number
2. An insertion into the list ordered by last name

For each new passenger, a single record is dynamically allocated in heapspace, and the row number and name (along with any other passenger data) are then stored in this record. The first search must determine where in the linked list ordered by row number this node should be placed. The first insertion then adjusts the `ByRow` link fields accordingly. The second search and insertion does the same for the linked list ordered by name.

5.3 SEQUENTIAL STORAGE (ARRAY) REPRESENTATION OF THE ADT LINKED LIST

Throughout Section 5.2 we have been representing the ADT linked list using dynamic allocation. As we have seen, heapspace is a finite amount of internal memory in which variables may be allocated and deallocated dynamically via the standard `New` and `Dispose` procedures, respectively.

Nodes are linked together to form a chain or linked list by assigning to the link field of each node the heapspace address of the next node in the list and by assigning a `NIL` address to the link field of the final node.

Intead of using the heapspace to hold linked list nodes, we can use another kind of finite memory space—an array—to serve as a **pseudoheapspace.** And instead of using a heapspace memory address, we can use an array index value to point to a node; an index value of zero will serve as a **pseudo-`NIL` value**. With dynamic allocation, a Pascal compiler generates the appropriate object code to manage the use of the heapspace whenever it encounters calls to `New` and `Dispose` in the source code. With the array representation, however, it is the *programmer's responsibility* to include the source code instructions explicitly in order to manage available array elements so that such elements are allocated and deallocated efficiently. (As we shall see, this is best accomplished by maintaining a separate linked list of such available nodes.) You may refer back to Figure 5.5, which distinguishes the dynamic allocation and sequential storage representations of a linked list.

The sequential storage strategy for a linked list is summarized as follows:

1. Each node is a record, and the entire pseudoheapspace is an array of such records.
2. As usual, each node consists of a *data* section plus a *link field*. The link field contains the array index of the next node in the list or else some special key value that, like `NIL`, is used to indicate that no other nodes follow in the list.
3. A linked list of nodes is referred to as the **active list.** As usual, a *list head variable* contains the array index of the first (active) node.
4. All unused records in the array are linked together in a linked list referred to as the **free list.** A new node for the active list is obtained by deleting the next node from the free list and inserting it into the appropriate place in the active list. Conversely, whenever a node is deleted from the active list, it is inserted at the head of the free list. A list head variable, usually named `Free`, holds the array index of the first available node in the free list.

Two types of linked lists must therefore be maintained:

- The *active list(s)* of nodes in use, with one list head variable per list
- The *free list* of nodes *available* for use, with one list head variable

A set of generic declarations for the sequential storage of a linked list follows (refer ahead to Figure 5.39 if necessary):

```
CONST
  Null      =  0;   {Analogous to NIL, indicating "no more active nodes"}
  MaxNodes  =  ??;  {Positive integer; maximum number of nodes allowable}

TYPE
  KeyType   =  ??;
  InfoType  =  RECORD;
                 Key    : KeyType;    {Key value}
                 {Other fields as necessary for the application}
               END;

  NodePtr   =  Null..MaxNodes;
  Node      =  RECORD
                 Data   : InfoType;   {Data portion of an active node}
                 Next   : NodePtr     {Array index of next active node}
               END;

  PHeapType =  RECORD
                 Items  : ARRAY [ 1..MaxNodes ] OF Node;
                 Free,                {Array index of next available node}
                 FCount : NodePtr     {Count of all free (unused) nodes}
               END;

  LListType =  RECORD
                 Head   : NodePtr;    {Index of 1st active list node}
                 Count  : Integer     {Count of nodes in an active list}
               END;

VAR
  PseudoHeap : PHeapType;             {Entire array}
  LList      : LListType;             {One active linked list}
```

The domain and fundamental operations of ADT linked list remain the same, whether the list is represented using dynamic allocation or a static array. Of course, the primitive routines we developed for the dynamic representation must be modified. As an example, for the sequential storage representation we must have a `PHeapInit` procedure that is called initially to link together *every* record in the array to form the free list of available nodes.

As a simple example of a sequential storage representation of a linked list, we assume that the data type of each node key is character and `MaxNodes` is 7. Figure 5.39 depicts the pseudoheapspace array after the `LLInit` routine is executed and several insertions and deletion operations are performed. Carefully examine the guide to the lines and symbols that appears at the top of the figure. For simplicity, `Data` fields of each node in the free list are always shown as blank, even though they may actually contain the data of deleted nodes. Also for simplicity, the active and free lists in Figure 5.39 do not contain header nodes; however, header nodes may be used to simplify the algorithms for insertion and deletion operations, as discussed in Section 5.2.

With the dynamic allocation representation of a linked list, an `LLFull` function (the corollary of the `LLEmpty` function) is rarely used, since a computer's heapspace is typically large enough to accommodate most applications. In the sequential storage representation, however, the pseudoheap-

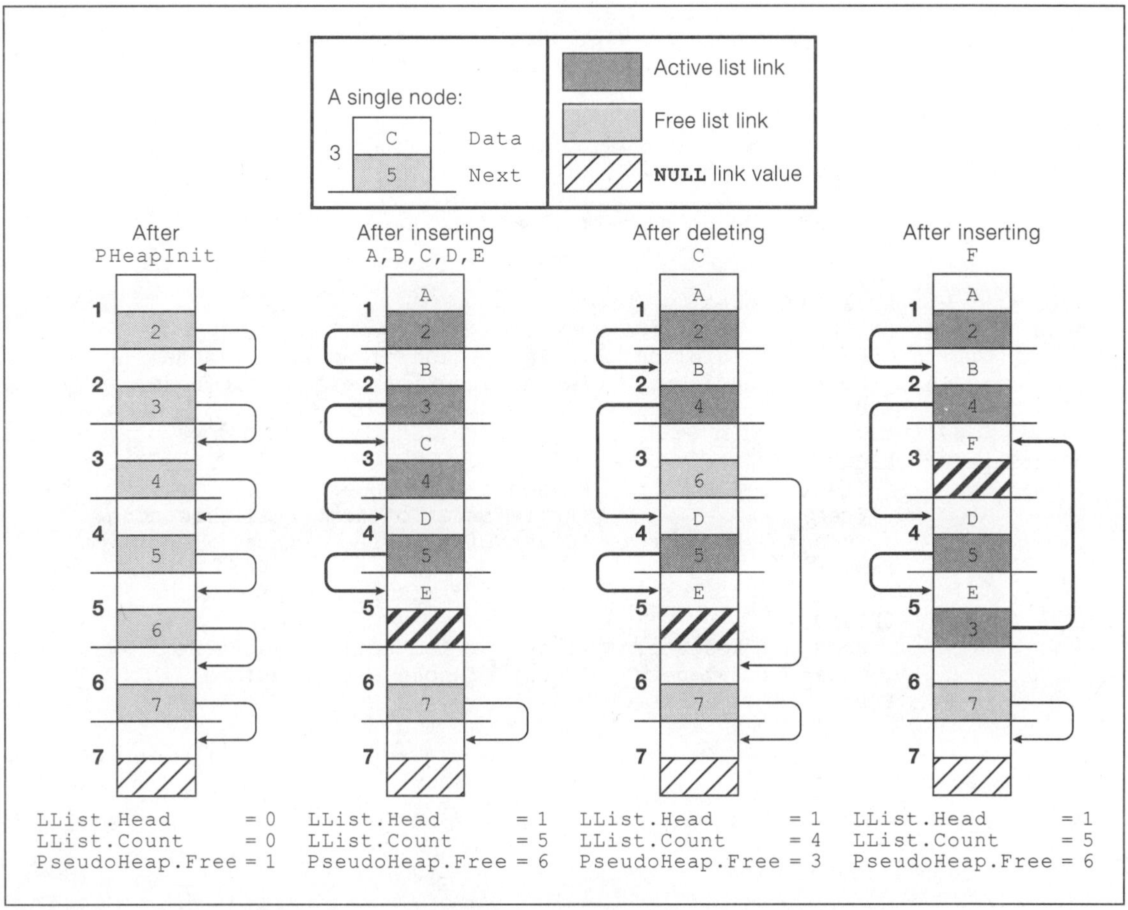

FIGURE 5.39 Sequential Storage Representation of a Linked List

space array is typically much smaller than the real heapspace, so an `LLFull` function is very important:

```
FUNCTION LLFull ( VAR LList : LListType ) : Boolean;

BEGIN
LLFull := LList.Count = MaxNodes
END;
```

`MaxNodes` is a global named constant set to the total number of nodes the pseudoheapspace array may hold—i.e., the sum of all nodes contained in the free list and all active lists.

Also important is a procedure that is analagous to the standard `New` routine, which only works for dynamic allocation in the real heapspace. Procedure `NewNode` returns the address (i.e., array index) of the next available record element in the free list; then it updates the free list appropriately. If the free list is empty, a null `NodePtr` value is returned in parameter `P`.

```
PROCEDURE NewNode ( VAR PseudoHeap : PHeapType; VAR P : NodePtr );

BEGIN
WITH PseudoHeap DO
  BEGIN
  P := Free;                        {Assign to P the address of next free node}
  IF FCount <> 0 THEN               {IF there are free nodes available...}
    BEGIN
    FCount := FCount - 1;           {  Decrement count of free nodes}
    Free := Items [ Free ].Next {   Advance Free to point to next free node}
    END
  END
END;
```

Once again, do not confuse the *simple sequential representation of a (non-linked) list* with the *sequential storage representation of a linked list.* As summarized in Figure 5.5, both involve arrays but in fundamentally different ways. The implementation of all fundamental linked list operations for the sequential storage representation of a linked list are left as exercises.

> *At this time, examine the sequential storage representations of the following routines in Appendix D.*

```
PROCEDURE PHeapInit ( VAR PseudoHeap : PHeapType );

PROCEDURE LLInit ( VAR LList : LListType );

FUNCTION LLEmpty ( VAR LList : LListType ) : Boolean;

FUNCTION LLFull ( VAR LList : LListType ) : Boolean;

PROCEDURE LLSearch ( VAR PseudoHeap : PHeapType;  VAR Key : KeyType;
                     Start : NodePtr;  VAR Previous : NodePtr;
                     VAR Found : Boolean );

PROCEDURE NewNode ( VAR PseudoHeap : PHeapType; VAR P : NodePtr );
```

5.4 DEBUGGING LINKED LIST ALGORITHMS

Debugging a routine is more challenging when dynamic allocation is involved because pointer values cannot be displayed via `Write` or `Writeln` statements; e.g., the following is illegal:

```
New ( P );                                {P is a pointer variable}
Writeln ( 'The value of P is ', P );      {ILLEGAL}
```

Even more frustrating is the fact that the attempted use of a pointer variable that does not contain a valid heapspace address will typically crash not only the user program but the operating system program as well.

Common bugs in linked list routines involving dynamic allocation include the following:

- A list head variable is not initialized to **NIL**.
- The link field of the last node in a linked list is not assigned a **NIL** value.
- The link field is assigned a **NIL** value; however, a search, traversal, or other routine does not test for this value before using the field to reference a node. Typically, this error arises from either of the following:
  - Special cases are not handled properly, especially regarding empty lists and insertion at and deletion from the head of a list.
  - Statements are slightly out of place within the routine.
- There is improper use or assigning of a `Previous` type pointer variable, especially regarding `LLSearch`, `LLInsert`, and `LLDelete` type routines.
- There is incorrect node counting—e.g., forgetting to increment or decrement a `LList.Count` type variable.

It is especially important that you test your versions of the primitive linked list routines `LLInit`, `LLEmpty`, `LLSearch`, `LLInsert`, and `LLDelete` thoroughly before using them in a program.

As a routine is building a linked list, do not assume that the list is being built correctly. In the routine being tested insert a temporary call to your list traversal primitive to display the key value of each node in the list after each new node is inserted. Do the same whenever a node is deleted from the list. If your `LLSearch`-type routine does not seem to work, insert a temporary `Writeln` statement before the call to display the key value being sought. And although you cannot display the value of a pointer variable, you can display the fact that it does or does not contain a **NIL** value:

```
Write ( 'Within LLSearch, Current = NIL? ', Current = NIL );  {DEBUG}
IF Current <> NIL THEN                                        {DEBUG}
  Writeln ( '   Current^.Data.Key = ', Current^.Data.Key );   {DEBUG}
```

SUMMARY

Two representations of a linear list of items are the sequential storage and the linked list representations. In the sequential storage (simple array) representation, items (typically records) are stored in adjacent memory locations. In the linked list representation, records are not necessarily stored in adjacent memory locations. Therefore, each record must contain the address of the next record in the list. Such a linked list of records may be regarded as a data type itself.

ADT linked list is a structured data type forming a linear list of items; the list may or may not have its items ordered by key field values, depending on the application. Its domain consists of a collection of nodes, typically of record data type. Each node contains a data field, consisting of information relevant to the application, and a link field, as described previously. Fundamental operations include initializing the linked list as empty, testing for list emptiness, performing a linear search for a particular node, inserting or deleting a node, and traversing the entire list. In a Pascal program, linked lists are commonly represented using dynamic allocation in which each node is a dynamically allocated record and an address is a pointer value. Linked lists may also be represented within an array of records (sequential storage representation); most of Chapter 5 (and this summary) focuses on the dynamic allocation representation.

The responsibilities of creating and correctly linking the nodes of a linked list lie with the program/programmer. For example, a list head variable must be maintained to keep the address of the first node in a linked list; failure to do this may result in the program's having no way to access the list. By convention, programmers assign a **NIL** pointer value to the link field of the last node to indicate the end of the list, for the purposes of searching and traversing. Great care must be taken when inserting and deleting nodes so that list remains linked, with all nodes accessible from the head of the list. Care must also be taken when designing algorithms so that special cases are handled, such as deleting or inserting a node at head of the list. Drawing diagrams of the list during program design and debugging is most helpful.

Linked lists provide the advantage over arrays that (1) existing items do not have to be shifted when an item is inserted or deleted and (2) a list can actually grow or shrink in length in the heapspace as necessary. Searching a linked list is slower in the average case, however, because a linear search must be employed instead of the faster binary search on an ordered array. If a linked list is ordered by key value, a search algorithm must be used to find a particular node or to find the point of insertion or deletion prior to inserting or deleting a node. Using a header node increases the average efficiency of insertion and deletion Pascal routines.

When a linked list is saved in a binary file, only the data portion of each node should be written, since link field values—like all pointer values—are valid only during the execution of the program during which those values are obtained.

In a circular linked list, the link field of the final node contains the address of the first node rather than a **NIL** value, thereby creating a ring. While each node in a singly linked list contains one link field that points to the next node in list, each node in a doubly linked list contains a second link field that points to the previous node. Application 5.5 illustrates how several different linked lists may share the same physical resources via different sets of link fields. It also shows how a program can index into different points of a linked list to access a particular node or sequence of nodes without having to always commence searching at the head of the list.

The sequential storage representation of a linked list uses an array of records as a pseudoheapspace in which linked lists may be created and manipulated. Again, each node consists of a data section plus one or more link fields. Here, a node address is an array index, typically of integer data type, with a zero value used commonly in place of **NIL**. The linked list of data nodes is referred to as the active list and all unused nodes in the array form a second linked list referred to as the free list; both lists require list head variables. It is the responsibility of the program/programmer to build and maintain these lists as well as write procedures to replace the `New` and `Dispose` routines, which apply only to dynamically allocated variables in heapspace.

Debugging a routine is more challenging when dynamic allocation is involved because pointer values cannot be displayed via the standard procedure `Writeln` and because the attempted use of a pointer variable that does not contain a valid heapspace address will typically crash both the user program and the operating system. Section 5.4 provides debugging guidelines.

KEY TERMS

Active list
ADT linked list
Circular linked list
Data field
Doubly linked list
Free list
Header node
Linear search
Link field
List head variable
List tail variable
NIL link field value
Nonlinear structure
Node
Primary key
Pseudo **NIL** value
Pseudoheapspace
Runtime dependent
Secondary key
Sequential storage representation
Singly linked list
Sparse matrix
Traversal
Trie structure

REVIEW QUESTIONS

1. Describe ADT linked list, including the domain, fundamental operations, and structure. What are the two components of any linked list node? When represented using Pascal, is the linked list data type standard or programmer-defined?
2. Can a linked list be represented in any high-level language (e.g., FORTRAN)? What data type(s) must the language support, at a minimum, in order to support the linked list type?
3. Describe and compare the dynamic allocation and sequential storage (array-based) representations. What are the advantages and disadvantages of both representations?
4. Often, a programmer must decide whether to use a linked list or a simple array to store data items. What are the advantages and disadvantages of using a variable of either type? In what way do the advantages and disadvantages cancel each other out somewhat?
5. What is the role of a list head variable? Is it always necessary? What is **NIL** and what is its typical role? If `Ptr` is a pointer variable, what is the difference between `Ptr` being undefined and `Ptr` containing a **NIL** value?
6. In what three contexts might a search of a list be performed? The `LLSearch` procedure described in Section 5.2 has a Boolean parameter named `Found` and a parameter of pointer type named `Previous`. Upon return from a call to `LLSearch`, `Found` is either true or false, and `Previous` has either a **NIL** or a non **NIL** value. Explain the implication of the following combinations of `Found`, `Previous`, and `Previous^.Next` values upon return from a call to `LLSearch` for two linked lists—one with a header node and the other without a header node (state whether or not a particular combination is even possible):

Found	Previous	Previous^.Next
TRUE	NIL	-
TRUE	<>NIL	<>NIL
TRUE	<>NIL	NIL
FALSE	NIL	-
FALSE	<>NIL	<>NIL
FALSE	<>NIL	NIL

7. What are the advantages and disadvantages of using a header node? Which fundamental linked list operations are affected by the presence of a header node?

8. Describe the operations necessary for saving a linked list in a file and the operations for reconstructing a linked list from a file. What information is *not* saved and why?

9. What is the purpose of the nonlinear structure depicted in Figure 5.32? Does such a structure always require less memory than its two-dimensional array counterpart?

10. A circular linked list provides the convenience that a full traversal or search may begin anywhere in the list, without special handling when the "end" of the list is encountered. What problems are raised, however, by the circularity, and how may they be resolved?

11. Distinguish between singly and doubly linked lists. Can a doubly linked list be circular?

12. Explain how several linked lists may share the same data portions of a set of nodes, such as are depicted in Figure 5.38. What really distinguishes one linked list from another? What advantage is gained by storing the addresses of certain nodes of a linked list, as depicted in Figure 5.38?

13. In the sequential storage representation of a linked list, clearly an active list must be linked, but why must the free list of available nodes be linked as well? Let us assume that only one active list is allowed to be stored. As an alternative to keeping a `LList.Head` variable for this list, could we simply impose the rule that the first node in an active list is always to be kept in array element 1?

EXERCISES

1. The linked list in Figure 5.40 was built using the generic declarations given at the start of this chapter (`KeyType` = `Integer`). Execute each of the following code segments, one after the other ((a) then (b), etc.). After each code segment, redraw the list with appropriate `Key` field values and `Next` field arrows. Also draw arrows that clearly indicate to which nodes the `NodePtr` type variables `LList.Head`, `Q`, and `P` point.

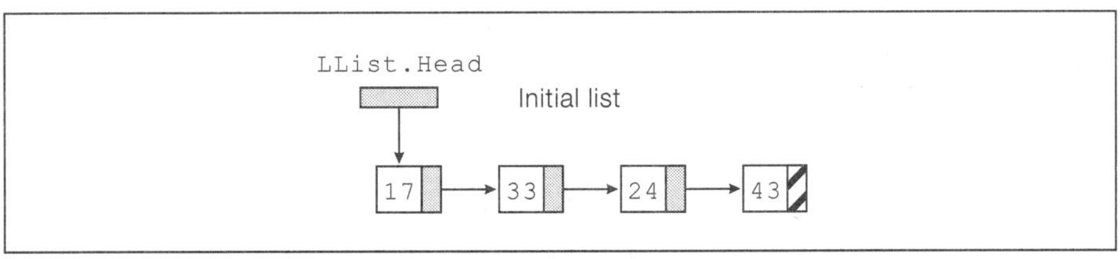

a.
```
P := LList.Head;
Q := P^.Next;
Q^.Data.Key := 54;
```

b.
```
P^.Data.Key := Q^.Data.Key;
```

c.
```
P := Q;
Q := P^.Next;
P^.Data.Key := 76;
```

d.
```
Q := P;
P := Q^.Next;
P^.Data.Key := 23;
```

e.
```
Q := P^.Next;
P := Q;
Q^.Data.Key := 99;
```

2. Assume that the following two linked lists have been built using the generic declarations given at the start of Section 5.1:

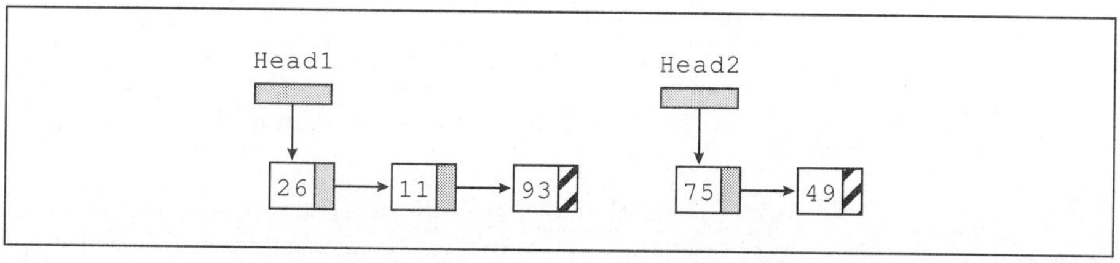

For both of the following code segments, hand-execute each of the following code segments and redraw the resulting lists. Start with the original lists as shown when hand-executing code segment (b). All variables are of `NodePtr` pointer type, as declared at the start of Section 5.2.

a.
```
P     := Head1;
Head2 := NIL;

WHILE P <> NIL DO
  BEGIN
  Head1   := P^.Next;
  P^.Next := Head2;
  Head2   := P;
  P       := Head1
  END;
```

b.
```
P     := Head1;
Head2 := NIL;

WHILE P <> NIL DO
  BEGIN
  New ( Q );
  Q^.Data.Key  := P^.Data.Key;
  Q^.Next      := Head2,
  Head2        := Q;
  P            := P^.Next
  END;
```

3. The following figure depicts a doubly linked list built using the generic declarations given in Section 5.2. `Current` is of type `NodePtr` and `KeyType` and `InfoType` are declared as follows:

```
KeyType   =  1..110;
InfoType  =  RECORD
               Key    :  KeyType;
               Rank   :  ( frsh, soph, midd, jun, sen )  {Age}
             END;
```

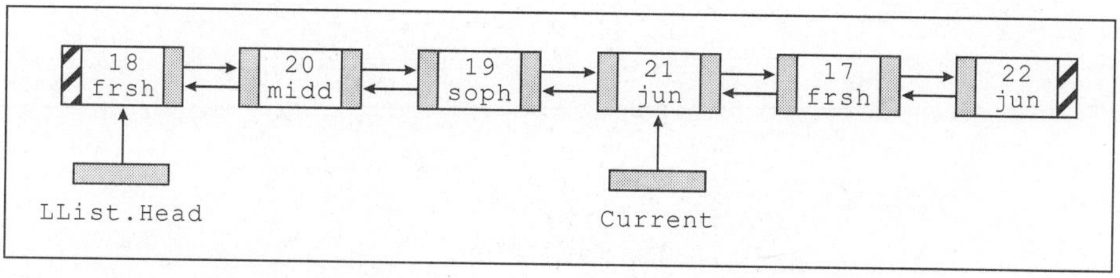

Write the output displayed when the following code segments are executed, or write "ILLEGAL" if the pointer reference is not valid. At the start of each code segment, assume that `Current` contains the address of the 21 node, as indicated in the diagram.

a.
```
Writeln ( Current^.Next^.Prev^.Data.Key );
```
b.
```
Current := LList.Head^.Prev;
Writeln ( Current^.Next^.Data.Key );
```
c.
```
Writeln ( Current^.Next^.Next^.Data.Key );
```
d.
```
Current^.Prev := LList.Head^.Next;
Current := Current^.Prev;
Writeln ( Current^.Next^.Data.Key );
```

4. The sparse matrix depicted in Figure 5.32 requires additional memory not required in its two-dimensional array counterpart, depicted in Figure 5.31. Assuming one word of memory is allocated for an integer variable and two words of memory are allocated for a pointer type variable, how large must the matrix be (in terms of the number of rows and columns—refer to Figure 5.31) so that the nonlinear linked list representation actually consumes less memory than is required by a simple two-dimensional array?

5. A linked list was built using the generic *sequential storage* declarations given in Section 5.3, with `KeyType = Char`. The following array diagram depicts the linked list after several insertions and deletions of nodes. The sole active list begins with element 2 and the free list begins with element 3; all nodes in the free list are shown with `Key` field.

	1	2	3	4	5	6	7	8	9
`Data.Key` fields:	K	G	space	H	J	L	N	space	space
`Next` fields:	6	4	8	5	1	7	0	9	0

Perform the following two operations; then redraw the array diagram appropriately and indicate the new values of `LList.Head` and `PseudoHeap.Free`.

a. Insert a new node with a `Key` field value of `M` such that it would be visited between the `L` and `N` nodes when the active list is traversed.

b. Delete the `G` node from the active list.

6. Write a function that returns a count of the number of nodes in a singly linked list, which was built using the global declarations given at the start of Section 5.1 but for which the `LList.Count` field was never updated.

7. Complete procedure `DeleteNode` such that it deletes the *N*th node in the linked list pointed to by parameter `Head`. You may assume that this list was built using the global declarations given at the start of Section 5.1, but the `LList.Count` field was never updated. A `Success` value of false should be returned if *N* is invalid (i.e., less than 1 or greater than the number of nodes in the list), and a true value should be returned otherwise. If the *N*th node can be deleted, its heapspace memory should be properly deallocated.

```
PROCEDURE DeleteNode ( VAR Head : NodePtr; N : Integer;
                       VAR Success : Boolean );
```

8. To select one soldier for a secret mission, General Josephus arranged all the soldiers in a large circle. Starting with one person, the general counted and removed every fourth person from the circle. By repeating this process, eventually all but one soldier was removed from the circle, and this person was sent on the mission.

   Assume that a circular linked list has been built using the generic declarations given at the start of Section 5.1, one node per soldier. A node's `Key` value is a soldier's name (use a nonstandard String type). Also assume that the `LList.Head` field already points to one soldier node in the list. Complete procedure `LastPerson`, which should display the name of the last person in the list. (Any node deleted from the list should be deallocated from heapspace using the standard `Dispose` procedure.)

```
PROCEDURE LastPerson ( VAR LList : LListType );
```

9. Complete the following two procedures, based on the global declarations for a dynamically allocated linked list given at the start of Section 5.1. `AppendItem` should append a node for a single `Item` to the end of the linked list pointed to by `LList.Head`. `AppendList` should append the entire linked list pointed to by `LList2.Head` to the end of the linked list pointed to by `LList.Head`. (Do not forget to update `LList.Count` in both cases.)

```
PROCEDURE AppendItem ( VAR List : LListType; VAR Item : InfoType );

PROCEDURE AppendList ( VAR LList, LList2 : LListType );
```

10. Complete procedure `CopyList`, which should make a copy of the dynamically allocated linked list pointed to by `Head`; the new list should be returned via parameter `LList`. You may assume that the list to be copied was built using the global declarations given at the start of Section 5.1 and may be empty.

```
PROCEDURE CopyList ( Head : NodePtr; VAR LList : LListType );
```

11. a. Complete procedure `MergeLLists`, which should merge the two dynamically allocated linked lists pointed to by `Head1` and `Head2` into a single linked list. `MergeLLists` should return (via parameter `Head3`) the address of the first node of this merged list. You may assume that the `Head1` and `Head2` lists were built using the global declarations given at the start of Section 5.1, with the nodes of each list ordered by *ascending integer key value* (a completed version of this procedure is given in Appendix D):

```
PROCEDURE MergeLLists ( Head1, Head2 : NodePtr; VAR Head3 : NodePtr);
```

b. Make `MergeLists` more versatile by adding the Boolean parameter `Circular` which has a true value in the call statement if both linked lists are circular. Even if circular, the nodes in both linked lists are ordered by ascending integer key value, and `Head1` and `Head2` each point to the node with the lowest key value in their respective lists. The resulting list should be circular as well.

12. Complete procedure `ReverseLinks`, which should reverse any existing single linked list; an example is depicted in the following figure. Assume that the list was built using the generic declarations given at the start of Section 5.1. `ReverseLinks` *should not call the standard* `New` *procedure.*

```
PROCEDURE ReverseLinks ( VAR LList : LListType );
```

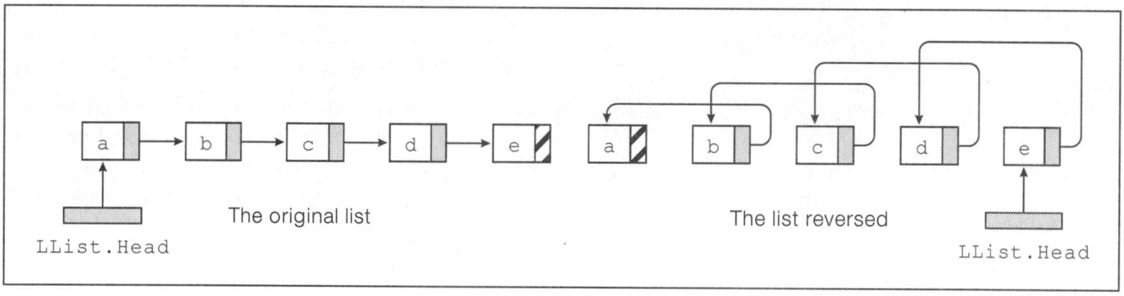

13. Complete function `MapCoords`, which operates on the sparse matrix structure described in Application 5.4. This function takes `Row` and `Column` values as arguments and evaluates to the heapspace address of the indicated element if located or else a **NIL** value if it is not located.

```
FUNCTION MapCoords ( VAR Matrix : MatrixType; Row, Column : Integer ) : NodePtr;
```

14. The elements of the standard Pascal set data type must be simple. Represent ADT set for *record elements,* each with an integer `Key` field. Use the global declarations given at the start of Section 5.1 to write the following three routines:

 a. `Member`: a Boolean function that tests for element membership
 b. `Union`: a procedure that performs a union operation on two such sets
 c. `Intersection`: a procedure that performs an intersection operation on two sets

15. a. Write all primitive routines for a dynamically allocated doubly linked list.
 b. Write the `LLInsert` and `LLDelete` primitive routines for a linked list represented using sequential storage.

16. Linked lists may be used to represent polynomials. The following declarations may be used to represent a polynomial of one variable:

```
TYPE
  NodePtr  =  ^Term;
  Term     =  RECORD
                Coefficient : Real;
                Exponent    : Integer
              END;
VAR
  Head1, Head2 : NodePtr;    {Addresses of first term nodes in
                              polynomials}
```

For example, the polynomial $4x^2 - 3x + 12$ is represented by the linked list in the following figure:

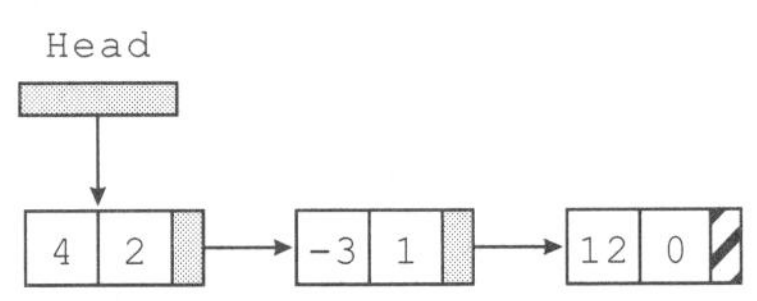

 a. Draw a linked list represent the polynomial $-5x^5 + 7x^3 + 2x^2 - 1$.
 b. Complete function `EvaluatePoly`, which should return the value of the polynomial pointed to by pointer-type argument `Head`.

```
FUNCTION EvaluatePoly ( Head : NodePtr; X : Real ) : Real;
```

 This requires your writing a function to raise a base value (`X`) to a power (`Exponent`). The designs of a recursive and nonrecursive function are discussed in Application 7.2. You may devise your own function or simply use the recursive function, `Power`, given in Appendix K.
 c. Complete function `AddSubPoly`, which either adds the two polynomials pointed to by arguments `Head1` and `Head2` if argument `Add` is true or subtracts them if `Add` is false. In either case, `AddSubPoly` creates a third linked list and should return the address of the first node in this list.

```
FUNCTION AddSubPoly ( Head1, Head2 : NodePtr; Add : Boolean ) : NodePtr;
```

d. Modify the declarations and the primitive routines to accommodate polynomials in three variables, *x*, *y*, and *z*. Typically, the terms in a multivariable polynomial are arranged *lexicographically*. That is, the terms are arranged based on decreasing values of the exponent on *x*, then terms with the same exponent on *x* are arranged based on decreasing values of the exponent on *y*, and then terms with the same exponent values on *x* and *y* are arranged based on decreasing values of the exponent on *z*. For example, the following polynomial is lexicographically correct:

$$2x^4yz + 7x^3y^3z - 4x^2y^4 - x^2y^2z^3 + x^2y^2z + 6xy^4 - y^2z^2 + y^2z - 12y$$

e. Write a procedure that prompts the user for each of the terms of a polynomial in one variable and then builds the appropriate linked list structure to represent it. Do the same for a three-variable polynomial, being careful to keep this list arranged lexicographically as you insert nodes.

17. Write an enhanced address/telephone directory program that supports the type of nonlinear structure depicted in Figure 5.27.

18. a. Add a sixth option to the electronic dictionary program of Application 5.3 to check the spelling of every word in a text file. The program should begin by prompting for the file name. The program should repeatedly read an entire line of text into a String variable and then extract and check the spelling of each word. The program should then display an error message each time it fails to find a word in the dictionary as well as displaying that word; then it should prompt the user to either enter a corrected spelling of the word or else indicate that the program should ignore the "misspelled" word. At the conclusion of the program, the file should contain all original text but with corrections. (*Hint:* use a second text file.)

b. Enhance your program further, as follows:

- Each time a "misspelled" word is found, the program should display the entire current line of text, with a caret (^) symbol positioned under the first character of the errant word. Seeing the context in which the word has been used may help the user decide whether or not to correct the spelling.
- When prompting the user for a corrected spelling, the program should allow the user to specify that this new spelling be added to the dictionary. The program also should allow the user to specify that all such misspellings of the word should (or should not) be automatically corrected when encountered in the remainder of the file.

19. Write an enhanced dictionary program that uses trie structures, as depicted in Figure 5.30.

20. Write a Game of Life program, as described in Application 3.1, but represent the colony array structures as sparse matrices, as described in Application 5.4.

21. Write a program that functions as a one-line text editor and is command-line driven (rather than menu-driven). It must support at least the following eight commands:

Command	Argument	Operation
Q		Quit the program
M	{1 to 70}	Move cursor ahead 1 to 70 characters or 1 character if no argument
M	-{1 to 70}	Move cursor back 1 to 70 characters or 1 character if no argument
F		Move cursor to first character on the line
E		Move cursor to the end of the line
I	{string}	Insert {string} before current cursor position
D	{1 to 70}	Delete 1 to 70 characters, starting with current character, or delete 1 character if no argument)
K		Delete entire line

The program should represent the line as a doubly linked list, based on the declarations given in Section 5.2, with `InfoType = Char`. The program should initialize the list as empty when the program begins and should display the entire line after performing each command, indicating the cursor position with a caret (^). You can enhance the program by adding cut and paste commands. A sample session follows (the display of the line is labeled `Text:`, and the user prompt for a command line is >):

```
Text:
     ^

>I ALine
Text: ALine
       ^

>D
Text: Line
       ^

>M 2
Text: Line
         ^
```

CHAPTER SIX

STACKS AND FIFO QUEUES

In this chapter you will learn about the linear stack and FIFO queue structured data types, whose items are arranged strictly by *time of arrival* (i.e., when items are inserted) rather than by *key value*. Each structure will be represented using both an array and a dynamically allocated linked list.

6.1 STACKS

Specifications for the ADT Stack

The **ADT stack** is a structured data type whose items form a linear list. An item is positioned in the list based solely on its time of arrival (i.e., when it is stored) according to the following last-in, first-out (**LIFO**) scheme:

> A new item is always **pushed** (added) at one end of the stack (the **stack top**), and an item already in the stack is **popped** (removed) from the same end.

Domain

The domain is items of any data type (typically records).

Fundamental Operations

1. *Initialize:* Initialize the stack as empty—i.e., containing no items [StackInit].
2. *Test for emptiness:* Determine if the stack is empty [StackEmpty].
3. *Test for fullness:* Determine if the stack is full [StackFull].
4. *Add an item:* Add an item to the top of the stack [Push].
5. *Remove an item:* Remove an item from the top of the stack [Pop].
6. *Make a copy of the top item:* Make a copy of the top item—i.e., the item to be removed next [InspectStack].

Figure 6.1 depicts an everyday example of this data structure. Cafeteria patrons can remove only a top dish and a cafeteria employee can add clean dishes only to the top as well.

Any dish *within* the stack remains buried and unretrievable until the dish above it is removed. The "younger" dishes (those added most recently) are closer to the top of the stack, whereas the "older" dishes (those added earlier) are closer to the table top. In computer programming, stack structures are useful for applications that process items in the *reverse order* in which the items are stored.

A stack may be represented using either a sequential storage (array) or linked list representation, as summarized in Figure 6.2.

Sequential Storage Representation of the ADT Stack

Special syntax is available to the programmer to specify that a particular operation is to be performed upon a variable of standard Pascal data type. For example, square brackets ([ ]) are used to access an array element or to specify the elements of a set, the period (.) is used to access a record field,

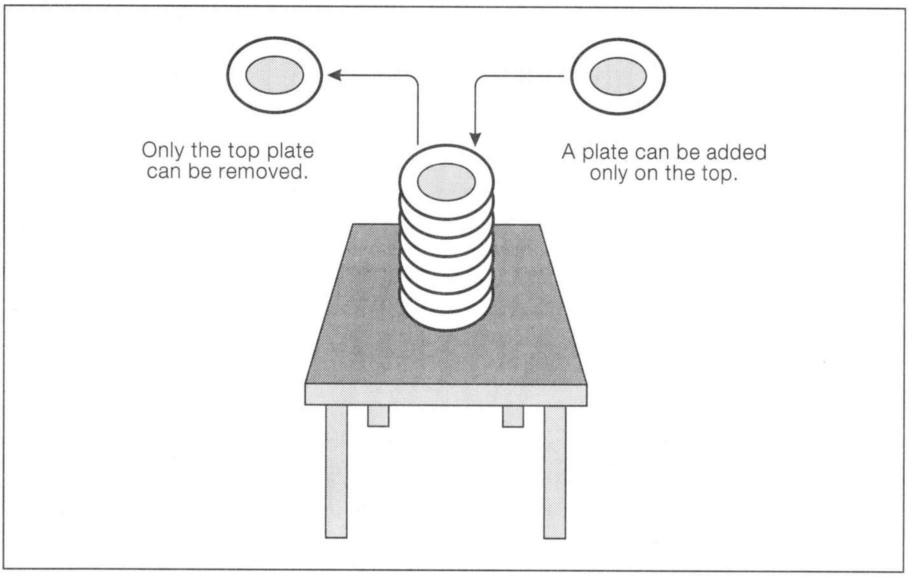

FIGURE 6.1 Cafeteria Dishes as an Example of a Stack Structure

and an asterisk (*) is used to multiply two numeric quantities or to obtain the intersection of two set data structures. There is no standard Pascal data type called *stack,* however. It is strictly a *programmer-defined* data type, as are all remaining data structures described in this textbook. Stacks are programmer-defined because the programmer must explicitly declare the structure (using one or more standard types) and must explicitly write procedures and functions to perform the operations. The programmer generally has the choice of using either sequential storage (array) or a linked list (yet another programmer-defined structure) to represent a programmer-defined structure. This reiterates an important point about the representation of *any* programmer-defined ADT:

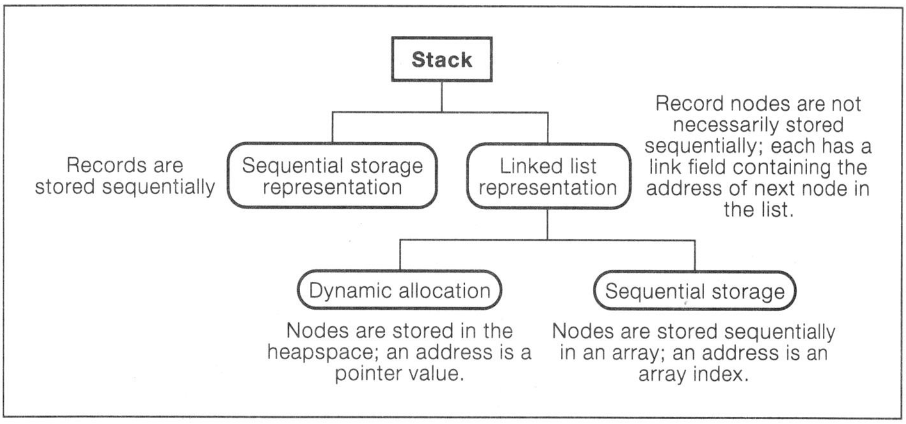

FIGURE 6.2 Different Stack Representations

> An array or linked list represents a particular programmer-defined ADT, such as a stack, when—and *only* when—its programmer-defined primitive routines manipulate the array or linked list *in a manner commensurate with the ADT specifications* of that ADT.

A compiler detects only syntax errors—it will not issue an error message if you include program instructions that insert an item to the *middle* of your stack structure rather than at the top. Upon such a violation of the ADT stack push operation, however, the structure ceases to be a true stack. (Of course, the coding for some applications can be simplified by using a structure as one data type and then later using that same structure as a different type!)

Let us start with a simple example: a stack of up to 16 character items, to be contained in an array of 16 elements (indexed from 1 to 16). An integer variable, `Top`, will contain the array index of the top stack item. The way in which the `Top` variable should be initialized depends on how we plan to update `Top` with each push (add) and pop (remove) operation. We will adopt the following scheme:

- To push an item, increment `Top` and assign the new item to this array element; this way, `Top` will always hold the index of the "youngest" item.
- To pop an item, copy the contents of the array element whose index is contained in `Top` and then decrement `Top`.

To initialize the stack as empty, we should therefore set `Top` to zero, as indicated in Figure 6.3 (in the figure, `T` represents the `Top` variable and is positioned under the index value it contains). The stack is *empty* when `Top` has the value zero and, looking ahead, the stack is *full* if `Top` has the value 16, the maximum number of items that may be contained in this array.

Figure 6.4 depicts the stack as its character items are pushed and popped. In this and future figures depicting stacks, the items are pushed in alphabetic order to help you differentiate the older and younger items, although such an ordering is not a requirement of stack structures. Also, when an item is popped and is therefore no longer in the stack (i.e., no longer accessible using valid stack operations), it is not shown in the diagram although the data are physically still in the array.

A set of generic declarations for a stack structure using sequential storage follows (note that `Stack.Top` also serves as a count of the items currently on the stack).

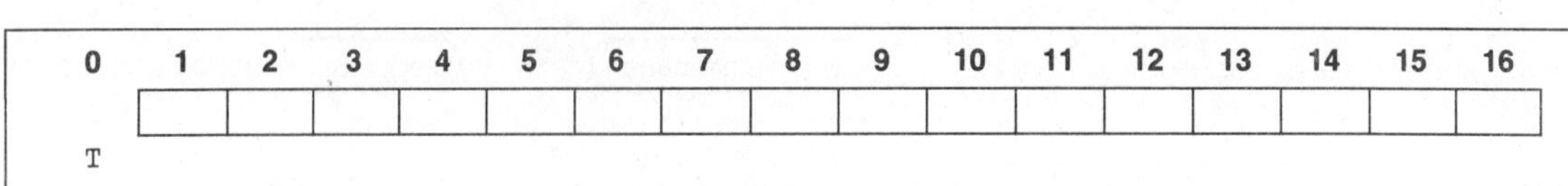

FIGURE 6.3 Sample Stack After Being Initialized as Empty

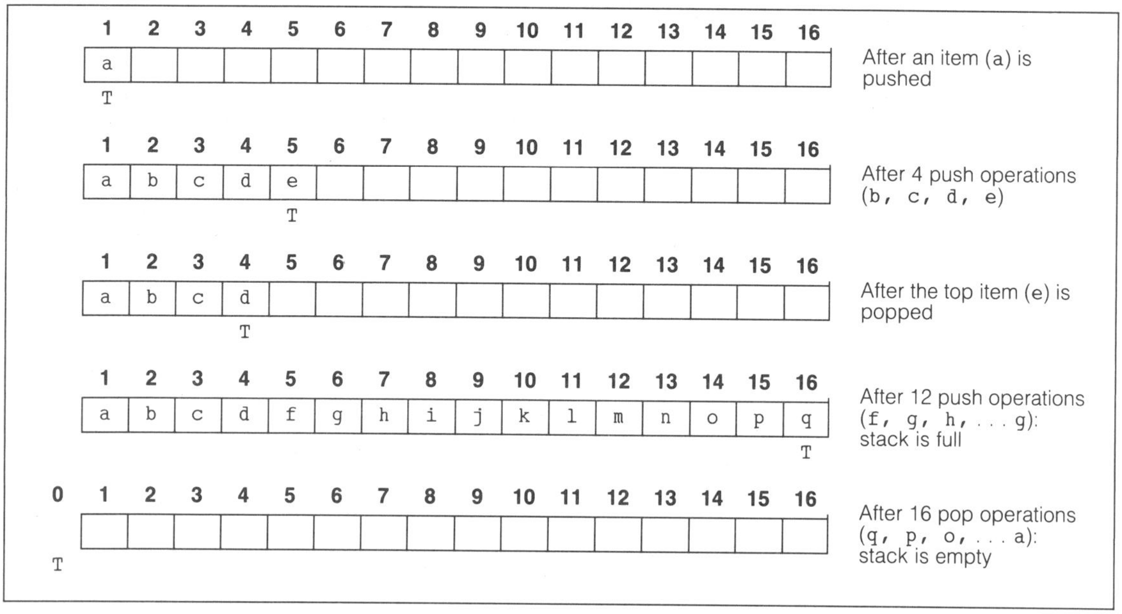

FIGURE 6.4 The Sample Stack After Several Push and Pop Operations

```
CONST
  MaxSItems  =  ??;                 {Maximum allowable number of items}

TYPE
  SInfoType  =  ??;                 {Application-dependent}

  StackType  =  RECORD
                  Items : ARRAY [ 1..MaxSItems ] OF SInfoType;
                  Top   : Integer    {Index of item just pushed}
                END;
VAR
  Stack  :  StackType;
```

> *At this time, examine the sequential storage representation of the following routines in Appendix E.*

```
PROCEDURE StackInit ( VAR Stack : StackType );

FUNCTION StackEmpty ( VAR Stack : StackType ) : Boolean;

FUNCTION StackFull ( VAR Stack : StackType ) : Boolean;

PROCEDURE Push ( VAR Stack : StackType; VAR Data : SInfoType );

PROCEDURE Pop ( VAR Stack : StackType;  VAR Data : SInfoType );

PROCEDURE InspectStack ( VAR Stack : StackType; VAR Data : SInfoType );
```

Linked List Representation of the ADT Stack

A sequential storage representation of a stack is appropriate if the maximum stack size is known at compile-time and is not prohibitively large and if the waste of memory stemming from any unused array elements does not pose a problem. The linked list representation overcomes all these limitations but does require that the program manage the creation, access, and disposal of heapspace records to hold the items.

We will now represent the stack using a linked list, which is itself represented using dynamic allocation. In the linked list representation, `Top` is a pointer variable (instead of an integer variable) and is initialized to **`NIL`** to indicate an empty stack. Accordingly, the `StackEmpty` function will consider the stack to be empty if `Top` has a **`NIL`** value. A set of generic stack declarations follows:

```
TYPE
  SInfoType  =  ??;                       {Application dependent}

  StackPtr   =  ^StackNode;
  StackNode  =  RECORD
                  Data : SInfoType;
                  Next : StackPtr
                END;

  StackType  =  RECORD
                  Top   : StackPtr;       {Address of item just pushed}
                  Count : Integer         {Number of items in the stack}
                END;

VAR
  Stack   :  StackType;
```

The implementations of the push and pop operations are slightly more complex for the linked list representation than for the sequential storage representation. Figure 6.5 shows two different "stacks" of character items

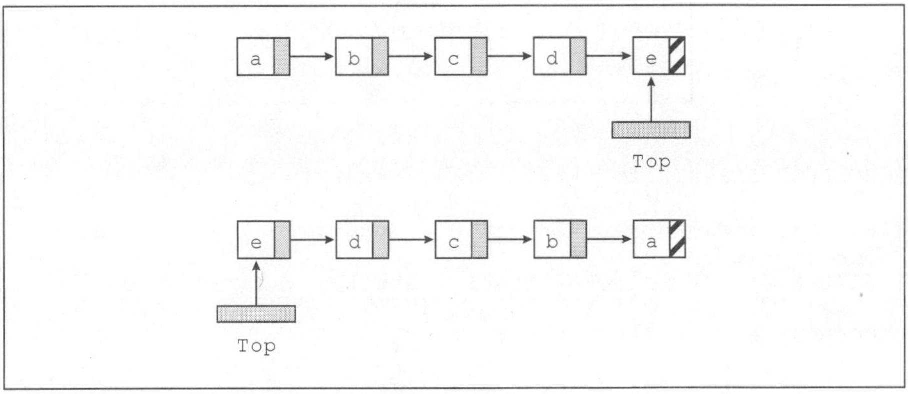

FIGURE 6.5 Two "Stacks" After Five Push Operations, Each Using a Different Push Strategy

after five push operations are performed, with each stack having been previously empty. (Again, the items have been pushed in alphabetic order *only* to reflect how long each has been in the stack—a, then b, then c, etc.)

To determine which of the two push strategies reflected in the figure is more useful, we must begin by considering two special cases:

- *Pushing onto an empty stack* is a special case because the link field of the new node must be assigned the value **NIL**.
- *Popping the last node in the stack* is a special case because the Top pointer variable must be assigned the value **NIL**.

Next, we must consider the mechanics of the algorithms themselves. A pseudocode algorithm for the pop operation follows:

```
ALGORITHM Pop ( VAR Stack : StackType; VAR Data : SInfoType );

BEGIN
Assign to parameter Data the data portion of the Top node;
IF the top node is the last node in the stack THEN
  Assign to variable Top the value NIL
ELSE
  Assign to variable Top the address in the top node's link field;
Dispose of the previously top node;
Decrement Stack.Count
END;
```

With the stack depicted by the top diagram of Figure 6.5, there is no way to perform a pop operation and update Top so that it points to the previous node (i.e., to the 'd' node). The *second stack* in the figure therefore employs the *correct* push strategy. The pseudocode algorithm for a push algorithm is

```
ALGORITHM Push ( VAR Stack : StackType; VAR Data : SInfoType );

BEGIN
Allocate heapspace memory for a StackNode type variable;
Store Data in the data portion of this new node;
IF this is the first node to be stored in an empty stack THEN
  Assign to its link field the value NIL
ELSE
  Assign to its link field the address of the top node;
Assign to variable Top the address of this new node;
Increment Stack.Count
END;
```

At this time, examine the linked list representation of the following routines in Appendix E.

```
PROCEDURE StackInit ( VAR Stack : StackType );

FUNCTION StackEmpty ( VAR Stack : StackType ) : Boolean;

PROCEDURE Push ( VAR Stack : StackType; VAR Data : SInfoType );

PROCEDURE Pop ( VAR Stack : StackType; VAR Data : SInfoType );

PROCEDURE InspectStack ( VAR Stack : StackType; VAR Data : SInfoType );
```

It is the responsibility of the calling routine to call `Pop` only if the stack is not empty rather than testing for emptiness within the `Pop` procedure:

```
IF NOT StackEmpty ( Stack ) THEN
  Pop ( Stack, Data )
ELSE
  ??
```

This way the appropriate *application-dependent* action may be taken in the calling routine if the stack is empty.

APPLICATION 6.1 Reversing a String

As a simple example of how stacks save information in reverse order, we will examine a program named `ReverseTheString`. This program displays a series of characters in the reverse order in which the characters are read from the keyboard.

Recall from the discussion of text files in Section 4.1 that all characters entered at the keyboard are stored in a special collection of memory cells known as the *input buffer,* from which they are accessible via the standard `Read` or `Readln` procedures. This buffer is maintained by the operating system with a special pointer indicating which character was just read from the keyboard. Because the input buffer is regarded by the operating system as a text file, a program may call the `Eoln` function to determine if this pointer is currently pointing to the special end-of-line indicator that is stored if the user presses the RETURN, or ENTER, key.

The code for program `ReverseTheString` follows:

```
PROGRAM ReverseTheString ( INPUT, OUTPUT );

{Insert global stack declarations here, with    SInfoType = Char;}
---------------------------------------------------------------------
{The following routines are defined in Appendix E}

PROCEDURE StackInit ( VAR Stack : StackType );

FUNCTION StackEmpty ( VAR Stack : StackType ) : Boolean;

PROCEDURE Push ( VAR Stack : StackType; VAR Data : SInfoType );

PROCEDURE Pop ( VAR Stack : StackType;  VAR Data : SInfoType );
---------------------------------------------------------------------
```

```
PROCEDURE Reverse;

VAR
  Stack : StackType;
  Ch    : Char;

BEGIN
StackInit ( Stack );
WHILE NOT Eoln ( INPUT ) DO
  BEGIN
  Read ( Ch );
  Push ( Stack, Ch )
  END;
Writeln;

WHILE NOT StackEmpty ( Stack ) DO
  BEGIN
  Pop ( Stack, Ch );
  Write ( Ch )
  END;
Writeln
END;

{***  Main  Routine  ***}

BEGIN
Writeln ( 'Enter a string of characters:' );
Reverse
END.
```

It is not clear from looking at either the code for procedure `Reverse` or at the main routine exactly which representation of the stack—sequential storage or linked list—is being used. `Reverse` is said to be **implementation independent,** which is a reflection of the routine's *versatility,* one of the characteristics of a well-written program (or program segment) discussed in Chapter 1. Implementation independence is desirable because the author of `Reverse` did not have to be concerned about issues related to the representation of the underlying data structure (the stack). High-level routines are free to become implementation independent when the primitive routines are written as generically as possible. Of course, a program's global declarations and the primitive routines themselves must reflect a particular representation, but these can be modified easily without having to modify the calling routines. In Application 7.2, we examine a recursive version of `ReverseTheString`.

APPLICATION 6.2 An Infix Expression Calculator Program

Expressions involving two operands and one operator may be formatted as either a prefix, infix, or postfix expression, depending on the relative positions of the operator and operands:

Expression form	Syntax			Example
Prefix notation	{**operator**}	{operand}	{operand}	− 3 5
Infix notation	{operand}	{**operator**}	{operand}	3 − 5
Postfix notation	{operand}	{operand}	{**operator**}	3 5 −

In this application, we design a program that serves as a simple calculator for evaluating *infix expressions*—i.e., expressions in a form we are used to in everyday life (in Application 7.8 we design a prefix expression calculator).

The evaluation of infix expressions poses an interesting challenge because of either or both of the following:

- *Operator precedence via parentheses.* An infix expression may have another parenthetic expression nested within it, and this parenthetic expression must be evaluated before evaluating the entire expression in which it is nested.
- *Natural precedence of operators.* In the absence of parentheses explicitly dictating the order of operations, multiplication and division (*high-order operations*) are performed before addition and subtraction (*low-order operations*). Expressions involving operators of the same precedence and without parentheses are evaluated from left to right.

Because some expressions must be evaluated before others, we will use stacks in our program to save operand values, intermediate arithmetic results, and operator symbols.

Our program will prompt the user to enter an infix expression, and the program then will evaluate that expression and display the result. The entire expression will be read into a nonstandard String variable and **parsed**; i.e., each character is examined. As with the development of any program, we will begin with a simple degree of functionality and will omit error checking on the user input. The program can always be enhanced at a later time to perform error checking and other operations. We will therefore assume that the user adheres to the following rules:

- The entire expression entered must be a syntactically correct infix expression.
- An operand may be a number or another infix expression.
- A numeric string operand is comprised of the character digits 0 through 9 with no embedded spaces. The converted integer value of the string must not exceed **MAXINT**.
- Only four operator symbols are allowed: +, −, *, /. Unary minus is not allowed—e.g., −5 must be entered as 0−5.
- Parentheses are allowed, including nested parentheses, but they must be balanced.
- Spaces are allowed except within a numeric string operand.

The program will prompt for an expression, which it reads into a String variable. The program will then call a function named `Evaluate`, which must parse and evaluate each string expression character by character until the end of the string, returning the value of the entire expression. `Evaluate` must manipulate the stacks to obtain a single real result for the entire infix expression entered by the user, and this final value is returned to the program's main routine. The user will input the character `Q` instead of an infix expression to terminate the program.

Because some operations in an infix expression must be postponed due to the natural precedence of the operators or the precedence imposed by parentheses, our program must maintain two stacks to save intermediate information:

- `Operands` stack. Each stack item is a single operand value or the numerical result of an expression, both of which will be stored as real numbers.
- `Operators` stack. Each stack item is a single operator character or parenthesis character.

We will develop the complete algorithm for `Evaluate` by examining a series of five expressions of increasing complexity, enhancing `Evaluate` appropriately each time.

Stage 1. Simple expression involving no operator precedence

Sample expression: 4 + 3

Since all four of the valid operators (+, −, *, /) are binary operators, two operands are needed before the indicated operation may be performed. In our sample expression, the 4 and the + characters must therefore be preserved in the `Operators` stack until the second operand, 3, is encountered. Each time a string of digits is parsed, `Evaluate` must convert it to a single integer value and then stored as a real number in the `Operands` stack. Figure 6.6 depicts the string-parsing and stack activity in the evaluation of this expression. In the figure, the vertical arrows point to the current string variable index—i.e., the character in the expression to be evaluated next.

The result is pushed onto the `Operands` stack because, looking ahead to more complex expressions, the value of one expression may itself be the operand of *another* expression. After any correctly written infix expression has been completely parsed and evaluated, the `Operators` stack will be empty and the `Operands` stack will contain a single value—the final result. Looking ahead a bit more, since the "operation" steps—popping the operand stack twice, popping the operator stack, performing the indicated operation, and then pushing the result onto the operand stack—will be done

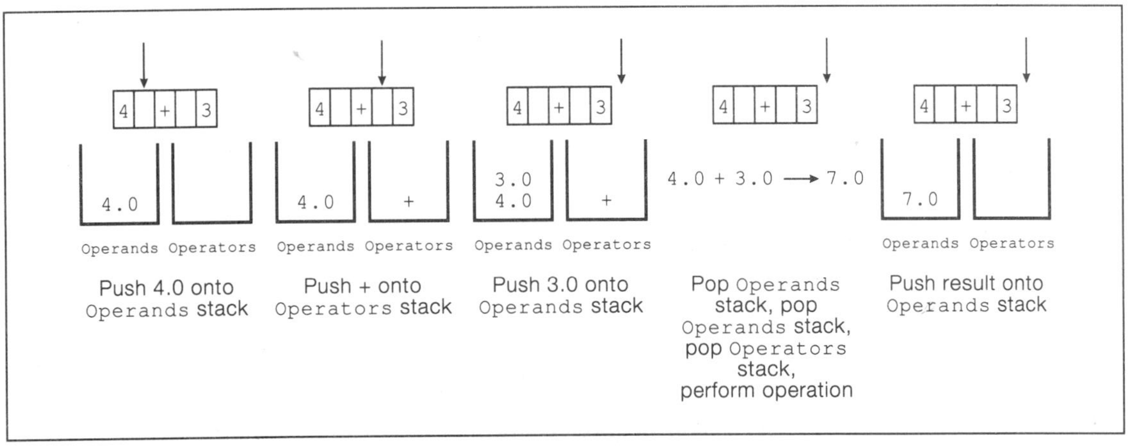

FIGURE 6.6 String-Parsing and Stack Activity in the Evaluation of 4 + 3

frequently, the program should include a procedure called `Operate` to perform these operations. A pseudocode algorithm for `Operate` follows:

```
ALGORITHM Operate ( VAR OperatorStack; VAR OperandStack );

VAR
  Operator : Char;
  Result, Operand1, Operand2 : Real;

BEGIN
Pop ( OperandStack, Operand2 );   {Pop 2nd operand}
Pop ( OperandStack, Operand1 );   {Pop 1st operand}
Pop ( OperatorStack, Operator );  {Pop operator character}
Perform indicated operation on Operand1 and Operand2, storing result in Result;
Push ( OperandStack, Result )     {Push Result onto OperandStack}
END;
```

Our simple evaluation algorithm thus far may be summarized as follows:

```
ALGORITHM Evaluate : Real;

BEGIN
REPEAT
  Obtain next character;
  CASE character OF
    '0'..'9'             :  BEGIN
                            Convert entire digit-string to a number;
                            Push number onto the Operands stack;
                            IF Operator stack is not empty THEN
                              Operate
                            END;

    '+', '-', '*', '/'   :  Push the operator onto the Operators stack
  END
UNTIL no more characters to evaluate;

Pop ( OperandStack, Value );
Evaluate := Value
END;
```

Hand-test a simple variation of our sample expression (4 + 3 − 2) to convince yourself that it is evaluated properly by our current version of `Evaluate`.

Stage 2. Simple operator precedence (no parenthesized expressions)

Sample expression: 4 + 3 * 2

In this sample expression, multiplication takes precedence over addition. Had the expression been 4 * 3 + 2 instead (or even 4 * 3 / 2), the first operation (multiplication) would have been performed immediately, since, in the absence of parentheses, the expression is evaluated from left to right (multiplication and division are both higher-order operators); i.e., there is no reason to postpone the multiplication operation. Our evaluation algorithm, as it is written thus far, will perform the addition as soon as the 3 is parsed; therefore, we must modify the algorithm so that it calls `Operate` immediately after a digit-string operand is encountered only if a high-order operator is the top operator on the `Operators` stack.

The cumulative strategy may be summarized as follows:

```
ALGORITHM Evaluate : Real;

BEGIN
REPEAT
  Obtain next character;
  CASE character OF
    '0'..'9'          :  BEGIN
                         Convert entire digit-string to a single integer;
                         Push the number onto Operands stack;
                         IF Operators stack is not empty THEN
                           IF top operator IN [ '*', '/' ] THEN
                             Operate
                         END;

    '+', '-', '*', '/'  :  Push operator onto Operators stack
  END
UNTIL no more characters to evaluate;

WHILE NOT EmptyStack ( OperatorStack ) DO
  Operate;
Pop ( Operands stack, Item );
Evaluate := Item
END;
```

Figure 6.7 depicts the string-parsing and stack activity for the current sample expression.

Notice that because the addition is postponed, the + operator is left in the `Operators` stack after the multiplication is performed. By adding the **WHILE** loop after the **REPEAT** loop, `Operate` is called repeatedly until the `Operators` stack is empty (i.e., until all stack operators have been used), as reflected in the steps of Figure 6.7.

Unfortunately, storing the low-order operators on the `Operators` stack, thereby giving the high-order operators precedence, creates a new problem. Consider the expression 5 − 3 − 2. The 5 is pushed, the first − is pushed, and, because the top operator is not high order, the 3 is pushed rather than the expression 5 − 3 being evaluated. The second − is then pushed and the 2 is pushed. The end of the expression has been reached, so our new loop calls `Operate` until the `Operators` stack is empty, resulting in an incorrect final value of 4.0.

We can correct this problem by calling `Operate` *before* pushing the second low-order operator. The following code segment replaces the single `'+','-','*','/'` case in the previous **CASE** statement:

```
'+', '-'  :  BEGIN
             IF Operators stack is NOT empty THEN
               Operate;
             Push operator onto the Operators stack
             END;

'*', '/'  :  Push operator onto Operators stack
END
```

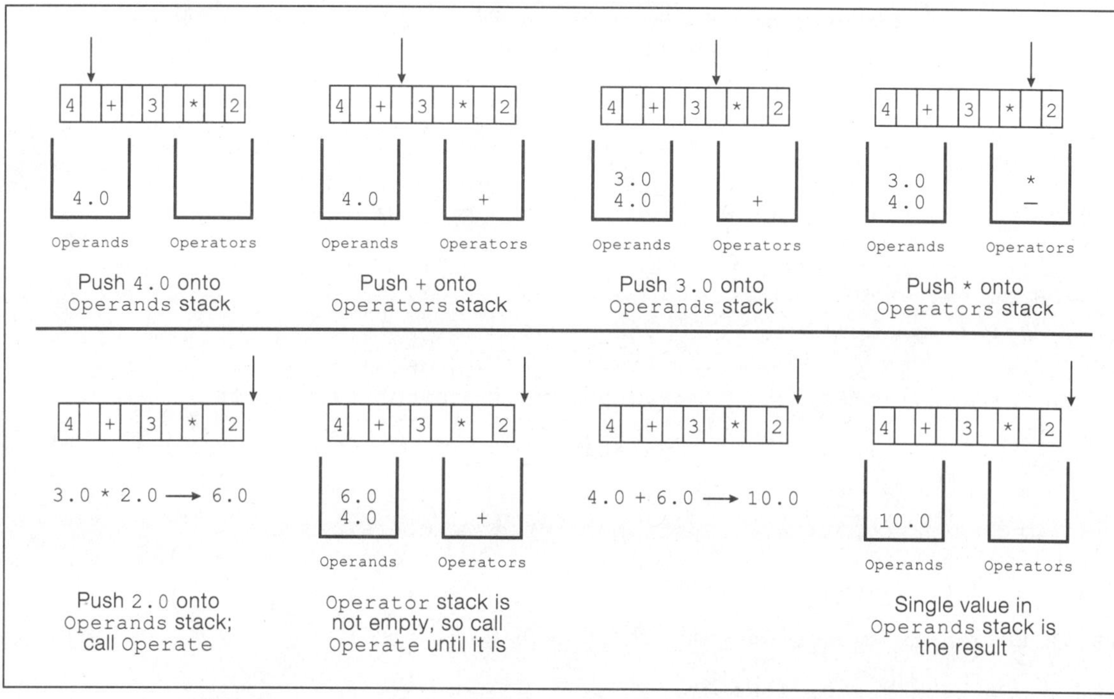

FIGURE 6.7 String-Parsing and Stack Activity in the Evaluation of 4 + 3 * 2

Stage 3. Simple operator precedence imposed by parenthesized expression

Sample expressions: 4 * (3 + 2)
4 * (3 * (3 + 2))

In the first sample expression of this stage of development, the parentheses supersede the natural precedence of operators, forcing the addition to be performed *before* the multiplication. The entire parenthetic expression is really just the second operand of the multiplication operator and must therefore be evaluated prior to multiplication. An expression delimited by parentheses is a self-contained expression, so that while it is being evaluated, any part of the overall expression is temporarily ignored.

As we saw in the last stage, it is possible to have low-order operators left on the `Operators` stack after an entire expression is parsed and evaluated. The Stage 2 remedy was to call `Operate` until the `Operators` stack is empty. If our algorithm encounters and pushes the (symbol onto the `Operators` stack, then when the next) symbol is encountered, marking the end of the parenthesized expression, our algorithm can call `Operate` until the top `Operators` stack operator is a (symbol; this character is then popped off. Notice how our treatment of the parenthetic expression is congruent to our treatment of the entire expression.

The following code can be added to the **CASE** statement to handle parenthesized expressions:

```
')'                   BEGIN
                      IF the Operators stack is NOT empty THEN
                        WHILE top operator <> '(' DO
                          Operate;
                      Pop operators stack to get rid of '('
                      END;

'*', '/', '('    :    Push ( Stacks, OperatorKind, Dummy, Ch );
```

Draw stack diagrams to hand-test the two sample expressions as well as the following expressions: 4 + (3 + 2) * 5 and 1 + (4 + 3) / (5 − 2).

Stage 4. Operator precedence within parenthetic expressions

Sample expression: (4 +3 * 2) / (5 * (6 − 1))

This sample expression involves operator precedence within parenthetic expressions in two ways: the natural precedence of high-order over low-order operators *plus* the precedence imposed by parentheses. These situations pose no new problems, however, and our algorithm developed thus far is sufficient. Hand-test this and similar expressions to convince yourself that this is true.

Stage 5. Operator precedence among and within parenthetic expressions

Sample expression: 4 + (7 / (2 + 3) * 8) / 6

This expression represents every kind of operator precedence situation. Draw stack diagrams to see that our algorithm will indeed evaluate this expression correctly. Think of other more complicated expressions to test.

Having developed that part of function `Evaluate`'s design dealing with the manipulation of the stacks, we can now finish the design by attending to the details of parsing the input string. `Evaluate` can increment an integer variable `Index` as it parses the string variable accessing characters. The main loop within `Evaluate` can therefore terminate when the value of `Index` exceeds the length of the string. `Evaluate` can call the `SeekChars` procedure (defined in Appendix K) to return in character variable `Ch`, the next nonblank character in the string, and increment `Index` one position beyond it. If `Ch` contains a character digit, marking the beginning of a "number," it will call the `StringToInteger` function (also defined in Appendix K), which parses further and converts the concatenation of the `Ch` and following characters to a single integer value.

Figure 6.8 illustrates the logic of function `Evaluate` using a **flowchart.** Unlike pseudocode, which offers a linear source code summary, a flowchart offers a two-dimensional, diagrammatic summary similar to the flow diagrams frequently used in this textbook to define Pascal syntax. The complete `InfixCalculator` program follows the flowchart. Again, this simple version assumes that the user will enter only a syntactally valid infix expression according to the rules enumerated at the start of this section. Figure 6.9 contains a module tree diagram for the calculator program.

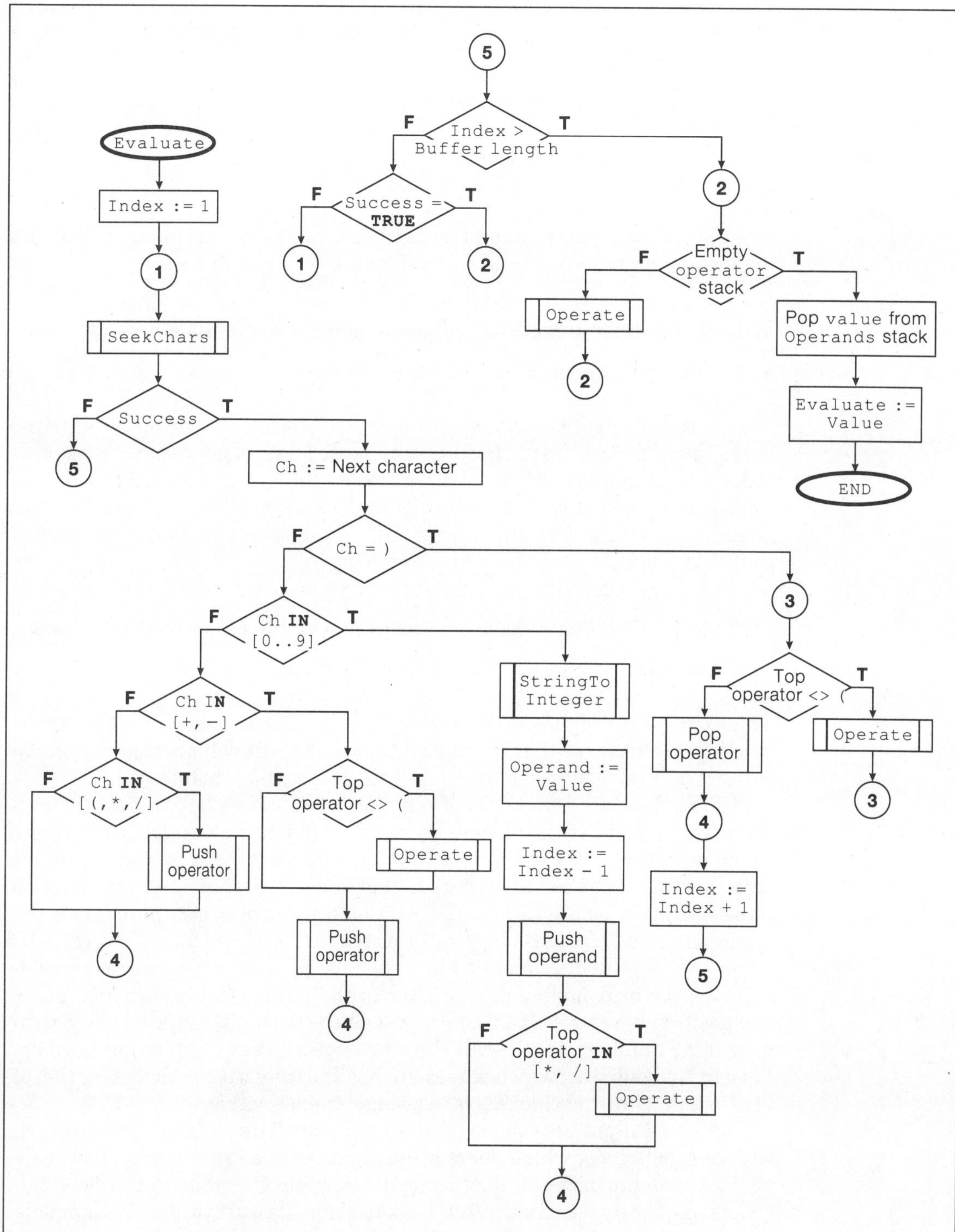

FIGURE 6.8 Flow Chart for Function `Evaluate`

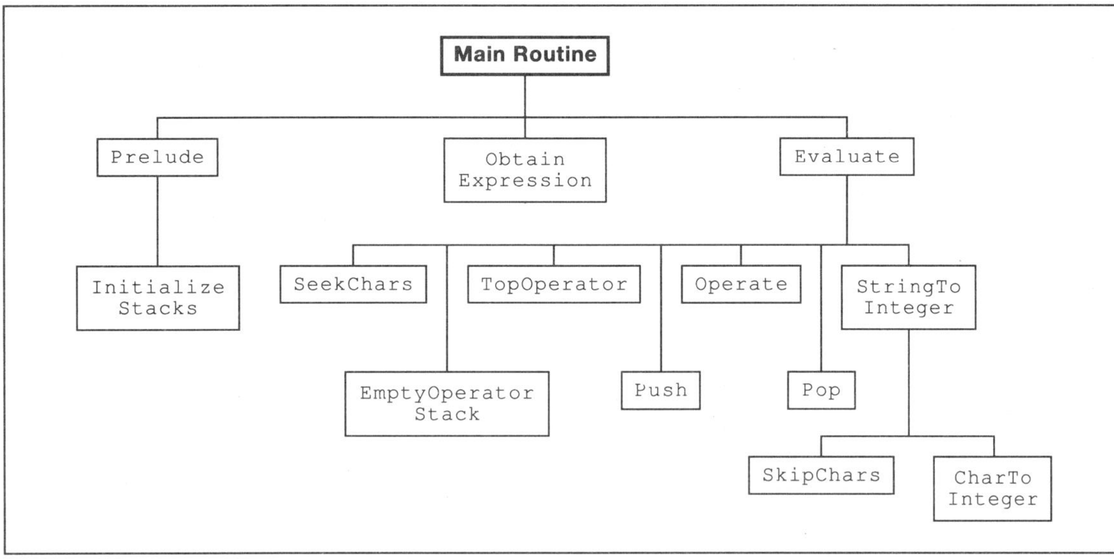

FIGURE 6.9 Module Tree Diagram for the `InfixCalculator` Program

```
{Program:  Infix Calculator
 Function: Evaluates a syntactically-correct prefix expression entered interactively
           after the prompt. Valid input:
           Operators:  +,-,*,/
           Operands:   Unsigned integer constants
           Other:      spaces,(,); Q terminates program}

PROGRAM InfixCalculator ( INPUT, OUTPUT );

CONST
  MaxChars    =  80;
  HalfMax     =  40;

TYPE
  StackType   =  RECORD
                   Operands      :  ARRAY [ 1..HalfMax ] OF Real;
                   Operators     :  ARRAY [ 1..HalfMax ] OF Char;
                   OperandTop,
                   OperatorTop   :  Integer
                 END;

  StackKind   =  ( OperandKind, OperatorKind );
  BuffType    =  String [ MaxChars ] ;
  CharSet     =  SET OF Char;

VAR
  Stacks  :  StackType;
  Buffer  :  BuffType;
  AnotherExpression  :  Boolean;
```

```
{The following procedures are defined in Appendix K}

PROCEDURE SeekChars ( VAR Buffer : BuffType; VAR Index : Integer;
                      SeekSet : CharSet;  VAR Success : Boolean );
```

```
PROCEDURE SkipChars ( VAR Buffer : BuffType; VAR Index : Integer;
                      SkipSet : CharSet;  VAR Success : Boolean );

FUNCTION CharToInteger ( Ch : Char ) : Integer;

PROCEDURE StringToInteger ( VAR Buffer : BuffType; VAR Index, Value : Integer;
                            VAR Success : Boolean );
```

```
PROCEDURE InitializeStacks ( VAR Stacks : StackType );

BEGIN
Stacks.OperatorTop  := 0;
Stacks.OperandTop   := 0
END;
```

```
FUNCTION EmptyOperatorStack ( Stacks : StackType ) : Boolean;

BEGIN
EmptyOperatorStack := Stacks.OperatorTop = 0
END;
```

```
{Push a real operand onto the Stacks.Operands stack or a char operator
onto the Stacks.Operators stack, depending on the value of WhichStack}

PROCEDURE Push ( VAR Stacks : StackType; WhichStack : StackKind;
                 Operand : Real; Operator : Char );
BEGIN
WITH Stacks DO
  IF WhichStack = OperatorKind THEN
    BEGIN
    OperatorTop := OperatorTop + 1;           {Increment stack top}
    Operators [ OperatorTop ] := Operator     {Store operator character}
    END
  ELSE
    BEGIN
    OperandTop := OperandTop + 1;             {Increment stack top}
    Operands [ OperandTop ] := Operand        {Store operand character}
    END
END;
```

```
{Pop a real operand from the Stacks.Operands stack or a char operator from the
Stacks.Operators stack, depending on the value of WhichStack}

PROCEDURE Pop ( VAR Stacks : StackType; WhichStack : StackKind;
                VAR Operand : Real; VAR Operator : Char );

BEGIN
WITH Stacks DO
  IF WhichStack = OperatorKind THEN
    BEGIN
    Operator := Operators [ OperatorTop ];   {Obtain top operator}
    OperatorTop  := OperatorTop - 1          {Decrement top}
    END
  ELSE
    BEGIN
    Operand := Operands [ OperandTop ];      {Obtain top operand}
    OperandTop := OperandTop - 1             {Decrement top}
    END
END;
```

```
FUNCTION TopOperator ( Stacks : StackType ) : Char;

BEGIN
WITH Stacks DO
  TopOperator := Operators [ OperatorTop ]               {Obtain top operator}
END;
```

```
PROCEDURE Operate ( VAR Stacks : StackType );

VAR
  Operator              :  Char;
  Result, Dummy,
  Operand1, Operand2    :  Real;

BEGIN
Pop ( Stacks, OperandKind, Operand2, Operator );         {Pop 2nd operand}
Pop ( Stacks, OperandKind, Operand1, Operator );         {Pop 1st operand}
Pop ( Stacks, OperatorKind, Dummy,   Operator );         {Pop top operator}

CASE Operator OF                                          {Perform operation}
  '+'  :  Result  := Operand1  +  Operand2;
  '-'  :  Result  := Operand1  -  Operand2;
  '*'  :  Result  := Operand1  *  Operand2;
  '/'  :  Result  := Operand1  /  Operand2
END;

Push ( Stacks, OperandKind, Result, Operator )            {Push result}
END;
```

```
PROCEDURE Prelude ( VAR Stacks : StackType );

BEGIN
Writeln ( '***  Simple  Infix  Expression  Evaluator  ***' );
Writeln;
Writeln ( 'Legal operands:  Unsigned integers between 0 and ', MAXINT );
Writeln ( 'Legal operators:  +, -, *, /' );
Writeln;
InitializeStacks ( Stacks )                            {Initialize stacks as empty}
END;
```

```
PROCEDURE ObtainExpression ( VAR Buffer : BuffType;
                             VAR AnotherExpression : Boolean );

BEGIN
Writeln;
Writeln ( 'Enter a syntactically-correct infix expression or Q to quit:' );
Write ( '  ' );
Readln ( Buffer );
AnotherExpression := NOT ( Buffer [ 1 ] IN [ 'Q', 'q' ] )
END;
```

```
FUNCTION Evaluate ( VAR Stacks : StackType; VAR Buffer : BuffType ) : Real;

VAR
  Index, Value      :  Integer;
  Success           :  Boolean;
  Ch, Dummy2        :  Char;
  Operand, Dummy1   :  Real;

BEGIN
Index := 1;
REPEAT
  SeekChars( Buffer, Index, [ '0'..'9', '+', '-', '*', '/', '(', ')' ], Success );
  IF Success THEN             {Needed in case of trailing blanks}
    BEGIN
    Ch := Buffer [ Index ];   {Obtain next character in expression}
    CASE Ch OF
      ')'             :  BEGIN
                         IF NOT EmptyOperatorStack ( Stacks ) THEN
                           WHILE TopOperator ( Stacks ) <> '(' DO
                             Operate ( Stacks );
                         Pop ( Stacks, OperatorKind, Dummy1, Ch )        {Pop '(' }
                         END;

        '0'..'9'      :  BEGIN
                         StringToInteger ( Buffer, Index, Value, Success  );
                         Index    := Index - 1;       {StringToInteger incremented Index}
                         Operand  := Value;
                         Push ( Stacks, OperandKind, Operand, Dummy2 );
                         IF NOT EmptyOperatorStack ( Stacks ) THEN
                           IF TopOperator ( Stacks ) IN [ '*', '/' ] THEN
                             Operate ( Stacks )
                         END;

      '+', '-'        :  BEGIN
                         IF NOT EmptyOperatorStack ( Stacks ) THEN
                           IF TopOperator ( Stacks ) <> '('  THEN
                             Operate ( Stacks );
                         Push ( Stacks, OperatorKind, Dummy1, Ch )
                         END;

      '*', '/', '('   :  Push ( Stacks, OperatorKind, Dummy1, Ch )

    END;

    Index := Index + 1
    END

UNTIL ( Index > Length ( Buffer )) OR NOT Success;

WHILE NOT EmptyOperatorStack ( Stacks ) DO
  Operate ( Stacks );
Pop ( Stacks, OperandKind, Value, Dummy2 );
Evaluate := Value
END;
```

```
{***  Main  Routine  ***}

BEGIN
Prelude ( Stacks );                                          {Initialize stacks}
REPEAT
  ObtainExpression ( Buffer, AnotherExpression );            {Read expression}
  IF AnotherExpression THEN
    Writeln ( '  =  ', Evaluate ( Stacks, Buffer ):9:7 ) {Evaluate expression}
UNTIL NOT AnotherExpression
END.
```

6.2 FIFO QUEUES

Specifications for the ADT FIFO Queue

The **ADT FIFO** (first-in, first-out) **queue** is a structured data type whose items form a linear list. Each item is positioned in the list based solely on its time of arrival (i.e., when it is stored) according to the following **FIFO** scheme:

> A new item is always **enqueued** (added) at one end, which is called the **queue back,** and an item already in the list is **served** (removed) from the opposite end, which is called the **queue front.**

Domain

The domain is items (usually records).

Fundamental Operations

1. *Initialize:* Initialize the queue as empty, i.e., containing no items [`QInit`].
2. *Test for emptiness:* Determine if the queue is empty [`QEmpty`].
3. *Test for fullness:* Determine if the queue is full [`QFull`].
4. *Enqueue (add) an item:* Add an item to the back of the queue [`Enqueue`].
5. *Serve (remove) an item:* Remove the item at the front of the queue [`Serve`].
6. *Make a copy:* Make a copy of the item to be served next [`QInspect`].

A common example of a FIFO queue is a line of people waiting to buy tickets at a movie theater. The person at the front of the line is processed by the ticket seller and then leaves the line. A new arrival must join the line at the rear and wait until each person already in the line is processed before leaving the line. (In Europe, such waiting lines are, in fact, called queues.) A FIFO queue therefore preserves the order in which data items are added, and the item that has been in the queue the longest is always the item that is removed next.

A FIFO queue is distinguished from another data structure referred to as a **priority queue**, for which each item is assigned a priority value; the stored item with highest priority is removed next. A common example of a priority queue is a hospital emergency ward waiting room, in which patients are seen according to the severity of their trauma or illness and not merely by how long they have been waiting. Both FIFO queues and priority queues are useful for computer simulations and for applications in which information is acquired faster than it can be processed, thereby requiring that certain information be temporarily saved in its original order.

Note: For the remainder of the textbook, the simple term *queue* implies a FIFO queue; priority queues are presented in Section 8.3.

A FIFO queue may be represented using sequential storage (i.e., a simple array) or a linked list, so Figure 6.2 applies to FIFO queues as well as to stacks. We begin with an examination of the sequential storage representation.

Sequential Storage Representation of the ADT FIFO Queue

A set of generic declarations for the sequential storage representation of a queue follows:

```
CONST
  MaxQItems  =  ??;                        {Application dependent}

TYPE
  QInfoType  =  ??;                        {Application dependent}
  QPtr       =  Integer;
  QueueType  =  RECORD
                  Items  : ARRAY [ 1..MaxQItems ] OF QInfoType;
                  Front,                   {Item to be served next}
                  Back   : QPtr;           {Item just enqueued}
                  Count  : Integer         {Number of items in queue}
                END;

VAR
  Queue : QueueType;
```

As with our discussion of stacks, we begin with a simple example: a queue of up to 16 character data items, to be contained in an array indexed from 1 to 16 as shown in Figure 6.10. How `Back` and `Front` should be initialized depends on how we plan to update `Front` and `Back` with each enqueue and serve operation. We will adopt the following queue initialization scheme:

- To *enqueue* an item, increment `Back` and assign the new item to this element; this way, `Back` will always hold the index of the youngest (last added) item in the queue.
- To *serve* an item, copy the contents of the element whose index is contained in `Front` and then increment `Front`; this way, `Front` will always hold the index of the oldest (next to be removed) item in the queue.

To initialize the queue as empty, we will therefore set `Back` to zero and `Front` to one, as indicated in Figure 6.10. (In the figure, `B` represents the

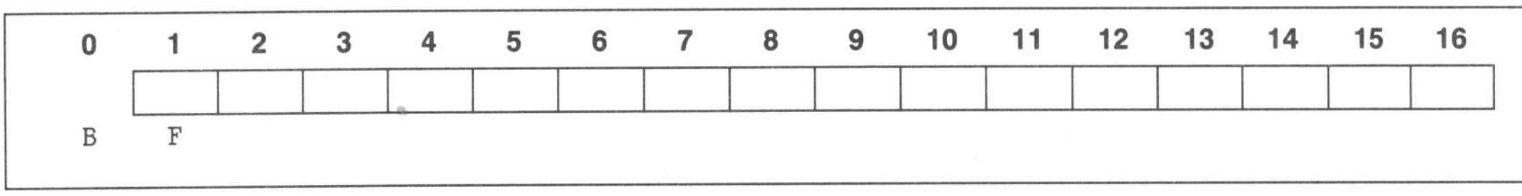

FIGURE 6.10 Sample Empty Queue

`Back` variable and `F` represents the `Front` variable, positioned under the index value each contains.)

Since the queue is empty, perhaps we can use the relative values of `Front` and `Back` as a test for queue emptiness:

```
QEmpty := Front > Back;       {TENTATIVE test for queue emptiness}

QFull  := Back = MaxQItems;   {TENTATIVE test for queue fullness}
```

Shortly, we will determine if these tests are always valid.

Figure 6.11 shows the queue as character items are enqueued and served. As with the stack diagram in Figure 6.4, in Figure 6.11 the character values are added in alphabetic order only to help you differentiate the "older" and "younger" items; items in queues need not be ordered this way. Also, when an item is served and is therefore no longer in the queue, it will not be shown in the diagram, although the data for that item are actually still in the array.

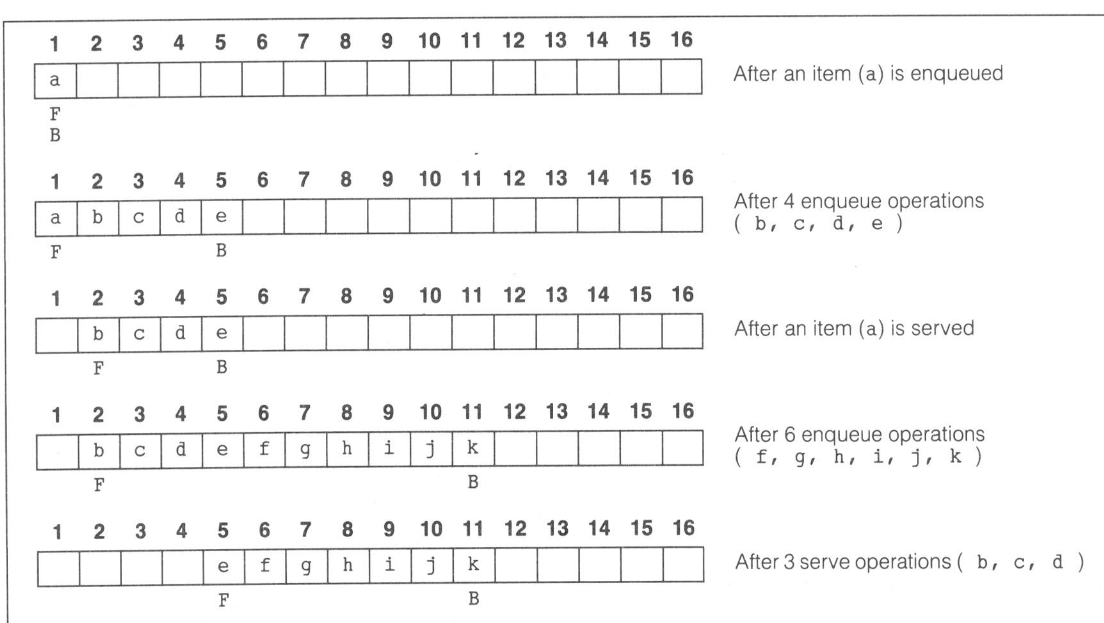

FIGURE 6.11 The Sample Queue After Several Enqueue and Serve Operations

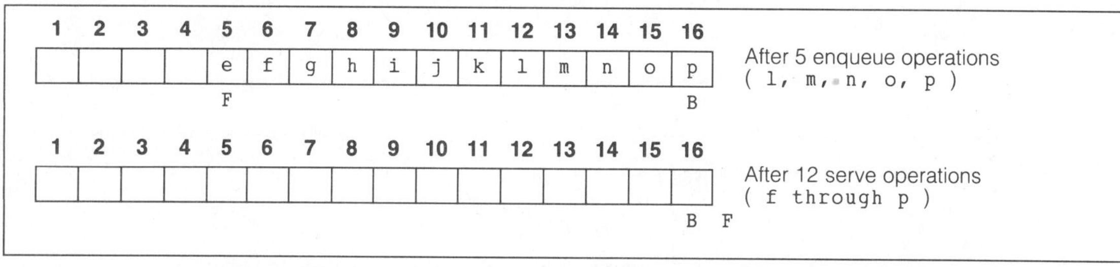

FIGURE 6.12 The Sample Queue After Several More Enqueue and Serve Operations

A strange phenomenon is happening—after several enqueue and serve operations, the contents of our queue are slowly drifting to the right within the queue! Figure 6.12 shows the queue after another five items are enqueued and again after all items are served.

The queue is now empty and our test for emptiness (`Front > Back`) holds. At the same time, however, the queue is technically full as well, since `Back` = `MaxQItems` (16) and no more items can be enqueued. Our queue is now quite useless, although all 16 array elements are unused! We could modify our enqueue and serve strategies in two different ways to make use of all available elements:

1. Whenever `Back` equals `MaxQItems`, the enqueue procedure can shift all items in the queue leftward (i.e., toward the low index end of the array) by `(Front - 1)` elements and assign `Front` the value 1. Referring to the top diagram of Figure 6.12, this means that items `e` through `p` would be shifted leftward four elements, leaving `e` in element 1 and `p` in element 11.
2. When either `Back` or `Front` are incremented off the high end of the array, **queue wraparound** to the front of the array should occur.

The first solution wastes execution time because the `Enqueue` routine must always perform a test to determine if `Back` equals `MaxQItems`. Also, whenever `Back` equals `MaxQItems` and `Front` is greater than 1, the `Enqueue` routine must shift all items to the low-index end of the array and shifting data within an array is relatively time consuming.

We will adopt the wraparound solution instead and will perform a simple arithmetic operation to update the `Back` or `Front` value. Wraparound queues are commonly referred to as **ring buffers,** or simply *rings.* Figure 6.13 depicts the queue as being (conceptually) circular.

This wraparound effect for `Back` is accomplished by the following assignment statements:

```
Back  := ( Back + 1 ) MOD MaxQItems;

Front := ( Front + 1 ) MOD MaxQItems;
```

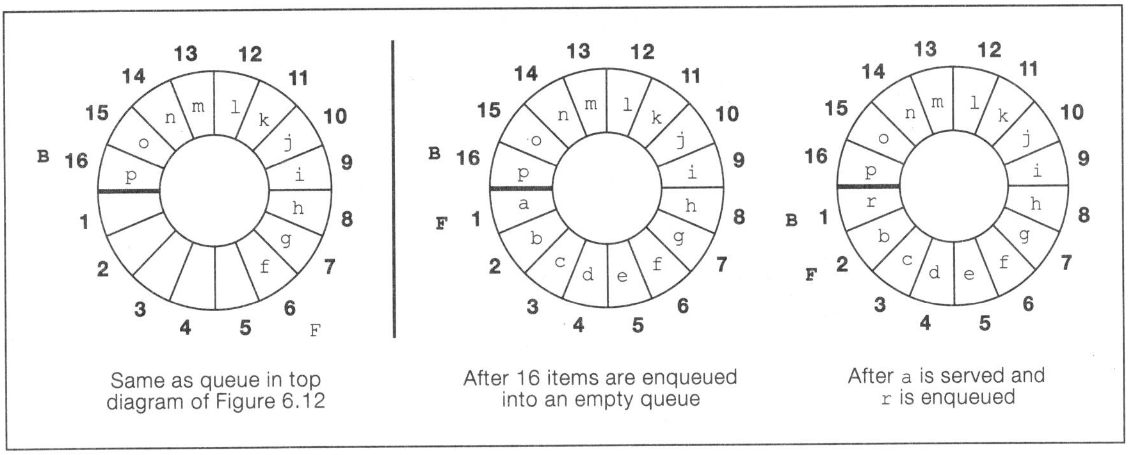

FIGURE 6.13 The Sample Queue Depicted as Rings

Now consider how to initialize `Back` and `Front` when initializing the queue as empty. Can we initialize `Back` to `MaxQItems` and `Front` to 1? Try enqueuing and serving a few items to convince yourself that this will indeed work.

Wrapping around makes optimal use of the array space but, in doing so, creates a new problem: Our previous (tentative) tests for emptiness and fullness are no longer valid. Look at the leftmost queue in Figure 6.13. Here, the expression `Front > Back` evaluates to a true value, yet the queue is not empty. Our tentative test for fullness (`Back = MaxQItems`) is valid in the case of the center queue but not the rightmost queue. Since the queue is truly full when `Back` lags behind `Front` by one element (since both "move counterclockwise"), would the test `Front – Back = 1` always evaluate to a true value if the queue is full? This works for the case of the right queue in Figure 6.13 but not for the center queue in that figure. Try devising new tests to determine queue emptiness and fullness before looking at the versions in Appendix F. (*Hint:* As in the case of the socks puzzle presented at the start of Chapter 1 in Puzzle 2, this is a situation for which the simplest solution is the best solution!)

At this time, examine the sequential storage representation of the following routines in Appendix E.

```
PROCEDURE QInit ( VAR Queue : QueueType );

FUNCTION QEmpty ( VAR Queue : QueueType ) : Boolean;

FUNCTION QFull ( VAR Queue : QueueType ) : Boolean;

PROCEDURE Enqueue ( VAR Queue : QueueType; VAR Data : QInfoType );

PROCEDURE Serve ( VAR Queue : QueueType; VAR Data : QInfoType );

PROCEDURE InspectQ ( Queue : QueueType; VAR Item : QInfoType );
```

Linked List Representation of the ADT FIFO Queue

A sequential storage representation is satisfactory if the maximum queue size is known at compile-time and is not prohibitively large and if the waste of memory stemming from any unused array elements does not pose a problem. The linked list representation overcomes all these limitations but does require that the program manage the creation, access, and disposal of records to hold the items. In this section we represent the linked list itself using dynamic allocation.

In the linked list representation, we could use two pointer variables named `Back` and `Front` rather than two integer variables and could initialize them both to **NIL** to indicate that the queue is empty. By making the linked list *circular,* however, we find that a single pointer variable—`Back`—is the only pointer variable we really need. Figure 6.14 depicts our simple queue of character items after five enqueue operations. Again, the character items are enqueued in alphabetic order *only* to reflect how long each has been in the queue; this is not a necessity with queues. If the list is circular, the program can always refer to the `Front` item using the link field of the node pointed to by `Back`. Figure 6.15 depicts the queue of Figure 6.15 twice: after an item is served and then after an item is enqueued.

The strategies for enqueuing and serving are slightly more complex for the linked list representation than for the array representation because of two special cases that arise if a list head node is not used:

- *Enqueueing into an empty queue* is a special case because the link field of the new node must point to *itself* rather than pointing to the node at the front of the queue; also, the former `Back` node must then point to the new `Back` node.
- *Serving the last remaining node in the queue* is a special case because the `Back` pointer must be assigned the value **NIL**, since there is nothing left to serve.

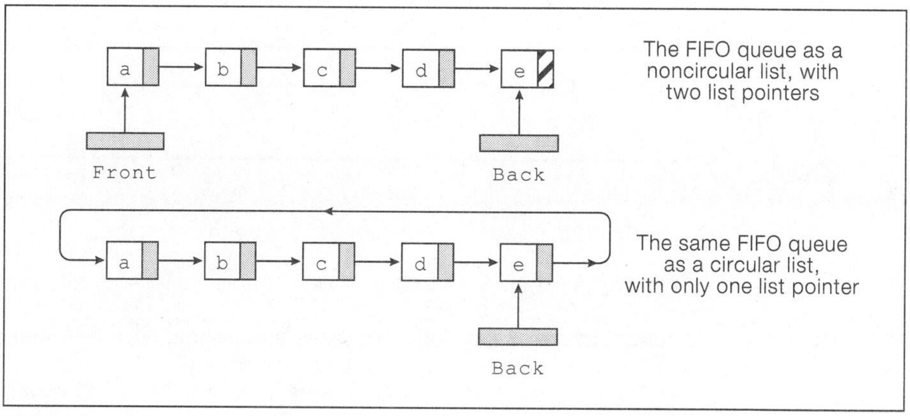

FIGURE 6.14 A Sample Queue Represented as a Noncircular and Circular Linked List

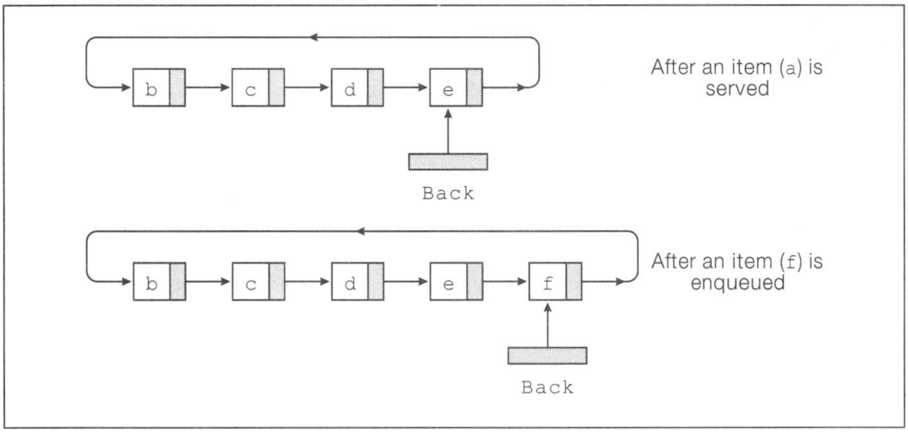

FIGURE 6.15 The Sample Queue After a Serve Operation and After an Enqueue Operation

The pseudocode algorithms for the linked list representation of the enqueue and serve operations follow.

```
{Both algorithms are applicable for a linked list without a header node}

ALGORITHM Enqueue ( VAR Queue : QueueType;  VAR Data : QInfoType );

BEGIN
Allocate heapspace for a new queue node;
Store Data in the data portion of this new node;
IF queue was empty THEN
  Assign to the new node's link field the address of itself
ELSE
  BEGIN
  Point the new node's link field to the front node (i.e., to Queue.Back^.Next);
  Point the former back node to the new back node
  END;
Queue.Back := address of this new back node;
Increment Queue.Count
END;
```

```
ALGORITHM Serve ( VAR Queue : QueueType;  VAR Data : QInfoType );

BEGIN
Assign to parameter Data the data portion of the front node;
IF front node is the only node in the queue THEN
  Queue.Back the value NIL
ELSE
  Assign to Queue.Back^.Next the address of node pointed to by the front node;
Dispose of the former front node;
Decrement Queue.Count
END;
```

Test these algorithms by drawing diagrams on paper and enqueuing several items, starting with an empty queue.

A set of generic declarations for the linked list representation of a queue follows:

```
TYPE
  QInfoType  =  ??;                        {Application dependent}

  QPtr       =  ^QNode;
  QNode      =  RECORD
                  Data  : QInfoType;       {Data portion of node}
                  Next  : QPtr             {Points to next node in the queue}
                END;

  QueueType  =  RECORD
                  Back  : QPtr;            {Points to the item just enqueued}
                  Count : Integer          {Number of items in the queue}
                END;

VAR
  Queue : QueueType;
```

At this time, examine the linked list representation of the following routines in Appendix E.

```
PROCEDURE QInit ( VAR Queue : QueueType );

FUNCTION QEmpty ( VAR Queue : QueueType ) : Boolean;

PROCEDURE Enqueue ( VAR Queue : QueueType; VAR Data : QInfoType );

PROCEDURE Serve ( VAR Queue : QueueType; VAR Data : QInfoType );

PROCEDURE InspectQ ( VAR Queue : QueueType; VAR Item : QInfoType );

PROCEDURE DeallocateQ ( VAR Queue : QueueType );
```

SUMMARY

ADT stack is a structured data type whose items form a linear list. An item is positioned in the list based solely on its time of arrival (i.e., when it is stored) according to the following last-in, first-out (LIFO) scheme: A new item is always pushed (added) at one end (the top) of the stack; an item already in the stack is popped (removed) from the same end. The domain of a stack includes items (typically records). Fundamental operations include initializing the stack as empty, testing the stack for emptiness or fullness, pushing and popping items, and making a copy of the top item.

In computer programming, stack structures are useful for applications that need to process items in the reverse order in which the items are stored. ADT stack may be represented in a program using either the sequential storage (simple array) or linked list representations. Both representations are programmer-defined; there is no native stack data type in standard Pascal.

ADT FIFO queue is a structured data type whose items form a linear list. Each item is positioned in the list based solely on its time of arrival (i.e., when it is stored) according to following first-in, first-out (FIFO) scheme: A new item is always enqueued (added) at one end (the back) of the queue and an item already in the queue is served from the opposite end (the front). The domain of a FIFO queue includes items (typically records). Fundamental operations include initializing the queue as empty, testing the queue for emptiness or fullness, enqueuing and serving items, and making a copy of the next item to be served.

In computer programming, queue structures are useful for applications that need to process items in the same order in which the items are stored. As with ADT stack, ADT queue may be represented in a program using either the sequential storage (simple array) or linked list representations. Both representations are programmer-defined; there is no native queue data type in standard Pascal. With the sequential storage representation, the contents may drift rightward within the queue when items are enqueued or served unless the algorithms for these operations are coded with a wraparound approach that regards the queue as a ring buffer.

KEY TERMS

ADT FIFO queue
ADT Stack
Enqueue
FIFO
Flowchart
Implementation independent
LIFO
Parse
Pop
Priority queue
Push
Queue back
Queue front
Queue wraparound
Ring or ring buffer
Serve
Stack top

REVIEW QUESTIONS

1. Describe ADT stack, including the domain, fundamental operations, and structure. When represented using Pascal, is the stack data type standard or programmer-defined? Give several everyday examples of a stack.
2. Distinguish between LIFO and FIFO. Which data structure is associated with each?
3. Distinguish between the time-of-arrival and key-value storage-retrieval methods. Which method is employed with a stack? With a FIFO queue? With a linked list?
4. Which structure—a stack or a queue—is best suited for storing and retrieving items that are to be processed (a) in order and (b) in reverse order of their storage?
5. Describe ADT FIFO queue, including the domain, fundamental operations, and structure. When represented using Pascal, is the queue data type standard or programmer-defined? Describe several everyday examples of a queue.
6. Distinguish between FIFO queue and priority queue.
7. Describe the *rightward drift* phenomenon with FIFO queues. With which representation (linked list or array) does it occur? How can this phenomenon be avoided and why does it not occur with stacks?
8. Describe how a queue can be represented when a back variable but no front variable is used.
9. How should the top variable for a stack be initialized when the stack is initialized as empty? How should the front and back variables for a queue be initialized when the queue is initialized as empty (assume both variables are used in both representations)?

EXERCISES

1. Assume that you have an empty FIFO queue and an empty stack, both capable of holding items of integer data type. Refer to the following eight operations:

(a) Add value 13	(e) Add value 9
(b) Add value 10	(f) Remove a value
(c) Remove a value	(g) Remove a value
(d) Add value 5	(h) Remove a value

   Perform these eight operations by hand on the empty *queue;* each time you remove a value, write it. Then, perform these eight operations by hand on the empty *stack;* again, each time you remove a value, write it.

2. You and your date race to the local movie theater for the last showing of your favorite movie only to find a long line of patrons waiting to purchase tickets.

   a. Before you join the line, are you hoping that the line behaves like a stack or a FIFO queue?
   b. Once you join the line, are you hoping that the line behaves like a stack or a queue?

3. Complete function `BalancedParentheses`, which parses the infix expression represented within `Buffer` (a String type variable) and returns a true value if the expression contains either no parentheses or else the proper nesting of left and right parentheses and a false value otherwise. For example, evaluation of the expression 5+(3 *(X + 2)−7) should return a true value, whereas evaluation of the expression 5+(3 *(4 + X) − 7)) / (Y / 2) should return a false value. `BalancedParentheses` should use a stack in its evaluation of the Buffer expression.

```
FUNCTION BalancedParentheses ( VAR Buffer : BuffType ) : Boolean;
```

4. Enhance the calculator program of Application 6.2 with the following features:

   a. The ability to detect any of the following syntax or logic errors and display an appropriate error message:
      - An illegal character
      - Unbalanced parentheses
      - Adjacent operators or operands
      - Division by zero
      - Arithmetic overflow and underflow

   b. The ability to allow the user to specify the precision of the next result displayed.
   c. The ability to properly evaluate expressions containing unary plus and minus operators—e.g., +5 − 7 and −(−3 * 6).
   d. The ability to evaluate expressions involving the multiplication of parenthetic expressions without operators, such as 3 + 7 (5 − 8 (−4)).
   e. The ability to evaluate assignment statements of the form

```
{identifier} = {infix expression}
```

   in which the identifier is any string of 1 to 4 characters, starting with a letter. Expressions containing identifiers. The program must maintain a *symbol table,* such as an array of records, which stores each identifier and its associated current value. When the program encounters an identifier within an expression, it must look up that identifier's current value to complete evaluation of that expression.

The program must also be robust enough to deal with invalid expressions that contain one or more identifiers which have not been previously assigned a value via a previous assignment statement.

5. A *double stack* is often used in computer hardware and software systems. For example, heapspace memory is typically managed as two stacks—a stack of operating system-managed, dynamically allocated activation records and a stack of program-managed, dynamically allocated variables—which start at opposite ends of heapspace and grow toward each other. This is depicted in both the generic memory layout diagram of Figure 2.4 and below (here, the diagram depicts six activation records and eight dynamically allocated variables, created by a user program):

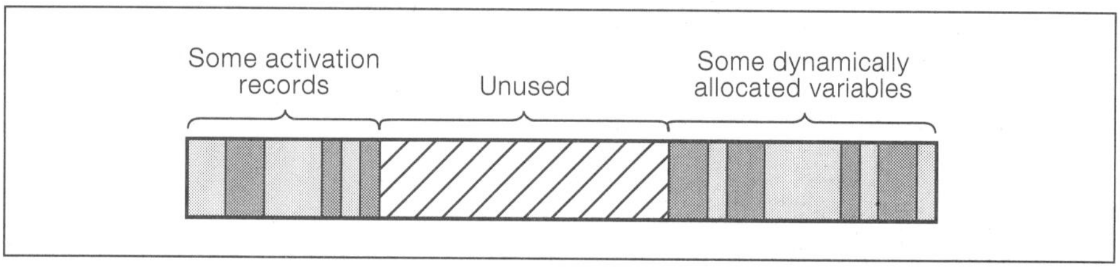

Complete the following global declarations to represent a double stack within a single array:

```
TYPE

  DStackType  =

VAR
  DoubleStack : DStackType;
  WhichStack  : Integer;
```

Rewrite the routines `InitStack`, `StackEmpty`, `StackFull`, `Push`, `Pop`, and `InspectStack` to accommodate a `DoubleStack` variable. Each routine should include a formal parameter named `WhichStack`, whose passed-in value indicates upon which stack the routine should operate.

6. A simple one-line text editor is being developed. The line, to be represented in a data structure named `Line`, may contain up to 80 characters, and # and \ are special characters: # effectively erases every preceding character in the line, whereas \ effectively erases the previous character.

   a. Give a set of global declarations for an appropriate `Line` data structure.

   b. Complete procedures `LoadLine` and `DisplayLine`.

```
PROCEDURE LoadLine ( VAR Line : ?? );

PROCEDURE DisplayLine ( VAR Line : ?? );
```

`LoadLine` should initialize the `Line` structure as empty, prompt the user to enter a string of characters at the keyboard, then read these characters and add them to the `Line` structure, in the exact order they were entered (including # and \ characters). `DisplayLine` should display the current contents of the `Line` structure, following the rules for the \ and # characters. For example, if the string `'abcd\e\\f\g'` is read and stored by `LoadLine`, then `'abg'` is displayed by `DisplayLine`; if `'a\bc\def#gh\ij'` is stored, `'gij'` is displayed.

7. Customers at Captain Nemo's Seafood Emporium (Application 4.1) are seated as they arrive; if no tables are available, customers must wait in line. You have been asked to computerize this wait-list process.

   a. Write global declarations for (i) a structure to contain values indicating the availability of each table, and (ii) a structure to contain names of persons waiting for a table (one 1–20 character name per party). Tables are numbered 1 to 28, are all the same size, and each day there is an unpredictable number of customers.
   b. Assume that the following two procedures already exist:

```
{If a table is available, Avail returns true, Number holds the table number}
PROCEDURE FindAvailTable ( VAR Avail : Boolean; VAR Number : Integer );

{Marks table Number as available if Avail is true or unavailable if Avail is fal
PROCEDURE UpdateTableStatus ( Avail : Boolean; Number : Integer );
```

   Write procedure `SeatCustomer` to handle either of the following situations:

   (i) *A customer just arrived.* If another customer is waiting for a table, prompt for a name to be added to the waiting list; otherwise, call `FindAvailTable` to look for an available table.
   (ii) *A table just became available.* Call `UpdateTableStatus`. If another customer is waiting for a table, the next party is removed from the waiting list and gets the table (display the appropriate name).

8. A *deque* (pronounced "deck") is a FIFO queue in which an item may be added or removed from either end—i.e., a double-ended queue. Further, a deque may be designated as *output-restricted* (an item may be removed only from one end) or *input-restricted* (an item may be added only at one end). Of course, a deque that is both output-restricted and input-restricted is simply a FIFO queue if the restrictions apply to opposite ends or a stack if the restrictions apply to the same end.

   a. Write versions of the `Enqueue` and `Serve` primitives for both the sequential storage and linked list representations of an output-restricted deque, an input-restricted deque, and a nonrestricted deque.
   b. Write Boolean function `APalindrome`, which prompts for a word or phrase and then uses a deque structure to determine if the word or phrase is a *palindrome* (a palindrome is a word or phrase that is spelled the same backwards—e.g., radar and Madam, I'm Adam). Your function should ignore spaces and grammatical characters, such as commas and apostrophes, and should be case-insensitive.

9. The Grand Funk Railroad Yard has sections of track called sidings, which allow the yardmaster to arrange and connect a series of railroad cars into a particular linear configuration. Shipping contracts inform the yardmaster of how a complete train leaving the yard on the track running out of the yard (the OutTrack) is supposed to be configured. The two sidings available for rearranging cars are depicted on the next page.

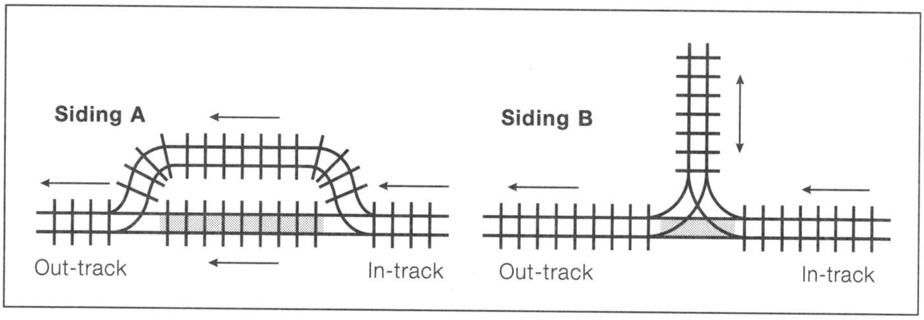

Cars on the in-track are numbered 1, 2, 3, and so on and can move only in the directions indicated by the arrows in the figure. Because Siding A and Siding B are physically located at opposite ends of the railroad yard, either *but not both* may be used to configure a particular train. Also, the sections that are shaded in the figure may be used only to move cars directly from the in-track to the out-track and may not be used to store cars in the configuration process.

Write a program named `ConfigureCars` to simulate the process of moving cars from the in-track to attain a desired configuration on the Out-Track, testing each siding. Assume that there is no limit on the number of cars that may be temporarily stored on a siding. An example of user input and program output follows:

```
Enter desired train configuration, leaving a space
between car numbers:

> 3 1 2

>>> Testing Siding-A <<<

1. Move car 1 from In-Track to Siding-A
2. Move car 2 from In-Track to Siding-A
3. Move car 3 from In-Track to Out-Track
4. Move car 1 from Siding-A to Out-Track
5. Move car 2 from Siding-A to Out-Track

Configuration can be achieved in 5 moves using Siding-A

>>> Testing Siding-B <<<

1. Move car 1 from In-Track to Siding-A
2. Move car 2 from In-Track to Siding-A
3. Move car 3 from In-Track to Out-Track

Configuration CANNOT be achieved using Siding-B
```

10. Although the Marlboro Airport is small, it is fairly busy. With its single runway, a plane may take off or land at random times, but no two planes may use the runway simultaneously. This means that some planes must hover above the airport, waiting in line to land, while other planes wait in line on the ground to take off; a plane waiting to land has precedence in its use of the runway over a plane waiting to take off.

Write a program that performs a *time-driven simulation* of the control tower management of the runway. Two waiting lines should be represented as queues, in which each airplane waiting to land or take off is represented by a seven-character identification code (your design). Assuming that it takes 5 minutes for an airplane to clear the runway after using it either to land or to take off, your program should examine the fronts of the queues every 5 minutes to determine if an airplane should be allowed to leave its waiting line. When your program is not managing take-offs and landings, it can process requests for take-offs and landings (i.e., adding airplanes to the waiting lines) either interactively or by using a random-number generator (a particular range of random numbers can signal the request for a landing or a take-off or indicate "no request").

CHAPTER SEVEN

RECURSION

In this chapter, you will learn about a powerful and elegant technique for solving problems and defining sets of objects. Recursive definitions and algorithms always involve self-reference, producing a looping efect. As a problem-solving strategy, recursion is best suited for problems that can be divided into a series of smaller, similar subproblems, each of which is solved in terms of the previous solution. Recursion is therefore fully commensurate with the principles of top-down, modular program design and often provides a shorter and more natural solution than its nonrecursive counterpart.

7.1 PRELIMINARIES

Recursive Definitions and Algorithms

As a prerequisite to understanding recursion, you must understand the relationship between definitions and algorithms. As an example, two methods of defining the same set of numbers follow:

1. The set of integers between 0 and 9, inclusive
2. {0, 1, 2, 3, 4, 5, 6, 7, 8, 9}

Definition 1 provides a summary description of a set of objects (integers), whereas definition 2 lists the actual set members themselves. There is yet a third way of defining the same set:

3. The set of integers, starting with 0, generated by successively adding 1 to the previous integer, up to and including 9

Unlike definitions 1 and 2, which provide "after-the-fact" descriptions, definition 3 is really an algorithm for generating the set. Recall that an *algorithm* is a finite series of operations intended to produce a desired result or solution. When the instructions of an algorithm are clear, concise, and complete, the algorithm itself may serve as an effective description of the result it is supposed to produce.

Let us devise a general definition of the syntax of a decimal-based, unsigned integer constant. Since there are too many of them to list explicitly, we need to devise an algorithm for generating such integer constants. (Note that a complete definition of a set may be used both to *generate members of the set* or, conversely, to *test an object for membership*.) In devising algorithms to generate members of any set, it is useful to begin with simple examples and look for similar characteristics. Sample unsigned integer constants follow:

158 94 32767 2 0 1000000 0008

The following sequence of observations leads us to the algorithm for building and testing an integer:

1. The samples involve the digits 0, 1, 2, 3, 4, 5, 6, 7, 8, and 9, since we are using the decimal system.
2. Each sample has differing quantities of these digits; i.e., each digit may be followed by another group of digits or may be followed by nothing.
3. An integer may therefore be defined as either a single digit followed by nothing or a single digit followed by a group of one or more digits, which themselves form an integer.

Hence, the syntax of an unsigned integer constant is as follows:

- A single digit followed by nothing, or else
- A single digit followed by another unsigned integer

Let us use this definition to determine if 158 is an unsigned integer (hereafter in this exercise, we use the simple term *integer* to imply an unsigned integer). 158 consists of the digit 1 followed by an integer, 58. But is 58 really an integer? 58 consists of the digit 5 followed by a digit, 8, and 8 is an integer because it is a digit followed by nothing. Working backward, 58 is therefore an integer, as is 158.

Is 15X an integer? 15X comprises the digit 1 followed by the integer 5X. But is 5X really an integer? 5X consists of a 5 followed by an X. According to our definition, 5X is an integer only if X is an integer. X is not an integer, however, because it is not a single digit, so 5X is not an integer, and therefore 15X is not an integer.

Our definition of the syntax of an integer constant is a **recursive definition** because the word *integer* was partially defined in terms of itself. 158 is an integer only if the digit 1 is followed by an integer—i.e., if 58 is an integer. To determine if 58 is an integer, we reapplied the same two criteria as were applied to 158. This self-reference creates a loop in which we reapply the same operations to different data (smaller and smaller portions of the original data). The loop stops when we have a digit followed by nothing or followed by a nondigit. This nonrecursive (i.e., nonlooping) provision is called the terminal condition.

Recursive definitions are powerful and elegant because they can describe an infinite set of items using just a few statements. Consider the following definitions of the two levels of divisibility for Pascal data types, noticing that the second definition is recursive because it contains a self-reference:

- *Simple data type:* A nondecomposable type capable of specifying a single value—e.g., integer, real, character, or Boolean.
- *Structured data type:* A decomposable type capable of specifying a collection of values, in which each value is of either a simple or structured data type—e.g., array, record, linear linked list.

Self-reference may create an interesting logical **paradox**—i.e., a self-contradiction. Consider the following (unrelated) "self-devouring" statements:

1. There is an exception to every rule.
2. This statement is false.

Statement 1 is a rule itself and, since there is an exception to every rule, there must be an exception to this rule as well. The exception to rule 1 means that there is not an exception to every rule—rule 1, therefore, contradicts itself. Statement 2 claims to be false; i.e., "This statement is false" is itself a false statement. Therefore statement 2 is not false—again, the statement contradicts itself.

APPLICATION 7.1 Factorial Function

Many algorithms require that an operation or set of operations be repeated until some condition becomes true. For example, calculating the factorial of 4 involves multiplying 4 times 3, multiplying this product by 2, and then multiplying that product by 1. The multiplication continues until the multiplicand is 1:

$$\begin{aligned} 4! &= 4 \times (4 - 1) \times (4 - 2) \times (4 - 3) \\ &= 4 \times 3 \times 2 \times 1 \\ &= 24 \end{aligned}$$

Given the fact that 0! is 1, the following function may be called to compute the factorial of a positive integer. For example, this function would be called by `IFactorial ( 4 )` to compute 4!.

```
FUNCTION IFactorial ( N : Integer ) : Real;

VAR
  Product  :  Real;
  K        :  Integer;

BEGIN
Product := 1;
FOR K := N DOWNTO 1 DO
  Product  := Product * K;
IFactorial := Product
END;
```

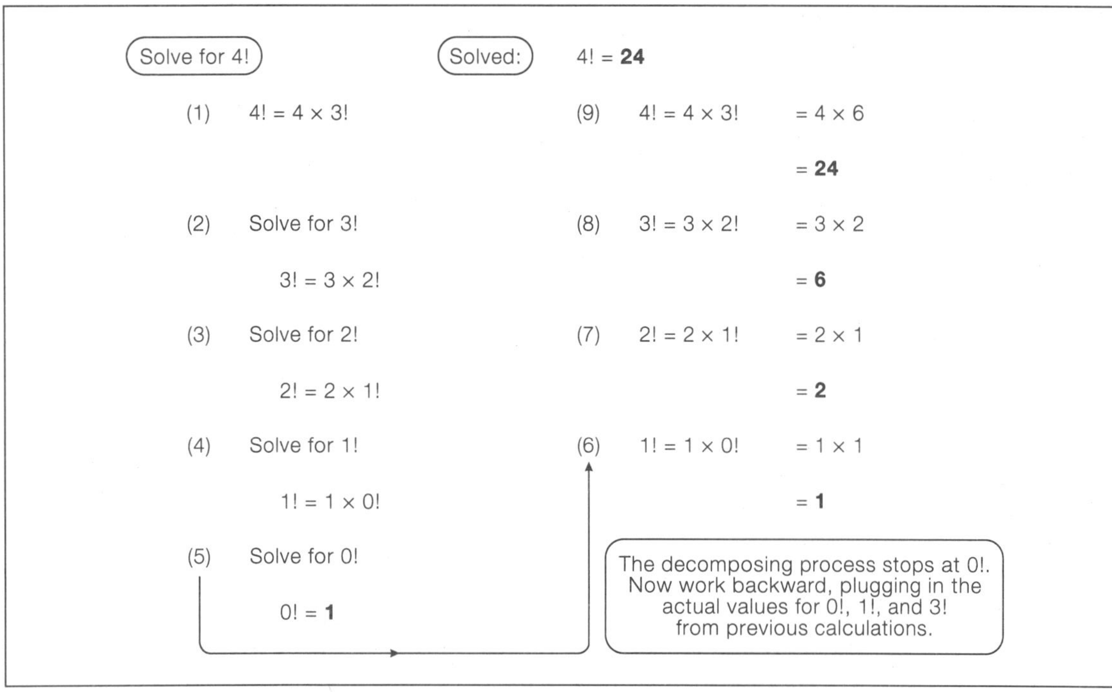

FIGURE 7.1 Steps Taken to Compute 4! Recursively

It is also possible to define 4! as $4! = 4 \times 3!$. If we knew the value of 3!, we could substitute that value for 3! and complete the computation for 4!. 3! can be defined as $3 \times 2!$, 2! defined as $2 \times 1!$, and 1! defined as $1 \times 0!$, where 0! always has the value 1. Therefore, before we can solve for 4! we must solve for 3!, then for 2!, and then for 1!, with the process stopping at 0!. We can then work backward and substitute the appropriate values to solve for 4!; Figure 7.1 summarizes these steps.

This approach may be summarized recursively by the following two equations:

$$0! = 1$$
$$N! = N \times (N - 1)!$$

The second equation creates a loop, since solving for $(N - 1)!$ requires reapplying the second equation, in which $N!$ is really $(N - 1)!$. When N is initially 4, the following equations hold:

$$0! = 1$$
$$4! = 4 \times (4 - 1)!$$

To solve for $(4 - 1)!$, we must reapply the equation $N! = N \times (N - 1)!$, substituting $(N - 1)$ as the new value for N. $(4 - 1)$ is 3, so we reapply the second equation using 3: $3! = 3 \times (3 - 1)!$. This process of *substitution* and *reapplication* continues until the new value of N is 0, at which time we apply the first equation and not the second. Since 0! has a constant value of 1, we work backward, substituting 1 for 1!, substituting 2 for 2!, and then substituting 6 for 3!. The value of 4! is then calculated as 4×6, or 24.

Pascal function `IFactorial` is an *iterative algorithm,* whereas this approach reflects a *recursive algorithm.*

- An **iterative algorithm** is an algorithm involving a single loop and no self-reference; it is represented in Pascal using a **WHILE**, **REPEAT**, or **FOR** statement.
- A **recursive algorithm** is an algorithm defined in terms of itself, effectively creating a loop; it is represented in Pascal by having a procedure or function repeatedly call itself until a terminal condition, tested in the procedure or function prior to a recursive call, evaluates to a true value.

In the recursive factorial approach, the looping process resulted by substituting $(N - 1)$ for the new N and reapplying the second equation, but this looping did not continue indefinitely. It terminated when N became 1 and we solved for $(1 - 1)!$, or 0!, which is known to be 1. $N = 0$ is therefore the terminal condition for the recursive factorial algorithm, marking the end of recursive looping and the start of the return path from each recursive call, a process referred to as **unwinding.**

All recursive algorithms consist of two basic parts:

1. The **terminal condition** by which recursive looping is halted.
2. The **base operation(s)** performed repeatedly until the terminal condition is met.

In the case of a recursive function that computes a value or generates members of a list, these two criteria often can be described succinctly by a **recurrence relation.** The recurrence relation to recursively compute the value of N! is as follows:

1. $0! = 1$ {Terminal condition}
2. $N! = N \times (N - 1)!$ for all $N \geq 0$ {Recursive base operation}

This translates easily into a recursive version of the `IFactorial` function:

```
FUNCTION Factorial ( N : Integer ) : Real;

BEGIN
IF N <= 0 THEN                               {Terminal condition}
  Factorial := 1
ELSE
  Factorial := N * Factorial ( N - 1 )  {Recursive base operation}
END;
```

`Factorial` calls *itself,* creating a loop. Notice the similarity between the recurrence relation and the actual Pascal code. Again, to compute the value 4!, this function would be called initially by `Factorial ( 4 )`.

Pascal Implementation of Recursion

It may seem strange that a function can call itself. How can the same code be "reexecuted"? Once the terminal condition becomes true, how does the computer "remember" where to return? This section describes how Pascal recursion works and describes a verification or debugging technique for tracking the execution of any recursive function or procedure.

Recall that a Pascal compiler program transforms Pascal source code into a 1s and 0s representation of source code referred to as the machine code or object code. The Pascal linker program forms an executable image that includes enough space to store static global variables whose memory requirements are determined during compilation. To complete the executable image, the linker then merges Pascal library code with the user-program object code. As explained in Section 4.2, internal memory contains a section called the *heapspace,* which is available for use and reuse (allocation and deallocation) during the execution of a program, to store dynamically allocated variables and activation records. (Briefly refer back to Figure 4.8.)

Recall also that an activation record is allocated by the operating system whenever a procedure or function is called. Conversely, when a procedure or function is exited, its activation record is deallocated. Activation records store the following information (and possibly other information not relevant to this discussion):

- *Local variable values.*
- *Formal parameter values:* A **VAR** parameter holds the *address* of the actual parameter; a non-**VAR** parameter holds a *copy* of the actual parameter value.
- *The return address*—i.e., the address of the statement following the calling statement.
- *Current value of the function* for recursive functions.

Figure 7.2 is a reprinting of Figure 4.9, depicting sample activation activity for sample routines W, X, Y, and Z, traced using **heapspace diagrams.** Heapspace diagrams are useful in tracing the execution of recursive Pascal

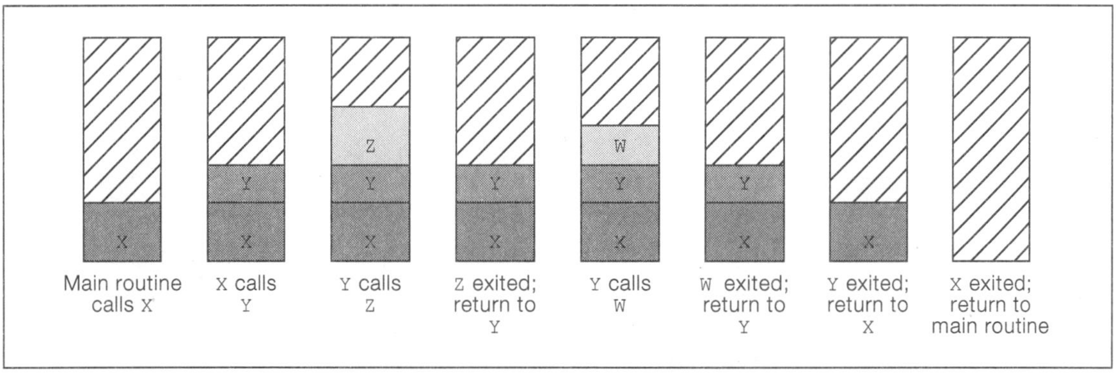

FIGURE 7.2 Depiction of Activation Record Allocation and Deallocation

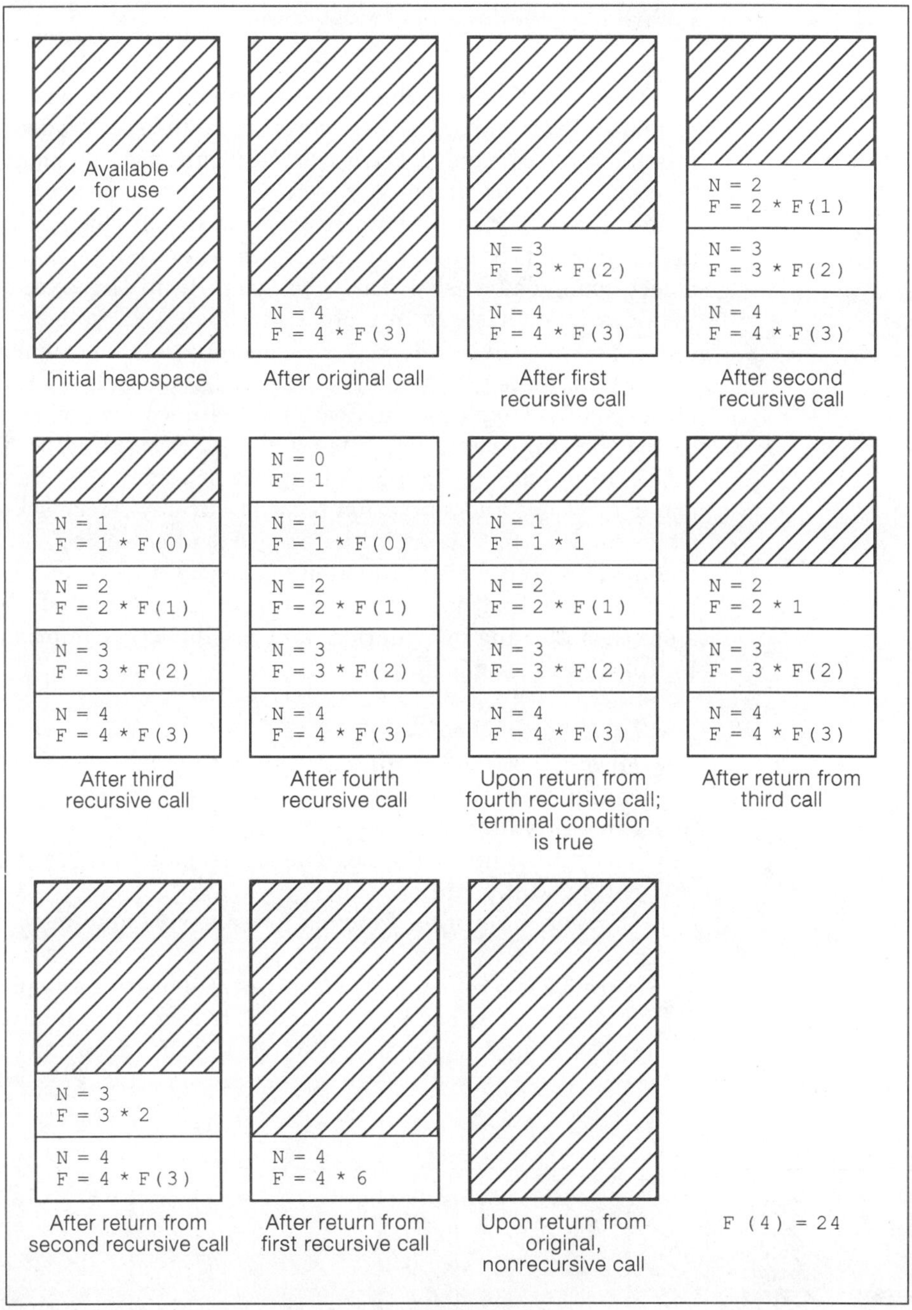

FIGURE 7.3 Heap Diagrams for `Factorial(4)`

routines with local variables and parameters and will be used extensively in our early discussion of recursion.

As an example of tracing execution flow with a recursive routine, we reexamine the recursive `Factorial` function. Figure 7.3 shows the heap diagrams depicting activation record activity generated by the initial call, `Factorial ( 4 )`, which computes 4!. In the figure, `Factorial` is abbreviated as `F` and the heapspace activation record pointer is omitted. Also, for simplicity, activation records are not depicted within the heapspace rectangle after they are deallocated—i.e., upon return from the function.

Each recursive function call results in the creation of an activation record, stacked "above" the other activation records in the heapspace. The terminal condition **IF** N <= 0 **THEN** evaluates to a true value and no more recursive looping occurs. The function is then assigned the value 1 before execution flow exits the function and returns to the call statement. Note that the heapspace need not be empty before the first function call is made; it is depicted as empty here to simplify the diagram.

There are no duplicate copies of the instructions of recursive functions and procedures; these instructions are compiled once and stored within the program's executable image. Recursive calls result in the reexecution of exactly the same code path—the only thing unique about each call is the activation record allocated for that procedure or function when the call is made.

APPLICATION 7.2 Program Reverse-The-String, Application 6.1 Revisited

As a simple but illustrative example of how activation records "save" local values for processing during unwinding, we will examine a recursive version of procedure Reverse, which was given in the ReverseTheString program of Application 6.1. Recall that this program prompts the user for a string of characters and then calls procedure Reverse, which reads each character and displays the entire sequence of characters backward:

```
PROGRAM ReverseTheString (INPUT, OUTPUT);

  PROCEDURE Reverse;

  VAR
    Ch : Char;

  BEGIN
  Read ( Ch );
  IF NOT Eoln ( INPUT ) THEN
    Reverse;
  Write ( Ch )
  END;

{***  Main routine for ReverseTheString  ***}

BEGIN
Writeln ( 'Enter a string of characters:' );
Reverse
END.
```

Figure 7.4 shows the input buffer and activation record activity that results when the user enters the string West and then presses the RETURN or ENTER key. In the figure, the shaded region of the input buffer represents the end-of-line indicator and the arrow represents the input buffer pointer.

Note: As in Application 6.1, this is a greatly slowed down depiction of input buffer activity. In actual practice, a character would be extracted from the input buffer via a Read statement immediately after the character

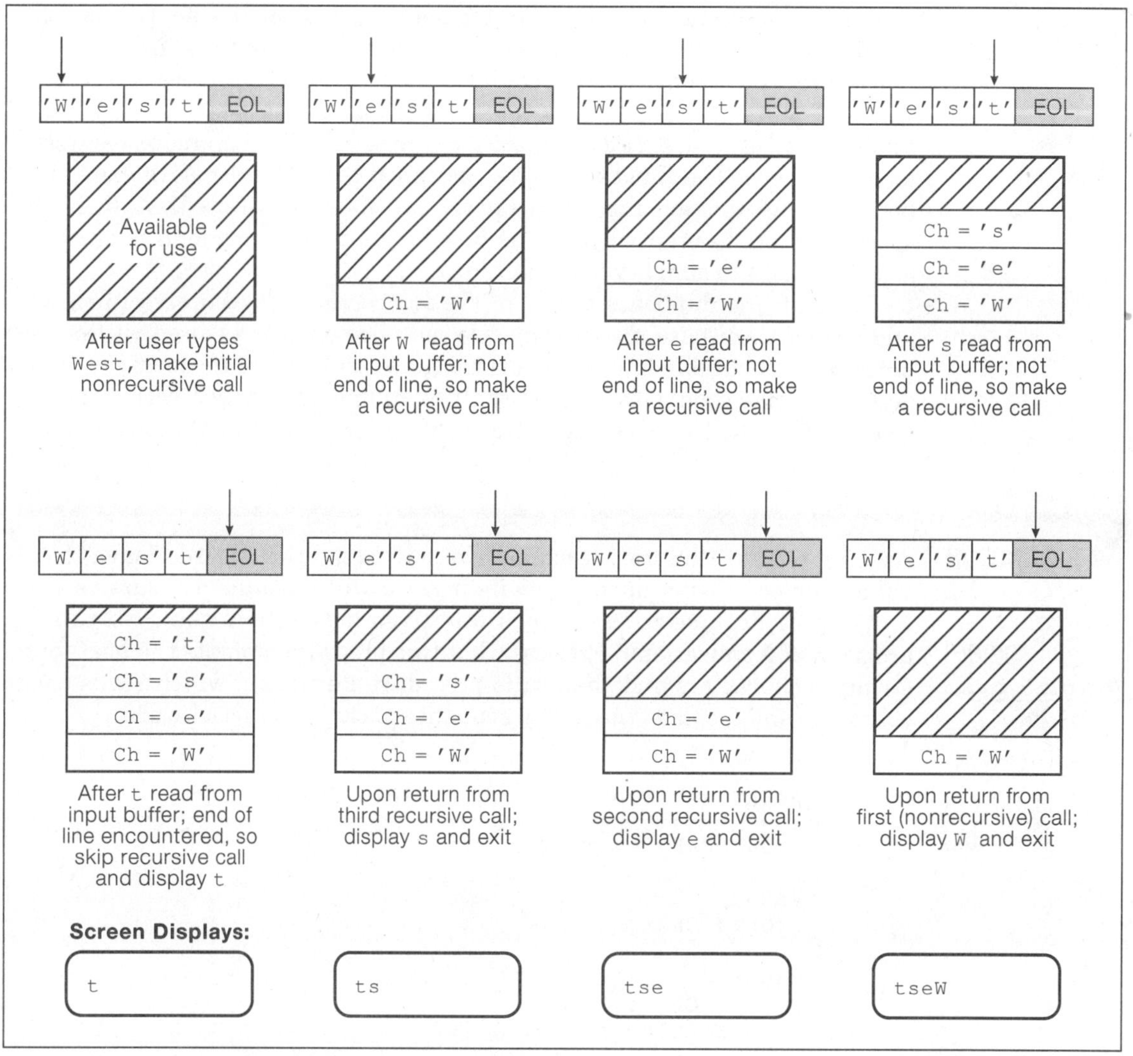

FIGURE 7.4 Input Buffer, Heapspace Diagrams, and Screen Displays for Procedure `ReverseTheString`

is typed and long before the RETURN key is pressed. At most, only a single character would sit in the buffer and for a very brief time. The diagrams depict the buffer as a text file only for visual clarity. The activation record buildup is correct as shown.

After the `'W'` is displayed, execution flow returns from the original call. Notice how the local versions of variable `Ch` are saved in the operating system controlled stack of activation records. Each `Ch` is a separate variable with its own memory space. (If the **`IF/THEN`** statement were replaced by an **`IF/THEN/ELSE`** statement, with the `Write` statement associated with the **`ELSE`**, the only screen display would be `'t'`.) This process of storing local values for later processing in reverse order is the foundation for many recursive techniques, such as *backtracking* and *recursive traversal* routines (discussed later in the chapter), which operate on the local values while unwinding back to the original call statement.

ReverseTheString illustrates how activation records for procedure Reverse are *stacked up* when Reverse calls itself recursively, one recursive call per character read and one activation record per call. Each character value is saved in local variable Ch before each recursive call. During the unwinding process, Reverse displays the value of the local variable, resulting in the series of characters being displayed in reverse order.

Recursion is permitted by Pascal compilers because the compilers generate the code to push a new activation record onto the stack of activation records in heapspace each time a procedure or function is called. Any recursive algorithm can be rewritten *nonrecursively* by having the program maintain its own stack to save information in reverse order; this was done in the Application 6.1 version of ReverseTheString. Many recursive routines, such as the Factorial function of Application 7.1, do not involve saving and processing information in reverse order; removing this type of recursion does not even require a program-maintained stack. Section 7.7 discusses in greater detail the mechanics of removing both types of recursion.

Terminating Recursion

In any recursive procedure or function, some terminal condition should be tested prior to making a recursive call. The code should be written such that when a terminal condition evaluates to a true value, the recursive call statement is bypassed and execution flow reaches the end of the routine and returns to the calling statement. Examine procedures P1 and P2, which follow. They are intended to display recursively the first ten powers of 2 when called initially by P1 (2) or P2 (2). Can you see why they do not work?

```
PROCEDURE P1 ( K : Integer );

BEGIN
Writeln ( K );
K := K * 2;
P1 ( K )
END;
```

```
PROCEDURE P2 ( K : Integer );

BEGIN
K := K * 2;
P2 ( K );
IF K <= 1024 THEN
  Writeln ( K )
END;
```

With no terminal condition being tested, the recursive looping via the calls made in P1 continues "indefinitely." Procedure P2 is no better. What looks like some kind of terminal condition testing occurs after the recursive call statement, so it is never executed. Now examine procedure P3.

```
PROCEDURE P3 ( K : Integer );

BEGIN
Writeln ( K );
K := K * 2;
IF K <= 1024 THEN          {Terminal condition }
  P3 ( K )
END;
```

In P3, the recursive call is made only if K is less than or equal to 1024, in which case the just-multiplied value of K is passed. After the K value 1024 is displayed, `K` is assigned the value `2048`. Since 2048 is greater than 1024, the Boolean expression `K <= 1024` evaluates to a false value, the recursive call is bypassed, and the procedure is exited. But to where does the execution flow return? Remember:

- Recursion involves execution of the *same code path* but the accessing of *different activation records.*
- Upon exiting any procedure or function, execution flow *always* returns to its call statement.

In this case, execution flow returns to the call `P3 ( 1024 )`. There is only one copy of procedure `P3` in the executable image, whereas there are multiple activation records on the heap (one per call to `P3`), each of which stores a value for parameter `K` along with the address of the call statement.

What happens if `P1` and `P2` are actually compiled and executed? Recall that a new activation record is stacked in the heapspace each time a procedure or function (recursive or not) is called. Based on the model of internal memory depicted in Figure 4.8, the stack of activation records can grow until it either collides with the stack of dynamically allocated variables or, if there are no such variables, until it collides with the boundary of the heapspace. In response to such a collision, the operating system terminates program execution and displays an appropriate message, such as *heapspace exceeded* or *stack overflow.* Both procedures `P1` and `P2` can be regarded as producing infinite loops even though the operating system provides its own terminal condition!

A temporary `Writeln` statement may be placed in any recursive routine suspected of being trapped in an infinite loop. For example, if the following statement is inserted as the first executable statement in `P1`, output is displayed repeatedly until the entire program crashes:

```
Writeln ( 'PROCEDURE P1, K = ', K );
```

(When the `K` value exceeds **`MAXINT`**, it becomes negative.) If a recursive routine is trapped in an infinite loop and no input/output operations are being performed in that routine, the keyboard may appear "frozen" (i.e., unresponsive). If this happens, you can try pressing the CTRL and C keys simultaneously to terminate execution of the program or, in a time-sharing environment, have the system manager terminate the process.

There is no "quick" way to return to the original call statement when several recursive calls have been made. Since another activation record is stacked up with each recursive call, the algorithm must unwind gracefully, deallocating each activation record, until execution flow returns to the original call statement. For some complex recursive algorithms, proving beforehand that an algorithm will actually terminate at some point—given a particular set of initial data—may be difficult. Recursive algorithms should be designed such that, by the totality of all recursive calls, the terminal condition is gradually approached and eventually reached.

`P3` and `Reverse` are examples of recursive procedures, whereas `Factorial` is an example of a recursive function. The process of recursing is identical for functions and procedures except, of course, that a function returns a single value. Any function call must be evaluated before the statement in which it appears can be completely evaluated, unlike a procedure statement that "stands alone." As an example, the statement from function `Factorial` containing the recursive call follows:

```
Factorial := N * Factorial ( N - 1 )
```

The function identifier `Factorial`, to the left of the assignment operator, cannot be assigned a value until the expression `N * Factorial ( N - 1 )` is evaluated, and this is not possible until the call `Factorial ( N - 1 )` is made, returning a value. Remember the basic rule for any procedure or function (recursive or not) stated earlier: When the procedure or function is completed, execution flow returns to the calling statement. *Recursion involves executing the same code path repeatedly but accessing different activation records in the process.*

Recursion with VAR and Non-VAR Parameters

Recall that when a **VAR** appears before a formal parameter, the memory address of the actual parameter is passed to that formal parameter (e.g., stored in the activation record). When **VAR** does not appear before a formal parameter, a copy of the actual parameter is passed to that formal parameter. As an example, study the code and output of procedure `Guess`, which follows, *with* and *without* the **VAR** before the formal parameter, `N`. Assume that the initial call to `Guess` is as follows (`K` is an integer variable):

```
K := 3;
Guess ( K ):

PROCEDURE Guess ( VAR N : Integer );

BEGIN
IF N > 0 THEN
  BEGIN
  Write ( N:4 );
  N := N - 1;
  Guess ( N );      {Recursive call}
  Write( N:4 )
  END
END;
```

The output without **VAR**:	3	2	1	0	1	2
The output with **VAR**:	3	2	1	0	0	0

The `Write` before the recursive call statement is executed as the procedure recurses ahead, whereas the `Write` following the recursive call is executed during the unwinding process, upon each return from a recursive call. Without the **VAR**, parameter `N` behaves as a local variable so that the different values (1 and 2) stored while recursing are redisplayed during the unwinding. With the **VAR** parameter, the last value of `N` (zero) is effectively "brought back" and displayed during the unwinding process. You can draw heapspace diagrams to confirm these results.

As an interesting example of the use of a **VAR** parameter, procedure `CreateLList`, which follows, builds a singly linked list in an unusual manner: The nodes of the list are allocated and their data fields are assigned values while recursing ahead but are linked during the unwinding process. Necessary global declarations precede the procedure. (To simplify the code in this example, no node counting is performed as the list is built.)

```
{Global declarations}

TYPE
  NodePtr   =  ^Node;
  Node      =  RECORD
                 Data : Integer;
                 Next : NodePtr     {Assigned during unwinding process}
               END;

VAR
  Head : NodePtr;                   {Points to first node after the list is built}
```

```
PROCEDURE CreateLList ( VAR Ptr : NodePtr;  N : Integer );

BEGIN
New ( Ptr );
Ptr^.Data := N;
Ptr^.Next := NIL;
N := 2 * N;

IF N <= 16 THEN                     {Terminal condition}
  CreateLList ( Ptr^.Next, N )
END;
```

Notice that the value of `Head` is irrelevant when `CreateLList` is called initially. Upon return from this call, however, `Head` is assigned the address of the first node and the `Next` field of the final node contains a **NIL** value (as indicated by the stripe-filled link field). Figure 7.5 depicts the list that results from the initial call `CreateLList ( Head, 2 )`.

The `Next` link fields are given values upon returning from the recursive calls. This happens because the formal parameter, `Ptr`, is a call-by-reference (**VAR**) parameter and the corresponding actual parameter in the recursive call statement is `Ptr^.Next`. Upon return from each call to

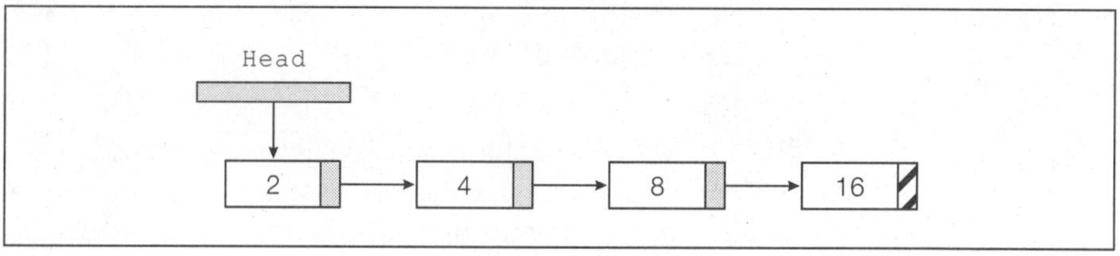

FIGURE 7.5 Linked List Produced by `CreateLList(2)`

`CreateLList`, the `Next` field of the previous node (the actual parameter) gets the address of the formerly current node.

Developing Recursive Algorithms

Five steps are recommended in the development of any recursive algorithm:

1. *Determine whether or not recursion is a better strategy than is simple iteration.* The section at the end of this chapter provides a full discussion of advantages and disadvantages of recursion and iteration. Generally, recursion is appropriate if the problem can be expressed as a series of smaller, nearly identical subproblems. By substituting solutions of each subproblem, the entire problem is eventually solved. If possible, try to state the algorithm as a succinct recurrence relation.
2. *Clearly define the base operation(s),* each of which solves a smaller but similar subproblem.
3. *Clearly define the terminal condition* that halts the recursion. Ensure that this condition is tested before each recursive call is made.
4. *Ensure that, with each recursive call, the algorithm moves closer to the terminal condition and to a solution.*
5. *Ensure that the algorithm handles special cases,* if any, in addition to the terminal case.

For example, recursion is a viable approach in computing a factorial because the overall problem ($N!$) is divisible into successively smaller subproblems $(N - 1)!$ Both the terminal condition, `N = 0`, and the base operation, `Factorial := N * Factorial (N - 1)!`, are clearly defined, and repeated execution of the base condition moves the execution flow closer and closer to the terminal condition. We handled the special case of a negative number by making the calling routine responsible for initially passing a positive value for N.

7.2 GENERAL RECURSIVE COMPUTATIONS

APPLICATION 7.3 Power Functions

A Simple Power Function

Recall that exponentiation is nothing more than multiplication, with the value of the exponent specifying that the base is multiplied by itself |exponent| − 1 times. Figure 7.6 summarizes the different cases to consider, based on the value of the base and exponent.

As a review, sample powers of 5 follow:

$$5^{-2} = \frac{1}{5 \times 5} = \frac{1}{25} \qquad 5^0 = 1 \qquad 5^2 = 5 \times 5 = 25$$

$$5^{-1} = \frac{1}{5} \qquad 5^1 = 5 \qquad 5^3 = 5 \times 5 \times 5 = 125$$

Base (b)	Exponent (y)	Value of expression
0	0	0
≠0	0	1
≠0	<0	$\frac{1}{b^{-y}}$
≠0	>0	$b^y = \underbrace{b \times b \times .. \times b}_{\text{y number of multiplicands}}$

FIGURE 7.6 Different Cases in Calculating a Power

The base operation involves multiplying the base by the accumulated product an |exponent| − 1 number of times. The exponent value therefore manages the number of repetitions, controlled by decrementing this value by 1 after each looping. Since the value of any base greater than zero raised to the zeroth power is 1, testing whether or not the exponent is 1 promises to be a viable terminal condition. Also note that whether the exponent is positive or negative, the value of the base raised to a positive exponent must be calculated. Both the iterative and recursive versions of a Pascal function to calculate a power follow:

```
{*** Iterative Power Function ***}

FUNCTION IPower ( Base : Real; Exponent : Integer ) : Real;

VAR
  K       : Integer;
  Product : Real;

BEGIN
IF Base = 0 THEN
  IPower := 0
ELSE
  BEGIN
  Product := 1;
  FOR K := 1 TO Abs ( Exponent ) DO
    Product := Product * Base;

  IF Exponent >= 0 THEN
    IPower := Product
  ELSE
    IPower := 1 / Product
  END
END;
```

```
{*** Recursive Power Function ***}

FUNCTION Power ( Base : Real; Exponent : Integer ) : Real;
```

```
  FUNCTION CalcPower ( Exponent : Integer ) : Real;

  BEGIN
  IF Exponent = 0 THEN              {Terminal condition}
    CalcPower := 1
  ELSE
    CalcPower := Base * CalcPower ( Exponent - 1 )
  END;
  ____________________________________________________________
{*** Main routine for Power ***}

BEGIN
IF Base = 0 THEN
  Power := 0
ELSE
  IF Exponent >= 0 THEN
    Power := CalcPower ( Exponent )
  ELSE
    Power := 1 / CalcPower ( -Exponent )
END;
```

If the exponent is negative, `Power` returns the value of one divided by the value of the base raised to the *positive* exponent. The real "work" is therefore performed when the exponent is positive. Notice that if the exponent is initially negative, the call in the following expression is made only once:

```
1 / Power ( Base, -Exponent )
```

Therefore, with exponent being positive, all recursive calls will be made by the following call:

```
CalcPower ( Base, Exponent - 1 )
```

Figure 7.7 shows the heapspace diagrams for the following initial call to `Power`:

```
Writeln( '7 to the 3rd power is ', Power ( 7, 3 ):5:1 );
```

In the figure, `Power` is abbreviated as `P`, `Base` is abbreviated as `B`, and `Exponent` is abbreviated as `E`.

A More Efficient Power Function

Although the strategy just presented for evaluating a power is straightforward, the total number of multiplications increases as the value of exponent increases. This means that overall execution time increases as the value of the exponent increases. A better strategy is the *halving and squaring* technique, which takes a shortcut. To evaluate 5^{12} using this technique, for example, rather than multiplying 5 by itself 12 − 1 times (11 multiplica-

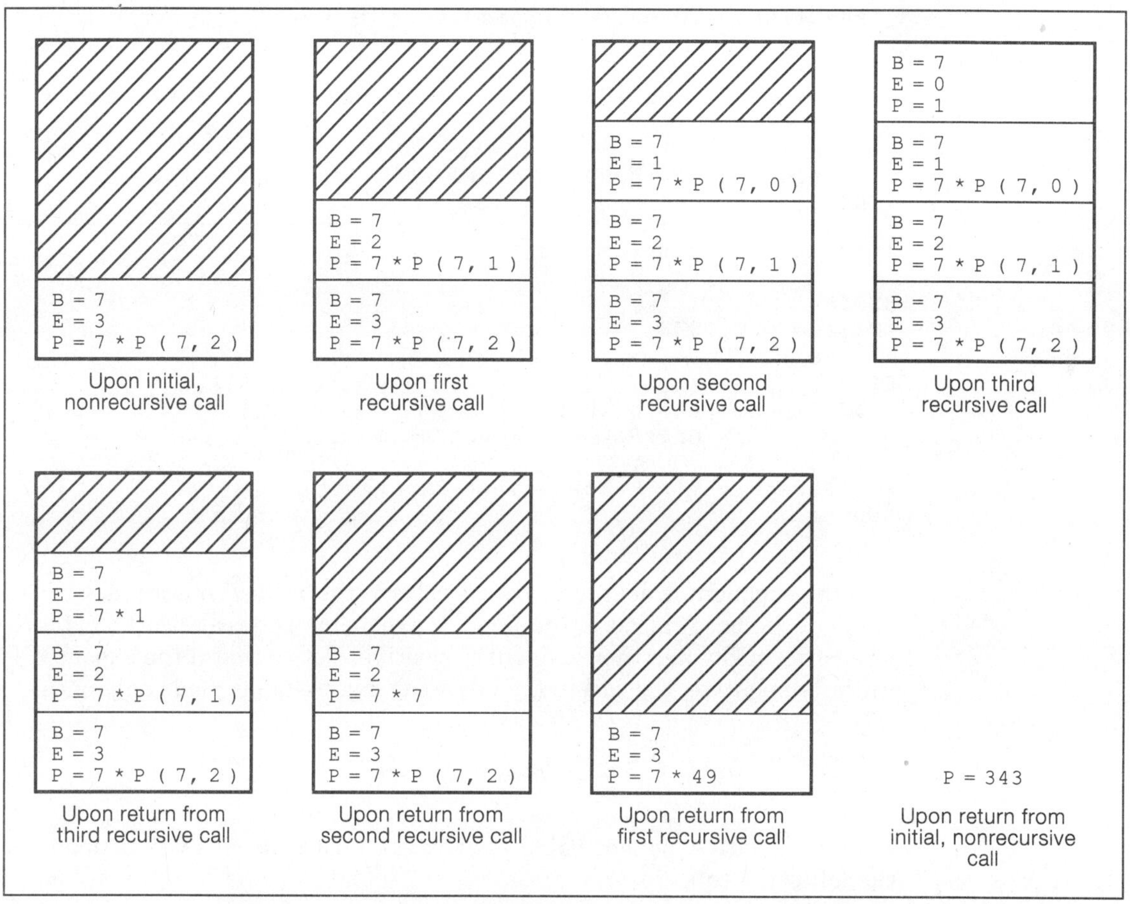

FIGURE 7.7 Heapspace Diagrams for `Power( 7, 3 )`

tions), we would calculate 5^6 and then square this value (a total of seven multiplications).

The formulas for exponentiation, based on the values of base and exponent, are summarized in the table of Figure 7.8. An even exponent can be halved with no remainder; e.g., $5^{12} = 5^6 \times 5^6$. An odd exponent leaves a remainder of 1 when it is halved, requiring one more multiplication by the base; e.g., $5^{13} = 5^6 \times 5^6 \times 5$.

Exponent (*y*)	Base (*b*)	Value of expression
> 0	0	0
0	$\neq 0$	1
< 0	$\neq 0$	$b^{1/-y}$
Even, > 0	$\neq 0$	$(b^{(y\ \mathbf{DIV}\ 2)})^2$
Odd, > 0	$\neq 0$	$(b^{(y\ \mathbf{DIV}\ 2)})^2 \times b$

FIGURE 7.8 The Halving and Squaring Technique

A Pascal version of the halving and squaring power function follows (note that the main routine section of `Power` is identical to the main routine section of the previous version of `Power`):

```
FUNCTION Power ( Base : Real; Exponent : Integer ) : Real;

    FUNCTION CalcPower ( Exponent : Integer ) : Real;

    BEGIN
    IF Exponent = 0 THEN          { Terminal condition}
      CalcPower := 1
    ELSE
      IF Odd ( Exponent ) THEN
        CalcPower := Sqr ( CalcPower ( Exponent DIV 2 )) * Base
      ELSE
        CalcPower := Sqr ( CalcPower ( Exponent DIV 2 ))
    END;

{*** Main Routine For Power ***}

BEGIN
IF Base = 0 THEN
  Power := 0
ELSE
  IF Exponent >= 0 THEN
    Power := CalcPower ( Exponent )
  ELSE
    Power := 1 / CalcPower ( Exponent )
END;
```

7.3 RECURSIVE TRAVERSALS

Traversals involve two base operations: processing the current item and advancing to another item. The data structure may be a *linear list,* such as a simple array or a linear linked list, in which all items are aligned sequentially. (While routines to traverse linear lists provide excellent educational examples and so are included here, the memory required for activation records and the time required to allocate and deallocate the records may render them impractical for very long lists.) The data structure may instead be *nonlinear,* such as a tree or graph structure, in which it may be possible to move from one item to several other items in the list rather than merely to the next (or previous) item. Traversals of nonlinear lists are discussed in Section 8.2 (binary search trees), Chapter 9 (graphs), and Sections 10.1 (2-3 trees) and 10.3 (B-trees).

Traversing Arrays and Linear Linked Lists

Given the following global declarations, try writing a recursive procedure that traverses an array of integers and displays the value of each element from the low-index end of the array to the high-index end:

```
CONST
  UpperBound  =  ??;   {Application dependent}

TYPE
  InfoType  =  Integer;
  ListType  =  ARRAY [ 1..UpperBound ] OF InfoType;

VAR
  List : ListType;
```

The base operation of the traversal algorithm is the display of the element contents and the terminal condition is an array index value greater than the index of the last array element; i.e., the traversal has reached the end of the array. A recursive version of the traversal algorithm follows; the initial call to traverse the entire array would be `ArrayTraverse ( List, 1 )`:

```
PROCEDURE ArrayTraverse ( VAR List : ListType; K : Integer );

BEGIN
IF K <= UpperBound THEN  {Terminal condition}
  BEGIN
  Writeln( 'Element ', K, ' contains ', List [ K ] );
  ArrayTraverse ( List, K + 1 )
  END
END;
```

For practice, modify this procedure so that it displays the elements in the *reverse order*—i.e., from the high-index end of the array to the low-index end.

Refer back to the basic global declarations for a dynamically allocated singly linked list, which preceded the `CreateLList` procedure in Section 7.1. Notice that the data structure declaration itself is inherently recursive: `Node` is defined in terms of `NodePtr`, which is a pointer to a `Node` record. That is, the declaration of `Node` contains a self-reference (`NodePtr`). Recursive data structures easily lend themselves to recursive algorithms.

Assume that the linear linked list shown in Figure 7.9 has already been built using these declarations and that list head variable `Head` points to the first node. Try writing a recursive procedure that visits every node, displaying the value of each `Data` field in ascending order, and then displays the same values in descending order during the unwinding process (a version of such a procedure will follow shortly).

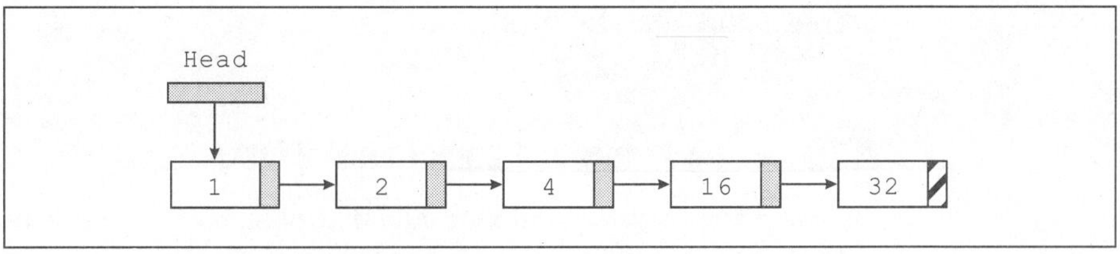

FIGURE 7.9 Sample Linked List

The base operations include displaying the current node's `Data` field and advancing a pointer variable to point to the next node. The recursion should continue until the pointer variable is assigned the value **NIL** when attempting to advance from the final node. Write a procedure that displays the `Key` values 1, 2, 4, 8, 16, and 32 while it recurses ahead and then outputs the values 32, 16, 8, 4, 2, and 1 as it is unwinding back to the initial call (the initial call should be `LLTraverse ( Head )`). A version of such a routine follows:

```
PROCEDURE LLTraverse ( Current : NodePtr );

BEGIN
IF Current <> NIL THEN                  {Test for terminal condition}
  BEGIN
  Write ( Current^.Data.Key, '   ' );   {Write in order, first node to last}
  LLTraverse ( Current^.Next );         {Recursive call to traverse ahead}
  Write ( Current^.Data.Key, '   ' )    {Write in reverse order, last node to first}
  END
END;
```

As with procedure `Guess` of Section 7.1, the `Writeln` before the recursive call statement is executed as the procedure is recursing, whereas the `Writeln` following the recursive call is executed upon each return from a recursive call. A **VAR** placed before the formal parameter `Current` would result in a runtime error because `Current` is set to **NIL** upon attempting to advance from the final node; this condition terminates the recursion. With **VAR**, a **NIL** `Current` value would be passed back from each call, and execution of the statement `Write ( Current^.Data.Key, '  ' )` would, therefore, crash the program.

As a variation of the traversal algorithm, try writing a recursive procedure that deallocates every node in the list. The procedure should have a single formal parameter of type `NodePtr` data, with the address of the first node in the list passed to it upon the initial call. A version of such a procedure follows:

```
PROCEDURE DeAllocateAll ( Current : NodePtr );

BEGIN
IF Current <> NIL THEN
  BEGIN
  DeallocateAll ( Current^.Next );
  Dispose ( Current )
  END
END;
```

As `DeAllocateAll` recurses ahead, it saves in each activation record the address of each node (without a **VAR**, parameter `Current` behaves like a local variable). During the unwinding process, `DeAllocateAll` disposes of the node currently being pointed to by `Current`. For practice, hand--execute this procedure to the linked list of the previous case, drawing heap diagrams. Omitting the **BEGIN** and **END** statements would produce a runtime error: Upon attempting to advance from the last node, `Current` is set to **NIL**, so after recursing a final time, the recursive call is bypassed and the attempted execution of `Dispose ( Current )` crashes the program.

APPLICATION 7.4 Counting Vowels

Given the following global declarations and assuming variable `Line` contains text characters, try writing a recursive function named `CountVowels` to count the number of vowels in `Line`. Try writing an initial call to the function as well. Figure 7.10 contains a sample `Line` array (an empty square indicates a space character).

```
CONST
  MaxChars = 80;

TYPE
  LineType = String [ MaxChars ];

VAR
  Line : LineType;
```

A version of the first vowel-counting function, `ACountVowels`, follows:

```
FUNCTION ACountVowels ( VAR Line : LineType; Len, K, Sum : Integer ): Integer;

BEGIN
IF K > Len THEN                          {Terminal condition}
  ACountVowels := Sum
ELSE
  BEGIN
  IF Line [ K ] IN [ 'A','a','E','e','I','i','O','o','U','u' ] THEN
    Sum := Sum + 1;
  ACountVowels := ACountVowels ( Line, Len, K + 1, Sum )
  END
END;
```

A sample initial call for the function `ACountVowels` follows:

```
Writeln( 'Vowel count: ', ACountVowels ( Line, Length ( Line ), 1, 0 ));
```

The base operations involve (1) adding 1 to `Sum` if the *K*th element of `Line` is a vowel and then (2) incrementing array index variable *K*. The vow-

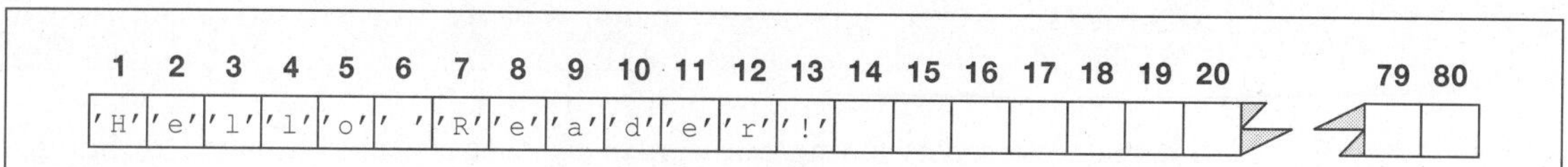

FIGURE 7.10 Sample Contents of Array `Line`

els are counted as the function recurses toward the terminal condition, passing Sum ahead with each recursive call. When the terminal condition becomes true, this sum is assigned to the function identifier, ACountVowels, and the process unwinds uneventfully back to the original call.

A more interesting version follows:

```
FUNCTION BCountVowels ( VAR Line : LineType; Len, K : Integer ): Integer;

BEGIN
IF K > Len THEN                    {Terminal condition}
  BCountVowels := 0
ELSE
  IF Line [ K ] IN [ 'A','a','E','e','I','i','O','o','U','u' ] THEN
    BCountVowels := BCountVowels ( Line, Len, K + 1 ) + 1
  ELSE
    BCountVowels := BCountVowels ( Line, Len, K + 1 )
END;
```

A sample initial call for the function BCountVowels is

```
Writeln( 'Vowel count: ', BCountVowels ( Line, Length ( Line ), 1 ));
```

Unlike ACountVowels, in which the counting is done during the recursing process, in BCountVowels, the counting is done during the unwinding process. The recursion sets up the *unwinding path*—i.e., the path along which the execution flow returns from each recursive call. Here the path is very important, since 1 may or may not be added to the cumulative count upon return from each call, depending upon which statement made the recursive call. The count is carried back from the terminal condition to the original call via the function identifier, so no Sum like additional parameter is needed, as it was in procedure ACountVowels.

To trace the execution flow of this function during unwinding, we must remember to which of the two recursive calls execution flow must return. As an alternative to heap diagrams, a **call-number technique** may be used:

```
IF K > Len THEN                                        {Terminal condition}
  BCountVowels := 0
ELSE
  IF Line [ K ] IN [ 'A','a','E','e','I','i','O','o','U','u' ] THEN
    BCountVowels := BCountVowels ( Line, K + 1 ) + 1{ 2,5,8,9,11 }
  ELSE
    BCountVowels := BCountVowels ( Line, K + 1 )    { 1,3,4,6,7,10,12,13 }
```

Notice the list of numbers to the right of each recursive call, which would be *handwritten* within the { } symbols on a hard-copy listing of the source code. These numbers reflect the order in which the calls are made; the actual values shown are based on the sample contents of array Line, as depicted in Figure 7.10. The character in element 1 is 'H', that is, not a vowel—so the first recursive call is made by the function call immediately *following* the second **ELSE**. The character in element 2 is 'e', which is a vowel, so the second recursive call is made by the function call immediately *before* the second **ELSE**, and so forth. During the unwinding process, the execution flow returns to calls in *reverse order* of these numbers.

`ACountVowels` is an example of **preorder recursion** because the base operation is performed *before* each recursive call. `BCountVowels` is an example of **postorder recursion** because the base operation occurs *after* the recursive call—i.e., upon return from each recursive call. (Procedure `LinearLLTraverse`, presented earlier in this section, involved both preorder and postorder recursion.) `BCountVowels` is also an example of **tail recursion** because the last action taken in the procedure is always a recursive call. Tail recursive is the easiest form of a recursion to replace with iteration, as is described in Section 7.7.

7.4 RECURSIVE SEARCHING

Every recursive algorithm takes a top-down, divide-and-conquer approach because it divides the original problem into smaller, similar problems. Each of these subproblems is then solved in terms of previous solutions. This strategy is especially salient in the *binary search* and *quicksort* algorithms. We examine the binary search algorithm in this section and the quick sort algorithm in Section 11.3.

APPLICATION 7.5 Binary Search

Assume that we wish to look up the telephone number for Herman Hollerith in the greater metropolitan Boston telephone book. There may be, of course, one, several, or no "Hollerith, Herman" listings in the book. Using a linear search strategy, we would start on page 1, line 1, and examine each listing. After page 1, we advance to page 2, then to page 3, and so forth. Although this technique would eventually reveal whether or not Herman Hollerith is listed, the process is certainly tedious. Another strategy is to repeatedly open the telephone book at random and scan a page in a linear search manner. This approach is not only tedious, but worse, it does not guarantee that we will ever find Herman's telephone number or confirm that he does not have a listing in the book.

A more reliable and efficient strategy would take advantage of the fact that the telephone book is ordered by last name. We could thus begin by opening the book to the middle and examining the first listing on a page. Suppose the first name listed is "Newton, Isaac". Since "Hollerith" would come before "Newton" in the telephone book, we can assume that the listing we are looking for must be in the *first half* of the book (if it is in the book at all), and we can ignore the last half. We then perform exactly the same search technique on the first half that we just applied to the entire book—we open *this* half to the middle and examine the first listing on the left page. Suppose the name listed here is "Galileo, G." Since "Hollerith" would come after "Galileo" in the telephone book, we can assume that the Hollerith listing would be in the *last half* of this sublist. The process continues until we get down to a single page, on which we could use a similar process or degenerate to a linear search.

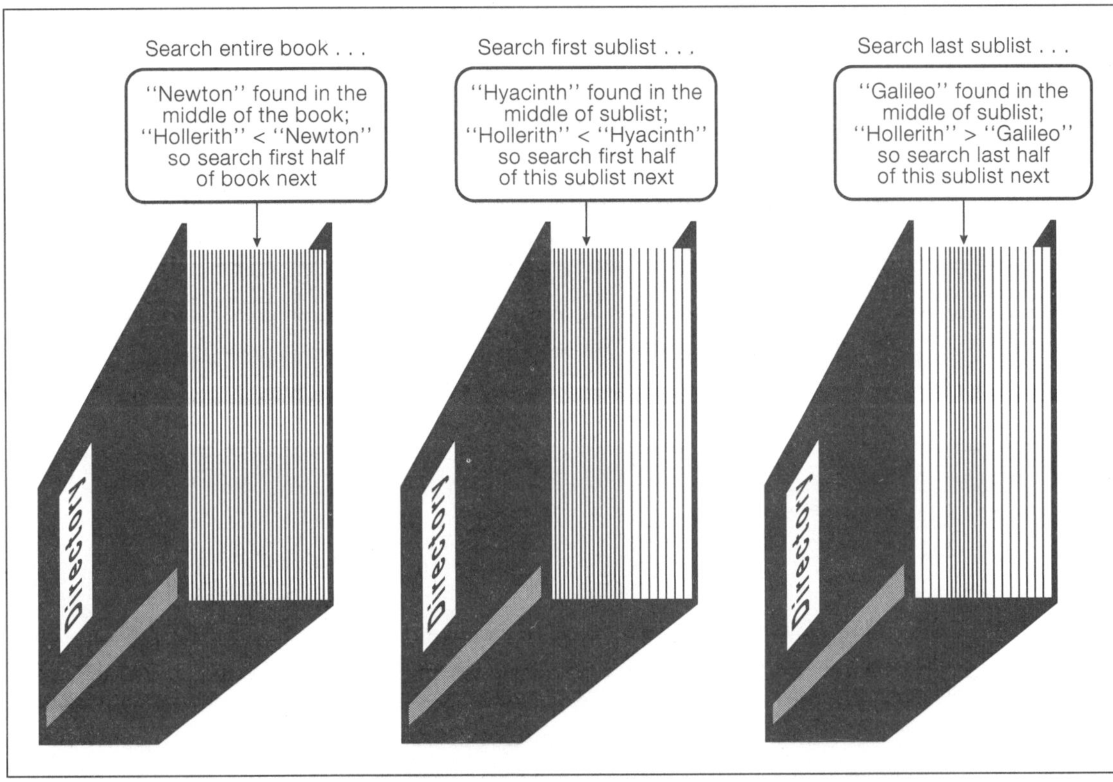

FIGURE 7.11 Initial Comparisons in a Binary Search for "Hollerith" in a Telephone Book

Figure 7.11 depicts views of the closed telephone book with that portion currently being searched shown as darker pages.

The search here consists merely of selecting the middle page of a section and comparing "Hollerith" to the first listing there. "Hollerith" is either equal to, less than, or greater than the listing. This process is reapplied until we either find a match or else run out of pages. Notice that the *same search process* is reapplied to successively smaller portions (sublists) of the entire telephone book (list). Such a searching scheme is called a **binary search** because the size of the portions decrease by a factor of 2: ½ of the original list, then ½ of that list (which is ¼ of the original list), and so forth.

How can we represent this binary search algorithm in Pascal? Since we must repeatedly advance to the middle of the list, the algorithm should be designed to operate on a list stored in an array. A procedure is appropriate that returns a Boolean parameter called `Found`, which is assigned a true value if the desired item is found and a false value otherwise. If the desired item is found, the procedure should also return its array index. A binary search routine is inherently recursive because it repeatedly performs the same base operation on smaller and smaller versions of the original list:

> Compare the key value of the desired item with the key value of the item in the middle element of the current list. If a match is not found, search the appropriate half of the current list next; this portion becomes the current list next.

Upon the first call to the procedure, the list is the entire array; with each recursive call, the list is actually a sublist of the previous list. A particular list may be specified by passing the entire array along with the array index of the lower bound of the list and the index of the upper bound. There are two terminal conditions for any kind of search, whether recursive or iterative:

1. Either the key value is found in an element of the list, or else
2. There are no more elements left to search; i.e., the remaining list is empty.

Try writing iterative and recursive versions of a `BinarySearch` procedure.

> *At this time, examine the following routine in Appendix K.*

```
PROCEDURE Binary Search ( VAR List : ListType; Low, High : Integer;
                          VAR Key : KeyType; VAR Mid : Integer;
                          VAR Found : Boolean );
```

Figure 7.12 traces the recursive execution of `BinarySearch` based on the following initial call (a search for key value 59):

```
BinarySearch ( List, 1, 20, 59, Index, Found );
```

1	2	3	4	5	6	7	8	9	10	11	12	13	14	15	16	17	18	19	20
31	37	45	45	45	52	53	59	62	64	67	68	73	75	79	81	85	85	94	96
L									M										H

`59 < List [ Mid ].Key` so make a recursive call:
`BinarySearch (List, Low, Mid-1, 59, Index, Found )`

1	2	3	4	5	6	7	8	9	10	11	12	13	14	15	16	17	18	19	20
31	37	45	45	45	52	53	59	62	64	67	68	73	75	79	81	85	85	94	96
L				M				H											

`59 > List [ Mid ].Key` so make a recursive call:
`BinarySearch (List, Mid+1, High, 59, Index, Found )`

1	2	3	4	5	6	7	8	9	10	11	12	13	14	15	16	17	18	19	20
31	37	45	45	45	52	53	59	62	64	67	68	73	75	79	81	85	85	94	96
					L	M		H											

`59 > List [ Mid ].Key` so make a recursive call:
`BinarySearch (List, Mid+1, High, 59, Index, Found )`

1	2	3	4	5	6	7	8	9	10	11	12	13	14	15	16	17	18	19	20
31	37	45	45	45	52	53	59	62	64	67	68	73	75	79	81	85	85	94	96
							L M	H											

`59 = List [ Mid ].Key`, so the assignment statement `BinarySearch := Mid` is executed and no more recursive calls are made; execution flow merely unwinds back to the original (nonrecursive) function call

FIGURE 7.12 A Binary Search for the Item with Key Value 59

In the figure, the sublist currently being searched is indicated with a heavier border, `L` denotes the `Low` element, `M` denotes the `Mid` element, and `H` denotes the `High` element. `L`, `M`, and `H` are shown below the index value they contain.

Had the key value been 62 instead of 59, another recursive call would have been made. `Low` would then equal `High`, a comparison would be made the key value and `List [ Low ].Key` (i.e., `List [ 9 ].Key`, which contains 62), and a match would have been found. Trace the execution flow in the search for items with key values 63, 30, and 100.

Analysis of the Binary Search Algorithm

Section 3.7 provided an introduction to the analysis of algorithms by deriving the growth-rate functions for the worst and average cases of the linear searching algorithm. In this section we will derive growth-rate functions for the worst and average cases of the binary search algorithm. As with the linear search algorithm, we will count key value comparisons as a gauge of algorithm efficiency.

In the *worst case* of any search algorithm, the item sought is not found. The linear search algorithm must examine every item before reaching this conclusion. Intuitively, we would expect that the binary search algorithm can reach such a conclusion in less time because it skips groups of items during the search process, and we can prove mathematically that this is indeed the case.

To derive the worst-case growth-rate function for the binary search algorithm, we must calculate the maximum number of comparisons the algorithm will ever make for a list of N items. Since each comparison results in halving the previous list, calculating the maximum number of comparisons becomes a question of how many times a list of N items can be halved. If a list of N items can be halved K times, we can solve for N as follows:

$$N = 2^K$$

$$K = \log_2 N$$

But this is true only for lists of N items where N is an even multiple of 2. To handle *all* lists accurately, we must employ a ceiling function:

$$\text{Search time} = \lceil \log_2 N \rceil = O(\log N)$$

The *ceiling function,* as indicated by $\lceil\ \rceil$ produces the smallest integer that is greater than or equal to $\log_2 N$. In the worst case, binary search is therefore $O(\log N)$. (Recall from Section 3.7, in big O notation the base of the log function is usually omitted.) To verify this function, Figure 7.13 contains three sample lists and calculations of the number of comparisons made by the algorithm in the worst case.

The average-case growth-rate function is approximately equal to its worst-case function, so the binary search algorithm is $O(\log N)$ in the average case as well. Although binary search is one of the fastest searching algorithms in both the worst and average cases, it may be employed only if the following two conditions are met:

3	5	6	10	13	17	19			$\lceil \log_2 7 \rceil = \lceil (2 < \text{some value} < 3) \rceil = 3$
3	5	6	10	13	17	19	20		$\lceil \log_2 8 \rceil = 3$
3	5	6	10	13	17	19	20	23	$\lceil \log_2 9 \rceil = \lceil (3 < \text{some value} < 4) \rceil = 4$
1	**2**	**3**	**4**	**5**	**6**	**7**	**8**	**9**	

FIGURE 7.13 Three Sample Lists and Their Worst-case Calculations

1. *The algorithm must have direct access to the item occupying the middle of the current sublist.* This confines the use of binary search to a list represented using an array rather than a linear linked list.
2. *The list must be sorted* in order of the key value being used to search. As we saw in Application 5.2, insertion and deletion of items from an ordered array is typically very time-consuming, since other items must be shifted.

Binary searching is therefore appropriate for an application involving relatively few insertion and deletion operations.

7.5 RECURSIVE BACKTRACKING

Many programming tasks must be solved using a general problem-solving approach, in which an algorithm seeks a solution by careful trial and error rather than plugging values into some formula or recurrence relation. As with all recursive algorithms, the overall problem is decomposed into a finite number of subproblems, each of which is solved until a complete solution is found. The operative word here is *careful,* since the algorithm must be systematic and thorough enough to test a uniform sequence of possible solutions for each subproblem without repeating any test.

Backtracking is a general problem-solving technique in which the subproblems are ordered such that a solution to the Kth subproblem enables the algorithm to advance and seek a solution to the $(K + 1)$st subproblem. Upon the failure to solve a particular subproblem, the algorithm returns to the previous successful subproblem and then seeks a solution to the next (previously failed) subproblem. If each subproblem can be solved, the original problem can be solved; otherwise, the algorithm backs up all the way to the initial situation, from which point there is no way to solve the first subproblem such that other successes will follow.

Recursion is the natural approach for backtracking algorithms because the following are true:

1. *The same basic test is applied to each subproblem.*
2. *Local information must be saved in reverse order* of appearance, since the algorithm must return to the previous success upon the failure to solve a subproblem.

If necessary, review the `ReverseTheString` procedure in Application 7.2 as an example of saving local variable values for reverse-order processing.

APPLICATION 7.6 In Search of the Golden Floppy

Imagine that we have just landed our small airplane upon a mysterious island somewhere in the South Pacific in search of the elusive Golden Floppy. We do not know exactly where it is on the island, but we are determined to find it even if we must comb the entire island. Of course, there are plenty of obstacles to avoid, such as piranha-infested rivers, deep gorges, steep mountains, dense thickets, perilous quicksand, the edge of the island itself, and some fairly user-unfriendly cannibals! In fact, it is entirely possible that we cannot ever reach the Golden Floppy at all because of these obstacles.

We will represent the island as a two-dimensional array of char characters called `Island`. Each array element contains one of the following eight characters:

`@` = the Golden Floppy	`~` = water	`#` = thicket	`v` = gorge
space = safe walking area	`*` = quicksand	`/` = mountain	`!` = cannibals

In Application 3.1, the Game of Life, a border of lifeless cells surrounding the bacterial colony simplified the neighbor-counting algorithm, since counting the neighbors of cells along the perimeter of the colony would otherwise pose a special case. Similarly, we will enclose the island itself in a border of water characters. Two global declarations for our sample island follow:

```
VAR
  Island    : ARRAY [ 0..11, 0..11 ] OF Char;  {Rows 0, 11 & columns 0, 11 are water}
  PathFound : Boolean;
```

For simplicity, we will assume that a search begins with the element `Island [ 1, 1 ]`, which always contains a blank character—i.e., a safe walking area. (The program could be later modified to prompt the user for the start element and then test the specified element to determine if it is a safe area to begin.) We must abide by three rules when searching:

1. We can move into any *adjacent* element along the current *row* or the current *column*. We cannot move diagonally or skip elements.
2. We can move only into an element that contains a blank (`' '`) or the beloved Golden Floppy (`@`); we cannot leave the island during the search or move into any element containing an obstacle character (`~`, `*`, `#`, `/`, `v`, or `!`) or a period (`.`)—the placement of periods is explained in rule 3.
3. We must leave a trail of periods in the array to represent a path to the Golden Floppy if such a path is found; otherwise, we must leave the island as we found it.

After a successful search is completed, the entire island should be displayed, with periods marking the trail. Depicted in Figure 7.14 are two sample islands and the results of searching them (the starting location, golden floppy and path—if found—is outlined in boldface).

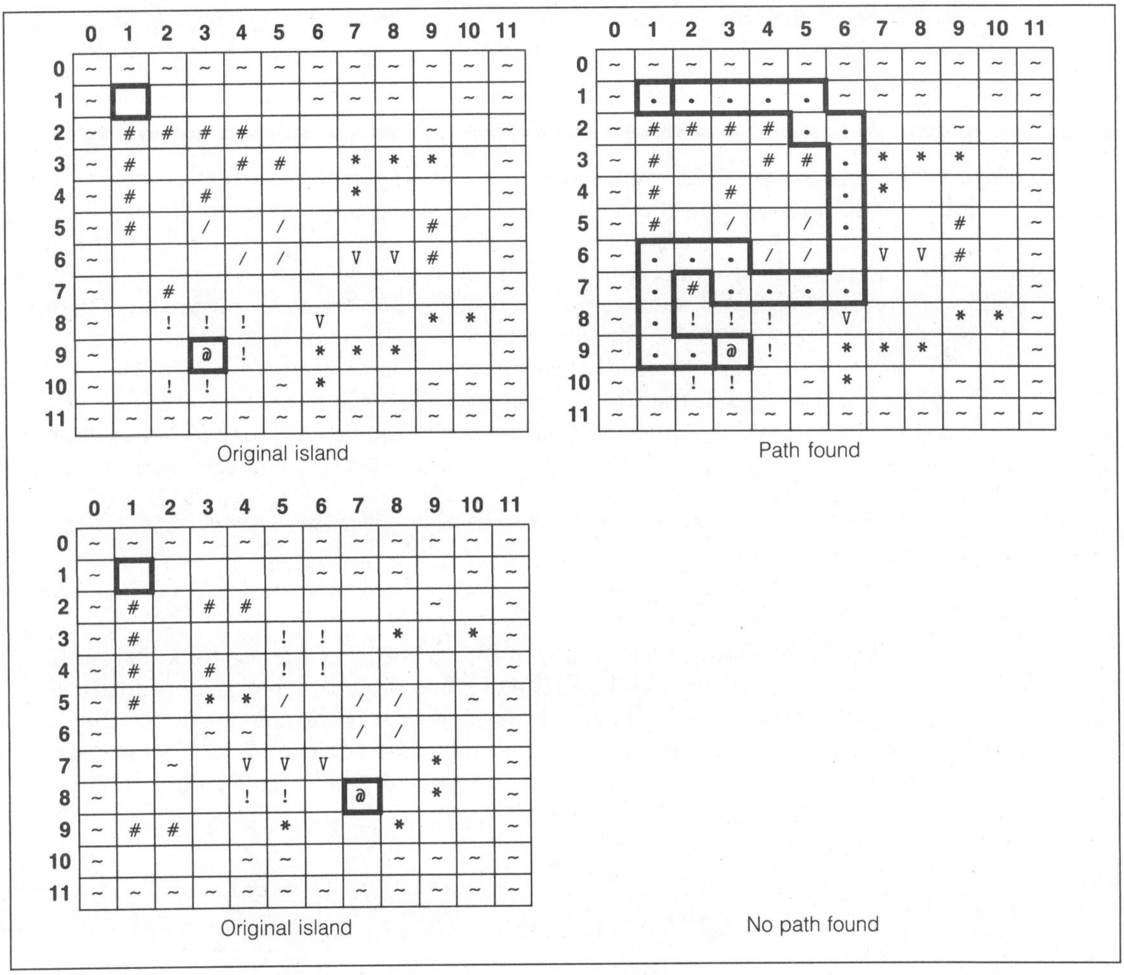

FIGURE 7.14 Searching Two Sample Islands

The `Island` array can be initialized by reading characters from a text file, one array row per line. Since many recursive calls will be made, this is an application in which the `Island` array will simply be used as a global variable rather than passing its address upon each call .

The overall problem here is to find a path from the starting element (element `Island [ 1, 1 ]` in these examples) to the element containing the Golden Floppy. A complete success occurs when we are able to move to the element containing the `@` character. A complete failure occurs when, upon successive failures, we have backtracked all the way to the start element and are unable to find a successful path in any direction from there.

In designing our recursive algorithm, we must choose the fixed order in which we will examine adjacent elements. The algorithm will employ a particular probe order—i.e., the order in which four adjacent elements will be tested. If there is but a single path to the Golden Floppy, any of the 24 different probe orders will yield this path. If several paths are possible, however,

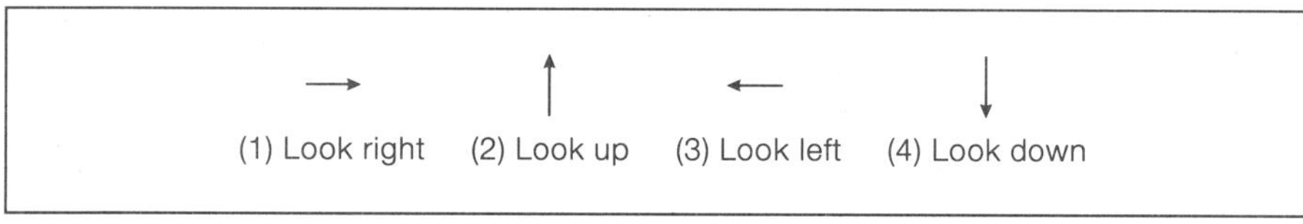

FIGURE 7.15 Probe Order Used for the Islands of Figure 7.14

different probe orders may produce different paths. The probe order used to find the path in Figure 7.14—and the one we will use in our discussion is counterclockwise—is shown in Figure 7.15.

Each time we advance to another element this same probe order is employed, beginning with "look right." We keep on advancing (i.e., recursing) as long as it is successful. Upon a failure to advance, we will return to the previous element where we placed a period and attempt to move in the next direction from there, again using this same probe order.

In designing the search algorithm we must also be careful about exactly when a period is stored and when an existing period is overwritten with a space character. And if a path is found, the algorithm must unwind "gracefully" from all recursive calls—i.e., it should not overwrite the stored periods along the path back to `Island [ 1, 1 ]`.

Here is how the successful (manual) search of the first island in Figure 7.14 begins:

1. From `Island [ 1, 1 ]` we look right, since it is the first direction in the probe order. `Island [ 1, 2 ]` contains a space, so we can move there and place a period.
2. From `Island [ 1, 2 ]` we start the probe order all over again; i.e., we look right. We are able to advance by looking right until we get to element `Island [ 1, 5 ]`. Here we look right (no space or @), look up (island/array border), look left (no space or @), then look down to find a space and move there (`Island [ 2, 5 ]`).
3. From `Island [ 2, 5 ]` we again advance element by element until `Island [ 2, 8 ]`, which is a dead end. Since we cannot advance, we must replace the period at `Island [ 2, 8 ]` with a space and backtrack (return) to the last "success," which is at `Island [ 2, 7 ]`.
4. The last time we were at `Island [ 2, 7 ]`, we looked right and advanced to `Island [ 2, 8 ]`. This resulted in failure, so we now look up from element `Island [ 2, 7 ]`, left, and then down before concluding that moving to `Island [ 2, 7 ]` also resulted in failure.
5. Upon backtracking to `Island [ 2, 6 ]`, we look up, left, and then down to find a space at `Island [ 3, 6 ]`. We move to `Island [ 3, 6 ]` and store a period.

A pseudocode recursive algorithm for finding the first path, based on the aforementioned counterclockwise probe order, follows.

```
ALGORITHM FindPath ( Row, Column : Integer; VAR PathFound : Boolean )

BEGIN
IF Island [ Row, Column ] contains the Golden Floppy THEN
  PathFound := TRUE
ELSE
  Island [ Row, Column ] := '.';

IF (path not yet found) AND (can move right) THEN
  Make a recursive call to move right:  FindPath ( Row, Column + 1, PathFound );

IF (path not yet found) AND (can move up) THEN
  Make a recursive call to move up:  FindPath ( Row - 1, Column, PathFound );

IF (path not yet found) AND (can move left) THEN
  Make a recursive call to move left:  FindPath ( Row, Column - 1, PathFound );

IF (path not yet found) AND (can move down) THEN
  Make a recursive call to move down:  FindPath ( Row + 1, Column, PathFound );

IF path not yet found THEN
  Replace '.' at Island [ Row, Column ] with ' '
END;
```

It is important to note that, because **VAR** does not appear before `Row` and `Column`, these parameters preserve the locations of safe squares where periods were placed. Also note that to find a path it is not necessary to leave some kind of special character in every element that is visited but is not in the path. (Study the algorithm and the island examples to convince yourself that this is true.) Leaving a special character, however, will speed up the searching process by ensuring that the same safe-walking-area element is never visited twice. This is especially important for larger sections of the island that contain safe-walking areas. For example, the elements `Island [ 7, 7 ]`, `[ 7, 8 ]`, `[ 8, 7 ]`, and `[ 8, 8 ]` in the top sample island of Figure 7.14 will be visited a number of times after advancing rightward from `Island [ 7, 6 ]`. To improve the efficiency of our search we will therefore substitute the following **IF** statement for the final **IF** statement in pseudocode algorithm FindPath.

```
IF Path not yet found THEN
  Replace . at Island [ Row, Column ] with x
```

The `x` character will be regarded as an obstacle character, signaling that the element has already been examined and therefore should not be reexamined. If a path is found, the routine redisplaying the island must be designed so as to not display any `x` characters stored.

Do you see why the algorithm must test for a complete success before testing adjacent elements for "walkability" and before replacing the `.` with an `x` upon a failure? Remember that execution flow here will return from any given recursive call for either of two reasons: Either the algorithm failed to advance from a square and must therefore *backtrack* to the previous safe walking area to attempt a different direction from there, or else the Golden Floppy was found. In the latter case, the algorithm must simply return gracefully from all the recursive calls, being careful not to disturb the path or to continue searching en route back to the original call.

When the Golden Floppy is reached, there will probably be many activation records stacked in the heap (one per period stored), and there is no shortcut back to the original call statement; the algorithm must, instead, unwind from all recursive calls, as with any recursive algorithm. If a path were found and we did *not* test for such a success before testing each adjacent element for safety or before replacing the space, upon unwinding each . would simply be replaced with an x, erasing the entire path (remember that x characters should not be displayed when the entire island is redisplayed).

The Pascal version of algorithm FindPath and a simple main routine follows.

```
{Global declarations}
VAR
  Island    : ARRAY [ 0..11, 0..11 ] OF Char:  {Rows 0,11 & columns 0,11 are water}
  Pathfound : Boolean;
```

```
PROCEDURE  FindPath ( Row, Column : Integer;  VAR PathFound : Boolean );

BEGIN
IF Island [ Row, Column ] = '@' THEN
  PathFound := TRUE                                    {Set flag for overall success}
ELSE
  Island [ Row, Column ] := '.';                       {Leave marker in this "safe" area}

IF NOT PathFound AND ( Island [ Row, Column + 1 ] IN [ ' ', '@' ] ) THEN
  FindPath ( Row, Column + 1, PathFound );                                 {Move right}

IF NOT PathFound AND ( Island [ Row - 1, Column ] IN [ ' ', '@' ] ) THEN
  FindPath ( Row - 1, Column, PathFound );                                 {Move up}

IF NOT PathFound AND ( Island [ Row, Column - 1 ] IN [ ' ', '@' ] ) THEN
  FindPath ( Row, Column - 1, PathFound );                                 {Move left}

IF NOT PathFound AND (Island [ Row + 1, Column ] IN [ ' ', '@' ] ) THEN
  FindPath ( Row + 1, Column, PathFound );                                 {Move down}

IF NOT PathFound THEN                      {Unable to move from Island [Row, Column]}
  Island [ Row, Column ] := 'x'            {  so replace . with x}
END;
```

```
{***  Main Routine  ***}

BEGIN
{Call a programmer-defined procedure to initialize the Island array}
{Call a programmer-defined procedure to display the Island array}

PathFound := FALSE;
FindPath ( 1, 1, PathFound );

IF PathFound THEN
  BEGIN
  {Call the procedure to display the Island array--do not display x characters}
  Writeln ( 'Path Found!' )
  END
ELSE
  Writeln ( 'No Path Found!' )
END.
```

APPLICATION 7.7 The Eight Queens Problem

As the most powerful piece in chess, a queen may attack any piece in its same column or row or along either diagonal. In the classic Eight Queens Problem, we attempt to place eight queens on a chessboard such that no queen is in a position to attack another queen. Figure 7.16 illustrates the power of a single queen (indicated by a Q character) along with showing two unique solutions to the problem.

As with the island-searching algorithm in Application 7.6, the Eight Queens Problem must be solved using a careful trial-and-error, *backtracking* approach. You may be surprised to learn that there are actually 92 solutions, 12 of which are unique (the others are merely symmetrical duplicates). Of course, it is not possible to place more than eight nonattacking queens on a chessboard.

In the worst case, how many different board configurations might an algorithm have to test? There are 4,426,165,368 different ways of arranging eight queens on a chessboard (i.e., selecting 8 squares out of 64). This staggering number can be immediately reduced to 40,320 or 8!, since no two queens may share a column or row. And this quantity is significantly reduced further by the fact that, with backtracking, a failure along a particular path of investigation will preclude any further (useless) attempts along the same path.

As with the island-searching problem, a testing algorithm should recurse ahead upon each success, or, upon a failure, should return to the last success and attempt further successes from there. In this problem, success is defined as the ability to place a queen on the board, whereas a failure is defined as the inability to place a queen, leading to the removal of the previously placed queen. Again, the attempts must be uniform rather than random to preclude testing the same configuration twice or overlooking a possible successful configuration.

We will represent the chessboard using a two-dimensional character array of eight rows by eight columns, as specified by the following global Pascal declaration:

```
VAR
  Board      : ARRAY [ 1..8, 1..8 ] OF Char;
  QueenCount : Integer;
```

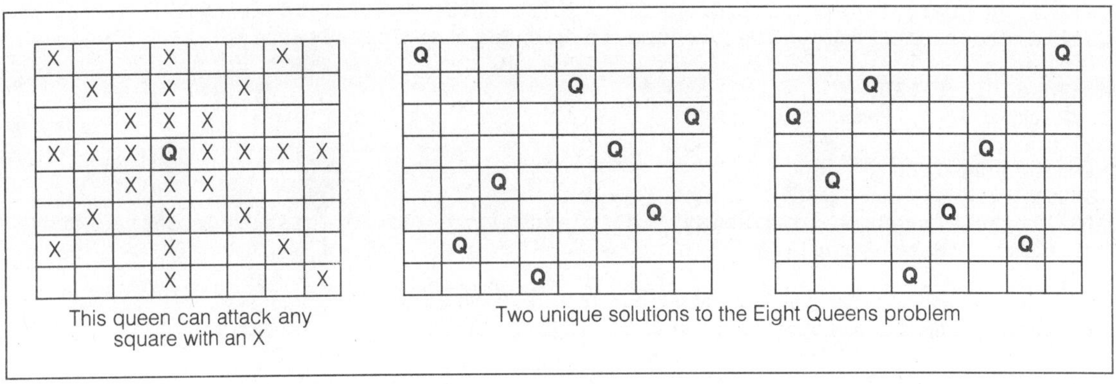

FIGURE 7.16 The Eight Queens Problem

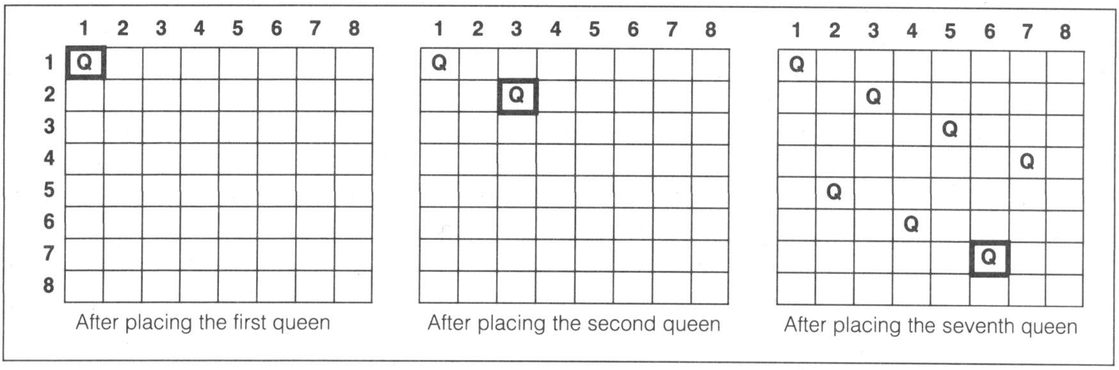

FIGURE 7.17 The Chessboard after Placing One, Two, and Seven Queens

We can begin by placing the first queen at position Board [1, 1]. From Board [1, 1] we can examine each position, Board [1, 2], [1, 3], . . ., Board [1, 8], Board [2, 1], Board [2, 2], until element Board[2, 3] is found to be "safe" and the second queen is placed, as shown in Figure 7.17. From the Board [2, 3] success, the search continues in the same way (Board [2, 4], [2, 5], . . . , Board [3, 1], . .) until Board [3, 5] is found to be safe. This continues until seven queens have been placed.

Testing each square from Board [7, 7] until Board [8, 8], however, we can find no safe positions for the eighth queen. Upon this failure, we backtrack to the last success (the seventh queen at Board [7, 6]), remove this queen, and then attempt to place it at the next safe position, which is at Board [8, 5], as shown in Figure 7.18. From Board [8, 6] we are again unable to place the eighth queen, so the seventh queen is removed and, since we cannot replace the seventh queen, we must backtrack to the sixth queen. The sixth queen must be removed and replaced at the next safe position, from which we again attempt to place the seventh and eighth queens. These steps are depicted in Figure 7.18.

Notice that, upon a failure, we backtrack only to the *previous* queen for removal and replacement. This ensures that no configuration is ever re-

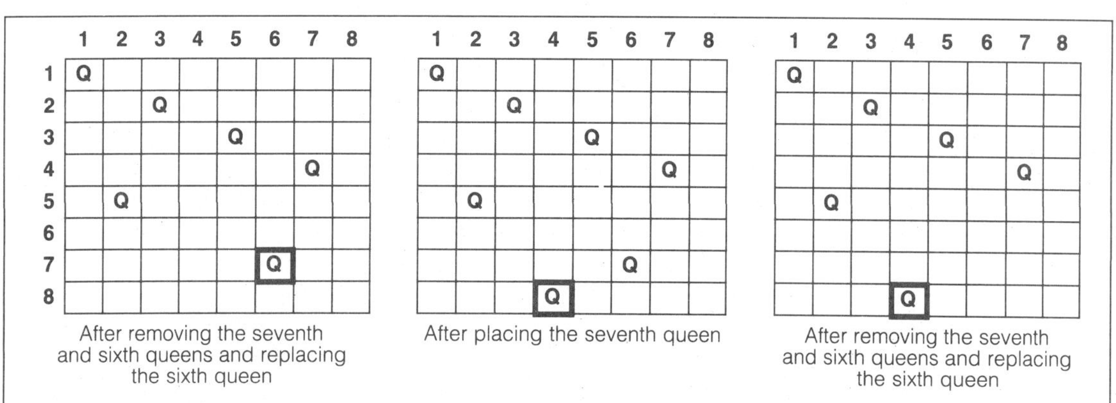

FIGURE 7.18 Some Intermediate Trials in the Eight Queens Problem

peated or overlooked. The process could conceivably continue until we have backtracked all the way to the queen at `Board [ 1, 1 ]`, which would then be removed and replaced at `Board [ 1, 2 ]`. A pseudocode algorithm for deriving the first solution to the Eight Queens Problem follows. It has been written based on the following initial call:

```
QueenCount := 0;
EightQueens ( 1, 1, QueenCount ).
```

Because so many recursive calls to `EightQueens` will be made, we will use the `Board` array as a global array rather than passing it as a parameter. (As you examine this simple version, consider how you would modify it to reduce total execution time.)

```
ALGORITHM EightQueens ( Row, Column : Integer;  VAR QueenCount : Integer );

BEGIN
REPEAT
  Look for next safe position starting with Board [ Row, Column ], setting Row
    and Column to the safe position;

  IF a safe position was found (at Board [ Row, Column ]) THEN
    BEGIN
    Place queen at Board [ Row, Column ];
    Increment QueenCount;
    IF QueenCount < 8 THEN
      Try to place next queen:   EightQueens ( Row, Column, QueenCount );

    IF QueenCount < 8 THEN
      BEGIN
      Remove queen at Board [ Row, Column ];
      Decrement QueenCount;
      Change Row and/or Column to examine next board position, if possible
      END
    END

UNTIL  (QueenCount = 8)  OR (no more Board positions for current configuration)
END;
```

Study this algorithm very carefully, since it involves both recursion and iterative looping (via the **REPEAT** statement). A recursive call is made after each successful placement of a queen if an eighth queen has not yet been placed. As in the island-searching problem of Application 7.8, a return from a recursive call indicates that one of two events has happened: In the failure case, the algorithm failed to place the next queen and must therefore backtrack to the last-placed queen, remove it, place it at the next safe board position, and then look for the next safe board position for the next queen. In the success case, the algorithm just placed all eight queens and must now unwind gracefully from all recursive calls without attempting to place other queens or disturbing already-placed queens.

The Pascal representation of the pseudocode algorithm follows; it was written based on the following three assumptions:

1. `Board` is initialized to all blank characters.
2. The initial call is (again) as follows:

```
QueenCount := 0;
EightQueens ( 1, 1, QueenCount ).
```

3. The programmer-defined procedure `FindSafePosition` *already exists;* it finds the next safe position starting with the current board position, `Board [ Row, Column ]` passed to it. If `FindSafePosition` does not find a safe position, it returns a false value in Boolean parameter `FoundSafePosition`; otherwise it returns a true value as well as the row and column coordinates of the safe position in parameters `Row` and `Column`.

```
PROCEDURE EightQueens ( Row, Column : Integer; VAR QueenCount : Integer );

VAR
  FoundSafePosition : Boolean;

BEGIN
REPEAT
  FindSafePosition ( FoundSafePosition, Row, Column );

  IF FoundSafePosition THEN
    BEGIN
    Board [ Row, Column ] := 'Q';       {Store queen symbol}
    QueenCount := QueenCount + 1;       {Increment queen count}
    IF QueenCount < 8 THEN
      EightQueens ( Row, Column, QueenCount );

    IF QueenCount < 8 THEN              {Return here means failure to place queen}
      BEGIN
      Board [ Row, Column ] := ' ';     {Remove queen}
      QueenCount := QueenCount - 1;     {Decrement queen count}

      Column := Column + 1;             {Preparation for call to FindSafePosition}
      IF Column > 8 THEN                {Wrap around to next row if necessary}
        BEGIN
        Column := 1;
        Row    := Row + 1
        END;
      FoundSafePosition := Row <= 8     {Flag to continue searching}
      END    {IF QueenCount < 8 THEN}

    END      {IF FoundSafePosition THEN}
UNTIL  (QueenCount = 8)  OR NOT FoundSafePosition
END;
```

7.6 RECURSIVE DESCENT

Recursion is a convenient tool for defining the syntax of a language and for designing algorithms, which must parse a string of characters in order to evaluate it. In the latter application, the string may represent a numeric expression, a command line for a program, or even a high-level programming language statement to be evaluated by a compiler. As an example of using recursion to both define and evaluate expressions, in our next application we design a function to evaluate an arithmetic prefix expression using a technique called *recursive descent.*

APPLICATION 7.8 A Prefix Expression Calculator

Recall from Application 6.3 that expressions involving two operands and one operator may be formatted as either a prefix, infix, or postfix expression, depending on the relative positions of the operator and operands:

Expression form	Syntax			Example
Prefix notation	**{operator}**	{operand}	{operand}	− 3 5
Infix notation	{operand}	**{operator}**	{operand}	3 − 5
Postfix notation	{operand}	{operand}	**{operator}**	3 5 −

Although infix notation is the most common form in daily life, prefix notation provides the advantage that no parentheses are necessary (if the expression is written correctly) to indicate the hierarchy of addition and subtraction operations over multiplication and division operations. Several examples to show equivalent infix and prefix expressions follow, using five variables of real data type (A, B, C, D, and E):

Infix Notation	Equivalent Prefix Notation	Result
A = 3 + 10	A = + 3 10	13
B = 3 × (10 + 5)	B = × 3 + 10 5	45
C = 3 × (10 + 15) − 17	C = − × 3 + 10 15 17	58
D = (C − B) × A	D = × − C B A	169
E = A × B + C + D	E = + + × A B C D	812

Notice that a prefix expression consists of an operator followed by two operands, each of which may be a constant, variable, or another prefix expression. *Evaluating a prefix expression requires the repeated application of the prefix syntax rule.* The expression + 3 10 indicates a + operator followed by its two operands, 3 and 10, and the result is 13. The expression × 3 + 10 5 indicates a × operator followed by its two operands, 3 and the expression + 10 5. Again we employ the prefix syntax rule and find that the subexpression + 10 5 consists of a + operator followed by its two operands, 10 and 5, and the result is 15. The × operator now has its first and second operands, 3 and 15, and the result is 45.

We will write a recursive function named `Eval` to parse a string of characters representing a valid prefix expression and return the value of that expression. The base operation involves parsing ahead enough to evaluate an expression of the form:

```
{operator} {operand 1} {operand 2}
```

Our program will prompt the user to enter an infix expression, and will then evaluate that expression and display the result. The entire expression will be read into a nonstandard String variable and parsed. As usual, we will begin with a simple degree of functionality and will omit error checking on the user input. The program can always be enhanced at a later time to perform error checking and other operations. We will assume that the user adheres to the following rules:

- The entire expression entered must be a syntactically correct prefix expression.
- An operand may be a number or another infix expression.
- A numeric string operand is comprised of the character digits 0 through 9 with no embedded spaces. The converted integer value of the string must not exceed **`MAXINT`**.
- Only 4 operator symbols are allowed: +, −, *, /. Unary minus is not allowed; e.g., −5 must be entered as 0−5.
- Parentheses are allowed, including nesting parentheses, but must be balanced.
- Spaces are allowed except within a numeric string operand.

The program will prompt for an expression, which it reads into a String variable. The program will then call a recursive function named `Eval`, which must parse and evaluate each string expression character by character until the end of the string, returning the value of the entire expression. The user will input the character `Q` instead of a prefix expression to terminate the program.

The expression will be passed to the `Eval` function in a variable called `Buffer`, of data type `String[80]`. As an example, Figure 7.19 depicts the sample expression − * 3 + 10 5 17 already stored in the `Buffer` structure.

An operator character, encountered by `Eval` as it parses the string, marks the start of a prefix expression. This is where the recursion is used:

> Each time an operator is encountered, `Eval` recurses ahead to parse and evaluate its operands. When both operands are evaluated, the execution flow returns, and `Eval` applies the appropriate operation to the operands.

Of course, an operand may, itself, be another prefix expression to be evaluated.

A simple version of a program follows. The program prompts the user for a syntactically correct prefix expression; then function `Eval` is called to evaluate the expression, and the result is displayed upon return to the main routine. Procedure `SeekChars` increments `Index` until it encounters a `SkipSet` character in `Buffer` string or else `Index` exceeds the length of `Buffer`.

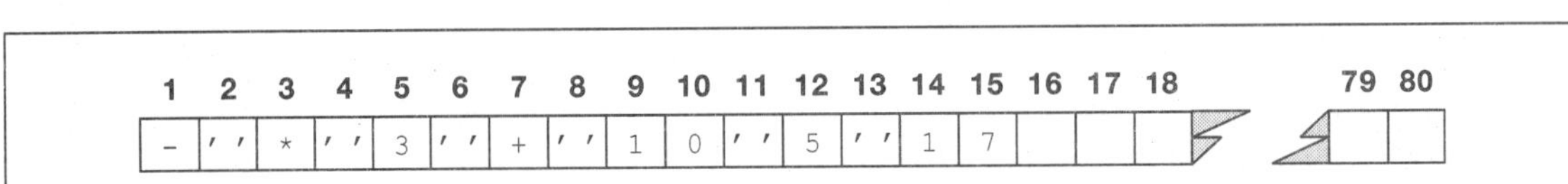

FIGURE 7.19 **Sample Prefix Expression − * 3 + 10 5 17 Stored Within `Buffer`**

```
{Program:   PrefixCalculator

 Function:  Evaluates a syntactically-correct prefix expression entered
            interactively after the prompt.  Valid input:
            Operators:  +, -, *, /
            Operands:   Unsigned integer constants
            Other:      Spaces,(,); Q terminates program  }

PROGRAM  PrefixCalculator ( INPUT, OUTPUT );

TYPE
  BuffType   =  String [ 80 ] ;
  CharSet    =  SET OF Char;

VAR
  Buffer               :  BuffType;            {Holds the entire prefix expression}
  Index                :  Integer;
  AnotherExpression    :  Boolean;             {Becomes false when user enters Q}
```

```
{The following 4 procedures are defined in Appendix K}

PROCEDURE SeekChars ( VAR Buffer : BuffType; VAR Index : Integer;
                      SeekSet : CharSet;  VAR Success : Boolean );

PROCEDURE SkipChars ( VAR Buffer : BuffType; VAR Index : Integer;
                      SkipSet : CharSet;  VAR Success : Boolean );

FUNCTION CharToInteger ( Ch : Char ) : Integer;

PROCEDURE StringToInteger (  VAR Buffer : BuffType; VAR Index, Value : Integer;
                             VAR Success : Boolean );
```

```
FUNCTION Eval ( VAR Buffer : BuffType; VAR Index : Integer  ) : Real;

VAR
  Ch        :  Char;
  Success   :  Boolean;
  Value     :  Integer;

BEGIN
SeekChars ( Buffer, Index, [ '0'..'9', '+', '-', '*', '/' ] , Success );
                                                      {Success is assumed}
Ch := Buffer [ Index ] ;                              {Obtain next character}
IF Ch IN [ '0'..'9' ] THEN
  BEGIN
  StringToInteger ( Buffer, Index, Value, Success );  {Success is assumed}
  Eval := Value
  END
ELSE                                                  {An operator character}
  BEGIN
  Index  := Index + 1;
  CASE Ch OF
    '+'  :  Eval := Eval ( Buffer, Index )  +  Eval ( Buffer, Index );
    '-'  :  Eval := Eval ( Buffer, Index )  -  Eval ( Buffer, Index );
    '*'  :  Eval := Eval ( Buffer, Index )  *  Eval ( Buffer, Index );
    '/'  :  Eval := Eval ( Buffer, Index )  /  Eval ( Buffer, Index )
  END
  END
END;
```

```
PROCEDURE Prelude;

BEGIN
Writeln ( '***  Simple  Prefix  Expression  Evaluator  ***' );
Writeln;
Writeln ( 'Legal operands:   Integers between 0 and ', MAXINT, ' (inclusive)' );
Writeln ( 'Legal operators:  +, -, *, /' );
Writeln
END;
```

```
PROCEDURE  ObtainExpression ( VAR Buffer : BuffType;
                              VAR AnotherExpression : Boolean );
BEGIN
Writeln;
Writeln ( 'Enter a syntactically-correct prefix expression or Q to quit:' );
Write ( '              ' );
Readln ( Buffer );
AnotherExpression := NOT ( Buffer [ 1 ] IN [ 'Q', 'q' ] )
END;
```

```
{***  Main  routine for PrefixCalculator  ***}

BEGIN
Prelude;                                  {Welcome user, display rules of syntax}
REPEAT
  ObtainExpression ( Buffer, AnotherExpression );
  IF AnotherExpression THEN
    BEGIN
    Index := 1;
    Writeln ( 'Value = ', Eval ( Buffer, Index ):9:7 )
    END
UNTIL NOT AnotherExpression
END.
```

`Eval` obtains the next character and determines if it is a digit or an operator. If it is a digit, then that digit and any others immediately following it are converted from characters to a single integer value by our programmer-defined procedure `StringToInteger`; this value is then assigned to the function identifier, `Eval`. An operator character, on the other hand, indicates the start of a prefix expression. To evaluate this expression, `Eval` will **CASE** on the operator value to execute one of four statements. Each of these statements applies a Pascal operator to two operands obtained; a recursive call is made to obtain the value of each operand before the operator is applied. When both operand values are obtained and the operator is applied, the result is assigned to the `Eval` function identifier.

The prefix expressions comprise two key items: Nondecomposable entities called *tokens* (integer operands and operators) and decomposable entities (other whole prefix expressions). Tokens may be evaluated directly, whereas prefix expressions must be broken down into an operator (token) and two operands (each of which may be an integer token or another decomposable prefix expression). Eventually all decomposable operands are broken down into tokens. This process of parsing/decomposing/evaluating is referred to as *recursive descent: recursive* because the same evaluation is reapplied repeatedly and *descent* because the recursion takes the evaluation process deeper and deeper in the recursive search for integer tokens (i.e., higher and higher into heapspace, based on depiction of heapspace in Figure 4.8).

7.7 RECURSION VERSUS ITERATION

In deciding whether to design and represent an algorithm recursively instead of iteratively, three issues must be considered:

1. Can the algorithm be written recursively?
2. Is recursion a "natural" approach? Does the recursive representation result in code that is easier to write, understand, and test?
3. Does the recursive representation require an acceptable amount of heap-space and execution time?

Discussion of each of these issues follows.

Some problems naturally lend themselves to recursive solutions, whereas others do not. Recursion is appropriate if the problem can easily be divided into similar parts, each of which may be solved by (recursively) applying an identical set of operations and using information from the solution of a previous subproblem. Each subproblem must be congruent to the original problem, as in the binary search (Application 7.5) or prefix expression evaluation (Application 7.8), so that solving each subproblem in turn results in a solution to the original problem. Both recursive and iterative loops require that the terminal condition or conditions become true at some point to halt the looping. Problems that naturally call for recursive looping can often be expressed using a recurrence relation, as in the factorial algorithm (Application 7.1).

Some problems require that values be saved during the recursing, to be processed while unwinding. The string-reversing problem (Applications 6.1 and 7.2) and the Eight Queens problems (Application 7.7) are examples of this. Recursion is useful because such values can be saved in the recursive routine's local variables, to be accessed as needed upon returning from recursive calls. Such postorder recursion could be simulated by an iterative routine that maintains its own stack of values in lieu of an operating system-controlled stack of activation records. This shifts the burden of storing and retrieving values from the operating system to the programmer, resulting in a longer program code and thereby requiring more time for program design, coding, and testing.

Recursive algorithms involving *tail recursion,* where the last statement executed involves a recursive call, are even easier to convert. The general conversion strategy is as follows (for simplicity, a single integer parameter is assumed).

If a recursive routine `R ( X : Integer )` has as its last executable statement a call to itself, `R ( Y )`, the recursion can be eliminated by doing the following:

1. Enclose all executable statements in the routine within a **WHILE**, **REPEAT**, or **FOR** statement.
2. The terminal condition for the recursive implementation (or its logical inverse) now becomes the terminal condition for the **WHILE** (or **REPEAT** or **FOR**) statement.
3. Derive the value of `Y` as in the recursive version, then substitute the recursive call with the assignment statement `X := Y` as the last statement inside the **WHILE**, **REPEAT**, or **FOR** loop.

A recursive approach offers both advantages and disadvantages. A recursive algorithm involving postorder recursion typically requires fewer statements than does its iterative counterpart, which must include the instructions and data structures to maintain its own stack of values. Recursive algorithms often reflect a natural, or intuitive, solution that is more readily understandable than is its iterative counterpart. Even so, developing and verifying a nonrecursive version of an algorithm may take more time. Recursive functions are often easier to verify mathematically than are iterative functions by representing the algorithm as a recurrence relation and employing a *proof by induction*. Because a recursive routine calls itself repeatedly, resulting in the reexecution of the same code path, algorithm testing may seem a little confusing to novice programmers, who must determine not only *where* a particular bug occurred but *when* (i.e., upon which recursive call) it occurred as well.

Remember that one activation record is allocated in heapspace each time a procedure or function is called. A procedure or function that must make many recursive calls will expend time in the overhead of each call and may attempt to consume more heapspace than is available. In this regard, an iterative algorithm will typically prove more efficient than will its recursive counterpart, even if a stack is being directly maintained. For some applications, the choice between recursion and iteration boils down to a choice between computer runtime efficiency and programmer efficiency. On the other hand, there are problems for which recursion is decidedly not a sound choice. As an example, we consider the famous Fibonacci series.

APPLICATION 7.9

Calculating the Nth Value of the Fibonacci Series

In 1202, Italian mathematician Leonardo Fibonacci wondered how many pairs of rabbits would inhabit an island after 1 year, based on the following simple scenario:

> A pair of rabbits requires a month to mature, after which time they will produce a pair of baby rabbits every month, with no rabbits dying within the year.

He assumed the existence of a single pair of rabbits in the first month. In the second month, there is still only one pair but they have matured and produce a new pair of rabbits in the third month (there are now two pairs on the island). In the fourth month, while the just-born pair are as yet sexually immature, the original pair of rabbits give birth to another pair (there are now three pair of rabbits). In the fifth month, the rabbits born in the third month have matured and now give birth to a pair, along with the original rabbits who produce yet another pair (there are now 5 pairs on the island). The number of rabbit pairs continues to grow as follows:

Month:	1	2	3	4	5	6	7	8	9	10	11	12 . . .
Pairs:	1	1	2	3	5	8	13	21	34	55	89	144 . . .

Notice that after the second month, a specific count of rabbit pairs may be calculated as the sum of the counts from the two previous months.

The sequence generated in counting the number of rabbit pairs is called the **Fibonacci series** and is used in a variety of mathematical applications.

The recurrence relation for generating this series may be written as follows (here, Fibonacci is abbreviated as Fib):

Fib (1) = 1

Fib (2) = 1

Fib (N) » Fib (N – 2) + Fib (N – 1) {for $N \geq 3$}

N is the ordinal position of a term of the series and Fib (N) is the value of the Nth term, commonly referred to as the Nth Fibonacci number. For example, the eleventh Fibonacci number is computed as follows:

$$\begin{aligned}\text{Fib (11)} &= \text{Fib (9)} + \text{Fib (10)}\\ &= 34 + 55\\ &= 89\end{aligned}$$

The recurrence relation may be represented easily in Pascal as a recursive function. The following version was written based on the assumption that a positive initial value for parameter N is passed on the initial call):

```
FUNCTION Fib ( N : Integer ) : Integer;

BEGIN
IF N <= 2 THEN
  Fib := 1
ELSE
  Fib := Fib ( N - 1 ) + Fib ( N - 2 )
END;
```

Each call with N greater than 2 results in the execution of a statement containing more than one recursive call. This is an example of **nonlinear recursion** because the total number of recursive calls grows exponentially. In function Fib, any Fib (N – 1) expression must be evaluated completely before its value can be added to the associated Fib (N – 2) expression, which also must be evaluated completely. Every other application in this chapter has involved **linear recursion,** in which case the total number of calls increases at a slower, linear rate based on problem size. Whereas *heapspace diagrams* are useful for tracing the values of variables during linear recursion, a **recursion tree** is useful in tracing the values of variables during nonlinear recursion. Figure 7.20 shows part of the recursion tree generated by the following initial call:

```
Writeln ( 'The 98th Fibonacci number is ', Fib ( 98 ));
```

Each level in the tree shows the subsequent recursive calls that result when Fib is called with a new value for N. At the top of the tree is the nonrecursive initial call that generates the two recursive calls shown on the next level.

To compute the value of the 98th Fibonacci number, the entire *left* side of this tree (which continues for another 94 levels) must be completely evalu-

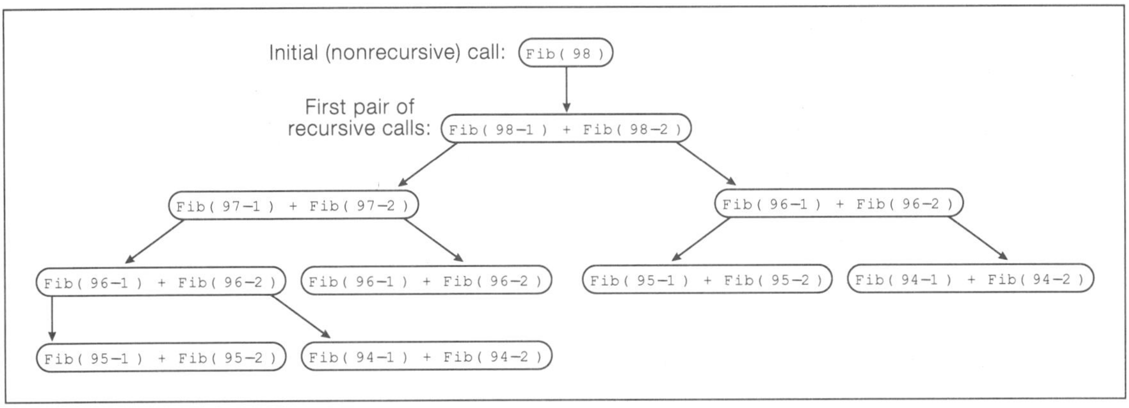

FIGURE 7.20 Partial Recursion Tree for `Fib(98)`

ated before the entire *right* side is evaluated. Although Figure 7.20 shows only a small part of the entire tree, two disturbing facts are readily apparent:

- Many recursive calls generate many activation records, which expends a great deal of heapspace.
- Many of the calls are redundant, thereby wasting both execution time and heapspace. For example, in just the fraction of the complete tree shown in Figure 7.20, the call `Fib ( 96 – 1 )` is made—i.e., `Fib ( 95 )` is calculated—three times.

The following iterative version of the algorithm is preferable because it requires only a single activation record and does not perform any redundant calculations:

```
FUNCTION IFib ( N : Integer ) : Integer;

VAR
  K, Temp,
  Prev1, Prev2 : Integer;

BEGIN
Prev1 := 1;
Prev2 := 1;
FOR K := 3 TO N DO
  BEGIN
  Temp  := Prev1 + Prev2;    {New term value}
  Prev2 := Prev1;            {New N-2 value for next Kth value}
  Prev1 := Temp              {New N-1 value for next Kth value}
  END;
Fib := Prev1                 {Last-calculated, new-term-value}
END;
```

The *N*th Fibonacci number may also be computed directly, using the following equation:

$$\text{Fib}(N) = \frac{1}{\sqrt{5}}(\delta^N - \phi),$$

where

$$\delta = \frac{1 + \sqrt{5}}{2} \approx -0.618$$

$$\phi = \frac{1 - \sqrt{5}}{2} \approx \ 1.618$$

We have just seen that the Nth Fibonacci number can be be calculated with greater efficiency using iteration rather than recursion. In contrast, as our final application of this chapter, we will examine the classic Towers of Hanoi puzzle, whose solution is best derived using a recursive approach.

APPLICATION 7.10

Towers of Hanoi

Towers of Hanoi is a puzzle in which there are three vertical pegs ("towers"), labeled A, B, and C, with a number of disks of increasing diameters stacked on peg A. The objective is to move the stack of disks to peg B, one disk at a time, following one simple rule: A disk may be moved onto an empty peg or on top of a larger disk but never onto a smaller disk or away from the pegs. The number of disks may be varied. Figure 7.21 shows an initial arrangement of three disks and the final arrangement upon solving the puzzle. Briefly look ahead to Figure 7.23, which shows the the intervening steps necessary to solve the puzzle with three disks, in a minimum number of disk moves.

Many legends surround the Towers of Hanoi puzzle. In one legend, the puzzle was posed by a Chinese emperor as a test of intellect for any man in the kingdom who wished to succeed the court's wise man, who had just died. In another legend, monks in a remote monastery in China believed the puzzle was invented by God at the dawn of time as a major task for humanity. They believed that in solving the puzzle for 64 disks, this task would be completed, thereby marking the end of the world. For simplicity (and just to be safe!), the example in our discussion involves only three disks, although the algorithm we will devise will work for any positive number of disks.

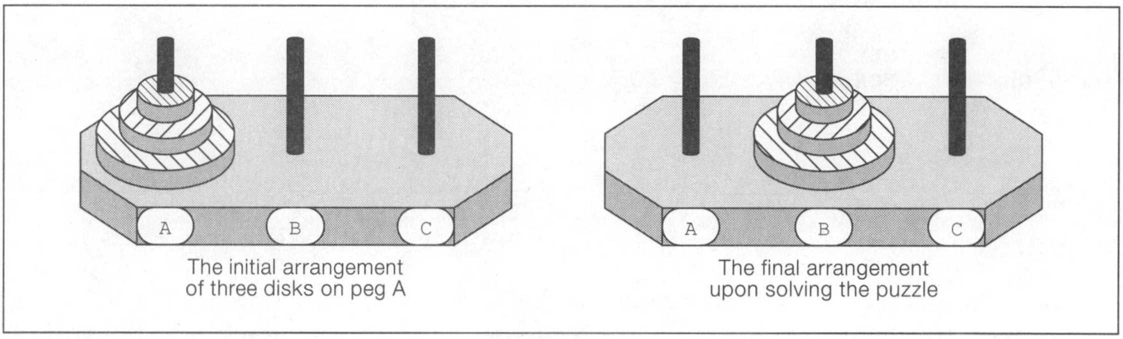

FIGURE 7.21 The Arrangement of Disks Initially and After the Puzzle is Solved

We will devise an interactive program that begins by prompting the user for the number of disks, then displays instructions directing the user to move a particular disk to a particular peg as the program solves the puzzle.

As you might expect, the puzzle increases in difficulty as a function of the number of disks; solving the puzzle with N disks requires a minimum of $2^N - 1$ disk moves; i.e., the algorithm is O (2^N). Solving the puzzle with three or four disks is fairly straightforward, but using five or six disks requires more thought. Solving the puzzle with ten disks is quite challenging, requiring at least 1023 moves. Solving it with 64 disks requires at least 2,518,687,446,509,551,615 moves—a series of *correct* moves made by hand one per second without stopping would take more than 79.9 billion years, more than six times the estimated age of the universe! (Of course, a computer can make many moves per second.) Through the power and elegance of recursion, the algorithm to solve the puzzle for any number of disks can be expressed in just five executable Pascal statements, as we shall see.

To derive an algorithm for solving the Towers of Hanoi puzzle, let us begin by breaking down the overall goal (i.e., moving the stack of disks from peg A to peg B) into three tasks. Let N be the quantity of disks, which are numbered 1 through N (disk 1 is smallest and disk N is largest):

1. Move disks 1 through $N - 1$ from the source to the free peg, leaving disk N on the source peg.
2. Move disk N from the source peg to the destination peg.
3. Move disks 1 through $N - 1$ from the free peg to the destination peg.

(Briefly looking ahead to Figure 7.23, the result of stage 1 is depicted in diagram 4, the result of stage 2 is depicted in diagram 5, and the result of stage 3 is depicted in diagram 8.) It is important to realize that the labels *source, destination,* and *free* are relative terms. Initially, peg A is the source, peg B is the destination, and peg C is free. During the act of solving the puzzle, these labels may be applied to other pegs because they are relative to the operation we are performing. For example, when the algorithm moves disks from peg A to peg C in step 1, peg C is the destination peg and peg B is the free peg. When it moves disks from peg C to peg B in step 3, peg C is the source and peg B is the destination.

Before moving disk N, we must first move disks 1 through $N - 1$. To move disk $N - 1$, we must first move disks 1 through $N - 2$, and so forth, until we have the simple task of moving only a single disk. Solving the puzzle for N disks therefore involves solving the same kind of puzzle for $N - 1$ disks, for $N - 2$ disks, etc.; i.e., the same algorithm is applied repeatedly to smaller and smaller collections of disks until the simple case of a collection of one disk occurs.

This approach is inherently recursive because we repeatedly solve subpuzzles, in which the number of disks to move is less than the original N value, by reapplying the steps. Eventually, the algorithm solves the puzzle for a single disk—the terminal condition—by simply moving a single disk from the source to the destination. Look ahead to procedure `Move` in the complete `TowersOfHanoi` program; the initial call to `Move` for the three-disk puzzle is `Move ( 3, 'A', 'B', 'C' )`.

Figure 7.22 contains a recursion tree mapping the execution of this algorithm when N is 3. In the tree, the order of the calls made are indicated by

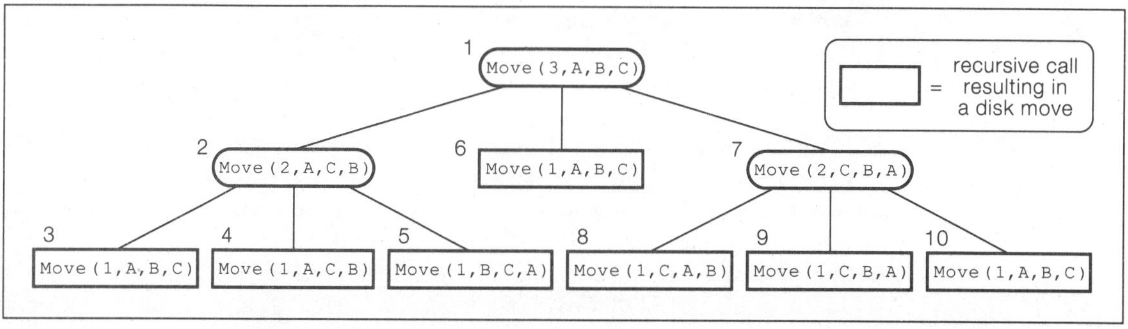

FIGURE 7.22 A Recursion Tree Mapping the Execution of Procedure `MoveDisks` for Three Disks

the number above each call. Examine the parameters for each call to see roles of *source, destination,* and *free* change as the algorithm progresses.

Figure 7.23 traces the seven disk moves that occur in solving the puzzle using three disks. In each diagram, the pegs are labeled appropriately as "Source", "Destination", or "Free." Also appearing above the pegs is the recursive call that resulted in the move shown, as well as the tree number, which refers to the recursion tree shown in Figure 7.22.

A complete, interactive Pascal program for solving the Towers of Hanoi puzzle for any number of disks follows:

```
PROGRAM TowersOfHanoi ( INPUT, OUTPUT );

VAR
  N : Integer;
------------------------------------------------------------------------
PROCEDURE Move ( N : Integer; Source, Destination, Free : Char );

BEGIN
IF N = 1 THEN
  Writeln ( 'Move a disk from peg ', Source, ' to peg ', Destination )
ELSE
  BEGIN {N      From ... To...       Temporary peg}

  Move ( N - 1, Source, Free,        Destination );  {Solve puzzle for N-1 disks}
  Move ( 1,     Source, Destination, Free );         {Solve puzzle for 1 disk}
  Move ( N - 1, Free,   Destination, Source )        {Solve puzzle for N-1 disks}
  END
END;
------------------------------------------------------------------------
{***  Main routine  ***}

BEGIN
Writeln ( '***  Towers  Of  Hanoi  ***' );  Writeln;
Write ( 'Enter the number of disks:  ' );
Readln ( N );
Move ( N, 'A', 'B', 'C' )
END.
```

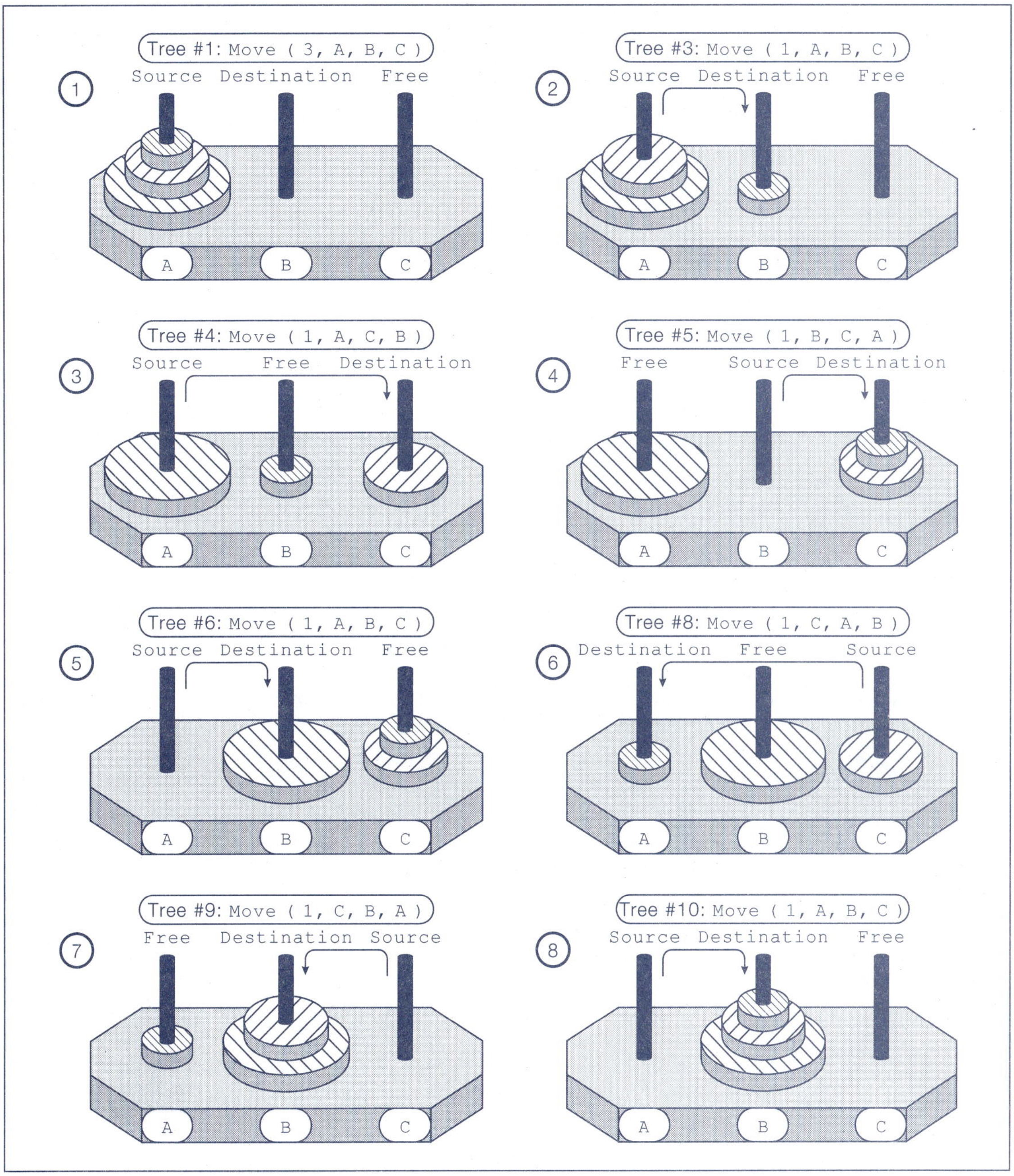

FIGURE 7.23 The Minimum Moves Necessary to Solve the 3-Disk Puzzle

7.8 DEBUGGING RECURSIVE ALGORITHMS

A programmer must be especially careful when debugging recursive routines because the element of time adds a new dimension of complexity. Since a recursive call results in the same code path of a routine to be executed, the programmer must determine not only *where* a bug occurred, but also *when;*

i.e., upon which recursive call. For runtime debugging, the intelligent use of the `Writeln` statement remains one of the most powerful tools for displaying the current values of variables and to track execution flow (in addition to any routine debugging aids provided by your own Pascal system). All such debugging output should be labeled appropriately, indicating where in the source code the display is being generated.

Common errors in recursive code include the following:

- An appropriate terminal condition is never tested by the routine.
- The terminal condition never evaluates to a true value, resulting in "infinite recursion," often because of the following:
  - Special cases are not handled properly.
  - The design of the solution did not properly divide the problem into smaller subsets of the problem.

The following techniques for tracking the execution of a recursive algorithm during development and debugging have been been presented in this chapter:

- *Heapspace diagrams.* A diagrammatic technique depicting activation records, useful for remembering the values of local variables—e.g., Applications 7.1 (factorial) and 7.2 (reversing a string).
- *Numbered call statements.* For algorithms that make multiple recursive calls (no more than one call per statement), useful for remembering to which call the execution flow returns when the call is completed—e.g., Application 7.4 (counting vowels).
- *Array-sectioning diagrams.* For algorithms that work with a section of an array upon each recursive call—e.g., Application 7.5 (binary search).
- *Tree diagrams.* For algorithms employing nonlinear recursion, to trace how each recursive call leads to other recursive calls—e.g., Application 7.9 (the Fibonacci series) and Application 7.10 (the Towers of Hanoi).

Another debugging tool is the **level counter technique,** which may be used in the runtime testing of any recursive procedure or function. This technique uses an integer variable to "remember" the current *level* of the recursion—i.e., how deep into the recursive process the algorithm currently is. (The integer value is equal to the number of activation records currently in the heap, that have been generated by the recursive process.) This technique may be employed to monitor the execution of generic, recursive routine `X` as follows:

1. Include `LevelCount` as a non-**VAR** integer formal parameter in the **PROCEDURE** or **FUNCTION** statement for `X`.
2. Pass a `LevelCount` value of zero on the initial (nonrecursive) call to `X`; pass `LevelCount` on each recursive call to `X`.
3. At the beginning of `X`, insert an assignment statement that increments `LevelCount` by one.
4. Each `Writeln` statement inserted in the routine for debugging purposes should display the current value of `LevelCount`, as well as other relevant information.

SUMMARY

Recursion is a powerful and elegant technique for solving problems and defining lists of objects. Recursive definitions and algorithms always involve self-reference, which produces a looping effect. As a problem-solving strategy, recursion is best suited for problems that can be divided into a series of smaller, similar subproblems, each of which is solved in terms of the previous solution. Often, the recursive form of an algorithm is much shorter than its nonrecursive counterpart.

In a recursive definition, the term being defined is used as part of the definition. A recurrence relation is a set of equations used to compute the numerical value of a function in terms of other values of that function. A recursive procedure or function contains a call to itself in place of a `WHILE`, `REPEAT`, or `FOR` (iterative) loop. This way, a base operation is performed repeatedly, as the algorithm calls itself recursively (recurses ahead), until a particular test—the terminal condition—becomes true; at this point, the execution flow unwinds back to the original call statement. An algorithm should always test the terminal condition before making a recursive call. As always, when execution flow exits any procedure or function it always returns to the statement following the call statement from which the procedure or function was called last (even if the routine calls itself recursively).

Many recursive algorithms are written such that they store information in local variables as the algorithm recurses ahead and then process this information in reverse order as the algorithm unwinds. This is possible because the heapspace is used by the operating system to build a stack of activation records, with the top record always serving as the activation record for the routine currently executing. Recursion involves execution of the same procedure or function code path but the accessing of different activation records.

When developing a recursive algorithm, (1) be sure that recursion is the better choice over iteration, (2) clearly define the base operation or operations, (3) clearly define the terminal condition, (4) ensure that, with each recursive call, the algorithm moves closer to the terminal condition, and (5) ensure that the algorithm handles special cases, if any.

A routine is using preorder recursion if the base operation (counting) is performed as the execution flow recurses ahead, or else it is using postorder recursion if the base operation is performed during the unwinding process. A routine is using tail recursion if the last action taken by the algorithm is always a recursive call.

An analysis of the binary search algorithm proves that it is substantially faster than a linear search, in the average case, for any ordered array of items.

Backtracking is a trial-and-error problem-solving technique in which the subproblems are ordered such that a solution to the kth subproblem enables the algorithm to advance and seek a solution to the $(k + 1)$st subproblem. Upon the failure to solve a particular subproblem, the algorithm returns to the previous successful subproblem and then seeks a solution to the next (previously failed) subproblem. If each subproblem can be solved, the original problem has been solved; otherwise, the algorithm backs up all the way to the initial situation. Recursion is a useful tool in backtracking because the same basic test is applied to each subproblem, and information about each subproblem must be saved in reverse order so that the algorithm can return to a previous subproblem, if necessary.

In choosing between recursion and iteration in the design of an algorithm, consider: (1) if the algorithm can be written recursively at all, (2) if recursion is a "natural" approach, resulting in Pascal code that is easier to write, understand by another programmer, and test, and (3) if the recursive representation requires an acceptable amount of heapspace and execution time. An algorithm is using nonlinear recursion if the total number of recursive calls grows exponentially; otherwise, it is using linear recursion. A recursive algorithm involving tail recursion is relatively easy to convert to a nonrecursive version, whereas recursive algorithms that must process information in reverse order, as with backtracking, are more cumbersome to convert.

Useful debugging techniques include heapspace diagrams, numbered call statements, array-sectioning diagrams, tree diagrams, and the level counter technique.

KEY TERMS

Backtracking
Base operation
Binary search
Call-number technique
Fibonacci series
Heapspace diagram
Iterative algorithm
Level counter technique
Linear recursion
Nonlinear recursion
Numbered call statement
Paradox
Postorder recursion
Preorder recursion
Recurrence relation
Recursive algorithm
Recursive definition
Recursion tree
Tail recursion
Terminal condition
Unwinding

REVIEW QUESTIONS

1. Distinguish between iterative and recursive algorithms; give examples not described in the chapter.
2. Distinguish between base operation and terminal condition.
3. How is recursion actually implemented by the computer? Why do some high-level languages, such as FORTRAN, not support recursion; i.e., what does a Pascal compiler do that a FORTRAN compiler does not?
4. What is a heapspace diagram, and how does it help to trace the execution of a recursive procedure or function?
5. Should a routine's terminal condition be tested *before* or *after* the next recursive call is made? What is the danger of not testing the terminal condition properly? How might the computer actually respond if a terminal condition is never tested?
6. Complete the following two sentences:

   Recursion involves execution of the ______ but the accessing of different ______.

   Upon exiting any procedure or function, execution flow always returns to ______.

7. Distinguish between the effects of placing a **VAR** before a formal parameter and not placing a **VAR** before a formal parameter in the **PROCEDURE** statement of a recursive procedure.

8. Describe the five steps recommended in the development of any recursive algorithm.
9. What is the terminal condition in recursively traversing (a) a linked list of nodes and (b) the elements in a simple array (not a linked list)?
10. Distinguish between preorder and postorder recursion. Can a tail recursive routine employ postorder recursion?
11. Describe the binary search algorithm. Why is it called *binary* search? Can this algorithm be applied to a linked list?
12. Define *backtracking* and give an everyday example of it that is not given in the chapter. In both Applications 7.6 and 7.7—In Search of the Golden Floppy and the Eight Queens Problem—the return from a recursive call implies that one of two events has just occurred. In general terms, what are these two events? In both applications, describe what the recursive routine should be careful not to do during the unwinding process?
13. In the Golden Floppy application, why must the same probe order be used each time the recursive routine attempts to advance across the island? What might happen if the recursive `FindPath` routine chose a probe order randomly each time it attempted to advance across the island? Describe what might result if a particular probe order is used for the first execution of the program, then a different probe order is used upon a second execution of the program, for the same island.
14. What three programming issues would you consider in deciding between an iterative approach and a recursive approach to solving a problem? Give examples of problems that may be solved by (a) either approach and (b) only an iterative approach. Why should a routine to calculate the Nth value of the Fibonacci series number not be written recursively? Could a problem exist that could *only* be solved recursively and not iteratively?
15. Describe how a tail recursive routine, such as the binary search function, can be converted to an iterative version. How might a nontail recursive routine such as the Eight Queens procedure be converted?
16. Describe a recursion tree. Under what circumstances might this technique be useful in tracing the execution of a recursive routine?

EXERCISES

1. a. Write the output generated by each of the following call statements (in the calling routines, `X` is an integer variable):

```
X := 1;              X := 0;              X := 5;
Enigma1 ( X, 0 );    Enigma1 ( X, 1 );    Enigma1 ( X, 3 );

PROCEDURE Enigma1 ( VAR X : Integer; Y : Integer );

BEGIN
IF Y > 0 THEN
  BEGIN
  X := X + 1;
  Y := Y - 1;
  Writeln ( 'Before call:  X = ', X, ' Y = ', Y );
  Enigma1 ( X, Y );
  Writeln ( 'After call:  X = ', X, ' Y = ', Y )
  END
END;
```

   b. Write an iterative version of this procedure.

2. Write the value returned by each of the following initial call statements:

```
Enigma2 ( 7, 3 )
Enigma2 ( 3, 2 )
Enigma2 ( 3, 1 )

FUNCTION Enigma2 ( X, Y : Integer ) : Integer;

BEGIN
IF Y = 1 THEN
  Enigma2 := X
ELSE
  Enigma2 := X + Enigma2 ( X, Y - 1 )
END;
```

3. Write the output displayed when procedure `BinVal` is called three times, with the initial `DecVal` values of 5, 19, and 0. Generally speaking, what does this procedure do?

```
PROCEDURE BinVal ( DecVal : Integer );

BEGIN
IF DecVal > 0 THEN
  BEGIN
  IF DecVal DIV 2 > 0 THEN
    BinVal ( DecVal DIV 2 );
  Write ( DecVal MOD 2 )
  END
END;
```

4. The following diagram depicts an array of integer values.

0	1	2	3	4	5	6	7	8	9	10	11	12	13
23	29	31	36	40	43	47	52	57	59	61	67	71	84

Use a binary search strategy to locate values 61, 42, 23, 22, 84, and 101. As you perform each of the searches, each time you make a comparison between the sought value and an element value, write the element value.

5. Ackerman's function is defined for the two integer values M and N as follows:

$$\text{Ackerman}(0, N) = N + 1 \qquad \{\text{for } N \geq 0\}$$

$$\text{Ackerman}(M, 0) = \text{Ackerman}(M - 1, 1) \qquad \{\text{for } M > 0\}$$

$$\text{Ackerman}(M, N) = \text{Ackerman}(M - 1, \text{Ackerman}(M, N - 1)) \qquad \{\text{for } M > 0 \text{ and } N > 0\}$$

a. Write recursive and iterative functions to compute the value of Ackerman's function for any two nonnegative integer arguments.

b. Compute the value returned from each of the following initial calls:

```
Ackerman ( 0, 0 )  Ackerman ( 3, 0 )  Ackerman ( 0, 3 )
Ackerman ( 2, 3 )  Ackerman ( 3, 2 )  Ackerman ( 4, 3 )
```

6. Function $Z(N)$ is defined as follows:

$$Z(N) = \frac{1}{3} \times \frac{2}{4} \times \frac{2}{5} \times \frac{3}{7} \times \frac{4}{10} \times \cdots \times \frac{N}{2N+1} \times \frac{N+1}{3N+1}$$

Write iterative and recursive real Pascal functions to compute $Z(N)$.

7. The function $F(X)$ is defined by the following recurrence relation:

$$F(0) = 1$$

$$F(1) = 2$$

$$F(N) = 2F(N-1) + NF(N-2) \qquad \{\text{for all } N > 1\}$$

a. Write a recursive function that computes the value of $F(N)$ for any $n \geq 0$.
b. Compute the values of $F(2)$ and $F(3)$.

8. The *greatest common divisor* (GCD) of two integers X and Y is the largest integer that divides X and Y evenly. For example, the GCD of 36 and 24 is 12, the GCD of 30 and 18 is 6, the GCD of 60 and 15 is 15, and the GCD of 31 and 13 is 1. Write a recursive integer function that returns the GCD of its two integer arguments. The general algorithm for computing GCD follows:

1. Divide X by Y, yielding the integer remainder, R.
2. If R equals 0, then Y is the greatest common divisor so **QUIT**.
3. Otherwise, because the GCD of X and Y is the same as the GCD of Y and X **MOD** Y, do the following:
   a. Set X equal to Y.
   b. Set Y equal to R.
   c. Repeat Steps 1 through 3, using the new values of X and Y.

9. a. Complete recursive function `ListLength`, which should return a count of the number of nodes in the linked list pointed to by `Current`. You may assume that the linked list was built using the global declarations given at the start of Section 5.2:

```
FUNCTION ListLength ( Current : NodePtr ) : Integer;
```

b. Write a recursive procedure that reverses the same linked list pointed to by `Current`.

10. Write five recursive functions, each of which operates on an integer array named `List`, with values already stored in no order in elements `List [ 1 ]` through `List [ Count ]`:
a. `Min ( List, Count )` returns the minimum element value.
b. `Max ( List, Count )` returns the maximum element value.
c. `Sum ( List, Count )` returns the sum of all element values.
d. `Mean ( List, Count )` returns the average element value.
e. `Product ( List, Count )` returns the (real) product of all element values.

11. Complete recursive function `StringToInteger`, which converts a string of digits in parameter `Buffer` into a single integer value and returns this value. You may assume that `Buffer` already contains a contiguous sequence of character digits representing an unsigned integer value, starting at element `Index` and delimited by either a nondigit character or the length of the string. You also may assume that the converted value will be less than or equal to **MAXINT**.

```
TYPE                                    {Necessary global declaration}
  BuffType = String [ 80 ];

FUNCTION StringToInteger (VAR Buffer : BuffType;
                          VAR Index : Integer ) : Integer;
```

12. Complete recursive function `IsPerfect`, which should return a true value if argument N is a *perfect* number and a false value otherwise. An integer is perfect if it is equal to the sum of its factors; e.g., 6 is perfect because it is equal to 3 plus 2 plus 1, each of which is a factor of 6.

```
FUNCTION IsPerfect ( N : Integer ) : Boolean;
```

13. a. Write the complete program to find and display a solution to the Eight Queens problem; it should call the `EightQueens` procedure from Application 7.7. This requires that you write the `FindSafePostion` procedure.
    b. Only 12 of the possible 92 solutions to the Eight Queens problem are "unique"; the others can be derived by reflections about axes or the center point on the board. Describe an algorithm for finding and displaying each of these 12 solutions.
    c. Design a nonrecursive version of the Eight Queens procedure.
    d. Design a more efficient version of the Eight Queens procedure.

14. a. Let us assume that in Application 7.6 we know the location of the Golden Floppy at the outset. Rewrite procedure `FindPath` so that, rather than employing a set probe order each time it attempts to advance to another element, it uses a probe order that always begins with the element *closest* to the element containing the Golden Floppy. Will this modification guarantee the shortest of all paths to the Golden Floppy? Will it even work?
    b. Rewrite procedure `FindPath` so that, rather than employing a set probe order each time it attempts to advance to another element, it chooses a direction *randomly*. Will this modification improve, worsen, or have no effect on the average number of elements examined?
    c. Rewrite the program so that it finds the shortest path to the Golden Floppy—if more than one path exists. (*Hint:* Use a FIFO queue. This technique is discussed in Section 9.2 in the context of finding the shortest path through a graph data structure, based on the number of intervening edges.)

15. *Knight's Tour Problem.* On a chessboard, a knight can move two squares along a column or row and then one square in a perpendicular direction. As an example, the knight (K) in the leftmost diagram of the following figure can move to any of the squares containing an x.

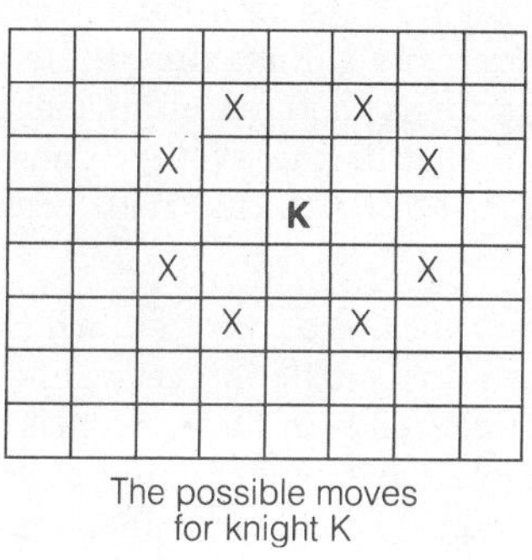

The possible moves for knight K

1	48	31	50	33	16	63	18
30	51	46	3	62	19	14	35
47	2	49	32	15	34	17	64
52	29	4	45	20	61	36	13
5	44	25	56	9	40	21	60
28	53	8	41	24	57	12	37
43	6	55	26	39	10	59	22
54	27	42	7	58	23	38	11

One solution to the Knight's Tour problem

Write a program that prompts the user for an initial knight position and then attempts to move the knight to each square on the board without visiting the same square twice. The program should number each move in a two-dimensional integer array, as shown in the sample solution depicted in the rightmost diagram, and then display the contents of the array if successful. (*Hint:* Use backtracking, as in the Eight Queens Problem.)

CHAPTER EIGHT

TREE STRUCTURES

In this chapter, you will learn about an important nonlinear data structure commonly used to represent a table, called a *tree*. A number of interesting variations are discussed.

8.1 PRELIMINARIES

Fundamental Tree Concepts

A *tree* is a *hierarchical* data structure in which data often are arranged according to the key values of the items. An item in a tree is said to have a *one-to-many relationship* with other items, unlike an item in a linear list, which has a one-to-one relationship with other items. Trees serve two related purposes:

1. *Trees preserve the hierarchical relationship among many items.* Trees of this purpose include *heaps* and *priority queues* (Section 8.3) and *game trees* (Section 8.4).
2. *A (balanced) search tree of items provides the average efficiency of binary searching plus the insertion and deletion efficiency of a linked list.* Search trees discussed in this textbook include *binary search trees* (Section 8.2), *2-3 trees* (Section 10.1), and *B-trees* (Section 10.3).

Although a general tree structure is a data type, it is introduced in this section through everyday examples and definitions of some fundamental terms rather than through an ADT specification. This section and Section 8.3 (priority queues and heaps) focus on the hierarchical character of trees; Section 8.2 covers the binary search tree in detail.

The structuring of data hierarchically is both natural and useful, and examples abound in daily life. Corporations, educational establishments, military forces, and entire governmental bodies often organize their members into different ranks of authority and responsibility. Genealogical (family) trees describe the lineage of a family over a particular number of generations, creating a nonlinear structure organized by both key value (name) and time of arrival (birth or marriage). In fact, most *stores of information* are organized in some hierarchical format, breaking down a complex entity

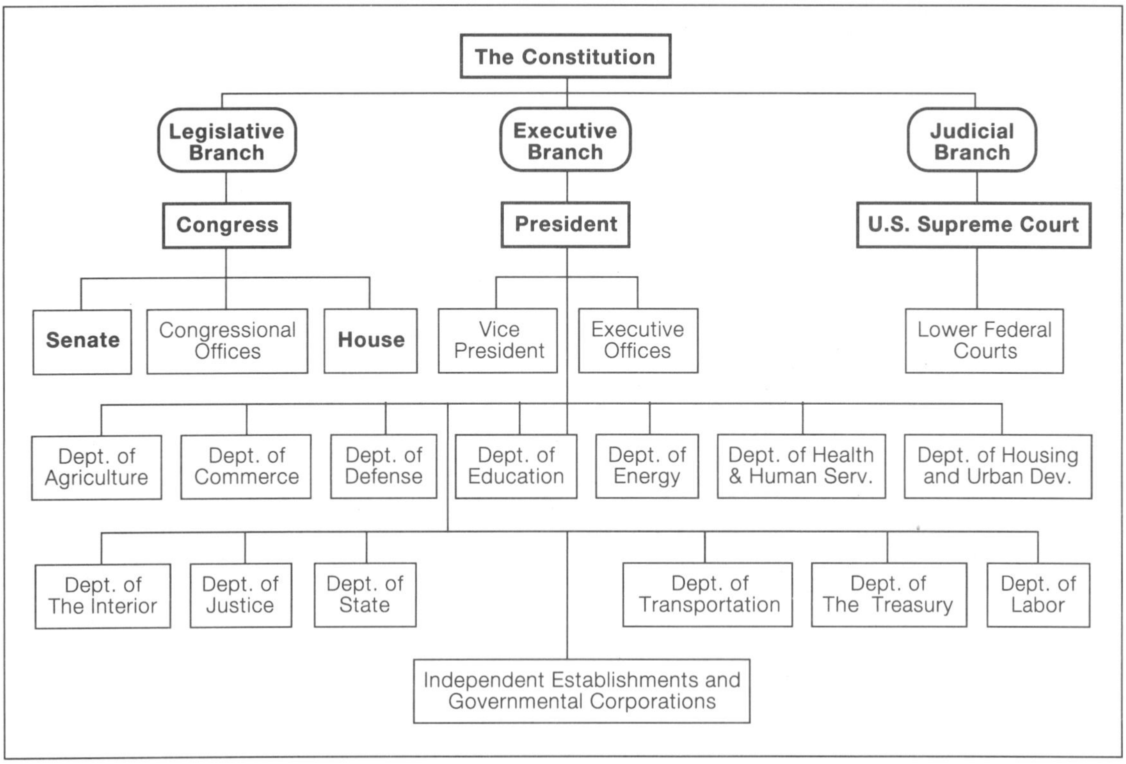

FIGURE 8.1 The Hierarchy of the Government of the United States

into simpler parts. The information in each chapter of this book, for example, is organized by sections and subsections, as described in the table of contents. As an example, Figure 8.1 illustrates the hierarchical organization of the top level of our federal government (the figure is based on a diagram in the 1986-87 version of the federal text *The United States Government Manual*).

Hierarchical organization extends to activities as well. The tree structure in Figure 8.2 describes a single-elimination collegiate basketball tournament of 16 teams, with the "action" (i.e., basketball games) indicated by a progression from left to right.

The theme running through all these examples is the **nonlinear, one-to-many,** or **hierarchical structure** among the events or items or information. This means that from a given point in the tree, there may be no, one, or several choices when advancing through the tree, unlike a linear list, which always offers no more than a single choice—forward or backward in the list. A tree is actually only one of several ways to represent a hierarchical organization, as illustrated in the diagrams of Figure 8.3.

The next section provides definitions of commonly used terms related to trees. Study these definitions carefully before advancing to Section 8.2.

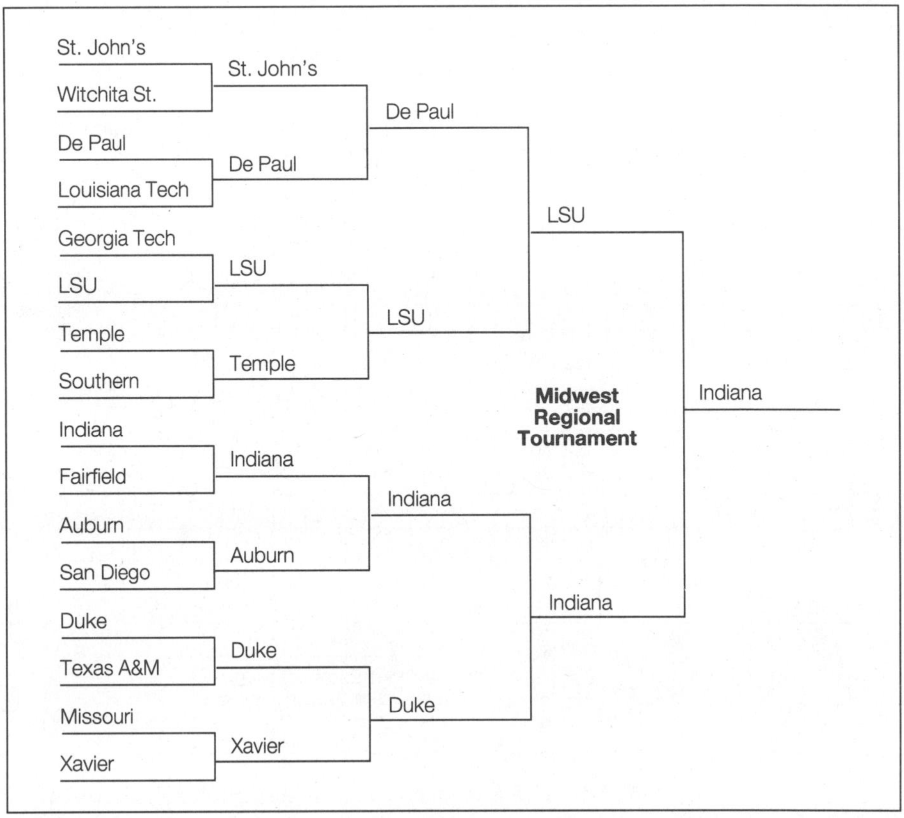

FIGURE 8.2 The Progression of a Basketball Tournament, Depicted as a Binary Tree

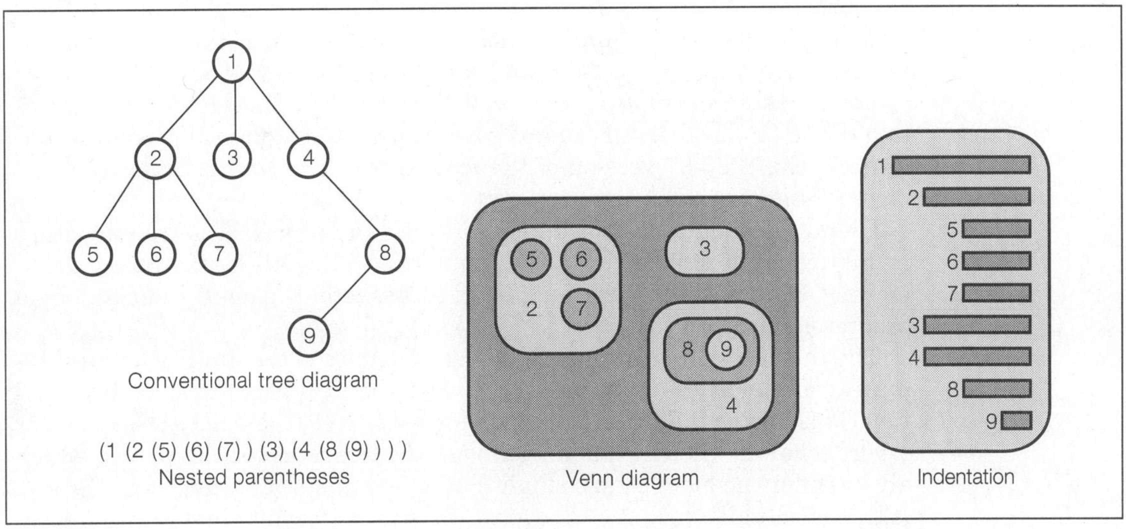

FIGURE 8.3 Four Ways of Depicting the Same Hierarchical Structure

Tree-Related Terminology

The terminology in this section is arranged conceptually, not alphabetically.

General Terms

Node, edge

Each item in a tree is called a **node,** or vertex. In diagrams depicting trees, each node is typically shown as a circle and may be connected to another node via a line called an **edge,** or branch. An edge reflects the relationship between the two nodes it connects, and there may be at most only one edge between any two nodes. Usually, only the key value of a node is shown within its circle. Figure 8.4 depicts a variety of trees.

Empty tree

A tree that contains no nodes is an **empty tree**.

Oriented tree

An **oriented tree** is a tree that is either empty (i.e., contains no nodes) or is nonempty, in which case the following is true:

- A particular node is designated as the root node of the tree.
- The remaining nodes are partitioned into disjoint sets called *subtrees,* each of which is an oriented tree.

Typically, the simple phrase *tree* refers to an oriented tree.

Tree root node

In a nonempty oriented tree, one particular node is designated as the **root node,** or apex of the tree. Oriented trees are usually diagramed as "growing" downward or sideways, away from the root node. In a **general tree,** or

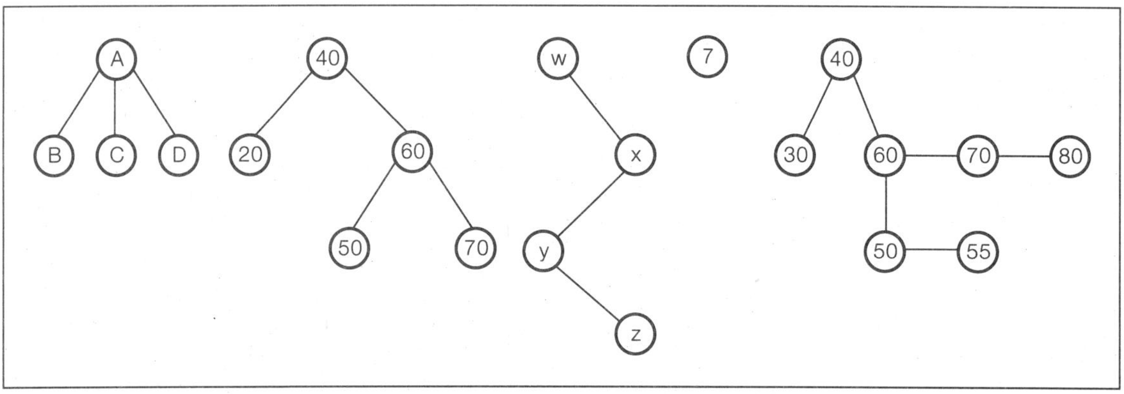

FIGURE 8.4 Five Sample Trees

free tree, there is no root node. (In Figure 8.4, both of the nodes labeled 40 are root nodes for their respective trees.)

Path, directed path, path length

The route from one node to another is a **path:** A path exists between node A and node B if an edge is connecting each pair of nodes between them. In an oriented tree, each path is a **directed path;** i.e., a routine can only advance along the path away from the root. The number of nodes along a path is the **path length.**

Cycle

A path that begins with and ends with the same node is called a **cycle.** A tree must not contain any cycles.

Parent, child, sibling

If an edge runs from node A to node B, then node A is the **parent** of node B and node B is the **child** of node A. In Figure 8.4, the B, C, and D nodes are **siblings**—all children of parent A.

Degree, leaf node, internal node

The **degree** (or more accurately, the **out-degree**) of a node is the number of children of that node. A node of degree zero (no children) is called a **leaf,** or terminal node. A node of degree one or more is called an **internal node.** In Figure 8.4, the nodes labeled B, C, D, 20, 50, 70, z, 7, 30, 55, and 80 are all leaves; all other nodes are internal.

Ancestor, descendant

In an oriented tree, all nodes along a path from node A to node B (excluding node A) are **descendants** of node A, and node A is the **ancestor** of all these nodes. In an oriented tree, the root is the ancestor of all other nodes; i.e., all nonroot nodes are descendants of the root, since a path connects the root to all other nodes. In Figure 8.4, the y and z nodes are descendants of the x node, and the 40 and 60 nodes are both ancestors of the 70 node in their respective trees.

Subtree

In an oriented tree, a **subtree** consists of a particular node (the root of the subtree), along with all its descendant nodes. Each subtree within an oriented tree is itself an oriented tree. Figure 8.5 depicts a tree with four of the possible subtrees enclosed within shaded triangles.

Level, Height

A given tier of a tree is called a **level.** Each level is designated by increasing integer values, with the root at level 1 (in some textbooks, the root is said to

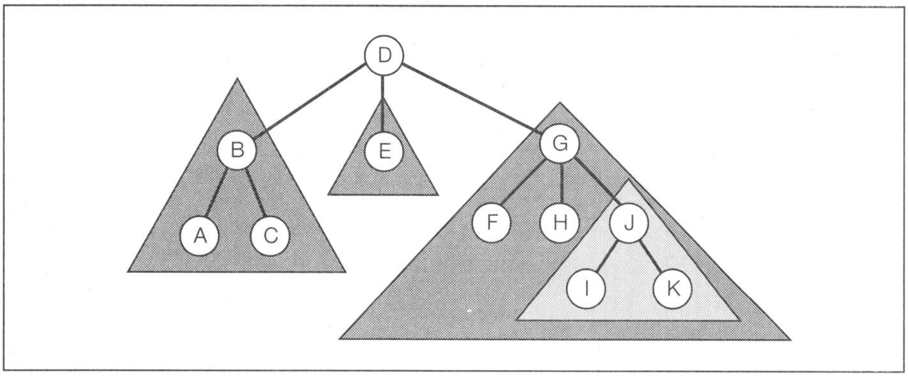

FIGURE 8.5 Four Sample Subtrees Enclosed Within Shaded Triangles

be at level 0). In Figure 8.5, the F node is at level 3 and the I node is at level 4. The **height** of a tree (or subtree) is the number of nodes along the *longest path* from the tree's root (or a subtree's root) to a leaf on the greatest level, inclusive of the root and leaf nodes. The height of the tree in Figure 8.5 is 4 and the height of that subtree whose root is node J is 2.

Tree traversal

The operation of visiting and processing each node in a tree in a particular order is called a **tree traversal.** In an oriented tree, commonly used traversals include preorder, in-order and reverse-order, postorder, and level-order traversals. Each of these is discussed in Section 8.2.

Types of Trees

Only a few types of trees are defined here; others are defined in later chapters.

General tree

A set of finite nodes that are connected by edges but contain no cycles is called a general tree, as opposed to an oriented tree, which designates one of the nodes as the tree's root.

Oriented tree

The oriented tree was defined earlier.

Ordered tree

An oriented tree in which each node is arranged hierarchically upon insertion, based on the node's key value, is called an **ordered tree.** In Figure 8.6, the leftmost tree is a general (nonoriented) tree but the two rightmost trees are oriented. The rightmost trees are unique if they are considered as being ordered, each ordered quite differently; they are identical if they are *not* considered as ordered.

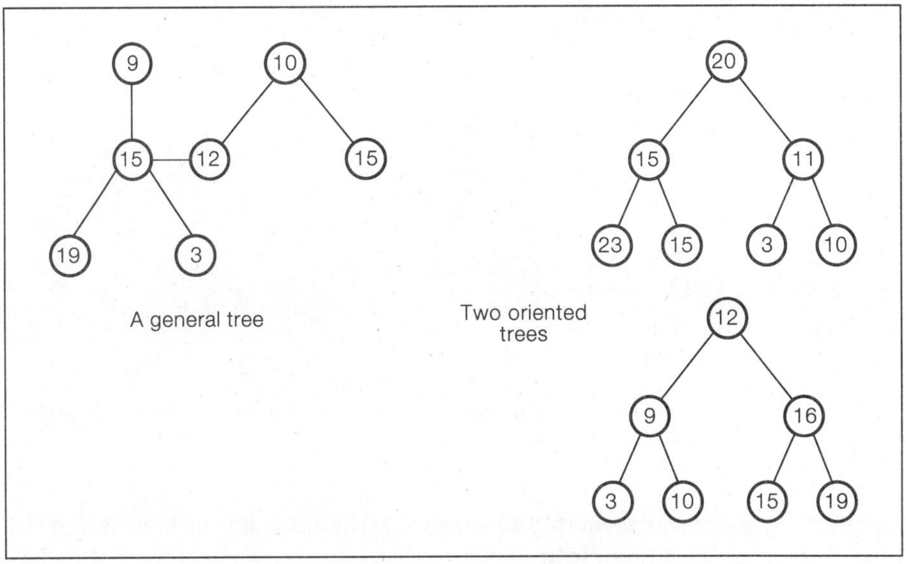

FIGURE 8.6 Examples of a General and Two Oriented Trees

Search tree

An oriented, ordered-tree representation of a table, designed to provide fast access to records of information, is called a **search tree.**

Binary tree

A **binary tree** is an oriented tree that is either

- Empty, or
- Nonempty, consisting of a root node plus a left and right subtree, each of which is a binary tree.

One of the most useful forms of a binary tree is the binary search tree, discussed at length in Section 8.2.

8.2 BINARY SEARCH TREES

Specifications for the ADT Binary Search Tree

The **ADT binary search tree** is an oriented, ordered tree used to represent the ADT table. It is either empty or the following are true:

- The tree consists of a root node and two subtrees (the left and right subtree) that are themselves binary search trees, as depicted in Figure 8.7.
- The relationships of Figure 8.8 exist for every node in the tree, each of which is considered as the root node of its two subtrees (of course, some subtrees will be empty).
  This rule determines the ordering of nodes throughout the tree.

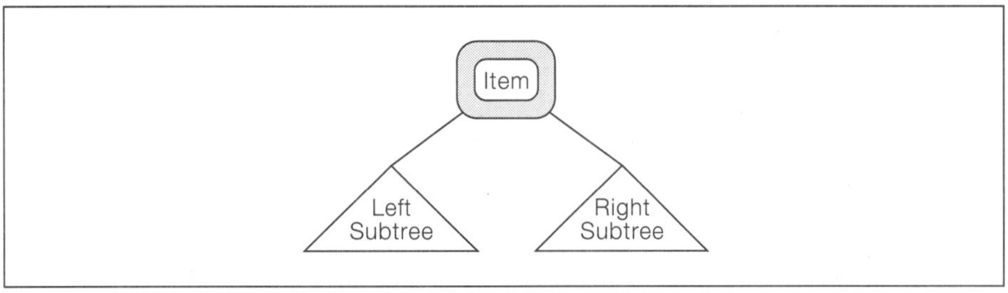

FIGURE 8.7 A Node and its Two Subtrees

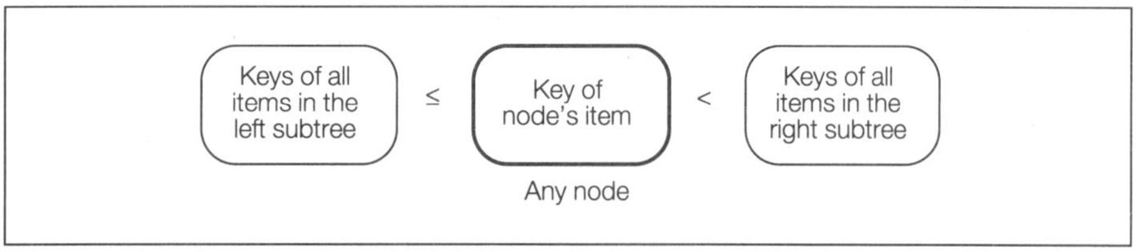

FIGURE 8.8 Orientation of a Node and its Left and Right Subtrees

Domain

The domain consists of nodes, usually of record data type; each node contains one item of data.

Fundamental Operations

1. *Initialize:* Initialize the tree as empty [`BinInitTree`].
2. *Test for emptiness:* Determine if the tree is empty [`BinTreeEmpty`].
3. *Search for an item:* Search for a particular item [`BinTreeSearch`].
4. *Add an item:* Add an item to the tree [`BinTreeInsert`].
5. *Remove an item:* Remove an item from the tree [`BinTreeDelete`].
6. *Traverse the tree:* Visit and process every item in a particular order: preorder, in-order, postorder, reverse inorder, and level-order traverses [`PreOrdTraverse`, `InOrdTraverse`, `PostOrdTraverse`, `ReverseOrdTraverse`, `LevelOrdTraverse`].

Figure 8.9 depicts a binary search tree in which each node has an integer key.

Note: In our discussion of binary search trees, we will use the terms *node* and *item* interchangeably; in Chapter 10, however, we see that other search trees, such as 2-3 trees and B-trees, may contain two or more items per node.

As usual with binary search tree diagrams, only the key values are shown, although there actually may be many other fields of information within each node.

Node `46` is the root of the entire tree. To prove that the second rule of the ADT specification is employed here, examine the tree carefully: `46` is greater

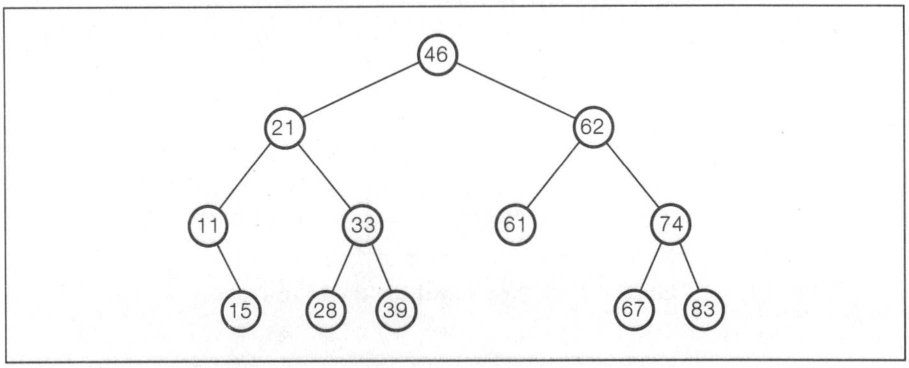

FIGURE 8.9 A Sample Binary Search Tree

than all key values of nodes in its left subtree and less than all key values of nodes in its right subtree. Accordingly, `21` is greater than all key values in its left subtree and less than all key values in its (or the root node's) right subtree. The required relationship between the key value of any node and the key values in both subtrees holds true for each node in the tree. Node `11` has an empty left subtree, which indicates that no node in the tree has a key value less than `11`.

Linked List Representation of the ADT Binary Search Tree

A set of generic, global declarations for a linked list version of a binary search tree follows:

```
TYPE
  BTKeyType    = ??;                            {Application dependent}
  BTInfoType   = RECORD
                   Key   : BTKeyType;           {Key value}
                   {Other fields, as necessary}
                 END;

  BTNodePtr    = ^BTNode;
  BTNode       = RECORD
                   Data  : BTInfoType;          {Data portion of node}
                   Left,                        {Left link field}
                   Right : BTNodePtr            {Right link field}
                 END;

  BinTreeType  = RECORD
                   Root  : BTNodePtr;           {Address of tree's root node}
                   Count : Integer              {Count of all nodes in the tree}
                 END;

VAR
  BinTree  :  BinTreeType;
```

After the tree is built `BinTree.Root` will contain either the address of the tree's root node or a **`NIL`** value if the tree is empty. Initializing the tree as empty therefore involves assigning a **`NIL`** value to `BinTree.Root` and assigning zero to `BinTree.Count`. A function determining if the tree is empty would return a true value if `BinTree.Root` is equal to **NIL** and a false value otherwise.

> *At this time, examine the following routines in Appendix G.*

```
PROCEDURE InitBinTree ( VAR BinTree : BinTreeType );

FUNCTION BinTreeEmpty ( VAR BinTree : BinTreeType ) : Boolean;
```

Searching and Inserting into a Binary Search Tree

As in any search for an item among a collection of items, an algorithm searching a binary search tree stops when either of the following is true:

- *Success—Item is found.* A match is found between the sought key value and the key value of one of the nodes.
- *Failure—No more items to examine.* There are no more nodes in the search path to examine.

Starting with the root node as the current node, each time a node is visited, the sought key value is compared to the "current" node's key value, as indicated by the following pseudocode:

```
IF link field to be followed = NIL THEN
  Search concludes unsuccessfully
ELSE
  IF the keys match THEN
    Search concludes successfully
  ELSE
    IF target key < the node's key  THEN
      Follow left link; i.e., left child becomes the current node
    ELSE  {the target key > the node's key}
      Follow right link; i.e., right child becomes the current node
```

Let us assume that the binary search tree depicted in Figure 8.9 already exists (it is redrawn in Figure 8.10). A search usually begins with the root node, pointed to by `BinTree.Root`, and advances node by node toward the leaves. A search routine needs a variable of type `BTNodePtr`, which we can name `Current`, to hold the address of the node whose key field is currently being examined:

```
Current := BinTree.Root;  {Node 46 is now the current node}
```

The searching algorithm advances to another node by following a particular link field of the current node. For example, if the algorithm were looking for a node containing key value 74, it would advance `Current` from node 46

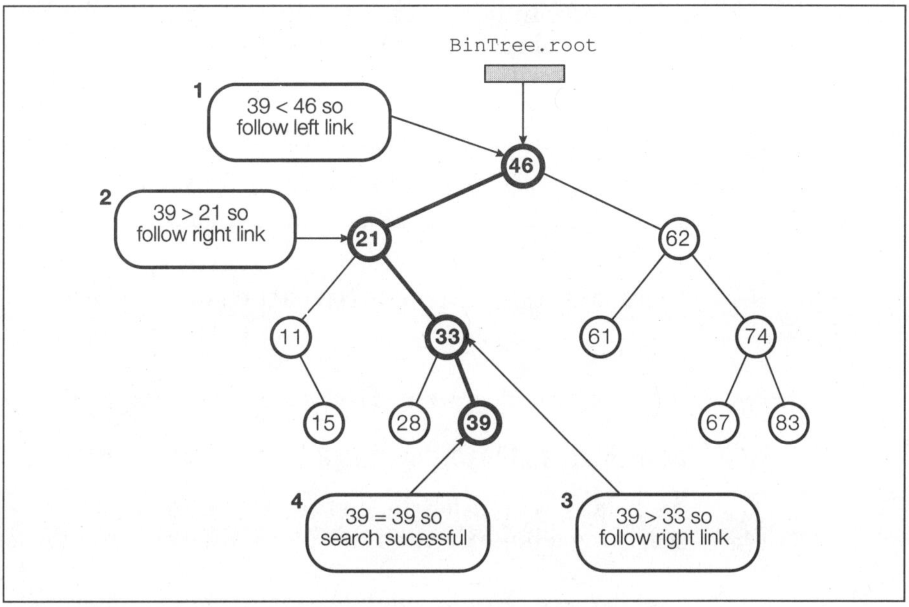

FIGURE 8.10 Searching for the Node with Key Value 39

(the tree's root node) to node 62 (since 74 is greater than 46) by following the right link of node 46:

```
Current := Current^.Right;  {Node 62 is now the current node}
```

As an example of tree searching, Figure 8.10 traces a search for the node that contains key value 39 (the **search path** is shown in boldface).

If a node with a key value of 40 is sought, the search path is the same but with a different step 4:

> **4.** 40 > 39 and the right link is **NIL**, which means there are no other nodes to search, so the search ends in failure

Try searching for nodes with the key values 21, 67, 60, 46, and 10 as well.

As in the search performed on an ordered linear linked list, the search operation performed on a binary search tree (which, by definition, is also ordered) is necessary in three different contexts:

- *Simple searching.* The algorithm must determine if a particular node is in the tree, returning its location (heapspace address) if found.
- *Prerequisite to insertion.* Before inserting a new node, the searching algorithm must be called to locate the parent node, to which the new node will be connected.
- *Prerequisite to deletion.* Before deleting an existing node, the searching algorithm must locate the node to be deleted (as well as its parent node, which, as we see in Section 8.2, is also necessary).

Each of these three contexts may require that the searching algorithm return different information. Rather than design three different search algorithms, we will design a single versatile algorithm named `BinTreeSearch`, which may be called in any of the three contexts. We will begin by determining what information our search algorithm must return in each context.

For *simple searching,* `BinTreeSearch` should return a Boolean value indicating whether or not the sought node has been found and, if it has been found, the heapspace address of the node. For *deletion,* `BinTreeSearch` should return a Boolean value indicating whether or not the node has been found and, if it has been found, the address of the node *plus* the address of the node's parent, if the node is not the root node. (Again, the reason for this additional datum will become clear in our discussion of the deletion operation in Section 8.2.)

To determine what information is needed from `BinTreeSearch` as a prelude to *insertion,* we must first understand how new nodes are inserted in a binary search tree. Let us temporarily suspend our discussion of searching and focus on node insertion. We will design a procedure named `BinTreeInsert` to insert a new node in a binary search tree. For simplicity, we will assume that all nodes have unique key values, but upon return to our discussion of searching, you are encouraged to consider what modifications are necessary to accommodate duplicate key values, as is required in some applications.

A new node is always inserted as a leaf and never among the internal nodes of a binary search tree. Prior to the actual insertion process, procedure `BinTreeSearch` must be called to determine from which existing parent node to "hang" (i.e., connect) the new node. The algorithm will search for a node containing the new node's key value. If the key value sought is never encountered and a **NIL** link field is eventually encountered instead, the *last* node visited is the node that must now point to the new node (via its `Left` or `Right` link fields). Exactly *which* of that node's link fields to use can be determined by a simple comparison of its key to the new node's key upon return from the search. If the sought key value is found, the insertion process is terminated (again, we are assuming that only unique key values are allowed in the tree). The following pseudocode summarizes this algorithm:

```
IF a matching key value is found THEN  {Failure -- node already in tree}
  Terminate the insertion process
ELSE                                   {Success -- can insert new node}
  IF new node's key < last-visited node's key THEN
    Last-visited node's Left link field  := Address of new node
  ELSE
    Last-visited node's Right link field := Address of new node
```

Figure 8.11 shows the sample tree after five new nodes are inserted (the new nodes and edges are shown in boldface).

`BinTreeInsert` therefore requires that the search routine return the address of the last-visited node—the soon-to-be parent of the new node. `BinTreeSearch` also should return a Boolean parameter with a true value if a node with the new key value already exists in the tree and a false value otherwise.

We can now return to the business of designing the `BinTreeSearch` algorithm. Based on the needs of `BinTreeInsert` and `BinTreeDelete` (which deletes a node), `BinTreeSearch` should therefore return three val-

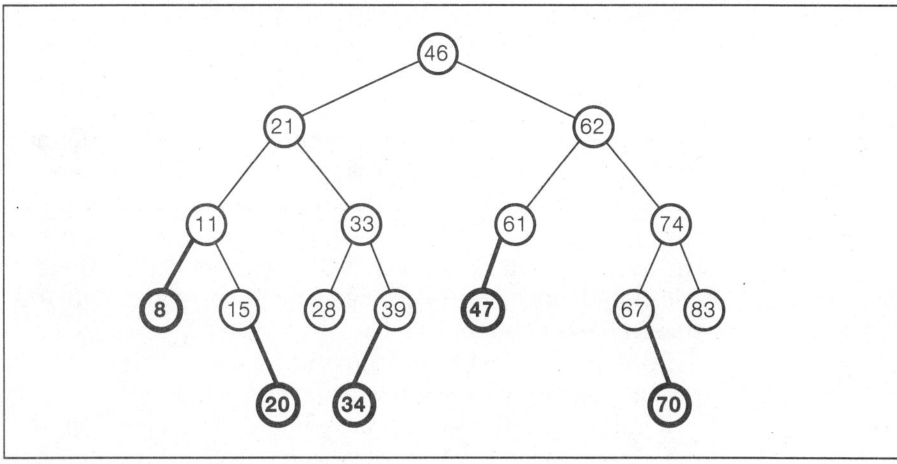

FIGURE 8.11 The Sample Tree after Inserting Five Nodes

ues via the parameters `Found`, `LastNode`, and `Parent`, as summarized in the chart of Figure 8.12.

Now that we have established the values of `Found`, `LastNode`, and `Parent` that should be returned by `BinTreeSearch` upon a successful or failed search, this chart can be condensed, as shown in Figure 8.13.

In addition to parameters `Found`, `LastNode`, and `Parent`, which *return* data, `BinTreeSearch` needs two data items passed in, via two more parameters: the address of the tree node where searching is to begin (typically, the address of the tree's root node) and the key value of the node sought. Try writing your own Pascal version of the versatile `BinTreeSearch` algorithm, either recursively or iteratively.

Context	Result of search	Parameter values returned: Found	LastNode	Parent
Simple search	Node found	**TRUE**	Address of found node	———
	Node not found	**FALSE**	———	———
Before Insertion	Node found	**TRUE**	———	———
	Node not found	**FALSE**	Address of last node visited	———
Before Deletion	Node found	**TRUE**	Address of found node	Address of node's parent
	Node not found	**FALSE**	———	———

FIGURE 8.12 Summary of the Relevant Data Returned by `BinTreeSearch`

Found	LastNode	Parent
TRUE	Address of found node	Address of node's parent
FALSE	Address of last node visited	———

FIGURE 8.13 Condensed Summary of the Data Returned by `BinTreeSearch`

At this time, examine the following routine in Appendix G.

```
PROCEDURE BinTreeSearch ( VAR Key : KeyType; Current : BTNodePtr;
                          VAR LastNode, Parent : BTNodePtr;
                          VAR Found : Boolean );
```

Any of three cases may arise when searching a binary search tree prior to inserting a node:

1. The tree is empty.
2. The key is already in a node in the tree (an error if multiple keys are not allowed).
3. The tree is not empty and the key of the new node is not already in the tree.

Insertion into an empty tree is a special case because the root pointer, `BinTree.Root`, must have its value changed from **NIL** to the address of the new node.

In our discussion of the `LLInsert` algorithm of Section 5.2, we found that if a special header node is stored as the first node and is never deleted, then insertion at the head of the list and insertion into an empty list are not special cases, since the content of the list head variable never changes (it always contains the address of the header node). This strategy may be applied to trees as well. Although the strategy requires the expenditure of more memory (another `BTNode` type record for the header node), it results in a slightly shorter and faster-executing `BinTreeInsert` procedure, which does not need to determine if the list head variable must be assigned a new value. Figure 8.14 depicts the tree of Figure 8.10 with an additional header node (the decision to have the header node's left link field point to the rest of the tree rather than the right link field was arbitrary). With a header node, the call to `BinTreeSearch` to search the entire tree for a particular node would pass `BinTree.Root^.Left` rather than `BinTree.Root`. The use of a header node also requires that the `InitBinTree` procedure be modified to create the header node when it initializes the tree as empty. Because the use of header nodes is strictly an implementation-dependent issue and for the sake of visual simplicity, future diagrams depicting trees will not contain header nodes.

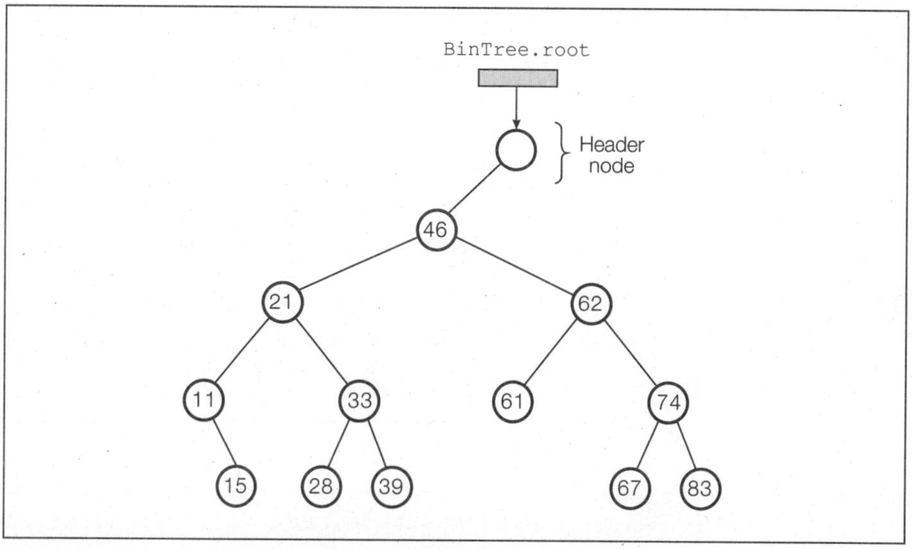

FIGURE 8.14 The Tree of Figure 8.9 with a Header Node

At this time, examine the following routine in Appendix G.

```
PROCEDURE BinTreeInsert ( VAR BinTree : BinTreeType; VAR Data :
                          BTInfoType; Parent : BTNodePtr );
```

The operation of deletion from a binary search tree is examined following the discussion of tree traversals.

Binary Tree Traversals

Recall from Chapter 5 that the operation of traversing a structure involves visiting and "processing" every node in the structure in a particular order, beginning at the tree's root node. Processing may entail any operation upon that node, such as displaying its key value or writing the entire data portion of the node to a file. In a linear list represented using an array or a linked list, the two common traversal orders are first-to-last and last-to-first. For any binary tree (not just binary search trees), there are two types of traversals, for a total of seven different traversal orders commonly used:

- A **depth-first traversal** algorithm advances as far into the tree as possible (i.e., toward the leaves), then backtracks to a previously visited node, then again advances as far as possible, and so on. Depth-first traversals include *preorder, in-order,* and *postorder traversals* plus the reverse order of any of these. The most commonly used reverse order traversal is the reversal of in-order, which we shall simply call *reverse-order traversal.*
- A **breadth-first traversal** algorithm processes nodes from left to right, level by level toward the leaves (based on conventional oriented tree

diagrams, such as Figure 8.14), spanning the breadth of the tree. The sole breadth-first traversal is the *level-order traversal* (sometimes referred to as the breadth-order traversal).

We will now examine the various depth-first and breadth-first traversals.

Depth-First Traversals

The operation of selecting which node to process next during a depth-first traversal is defined by a unique set of *visitation rules* for each traversal algorithm, which are applied each time a node is visited. As you can see in the following table, the **in-order** and **reverse-order traversal** algorithms are nearly identical; the only difference lies in *when* the left and right subtrees of a given node are processed relative to when *that* node is processed.

In-order Traversal	Reverse-order Traversal
1. Traverse left subtree	1. Traverse right subtree
2. Process node	2. Process node
3. Traverse right subtree	3. Traverse left subtree

Figure 8.15 indicates the order in which nodes are processed during in-order and reverse-order traversals of the same binary search tree with character key values. Remember that merely *visiting* a node is not the same as *processing* that node. As the entire tree is traversed, each node may be visited several times en route to another node, but each node is processed only once (refer back to the visitation rules).

An in-order traversal of the tree of Figure 8.15, displaying the character key value of each node processed, produces `a b c d f g`. A reverse-order traversal produces `g f d c b a`. In a binary search tree, an in-order traversal always processes the nodes in *ascending key-value order,* and a reverse-order traversal always processes the nodes in *descending key-value order.* Try performing in-order and reverse-order traversals on the tree of Figure

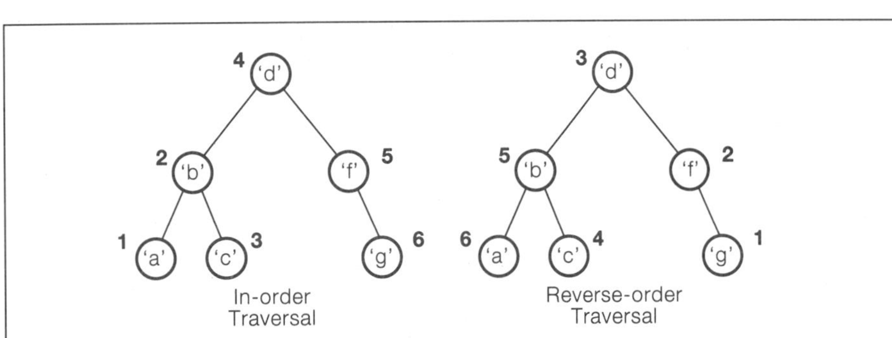

FIGURE 8.15 The Order in Which Nodes Are Processed During In-Order and Reverse-Order Traversals

8.11 to display the key value of each node. The display from such traversals follows:

```
Inorder:        8 11 15 20 21 28 33 34 39 46 47 61 62 67 70 74 83
Reverse-order: 83 74 70 67 62 61 47 46 39 34 33 28 21 20 15 11  8
```

As you examine the recursive Pascal representations of the inorder and reverse-order traversal routines that follow, refer back to the visitation rules as necessary. The address of the tree's root node is passed on the initial call to both routines.

```
PROCEDURE InOrdTraverse ( Current : BTNodePtr );

BEGIN
IF Current <> NIL THEN
  BEGIN
  InOrdTraverse ( Current^.Left );        {Traverse left subtree}
  Process ( Current );                    {Programmer-defined}
  InOrdTraverse ( Current^.Right )        {Traverse right subtree}
  END
END;
```

```
PROCEDURE ReverseOrdTraverse ( Current : BTNodePtr );

BEGIN
IF Current <> NIL THEN
  BEGIN
  ReverseOrdTraverse ( Current^.Right );  {Traverse right subtree}
  ReverseOrdTraverse ( Current^.Left );   {Traverse left subtree}
  Process ( Current )                     {Programmer-defined}
  END
END;
```

These procedures are written recursively, since the *same* visitation rule is applied each time a node is visited, and the decision of which node to visit next is based upon which nodes have already been visited. Upon return from a recursive call, the previous invocation of the rule is continued with the current node.

In-order and reverse-order traversals are especially useful with binary search trees. For other applications, the **preorder** or **postorder traversals** are more useful. For example, later in this chapter we see that a preorder traversal is useful for saving a binary search tree to a file in a manner that allows the program to read the file sequentially and reconstruct the original tree later. The visitation rules for preorder and postorder traversals follow.

Preorder Traversal	Postorder Traversal
1. Process node	1. Traverse left subtree
2. Traverse left subtree	2. Traverse right subtree
3. Traverse right subtree	3. Process node

Figure 8.16 indicates the order in which nodes are processed during a preorder and postorder traversal of the same binary tree (refer back to the visitation rules). Again, the tree root is always the first node visited.

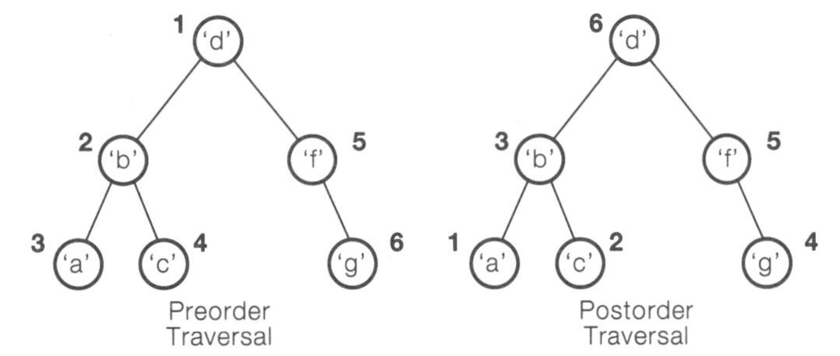

FIGURE 8.16 The Order in Which Nodes Are Processed During Preorder and PostOrder Traversals

A preorder traversal of this tree, displaying the key value of each node processed, produces `d b a c f g`. A postorder traversal produces `a c b g f d`. Try performing preorder and postorder traversals on the tree of 8.11 to display the key value of each node. Output from these traversals follows:

Preorder: 46 21 11 8 15 20 33 28 39 34 62 61 47 74 67 70 83
Postorder: 8 20 15 11 28 34 39 33 21 47 61 70 67 83 74 62 46

Carefully examine the following recursive Pascal representations of the preorder and postorder traversal algorithms, and compare them to the visitation rules for these traversals. Again, the address of the tree's root node is passed upon the initial call to both procedures.

```
PROCEDURE PreOrdTraverse ( Current : BTNodePtr );

BEGIN
IF Current <> NIL THEN
  BEGIN
  Process ( Current );                    {Programmer-defined}
  PreOrdTraverse ( Current^.Left );       {Traverse left subtree}
  PreOrdTraverse ( Current^.Right )       {Traverse right subtree}
  END
END;
```

```
PROCEDURE PostOrdTraverse ( Current : BTNodePtr );

BEGIN
IF Current <> NIL THEN
  BEGIN
  PostOrdTraverse ( Current^.Left );      {Traverse left subtree}
  PostOrdTraverse ( Current^.Right );     {Traverse right subtree}
  Process ( Current )                     {Programmer-defined}
  END
END;
```

One application of preorder and postorder traversing involves an **expression tree**. An expression tree is the binary tree representation of an arithmetic expression. For example, when a Pascal compiler parses a line of source code, it may generate an expression tree to represent the state-

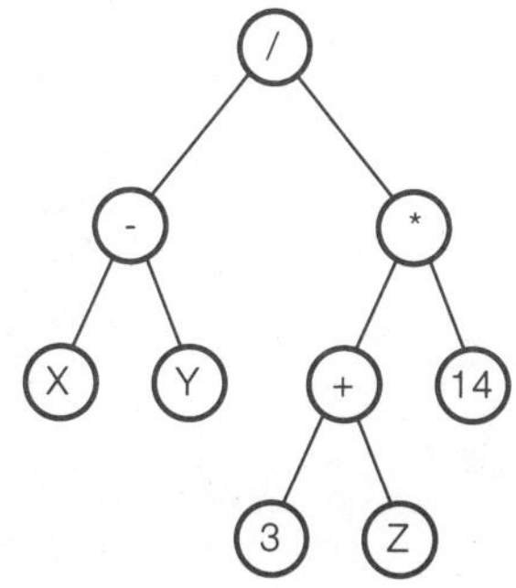

FIGURE 8.17 Sample Expression Tree

ment in a form that is easier to translate into machine code. In an expression tree, each node contains either an operand (constant value or variable address) or an operator symbol. Figure 8.17 depicts a sample expression tree (using variable identifiers instead of addresses) for the Pascal expression `( X - Y ) / ( ( 3 + Z ) * 14 )`.

After generating such a tree, the compiler can perform either a preorder or a postorder traversal to evaluate the expression in preorder or postorder fashion, respectively, *just as the expression was originally intended,* without having to store any parentheses.

Preorder: `/ - X Y * + 3 Z 14` (Correctly reconstructed prefix expression.)

Postorder: `X Y - 3 Z + 14 * /`

Performing an in-order traversal, however, does not result in an evaluation that is commensurate with the original expression, since nothing stored in the tree reflects the structure of the subexpressions:

In-order: `X - Y / 3 + Z * 14`

Breadth-First Traversal

As with the four depth-first traversals, the breadth-first level-order traversal may be used with *any* binary tree and not merely with binary search trees. An entirely different strategy must be employed for this kind of traversal, however. The simple tree used in the previous traversal examples of Figures 8.15 and 8.16 is depicted in Figure 8.18, here showing the order in which the nodes are processed for a **level-order traversal.**

As with the previous traversals, the level-order traversal starts at the root. A level-order transversal of the tree, displaying the key value of each node processed, produces `d b f a c g`. From the root it is relatively easy to process nodes `d`, `b`, and `f` but how can the algorithm then process nodes `a` and `c`, which are the children of node `b`? Even if the algorithm is able to process node `c`, how can it then "jump across" to process node `g`? This problem of spanning the gap between subtrees seems to worsen as the traversal

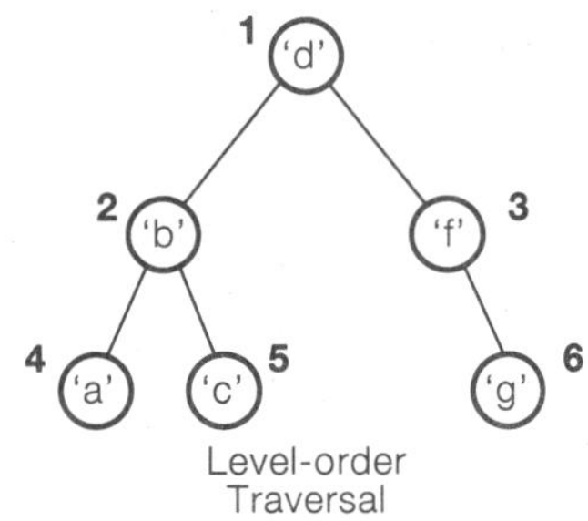

FIGURE 8.18 The Order in Which Nodes Are Processed During a Level-Order Traversal

progresses toward the highest tree level. Rather than concocting a complex algorithm in which the traversal path must backtrack constantly to the root and flow all the way down to the appropriate level on the opposite side of the tree (assuming that such an algorithm can even be written), a simple strategy is sufficient:

> When processing a parent, store the addresses of its children.

A circular FIFO queue can be used to store these addresses, as indicated in the following pseudocode algorithm:

```
ALGORITHM LevelOrdTraverse ( Root );

BEGIN
Create an empty FIFO queue;
Enqueue the address of the root node;
WHILE the queue is NOT empty DO
  BEGIN
  Serve the front address and process its node;
  Enqueue the non-NIL address(es) of its left and right children, if any
  END
END;
```

At this time, examine the following routine in Appendix G.

```
PROCEDURE LevelOrdTraverse ( Root : BTNodePtr );
```

Figure 8.19 depicts the queue activity during a level-order traversal of the tree of Figure 8.18 using a dynamically allocated linked list representation of the queue and no header node. In the figure, a nonstandard Pascal notation is used to represent heapspace address. For example ^d means "the address of the node with key value d." Refer back to Figure 8.18 as you examine these steps.

1. Enqueue address of root node into an empty queue.

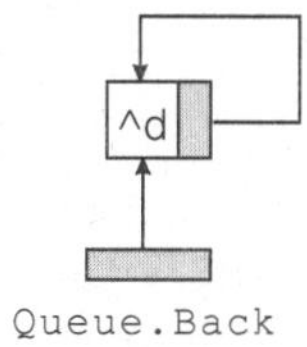

2. Inspect the queue node to be served next (the node for `'d'`); enqueue the addresses of its left and right children, which contain key values `'b'` and `'f'`, and then serve the next queue node (`'d'`):

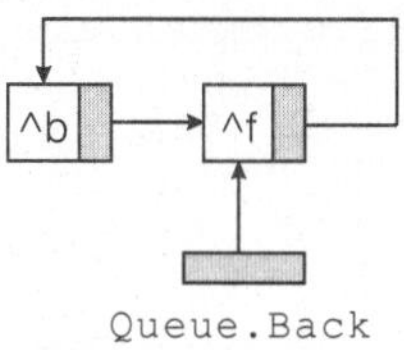

3. Inspect the queue node to be served next (the node for `'b'`); enqueue the addresses of its left and right children, which contain key values `'a'` and `'c'`, then serve the next queue node (`'b'`):

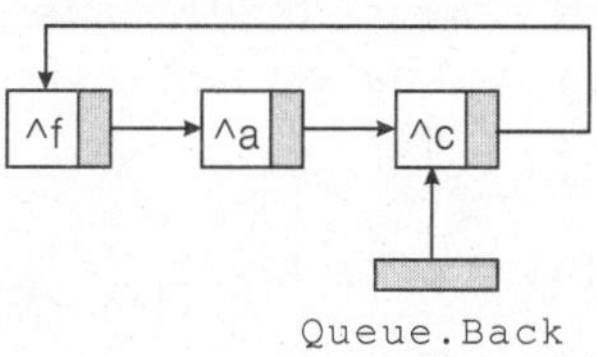

4. Inspect the queue node to be served next (the node for `'f'`); enqueue the addresses of its right child, which contains key values `'g'`, and then serve the next queue node (`'f'`):

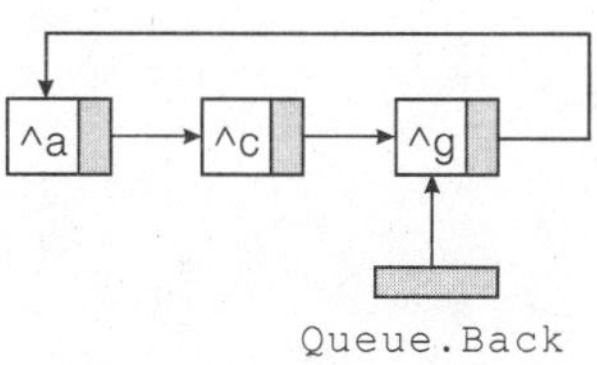

5. Inspect the queue node to be served next (the node for `'a'`); enqueue nothing since it has no children, and then serve the next queue node (`'a'`):

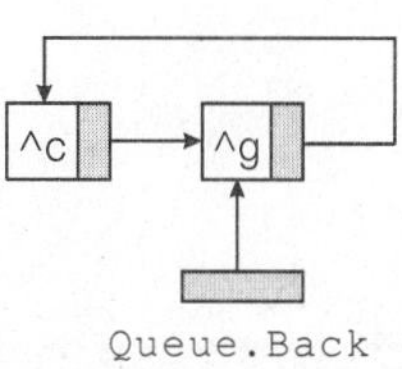

6. Inspect the queue node to be served next (the node for `'c'`); enqueue nothing since it has no children, and then serve the next queue node (`'c'`):

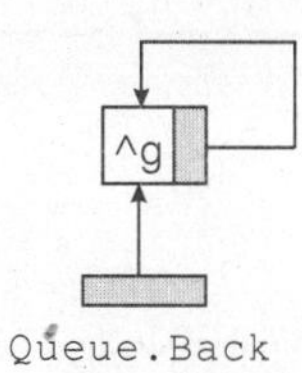

7. Inspect the queue node to be served next (the node for `'g'`); enqueue nothing since it has no children, and then serve the next queue node (`'g'`). The queue is now empty and the traversal is complete.

FIGURE 8.19 Queue Activity During a Level-Order Traversal of the Tree in Figure 8.18

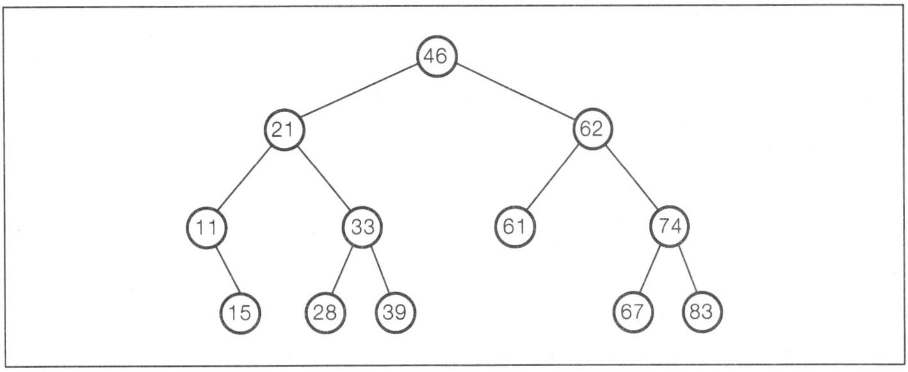

FIGURE 8.20 The Sample Binary Search Tree

Deletion from a Binary Search Tree

Figure 8.20 redisplays the tree of Figure 8.9. The process of inserting a new node in a binary search tree is fairly straightforward because new nodes are always attached as leaves. Deletion is somewhat more complex because *any* node in the tree may be deleted, including the tree's root node. The different cases for deletion include the following:

1. Easy case: Node has degree 0 (a leaf): nodes 15, 28, 39, 61, 67, or 83
2. Easy case: Node has degree 1 (1 child): node 11
3. Difficult case: Node has degree 2 (2 children): nodes 21, 33, 46, 62, or 74

In addition, the node to be deleted may be the tree's root node, in which case the root-pointer variable must be assigned a new value.

A deletion algorithm can determine if the node to be deleted is the tree's root by comparing the address of the node with the address stored in the tree's root-pointer variable (`BinTree.Root`). When such a deletion is completed, the root-pointer variable is merely assigned the address of the *new* tree root. The operations required for deleting either of the easy cases are fairly straightforward (recall that our `BinTreeSearch` procedure will return the address of the node's parent as well as the address of the node to be deleted):

If the node is of degree 0:

```
IF this is the root node THEN
  BinTree.Root := NIL
ELSE
  Appropriate link field of the node's parent := NIL;
Dispose of the node;
```

If the node is of degree 1:

```
IF this is the root node THEN
  BinTree.Root := address of the node's child
ELSE
  Appropriate link field of the node's parent := address of the node's only child;
Dispose of the node;
```

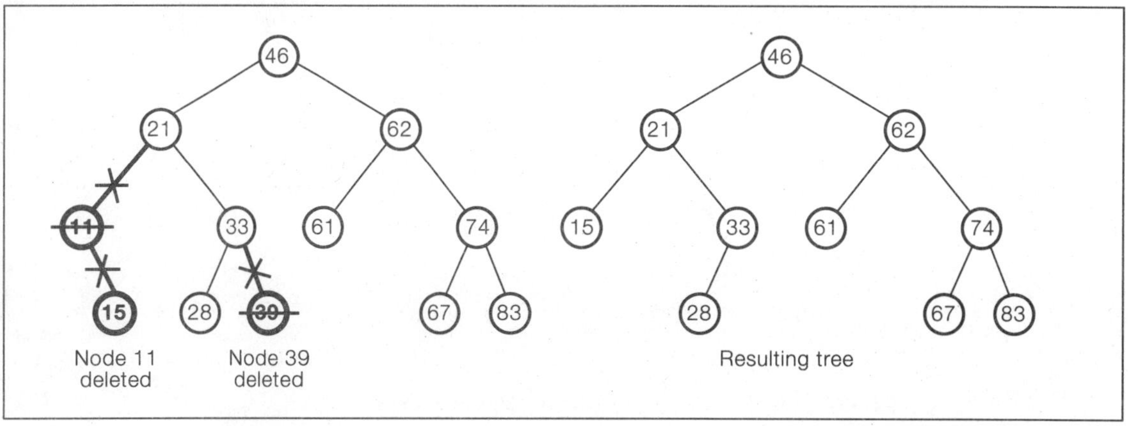

FIGURE 8.21 Examples of Deleting Nodes of Degree 1 (Node 11) and Degree 0 (Node 39)

When disposing a node of degree 1, the deletion algorithm effectively "moves up" the lone child one level closer to the tree's root. For example, Figure 8.21 illustrates that when a node of degree 1 (node 11) is deleted, its right child (node 15) becomes the new left child of node 11's parent, node 21.

If the node has degree 2, the deletion algorithm cannot simply move up a child one level because *that* node may have two children itself. Our general deletion strategy will be to transform this difficult case into one of the two easy cases, based on two facts:

1. The **in-order successor** (or predecessor) of a node with degree 2 is always a node with degree 0 or 1. The in-order successor of the node is the leftmost node of the right child's left subtree (based on the visitation rule for an inorder traversal).
2. The key value of the in-order successor of a node, P, in a binary search tree is greater than all nodes in P's left subtree and less than all other nodes in P's right subtree. Therefore, if it is moved to P's position in the tree, the tree will still be a binary search tree. (The proof for the in-order predecessor of P is parallel to this proof.)

For example, the in-order successor of node 46 in the tree of Figure 8.22 is node 61. The deletion operation for a node of degree 2 may therefore be summarized as follows. *If the node has degree 2:*

1. Locate the in-order successor (or predecessor) of the node.
2. Copy the successor's node's data field into the node's data field.
3. Delete the original successor node (this is always one of the two easy cases).

Apply this algorithm yourself to see that the in-order successor of node 46 is, indeed, node 61 and the in-order successor of node 74 is node 83. This algorithm for locating an in-order successor of a nonleaf node with two children may be summarized in more detail as follows:

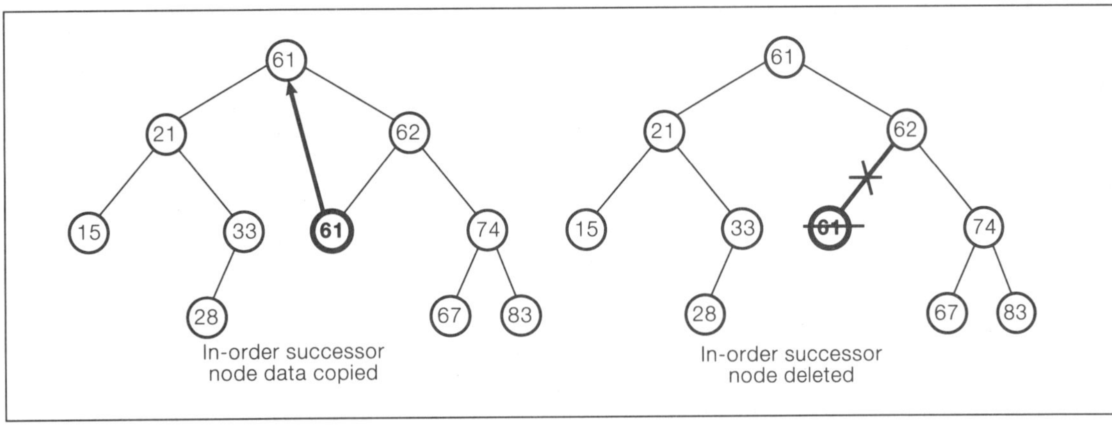

FIGURE 8.22 Examples of Deleting a Node of Degree 2—the Tree's Root Node (Node `61`)

1. Follow the node's right link to the node's right child.
2. From this node, follow all the left links—the last node visited before a **`NIL`** link field is encountered in the in-order successor.

(In an algorithm for locating the in-order predecessor, the word *left* is replaced with *right* and vice versa.)

As an example of deleting a node of degree 2, Figure 8.22 depicts the deletion of the tree's root node.

Deletion of a tree's root node is a special case for deletion just as insertion of a node into an empty tree is a special case for insertion; in both cases, `BinTree.Root` must be assigned a new address value. If a header node node is used, neither is a special case, and the respective algorithms are shortened slightly.

> *At this time, examine the following routine in Appendix G.*

```
PROCEDURE BinTreeDelete ( VAR BinTree : BinTreeType;
                          Current, Parent : BTNodePtr );
```

Accessing Information Using Different Keys

It is often useful to be able to access information using any of several key types rather then being limited to only one key type. As an example, Figure 8.23 shows the diagram of a binary search tree containing information about telephone company customers. The entire tree is structured using a portion of a telephone number as the key value (as usual, only key values are shown, but other information such as customer name, address, business versus residence, number of lines, outstanding balance, etc., are stored within each node as well). Different trees could be used for different three-

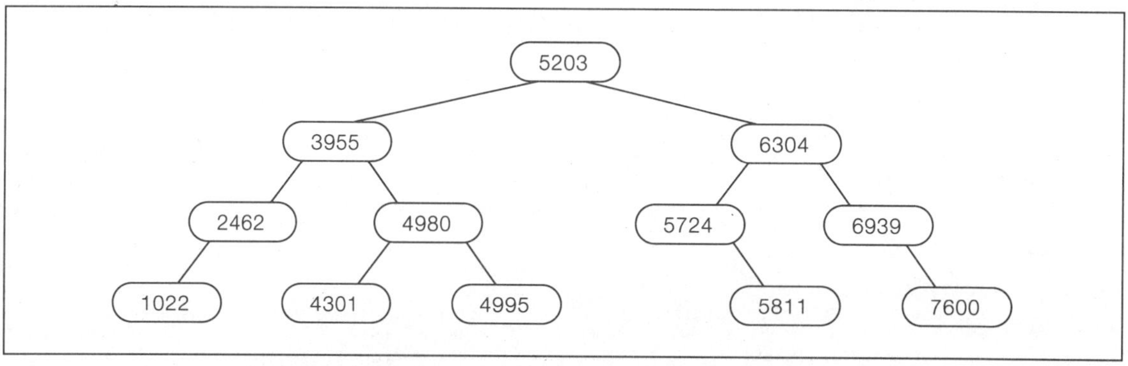

FIGURE 8.23 A Binary Search Tree of Information about Telephone Company Customers

digit extensions, all within the same area code. For example, the tree of Figure 8.23 might be a tree for customers with a 617 area code and 437 exchange (the root node telephone number would therefore be 617-437-5203).

The telephone number is the key by which a telephone company operator can access the node for a particular customer; i.e., the tree has been structured using telephone numbers, so any customer record can be located within a reasonable time using the search algorithm presented in Section 8.2. An operator may wish to access customer information using a name or address value instead. For example, the operator may wish to display the telephone number of all Drakes in a given city (i.e., given a set of trees), look up the number of a particular Drake, or display the names and telephone numbers of all accounts on a given street in a given city. All such searches for nonkey values must be made using the slower linear search via an in-order traversal rather than a binary search since the values are distributed randomly among the nodes.

> Any search tree is organized using one particular key type (e.g., telephone number, name, address, etc.). Accessing a record using a particular type of key requires a search of the tree that has been organized using that type of key. *The ability to access a particular record using any of N different keys therefore requires the maintenance of N different search trees.*

As was pointed out in Application 5.5 (the Sky-High Airlines passenger list), however, maintaining *N* redundant copies of *nonkey information* in different trees not only requires *N* times as much memory but also will require a greater expenditure of program-execution time: If a modification is made to a node's nonkey information in one tree, the corresponding nodes in the other search trees must be modified as well.

> The main purpose of any search tree is to provide quick access to a particular node. Therefore, the key is the only data that need be stored; associated nonkey information can be stored elsewhere, such as in heapspace if the tree node contains the address of the heapspace record.

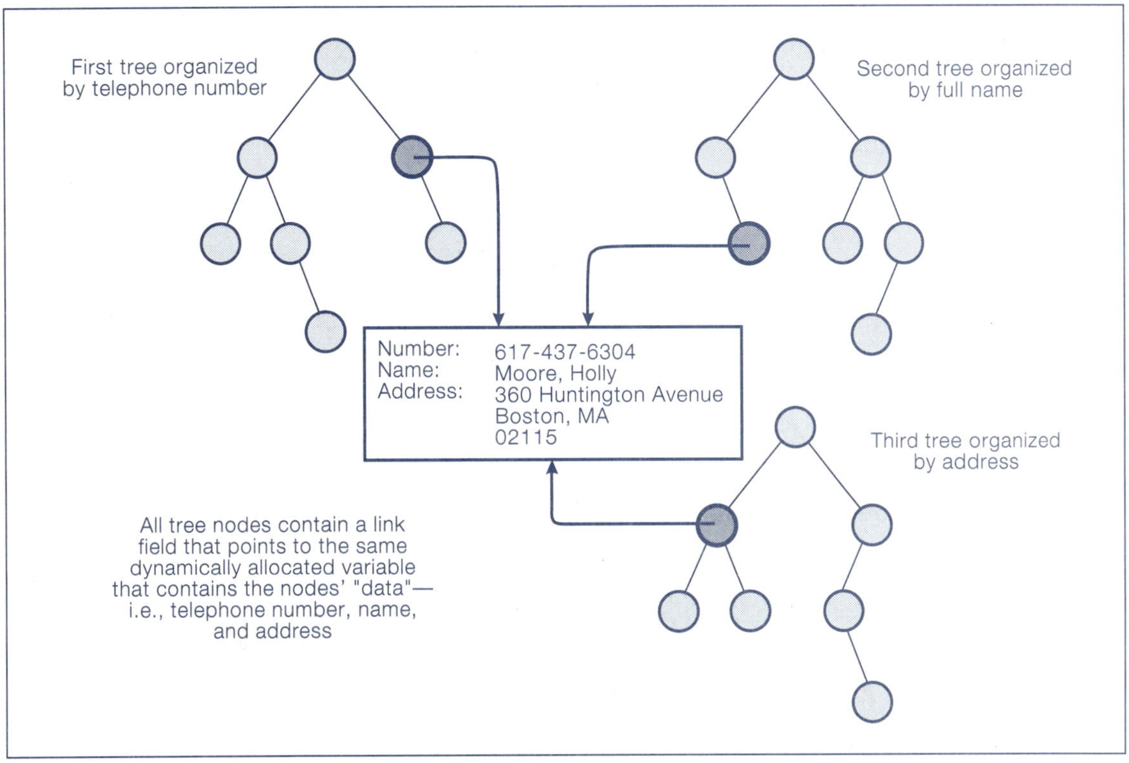

FIGURE 8.24 Three Search Trees Are Required to Access a Record Using Any of Three Keys

Although we cannot avoid using *N* different search trees to support a search using any of *N* different types of key, we can avoid keeping *N* identical copies of each node's nonkey data. We can add to each node a pointer variable to hold the heapspace address of a dynamically allocated record containing that node's nonkey data. As a simple example of this, Figure 8.24 depicts portions of three search trees structured using telephone number, name, and address value as the respective key.

This way, the modification of any nonkey data field requires only one change in the data base—a modification of the data field within its dynamically allocated record. This technique of storing data records separately from the linked structure used to access the data is useful in *many* contexts and not just with search trees. Some of the best sorting and hashing algorithms work this way.

Analysis of the Binary Search Tree Search

In Section 3.7 we analyzed the efficiency of the linear search algorithm for both sorted and unsorted lists, and in Section 7.4 we analyzed the efficiency of the binary search algorithm for an ordered linear list stored in an array. In this section we analyze the search algorithm for a binary search tree, deriving growth rate functions for the worst and average cases. We also examine how tree height and shape affect searching efficiency. As before, we will count key value comparisons as a gauge of algorithm efficiency; i.e., efficiency decreases as the number of comparisons increases.

Unlike the efficiency of linear and binary searches that are performed on linear lists, the efficiency of a search performed on a binary search tree is affected profoundly by the particular *shape* of the tree—i.e., how balanced it is:

- A **height-balanced** tree (or simply, **balanced tree**) is one in which, for every node, the heights of its two subtrees differ by no more than one level. A balanced tree is a **tree of minimal height** for the number of nodes it contains.
- A **full tree** is not only balanced, it has all its leaves on the same level. A full tree contains the *maximum* number of nodes for a tree of its height.
- A **degenerate tree** contains one node per level; i.e., it is completely *unbalanced.* A degenerate tree contains the *minimum* number of nodes for a tree of its height and is therefore a **tree of maximum height** for the number of nodes it contains.

Figure 8.25 depicts examples of these types of trees.

> A search tree of minimum height requires the *minimal* average searching time (best efficiency), whereas a tree of maximum height (i.e., a degenerate tree) requires the *maximum* average searching time (worst efficiency).

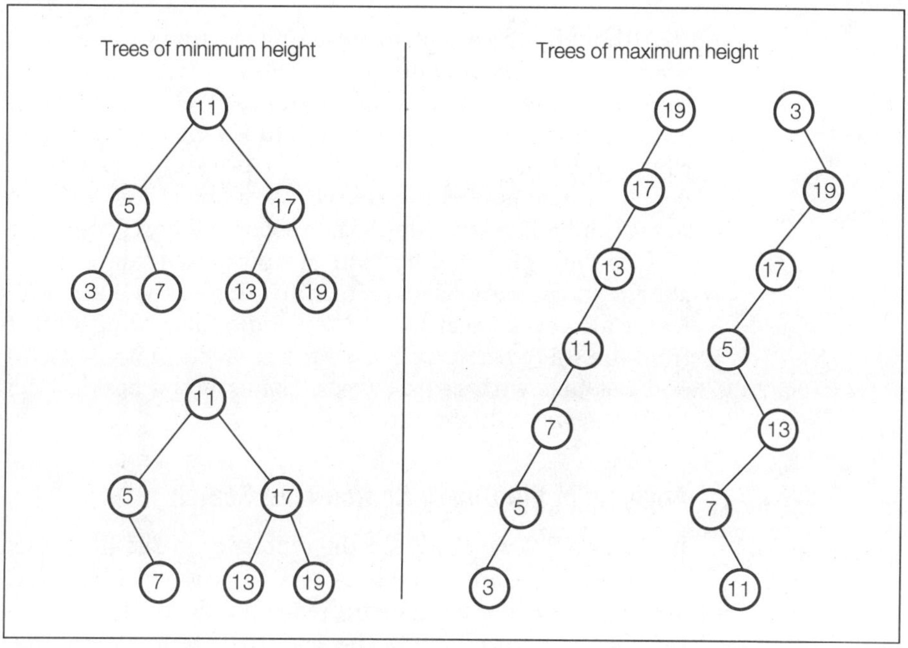

FIGURE 8.25 Sample Trees of Minimum and Maximum Height

This makes sense when you consider that for a binary search tree, the searching algorithm will make a key comparison at each level until either a match is found (success) or no more nodes are found along that path (failure).

As with the binary search, each time a node in a *full* binary search tree item is visited and a comparison to the item's key value is made and fails, the total number of items remaining to be searched is reduced by a factor of 2. Therefore, *the search of a minimal height binary search tree has the same worst-case efficiency as does the binary search on an ordered linear list:*

$$\lceil \log_2(N + 1) \rceil = O(\log N)$$

The average case growth-rate function is approximately equal to its worst case function, so the tree search algorithm is O (log N) in the average case as well.

A degenerate tree is effectively just a linear list with a growth rate function of $N/2$, which is O (N). In describing the efficiency of a tree search, we must therefore state a *range* of efficiency for all tree shapes, from a minimum height tree to a maximum height tree. The worst case for the time required for tree searches is rated as follows:

$$\text{Time}_{\text{minimum height}} = O(\log N)$$
$$\text{Time}_{\text{maximum height}} = O(N)$$

The relationship between tree shape or balance and searching efficiency for a tree of N nodes is summarized in Figure 8.26. The search of a balanced binary search tree of N nodes performs with the same average-case and worst-case efficiency as for a binary search in an array: log N.

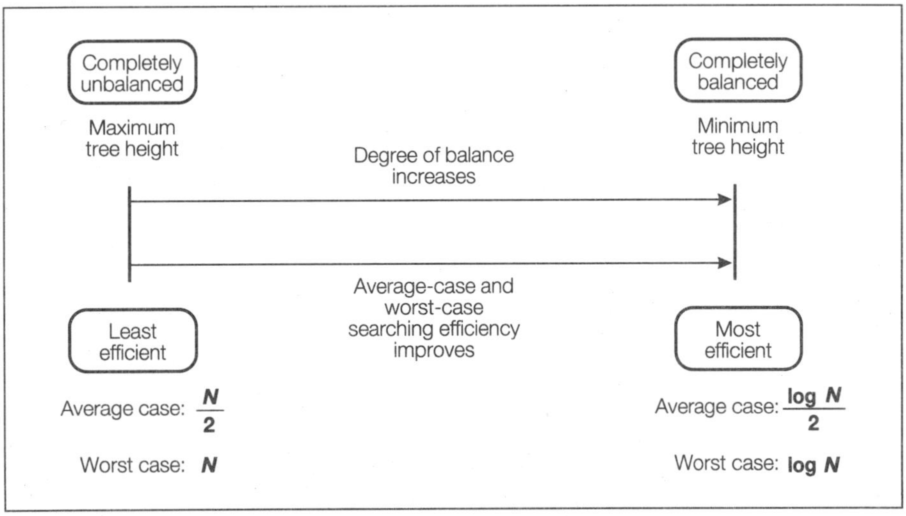

FIGURE 8.26 The Relationship Between Tree Shape and Average Searching Efficiency

For a full binary tree, the following equations describe the relationships between the total number of nodes in a tree (N) and either the tree's height (H) or the number of leaves:

$$\text{Height}_{\text{minimum}} = \log_2(N + 1) \qquad \text{Number of leaves} = \frac{N+1}{2}$$

$$N = 2^H - 1 \qquad \text{Number of leaves} = 2^{(H-1)}$$

Given a tree (whether full or not full) of N nodes, what are the maximum and minimum heights possible? A tree of *maximum height* is merely a degenerate tree, so the height value is simply N:

$$\text{Height}_{\text{maximum}} = N$$

Knowing the *minimum possible height* of a tree helps to predict search performance, although the calculation of this value may not be quite as obvious in a nonfull tree as the calculation of the maximum height. For example, a tree of height 3 can hold three to seven nodes, as illustrated in the sample trees of Figure 8.27. Since no more than $2^H - 1$ nodes will fit in a tree of N nodes, we must find the smallest H such that $N \leq 2^H - 1$ (the $\leq$ operator is used because the tree may not be full):

$$\begin{aligned} N &\leq 2^H - 1 \\ N + 1 &\leq 2^H \\ \log_2(N + 1) &\leq H \end{aligned}$$

If $(N + 1)$ is a power of 2, then H will be a positive integer value; a height value must be an integer, since a tree cannot have a fractional height. But $(N + 1)$ may *not* be a power of 2, in which case the expression $\log_2(N + 1)$ must be rounded *upward* using a ceiling function (indicated by $\lceil\ \rceil$):

$$\text{Height}_{\text{minimum}} = \lceil \log_2(N + 1) \rceil$$

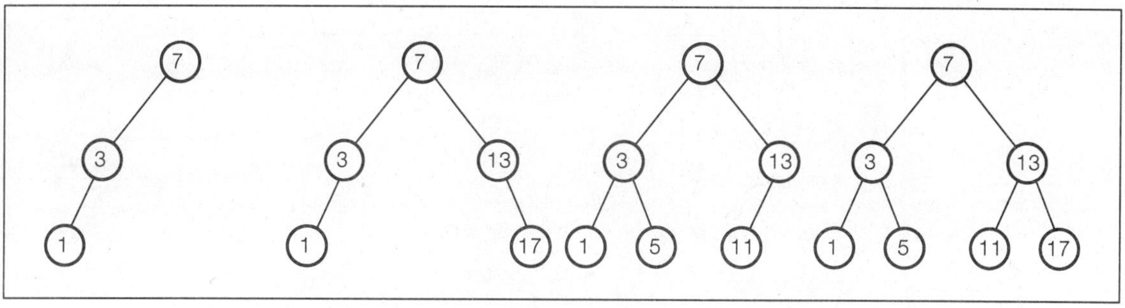

FIGURE 8.27 A Tree of Height 3 Can Hold Three to Seven Nodes

For example, the minimum height of a tree to hold 11 nodes is 4, calculated as follows:

$$\lceil \log_2(11 + 1) \rceil = 4$$

If a tree of 11 nodes has a height *greater* than 4, it will not provide the maximum average searching efficiency—i.e., minimum search time.

Try writing a recursive integer function named `FindHeight` that returns the height of a binary search tree, which may or may not be full, whose root address is passed as an argument.

> *At this time, please examine the Pascal implementations of the two* `FindHeight` *algorithms in Appendix G.*

```
FUNCTION FindHeight ( Root : BTNodePtr ) : Integer;
```

Saving a Binary Search Tree in a File, Rebuilding a Tree

As with a linear linked list, many applications require that a binary search tree, which is created and manipulated by a program, be preserved in a file between program runs. When the program is reexecuted, records of information can be read and the original tree rebuilt. Pseudocode algorithms for the two operations of saving and rebuilding follow:

```
ALGORITHM WriteTree ( VAR BinTree : BinTreeType );

BEGIN
Open the file for writing;
Perform a traversal: processing a node involves writing the node to the file;
Close the file
END;
```

```
ALGORITHM ReadTree ( VAR BinTree : BinTreeType );

BEGIN
Open the file for reading;
Initialize the binary search tree as empty;
WHILE the file is NOT empty DO
  BEGIN
  Read a node record from the file;
  Insert that node record in the tree
  END;
Close the file
END;
```

As with dynamically allocated linked lists, only the data portion of each node is saved; pointer values are *never* saved in a file because these values are runtime dependent. The `WriteTree` algorithm involves a tree traversal in which each node is processed by writing its data portion to the file.

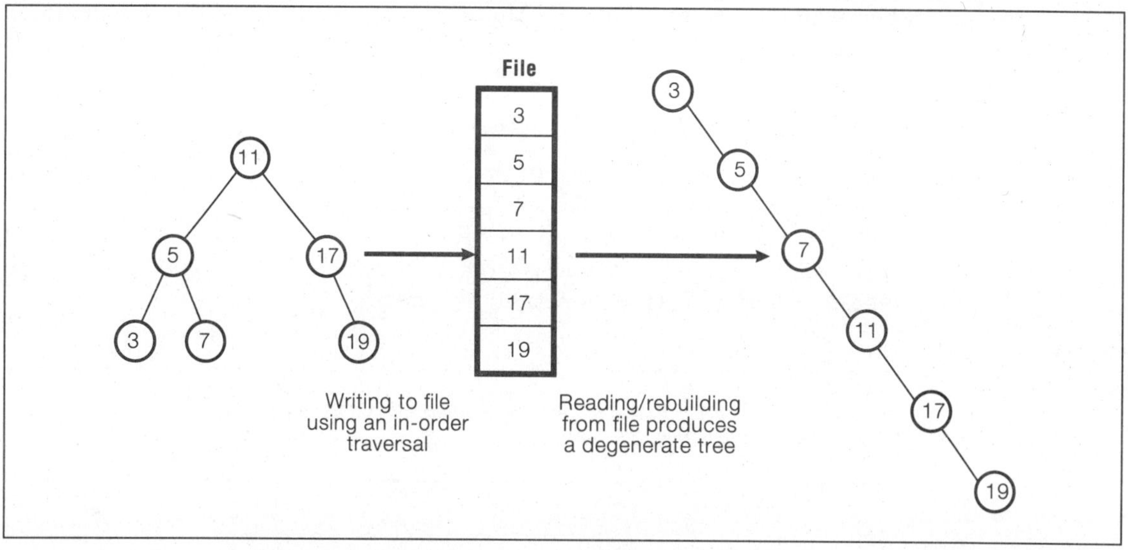

FIGURE 8.28 Saving a Binary Search Tree Using an In-Order Traversal

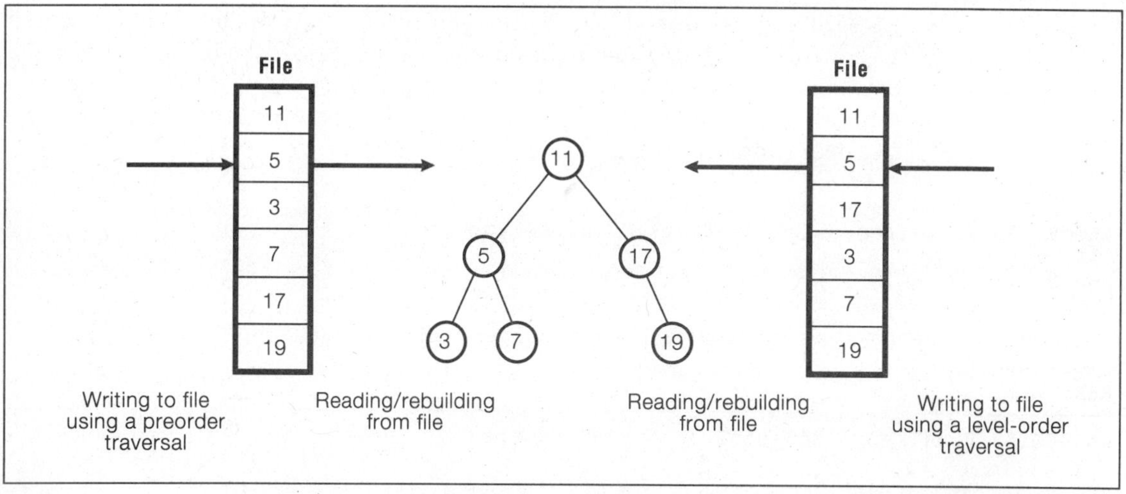

FIGURE 8.29 Saving the Same Binary Search Tree Using Preorder and Level-Order Traversals

Which tree traversal should be used? Not just any traversal will do; Figure 8.28 depicts a balanced binary search tree saved to a file using an in-order traversal and then rebuilt using the `BinTreeInsert` algorithm to produce a degenerate tree! (Saving via a reverse-order traversal produces a similar result.) Saving the same tree using either a preorder or level-order traversal, on the other hand, will permit the tree to be rebuilt to its original shape when records are read sequentially from the file.

Figure 8.29 depicts the reconstruction of the tree by reading records from this file.

APPLICATION 8.1 Building an Identifier Index for a Source Program

When developing and debugging large computer programs, it is often useful to be able to locate a particular identifier quickly. For example, when debugging a procedure called `GetData`, it may prove helpful to find every call to `GetData`. In this application we will devise a Pascal program that creates a line-number index of all identifiers for any Pascal source-code program contained in a text file, which we will refer to as the *input program*. Our program will build a binary search tree of such identifiers, with a singly linked list emanating from each tree node to hold line numbers for that identifier. By performing an in-order traversal of the tree, our program can display all identifiers in alphabetical order, as well as displaying the line numbers for each identifier (via a traversal of each linked list). The program will be versatile enough to generate an index of *all* identifiers in the input program or, at the user's request, will exclude a particular set of identifiers.

The program should be robust enough to exclude from the index any identifier appearing within literal strings and comments. At the user's request, the index also could exclude Pascal special identifiers, such as **MAXINT** and **FALSE**, and the identifiers of native routines, such as `Close` and `Sqr`. For example, assume that the following has just been read by our index program as one long string from line 314 of the input program:

```
Writeln ( 'Result =', Total:4:2, 'Mean =', (Total / N ):4:2 );   {Debugging line}
```

The identifier `Writeln` are excluded from the index because it is the name of a predefined procedure. The strings `'Result'` and `'Mean'` are excluded, since they appear within a literal string, and the strings `'Debugging'` and `'line'` are excluded, since they appear within a comment. The identifiers `'Total'` and `'N'` are inserted in the index tree—but only *if they are not already in the tree*. (They *should*, in fact, already be in the tree, having appeared earlier in the input program in one of the declaration sections.) A line-number node containing the value 314 is added to each of the linked lists emanating from the index tree node containing the identifier `'Total'` and the identifier `'N'`. Although `'Total'` appears twice on line 314 of the input file, only one line number node is added to its linked list.

Users of our index program must furnish a text file containing any identifiers they wish to exclude from the index (if any); the program will build a separate binary search tree to hold them. This text file will likely contain all standard Pascal reserved words, predefined constants, and predefined procedure and function names but certainly may contain any other word as well. Our program will assume that such a text file contains one identifier per line and that the identifiers are *not* ordered alphabetically, as this would result in a degenerate binary search tree when the words are read sequentially from the file.

One or two binary search trees are therefore used in building the identifier index:

- *Index tree.* Holds each identifier currently in the index, as well as the line number linked list for each identifier.
- *Exclusion tree* (Optional). Holds identifiers that are explicitly *excluded* from the index.

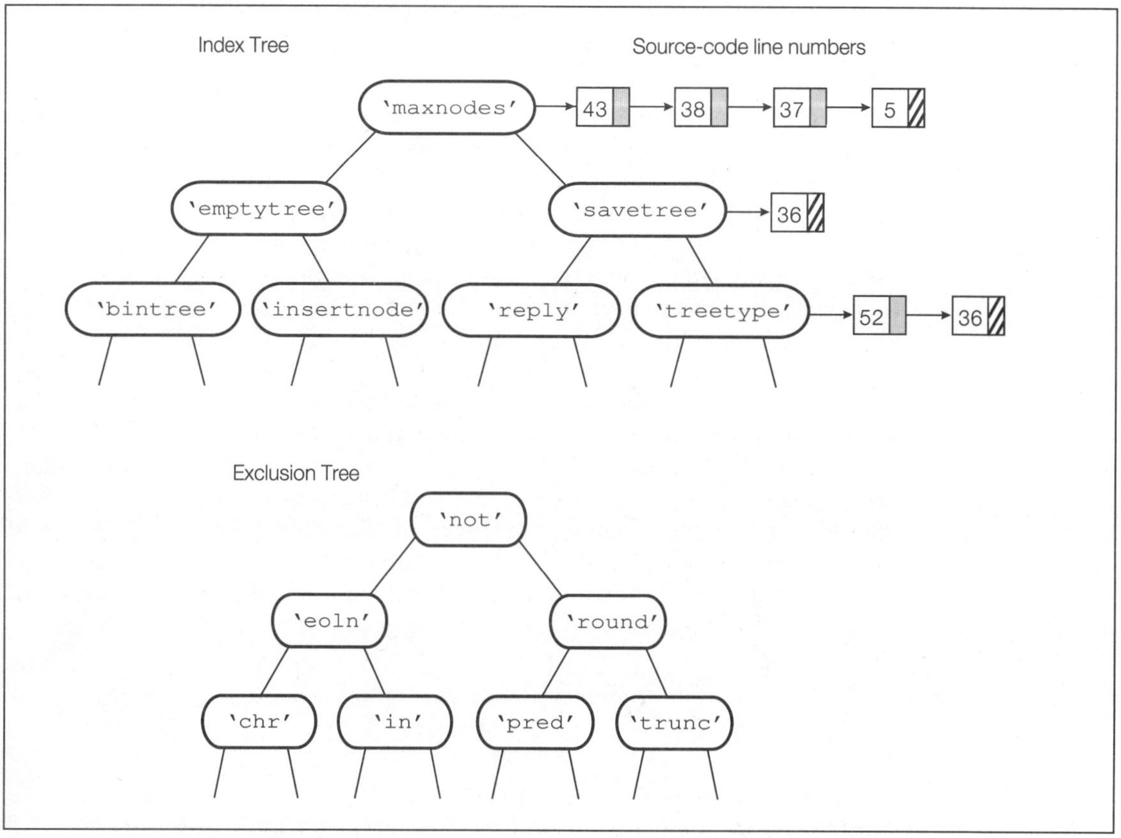

FIGURE 8.30 First Three Levels of Sample Index and Exclusion Trees

Figure 8.30 depicts the first three levels of an index tree and an exclusion tree used to create an index for an imaginary input program (only three linked lists of line numbers are shown). Notice that a new line number node is always inserted at the *beginning* of a linked list. If each new line number node were always inserted at the *end* of a linked list instead, time would be wasted traversing the list to find the end, or an additional pointer variable would have to be stored in each tree node to point to the last linked list node, thereby wasting memory. A linked list header node does not provide any advantage and is therefore not used.

The index itself will be written to a text file, with identifiers appearing in alphabetical order and line numbers appearing in ascending order. (Think about how each list of line numbers can be written in *ascending order* if they are stored in *descending order!*) Three sample lines of output for an imaginary input program follow:

```
lastnode  123, 126, 129, 130, 135, 138, 145
m         120, 126, 127, 128, 134, 135, 139, 254, 257, 278, 281, 283
maxnodes    5,  37,  38,  43
```

A pseudocode algorithm for the entire index tree building process follows; the Pascal representation of this algorithm would actually be distributed among many routines.

```
ALGORITHM BuildIdentifierIndex;

BEGIN
Open the input program file for reading;
Ask the user if she has provided an additional text file of identifiers
  to be explicitly excluded;

Initialize the exclusion and index trees as empty;

WHILE NOT Eof ( Source code program file ) DO
  BEGIN
  Read the next line from file;

  WHILE other characters in the line just read DO
    BEGIN
    Extract the next identifier from line;

    IF an exclusion tree THEN
      Search for a matching identifier in the exclusion tree;

    IF NOT ( an exclusion tree ) OR
      (( an exclusion tree ) AND ( no matching identifier found )) THEN
      BEGIN
      Search the index tree;
      IF no match found THEN
        Insert the new node for this identifier;
      IF no line number node for current line number THEN
        Add a node, at head of list emanating from the identifier node
      END
    END  {WHILE other characters ... }
  END;

Close the input file
END;
```

As with any program, our index program should be developed in stages. All code for a particular stage should be tested fully before the development process advances to the next stage. Six recommended stages of development for the index-building program follow. In stages 1 through 4, a small source-code file that does not contain any literal strings or comments should be used. As you read the description of each stage, consider how you would actually implement the operations described.

Stage 1 *Correct extraction of identifiers.* Prompt for the name of a source code file and then open this file for reading. Read each line of the file into a String variable and simply extract and write all identifiers to a text file, one identifier per line. (Always display an informative message to the user before and after reading all lines from the input file.) Examine the output text file to ensure that all identifiers were extracted from the line correctly.

Stage 2 *Correct building/searching of index tree.* Initialize the index tree as empty. Rather than writing each identifier to the output text file immediately, search for it in the index tree, and then insert it if it is not already there. (Do not bother excluding any identifiers at this stage.) After each insertion, write *every* identifier via an in-order traversal; examine this file for accuracy.

Stage 3 *Correct linked list insertion of line numbers*. For each identifier extracted, add its line number to the linked list of numbers for that identifier in the tree. Add the code to write the complete index (i.e., each identifier and its list of line numbers) to a text file.

Stage 4 *Correct building/use of exclusion tree*. Begin by prompting the user for the name of a text file containing identifiers to be excluded from the index, one identifier per file line. Open this file for reading and insert all identifiers in a separate binary search tree. Write every identifier via an in-order traversal and then examine this file for accuracy. Add the code to search this tree after extracting each identifier from the current line; your program should exclude the identifier from the index if it is found in the exclusion tree. After each insertion, display a message indicating the result of searching the exclusion tree and indicate whether or not it was inserted in the index tree.

Stage 5 *Correct exclusion of literal strings*. Modify the program to ignore anything within literal strings. Perform an in-order traversal of the index tree, writing each identifier to a text file and then examine this file for accuracy.

Stage 6 *Correct exclusion of comments*. Modify the program to ignore anything within comments. Remember that either `{ }` or `(* *)` may be used in the source code input to delimit comments. Perform an in-order traversal of the index tree, writing each identifier to a text file; examine this file for accuracy.

The Pascal coding of program `BuildIndentifierIndex` is left as exercise, and Figure 8.31 contains a possible module tree diagram for it.

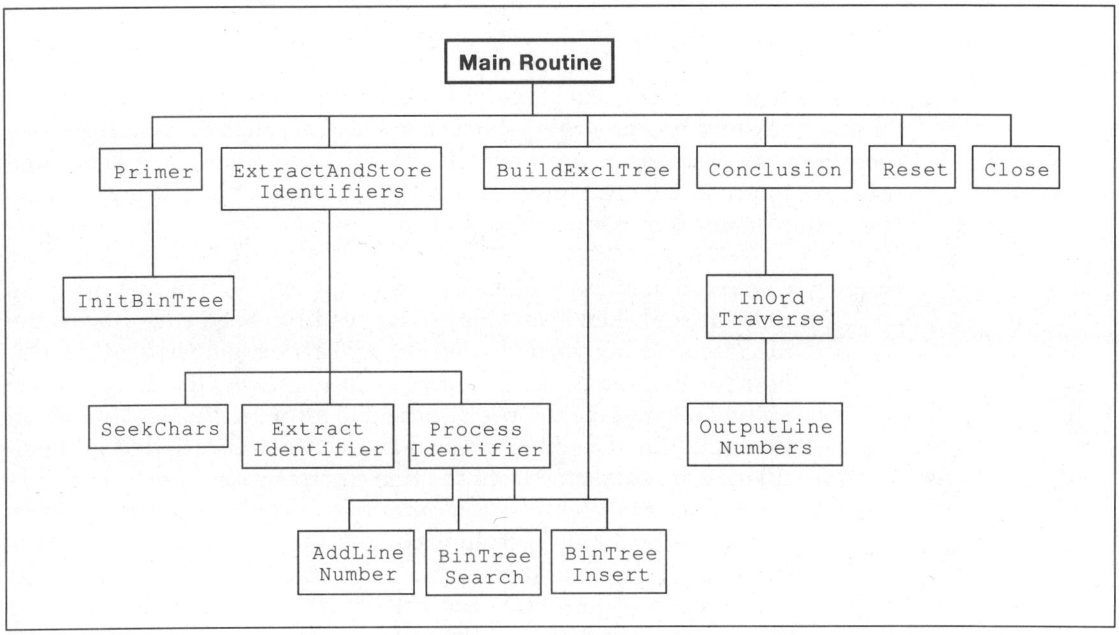

FIGURE 8.31 **A Module Tree Diagram for Program `BuildIdentifierIndex`**

Sequential Storage Representation of the ADT Binary Search Tree

The ADT binary search tree can be represented within an array rather than using heapspace. As with the sequential storage representation of a linked list, the array behaves as a "pseudoheapspace." And, as with any sequential storage representation, the usual disadvantage of a fixed maximum size arises. However, it *does* offer two interesting advantages over the dynamic allocation representation, as we shall see:

- No link fields are necessary.
- Immediate access from a node back to its parent is provided.

In Section 8.3 we represent a *priority queue* data type using a tree structure called a *heap* (not to be confused with heapspace) that is, itself, represented as a binary tree using sequential storage. A set of generic global declarations for the sequential storage representation of any binary search tree follows:

```
CONST
  Null          =  ??;        {Unusual BTKeyType value to indicate "no node"}
  MaxBTNodes    =  ??;        {Maximum number of nodes allowable}

TYPE
  BTNodePtr     =  Integer;
  BTKeyType     =  ??;        {Application-dependent}
  BTInfoType    =  RECORD
                     Key  :  BTKeyType;
                     {other fields, as necessary}
                   END;

  BinTreeType   =  RECORD
                     BTNodes   :  ARRAY [ 1..MaxBTNodes ] OF BTInfoType;
                     Count     :  Integer
                   END;

VAR
  BinTree   :  BinTreeType;
```

The following rules are employed with this representation:

1. The tree can be initialized as empty by merely assigning a zero value to `BinTree.Count`.
2. The tree's root node always occupies the first array element.
3. As with any array element, a particular node is referenced using its array index: `BinTree.BTNodes [ {node index} ]`.
4. The array index of the left child, right child, and parent for a node in element `{node index}` may be calculated as follows:

   Index of left child of node P = P index × 2
   Index of right child of node P = P index × 2 + 1
   Index of parent of node P = P index **DIV** 2

5. The absence of a node is indicated if the calculated array index is beyond the bounds of the array or else the element contains a `Null` key value.

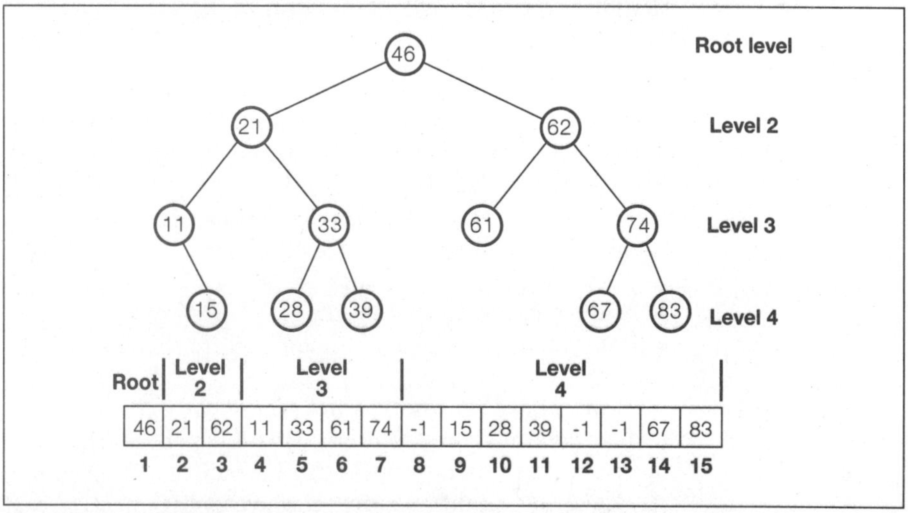

FIGURE 8.32 A Binary Search Tree and Its Sequential Storage Representation

Figure 8.32 shows the sample binary search tree of Figure 8.19, along with a diagram depicting its corresponding array representation (here, `Null` is −1).

A distinct *disadvantage* of this representation is that it may waste a significant amount of memory. A full tree of N elements requires N elements. A completely degenerate tree (one node per tree level), on the other hand, may require as many as $2^N - 1$ elements, with only N of these elements actually being used. For example, reexamine the two degenerate trees of Figure 8.25. Nodes `19`, `17`, `13`, `11`, `7`, `5`, and `3` of the left tree would occupy elements 1, 2, 4, 8, 16, 32, and 64, respectively. Nodes `3`, `19`, `17`, `5`, `13`, `7`, and `11` of the right degenerate tree would occupy elements 1, 3, 7, 15, 31, 63, 127. The latter tree requires 127 array elements, of which only 7 are actually used!

8.3 PRIORITY QUEUES AND HEAPS

Priority Queues

In Section 7.2, the FIFO queue is introduced as a data structure in which an item is stored (and later accessed) solely on the basis of *when* that data item was stored—i.e., its time of arrival. The data items are merely enqueued at the back end of the list and served at the front end, with no regard to the item's key value (if it even has a key value). The item that has been stored the longest, relative to all other items currently in the queue, is always the item to be served next.

In a *priority queue,* each item does have a key value, which is regarded as a **priority value** relative to the other items in the queue. The priority/key value of each item determines *where* the item is positioned within the structure, and the item with the highest priority/key value in the queue is served next. A line of movie theater patrons waiting to buy tickets behaves typically as a FIFO queue, but a group of persons waiting to be seen in a hospital's emergency ward characterizes a priority queue, since persons with more serious injuries are given higher priority and are attended to sooner than those with less serious injuries. The specifications for the ADT priority queue follow.

Specifications for the ADT Priority Queue

The **ADT priority queue** is a structured data type whose items belong to the same type, yet no ordering is imposed by the structure other than the fact that the item with the greatest priority value (relative to the other items) is always the next item to be removed. Each item is independent of other items, so the concept of linearity does not apply.

Domain

The domain consists of items, usually of record data type. Each item has a key value, which is regarded as a priority value relative to other items in the queue. Priority values need not be unique among items.

Fundamental Operations

1. *Initialize:* Initialize the priority queue as empty—i.e., a queue with no items.
2. *Test for emptiness:* Determine if the priority queue is empty.
3. *Test for fullness:* Determine if the priority queue is full.
4. *Enqueue:* Enqueue (add) an item.
5. *Serve:* Serve (remove) an item.

Pascal Representations of the ADT Priority Queue

How shall we actually represent this data type using Pascal? A priority queue of items could be represented by merely storing the items in an array as a simple linear list. We can eliminate the time required to search for the next item to serve by maintaining the structure of the array items in *descending priority value order;* this way, the next item to be served will always reside in element 1. Unfortunately, the usual inefficiencies that accompany array insertions and deletions of items arise. During an enqueue operation, for example, the point of insertion can be found quickly using a binary search; however, existing items with a lower priority must then be shifted toward the high-index end of the array to "make room" for the new item. Conversely, upon serving the item in the first element, all remaining items must be shifted toward the lower-index end of the array to fill in the "gap" left by the removal of the item in element one. Another disadvantage with the array representation is that the size of the queue is fixed at compile-time.

From the simple array representation we can consider the linked list as a possible representation. We can again maintain the structure in *descending priority-value order* so that the next item to be served will always reside in the first node. The efficiency of enqueuing and serving improves, since there is no shifting of items; however, the efficiency of the enqueue operation suf-

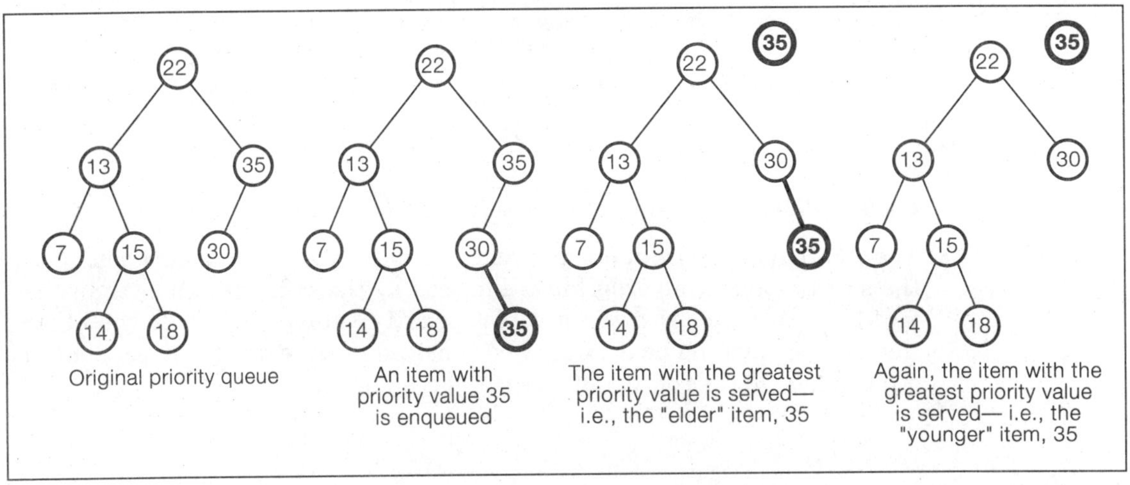

FIGURE 8.33 Representing a Priority Queue Using a Binary Search Tree

fers from the fact that the appropriate point of insertion must be located using a linear search rather than a binary search.

To maximize searching efficiency while preserving the insertion/deletion benefits of a linked list, we then progress to a binary search tree representation using dynamic allocation. Now the appropriate point of insertion can be located with reasonable efficiency (*maximum* efficiency, in fact, if the tree is balanced), and the dynamic allocation simplifies the enqueueing and serving of items. But how can we locate the item to be removed next? Although a full in-order traversal will eventually reach the item with the greatest priority, a faster approach is to *access the last node in the path starting with the root and following all right links*. This technique is illustrated in Figure 8.33.

Of course, any binary search tree may become unbalanced, as does the sample tree of Figure 8.33. While the lack of balance will not prohibit priority queue operations, it will slow the enqueueing and serving operations, since they rely heavily upon the tree-search operation.

Heaps

We now examine yet another alternative: a *heap* (not to be confused with *heapspace* memory), whose enqueue and serve operations *always* perform with maximum efficiency. Before considering the specifications for the ADT heap, the concept of a *nearly-full tree* must be discussed.

A **nearly full tree** is an oriented, balanced tree with the following properties:

- The tree has the *minimum possible height* for as many nodes as it contains.
- The tree is *full from level 1 through level (tree-height − 1)*.
- At the leaf level of the tree *all leaves are in the leftmost positions,* based on conventional tree diagrams.

Figure 8.34 depicts examples of full trees and nearly full trees.

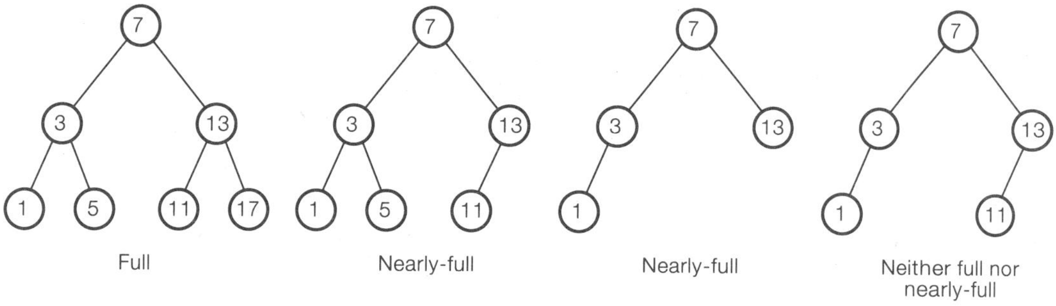

FIGURE 8.34 **Examples of Trees That Are Full, Nearly Full, or Neither**

Specifications for the ADT Heap

The **ADT heap** is a *full or nearly full binary tree* in which the relationship shown in Figure 8.35 holds true for every node in the tree (each of which is considered as the root node of its two subtrees):

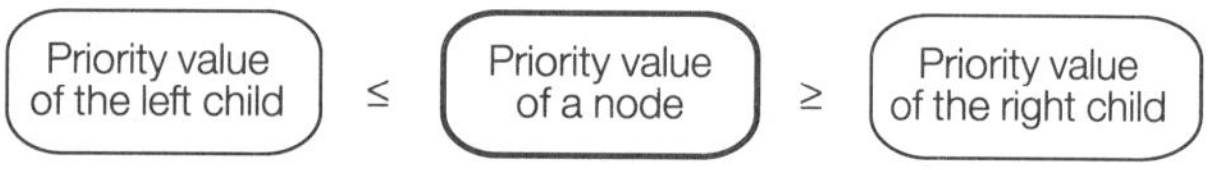

FIGURE 8.35 **Relationships among Priority Values in a Heap**

Some applications may require that the opposite relation holds; i.e., the priority value of a node is less than or equal to the priority value of either child.

Domain

The domain consists of items called *nodes,* usually of record data type. Each item has a key value regarded as a priority value; priority values need not be unique among items.

Fundamental Operations

1. *Initialize:* Initialize the heap as empty; i.e., containing no items [`InitHeap`].
2. *Test for emptiness:* Test the heap for emptiness [`HeapEmpty`].
3. *Test for fullness:* Test the heap for fullness [`HeapFull`].
4. *Add an item:* Add an item [`HeapInsert`].
5. *Serve an item:* Serve (remove) an item [`HeapDelete`].
6. *Make a copy:* Make a copy of (but do not remove) the item that is to be served (removed) next [`HeapInspect`].

Pascal Representation of the ADT Heap

We will represent the heap using the sequential storage representation of a binary tree. Figure 8.36 depicts the sample heap we will use in our discus-

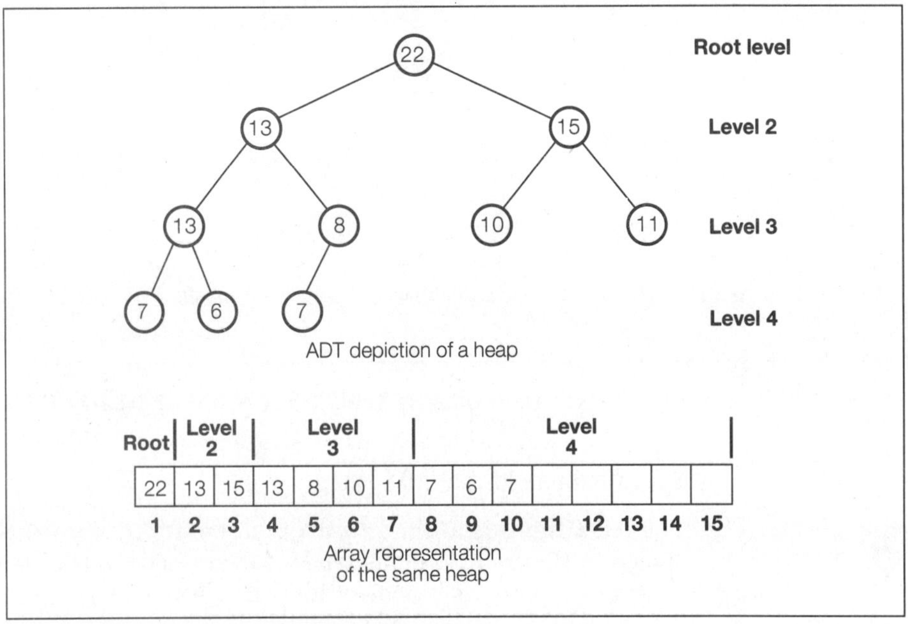

FIGURE 8.36 A Sample Heap

sion of priority queues, along with a diagram depicting its array representation. (As a reminder of how binary trees are represented using arrays, tree level numbers also are shown in the figure.)

A set of generic, global declarations for a heap structure follow:

```
CONST
  MaxHItems   =  ??;       {Maximum number of items allowable}

TYPE
  HKeyType    =  ??;       {Application-dependent}
  HInfoType   =  RECORD
                   Key   :  HKeyType;
                   {Other fields, as necessary}
                 END;

  HeapType    =  RECORD
                   Items  :  ARRAY [ 1..MaxHItems ] OF HInfoType;
                   Count  :  Integer
                 END;

VAR
  Heap  :  HeapType;
```

A heap must be a full or nearly full binary tree so that all nodes occupy contiguous elements at the low-index end of the array, with all unused nodes occupying contiguous elements at the high-index end of the array. The `Heap.Count` field value provides both a count of the items in the queue as well as the array index of the last node in the heap. The last node is the rightmost leaf at the highest level of a heap, based on conventional tree diagrams. In the sample heap of Figure 8.36, the rightmost node `7` is the last node.

At this time, examine the following routines in Appendix H.

```
PROCEDURE HeapInit ( VAR Heap : HeapType );

FUNCTION HeapEmpty ( VAR Heap : HeapType ) : Boolean;

FUNCTION HeapFull ( VAR Heap : HeapType ) : Boolean;

PROCEDURE InspectHeap ( VAR Heap : HeapType; VAR Item : HInfoType );
```

Insertion into a Heap

In a heap insertion operation, `Heap.Count` is incremented and the item is inserted as the new last item. The item is then "moved up" the tree into its appropriate location—i.e., to the location where its key value is less than or equal to that of its parent or until it becomes the heap root (with no parent, in element one of the array). Figure 8.37 traces the insertion operation of an item with integer priority value `14`. In the figure, the value of `Heap.Count` field is indicated by the **C** character.

Pseudocode algorithms for the insertion of an item into a heap follow. Here, the algorithm for insertion is made slightly more efficient than the process depicted in Figure 8.37 by deferring assignment of the new item to any array element until its final location is determined (in the figure, the new item and its parent are swapped as the new item is moved up in the heap):

```
{Moves item in Heap.Items [ Hole ] up in the heap, to its appropriate location}

ALGORITHM AdjustUp ( VAR Heap : Heaptype; Hole : Integer );

VAR
  Item   : HInfo Type;              {The item to be adjusted upward}
  Parent : Integer;

BEGIN
Item    := Heap.Items [ Hole ];     {HeapInsert stored new item in array}
Parent  := Hole DIV 2;

WHILE Parent >= 1 DO                {WHILE there is a parent to examine DO}
  BEGIN
  IF Item's key > key of its parent THEN
    BEGIN
    Copy its parent item to element Hole;
    Hole := Parent
    END;

  Parent := Parent DIV 2            {Parent := parent of the current parent}
  END;

Store Item in element Hole          {Finally, store new item!}
END;
```

```
ALGORITHM HeapInsert ( VAR Heap : HeapType; VAR NewItem : HInfoType  );

BEGIN
Increment Heap.Count;
Store NewItem in element Heap.Count;
AdjustUp ( Heap, Heap.Count )      {Move NewItem up in heap as necessary}
END;
```

At this time, examine the following routines in Appendix H.

```
PROCEDURE AdjustUp ( VAR Heap : HeapType; Hole : Integer );

PROCEDURE HeapInsert ( VAR Heap : HeapType; VAR NewItem : HInfoType );
```

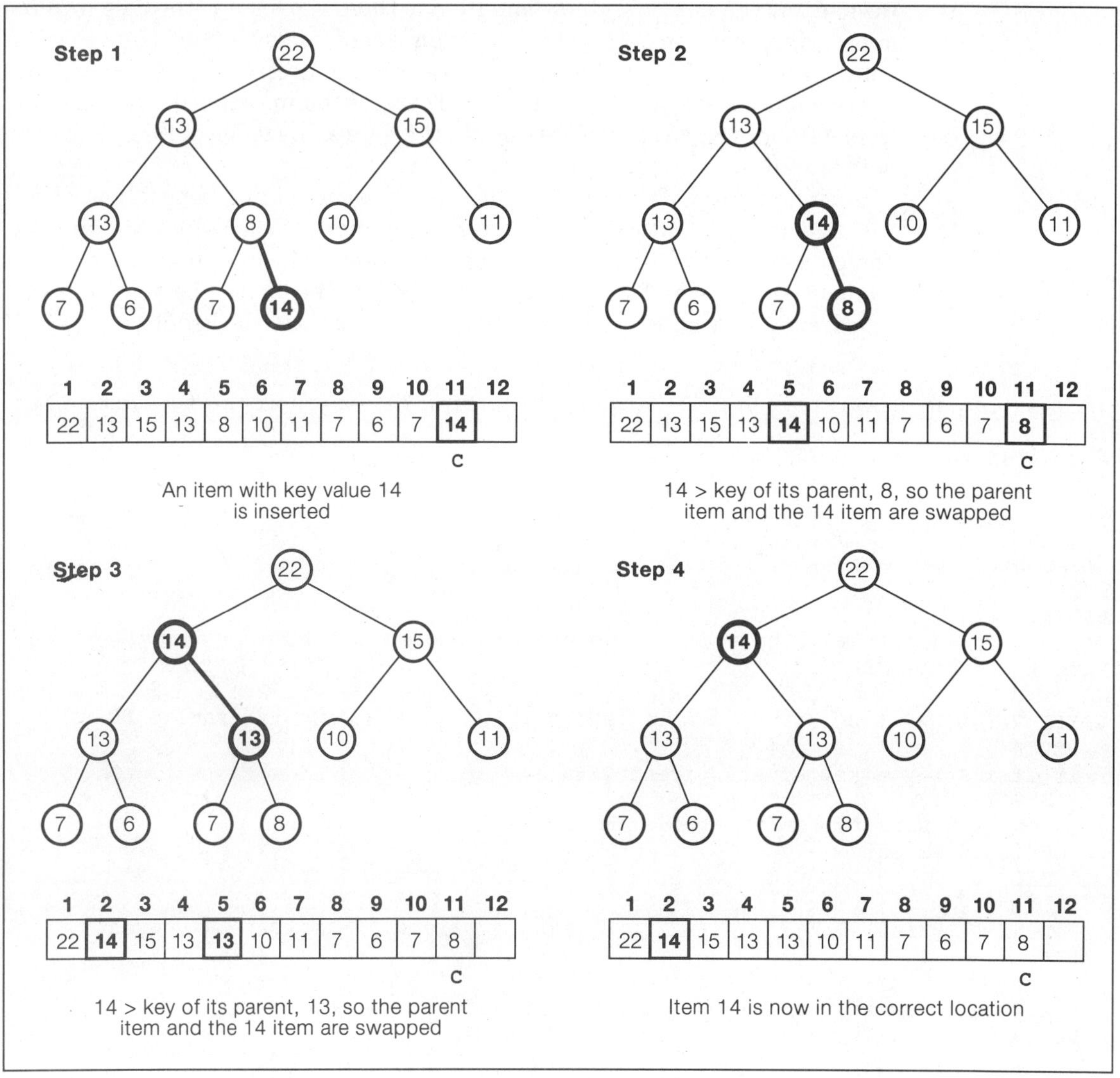

FIGURE 8.37 Inserting an Item with Priority 14 into a Heap

Deletion from a Heap

Since every heap item has a priority value greater than or equal to the priority value of either child, the tree's root node will always contain the item with the greatest priority value of all items—i.e., the item to be removed next. Once the root item is "removed" (actually, just a copy of it is returned), the last heap item is copied to element 1 and `Heap.Count` is decremented. The item in element 1 is then moved *down* the heap to its appropriate location—i.e., until its key value is greater than or equal to the keys of either child or until it is placed in a location with no children. Figure 8.38 traces the deletion operation of an item from the heap, using these algorithms. In the figure, the value of `Heap.Count` field is indicated by the C character.

Pseudocode algorithms for the deletion of an item from a heap follow. As with the insertion pseudocode algorithms given earlier, the algorithm for deletion is made slightly more efficient than the process depicted in Figure 8.38 by deferring assignment of the new item to any array element until its final location is determined (in the figure, the new item and a child are swapped as the new item is moved down in the heap):

```
{Moves the root item down in the heap, to its appropriate location}

ALGORITHM AdjustDown ( VAR Heap : HeapType );

VAR
  Item          : HInfoType; {The item to be adjusted downward}
  Parent, Child : Integer;

BEGIN
Parent := 1;
Item   := Parent;              {Heap.Items [ 1 ]}
Child  := 2;                   {Left child of root}

WHILE there is a child of Parent node left to examine DO
  BEGIN
  Child := index of that child of Parent with the greater key;

  IF Item's key < key of Child node THEN
    BEGIN
    Copy Child to Item node;
    Parent := Child;
    Child  := Parent * 2       {Child is the right child of Parent item}
    END
  END;

Store Item in element Parent
END;
```

```
ALGORITHM HeapDelete ( VAR Heap : HeapType; VAR Item : HInfoType  );

BEGIN
Item := Root item;
Copy to the root element the item in element Heap.Count;
Decrement heap count;
AdjustDown ( Heap )            {Move root item down in heap as necessary}
END;
```

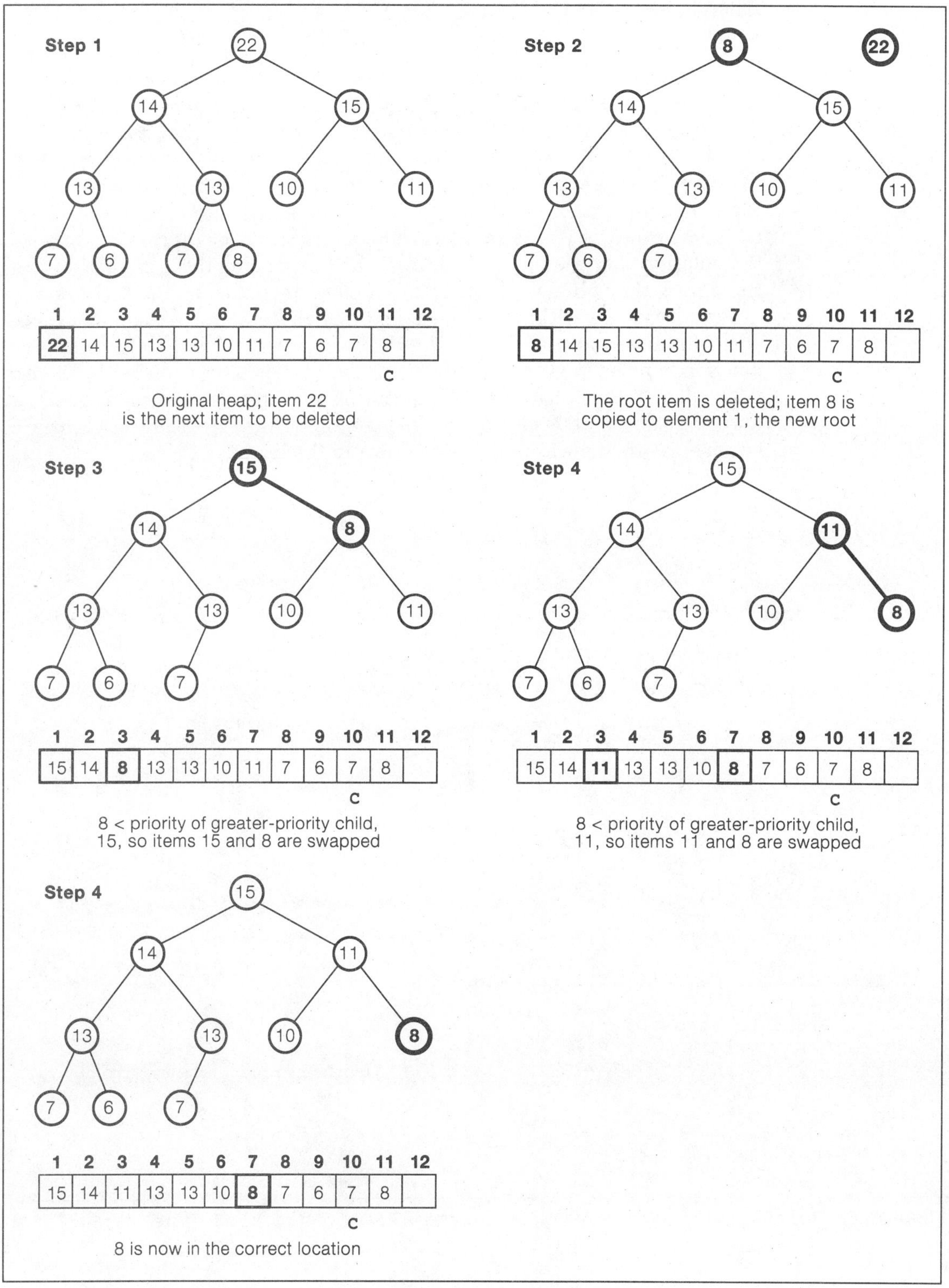

FIGURE 8.38 A Heap Deletion Operation

At this time, examine the following routines in Appendix H.

```
PROCEDURE AdjustDown ( VAR Heap : HeapType );

PROCEDURE HeapDelete ( VAR Heap : ListType; VAR Item : HInfoType );
```

8.4 GAME TREES

Artificial intelligence (AI) is a rapidly expanding discipline of computer science in which algorithms are designed to solve problems by modeling human problem-solving techniques. Designing algorithms to play interactive games competently has been a traditional application of AI; the rules of play are few enough for the degree of problem solving to be manageable, yet complex enough to require problem-solving capabilities fundamental to most AI applications. The desire for an unbeatable chess game, for example, has been a driving force in establishing fundamental AI principles. In Application 8.2 we examine the principles involved in developing an interactive tic-tac-toe game.

APPLICATION 8.2 A Game Tree for Tic-Tac-Toe

As you may recall, tic-tac-toe is played on a three-cell-by-three-cell grid (initially empty) in which the two players alternate turns, the X player placing an X in any empty cell and the O player then placing an O in any empty cell. The X player wins when three X's have been placed in the same row, or in the same column, or in the same major or minor diagonal. The O player wins by attaining any of the same configurations with Os. A draw results when all nine cells have been filled and neither player has won.

Human Interface and Bookkeeping Issues

Before we consider how to write a computer program that behaves as a competent player against the human user, we will digress a bit to consider several basic programming issues, such as the human interface. After all, to provide maximum enjoyment, computer games must be easy to use and visually pleasant. The program is therefore also charged with the responsibilities of not only deciding upon its move but also providing appropriate screen displays and obtaining the user's choice of move during the user's turn.

How should the program obtain the user choice? One technique, suggested in Exercise 2 at the end of Chapter 2, is to display a matrix of numbers from 1 to 9 next to the grid, and then prompt the user for one of these numbers, as indicated in Figure 8.39 for a game already in progress. The figure also shows how the program can display other useful information (D for Game Wins represents a draw).

To represent the grid internally, a two-dimensional array of character elements may seem the obvious choice. However, using integer elements provides an interesting advantage. By representing the X piece with the value 1, the O piece with the value 4, and a free space with the value 0, values in each row, column, and diagonal can be summed to determine if a win has occurred or is about to occur. Figure 8.40 depicts a two-dimensional array named `Grid`, which represents the current state of the game shown in Figure 8.39. The figure also depicts a second integer array named `Sums` and

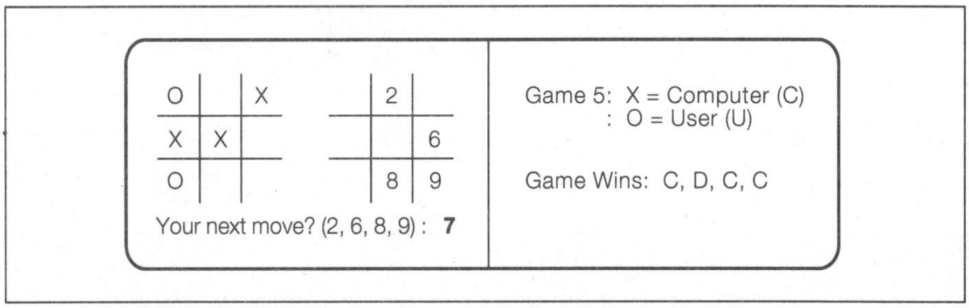

FIGURE 8.39 Prompting the Human User for the Next Move

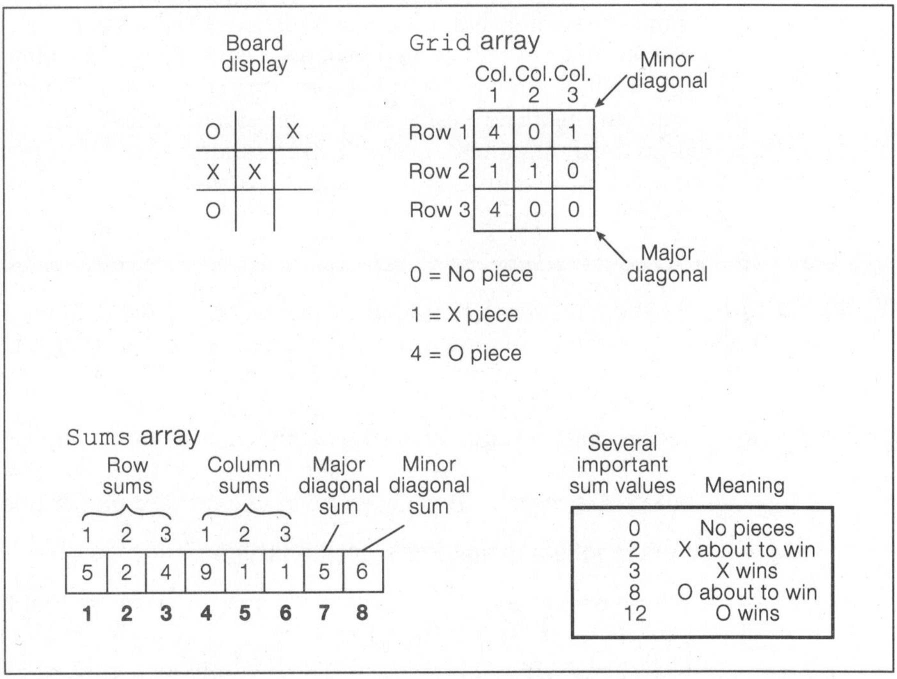

FIGURE 8.40 Representing Pieces Numerically, Summing Rows, Columns, and Diagonals

describes the five interesting sum values. Each time a player places an X or O on the grid, the program must store its associated integer value in `Grid` and then sum each row, column, and diagonal of integer values and assign each sum value to its designated `Sums` element. The values 0, 1, and 4 are used because they are capable of producing the sums 0, 1, 2, 3, 4, 5, 6, 8, 9, and 12, each of which represents a unique game state. For example, the sum of 5 in row 1 is attainable only by the presence of an X, an O, and a free space in row 1; no other combination of pieces will result in a sum of 5.

Selecting Appropriate Moves

There are two fundamental ways of designing the portion of the program that selects the next move taken by the computer during game play:

- **Rote evaluation.** *Before* the program is compiled and run, all possible game states are identified and "hard-coded" by the programmer, along with all appropriate responses. The computer makes a decision by searching a data base of stored game scenarios for the scenario that matches the current game state and then selects the response associated with this scenario.
- **Heuristic search.** *During* runtime, the program examines the current game state and generates representations of all game states resulting from each of several potential moves; i.e., it "looks ahead." The program then uses a set of rules (heuristics) to choose the best move. The ability to evaluate a current game state is coded in Pascal at *compile-time,* but specific responses to individual game states are determined at *runtime.*

With the rote evaluation strategy, every unique configuration of tic-tac-toe pieces can be designated by a unique integer value (a game state number). After the human player makes a move, the program updates the internal representation of the grid and then carefully examines the entire grid to obtain the game state number. The program then uses this number as an index into an array of stored responses to determine which move to make next on the grid. In games as simple as tic-tac-toe this configuration number or table of stored-responses system could even be replaced entirely by a complex set of `IF` statements. This way, the program would propagate through the `IF` statements until the current game state is identified; again, the appropriate response is already stored, this time embedded in the source code itself rather than stored in a table data structure.

This mechanical style of decision-making based on prestored knowledge may be likened to instinctive and habitual or reflexive behavior in people and animals. However, rote evaluation is not sufficient for complex games that have a very large number of unique configurations of game pieces or with other applications involving a truly infinite number of possible configurations of parameters. For these games, identifying all configurations and storing all appropriate responses would require a prohibitive amount of programmer effort, program instructions, memory, and program execution time just searching through the stored game states. For example, it has been calculated that with approximately 10,120 different possible chess games, if every atom in the universe were itself a computer that had begun analyzing all board positions at picosecond speeds since the Big Bang some 15 billion years ago, the complete analysis would barely be underway by now! (Even games as complex as chess begin with a standard set of opening moves, however, so the rote evaluation strategy *may* be applicable at the start of the game or in certain game states.)

In contrast to relying solely upon prestored knowledge, on-the-spot reasoning—typically associated with intelligent decision making—is embodied in the heuristic search strategy. Here, the program takes a "snapshot" of the current game configuration and then considers possible moves it *might* make next. Each of these potential moves would render a new game state, to which the human opponent will respond (unless a win is imminent), creating yet another game state. The program continually looks ahead and evaluates each game state rendered by a given move—its next move, the opponent's next move, its next move, etc.—for a particular number of moves (**look-**

ahead levels). By examining resulting game states and making guesses as to which moves the opponent will likely make when confronted with a given state, the program can solve its original problem—deciding which move to make next—by choosing the move most likely to produce a favorable game state one or several moves later. The resulting tree structure of configurations resulting from each potential move is called a **game tree,** and the heuristic search algorithm for analyzing the game tree and selecting the best next move for a given player is the *MiniMax method.*

As an essential primitive operation, the program must be able to compare any two different game configurations to determine which is better for the computer player—i.e., resulting in a configuration for which the game is more winnable for the computer player than for the human player. We will assume the existence of a function named `Evaluate`, as suggested by Tenenbaum (1981), which takes a particular configuration and returns an integer value that is a relative measure of quality (parameter `Player` indicates for which player—either the computer or the human—the evaluation is being performed):

```
Evaluate ( CurrentConfig, Player ) :=  the total number of rows, columns, and
                                       diagonals the Player can still claim

                                MINUS  the total number of rows, columns, and
                                       diagonals that the Player's opponent can
                                       still claim
```

Alternatively, `Evaluate` will return a special value, such as **`MAXINT`**, if `Player` has just won and another special value such as **`-MAXINT`** if `Player` just lost. This process of deriving the quality value of a given configuration, using no information other than the positions of pieces in the configuration, is a **static evaluation.**

Parameter `CurrentConfig` is a data structure representing a particular configuration of Xs and Os. One player can claim a row, for example, if there are, as yet, none of the opponent's pieces in that row. This formula for measuring configuration quality makes intuitive sense, since the probability of a win is reflected by the number of different opportunities still remaining for a win. As an example, Figure 8.41 shows a current configuration just after player O has made a move; player X can now make any of five different moves. The number of legal moves a player can choose to make is the **branching factor.** (In artificial intelligence parlance, the action of one player making a move is a *ply* and two ply comprise a *move,* or a *complete move;* in our discussion, we will simply refer to each player move as a move rather than a ply, or half-move.) The figure also shows each subsequent configuration and its quality value resulting from each of these moves.

Notice that, strangely enough, one of the best moves for player X is the one for which the quality rating (1) is lowest, even though this move guarantees that player X can win, regardless of player O's next move. A quick solution to this anomaly is to enhance the `Evaluate` function to return a special value, such as 9, if a win for `Player` is imminent and −9 if `Player` is in immediate danger of losing. This way, the first two resulting configurations would both yield quality ratings of 9 rather than 2 and 1, respectively, signaling that they are the best moves for `Player`. This fix is useful only

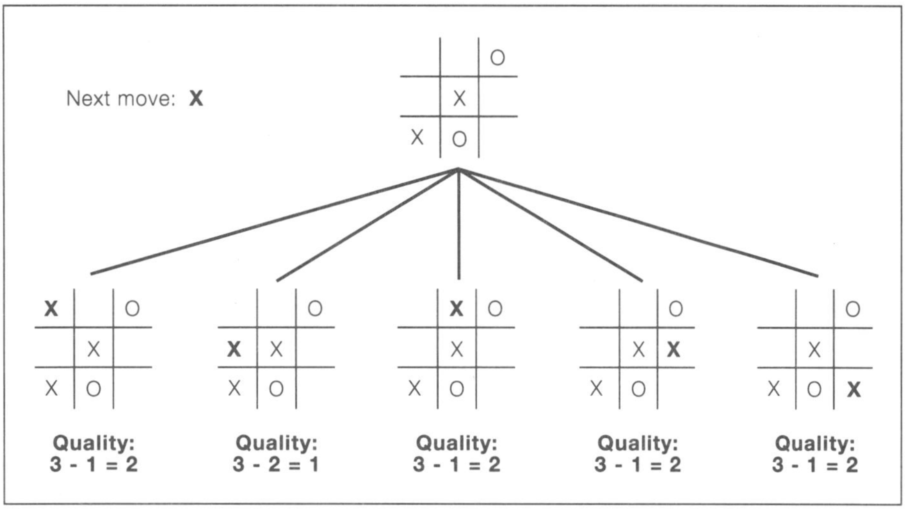

FIGURE 8.41 (X's Turn) Sample Configuration and Five Possible Resulting Configurations

near the conclusion of a game, however, and most games, such as chess, are complex enough that looking ahead only one move—i.e., a static evaluation of leaves—is not sufficient to determine the best move for the program to make. The program must look ahead two or more moves and, to no surprise, as the number of look-ahead levels increases, the quality and accuracy of the move-selection process itself improves.

As an example of looking ahead two moves, Figure 8.42 shows a game tree for determining which opening move player X should make by looking ahead two moves. (Only unique moves by either player are stored in the tree; other possible moves are symmetrically identical to those shown.) Each tree level corresponds to a player's turn, so the height of any game tree is the number of look-ahead levels plus 1 (for the root); the height of the tree of Figure 8.42 is 3. Each level beyond the root is designated as a + level for an opponent's turn or a − for the current player's turn. The root node contains the current configuration, an empty tic-tac-toe grid in the tree of Figure 8.42. Player X may make any of three unique moves. The configurations resulting from each of these three moves are stored in the three nodes of tree level two. Leaf nodes contain configurations resulting from each of player O's responses. All quality values in the figure are computed for player X.

The MiniMax Algorithm

We can now apply the **MiniMax technique** to determine the best opening move for player X. Presumably, each player will always choose the move that maximizes the chances of winning while minimizing the opponent's chances. This means that for each of the three groups of responses at the leaf level, *player O would choose the response that yields the minimum quality value:* −2 (leftmost group), or 1 (middle group), or −1 (rightmost group). The quality value of player X's first choice (leftmost node, tree level two) is −2, 1 for the second choice, and −2 for the third choice. Therefore, *player X should choose the move that yields the maximum quality value*—namely, the center square.

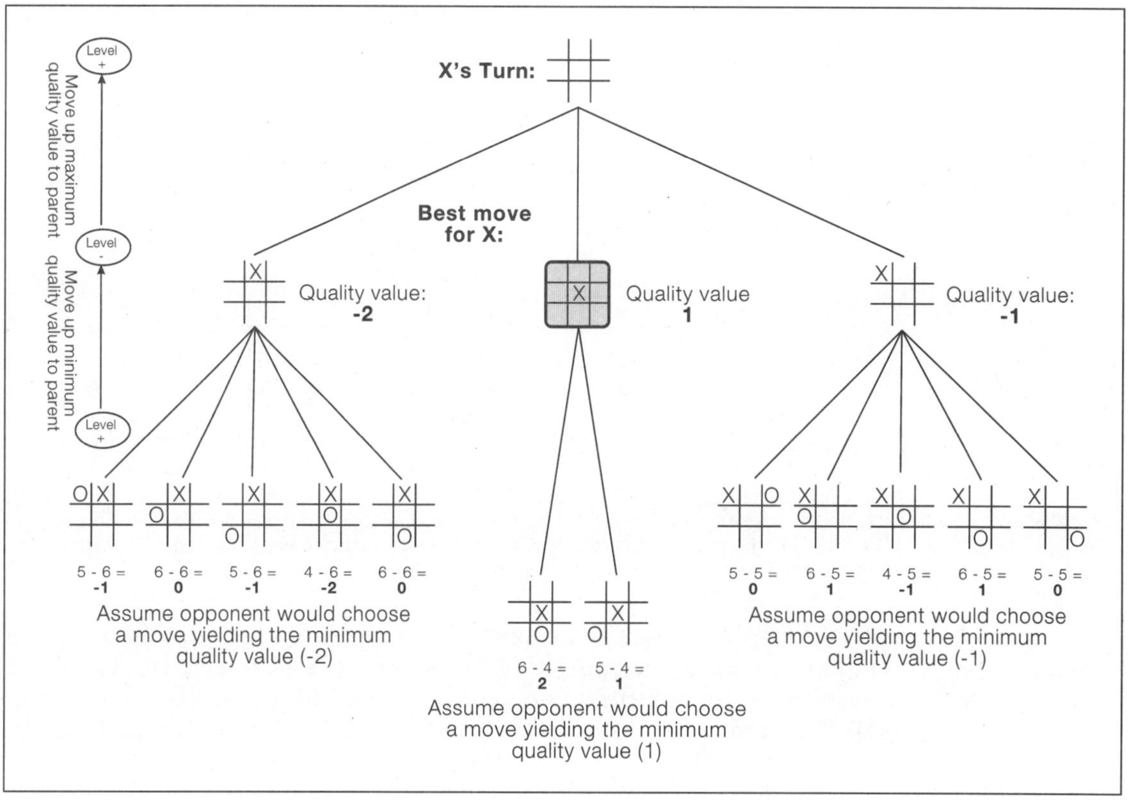

FIGURE 8.42 Game Tree for Player X's Opening Move (2 Look-Ahead Levels)

This technique is called MiniMax because, at each tree level in the progression from the leaves to the root, we alternate between choosing the *Mini*mum quality (at + levels beyond the root level) value and the *Max*imum quality value (at − levels). The MiniMax technique for choosing the best next move for a given player (`Player`) in a game tree of any number of look-ahead levels may be summarized as follows:

```
ALGORITHM FindBestMove ( VAR CurrentConfig; Player; LookAheadLevels );

  ALGORITHM MiniMax ( Current level );

  BEGIN
  IF Current level = + level THEN                        {Opponent's move}
    Move minimum quality value from each group of siblings to parent
  ELSE                                                   {Player's move}
    Move maximum quality value from each group of siblings to parent;

  IF Current level > root level THEN
    Minimax ( Current level - 1 )
  ELSE
    CurrentConfig := that configuration among the root's children with the
                     greatest quality value
  END;
```

```
{*** Main routine for FindBestMove ***}

BEGIN
Construct a game tree of height (LookAheadLevels + 1), with CurrentConfig
  in the root node;

Perform a static evaluation of each leaf, using function Evaluate;

MiniMax ( Leaf level )
END;
```

Improving the Efficiency of MiniMax

In the algorithm described, each time the program must select a move it builds a new game tree based on the current grid configuration. As the game progresses, identical portions of the tree are rebuilt, thereby wasting execution time. Instead, once the program selects its next move, it should preserve that subtree emanating from the node containing this move; this node will serve as the root of the *next* game tree.

Of course, we could construct a complete game tree of all possible moves for player X and player O, thereby precluding the need to generate (partial) game trees during the game. This rote evaluation approach is feasible only with the simplest of games, such as tic-tac-toe, and not with more interesting and complex games, such as chess and backgammon. How many moves should the program look ahead? Certainly, we will want to strike an acceptable balance between accuracy in choosing a next move and the execution time for making this calculation. Software games typically offer different "levels of difficulty" that reflect how many moves ahead are analyzed and, inversely, how quickly the program will determine its next move.

Adding just a single look-ahead level can drastically increase execution time. For the game of chess, it has been calculated that since a player typically has about 20 legal moves from which to choose on each turn, looking ahead 6 moves (including 3 for the opponent), the MiniMax algorithm must evaluate about 3,200,000 leaves and 168,421 interior nodes. The best chess programs on the fastest computers may still require more than 22 seconds to make a decision (approximately 160,000 evaluations per second). Extending the heuristic search by just one more move increases the execution time to about 7 minutes! (In tournament chess, each player is required to make a move within 3 minutes.)

Although nodes cannot be omitted in the construction of a given game tree, total heuristic search time *can* be reduced if the minimax algorithm can *avoid any unnecessary evaluations*. Look back at Figure 8.42. After a static evaluation of the five leftmost leaves (opponent moves), the minimum quality value is -2 (associated with the move that the opponent will likely make), which is moved up to the parent node. A static evaluation of the middle two leaves finds a minimum quality value of 1, which is moved up to the parent node. The 1 value is better than the -2 just moved up, since the program is choosing the maximum quality value among the nodes of the parent (second) tree level. Now, a static evaluation performed on the first node of the rightmost five leaves renders a quality value of zero. 1 is the largest value (the threshold value) moved up from this level to a parent thus far. Zero is less than the 1 just moved up, so there is no point in performing any more static evaluations of its sibling leaves in the rightmost five leaves.

For the sample tree in Figure 8.42, such automatic elimination of evaluations at a + (minimizing) level may be summarized as follows:

- Nodes whose quality values are greater than or equal to zero may be ignored, since only the minimum value among siblings is moved up to the parent.
- The minimal value found among its siblings, including the zero itself (e.g., −1), *would* be moved up in the standard MiniMax technique, except that all such values will be less than the largest value already moved up to a parent from this tree level. These values will therefore not be selected when the maximum value at the parent level is selected. All nodes less than or equal to zero may therefore be ignored as well.

In this simple example of Figure 8.42, the *pruning* of unnecessary nodes occurs at a minimizing tree level—i.e., at a level in which the minimum quality value among each set of siblings is sought and moved up to their respective parent. In a larger tree for which more look-ahead levels are considered, unnecessary nodes at a maximizing level may be pruned from further consideration as well. Slightly more bookkeeping will be required by the MiniMax algorithm, however, to "remember" the best quality values already moved up to the parent level from the current level. (The term *parent level* is relative to the current level.) This MiniMax refinement is called **alpha-beta pruning** because, for any game tree, it involves two types of threshold values, alpha and beta:

- At a maximizing level, the *alpha value* is the smallest value moved up to the parent level thus far.
- At a minimizing level, the *beta value* is the greatest quality value moved up to the parent level thus far.

In Figure 8.42, the alpha values moved from level 3 to level 2 are −2, 1, and −1. The beta value moved from level 2 to the tree root is 1.

Alpha-beta pruning for any game tree may be summarized as follows:

- *Alpha pruning.* At a minimizing + level, when a node with a quality value *less than alpha* has been encountered, its remaining sibling nodes are ignored.
- *Beta pruning.* At a maximizing − level, when a node with a quality value *greater than beta* has been encountered, its remaining sibling nodes are ignored.

In the simple example of Figure 8.42, this pruning of the tree saves only four static evaluations. In a much larger tree for a more complex game, in which many more look-ahead levels are considered, the accumulated savings in evaluations and time can be significant because the evaluation of entire subtrees may be eliminated.

Pascal Representation of a Game Tree

In a binary tree, any node may have, at most, two children; thus we can declare a node as a record with a data portion and two link fields. This simple approach will not work with a game tree, since the internal nodes of a game tree may have a variable number of children. Instead, we must represent the tree in a very different way, as a *graph structure*, the topic of the next chapter. As you read the chapter, consider how you might design a graph to represent a game tree.

SUMMARY

A tree is a structured data type in which data often are arranged according to key values of the items. Trees preserve the hierarchical (one-to-many) relationship among items (nodes), since it may be possible to advance from one item to one or more other items via the edges that connect them. A search tree may provide the efficiency of a binary search plus the insertion and deletion efficiency of a linked list. (Review the list of definitions at the beginning of the chapter.)

The ADT binary search tree is an oriented, ordered tree used to represent the ADT table. It is either empty or else the following are true: (a) It consists of a root node along with left and right subtrees, both of which are binary search trees, and (b) the key value of each node is greater than (or equal to) key values in the left subtree and less than key values in the right subtree (this rule determines the ordering of all nodes). The domain of a binary search tree includes items (nodes). Fundamental operations include initializing the tree as empty, determining if the tree is empty, searching for a particular node, adding or removing nodes, and traversing the tree. A binary search tree may be implemented using either a linked list or a sequential storage representation.

A new node is always added as a leaf. Traversal algorithms include preorder, in-order, postorder, and reverse-order, and level-order algorithms. An expression tree is the binary tree representation of an arithmetic expression.

Any search tree is organized using one particular key type. The ability to access a particular tree item (whose data portion is a record) using any of N different keys requires the maintenance of N different search keys. The main purpose of any search tree is to provide quick access to a particular node, in which the key is the only data that need be stored; associated nonkey information can be stored elsewhere, such as in heapspace.

The efficiency of a tree search performed on a binary search tree is affected profoundly by the particular shape of the tree. A balanced tree is one in which, for every node, the height of its two subtrees differs by no more than one level. For each node in a height-balanced or balanced tree, the heights of its subtrees never differ by more than one. A balanced tree is a tree of minimal height for the number of nodes it contains. A full tree is balanced and contains the maximum number of nodes for a tree of its height. In contrast, a degenerate tree contains the minimum number of nodes for a tree of its height, one per level, and is therefore a tree of maximum height for a given number of nodes. A nearly full tree is balanced, is full from level 1 through level (tree-height − 1), and has all leaves in the leftmost position based on conventional tree diagrams (refer to Figure 8.34).

For searching, a tree of minimum height has a worst-case rating of $O(\log N)$, which is as efficient as a binary search on an array, whereas a tree of maximum height (a degenerate tree) has a worst-case rating of $O(N)$—effectively, a linear search. In any tree of N nodes, the maximum height is computed as N and the minimum height as $\lceil \log_2(N + 1) \rceil$.

A binary tree may be preserved in a binary file via a preorder or level-order traversal; this way, the tree can be rebuilt subsequently by reading file items linearly.

The sequential storage representation of a binary tree provides two advantages: no link fields are necessary and there is immediate access from a node back to its parent. An array of records replaces the heapspace of dynamically allocated records, with index values serving as addresses. The index of the left child of node P is (P's index × 2), the index of the right child is (P's index × 2 + 1), and the index of P's parent is (P's index **DIV** 2).

The ADT priority queue is a structured data type in which the item with the greatest priority value (relative to the other items) is always the next item to be removed. The domain consists of items (usually records), each with a key priority value, which need not be unique. Fundamental operations include initializing the priority queue as empty, determining if the queue is empty or full, and enqueuing (adding) and serving (removing) an item. The ADT heap (not to be confused with heapspace) is typically used to represent a priority queue.

The ADT heap is a full or nearly full binary tree used to represent a priority queue. The domain and fundamental operations are the same as for the ADT priority queue.

In the computer science discipline of artificial intelligence (AI), algorithms are designed to solve problems, such as interactive game-playing, by modeling human problem-solving techniques and capabilities. One strategy for designing how a program selects its next move is rote evaluation, in which all possible game moves by players are prestored by the programmer and the program merely chooses among them. More complicated games require a heuristic search strategy, in which the computer builds a game tree representing the current game state along with the game states resulting from each of several potential moves (i.e., the program looks ahead), and then uses the MiniMax method of choosing the best move. The efficiency of MiniMax can be improved through alpha-beta pruning.

KEY TERMS

ADT binary search tree
ADT heap
ADT priority queue
Alpha-beta pruning
Ancestor
Balanced tree
Binary tree
Branching factor
Breadth-first traversal
Child
Cycle
Degenerate tree
Degree
Depth-first traversal
Descendant
Directed path
Edge
Empty tree
Expression tree
Full tree
Game tree
General or free tree
Height
Height-balanced tree
Heuristic search
Hierarchical structure
In-order successor
In-order traversal
Internal node
Leaf node
Level
Level-order traversal
Look-ahead levels
MiniMax technique
Nearly full tree
Node
Nonlinear structure
One-to-many structure
Ordered tree
Oriented tree
Out-degree
Parent
Path
Path length
Postorder traversal
Preorder traversal
Priority value
Reverse-order traversal
Root node
Rote evaluation
Search path
Search tree
Sibling
Static evaluation
Subtree
Tree of maximum height
Tree of minimal height
Tree traversal

REVIEW QUESTIONS

1. Define the following:
   - Linear and nonlinear lists
   - One-to-one relationship and one-to-many relationship
   - Set, linear list, hierarchy
   - Table, array, linked list, binary search tree
2. Describe four ways of depicting a hierarchical structure visually. Describe two primary purposes of hierarchical structures. At most, how many children may a particular tree node have?
3. In terms of the efficiency of searching, insertion, and deletion of items, distinguish between (a) an ordered linear list represented in an array, (b) an ordered linear list of the same items represented within a linked list, and (c) the same items contained within a binary search tree.
4. Distinguish between the level and height of a tree. Contrast height-balanced, full, and nearly full trees. Is a height-balanced tree always full? Is a full tree always height-balanced?
5. Define the following:
   - Node, edge, and path
   - Parent, child, sibling, ancestor, and descendant
   - Oriented tree, ordered tree, and general or free tree
   - Free tree, binary tree, and binary search tree
6. Describe ADT binary search tree, including the domain, fundamental operations, and structure. For any node in a binary search tree, what is the relationship between that node's key and the keys in the left subtree? In the right subtree? For which fundamental table operation is the binary search tree intended to perform efficiently?
7. In what three contexts might a search be performed on a binary search tree? What address(es) should be returned by a tree search routine when it is called as a prerequisite to insertion and to deletion, as described in this chapter? How does a tree search routine recognize a failed search?
8. In a binary search tree where are nodes inserted? Where are they deleted? Which algorithm is more complicated, an algorithm to insert a node or an algorithm to delete a node, and why? How may a header node be used with a binary search tree, and what advantages and/or disadvantages would it provide, if any?
9. Name the four commonly used traversal algorithms for a binary search tree. Can they be applied to any binary tree or only to a binary search tree? Give the visitation rules for each. Distinguish between a *depth-first traversal* and a *breadth-first traversal,* and give examples. Which traversal must be used to evaluate an expression tree correctly, as described in this chapter? Describe the level-order traversal algorithm.
10. Describe the binary search tree deletion algorithm—what are the two "easy" cases and the one "difficult" case? Describe the algorithms for locating (a) an in-order successor node and (b) an in-order predecessor node from a current node. Will these algorithms find the in-order successor or predecessor of *any* node in a binary search tree?
11. It is often useful to be able to access information using any of several key types rather than using only a single key type. Describe what must be done to support the lookup of an item using any of N different key types per item.

12. State the growth-rate functions and the corresponding big O notation form of the function for the best, worst, and average cases of searching a binary search tree. What characteristic of a tree (unlike any linear list) affects searching efficiency? What types of tree provide (a) minimum average search time and (b) maximum average search time?
13. State the exact formula to calculate each of the following:
    - The minimum height for any binary tree of N nodes
    - The maximum height for any binary tree of N nodes
    - The height of a full binary tree of N nodes
    - The number of leaves in a full binary tree of N nodes
    - The number of nodes in a full binary tree of height H
    - The number of leaves in a full binary tree of height H
14. What two traversals may be performed to save a binary tree to a file so that the tree can be rebuilt exactly by subsequently reading from the file? What results if an in-order traversal is used to save the tree? What portion of each node is saved and what portion is never saved?
15. Describe how a binary search tree can be represented using sequential storage rather than dynamic allocation. What are the advantages and disadvantages of both representations? Will the sequential storage scheme work with any binary tree or only with binary search trees? Give the exact formula to calculate each of the following for a binary search tree represented using an array:
    - Left child of the node in element K
    - Right child of the node in element K
    - Parent of the node in element K
16. Describe the ADT priority queue. Could two items in a priority queue have the same priority value? Describe several structures and accompanying schemes for representing the ADT priority queue in Pascal. Why is a heap a good choice for representing a priority queue?
17. Describe the ADT heap, including the domain, fundamental operations, and structure. Distinguish between a priority queue and a FIFO queue.
18. Describe algorithms for heap insertion and deletion. Is traversal a fundamental operation for heaps? Could any of the four commonly used traversals for a binary search actually be applied to a heap? Describe an algorithm for saving a heap to a file.
19. Describe game trees and the MiniMax method in the context of simulating the game, tic-tac-toe. Describe how the process of choosing a move can be hastened via alpha-beta pruning.

EXERCISES

1. Draw the binary search tree that results from inserting nodes with the following key values into an empty tree. Insert in the order shown—e.g., 29, then 21, then 43, etc.

   Key values: 29, 21, 43, 17, 10, 25, 30, 35, 45, 23

2. Questions 2(a) through 2(l) refer to the binary search tree on the next page.

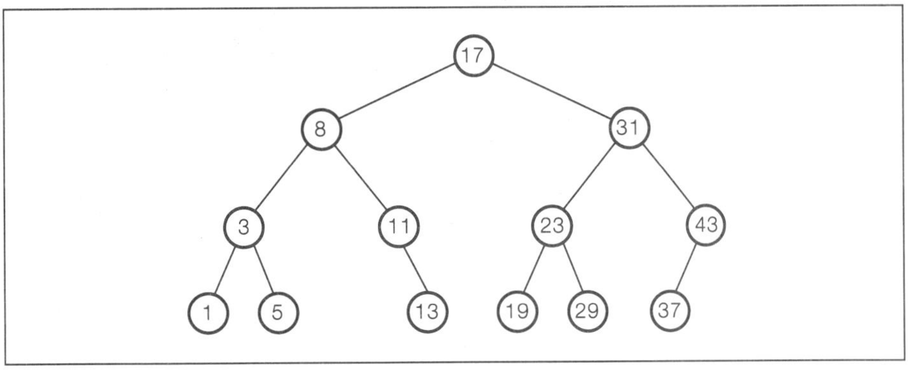

a. What is the height of the subtree with node 31 as its root?
b. What are the key values of the nodes visited during a search for a node 20?
c. What is (are) the descendant(s) of node 11?
d. List all keys using preorder and postorder traversals.
e. Is the tree full, nearly full, or neither?
f. Node 31 is at what level?
g. What is the postorder successor of node 23?
h. What is (are) the key value(s) of the sibling(s) of node 29, if any?
i. How many leaves are in the tree?
j. What tree traversal(s) might be used to save this tree to a file of records, such that the exact same tree could be rebuilt later by reading each record sequentially and performing an insertion operation?
k. Draw an array diagram depicting the tree stored using sequential storage representation.
l. Delete node 29, then node 43, and then node 8, and draw the resulting tree.

3. What are the maximum and the minimum possible heights of a binary tree of 64 nodes? 134 nodes? 31 nodes? N nodes?

4. Assume that a binary tree (not a binary search tree) with character key values has already been built. If in-order and preorder traversals are performed, processing each node by displaying its key value, the following characters are displayed:

In-order traversal: `E V R S Y I U O G T I H`
Postorder traversal: `E R V Y S U G O I H T I`

a. Given this information, draw the binary tree.
b. Perform a preorder traversal by hand, processing each node by writing its key value. What is the message?

5. a. Draw a tree diagram representing the heap that results from inserting items with the following priority values into an empty heap. Insert in the order shown; e.g., 7, then 11, then 5, etc.—the *smaller* the value, the *greater* the priority:

7, 11, 5, 91, 7, 10, 4, 6

b. Draw an appropriate array diagram representing this heap; leave an element empty to indicate the absence of a heap item.
c. Perform a deletion operation on the heap and redraw the tree diagram.

6. Complete procedure `DisplayAncestor`, which should display the integer key value of each ancestor of the node whose key value is passed in. If no node containing the sought key value is found, `DisplayAncestor` should display an error message; otherwise, it should display these ancestor values in reverse order (i.e., the root node's key value should be displayed last). Assume that the tree was built using the global declarations given at the start of Section 8.2.

```
PROCEDURE DisplayAncestor ( VAR BinTree : BinTreeType;
                            VAR Key : KeyType );
```

7. Complete function `CountNodes`, which should return the number of nodes in a tree built using the declarations given at the start of Section 8.2.

```
FUNCTION CountNodes ( Root : BTNodePtr ) : Integer;
```

8. Complete function `LeafCount`, which should return a count of the number of leaves in binary tree `BinTree`, which was built using the declarations given at the start of Section 8.2:

```
FUNCTION LeafCount ( BinTree : BinTreeType ) : Integer;
```

9. Complete function `FindLevel`, which should search the tree for a node containing key value `Key` and return the value of the tree level where this node is found or else zero if such a node is not found. The address of a tree's root node is passed into `Root` initially. Assume that the tree was built using the global declarations given at the start of Section 8.2.

```
FUNCTION FindLevel ( VAR Key : BTKeyType; Root : BTNodePtr ) : Integer;
```

10. Complete function `Identical`, which should return a true value if the binary trees `BinTree1` and `BinTree2` are identical and a false value otherwise. The trees are identical if they contain the same number of nodes with the same key values and both trees have exactly the same shape. You may assume that both trees were built using the declarations given at the start of Section 8.2.

```
FUNCTION Identical ( BinTree1, BinTree2 : BinTreeType ) : Boolean;
```

11. Rewrite the `InOrdTraverse` function of Section 8.2 using a stack instead of recursion.

12. Write the following Pascal routines for a binary search tree represented using sequential storage:
    a. Functions to perform in-order and preorder traversals.
    b. `BinTreeInsert`
    c. `BinTreeDelete`

13. You purchased a Pascal compiler on sale, only to discover it does not have a standard set data type, so you decide to represent this ADT *for integer elements* using a binary search tree, based on the generic declarations given at the start of Section 8.2. Write the following routines in Pascal:
    a. A Boolean function to test for set membership
    b. A procedure to perform a union operation on two sets
    c. A procedure to perform an intersection operation on two sets
    d. A procedure that makes a particular set empty (deallocate nodes using `Dispose`)

14. Modify the heap routines and, if necessary, the global declarations, given in Appendix H so that, if a heap contains two or more items with the *same* priority, the item that has been stored in the heap longest is always removed before other items of the same priority.

15. Design a procedure that combines two priority queues to form a third priority queue.

16. a. Give a set of global Pascal declarations that may be used to build a binary expression tree. Assume that each operator (+, −, *, /) and each variable identifier is represented by a single character and that each constant is an integer number. (*Hint:* Use a variant record.)

b. Draw a diagram representing the binary expression tree for the following expression:

$$3 * (4X + 7Y) / 5 - Z$$

c. Complete function `BuildExpressionTree`, which should build a binary expression tree to represent the prefix expression stored in parameter `Buffer` (`BuffType` is of type `String [ 80 ]`) and it returns the address of the tree's root node. You may assume that the expression in `Buffer` is syntactically correct and adheres to the simple syntax described in (a) (any spaces within the expression should be ignored).

```
FUNCTION BuildExpressionTree ( VAR Buffer : BuffType ) : BTNodePtr;
```

d. Complete the code for real function `EvalTree`, which should evaluate to the value of an expression represented correctly by an expression tree, built using your declarations of (a) and procedure of (c). Assume that a function, `Value (Ident)`, has already been written; it returns the *real value* of the variable whose character identifier is passed as an argument. Assume further that the address of the tree's root node is passed to parameter `Root` upon the initial call to `Eval`:

```
FUNCTION EvalTree ( Root : BTNodePtr ) : Real;
```

17. Write a Pascal program that builds and maintains a binary search tree of country name/population pairs, with country name as the key value for each node. The program should support the following operations:

- Add records to the existing tree from a file, or save all records to a binary file
- Add, delete, or modify a single record
- Display information about a particular country or about all countries

After each full screen display or the final screen display, the program should prompt the user to press either (a) the RETURN key to continue or (b) the Q key and then the RETURN key to preclude further displaying. Population values should be displayed with embedded commas. If a desired country name is not found in the tree, the program should display an error message and then display the names and populations of the *nearest below country* (if any) and the *nearest above country* (if any), based on country name. The screen display from a sample interactive session follows:

```
>>  Enter country name: Afghanistan  [RETURN]

    Afghanistan not found ...
      Nearest below:  None
      Nearest above:  Algeria  19,270,000
```

Possible enhancements: Allow the user to modify the spelling of a country name or to specify a population value as a key rather than a country name. Allow the user to enter a range of populations and then display all country names and population pairs for countries whose populations lie within this range.

18. Any dynamically allocated binary search tree with N nodes has $N + 1$ empty subtrees—i.e., $N + 1$ **NIL** link fields. These **NIL** values can be replaced with the addresses (*threads*) to other nodes in the tree, thereby creating a *threaded* *binary search tree*. The left thread of a node points to that node's in-order successor, and the right thread points to that node's in-order predecessor. A threaded tree may have only left threads, only right threads, or both.

Threaded trees usually contain a header node to avoid the special case of inserting into an empty tree or deleting the last node. Threads are installed whenever a node is inserted or deleted; exactly *where* a particular thread will point depends on the kind of traversal the threads are intended to facilitate. A sample tree with inorder successor and predecessor threads and with preorder successor threads is shown below (threads are shown using boldface arrows).

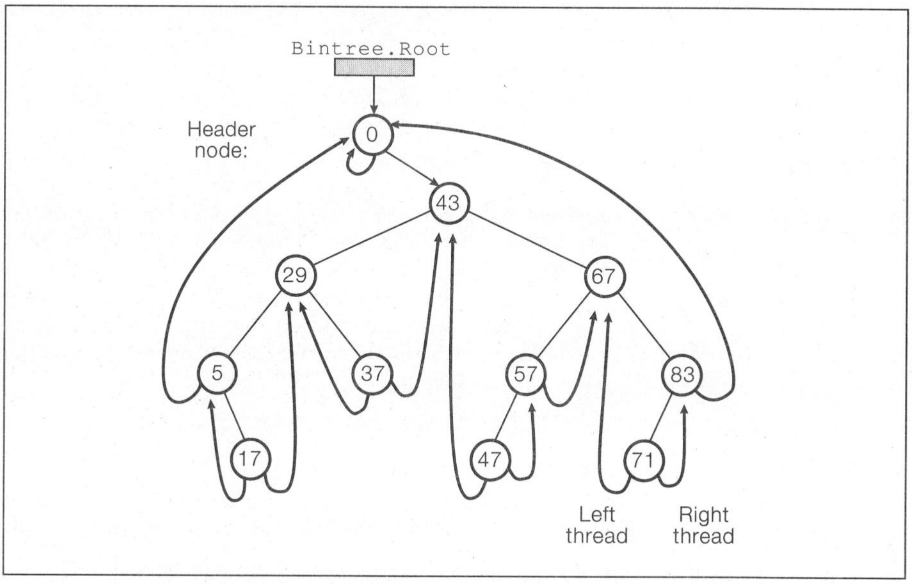

A threaded tree supports traversals without recursion or a program-maintained stack merely by following right threads; unlike a nonthreaded tree, a traversal may begin *anywhere in the tree* and not merely at the tree's root node. Another benefit is that if in-order predecessor threads are included in the tree, the traversal algorithm may move immediately from any node to that node's in-order predecessor and not merely its successor.

a. Redraw the sample tree with only preorder successor threads.
b. Give a set of global declarations for a threaded binary search tree, based on a dynamic allocation representation. (*Hint:* A program using such a tree must be able to distinguish threads from regular links.)
c. Write a pseudocode algorithm for searching, traversing, and inserting a new node for a binary search tree that has inorder successor and predecessor threads.

19. The ancient game of *Nim* is played by two players as follows: Fifteen sticks are placed in a pile. The players take alternate turns, each choosing to remove either one or two sticks from the pile. The player who is left with a single stick in the pile to remove is the loser. Describe how a computer program for Nim may be devised in which a human player plays against the computer using (a) a rote evaluation strategy (hard-coding all responses and remembering previous games) and using (b) a game tree strategy.

CHAPTER NINE

GRAPH STRUCTURES

In this chapter, you will learn about a nonlinear data structure called a *graph*. As one of the most versatile of data structures, a graph can be designed to represent electrical circuits, aqueduct systems, maps, project tasks, or virtually any *set of relationships*. This section offers an introduction to graphs by examining fundamental graph operations and several interesting applications.

9.1 PRELIMINARIES

Fundamental Graph Concepts

Recall from Chapter 3 that each item in a *linear list structure* has a one-to-one relationship with other items—i.e., at most, one distinct successor and predecessor. This concept is expanded with a *hierarchical (tree) structure,* whose items have a one-to-many relationship with other tree items—i.e., at most, a single predecessor (the parent) but possibly many successors (children). A *graph* is a **network structure** in which data are usually arranged

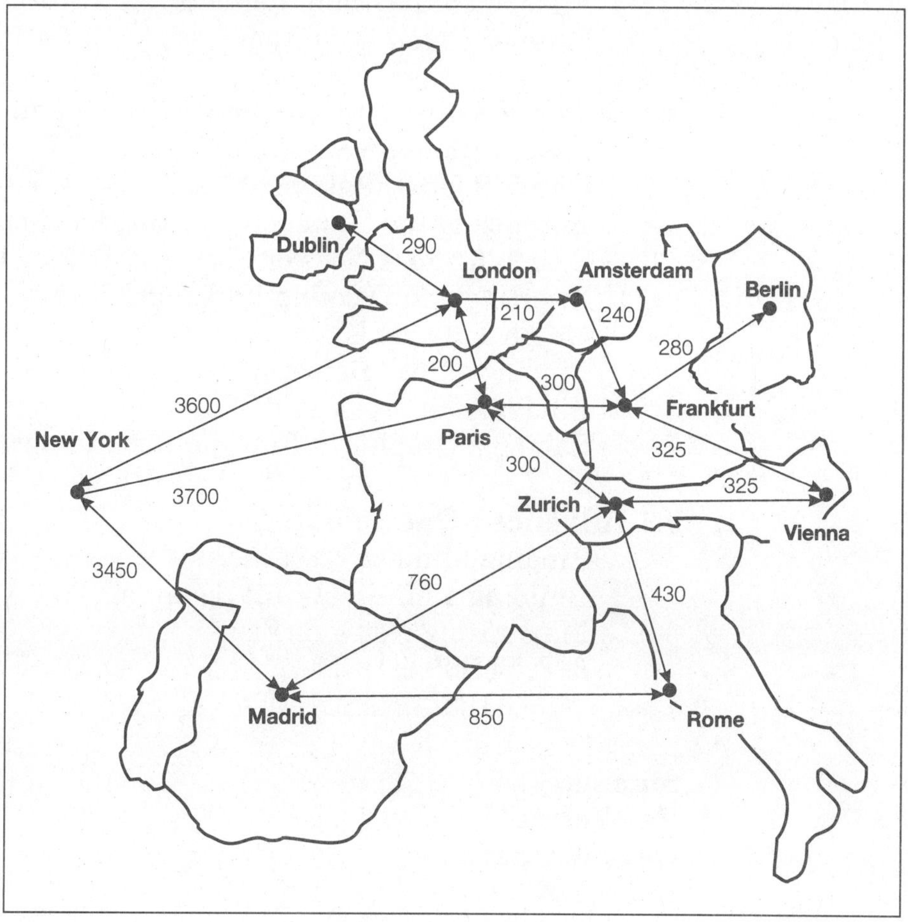

FIGURE 9.1 Airline Routes for Sky-High Airlines

according to the key values of their items. In a graph structure, each item has a many-to-many relationship with other graph items. That is, in a graph of N items, each item may have N successors *and* N predecessors. A graph is, therefore, a useful structure for representing a complex set of relationships.

Figures 9.1, 9.2, and 9.3 illustrate several interesting graph applications. Figure 9.1 depicts a set of European airline routes for Sky-High Airlines, along with air-mile distances and terminal cities. (Figure 9.7 contains a more succinct depiction of these routes and cities.)

Figure 9.2 depicts a portion of a Boston city map and its graph representation. In the graph, each circle (*node*) represents an intersection (for simplicity, a Cartesian-like coordinate system is employed to identify the streets and intersections). For example, a node with key values 6, 4 represents the intersection of Dartmouth Street (6) and Marlborough Street (4). Each arrow (*edge*) represents a portion of a street between two intersections. The *directionality* of the edges reflects the directionality of street traffic.

In Figure 9.3, the structure of a phenothiazine molecule is represented by an *undirected graph*. Here, each node represents an atom and each edge represents an ionic bond between two atoms. The graph is also said to be weighted because a value (the edge weight) is associated with each edge; this value reflects the number of chemical bonds between the two atoms connected by that edge.

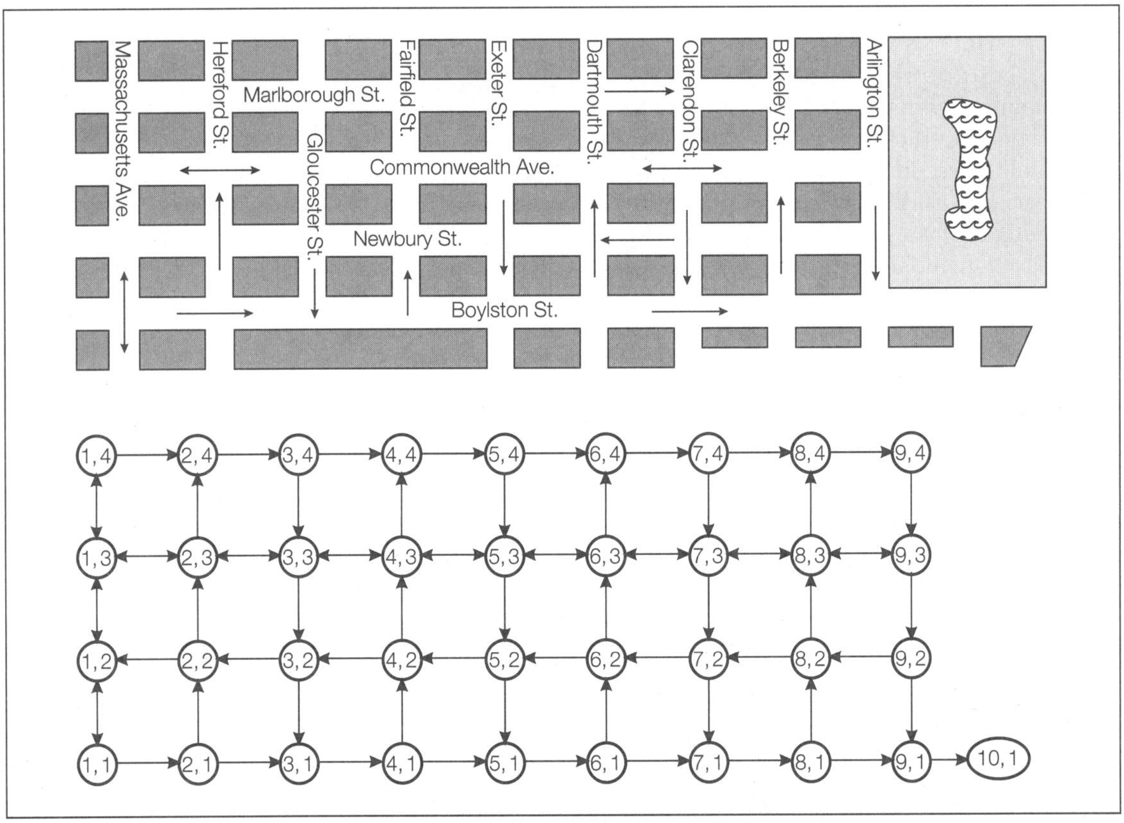

FIGURE 9.2 Portion of a Boston City Map and a Graph Representation

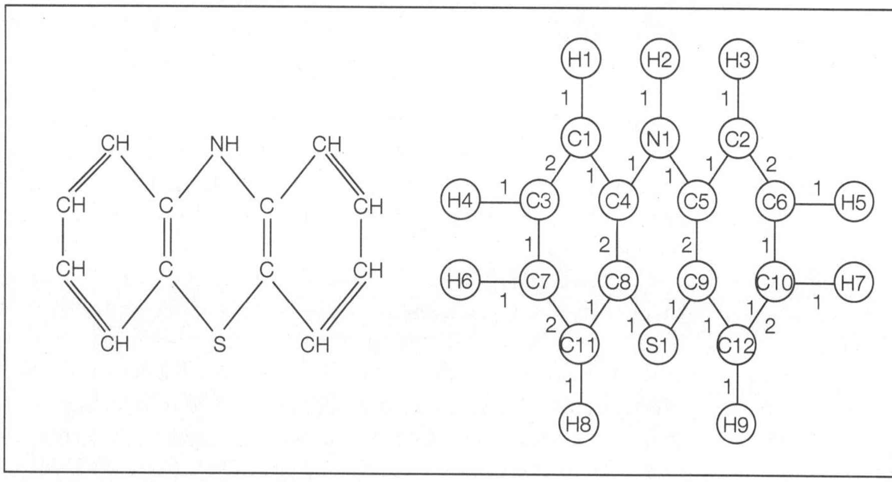

FIGURE 9.3 Molecular Diagram and Its Weighted Graph Representation

Graph-Related Terminology

The terminology is arranged conceptually, not alphabetically.

General Terms

Nodes, edges

Each item in a graph is called a **node,** or vertex. In diagrams depicting graphs, a node is typically shown as a circle and may be connected to another node via a line called an **edge.** There is at most a single edge between any two nodes. In graph diagrams, only the key value of a node is typically shown within the circle. Figure 9.4 depicts three graphs.

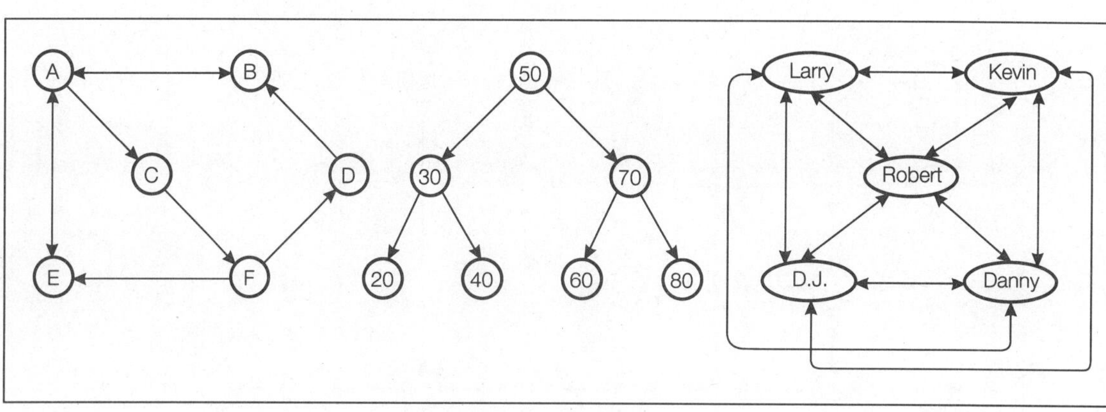

FIGURE 9.4 Depictions of Three Graphs

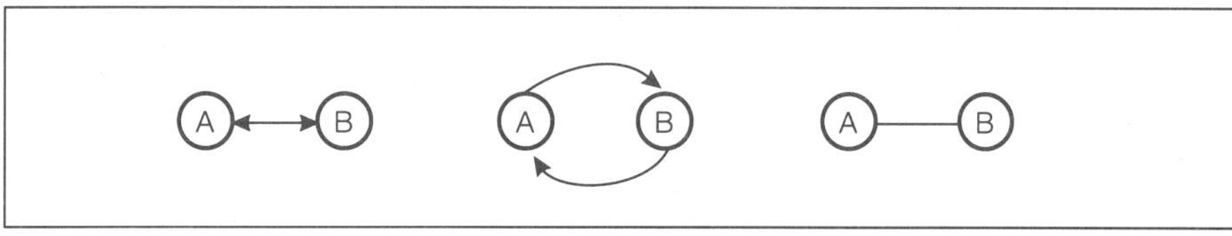

FIGURE 9.5 Functionally Equivalent Notations

Directed edge, undirected edge

If an edge connects node X and node Y and it is possible to advance in only *one* direction, the edge is **directed;** otherwise it is **undirected** or **bidirectional.** In Figure 9.4, edges (A, C) and (F, D) are directed, whereas edges (A, B) and (A, E) are undirected. The notations in Figure 9.5 are functionally equivalent.

Parent, child, neighbors

If there is an edge from node X to node Y, node X is the **parent,** or initial point, and node Y is the **child,** or **endpoint.** In Figure 9.4, node 30 is the parent of nodes 20 and 40, and node 20 is a child of node 30. The term **neighbor** is synonymous with the term child.

Adjacent, incidental

A child node is **adjacent** to its parent node—i.e., it is a **neighbor**—and a parent node is **incidental** to a child node.

In-degree, out-degree, isolated node

The **in-degree** of node X is the number of nodes incident to node X—i.e., the number of edges leading into node X. The **out-degree** of a node is the number of children that node has—i.e., the number of edges heading out of it. An **isolated node** has an in-degree of zero. In Figure 9.4, the in-degree of node A is 2, whereas the in-degree of node 50 is zero, making it isolated. The out-degree of node 50 is 2 and the out-degree of node 60 is zero.

Path, path length, source, destination

A **path** exists between node X and node Y if there is a sequence of nodes and edges connecting each pair of nodes between X and Y; i.e., if it is possible to advance along edges from X (the **source**) to Y (the **destination**). The **path length** is the number of edges along a path. In Figure 9.4, the length of the path from nodes D to F is 4, whereas the path length from C to F is only 1.

Circuit, cycle, acyclic

A **circuit** is a path that begins and ends with the same node. A circuit is a **cycle** if no edge or node (other than the source node) is repeated in the path. In Figure 9.4, the path (A, C, F, E, A) is both a circuit and a cycle. The center graph in Figure 9.4 contains no circuits or cycles and is therefore said to be **acyclic.**

Traversal

The operation of visiting and processing each node in a graph in a particular order is a **graph traversal.** As with trees, the two types of graph traversal are **depth-first traversal** and **breadth-first traversal.**

Types of Graphs

Directed graph, undirected graph

If all edges in a graph are undirected (or bidirectional), the graph is said to be an **undirected graph,** and all edges are typically depicted without arrows; i.e., the rightmost graph in Figure 9.4 could be drawn without arrows. A **directed graph** (or simply **digraph**), such as the leftmost graph of Figure 9.4, may contain only directed edges or both directed and undirected edges. In a directed graph, *all* edges are typically drawn with arrows. The simple term *graph* typically refers to an undirected graph or else a graph in which the concept of directionality is not addressed.

Weighted graph, weight

In a **weighted graph,** each edge has a special value (a **weight**) associated with it that reflects a relationship between the connected nodes such as distance. Typically, weight values need not be unique. Figures 9.1, 9.3, 9.10, 9.28, and 9.36 show examples of weighted graphs.

Simple graph

A **simple graph,** or **acyclic graph,** is a graph containing no cycles—e.g., the center graph of Figure 9.4.

Subgraph, connected graph, unconnected graph

A **subgraph** is a portion of a graph, just as a subtree is a portion of a tree. A **connected graph** contains a path between every pair of nodes; otherwise the graph is, to some degree, **unconnected** (i.e., consists of unconnected subgraphs). Figure 9.6 depicts both an unconnected and a connected graph.

Complete graph

A graph is **complete** if each node is adjacent to every other node. The rightmost graph of Figure 9.4 is complete.

Tree

A **tree** is a connected, directed, acyclic graph. The center graph of Figure 9.4 is a tree (more precisely, it is a *binary search tree*).

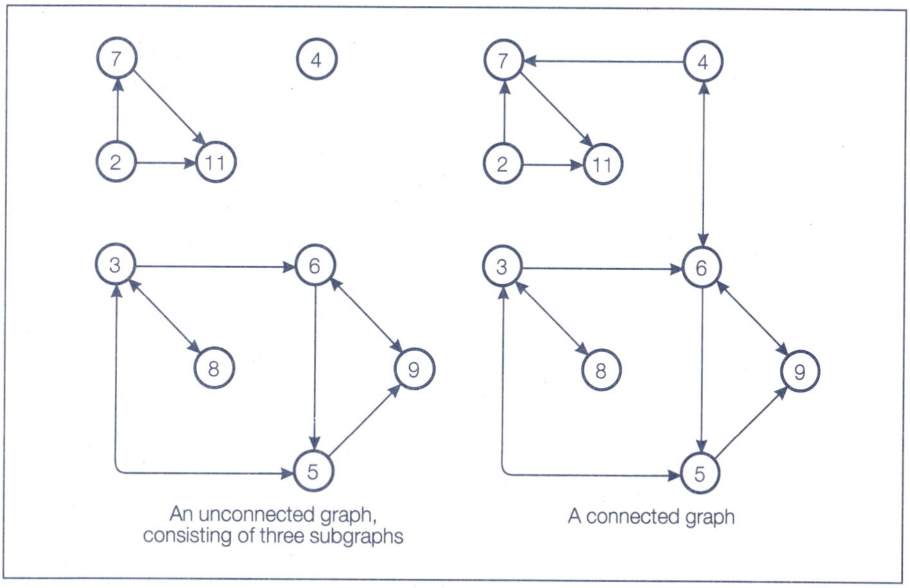

FIGURE 9.6 Unconnected and Connected Graphs

Sparse graph, dense graph

A **sparse graph** has relatively few edges, whereas a **dense graph** has relatively many edges.

DAG

DAG is an acronym for directed acyclic graph, such as the center graph of Figure 9.4.

Spanning tree

A **spanning tree** is a subgraph containing only the minimum number of edges of the original graph that are necessary to form a tree, as in Figure 9.27.

Minimal-cost spanning tree

A **minimal-cost spanning tree** is a spanning tree constructed from a weighted graph, whose total edge weights sum to the lowest total weight value of all possible spanning trees for that graph. An example is shown in Figure 9.28.

9.2 GRAPH REPRESENTATIONS AND FUNDAMENTAL OPERATIONS

Specifications for the ADT Graph

The **ADT graph** is a network data structure containing a collection of nodes and edges. A graph may or may not be arranged by node key value. Each node may have a many-to-many relationship with any other node in the graph.

Domain

The domain consists of nodes and edges, both typically of record data type.

Fundamental Operations

1. *Initialize:* Initialize the graph as empty; i.e., containing no nodes [GraphInit].
2. *Test for emptiness:* Determine if the graph is *empty* [EmptyGraph].
3. *Search for a particular node.*
4. *Search for a particular edge:* Search for a particular edge, returning the location of the edge if found.
5. *Insert a node.*
6. *Insert an edge:* Insert an edge between two particular nodes.
7. *Delete a node:* Delete a particular node, along with all edges for which the node is a parent or child.
8. *Delete an edge.*
9. *Traverse:* Traverse the graph using a depth-first visitation strategy [DFVisit] or a breadth-first visitation strategy [BFVisit].
10. *Test nodes for adjacency:* Determine if one node is *adjacent* to another.
11. *Find a path:* Find a path between two nodes, if possible, using a depth-first visitation strategy [DFVisit].
12. *Find a shortest path:* Find a path between two nodes that contains the fewest number of intervening edges (if such a path exists at all), using a breadth-first visitation strategy [BFVisit].

In Application 5.5 we discussed a program to manage a single passenger list for a Sky-High Airlines flight. Now we will examine all fundamental graph operations in the context of designing a route-manager program that travel agents for Sky-High Airlines may use to store and obtain information about its European flights. These routes and their terminal cities are depicted in Figure 9.1, along with the air-mile distance of each flight. The collection of routes can be represented as a single connected, weighted graph, with each city represented by a node in the graph, each route represented by an edge, and the indicated air-miles as the weight of each edge.

Such a route manager program should be able to perform the following functions:

- Determine if there is a route between any two cities, possibly via other cities.
- Determine the distance of any route.
- Find the shortest route between two cities, based on either the number of intervening routes or the total mileage of the complete route.
- Add or delete a city or add or delete a route.
- Output information about all cities and airports and routes.

Each of these operations corresponds to a fundamental graph operation. We will examine each operation, but the actual construction of the entire route-manager program is left as an exercise. In addition, we will devise algorithms to save the graph to a file and, conversely, to rebuild the graph from a file. Our discussion will frequently refer to the graph in Figure 9.7, which is a succinct depiction of the airline routes of Figure 9.1.

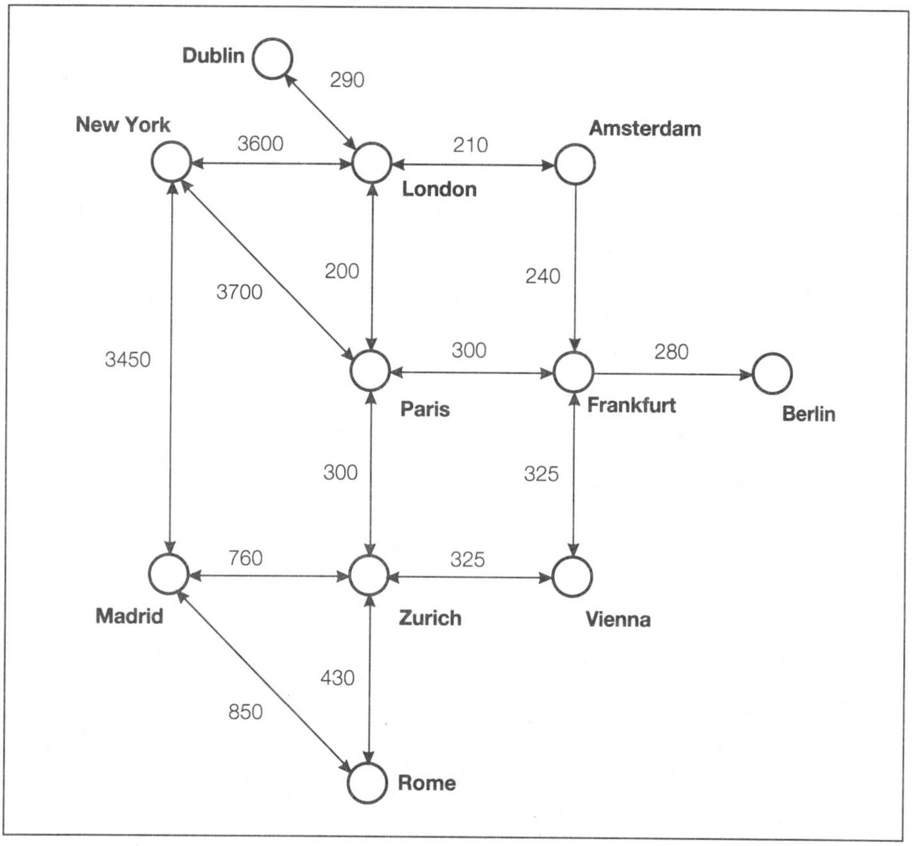

FIGURE 9.7 Graph Diagram Depicting the Sky-High Airlines European Routes of Figure 9.1

Graph Representations

Any internal memory representation of a graph must accurately describe all nodes and all edges. There are two common representations of a graph in internal memory:

- *Adjacency matrix.* Sequential storage (array) representation, best suited for dense graphs.
- *Adjacency list.* Linked list representation, best suited for sparse graphs.

Adjacency Matrix

An **adjacency matrix** is a two-dimensional array in which each row represents a parent node and each column represents a *potential* child node. The array element where a row and column intersect, ($node_{row}$, $node_{column}$), contains a value or values that represent the relationship between the row and column nodes—i.e., the edge from $node_{row}$ to $node_{column}$. If the graph is not weighted, this value could simply be Boolean: a true value if $node_{column}$ is *adjacent* to $node_{row}$ and a false value otherwise. If the graph *is* weighted (as

Graph.LTable		Graph.Matrix										
		1	2	3	4	5	6	7	8	9	10	11
'AMSTERDAM'	1	0	∞	∞	240	∞	∞	∞	∞	∞	∞	∞
'BERLIN'	2	∞	0	∞	∞	∞	∞	∞	∞	∞	∞	∞
'DUBLIN'	3	∞	∞	0	∞	290	∞	∞	∞	∞	∞	∞
'FRANKFURT'	4	∞	280	∞	0	∞	∞	∞	300	∞	325	∞
'LONDON'	5	210	∞	290	∞	0	∞	3600	200	∞	∞	∞
'MADRID'	6	∞	∞	∞	∞	∞	0	3450	∞	850	∞	760
'NEW YORK'	7	∞	∞	∞	∞	3600	3450	0	3700	∞	∞	∞
'PARIS'	8	∞	∞	∞	300	200	∞	∞	0	∞	∞	300
'ROME'	9	∞	∞	∞	∞	∞	850	∞	∞	0	∞	430
'VIENNA'	10	∞	∞	∞	325	∞	∞	∞	∞	∞	0	325
'ZURICH'	11	∞	∞	∞	∞	∞	760	∞	300	430	325	0

FIGURE 9.8 Adjacency Matrix for the Graph of Figure 9.7

in our present application), the array element contains the appropriate weight value(s) for the edge connecting $node_{row}$ and $node_{column}$:

- A **null weight** for elements along the major diagonal.
- An **infinite weight** indicating that $node_{column}$ is *not* adjacent to $node_{row}$.
- A nonnull, noninfinite weight, indicating that $node_{column}$ is adjacent to $node_{row}$.

Figure 9.8 depicts the adjacency matrix for the Sky-High Airline routes (refer back to Figure 9.7 if necessary). Each array element contains the integer mileage value between a parent city ($node_{row}$) and child city ($node_{column}$). A ∞ symbol represents *no adjacency* (infinite weight) to indicate that there is no direct flight from $node_{row}$ to $node_{column}$, and a zero represents *no distance*—i.e., a null weight. Infinity can be represented in the actual program data structure by an integer value greater than any legitimate mileage value, such as `MAXINT`.

The **lookup table** contains the name of each city (and perhaps other relevant information) and is used to map a particular city name to its corresponding matrix row or column index number or, conversely, map an index number back to an actual city name. For example, use of the lookup table and the matrix indicates that the route from London (5) to New York (7) is 3600 miles, whereas no direct route connects Dublin (3) to Madrid (6). The lookup table is represented using an ordered array (to support a binary search), although it could be represented as a search tree as well, with each node containing the city name, other information, and its associated matrix row index value.

A set of generic, global declarations for the adjacency matrix representation follows:

```
CONST
  MaxNodes        = ??;  {Maximum number of nodes}
  NullWeight      = ??;  {WeightType value < lowest weight that may arise}
  InfiniteWeight  = ??;  {WeightType value > highest weight that may arise}

TYPE
  KeyType     =  ??;                           {Application-dependent}
  InfoType    =  RECORD
                   Key  :  KeyType;            {Key value}
                   {Other fields, as necessary}
                 END;

  NodePtr     =  Integer;                      {Address of NodeType node}
  NodeType    =  RECORD
                   Data     :  InfoType;       {Data portion}
                   Visited  :  Boolean;        {Used in path-finding, traversing}
                   {Other fields as necessary}
                 END;

  WeightType  =  ??;                           {Edge weight; application-dependent}
  GraphType   =  RECORD
                   LTable  :  ARRAY [ 1..MaxNodes ] OF NodeType;
                   Matrix  :  ARRAY [ 1..MaxNodes, 1..MaxNodes ] OF WeightType;
                   NodeCount,                  {Count of all nodes stored}
                   EdgeCount  :  Integer       {Count of all edges stored}
                 END;

VAR
  Graph  :  GraphType;
```

Adjacency List

In the **adjacency list** representation, every parent node has a linked list associated with it. An empty list for node X would indicate that no nodes are adjacent to node X. A nonempty list, on the other hand, would indicate that there are one or more adjacent (i.e., child) nodes. Each of these nodes describes one adjacent node by key value, by lookup table index (if the lookup table is an array), or by a heapspace address (if the lookup table is a dynamically allocated structure). If the graph is weighted (as in our present case study), each of these nodes also must describe the edge weights.

The lookup table is a linked list of records, with each record containing a key field (the name of a city), a pointer to the next list item, and a pointer to the head of the linked list of adjacent nodes for a particular city. Figure 9.9 shows the adjacency list for the graph of Figure 9.7.

> In Figure 9.9 and throughout this chapter, nonstandard use of the caret symbol (^) is used to represent heapspace addresses of lookup table nodes; e.g., ^5 represents the address of the fifth node in the lookup table.

The four-node linked list emanating from the Paris record, for example, *does not represent a four-city path* from Paris to Zurich. Instead, it indicates that Frankfurt (^4), London (^5), New York (^7), and Zurich (^11) are each adjacent to Paris (children of Paris); i.e., direct flights connect Paris to each of these cities. For graphs containing many nodes, representing the lookup table as a search tree instead of a linked list improves the efficiency of searching the table for a particular node. *In this chapter, we will represent all fun-*

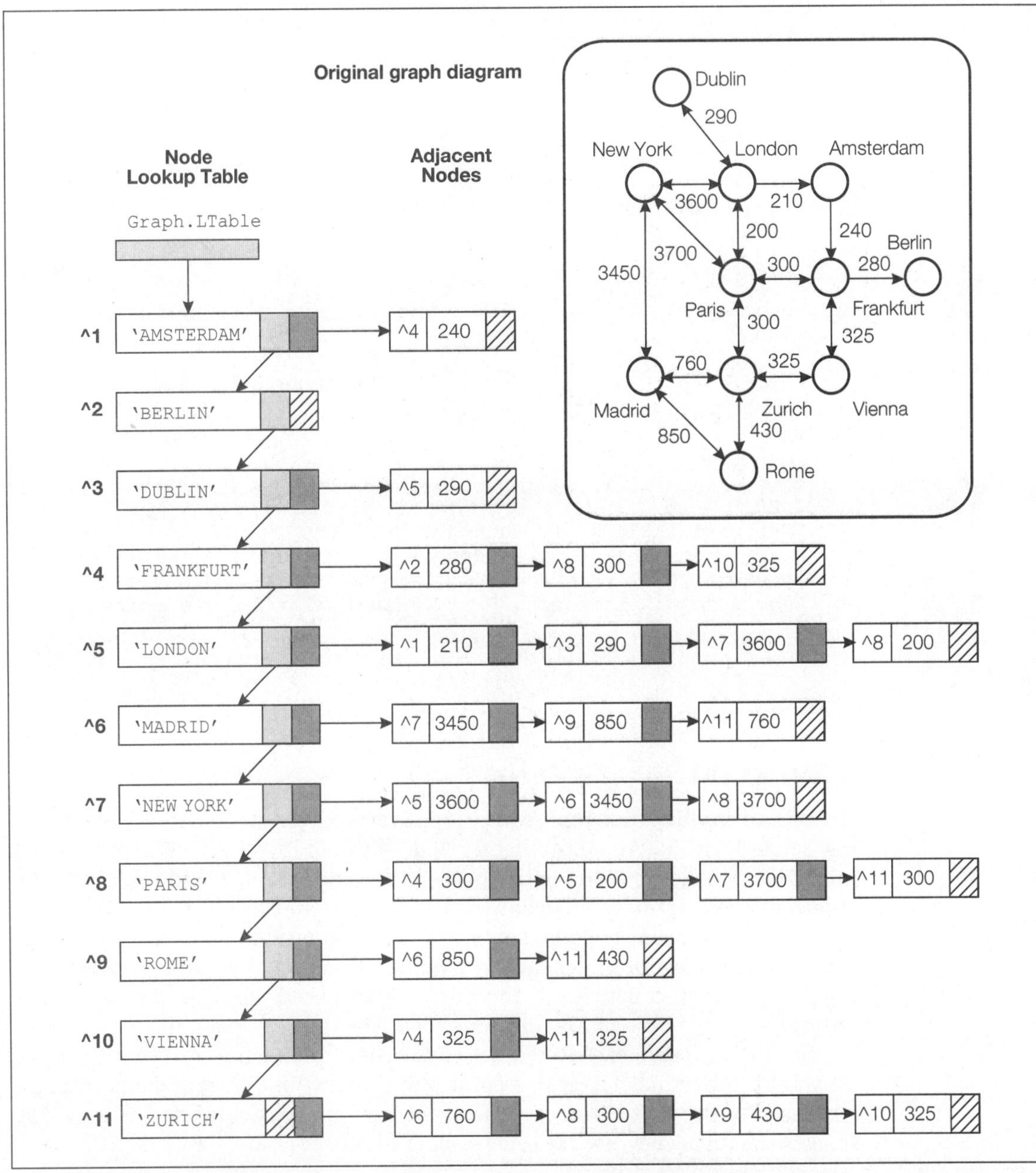

FIGURE 9.9 Adjacency List for the Graph of Figure 9.7

damental graph operations using an adjacency list representation of the airline route graph, as shown in Figure 9.9.

In both the adjacency matrix and adjacency list representations, the lookup table could be represented as an ordered, dynamically allocated linked list (as in the present application), an ordered array, or a search tree. As discussed in Section 5.2, a header node may be used with the linked list representation to simplify the insertion and deletion algorithms. For visual clarity, however, the diagrams of the lookup table for the present application will *not* contain a header node.

In an adjacency list representation, the lists of adjacent nodes may be represented as ordered, dynamically allocated linked lists, as ordered arrays, or as search trees. In the present application, the lists are represented as ordered, dynamically allocated linked lists; again, each of these lists could contain a header node, although the diagrams in this chapter will not display them.

A set of generic, global declarations for the adjacency list representation follows:

```
CONST
  NullWeight      =  ??;    {WeightType value < lowest weight that may arise}
  InfiniteWeight  =  ??;    {WeightType value > highest weight that may arise}

TYPE

  {***  Edge-node declarations  ***}

  NodePtr     =  ^NodeType;
  WeightType  =  ??;                        {Edge weight; application-dependent}
  EInfoType   =  RECORD                     {Information about an edge}
                   Child   :  NodePtr;      {Address of NodeType node}
                   Weight  :  WeightType    {Weight value of edge}
                 END;

  ENodePtr    =  ^ENodeType;                {Address of ENodeType edge node}
  ENodeType   =  RECORD                     {An edge/child node}
                   EInfo  :  EInfoType;     {Data portion of edge node}
                   Next   :  ENodePtr       {Next edge/child node}
                 END;

  {***  Lookup table declarations  ***}

  KeyType     =  ??;                        {Application-dependent}
  InfoType    =  RECORD
                   Key  :  KeyType;         {Key value}
                   {Other fields, as necessary}
                 END;

  NodeType    =  RECORD                     {Information about a node}
                   Data       :  InfoType;    {Data portion}
                   Visited    :  Boolean;     {Used in path-finding}
                   Head       :  ENodePtr;    {Points to 1st edge node in list}
                   Parent,                    {Used in representing paths}
                   Child      :  NodePtr;     {Used in TopologicalSort}
                   HeapIndx   :  Integer;     {Used in FindMCPaths, BuildMCSTree}
                   MinCost    :  WeightType;  {Used in FindMCPaths, BuildMCSTree}
                   Next       :  NodePtr      {Points to next lookup table node}
                 END;

  {***  Main graph structure declaration  ***}

  GraphType   =  RECORD
                   LTable     :  NodePtr;     {Points to 1st lookup table node}
                   NodeCount,                 {Count of nodes in graph}
                   EdgeCount  :  Integer      {Count of edges in graph}
                 END;

VAR
  Graph  : GraphType;
```

Initializing a Graph and Testing for Emptiness

Initializing a graph as empty, with either representation, involves setting the `NodeCount` and `EdgeCount` fields to zero and, for the adjacency list representation, setting the `Graph.LTable` field to **NIL**. Testing for emptiness involves comparing the `NodeCount` field to zero.

At this time, examine the following routines in Appendix I.

```
PROCEDURE GraphInit ( VAR Graph : GraphType );

FUNCTION GraphEmpty ( VAR Graph : GraphType ) : Boolean;
```

Searching for a Node or Edge and Testing for Adjacency

The search for a particular node involves looking through the lookup table of nodes, given the `KeyType` key value that uniquely identifies the desired node. Because a search procedure may be called for either simple searching or as a prelude to inserting or deleting a node (as with a binary search tree), it should return the appropriate parameters. If the lookup table is represented as an ordered, dynamically allocated linked list (as in the present application, the `LLSearch` routine presented in Section 5.2 may be used. If the lookup table is represented as an ordered array, the `BinarySearch` binary search routine in Application 7.5 and Appendix J may be used. If the lookup table is represented as a binary search tree instead, the `BinTreeSearch` routine in Section 8.2 and Appendix G may be used.

The algorithm to search for a particular edge from a parent node to a child node depends on the graph representation. In fact, for an adjacency matrix, no search is required at all; an edge may be referenced directly using the two appropriate array indices that correspond to the two nodes. Recall that in an adjacency list, the lists of nodes representing edges and adjacent nodes may be represented as ordered, dynamically allocated linked lists themselves (as in the present application), as ordered arrays, or as search trees. In the present application, the `LLSearch` algorithm of Appendix J may be used for searching such a list and, again, the lists may include header nodes, although the diagrams in this chapter will not show them. Again, the `BinarySearch` procedure may be used with arrays and the `BinTreeSearch` procedure may be used with binary search trees.

For some high-level operations, it is sufficient to test whether or not a particular (parent) node is merely adjacent to a particular (child) node. A Boolean function, perhaps named `Adjacent`, would therefore be useful. For the adjacency matrix representation, this function would return a false value if the array element representing the edge between two nodes contains a null or infinite value and a true value otherwise. For the adjacency list representation, this function would return a false value if the child node could not be found among the list of adjacent nodes of the parent node and a true value if it *is* found. The actual Pascal representation of function `Adjacent` is left as an exercise.

Inserting and Deleting Edges and Nodes

In an adjacency matrix, inserting an edge from node X to node Y involves merely assigning a nonnull, noninfinite value to array elements [X, Y]. In the adjacency list representation, inserting an edge from node X to node Y involves inserting an `ENodeType` node in the list of nodes emanating from parent node X—i.e., using the `LLInsert` routine (Appendix D) if the list is represented as a linked list (as in the present application), using the `BinTreeInsert` routine (Appendix G) if the list is represented as a binary search tree, or shifting other array elements toward the high-index end of the array to "make room" for the new edge-element. Because all three structures are ordered, an appropriate searching routine must be employed prior to insertion—`LLSearch`, `BinTreeSearch`, or `BinarySearch`, respectively. Deleting an edge requires the converse of the operations used to insert a new edge.

As an example of inserting edges, Figure 9.10 uses boldface lines to indicate *three* new routes.

Figure 9.11 depicts the changed portion of the adjacency list after these three edges are added. The new edge nodes are indicated by boldface lines, and vertical dots are shown in lieu of the remaining graph structure.

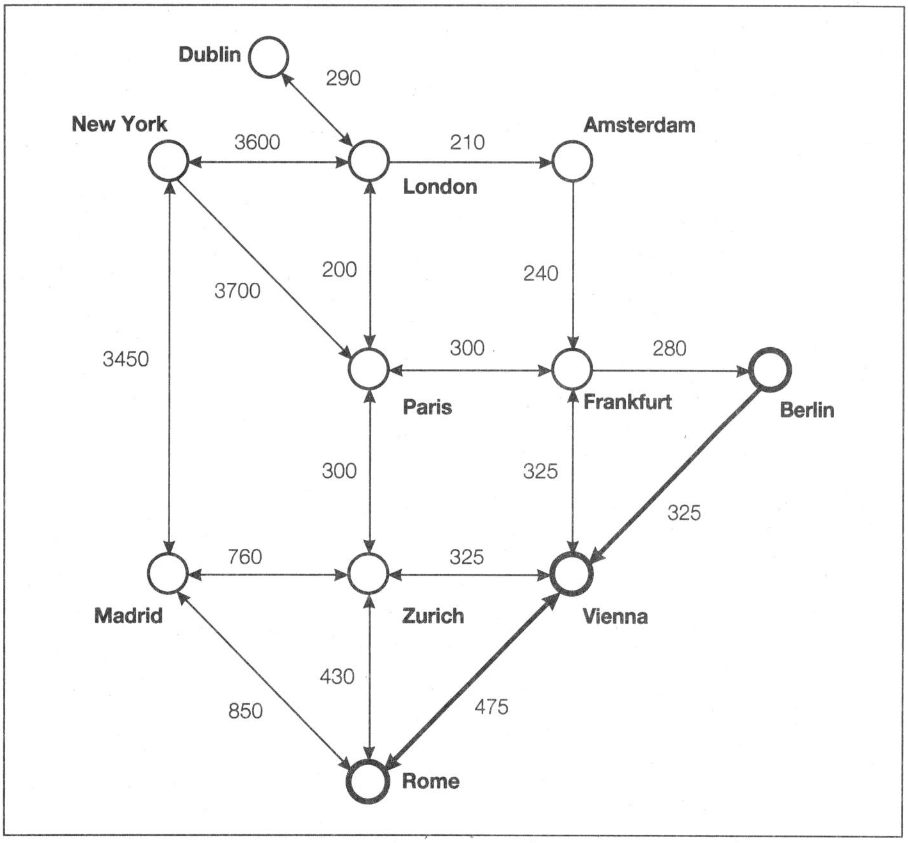

FIGURE 9.10 **Adding Three Routes by Inserting New Edges**

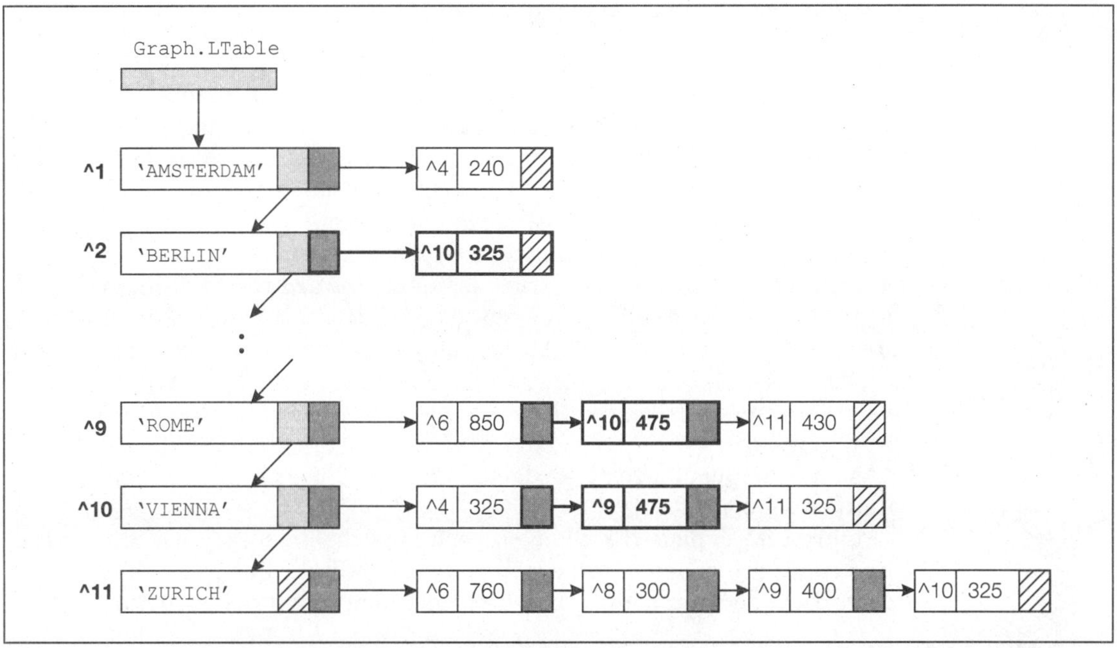

FIGURE 9.11 The Adjacency List after Three Edges Are Added (Indicated via Boldface Lines and Numbers)

For the adjacency matrix representation, inserting a new node is a relatively inefficient operation, requiring the shifting of array elements toward the high-index ends of the edges array in both dimensions to make room for the new row and column of elements associated with the new node. A new entry must be made to the lookup table as well. For the adjacency list representation, a search routine must be called first to determine the point of insertion in the lookup table; then the appropriate insertion routine must be called: `LLSearch` and `LLInsert` (both in Appendix D) for the linked list representation of the lookup table (as in the present application), `BinTreeSearch` and `BinTreeInsert` for the binary search tree representation, and `BinarySearch` for the ordered array representation. In the array representation a programmer-defined routine must be called to shift elements toward the high-index end of the array to make room for the new node.

For both the adjacency matrix and adjacency list representations, deleting a node involves the converse operations. In addition, when deleting node X, the adjacency list representation requires two operations:

1. *Delete all nodes representing edges from X;* i.e., all edge nodes in the linked list emanating from the lookup table node for X, representing outgoing edges from X to each of X's children, must be deleted.
2. *Delete all nodes representing edges to X;* i.e., all edge nodes in the linked lists emanating from other nodes in which X is specified as a child must be deleted.

The actual Pascal representations of the algorithms for edge and node insertion and deletion are left as exercises.

Graph Traversals

If we were writing a routine to visit and process every node in a meaningful order (e.g., in alphabetical order of city name), irrespective of the directionality of the edges, the routine could simply traverse the lookup table of node information. (As with any traversal, the exact set of operations involved in processing each node is application-dependent.) A traversal process is more complex, however, if the directionality of all edges is respected. As with tree structures, there are two types of traversal for visiting and processing each node of a graph if the directionality of edges is respected:

- *Depth-first traversal.* Advance as far into the graph as possible, backtrack to a previously visited node, then again advance as far as possible, and so forth.
- *Breadth-first traversal.* Visit all neighbors of the source node, then visit all neighbors of these neighbors, and so forth. This visitation path tends to fan out from the source, spanning the breadth of the graph and advancing more slowly into the graph than does the depth-first search.

Depth-First Traversal

We should begin by considering the mechanics of simply advancing from one node to the next. How can a depth-first traversal algorithm—`DFVisit`—advance from, say, Amsterdam to Frankfurt? Look ahead to the leftmost graph diagram of Figure 9.12 and assume the following declarations:

```
VAR
  Parent  : NodePtr;    {Lookup table address of a parent node}
  Edge    : ENodePtr;   {Address of an edge node in the list emanating from Parent^}
```

The lookup table can be searched to obtain the address of the Amsterdam (source) node in the table. Assuming that this address is assigned to variable `Parent`, the following statement assigns to pointer variable `Edge` the address of the first (and only) `ENodeType` edge node in Amsterdam's linked list:

```
Edge := Parent^.Head; {Edge := address of 1st edge-list node for Parent^}
```

(If `Parent` were, instead, the address of the Berlin node, `Edge` would be assigned the value **NIL**.) `DFTraverse` can advance to the Frankfurt node by using the `Child` field of the `Edge` node; `Child` contains the address of the Frankfurt `NodeType` node. The following assignment to `Parent` allows `DFVisit` to advance to Frankfurt:

```
Parent := Edge^.Child; {Parent := address of adjacent node}
```

Because the traversal algorithms we will design must be versatile enough to work for *any* configuration of nodes and edges, we must consider the three

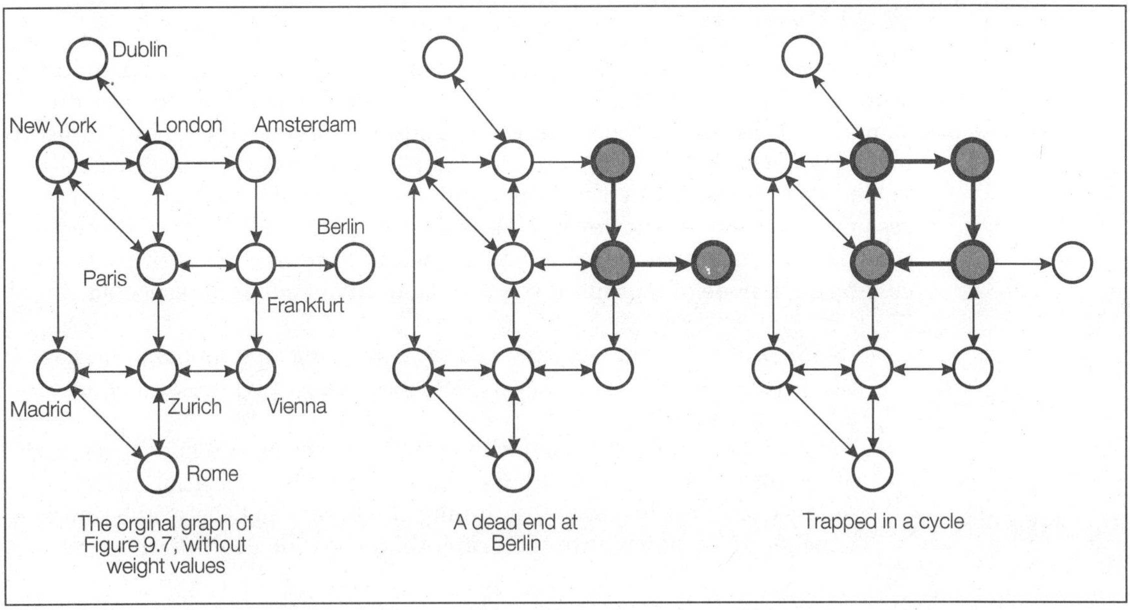

FIGURE 9.12 The Original Graph and Two Problematic Special Cases When Advancing from Amsterdam

possible special cases that may arise when advancing from one node to another:

- Multiple children from which to choose
- A **dead end** (an inability to advance)
- A cycle (a return to a previously visited node)

A particular node may be the parent of *several* adjacent nodes; e.g., from Paris, it is possible to fly directly to London, New York, Zurich, or Frankfurt. Therefore, the existence of *multiple adjacent nodes* is a special case, and `DFVisit` must make useful choices about which node to visit next from the current node. The center and rightmost diagrams of Figure 9.12 depict the two special cases that result in the failure to advance at all. The path (Amsterdam, Frankfurt, Berlin) results in a dead end, and the path (Amsterdam, Frankfurt, Paris, London, Amsterdam, Frankfurt, . . .) is an endless cycle. `DFVisit` must employ a consistent strategy for selecting the next node to visit as well as detecting and resolving dead ends and cycles.

To select which adjacent node to visit next, `DFVisit` can simply follow the ordering of the linked list emanating from the current node. This means that the first node visited from Frankfurt, for example, would be Berlin, since the first node in the linked list represents the edge from Frankfurt to Berlin.

A dead end results from either of the following:

- *No children.* The current node has no children, i.e., no adjacent node to which the traversal may continue.
- *No unvisited children.* The current node does have one or more children; however, they have already been visited during the traversal and therefore may not be visited again.

The solution to either type of dead-end problem is to *backtrack* to the previously visited node and then to advance to some other node. For example, if DFVisit begins at Amsterdam and advances to Frankfurt, it would then advance to Berlin, which is a dead end. The routine would escape this dead end by returning to Frankfurt and then advancing to a node other than Berlin, such as Paris.

To avoid being trapped in a cycle, we will impose the rule that DFVisit will advance only to those nodes not yet visited during the traversal. Being visited does not include backtracking to a previously visited node upon reaching a dead end. If the path thus far is (Amsterdam, Frankfurt, Paris), for example, it *does* mean choosing a child node from Paris other than Frankfurt. Notice in the global declarations for an adjacency list graph that each NodeType record contains a Visited field. DFVisit can begin by initializing each Visited field to a false value; then, each time a node is visited during the traversal, its corresponding Visited element is assigned a true value.

DFVisit may terminate successfully if it has visited and processed every node in the graph. Depending upon where the traversal begins in a directed graph, however, it may *not* be possible to visit all nodes. DFVisit must count the nodes it visits by using integer variable NCount. This count is compared to Graph.NodeCount when the traversal concludes to determine whether the traversal succeeded or failed:

- *Success:* All nodes in the graph have been visited; i.e., upon conclusion, NCount = Graph.NodeCount.
- *Failure:* In the course of trying all paths emanating from the source node, the backtracking eventually backs up to the source node, from which there are no more paths leading to unvisited children; i.e., upon conclusion, NCount < Graph.NodeCount.

The leftmost diagram in Figure 9.13 shows the order in which all nodes are visited during a depth-first traversal, starting at Amsterdam (1 means visited first, 2 means visited second, etc.). This order is based on the adjacency list structure shown in Figure 9.9, *selecting edges in the order they appear within the linked list of each node.* The DFVisit routine in Appendix I can perform either a depth-first traversal or path search, depending upon the value of parameter ATraversal.

At this time, examine the following routine in Appendix I.

```
PROCEDURE DFVisit ( VAR Graph : GraphType; Source, Destination : NodePtr;
                    VAR Success : Boolean; ATraversal : Boolean);
```

Breadth-First Traversal

In Section 8.2, a circular FIFO queue is employed to traverse a binary search tree in breadth-first order: The address of the root node is enqueued, then a loop begins in which the address at the front of the queue is inspected and processed, the addresses of its children are enqueued, and then the front address is served. This process repeats until the queue becomes empty.

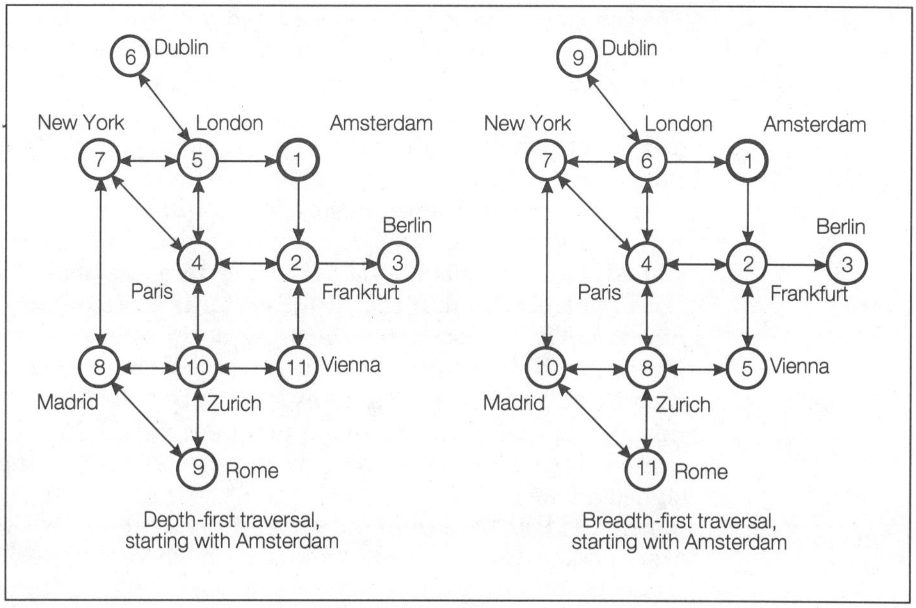

FIGURE 9.13 Depth-First and Breadth-First Traversals Starting at Amsterdam

Similarly, the algorithm for a breadth-first traversal, `BFVisit`, will employ a circular FIFO queue to control the order in which nodes are visited and processed. As with the depth-first traversal, to avoid being trapped in a cycle, the `Visited` field of each node is assigned a true value when it is visited and processed. Again, the traversal may succeed or fail, based on the directionality of the edges and with which node the traversal begins, requiring the traversal algorithm to maintain a count of nodes visited.

A pseudocode version of the `BFVisit` algorithm follows:

```
ALGORITHM BFVisit ( VAR Graph : GraphType; Source : NodePtr;
                    VAR Success : Boolean );
VAR
  NCount  :  Integer;
  Queue   :  QueueType;         {FIFO queue described in Appendix F}

BEGIN
Initialize each Visited field in the lookup table as FALSE;
Initialize the queue as empty;
NCount  := 0;                   {Initialize count of nodes visited thus far}
Success := FALSE;
Enqueue the Source node;
Mark the Source node as having been visited;

WHILE NOT QEmpty ( Queue ) DO
  BEGIN
  Serve a (parent) node from the front of the queue;
  Process this node;
  NCount := NCount + 1;
  Enqueue all unvisited children of the parent, marking each as visited
  END;

Success := NCount = Graph.NodeCount
END;
```

The rightmost diagram in Figure 9.13 shows the order in which all nodes are visited during a breadth-first traversal. This order is based on the adjacency list structure shown in Figure 9.8, selecting edges in the order they appear within the linked list of each node. The `BFVisit` routine in Appendix I can perform either a breadth-first traversal or path search, depending on the value of parameter `ATraversal`.

At this time, examine the following routine in Appendix I.

```
PROCEDURE BFVisit ( VAR Graph : GraphType; Source, Destination : NodePtr;
                    VAR Success : Boolean; ATraversal : Boolean );
```

Finding a Path Between Two Nodes

In this section we will devise an algorithm to search for a path from a particular node (the source) to another node (the destination) and return a representation of the path. The path-finding algorithm is really just a subset of the `DFVisit` algorithm. In both algorithms, the `Visited` field of each node must still be assigned a true value when that node is visited to preclude a cycle, and backtracking must be employed to escape a dead end. Two important differences distinguish the traversal and path-finding algorithms, however. The first difference pertains to *when* either routine may conclude. Recall that a *traversal* concludes when it has either visited all nodes (success) or is unable to visit any remaining unvisited nodes (failure). A depth-first *search* of a path, on the other hand, concludes when either of the following is true:

- *Success:* The destination node is encountered.
- *Failure:* The destination node has not been reached and no other nodes can be reached from the source node. (In the course of trying all paths emanating from the source node, the backtracking eventually returns to the source node.)

The second difference between the two algorithms is that the traversal algorithm must visit and process every node in the graph, whereas the path-finding algorithm must find a particular path and return a representation of that path. To preserve the path, each time the path-finding algorithm visits and processes a node, it will assign to its `Parent` field the address of its parent node. If the destination is reached, the entire path can be recovered by following these parent pointers *backward,* starting with the destination node. This recovery technique is illustrated in greater detail shortly.

Figure 9.14 traces the search for a path from Amsterdam to New York using this depth-first strategy. The algorithm will find the first possible path between the source and destination nodes, if a path exists, based on the structure of the adjacency list. (An upcoming algorithm finds the shortest path by counting the number of intervening edges, and the `FindMCPaths` algorithm presented later in this section finds the shortest path based on the sum of edge weights.)

The lookup table nodes in the adjacency list diagram of Figure 9.15 show `Parent` fields as they would be assigned at the successful conclusion of the search for the path from Amsterdam to New York. An explanation of how the path can be recovered follows the figure.

The backward path from the destination (New York) to the source (Amsterdam) may be recovered as follows:

1. New York (destination).
2. The parent of New York is at address ^5, London.
3. The parent of London is at address ^8, Paris.
4. The parent of Paris is at address ^4, Frankfurt.
5. The parent of Frankfurt is at address ^1, Amsterdam (source).

Therefore, the forward path is (Amsterdam, Frankfurt, Paris, London, New York).

A pseudocode algorithm for `DFVisit` follows:

```
ALGORITHM  DFVisit ( VAR Graph : GraphType;  Source, Destination : NodePtr;
                     VAR Success : Boolean );
           ________________________________________________________

  PROCEDURE DFT ( Parent : NodePtr );   {Recursive procedure}

  VAR
    Edge  :  Address of linked list node;

  BEGIN
  Determine if a path has been found;   {Success := Parent = Destination}
  IF a path has NOT been found THEN
    BEGIN
    Mark the Parent node as visited;
    Edge := Address of the 1st node in the linked list for Parent;

    WHILE  ( path has not been found ) AND ( other unvisited children ) DO
      BEGIN
      IF the next child of Parent is unvisited THEN
        BEGIN
        Child := NodePtr address of this unvisited child (stored in edge node);
        Parent field of the Child node := Parent's address;
        DFT ( Child )                   {Recursive call}
        END;
      Edge := Address of next child of Parent
      END
    END
  END;
           ________________________________________________________
{***  Main routine for DFVisit  ***}

BEGIN
Initialize each Visited field in the lookup table to FALSE;
DFFP ( Source )
END;
```

Notice that, because nested procedure `DFT` is recursive, the local variable `Edge` is used to retain the address of the linked list edge node last encountered before a recursive call is made. When the execution flow returns from

1. Mark Amsterdam as visited and assign **NIL** to its `Parent` field. Advance to its only child, Frankfurt.
2. Mark Frankfurt as visited and assign ^1 (address of Amsterdam node) to its `Parent` field. Advance to its first child, Berlin.
3. Mark Berlin as visited and assign ^4 (address of Frankfurt node) to its `Parent` field. This is a dead-end, so backtrack to Frankfurt.
4. Advance to Frankfurt's second unvisited child, Paris. Mark Paris as visited and assign ^4 to its `Parent` field. Advance to its second child, London (first child, Frankfurt, has been visited).
5. Mark London as visited and assign ^8 (address of Paris vertex) to its `Parent` field. Advance to its second child, Dublin (first child, Amsterdam, has been visited).
6. Mark London as visited and assign ^5 (address of London vertex) to its `Parent` field. This is a dead-end, so backtrack to London.
7. Advance to London's third child, New York. Mark New York as visited and assign ^5 to its `Parent` field. *Success:* Destination (New York) is reached.

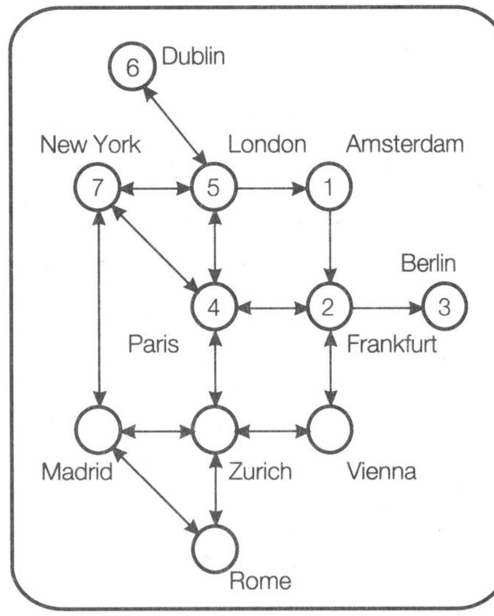

Order of visitation

FIGURE 9.14 Depth-First Searching for a Path from Amsterdam to New York

a recursive call to escape a dead end, the algorithm will advance from the current node to its next unvisited child by advancing `Edge`:

```
Edge := Edge^.Next;
```

An `Edge^.Next` value of **`NIL`** means there are no more children to visit from the current node; i.e., the present node represents a dead end and the algorithm must backtrack to the previously visited node.

At this time, examine the following routine in Appendix I.

```
PROCEDURE DFVisit ( VAR Graph : GraphType; Source, Destination : NodePtr;
                    VAR Success : Boolean; ATraversal : Boolean);
```

Finding a Shortest Path (Number of Intervening Edges)

In the previous section, an algorithm was designed to find a path between two nodes (if such a path exists), although not necessarily the *shortest* possible path. This algorithm employs a depth-first searching strategy, advancing as far into the graph as possible, then backtracking to a previously visited node upon encountering a dead end, then again advancing as far as possible, and so forth. In this section we will design an algorithm that em-

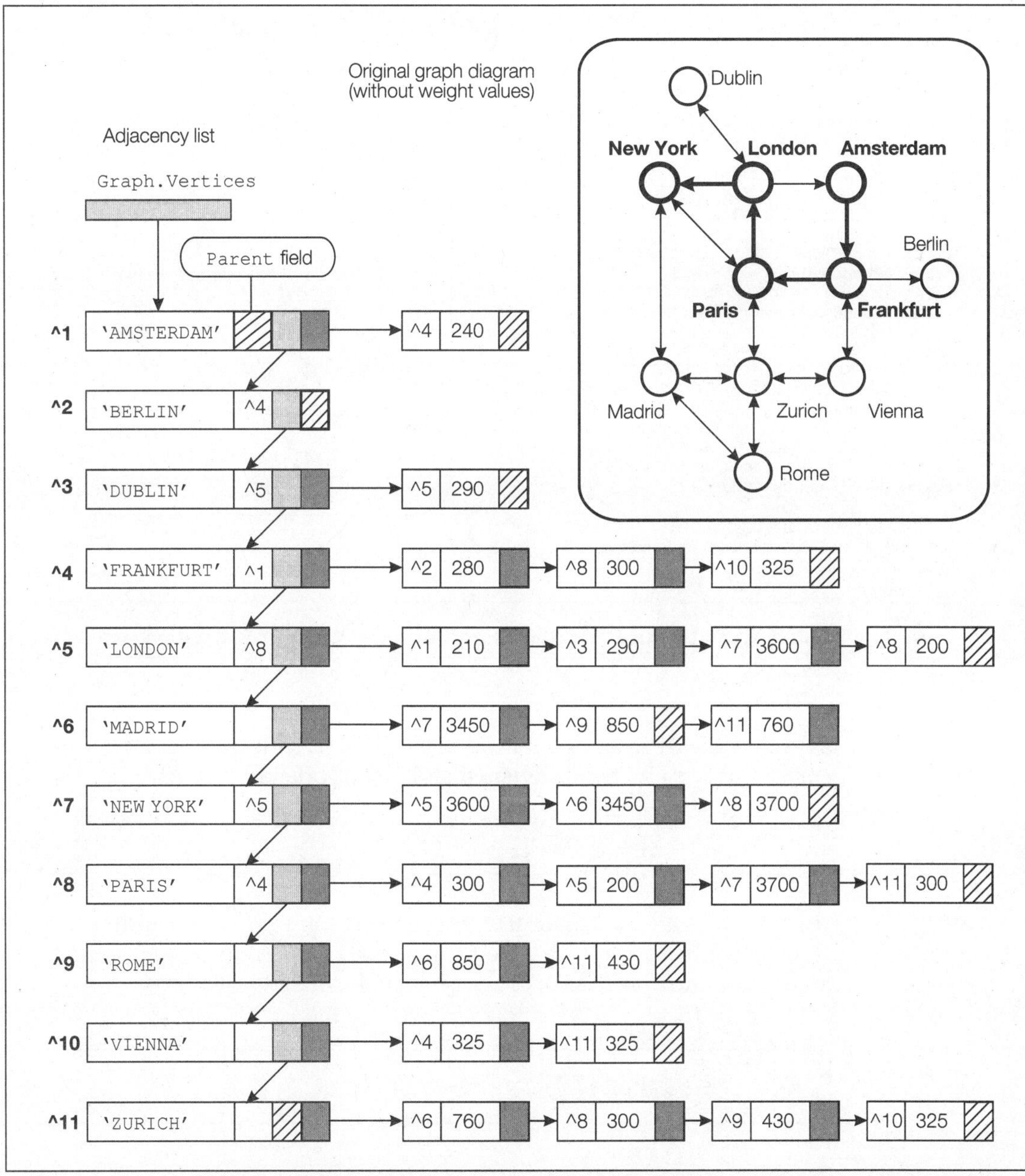

FIGURE 9.15 The Original Graph and Adjacency List, with `Parent` Field Values Shown

ploys a breadth-first searching scheme. This means that it must visit all neighbors of the source node, then all neighbors of these neighbors, and so forth. The search tends to fan out from the source node, spanning the breadth of the graph and advancing more slowly into the graph than does the depth-first search.

The breadth-first search provides the advantage of finding the shortest path between two nodes (if a path exists at all) in terms of the *number of intervening edges*. (The process of finding a shortest path in terms of total edge weights in a weighted graph—a minimal cost path—involves an entirely different algorithm named `FindMCPaths`, which will be presented in Section 9.3.)

This algorithm is really just a subset of the `BFVisit` traversal algorithm, and the two differences that distinguish depth-first traversal and path-finding algorithms arise here as well. As with the breadth-first traversal algorithm, the path-finding algorithm begins by enqueuing the `NodePtr` address of the source node. A loop then commences in which the front address is inspected, that node is processed, the addresses of *its* unvisited children are enqueued, and then the front address is actually served from the queue. The first difference between the algorithms relates to when each concludes. The path-finding algorithm concludes when either of the following is true:

- *Success:* The destination node is encountered.
- *Failure:* The queue becomes empty because there are no more unvisited children (of the nodes served) to enqueue.

The second difference between the two algorithms is that a traversal must visit and process every node in the graph, whereas a path-finding algorithm must find a particular path and store a representation of that path. Each time the path-finding algorithm visits and processes a node, it assigns to its `Parent` field the address of its parent node. If the destination is reached, the entire path can be recovered by following these parent pointers *backward,* starting with the destination node.

Figure 9.16 traces the steps and changes in the dynamically allocated, circular linked list structure in the search for a path from Amsterdam to New York.

The lookup table nodes in the adjacency list diagram of Figure 9.17 show `Parent` fields as they would be assigned at the successful conclusion of the search for the path from Amsterdam to New York. The path is shown again in boldface within the inset diagram and may be recovered from the `Parent` fields just as the path found by the `DFVisit` algorithm is recovered.

> *At this time, examine the following routine in Appendix I.*

```
PROCEDURE BFVisit ( VAR Graph : GraphType; Source, Destination : NodePtr;
                    VAR Success : Boolean; ATraversal : Boolean);
```

Saving a Graph in a File and Rebuilding a Graph

Preserving *any* data structure in a file involves the following:

1. Saving information about each item
2. Saving the relationships among the items

In a linear list, such as a linked list or a sequence of array elements, each pair of items has a one-to-one relationship, indicating their adjacency. As a

1. Enqueue the address of Amsterdam's unvisited child, Frankfurt. Mark it as visited and assign ^1 to its `Parent` field (the address of Amsterdam's node).

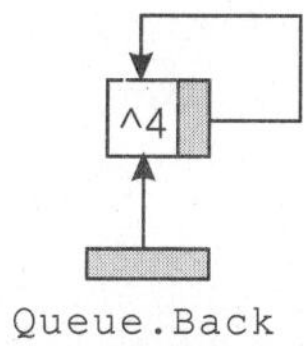

2. Inspect the queue node to be served next (^4, Frankfurt). Enqueue the addresses of Frankfurt's unvisited children, Berlin, Paris, and Vienna. Mark each as visited and assign ^4 to their `Parent` fields. Serve the next queue node (^4).

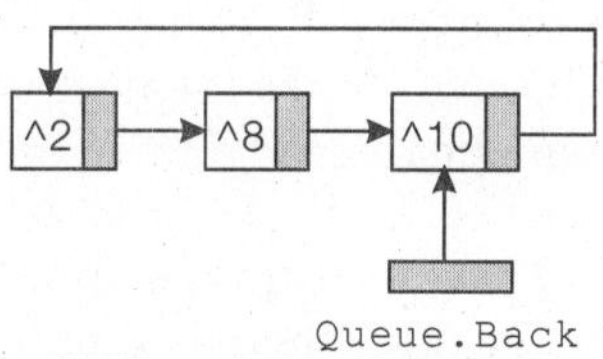

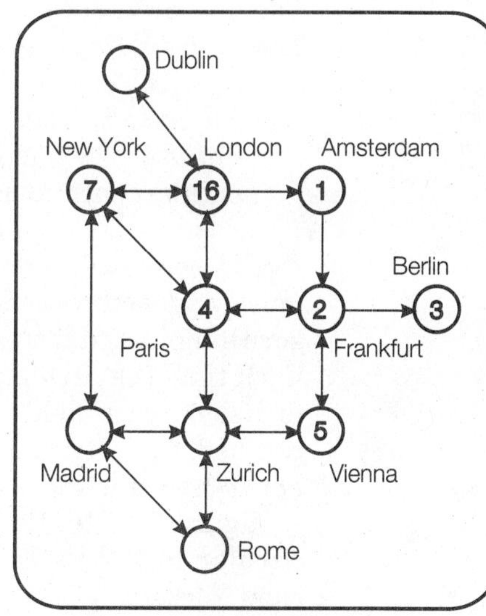

Order of visitation

3. Inspect the queue node to be served next (^2, Berlin). Enqueue nothing, since Berlin has no unvisited children. Serve the next queue node (^2).

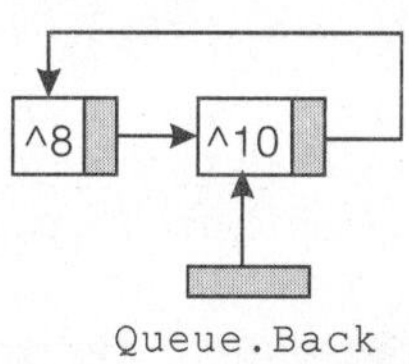

4. Inspect the queue node to be served next (^8, Paris). Enqueue the addresses of Paris's first two unvisited children, London and New York. Mark each as visited and assign ^8 to their `Parent` fields. Serve the next queue node (^8).

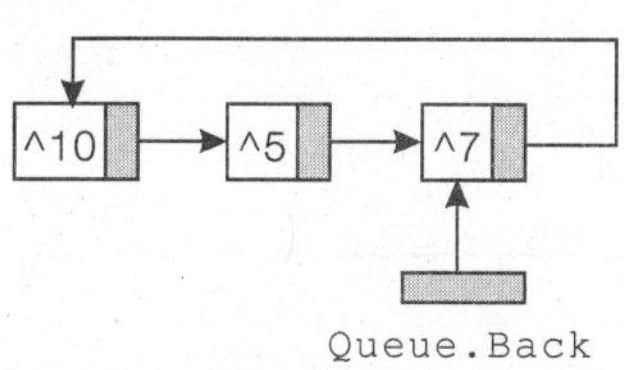

5. Inspect the queue node to be served next (^10). *Success*; The destination (New York) is reached.

FIGURE 9.16 Breadth-First Searching for a Path from Amsterdam (^1) to New York (^10)

linear structure, a file can be used readily to preserve the ordering of nodes in any linear list; a traversal algorithm simply traverses the list from beginning to end, writing the data portion of that element or node to the file. As we saw in Section 8.2, a (nonlinear) binary search tree can be preserved in a file by an algorithm that traverses the entire tree (using a preorder or level-order traversal) and writes the data portion of each node to the file. This

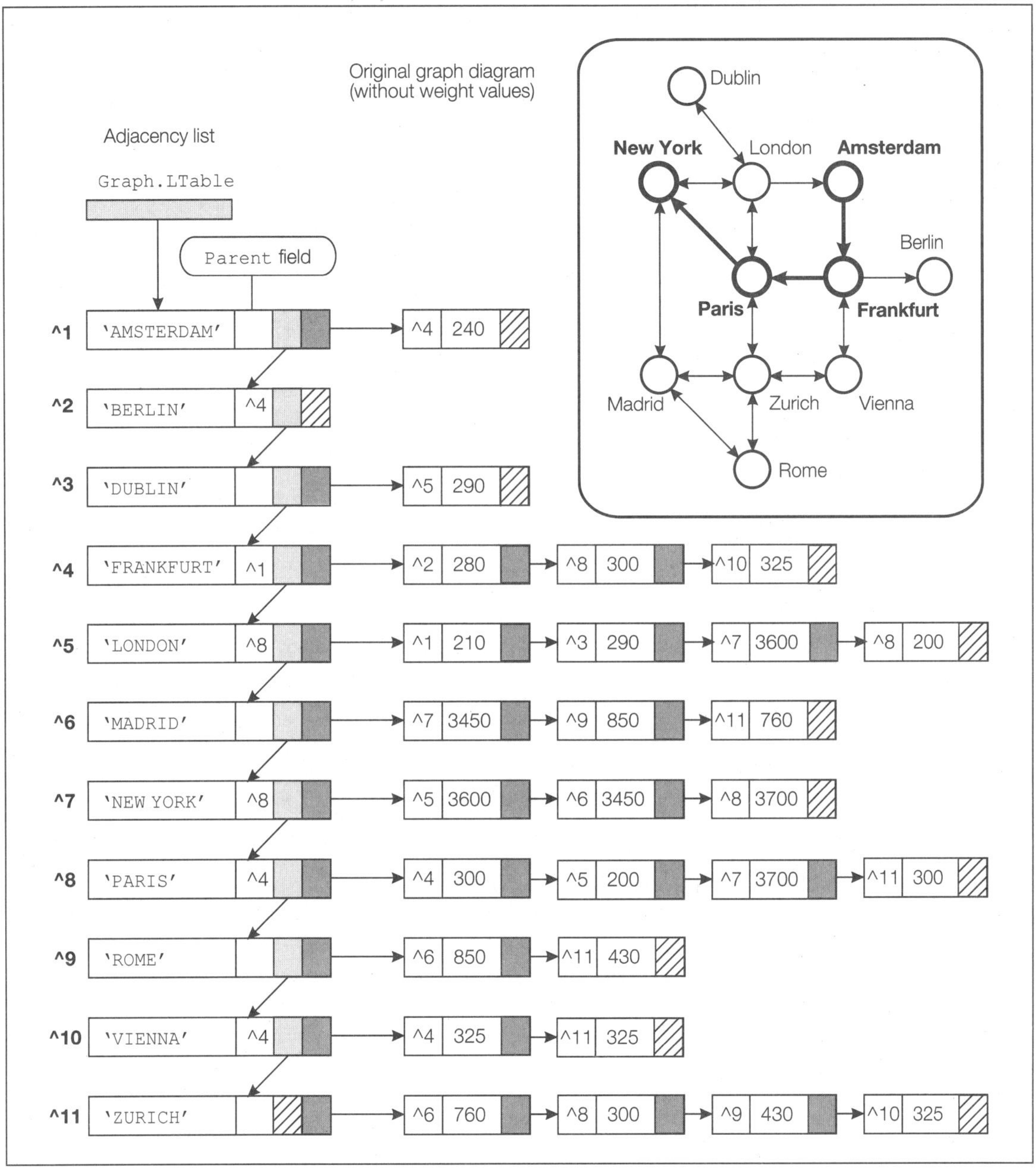

FIGURE 9.17 The Original Graph and Adjacency List, with Parent Field Values Shown

way, the relationships among the nodes are implied by the order in which these data portions are written to the file. By storing data portions in a particular order in the file, the original structure can be reconstructed later, by sequentially reading these items.

Because each node in a graph may have a many-to-many relationship with other nodes in the graph, the often complex relationships among nodes that result cannot be implied by the mere order in which the data portions of these nodes are written to a linear file. Therefore, to preserve a graph, *two types of file elements must be written to the file:*

- A file element that describes a particular node
- A file element that describes a particular edge (directed or undirected)

An algorithm to save a graph to a file must contain two loops. In the first loop, the lookup table is traversed and the data portion in each record is written to the file. In the second loop, each edge list is traversed and the data portion in each edge node is written to the file. For this strategy of saving the graph, the following variant record declaration may be added to the global declarations given earlier and used to write both types of information—parent data (lookup table data) and child data (edge list data).

```
TYPE
  GFileRec  =  RECORD
                 CASE AnEdge : Boolean OF
                   FALSE : ( Data        :  InfoType );    {Node descriptor}
                   TRUE  : ( ParentKey,                    {Edge descriptor}
                             ChildKey    :  KeyType;
                             Weight      :  WeightType )
               END;

  GFileType =  FILE OF GFileRec;

VAR
  GraphFile : GFileType;
```

These declarations are designed to store two separate edge descriptor records for a bidirectional edge between two nodes, an edge from node X to node Y and an edge from node Y to node X. Consider the advantages and disadvantages of adding a fourth Boolean field to the **TRUE** variant portion—`Bidirectional`—to save memory space in the file, requiring just one edge descriptor to be written for each bidirectional edge (this is one of the exercises at the end of the chapter). Be sure to consider the additional execution time necessary in assigning this field. (*Hint:* Must this Boolean `Bidirectional` field also be included in each edge node in the graph as well?)

Notice that each child node's key value is written to the file rather than its lookup table address, since heapspace addresses are never stored in a file. (Recall from Section 5.2 that a heapspace address used during one program run may not be valid during a subsequent run of the same program.) Notice also that all lookup table data are stored first; then edge data are stored so that lookup table data will be read before edge data when the graph is rebuilt later. If this were not done, an edge descriptor record might be read for a child node whose lookup table node has not yet been read, in which case the algorithm would not have a lookup table address to store in the edge node.

One of the chapter exercises asks you to write a Pascal procedure to read a graph from a file.

9.3 ADVANCED OPERATIONS

In this section, we examine algorithms for three advanced operations:

- Finding minimal-cost paths
- Building a minimal-cost spanning tree
- Maximizing total flow through a graph

We will continue to use the adjacency list representation for the first three operations. Before reading further, you may wish to review the global declarations for both representations of a graph. (The `FindMCPaths` and `BuildMCSTree` algorithms are based on algorithms designed by Dr. Richard Rasala of Northeastern University.)

Finding Minimal-Cost Paths

Many applications require finding the shortest path between two nodes in terms of the edge weights rather than merely in terms of the number of intervening edges. For example, a prospective Sky-High Airlines passenger may want to know the shortest flight path from London to Vienna in terms of total distance and not just the number of cities along the route. If edge weights depicting flying time and ticket cost were added to the graph, the shortest flying distance and time or lowest expense could be determined as well. An edge weight is commonly called a *cost,* and a path between two nodes with the smallest possible weight sum, of all possible paths between those nodes, is commonly called the **minimal-cost (MC) path.**

How can we devise an algorithm to find a minimal cost path between two nodes? Perhaps we should redesign the searching algorithm such that whenever it is about to advance from a node and must choose one of several outgoing edges, it should choose that edge with the smallest weight value. Unfortunately, this approach does not necessarily produce a minimal cost path. Look at Figure 9.7 again to see that, using this strategy, the resulting path from New York to Frankfurt would be (New York, Madrid, Zurich, Paris, London, Amsterdam, Frankfurt), which spans 5160 miles, rather than the shorter path (New York, Paris, Frankfurt), which spans only 4000 miles. Even worse, this strategy may result in a dead end. For example, the search for a path from Amsterdam to New York yields the path (Amsterdam, Frankfurt, Berlin).

Another strategy might be to find *every* path from the source node to the destination node while maintaining a description of the shortest path found. Although this strategy will work and is the strategy employed in Section 9.3 for finding a minimal-cost tour, it may prove prohibitively time-consuming with a large graph. We will instead devise a routine named `FindMCPaths`, which is based on the famous **Dijkstra's algorithm.**

Dijkstra's algorithm, named for Edsgar Dijkstra, who devised the algorithm in 1959, finds the minimum-cost paths between a source node and *all other reachable nodes* with the *same time efficiency* it would take to find the minimum-cost path between a source node and a particular other node. To examine how the algorithm works, we will use the small directed graph shown in Figure 9.18. (Again, nonstandard caret notation is used to indicate

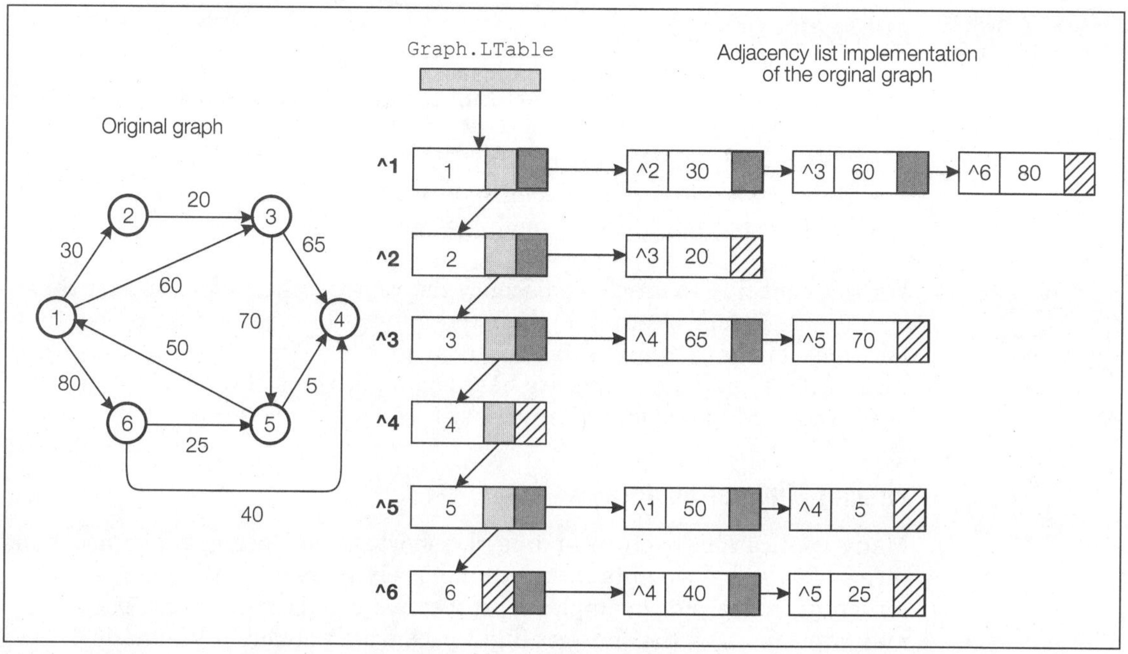

FIGURE 9.18 The Sample Directed Graph

heapspace `NodeType` addresses; e.g., ^2 represents the address of the second node of the graph.)

Our representation of Dijkstra's algorithm, `FindMinCostPaths`, requires an additional data structure:

```
NodePQ : HeapType: {Priority queue of nodes whose minimal cost paths are
                    currently being calculated}
```

`NodePQ` is a priority queue represented as a heap, so each `NodePQ` item is of type `HInfoType`:

```
TYPE
  HKeyType    =  WeightType;
  HInfoType   =  RECORD
                   Key   : HKeyType;  {Current minimum cost from Source to Node}
                   Node  : NodePtr    {Lookup table address of the node}
                 END;
```

Three fields within each `NodeType` record of node `p^` play important roles:

```
MinCost  : Integer;  {The current minimal integer cost of the path from the
                      source node to node P^}
HeapIndx : Integer;  {The index of the element in the NodePQ array that
                      represents the P^ node; used to locate this element if
                      P^.MinCost has changed, since the element must then be
                      repositioned within the queue}
Parent   : NodePtr;  {The NodePtr address of the parent of P^}
```

As it proceeds, the FindMCPaths algorithm extends paths from the source node to all reachable nodes. In the process of extending these paths, each node, P^, may be said to exist in one of three states (with the exception of the source, which is never enqueued in the NodePQ priority queue):

• No path cost determined:	• *Some* path cost determined:	• MC path determined:
P^ not yet enqueued in NodePQ	P^ currently in NodePQ	P^ already served from NodePQ
P^.MinCost = ∞	0 < P^.MinCost < ∞	0 ≤ P^.MinCost < ∞

Although the current cost of the MC path from the source to node P *could* be obtained from P^.MinCost, this value is stored in each queue item (the Key field) anyway. This allows FindMCPaths to use the heap primitive routines as they were designed in Section 8.4, with only a slight modification to the AdjustUp and AdjustDown primitives, which will be described shortly. All heap primitive routines are given in Appendix H.

The final set of paths between the source node and every other node will be preserved by the values of the Parent fields. As with the DFFindPath and BFFindPath algorithms, a path from the source to a node, P, will be recovered by tracing the path backward from P to the source: P, P^.Parent, P^.Parent^.Parent, etc.

To understand better the roles of the MinCost and Parent fields, let us examine their final states *after* FindMinCostPaths has already found all minimal-cost paths from node 1 (i.e., with node 1 as the source). Figure 9.19 shows the final states of the NodePQ priority queue and all MinCost and Parent fields (boldface arrows indicate the edges involved in the shortest paths to each node).

When FindMCPaths is completed, P^.MinCost contains the total cost of the minimal-cost path from the source node (node 1) to node P^. For example, the total minimum cost from node 1 to node 4 is 110, the minimum

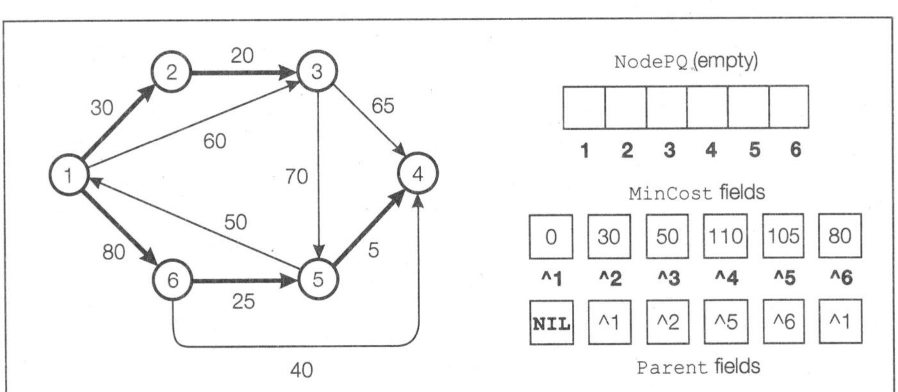

FIGURE 9.19 Node PQ and the MinCost and Parent Fields after Finding All Minimum Cost Paths from Node 1

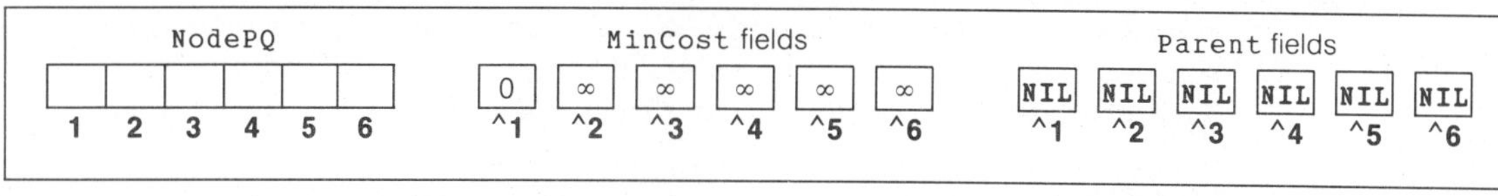

FIGURE 9.20 `NodePQ` **and the** `MinCost` **and** `Parent` **Fields, Initially**

cost to 6 is 80, and the minimal cost to 1 (itself) is 0. The path from node 4 back to the source node is 4, 5, 6, 1, so the forward path would be 1, 6, 5, 4.

Figure 9.20 shows the state of `NodePQ` (empty) and the `MinCost` and `Parent` fields after they are all initialized.

The cost of the path from the source (1) to itself is zero, whereas so far the paths to each of the other nodes all have an infinite cost. The cost of the paths from the source (1) to its children (nodes 2, 3, and 6) may now be computed. These costs are merely the weights of the edges (1, 2), (1, 3), and (1, 6), respectively. Figure 9.21 shows the updated priority queue and `MinCost` and `Parent` fields (as in Figure 9.19, boldface arrows indicate edges that are involved in the minimal cost paths to the nodes thus far).

The priority queue item for node 2 is at the front of the queue, indicating that the final minimal cost to node 2 is now known. There can be no path from the source to node 2 less costly than 30 (the `MinCost` field value for node 2). If there *were* such a path, it would have to pass through either nodes 3 or 6, so the cost from the source to 3 or to 6 would have to be less than 30. The entire alternate path to node 2, in fact, would have to be less than 30. The costs from node 1 to node 3 and to node 6 are both greater than the cost from the source to node 2, so that alternate paths to 2 (if any) must be more costly than 30.

The front queue item, the item for node 2, is served next. Does node 2 provide a less costly route from the source to its child, node 3? Yes—the current cost from the source to node 3 is 60 (`MinCost` for node 3), whereas the path via node 2 is 50 (`MinCost` for node 2 plus the weight of the edge from node 2 to node 3). The `MinCost` field value for node 3 is therefore reduced to

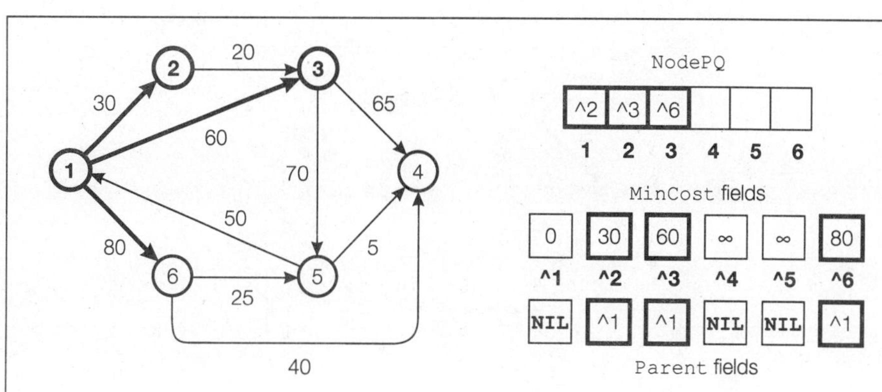

FIGURE 9.21 `NodePQ` **and** `MinCost` **and** `Parent` **Fields after Processing the Children of Node 1**

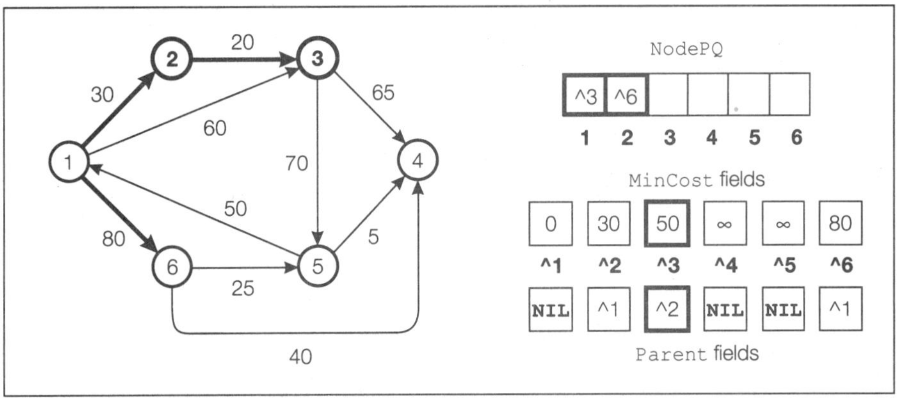

FIGURE 9.22 `NodePQ` and `MinCost` and `Parent` Fields after Processing the Children of Node 2

50, and node 2 is indicated as the parent of node 3. Figure 9.22 shows the updated priority queue and `MinCost` and `Parent` fields.

Recall that each priority queue item holds a lookup table node address and the current minimum cost (from the source) for that node. When the `MinCost` field for node 3 is reduced to 50, the priority queue item for node 3 must be updated as well. The `HeapIndx` field of each lookup table `NodeType` node contains the current array index in the `NodePQ` priority queue for that node. When an item is enqueued via a call to the `HeapInsert` primitive, `HeapInsert` calls the `AdjustUp` primitive to move the item up in the queue, as necessary. If the item is already in the priority queue and its current minimal cost has changed (as in the case of node 3), the `FindMCPaths` procedure just calls the `AdjustUp` procedure directly, in case the reduction in cost means that the item should be moved closer to the front of the queue.

Therefore, *two assignment statements must be added within* `AdjustUp` (which is nested within `FindMCPaths`) *to ensure that the* `HeapIndx` *field of each node is initialized and updated properly.* One relational operator must be switched as well, since a smaller cost represents a higher priority in the queue. Accordingly, two assignment statements must be added and two relational operators switched within procedure `AdjustDown`. Look ahead to the Appendix I representation of `FindMCPaths`, within which are nested the modified `AdjustUp` and `AdjustDown` procedures.

The front queue item—the item for node 3—is served next because its final minimum cost of 50 has been found; i.e., there is no path from the source to node 3 less costly than the path (1, 2, 3). Does node 3 provide a less costly route from the source to its children, nodes 4 and 5? Yes—the current cost from the source to both nodes is infinite, whereas the path (1, 2, 3, 4) has a cost of 50 plus 65, or 115, and the path (1, 2, 3, 5) has a cost of 50 plus 70, which is 120. The `MinCost` field value for node 4 is therefore reduced to 115, the `MinCost` field value for node 5 is reduced to 120, and node 3 is indicated as the parent of both in the `Parent` fields of nodes 4 and 5. Figure 9.23 shows the updated priority queue and `MinCost` and `Parent` fields.

The front queue item, the item for node 6, may now be served. Node 6 does not provide a less costly route to node 4, but it does provide one to node 5.

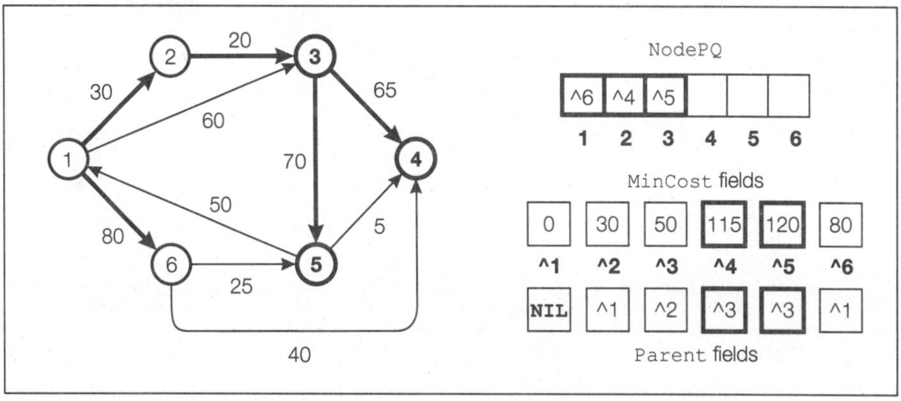

FIGURE 9.23 `NodePQ` **and the** `MinCost` **and** `Parent` **Fields after Processing the Children of Node 3**

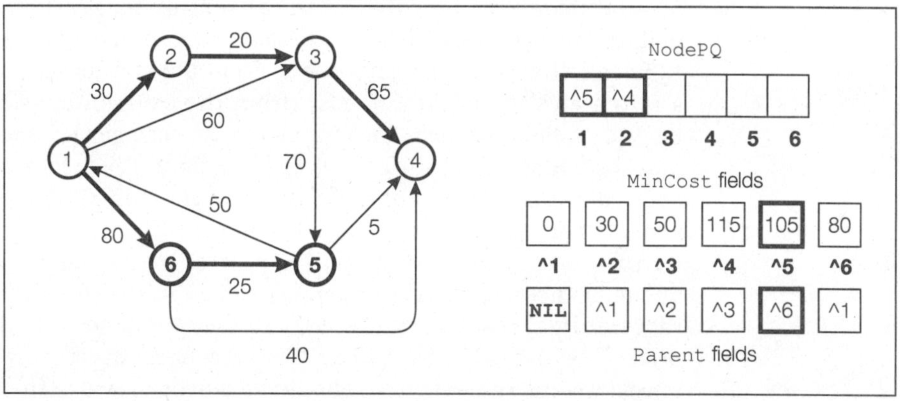

FIGURE 9.24 `NodePQ` **and the** `MinCost` **and** `Parent` **Fields after Processing the Children of Node 6**

The current cost of the path from the source to node 5 is 120, whereas the path (1, 6, 5) has a cost of 80 plus 25, or 105. Figure 9.24 shows the updated priority queue and `MinCost` and `Parent` fields.

The front queue item, the item for node 5, is served next. Node 5 does not provide a less costly route from the source (node 1) to itself, although a path via node 5 does exist (the current cost of the path from the source back to itself is zero, whereas the path via node 5 is 105 plus 50, or 155). Node 5 *does* provide a less costly route from the source to node 4, however. The current cost to node 4 is 115, whereas the path via node 5 is 105 plus 5, or 110. Figure 9.25 shows the updated priority queue and `MinCost` and `Parent` fields.

The remaining queue item—the item for node 4—is now served. Node 4 does not have any children and therefore cannot provide a less costly route to any other node. The emptiness of the priority queue signals the conclusion of the algorithm. Figure 9.26 traces all changes made to `NodePQ` and to the `MinCost` and `Parent` fields as `FindMCPaths` finds all minimal-cost paths from node 1 (the source node) in the sample graph.

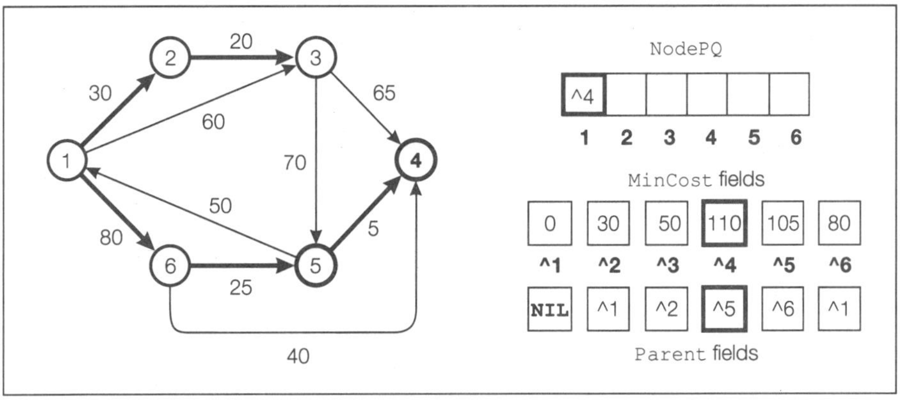

FIGURE 9.25 `NodePQ` and the `MinCost` and `Parent` Fields after Processing the Children of Node 5

At this time, examine the following routine in Appendix I.

```
PROCEDURE FindMCPaths ( VAR Graph : GraphType; Source : NodePtr;
                        VAR FoundPathsToAllNodes : Boolean );
```

Building a Minimal-Cost Spanning Tree

A spanning tree is an undirected, nonoriented tree representation of an undirected graph, consisting of *all nodes* of the graph but *only those edges necessary to connect the nodes*. This means that certain graph edges are omitted, so a variety of different spanning trees may be possible for a given graph.

A spanning tree can be constructed from a graph while performing either a depth-first or breadth-first traversal of the graph, producing either a **depth-first spanning tree** or a **breadth-first spanning tree**, respectively. During these traversals, each node is processed by inserting it into the tree, along with the edge that was followed to reach it. Figure 9.27 depicts a simple graph along with depth-first and breadth-first spanning trees. In constructing the trees shown in this figure, both traversals began by visiting and processing node 1 and then visiting and processing the other nodes in the order 2, 3, 4, 5, 6:

A minimal-cost spanning (MCS) tree has the *lowest total edge cost* of all possible spanning trees for a particular graph. This structure is particularly important for any networking application in which a common channel is used to service many end-user devices. For example, all rooms in a small college dormitory might have a common channel for water (pipes), for electricity (wiring), and for forced-air heat (air ducts). Many end-user devices will tap into these channels: Water devices include bathroom faucets and showers, electrical devices include outlets and lights, and heat devices include heat vents. These electrical, water, and heating systems can be represented using graphs, with each end-user device as a single node and all such nodes connected by undirected edges.

To minimize the total length of the pipe, wiring, or heating ducts used in the installation of these channels, a minimal-cost spanning tree could

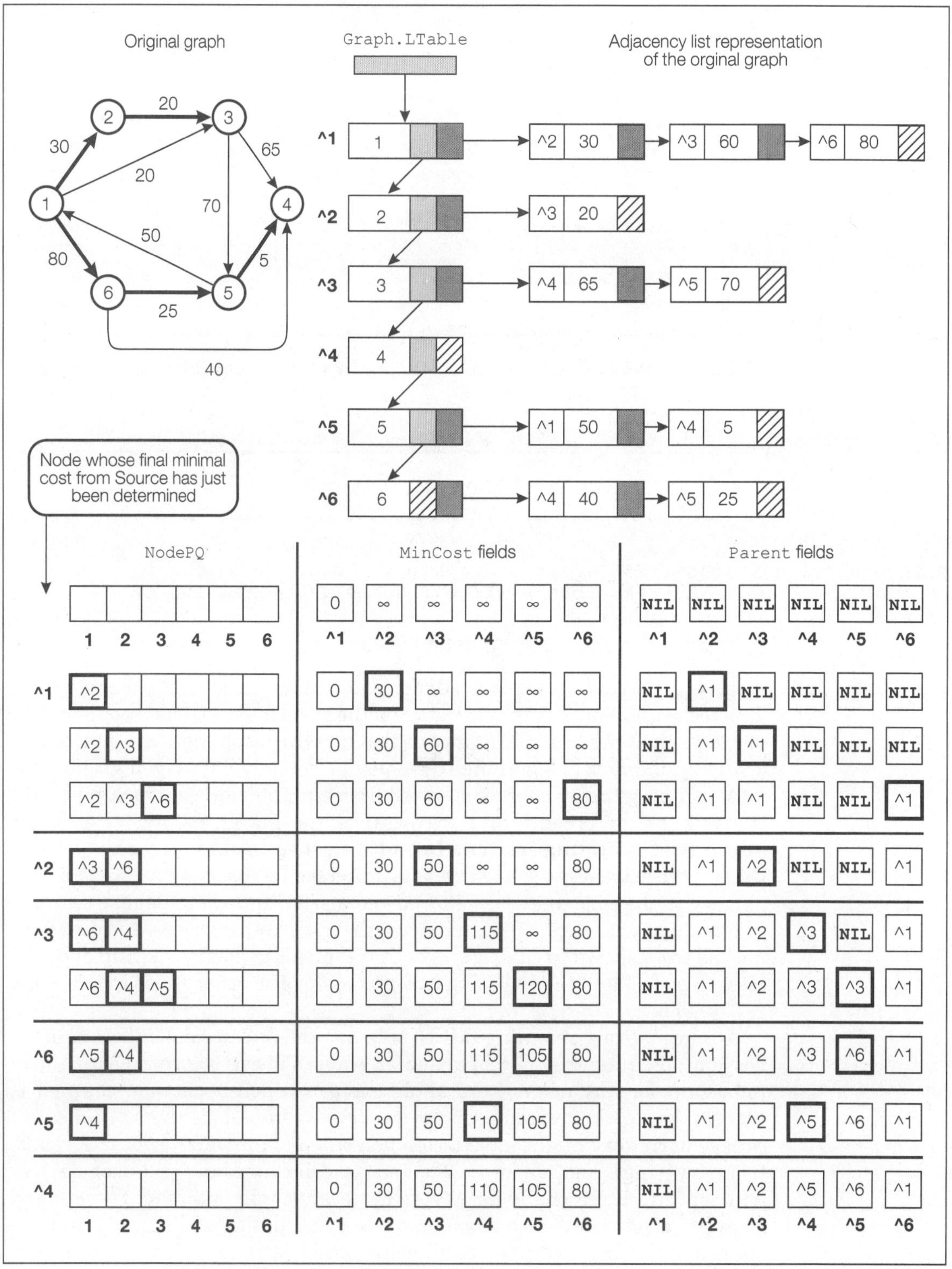

FIGURE 9.26 Applying `FindMCPaths` to Find the Minimal-Cost Paths from Node 1

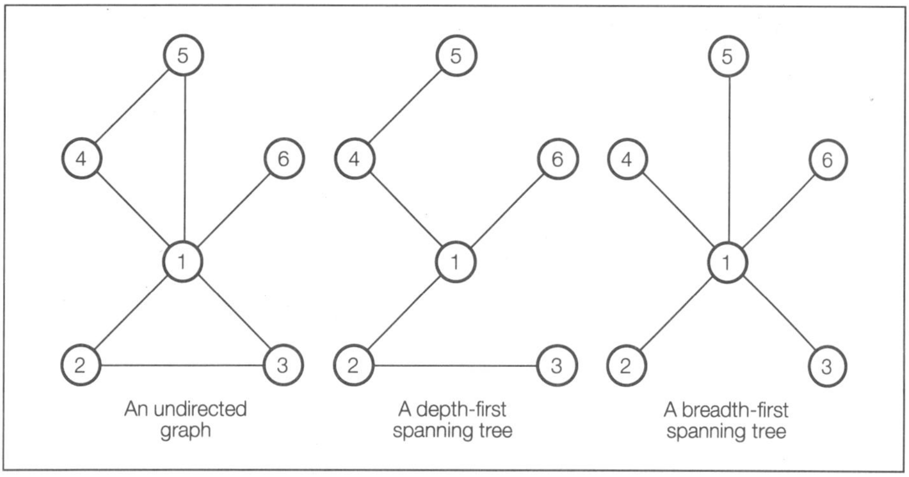

FIGURE 9.27 A Graph and Two of Its Many Possible Spanning Trees, Inserting 1, 2, 3, 4, 5, 6

be devised for each system. (Of course, other factors in the installation of these systems, such as the placement of walls, must be considered as well.) Minimal-cost spanning trees are especially important for communication systems that stretch over great distances, such as a network of computer workstations that access a central computer via a common data line (a *bus*) or a system of telephone lines for many homes and offices feeding into a single switching station. Figure 9.28 shows a sample undirected, weighted graph and two possible minimal-cost spanning trees whose total costs are both 115; i.e., it is not possible to construct any other spanning trees in which the sum of all edges is less than 115.

It may at first seem that simply applying our `FindMCPaths` version of Dijkstra's algorithm would be sufficient to construct an MCS tree, but this is not necessarily true. The rightmost diagram of Figure 9.28 depicts a tree containing all minimal-cost paths from node 1. The total cost of this span-

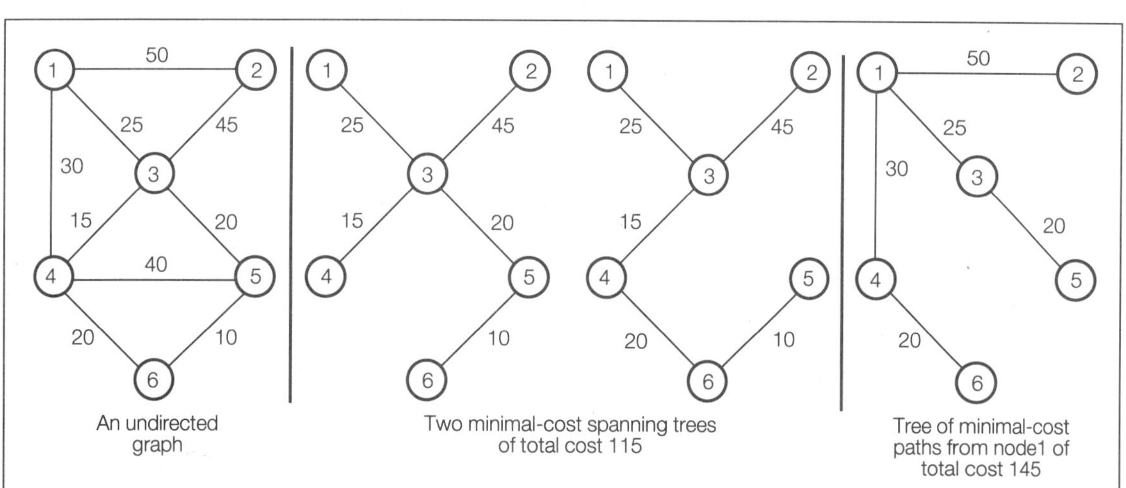

FIGURE 9.28 A Sample Weighted Graph, Two Possible MCS Trees, and a Tree of Minimal-Cost Paths

ning tree is 145, which is 30 more than the total cost of an MCS tree. This approach fails because, rather than simply minimizing the cost between each node and a particular node that has been designated as the source, *in constructing an MCS tree we must minimize the cost between each node and the MCS tree as a whole.*

Two famous algorithms have been developed for constructing an MCS tree from an undirected graph. In **Kruskal's algorithm**, proposed by J. Kruskal in 1956, an *edge* is selected from the original graph for inclusion in the growing MCS tree if both of the following are true:

- The edge has the lowest weight of all edges not yet considered for inclusion.
- Inclusion of the edge in the MCS tree does not produce a cycle.

Edges are selected and included in the tree until all nodes have been added to the MCS tree (success), or else not all nodes are included because their costs to the tree remain infinite (failure—the original graph is not connected).

In **Prim's algorithm**, independently proposed in 1956 by R. Prim, a *node* is selected from the original graph for inclusion in the growing MCS tree if the following is true:

- The node can be connected to the tree at the smallest cost of all nodes not yet in the tree.

Nodes are selected and included in the tree until all nodes are connected to the MCS tree (success), or else not all nodes are connected to the MCS tree because their costs to the tree remain infinite (failure—the original graph is not connected). This approach is actually very similar to that taken in Dijkstra's algorithm:

- *Dijkstra's algorithm.* Select a node (for inclusion in the set of nodes whose minimal cost has been determined) whose *cost from the source* is a minimum among all nodes not yet part of this set.
- *Prim's algorithm.* Select a node (for inclusion in the growing MCS tree) whose *cost from the tree* is a minimum, among all nodes not yet connected to the tree.

In this section we will devise an algorithm named `BuildMCSTree`, based on Prim's algorithm. Prim's algorithm is chosen over Kruskal's algorithm for two reasons: First, the concept and resulting Pascal representation are nearly identical to those for the `FindMCPaths` algorithm devised earlier in this section. Second, the Pascal representation of Prim's algorithm is somewhat simpler than that of Kruskal's algorithm, requiring fewer supporting data structures and a smaller heap structure (of `MaxNode` items rather than of `MaxEdge` items). To examine how the algorithm works, we will use the small directed graph shown in Figure 9.29. (Again, nonstandard caret notation is used to indicate heapspace `NodeType` addresses; e.g., ^4 represents the address of the fourth node of the graph.)

As with `FindMCPaths`, `BuildMCSTree` requires a priority queue named `NodePQ`, but the items in this structure will serve a slightly different purpose:

```
NodePQ : HeapType;  {Priority queue of nodes currently being considered for
                     connection to the tree; the next item removed is the
                     node with the smallest cost of connecting that node to
                     the tree}
```

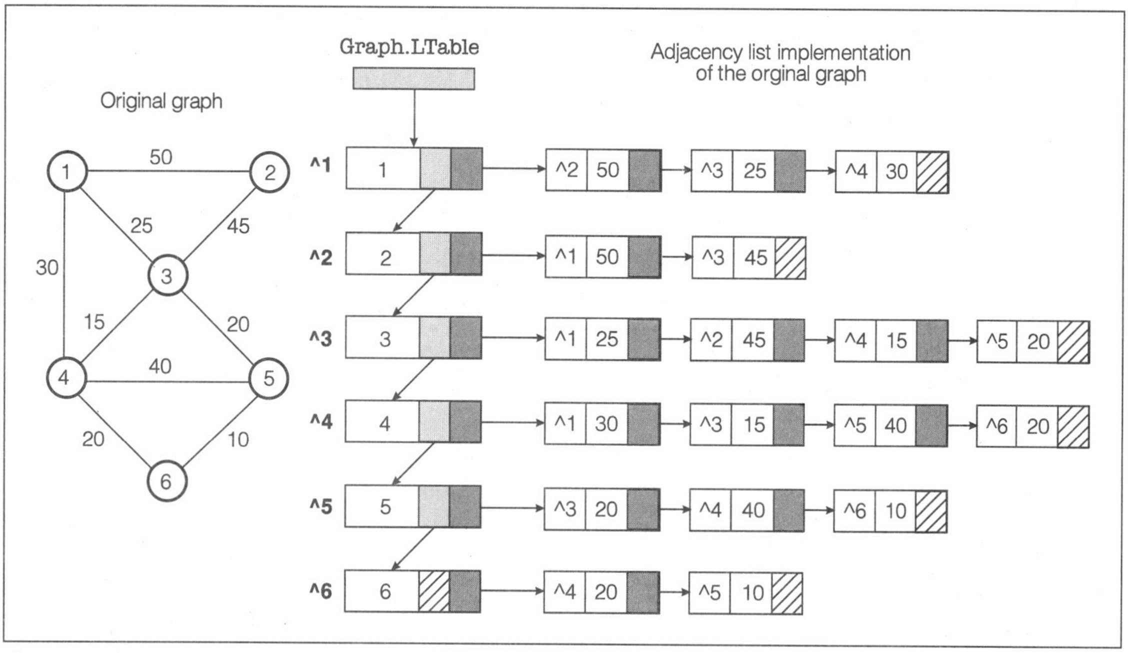

FIGURE 9.29 The Sample Undirected Graph and Its Adjacency List Representation

Each `NodePQ` item is, again, of type `InfoType` (as declared in Section 9.1 and in Appendix I), but the `Key` field of each will now contain the current minimum cost from its associated node to the growing MCS tree. Again, an additional assignment statement must be included as the last executable statement in the `AdjustUp` heap primitive, as described in Pascal representation of `BuildMCSTree` in Appendix I (all heap primitive routines appear in Appendix H).

As with the `FindMCPaths` algorithm, three fields of each `NodeType` (`P^`) node—`P^.MinCost`, `P^.HeapIndx`, and `P^.Parent`—also play important roles in the process of building an MCS tree. The only change for the `BuildMCSTree` algorithm is that *the* `MinCost` *field will contain the current minimal cost of connecting its associated node to the MCS tree* ("connection cost") rather than containing the minimal cost from some source node.

In the process of building an MCS tree, each `P^` node may exist in one of three states (with the exception of the source node with which the tree-building commences) and is never enqueued within `NodePQ`:

• No connection cost determined:	• A connection cost determined:	• Minimal connection cost determined:
`P^` not yet enqueued in `NodePQ`	`P^` currently in `NodePQ`	`P^` already served from `NodePQ`
`P^.MinCost` $= \infty$	$0 <$ `P^.MinCost` $< \infty$	$0 \leq$ `P^.MinCost` $< \infty$

The source node is automatically included in the tree. Every other node is included when it is served from the priority queue, and its `MinCost` value is assigned a zero value.

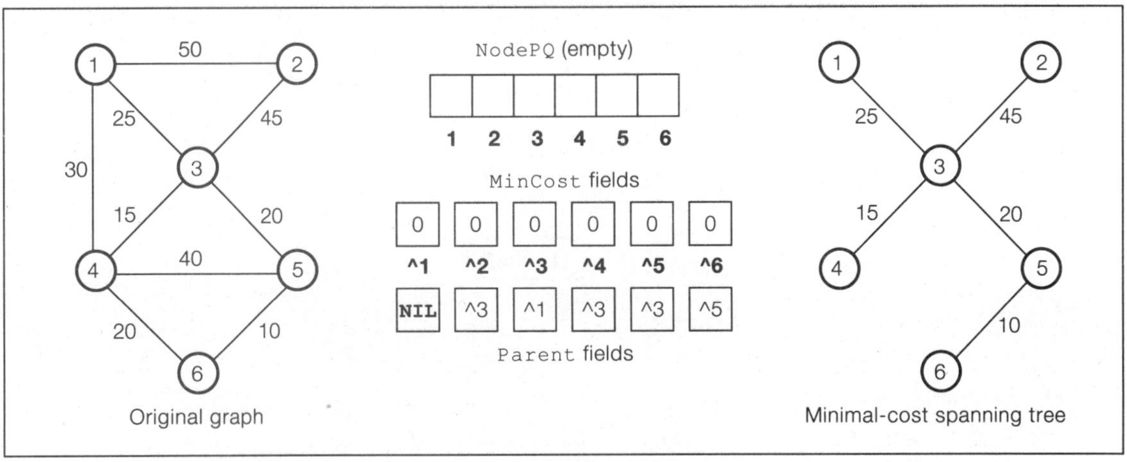

FIGURE 9.30 **`NodePQ` and the `MinCost` and `Parent` Fields, Initially**

To understand better the roles of the `MinCost` and `Parent` fields, let us examine their final states after `BuildMCSTree` has already built the MCS tree, starting with node 1. Figure 9.30 shows the final states of the `NodePQ` priority queue and all `MinCost` and `Parent` fields.

The final MCS tree is implied by the collective values of the `Parent` fields. In Figure 9.30, the collective `Parent` field values imply the MCS tree represented by the right tree diagram. The algorithm for converting this collection of values to an adjacency list or adjacency matrix representation is left as an exercise.

`BuildMCSTree` begins by regarding the first node of the original graph (node 1) as the sole node in the MCS tree. The cost of connecting node 1 to the tree is therefore zero, and each of the other nodes has an infinite connection cost thus far. The connection cost for each of the children of 1—nodes 2, 3, and 4—may now be computed; these costs are merely the weights of the edges (1, 2), (1, 3), and (1, 4), respectively. Figure 9.31 shows the original

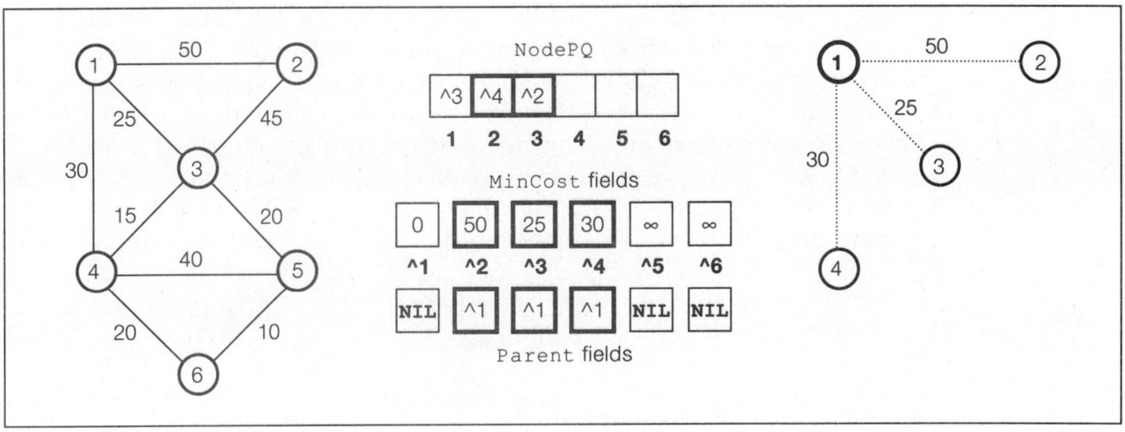

FIGURE 9.31 **`NodePQ` and the `MinCost` and `Parent` Fields after Processing the Children of Node 1**

graph, the updated priority queue and `MinCost` and `Parent` field values, and the budding MCS tree; only node 1 is included thus far. (In these MCS tree diagrams, a solid line indicates connections of nodes to the tree; a jagged line indicates potential connections):

The priority queue item for node 3 is at the front of the queue, indicating that the edge connecting node 3 to the existing tree at minimal cost is now known—namely, the edge with weight 25. The queue item for node 3 may now be served, and the tree grows to two nodes: nodes 1 and 3. The `MinCost` field for node 3 is assigned a zero value to indicate that it is now in the tree and to preclude adding any edge later that may produce a cycle. After all children of node 3 are processed, any edges to 3 from other nodes, such as (4, 1), will be ignored because the cost of connecting node 3 to the tree will already be at an absolute minimum—zero. Therefore, no other edge can provide a less costly connection.

Is there an edge between node 3 and any other node that is not yet in the tree (nodes 2, 4, 5, and 6) and provides a connection to the tree at a lower cost than the current (`MinCost`) connection cost? Yes; the current connection cost from node 2 is 50, whereas the edge (2, 3) has a weight of 45. Similarly, the current connection cost from node 4 can be reduced from 30 to 15, the weight of edge (3, 4), and the current connection cost from node 5 can be reduced from infinity to 20, the weight of edge (3, 5). Figure 9.32 shows the original graph, the updated priority queue and `MinCost` and `Parent` field values, and the tree thus far.

The front queue item, the item for node 4, is served next, since its final minimum connection cost of 15 has been found. (Had the edge (3, 5) been 10 instead of 20, the front queue item would have been an item for node 5 rather than for node 4.) Is there an edge between node 4 and any other node not yet in the tree (which currently consists of nodes 2, 5, and 6) that provides a connection to the tree at a lower cost than the current connection? Yes; the current connection cost from node 6 is infinite, whereas the edge (4, 6) is 20. The edges (4, 1) and (4, 5) do not reduce the connection costs of nodes 1 and 5 to the MCS tree. Figure 9.33 shows the original graph, the updated priority queue and `MinCost` and `Parent` field values, and the MCS tree thus far (again indicated with solid-line edges).

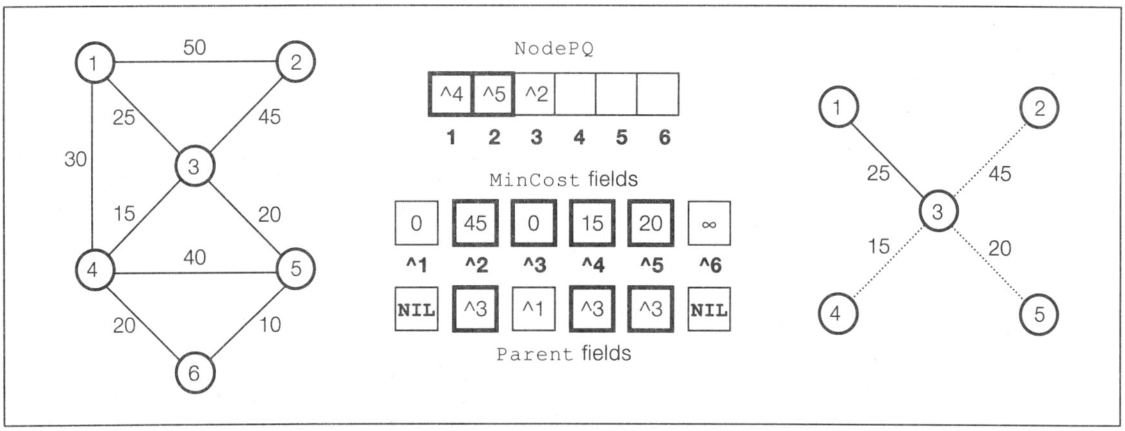

FIGURE 9.32 **`NodePQ` and `MinCost` and `Parent` Fields after Processing the Children of Node 3**

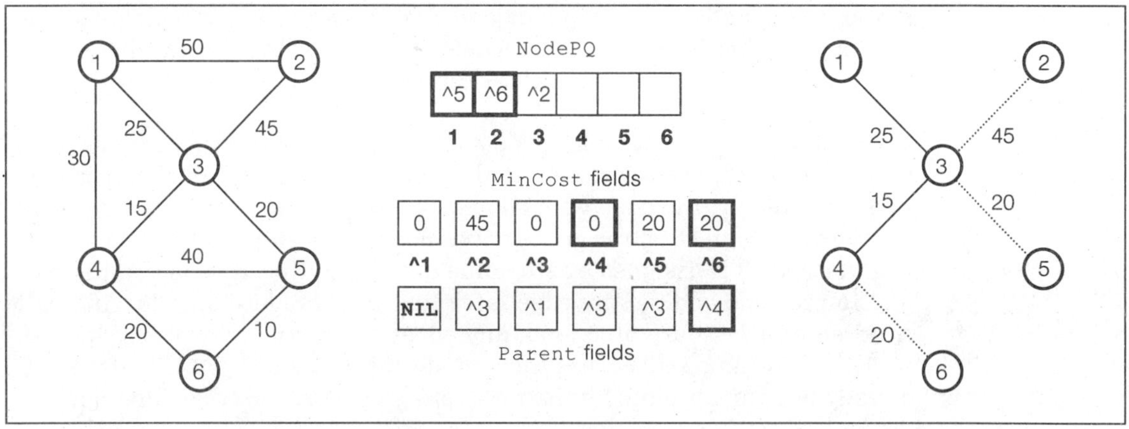

FIGURE 9.33 `NodePQ` **and** `MinCost` **and** `Parent` **Fields after Processing the Children of Node 4**

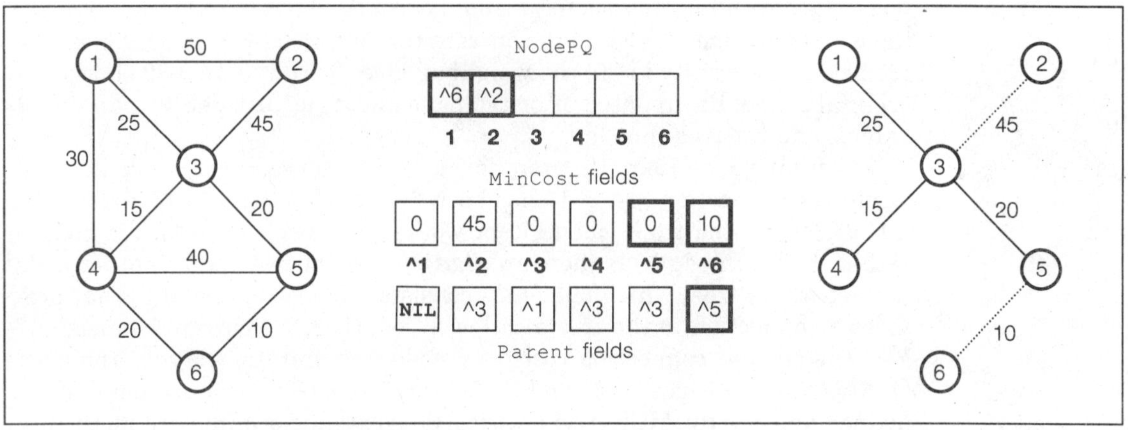

FIGURE 9.34 `NodePQ` **and** `MinCost` **and** `Parent` **Fields after Processing the Children of Node 5**

The front queue item, the item for node 5, may now be served. Node 5 provides a less costly connection for node 6. The current cost of connecting node 6 to the tree is 20, whereas the edge (5, 6) provides a connection cost of 10. Figure 9.34 shows the original graph, the updated priority queue and the `MinCost` and `Parent` field values, and the tree thus far.

The front queue item, the item for node 6, is served next. Node 6 does not provide a less costly connection for node 2, the only other node not yet connected to the tree. The final queue item, the item for node 2, is then served, and the algorithm concludes because the queue is empty. Node 2 is connected to the tree at a minimum cost of 45.

Figure 9.35 traces all changes made to the `NodePQ` priority queue and to the `MinCost` and `Parent` fields as `BuildMCSTree` builds an MCS tree, starting with node 1.

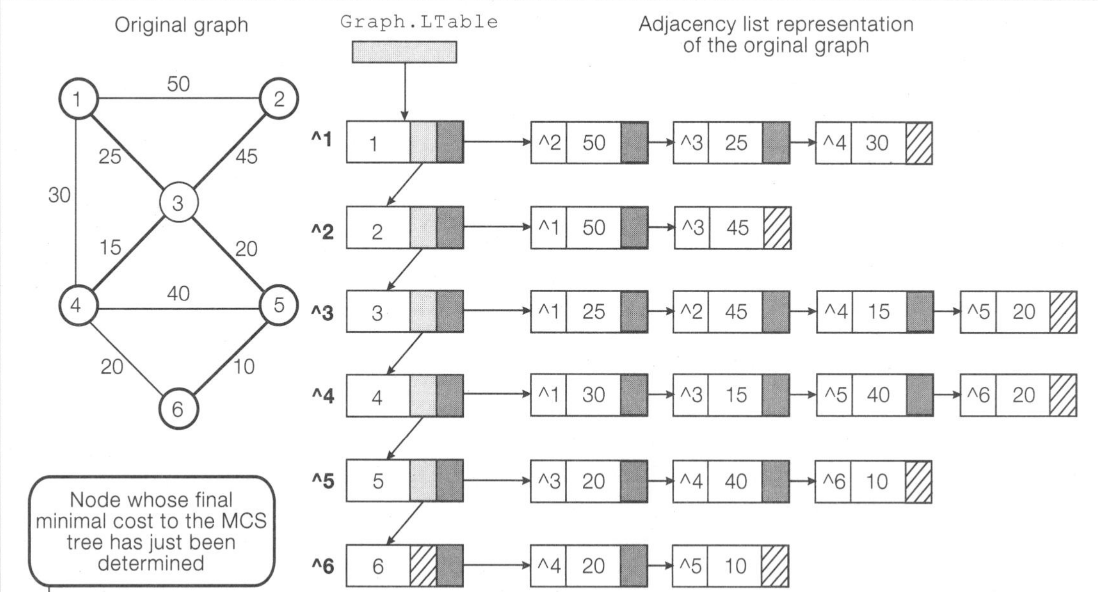

	NodePQ 1	2	3	4	5	6	MinCost fields ^1	^2	^3	^4	^5	^6	Parent fields ^1	^2	^3	^4	^5	^6
							∞	∞	∞	∞	∞	∞	NIL	NIL	NIL	NIL	NIL	NIL
^1	^2						0	50	∞	∞	∞	∞	NIL	^1	NIL	NIL	NIL	NIL
	^3	^2					0	50	25	∞	∞	∞	NIL	^1	^1	NIL	NIL	NIL
	^3	^4	^2				0	50	25	30	∞	∞	NIL	^1	^1	^1	NIL	NIL
^3	^4	^2					0	45	0	30	∞	∞	NIL	^3	^1	^1	NIL	NIL
	^4	^2					0	45	0	15	∞	∞	NIL	^3	^1	^3	NIL	NIL
	^4	^5	^2				0	45	0	15	20	∞	NIL	^3	^1	^3	^3	NIL
^4	^5	^6	^2				0	45	0	0	20	20	NIL	^3	^1	^3	^3	^4
^5	^6	^2					0	45	0	0	0	10	NIL	^3	^1	^3	^3	^5
^6	^2						0	45	0	0	0	0	NIL	^3	^1	^3	^3	^5
^2							0	0	0	0	0	0	NIL	^3	^1	^3	^3	^5

FIGURE 9.35 Applying the BuildMCSTree Algorithm, Starting at Node 1

At this time, examine the following routine in Appendix I:

```
PROCEDURE BuildMCSTree ( VAR Graph : GraphType; Source : NodePtr;
                         VAR AllNodesIncluded : Boolean);
```

Maximizing Network Flow

Weighted graphs are useful for representing networks in which any quantity (computer data, electric power, water, public transportation, telephone signals, etc.) flows from a single source (the source node), through the network to a particular end-user (the **sink** node). In this section we will examine how to represent such a network using a directed, weighted graph, and devise a procedure based on the **Ford-Fulkerson algorithm** to *maximize the total rate of flow* from the source to the sink nodes, by controlling the flow levels along the paths.

APPLICATION 9.1

Simulation of an Aqueduct System for Lost Wages, Nevada

As an example of a flow-maximization problem, we will model an aqueduct system that supplies water from Lake Yahoo to the desert town of Lost Wages, Nevada, some 350 miles away. The water is transported through a network of pipes and pumping stations, as depicted in Figure 9.36, in which node 1 is the source and node 7 is the sink. We can represent the entire aqueduct system as a weighted, directed graph in which the following are true:

- Each node represents a pumping station and is identified by a unique integer.
- Each edge represents a pipe with a fixed *capacity,* in hundreds of gallons of water per minute. Each pipe is also described in terms of its *current flow*—i.e., how much water per minute is actually flowing through the pipe at present. In the figures in this section, these weights are described using pairs of integers (current flow, capacity); e.g., (0, 5) means zero water flow through a pipe capable of carrying 500 gallons per minute.

Whereas pipe capacities are fixed, the current flows are controlled by the pumping stations. Figure 9.36 depicts one of many possible configurations of current flows (this particular configuration produces a total water flow of 1200 gallons per minute).

The total rate of 1200 gallons per minute can be improved by reconfiguring the current flows, however. Figure 9.37 depicts a slightly different configuration of current flows, producing an improved total rate of 1600 gallons per minute. This is the greatest rate possible, since the three incoming edges to the sink node are at maximum flow. Notice that this optimal flow is *not* found by simply pumping the maximum possible rate (1800 gallons per minute) from the source node.

In this application, we will design a procedure named `MaximizeFlow` to *maximize* the total rate of water flow from the lake to the town by calculating the appropriate flow levels for each pipe. Upon return from a call to

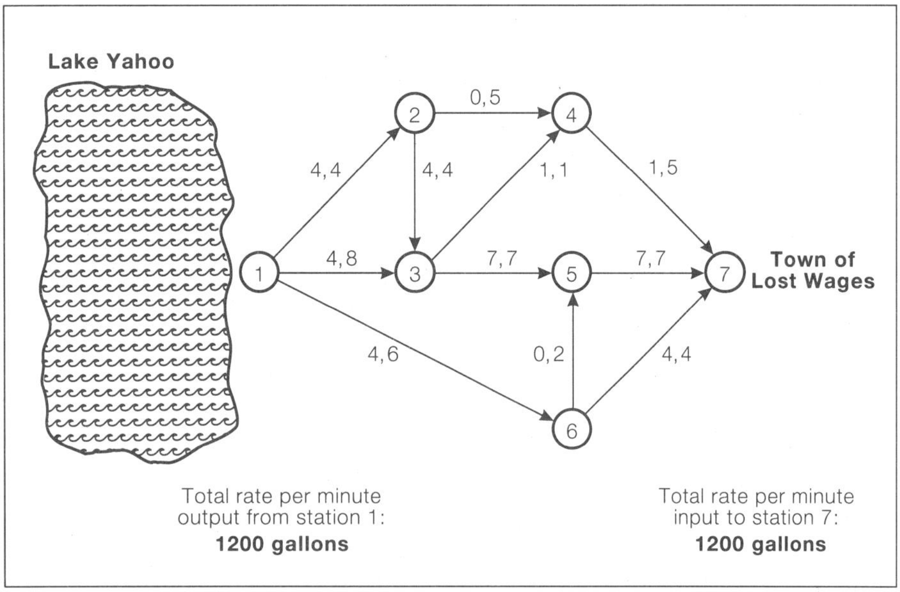

FIGURE 9.36 One Configuration of Capacity and Current Flows in the Aqueduct System

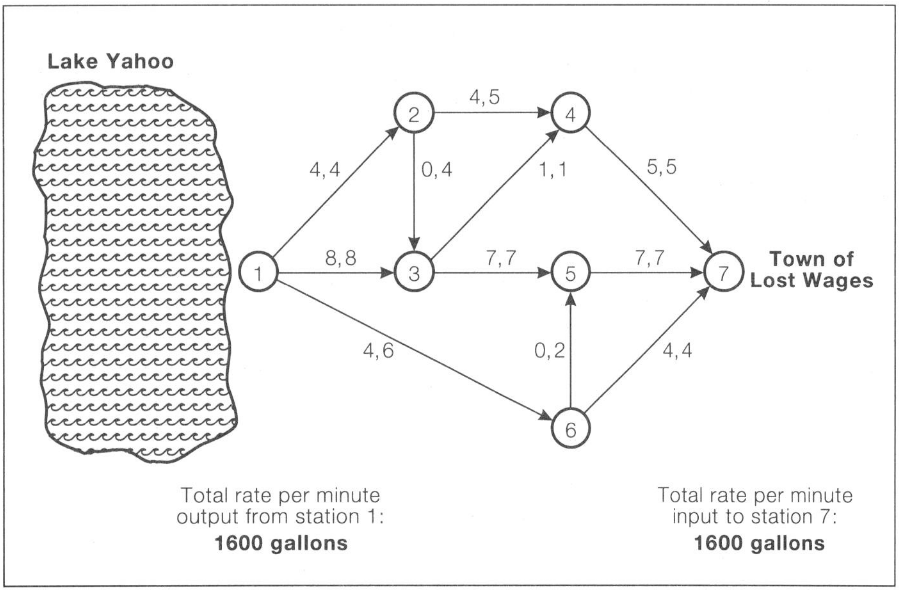

FIGURE 9.37 An Improved Configuration of Current Flows (a Complete Maximization)

`MaximizeFlow`, the program can display the capacity and current flow of each pipe. In our design, we will assume that no water is lost or consumed between source station and sink station, that the lake provides an "infinite" quantity of water, and that the town uses all water pumped into station 7. This implies that the total output from any station equals the input to that station and the total water pumped from the lake equals the total input into the town.

We will further assume that the current flow of water pumped into each pipe by a station may be varied (by that station) from zero flow to the capacity of that pipe. Therefore, for each pipe P, the following holds true:

$$0 \leq (P_{flow}) \leq (P_{capacity})$$

Also, a special valve in each station ensures that water always flows in only one direction, as indicated by the arrows in the figures. Finally, we will assume that the total pumping capacity of each pumping station exceeds the total capacity of all pipes leading into it; i.e., the pumps themselves do not impose a limiting factor.

Also important are the concepts of positive flow and negative flow:

- There is a **positive flow** from station X to station Y if water is flowing *from station X to station Y*—i.e., if flow > 0 in the pipe from station X to station Y.
- There is a **negative flow** from station X to station Y if water is flowing *from station Y to station X*—i.e., if flow > 0 in the pipe from station Y to station X.

Negative flow is an abstract concept that will prove useful in maximizing the total flow, as we shall see. Figure 9.37 shows a positive flow of 4 from station 1 to station 6, a negative flow of 4 from station 6 to station 1, and a zero flow from station 6 to station 5.

We will begin with a simple, preliminary maximization but may find that additional steps must be taken to produce a complete maximization. Figure 9.36 shows the flow values resulting from a preliminary optimization and Figure 9.37 shows the flow values resulting from a complete maximization. (Although our single procedure—`MaximizeFlow`, given later in this section—will encompass both maximization techniques, we will examine each technique individually.) A pseudocode algorithm for the preliminary maximization follows:

```
ALGORITHM PreliminaryOptimization ( VAR Graph : GraphType );

BEGIN
Set the flow of every pipe to 0;
REPEAT

  Find a path from the source node to the sink node in which, for each
  edge, (capacity - flow) > 0 while (a) remembering the smallest
  difference between capacity and flow in the path, and (b) marking each
  node as having been visited;

  IF the sink node is reached THEN
    Return to the source node by following the path backward, increasing
    the flow in each pipe by the smallest difference found in the path,
    and marking each node as unvisited

UNTIL there are no more such paths to the sink node
END;
```

Figure 9.38 shows the steps taken in the preliminary optimization of the aqueduct system, resulting in the current flows shown in Figure 9.36. The adjacency matrix implementation of the graph is used because there will

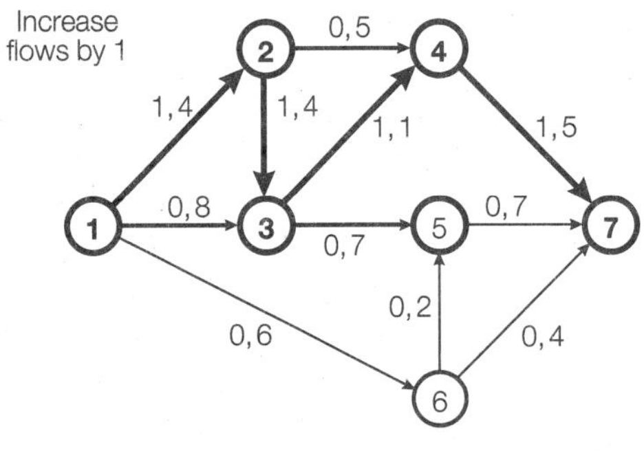

	1	2	3	4	5	6	7
1	0,0	1,4	0,8	0,0	0,0	0,6	0,0
2	0,0	0,0	1,4	0,5	0,0	0,0	0,0
3	0,0	0,0	0,0	1,1	0,7	0,0	0,0
4	0,0	0,0	0,0	0,0	0,0	0,0	1,5
5	0,0	0,0	0,0	0,0	0,0	0,0	0,7
6	0,0	0,0	0,0	0,0	0,2	0,0	0,4
7	0,0	0,0	0,0	0,0	0,0	0,0	0,0

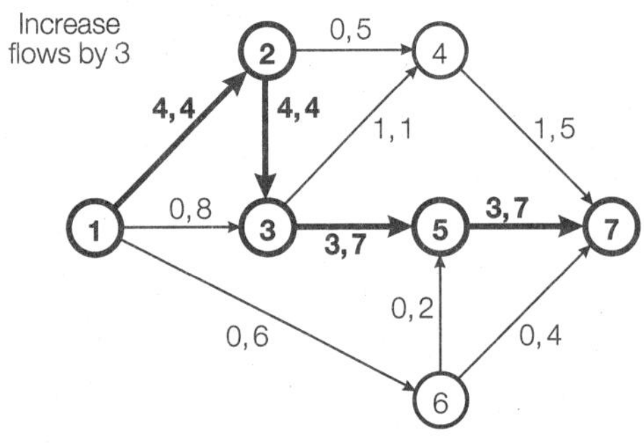

	1	2	3	4	5	6	7
1	0,0	**4,4**	0,8	0,0	0,0	0,6	0,0
2	0,0	0,0	**4,4**	0,5	0,0	0,0	0,0
3	0,0	0,0	0,0	1,1	**3,7**	0,0	0,0
4	0,0	0,0	0,0	0,0	0,0	0,0	1,5
5	0,0	0,0	0,0	0,0	0,0	0,0	**3,7**
6	0,0	0,0	0,0	0,0	0,2	0,0	0,4
7	0,0	0,0	0,0	0,0	0,0	0,0	0,0

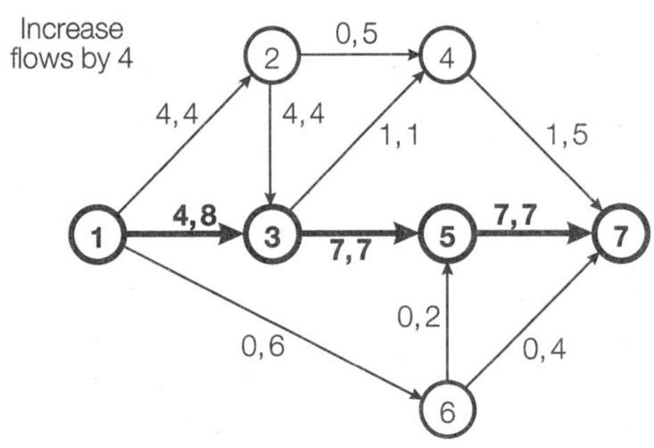

	1	2	3	4	5	6	7
1	0,0	4,4	**4,8**	0,0	0,0	0,6	0,0
2	0,0	0,0	4,4	0,5	0,0	0,0	0,0
3	0,0	0,0	0,0	1,1	**7,7**	0,0	0,0
4	0,0	0,0	0,0	0,0	0,0	0,0	1,5
5	0,0	0,0	0,0	0,0	0,0	0,0	**7,7**
6	0,0	0,0	0,0	0,0	0,2	0,0	0,4
7	0,0	0,0	0,0	0,0	0,0	0,0	0,0

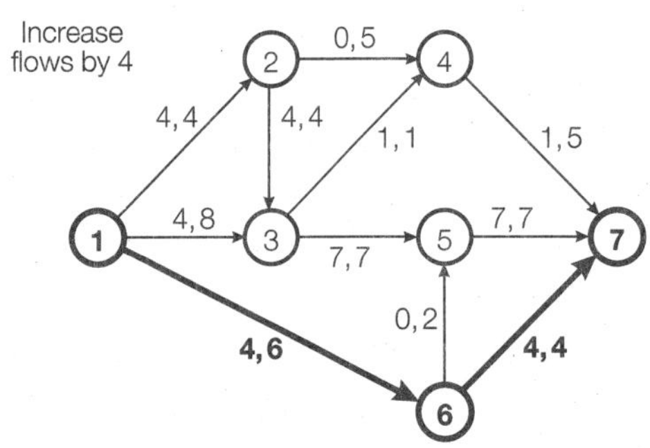

	1	2	3	4	5	6	7
1	0,0	4,4	4,8	0,0	0,0	**4,6**	0,0
2	0,0	0,0	4,4	0,5	0,0	0,0	0,0
3	0,0	0,0	0,0	1,1	7,7	0,0	0,0
4	0,0	0,0	0,0	0,0	0,0	0,0	1,5
5	0,0	0,0	0,0	0,0	0,0	0,0	7,7
6	0,0	0,0	0,0	0,0	0,2	0,0	**4,4**
7	0,0	0,0	0,0	0,0	0,0	0,0	0,0

FIGURE 9.38 Performing a Preliminary Maximization of the Aqueduct System

probably be few insertions or deletions of nodes in this application. It is also used because complete maximization also requires quick access to the parent node of any child node (as we shall see shortly), information not provided readily by an adjacency list representation. A depth-first searching strategy is employed to find each path from the source to the sink. In Figure 9.38, the current path is indicated in boldface and a nonzero capacity value indicates the presence of a pipe.

The preliminary maximization is complete when the algorithm cannot find another path from the source node to the target node in which the current flow is less than the capacity for each edge in the path. In the final diagram of Figure 9.38, edge (1, 2) cannot be followed, since the current flow equals the capacity. Similarly, the path (1, 3) cannot continue to nodes 4 or 5, and the paths (1, 6, 5) and (1, 6) cannot continue to node 7. Study the diagram to convince yourself that *given the strategy of the preliminary maximization,* the total flow of 1200 gallons per minute cannot be improved upon.

As Figure 9.37 has clearly illustrated, however, a reconfiguration of the flows *may* yield an even greater total rate of flow. The *secondary maximization* technique is similar to the primary maximization technique, except that, when it is not possible to advance from the current node because each outgoing edge has flow equal to capacity, an edge with a *negative flow* may be followed to continue the path. A negative flow from a child node to a parent node is indicated if `Graph.Matrix [Parent, Child].Flow` is greater than zero. Flows are subsequently altered in the path as follows:

> Upon returning from the sink to the source, *all positive flows are raised* and *all negative flows are lowered* by the *smaller* of the following values found along the path:
>
> - Smallest positive flow among all positive flows
> - Smallest negative flow among all negative flows

Figure 9.39 traces the steps taken when the complete maximization process is continued where the preliminary maximization process leaves off; i.e., it begins with the last configuration of Figure 9.38 and produces the configuration of Figure 9.37. The maximizing algorithm concludes when it is blocked from reaching the sink node because it encounters only positive-flow edges with flow equal to capacity, even considering negative flows. Changes to the graph are indicated with boldface lines.

Why does manipulating negative flows help to produce a complete maximization? The positive edges identified form part of a path along which flow can be increased. The node at which negative and positive links join is a place where part of the flow can be switched to go in another direction. The changes at node 2 mean that water entering the pumping station via edge (1, 2) now leaves the station via edge (2, 4) rather than edge (2, 3). The changes at node 3 mean that the water will be supplied by pipe (1, 3) rather than pipe (2, 3), but the same amount of water will arrive at node 3 and will satisfy the flows leaving node 3.

Each time the algorithm seeks a path from the source to the sink, it marks each node as visited to avoid being trapped in a cycle, as in any graph traversal–path-finding process. During the backtracking from the sink back to the source, the `Visited` field of each visited node in the path is reassigned a false value. Note that cycles are potential problems in following

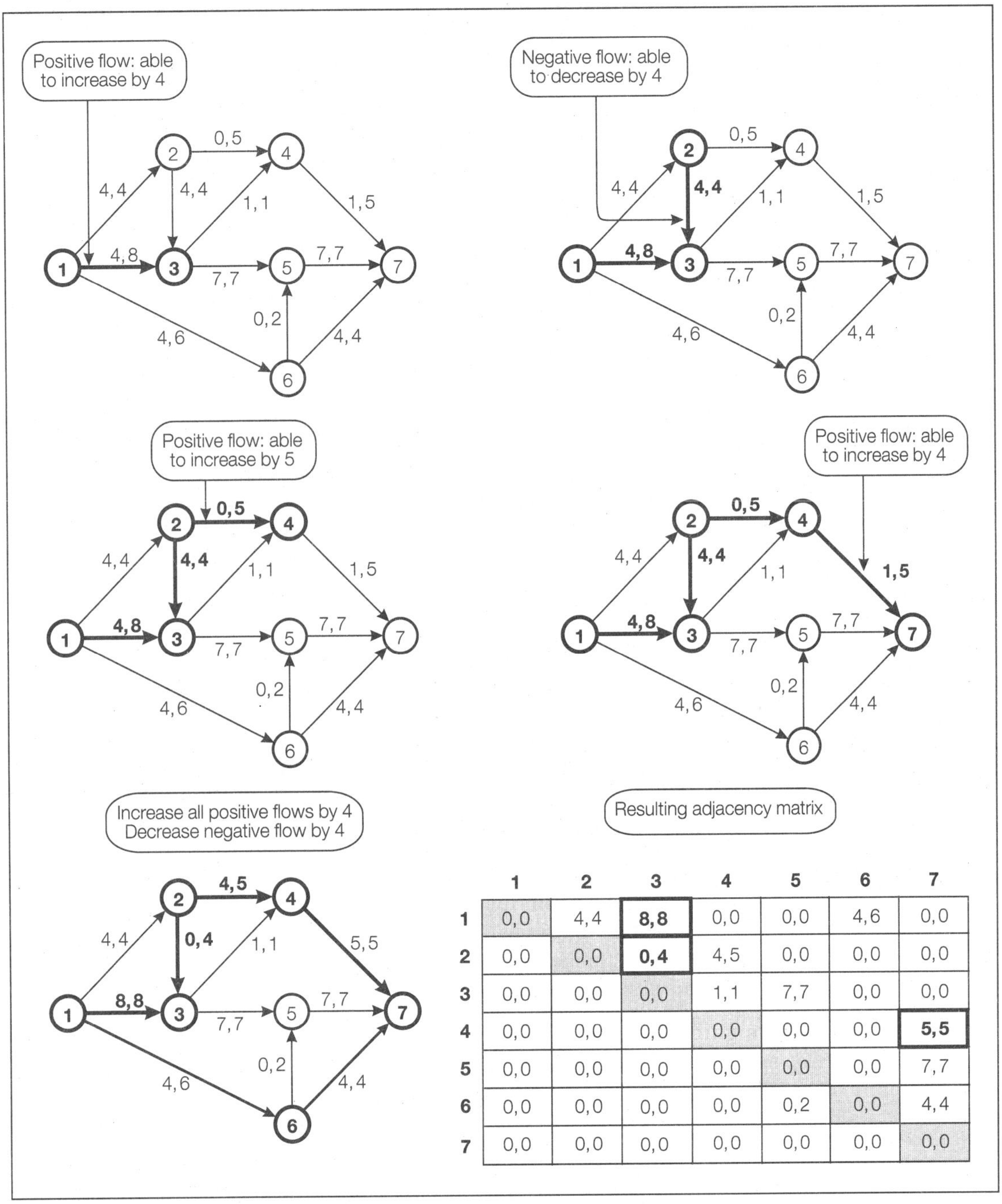

	1	2	3	4	5	6	7
1	0,0	4,4	**8,8**	0,0	0,0	4,6	0,0
2	0,0	0,0	**0,4**	4,5	0,0	0,0	0,0
3	0,0	0,0	0,0	1,1	7,7	0,0	0,0
4	0,0	0,0	0,0	0,0	0,0	0,0	**5,5**
5	0,0	0,0	0,0	0,0	0,0	0,0	7,7
6	0,0	0,0	0,0	0,0	0,2	0,0	4,4
7	0,0	0,0	0,0	0,0	0,0	0,0	0,0

FIGURE 9.39 Performing a Secondary Maximization to Produce the Configuration Shown in Figure 9.37

both positive and negative flows, as shown in the examples of Figure 9.40, in which potential cycles are indicated with boldface lines. The leftmost graph in Figure 9.40 indicates the potential positive-flow cycle (2, 4), (4, 3), (3, 2), (2, 4), etc. The rightmost graph contains several potential negative-flow cycles such as the one shown in boldface: (1, 3), (3, 2), (2, 1), (1, 3), etc. (the direction of the negative flow is indicated by the smaller arrows).

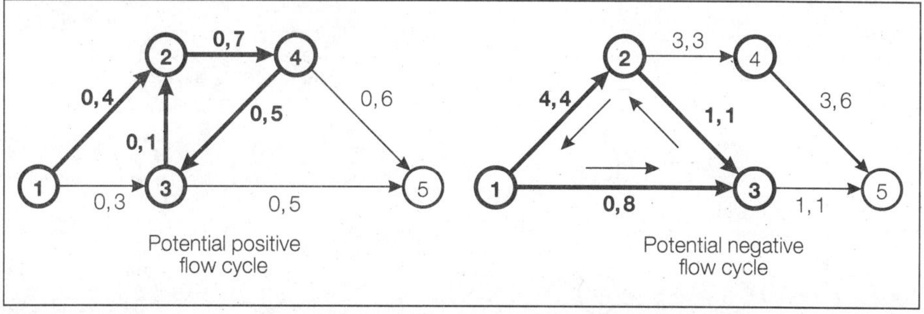

FIGURE 9.40 A Simple Graph Containing a Potential Cycle

A procedure to perform a complete maximization, `MaximizeFlow`, is given in Appendix I. For simplicity, the maximization process has been described thus far in two distinct phases: examining all positive flows (preliminary maximization) and then examining negative flows (complete maximization). In the `MaximizeFlow` procedure, to minimize the number of times each edge is followed, if there is no positive flow from a node X to a node Y, the negative flow from X to Y is examined *immediately*.

At this time, examine the following routine in Appendix I.

```
PROCEDURE  MaximizeFlow ( VAR Graph : GraphType;
                          Source, Sink : NodePtr; VAR TotalFlow : Integer );
```

SUMMARY

ADT graph is a network data structure in which data are usually arranged according to the key values of their items. Each item has a many-to-many relationship with other items; i.e., in a graph of *N* items, each item may have *N* successors and *N* predecessors. The domain consists of items (nodes), typically of record data type, connected by edges. An edge connects a parent node to an adjacent child node; if it is possible to advance only in one direction, the edge is said to be directed, otherwise it is undirected. A weighted graph contains edges with weight values; i.e., each edge has some value, such as length, associated with it. (Review other definitions at the start of the chapter.)

Fundamental graph operations include initializing the graph as empty, testing for emptiness, searching for a node or edge, inserting or deleting a node or edge, finding any path or the shortest path, testing for node adjacency, and traversal.

The two graph representations are the array-based adjacency matrix and the linked list based adjacency list. With an adjacency matrix, a lookup table may be used to map the key value of a node's item to its matrix row or column index; with an adjacency list, it may be used to point into each linked list of edge nodes.

A graph may be traversed or searched using either a depth-first or breadth-first traversal strategy. With either strategy, care must be taken in the design of the traversal or search algorithm to avoid being trapped in a dead end or a cycle. The breadth-first search has the benefit of finding the shortest path (in terms of the number of nodes visited) from the source node to the destination node. Lookup table `Parent` pointer fields are used to preserve a successful search path.

A graph may be saved to a file by writing information about each node and each edge; a variant record is useful to describe either.

A minimal-cost (MC) path is a path between two nodes in a weighted graph that has the smallest possible sum of edge-weight values. The algorithm presented for finding such a path is a derivation of Dijkstra's algorithm, and has the advantage of finding all minimal cost paths between the source node and all other reachable nodes in the process. `Parent` fields in the lookup table are used to represent all such paths.

A spanning tree is an undirected, nonoriented tree representation of an undirected graph, consisting of all nodes of the graph but only those edges necessary to connect the nodes. A variety of different spanning trees may be possible for a given graph. It may be constructed while performing either a depth-first or breadth-first traversal of the graph, resulting in a depth-first or breadth-first spanning tree, respectively. A minimal-cost spanning (MCS) tree has the lowest total sum of edge weights of all possible spanning trees for a given graph. It is particularly useful for any networking application in which a common channel is used to service many end-user devices where its "cost" (e.g., length) must be minimized. Two famous algorithms for constructing MCS trees are Kruskal's algorithm and Prim's algorithm. The algorithm presented is a derivation of Prim's algorithm, in which `Parent` fields in the lookup table are used to represent the tree.

Weighted graphs are useful for representing networks in which any quantity flows from a single source (the source node) through the network to a particular end-user (the sink node). Application 9.1 describes a derivation of the Ford-Fulkerson algorithm to maximize the total rate of flow from the source to the sink nodes in a weighted graph by controlling the flow levels along the paths. Here, each node represents a pumping station and each edge represents a conduit with a fixed capacity but a variable current flow, through which positive and negative flows are possible. The algorithm describes steps for both a preliminary and complete maximization of flows.

KEY TERMS

ADT graph
Acyclic
Acyclic graph
Adjacency list
Adjacency matrix
Adjacent node
Bidirectional edge
Breadth-first traversal
Breadth-first spanning tree
Child
Circuit
Complete graph
Connected graph
Cycle
Dead end
Dense graph
Depth-first traversal
Depth-first spanning tree
Destination
Digraph
Dijkstra's algorithm
Directed edge
Directed graph
Edge
Endpoint
Ford-Fulkerson algorithm
Graph traversal
In-degree
Incidental node
Infinite weight
Isolated node
Kruskal's algorithm
Lookup table (for a graph)
Minimal-cost path
Minimal-cost spanning tree
Negative flow
Neighbor
Network structure

Node
Null weight
Out-degree
Parent
Path
Path length
Positive flow
Prim's algorithm
Simple graph
Sink
Source
Spanning tree
Sparse graph
Subgraph
Tree
Unconnected graph
Undirected edge
Undirected graph
Weight
Weighted graph

REVIEW QUESTIONS

1. Distinguish among the structure types set, linear list, hierarchy, and network structures. Distinguish between the concepts of a one-to-many relationship and many-to-many relationship. Describe several everyday examples, not given in this chapter, of objects and organizations structured as a network.
2. Define the following (in the context of graph structures):
   - Parent, child, and neighbor
   - Directed and undirected graphs
   - Path, cycle, dead end, tour
   - Dense and sparse graphs
   - Directed and undirected graphs; simple and complete graphs; and trees
3. Describe the ADT graph.
4. Distinguish between the adjacency matrix and the adjacency list representations of a graph, citing the advantages and disadvantages offered by both. List the factors that might persuade you to choose one or the other.
5. Distinguish between a null weight and an infinite weight in a weighted graph represented using an adjacency matrix. What is the role of a lookup table in an adjacency matrix representation as opposed to the role of the matrix itself? Does the adjacency list representation require a lookup table structure separate from the adjacency list structure itself?
6. Describe an algorithm that determines if one node is adjacent to another and algorithms that search for a particular node or edge; do so for both graph representations.
7. Describe an algorithm to (a) insert an edge and (b) delete an edge; do so for both graph representations. Describe an algorithm to (a) insert a node and (b) delete a node in a graph; again, do so for both graph representations.
8. Distinguish between the concepts of depth-first traversal and breadth-first traversal of a graph. How does the directionality of a graph (i.e., whether it is directed or undirected) affect traversing? There are four commonly used depth-first traversals for a binary search tree; are there several types of depth-first traversal for a graph as well? For what two reasons may a traversal fail to visit every node in a graph?
9. Describe three special cases for an algorithm searching for a particular node in a graph. How may these problems be detected and either resolved or avoided? Do these special cases apply to traversing as well as searching?
10. How may a traversal algorithm be modified to find a single path between two nodes? Distinguish between the concepts of depth-first searching and breadth-first searching.
11. Describe how a graph may be saved to a file and subsequently reconstructed by reading from the same file. Give the declaration for a file element. Does either traversal strategy—depth-first or breadth-first—provide an advantage over the other?

12. What two connotations might the phrase *shortest path* have? Describe Dijkstra's algorithm for finding a minimal cost path between two nodes. Describe the role of the `MinCost` and `Parent` fields in each lookup table node and the role of the `NodePQ` priority queue. What useful side effect arises when this particular algorithm is employed? Will the algorithm work only with a directed graph, with an undirected graph, or with either?
13. Describe the technique of keeping `Parent` pointers to define a path from a target node back to a source node (this technique is employed in all algorithms that search for a path).
14. Distinguish between a spanning tree and a minimal-cost spanning tree. Describe two algorithms for building a spanning tree from a graph. Will these algorithms work only with a directed graph, with an undirected graph, or with either?
15. Describe some everyday applications, not given in this chapter, of a minimal-cost spanning (MCS) tree. Distinguish between Kruskal's algorithm and Prim's algorithm for building an MCS tree. Describe how Prim's algorithm is actually quite similar to Dijkstra's algorithm. Describe the role of the `MinCost` and `Parent` fields in each lookup table node and the role of the `NodePQ` priority queue.
16. Describe the Ford-Fulkerson technique for maximizing the flow through a network from a particular source node to a particular sink node; you may divide your description into a description of the preliminary and secondary maximizations. Are cycles and dead ends potential problems when maximizing flows in a graph? Under what circumstances does the correct modification of both positive and negative flows raise the total flow through the network, and why does this work?

EXERCISES

1. The following figure depicts the adjacency list representation of the graph to which parts (a), (b), (c), and (d) refer (this structure uses an array for the lookup table rather than a linked list). Each edge node describes a neighboring city (1–9) and distance to that city (175 to 1700 miles).

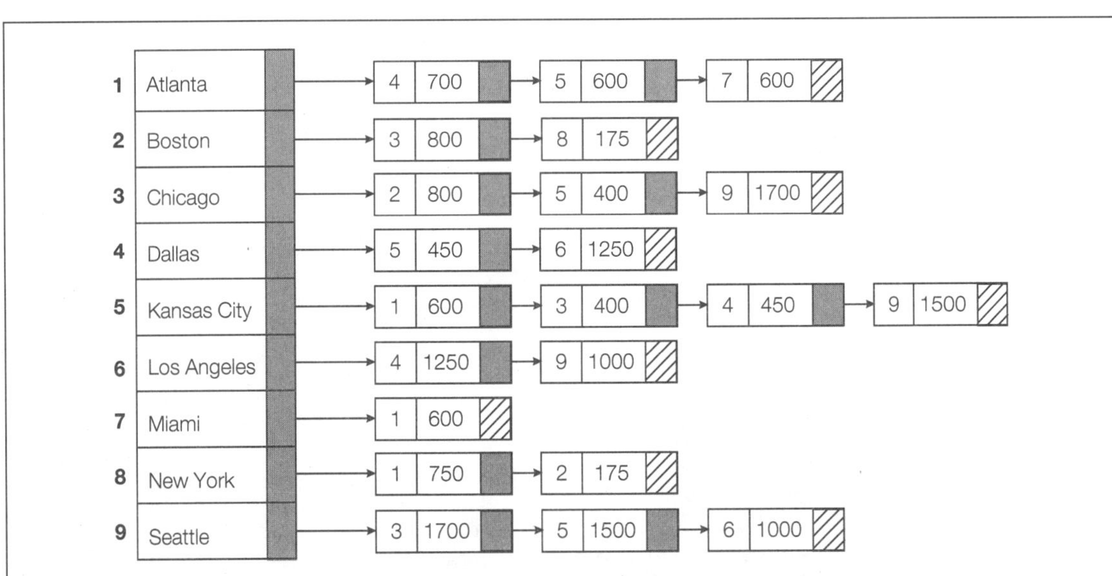

a. Correctly fill in the adjacency matrix diagram below, leaving an element blank to indicate the absence of adjacency.

	Lookup Table		1	2	3	4	5	6	7	8	9	
1	Atlanta	1	0									1
2	Boston	2		0								2
3	Chicago	3			0							3
4	Dallas	4				0						4
5	Kansas City	5					0					5
6	Los Angeles	6						0				6
7	Miami	7							0			7
8	New York	8								0		8
9	Seattle	9									0	9
			1	2	3	4	5	6	7	8	9	

b. Draw a diagram of the graph represented by the adjacency list.

c. Using your diagram of (b), perform a depth-first traversal starting at Seattle, numbering each node you visit (Seattle is 1, Chicago is 2, etc.). Given a choice of unvisited nodes to visit next, choose the node with the "smallest name," based on the ASCII character set.

d. Repeat part (d), but perform a breadth-first traversal instead.

e. Write a procedure to perform a depth-first traversal and another procedure to perform a breadth-first traversal for both the adjacency list graph representation and for the adjacency matrix representation, both based on the structures depicted in this exercise.

2. The following figure is used in parts (a) and (b):

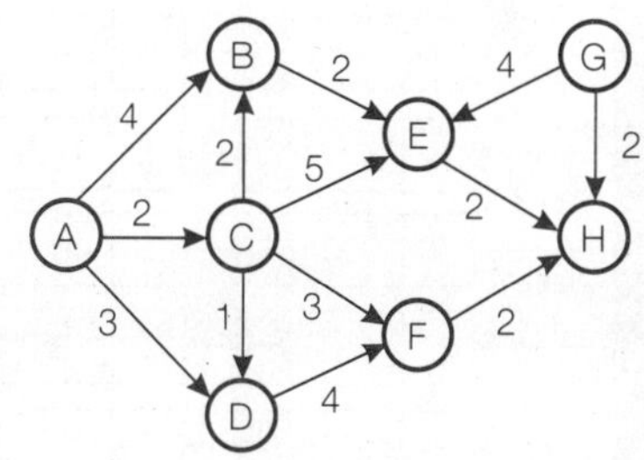

a. Use Dijkstra's algorithm to fill in the arrays in the figure at the top of the next page as follows: Element `MinCost [ K ]` should contain the final minimal cost from node A to some node `K` (write ∞ to indicate infinite cost if necessary). `Parent [ K ]` should contain the identifier of the parent of node `K` such that the minimal-cost path from node A to node `K` can be traced backward (if a path exists at all), starting with `Parent [ K ]`.

MinCost

A	B	C	D	E	F	G	H

Parent

A	B	C	D	E	F	G	H

b. Draw the graph diagram for an MCS (minimal-cost spanning) tree of this graph, starting from node A.

3. The following figure depicts a network of pumping stations (nodes) and pipes (edges), as described in Application 9.1. The weights of each edge are flow, capacity and each flow has already been initialized to zero.

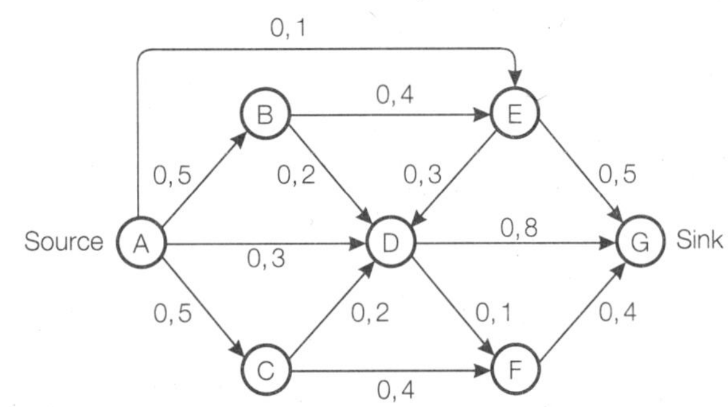

a. Use the Ford-Fulkerson algorithm to perform a *preliminary maximization* of the total rate of flow from the source to the sink node (do not consider negative flows), updating the flow levels of edges.
b. Perform a *secondary maximization*, again updating the flow level of each edge.

4. Give a set of declarations for a tic-tac-toe game tree (game trees and the MiniMax method were presented in Application 8.2).

5. Prove that the choice of starting node makes no difference in constructing an MCS tree.

6. Prove the following:
a. The sum of the degrees of all nodes in a connected graph is equal to twice the number of edges.
b. A connected graph contains an even number of nodes that have an odd degree.
c. The number of edges in a connected, complete graph with N nodes is

$$\frac{N(N-1)}{2}$$

7. Assume that a directed graph has already been built using either an adjacency list or adjacency matrix representation (your choice), based on the generic declarations given in this chapter. Complete function `CountNodes`, which should return a count of the number of different nodes that may be visited starting with the node whose location is passed to parameter `Start`. `StartType` is either of Pascal pointer type (`VNodePtr`) for the adjacency list representation or is of type integer for the adjacency matrix representation.

```
FUNCTION CountCities ( VAR Graph : GraphType; Start : ?? ) : Integer;
```

8. Complete Boolean function `Acyclic`, which should return a true value if the graph passed in the argument is acyclic and a false value otherwise:

```
FUNCTION Acyclic ( VAR Graph : GraphType ) : Boolean;
```

9. Design a procedure that builds a graph from a file of `GFileRec` records, the declaration for which was given at the end of section 9.2, Saving a Graph in a File. Assume that all node descriptor records are stored before edge descriptor records in the file, as just described. Assume further that *node descriptor records are ordered in the file,* as they should be in the lookup table, and that the *edge descriptor records for each parent node are ordered in the file,* as they should be in the linked list for that parent. These assumptions allow your procedure to simply append lookup table nodes and linked list nodes rather than searching for points of insertion, thereby saving execution time. Once your basic routine is written, you can modify it so that it is able to reconstruct the graph from the file regardless of the ordering of node and edge descriptor records in the file. Consider whether or not such a redesign would prove significantly less efficient than the basic design.

10. Write nonrecursive procedures that perform depth-first and breadth-first traversing of a graph (your choice of graph representation).

11. Rewrite procedure `FindPath` of Application 7.6, "In Search of the Golden Floppy," in order to find the *shortest path* to the beloved Golden Floppy, if a path exists at all. You must redesign the island structure as well.

12. In the flow-maximizing algorithm of Application 9.1, depth-first searching was performed to find each path from the source node to the sink node. Redesign procedure `MaximizeFlow` so it performs breadth-first searching instead, and consider which strategy may be more efficient (i.e., require fewer flow-capacity comparisons) in the average case.

13. A *Hamiltonian path* passes through each node in graph just once. A Hamiltonian path that begins and ends with the same node is called a *Hamiltonian circuit,* or *tour.* In a weighted graph, the tour that accrues the minimum total edge weight is called a *minimal-cost (MC) tour,* and the task of finding an MC tour for a weighted graph is called the *traveling salesperson problem,* in reference to a famous application of this task. In this application, a traveling salesperson attempts to find a single path that will lead him or her to every city within a set of cities and then back to the original city, while accruing the minimum total distance possible. This scenario can be generalized easily to *any* scenario requiring the tour of a weighted graph along a path involving the least total cost, and the edge cost may involve *any* kind of cost (distance, financial expense, time, etc.).

    As with the Eight Queens algorithm of Application 7.7, a trial-and-error approach must be taken; here, we must carefully test a uniform sequence of possible solutions while never producing or testing the path twice. There is an important difference between these two problems, however, which has a profound impact on the time requirements of the solving algorithms for each: Although both problems may involve a great many different configurations to test, the testing process in the eight queens problem concludes as soon as eight queens are placed, whereas the testing process in the traveling salesperson problem must test *every possible configuration* before concluding. The traveling salesman problem is said to belong to the class of *NP-complete problems* (for a large number of graph nodes). These are exponential-time problems for which a possible solution can be *tested* quickly to determine if it is indeed a solution, however, an algorithm to *find* a solution takes a prohibitive amount of time to execute.

a. Assuming that it takes 1 second for a computer program to generate a single tour of a graph of N nodes, what is the mathematical formula to approximate the total execution time?
b. Why does simply building an MCS tree for the graph not guarantee a minimal-cost tour?
c. Write a procedure that finds the minimal-cost tour of a weighted graph. If you design the procedure for a graph represented as an adjacency list, you may represent the tour using `Parent` fields. If you design the procedure for a graph represented as an adjacency matrix, you may represent the tour using a one-dimensional array of elements, each of which is used to indicate a graph node.

14. In 1736, Swiss mathematician Leonhard Euler published a paper describing his Koenigsberg bridge problem: The Prussian city of Koenigsberg was divided by a river in which there were two islands. Seven bridges connected the two sections of the city and the islands, as depicted below. The problem asks the following question: Is it possible to walk through the city, crossing each bridge just once?

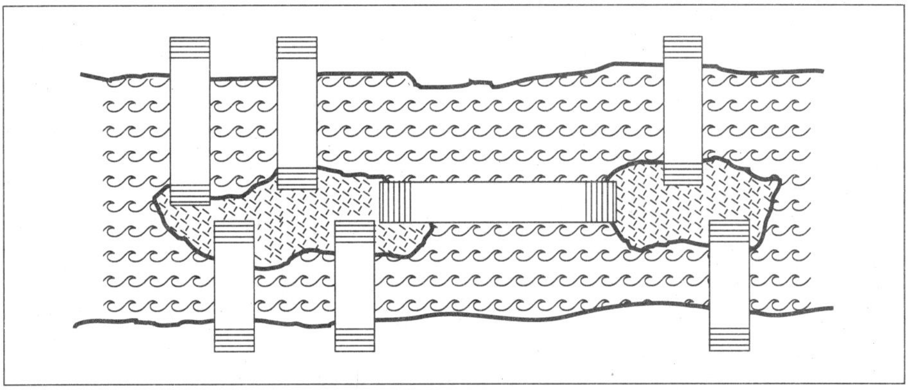

Think about whether or not such a path does exist and, if so, how to find it in a systematic fashion. Design a computer algorithm to search for such a path.

CHAPTER TEN

ADVANCED SEARCHING ALGORITHMS

In this chapter you will learn about a variety of new data structures and the search algorithms they support.

10.1 HEIGHT-BALANCED SEARCH TREES: 2-3 TREES

Preliminaries

In Section 8.2 we found that a balanced binary search tree provides superior searching efficiency in the average case. The search for an item in a balanced or nearly balanced tree of N nodes requires about log N key-value comparisons. This is as swift as a binary search performed on a sorted array and better than the average efficiency of a common linear search. The average search time worsens as the tree becomes more unbalanced, however. In the worst case—a degenerate tree—the search for a particular item performs with the average efficiency of a linear search, requiring N key-value comparisons if the item is not in the tree and about $N/2$ key-value comparisons if it is.

Section 8.2 described how saving an existing binary search tree to a file via a preorder or level-order traversal allows the program to reconstruct the original tree by reading the stored nodes from the file sequentially. Typically, a search tree must be constructed from a list already ordered by ascending key value, such as when a data base of records formerly kept on paper is transferred to an electronic, computer-based data base. The initial conversion from a paper representation to an electronic representation of the records often involves one of the following strategies:

- The program prompts the user for keyboard input for each record, or else
- The user enters information into a text file, using a text editor, and then the program reads this text file.

Either way, the user is likely to enter information about the records in order of ascending key value, since the records probably were stored that way on paper. And, as we saw in Section 8.2, inserting items into an empty binary search tree in key-value order produces the dreaded degenerate tree.

A tree is considered balanced if the two subtrees of every node never differ in height by more than one level. (In a perfectly balanced tree, all leaves are on the same level.) By its design and the rules for insertion and deletion operations, a **height-balanced tree** is a tree that is *always balanced.* This gain in efficiency is counterbalanced by the fact that the insertion and deletion operations for balanced trees tend to be more complex and time-consuming than for a regular binary search tree. (Of course, the efficiency of insertion and deletion operations is improved by the tree's balance, since the searching is always a prerequisite for both of these operations.) *A height-balanced tree is therefore useful for those applications involving significantly more simple searching than insertion and deletion.*

A **2-3 tree** is a height-balanced variation of the binary search tree in which each node may contain one or two items, so that a node containing one item has two subtrees and a node containing two items has three subtrees. The ADT specification for a 2-3 tree follows.

Specifications for the ADT 2-3 Tree

The **ADT 2-3 tree** is a height-balanced, oriented, ordered tree used to represent the ADT table, in which the following is true:

1. It is either empty, or else
2. One of the following is true:
   - It consists of a root node with one item along with two subtrees, which are 2-3 trees themselves (see Figure 10.1). In this case, the relationships among keys in Figure 10.2 holds.
   - It consists of a root node with two items along with three subtrees, which are 2-3 trees themselves (see Figure 10.3). In this case, the relationship among keys in Figure 10.4 holds.

In a 2-3 tree, all leaves are on the same tree level.

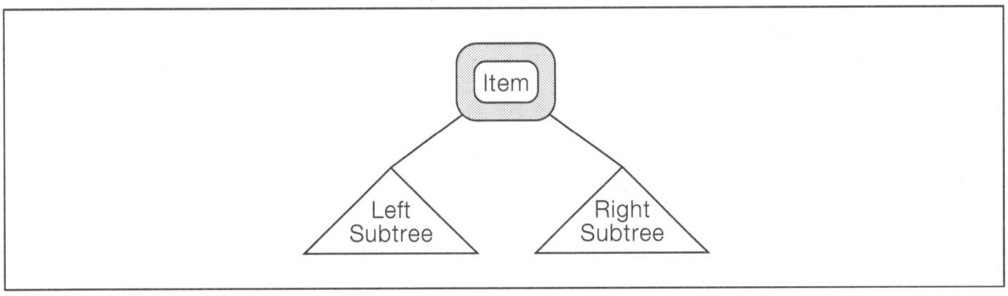

FIGURE 10.1 A One-Item Node and Its Two Subtrees

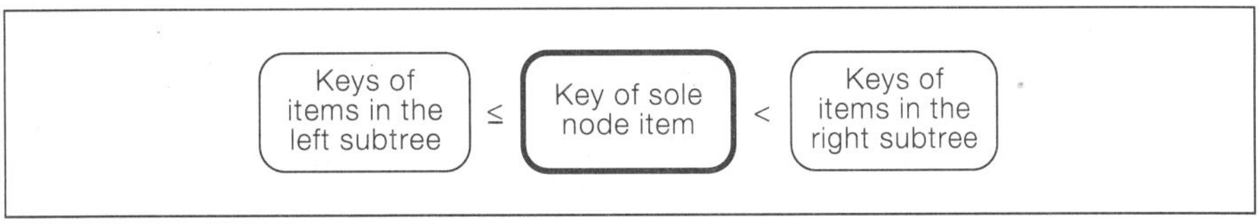

FIGURE 10.2 Orientation of a One-Item Node and Its Left and Right Subtrees

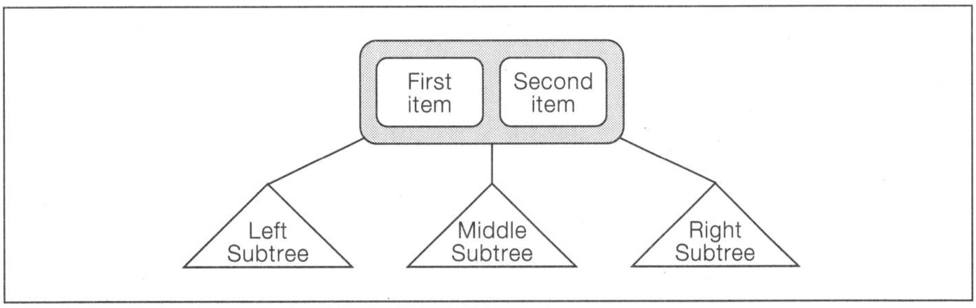

FIGURE 10.3 A Two-Item Node and Its Three Subtrees

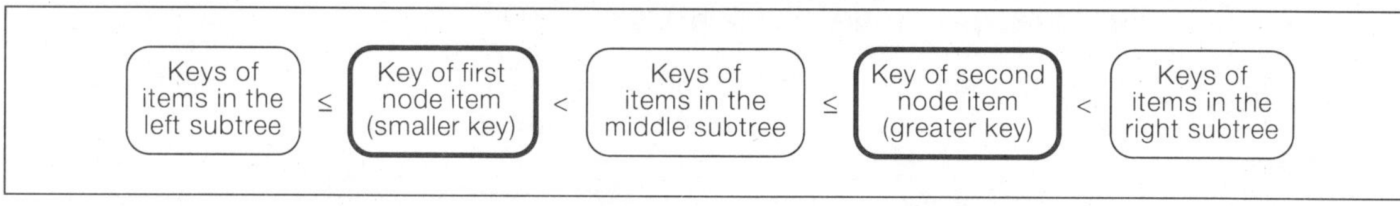

FIGURE 10.4 Orientation of a Two-Item Node and Its Three Subtrees

Domain

The domain is items, typically of record data type, contained within nodes. Each node contains either one or two items.

Fundamental Operations

1. *Initialize:* Initialize the 2-3 tree as empty; i.e., a tree with zero nodes.
2. *Test for emptiness:* Test the 2-3 tree for emptiness.
3. *Search for a particular item:* Search the 2-3 tree for a particular item.
4. *Insert an item:* Insert a new item in the 2-3 tree.
5. *Delete an item:* Delete an item from the 2-3 tree.
6. *Traverse:* Traverse the entire 2-3 tree, visiting and processing each item.

We begin with an abstract-level examination of the fundamental operations, and then we consider how to represent the structure using Pascal. Look ahead briefly to the figures in this section to see examples of 2-3 trees.

Searching a 2-3 Tree

The operation of searching for an item in a 2-3 tree is similar to the operation of searching for an item in a binary search tree. It is identical, in fact, when applied to a node containing a *single item.* If the searching algorithm encounters a 2-3 tree node containing *two items,* it compares the key sought to one of the node keys and, if no match is found, to checks the other node key. (In 2-3 tree diagrams, the smaller key value is always shown to the left of the larger key value.) If the key value sought does not match either of the node keys, the searching algorithm has a choice of up to three subtrees to search next—i.e., a choice of three edges to follow. The *left edge* is chosen if the desired key value is *less than the smaller* of the two node key values. The *right edge* is chosen if the desired key value is *greater than the greater* of the two node key values. The *middle edge* is chosen if the desired key value *lies between* the two node key values.

Figure 10.5 traces the searches for items with the integer key values 19, 34, 23, and 15 in a sample 2-3 tree, with the search paths and key values of items examined shown in boldface:

Insertion into a 2-3 Tree

As with a binary search tree, new nodes are inserted only at the leaf level of a 2-3 tree, so the search operation must be employed first to find the appropriate leaf for the insertion. A header node may be used, as was suggested for linked lists and binary search trees, so that insertion into an empty tree

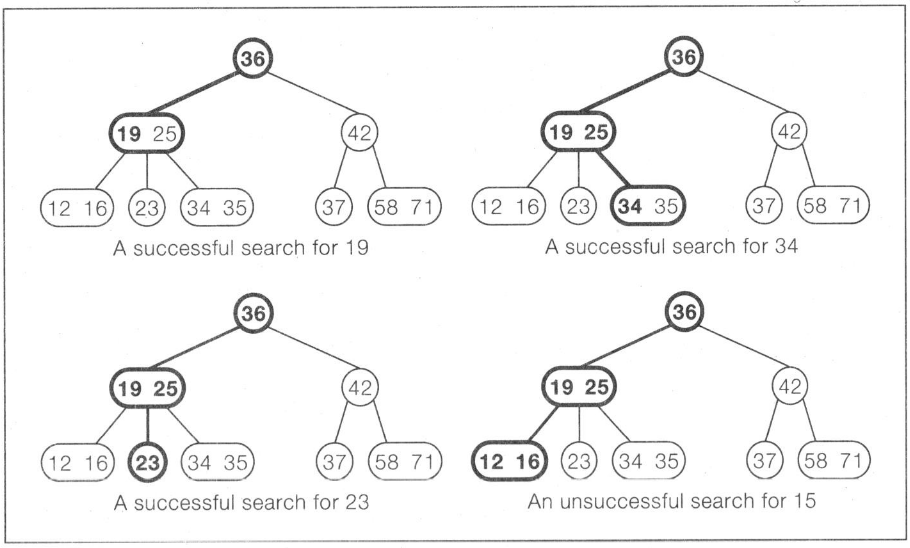

FIGURE 10.5 Searches for Items in a Sample 2-3 Tree

(and deletion of the root node) are not special cases requiring additional testing; however, the diagrams in this section do not show such header nodes.

If an item is inserted into a leaf already containing a single item, the node then contains two items, and the insertion process is complete. If the leaf last visited *already* contains two items, the insertion algorithm does *not* simply allocate a new node at a new level beyond the leaf level, as is done with a binary search tree, because the resulting structure would no longer be a 2-3 tree; i.e., not all leaves would be on the same level. Instead, the two-item leaf is split into two single-item nodes, and the middle item is "sent up" to the parent node.

If the parent node previously contained a single item, sending up a child item merely causes the node to have two items, and the insertion process is complete. If the parent node *already* contains two items, sending up a child item causes the node temporarily to have three items, and the node-splitting and sending-up process must be repeated. In fact, this process may be repeated many times until *either* of the following occurs:

- An item is sent up to a parent node that contains just a single item; this parent may or may not be the tree's root node, or else
- An item is sent up to the tree's root node, which already contains two items. In this case, a new tree root node is created, and the middle-valued item is sent up to a new node—the tree's new root node.

In the latter case, the tree gains one level of height *but does so uniformly,* with all leaves still on the same (highest) level.

As shown in Figure 8.28, inserting a series of items into an empty binary search tree in ascending (or descending) key-value order produces a degenerate tree. Let us determine if a 2-3 tree really does remain balanced regardless of the insertion order of the key values by testing this worst case. Figure 10.6 traces the process of inserting nodes with the integer key values

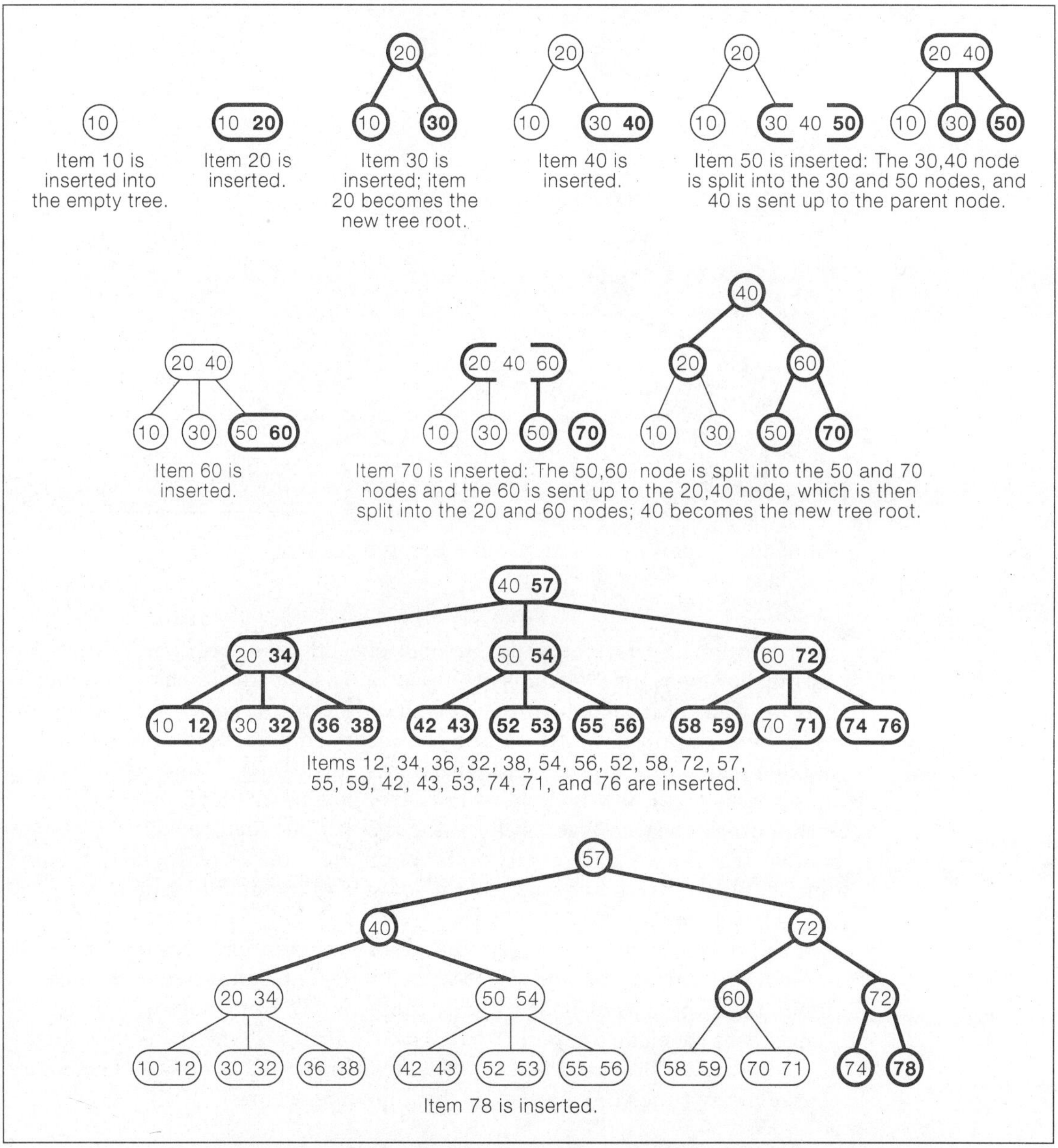

FIGURE 10.6 Inserting a Series of Items, in Ascending Key Value Order, into an Empty 2-3 Tree

10, 20, 30, 40, 50, 60, and 70 into an empty 2-3 tree. The figure also shows the tree after 19 more items are inserted, producing a 2-3 tree of height three, in which each node contains two items. The final diagram shows the tree after an item with key value 78 is inserted. In each diagram, a change from the previous diagram is indicated in boldface.

A pseudocode algorithm for insertion into a 2-3 tree follows. A search routine must be called first, returning the address of the appropriate leaf node into which the new node will be inserted (perhaps temporarily); the address of this leaf is passed to parameter `Current`.

```
ALGORITHM  Insert23 ( VAR Tree23 : ??; Data : ??; Current : ?? );
-----------------------------------------------------------------------------
  ALGORITHM SplitAndMoveUp ( Current : ?? );

  BEGIN
  Split Current node into 2 nodes -- Node_low and Node_high -- storing the lowest key
    item in Node_low and storing the highest key item in Node_high;

  IF the just-split node has a parent THEN
    BEGIN
    Send up middle key-value item to the parent of the Current node just split;
    Adjust parent node link fields to point to Node_low and Node_high as appropriate
      (parent may have to point to a total of 4 children temporarily);
    IF parent node now contains more than 2 items THEN
       SplitAndMoveUp ( address of parent node )
    END

  ELSE                    {New tree root node must be created}
    BEGIN
    Create new (tree root) node and store middle key-value item of the node just
      split;
    Adjust the left and right link fields of this node to point to Node_low and Node_low
      as appropriate;
    Assign to tree's root pointer variable the address of this new node
    END
  END;
-----------------------------------------------------------------------------
{***  Main routine for Insert23  ***}

BEGIN
Create a new item in the leaf node pointed to by Current;
Store Data in the new item;
Increment total node count;
IF the tree is empty THEN  {New tree root node just created}
  Assign to tree's root pointer variable the address of this new node
ELSE
  SplitAndMoveUp ( Current )
END;
```

Deletion from a 2-3 Tree

Inserting an item into a node already containing two nodes requires that the node be split and the item with the middle key value be sent up to the parent node. If the node just split was the root of the entire tree, a new root node is created that contains only the last item sent. With *deletion*, there are cases in which an item in a parent node is sent down to one of its children, and two nearest sibling nodes are merged. As with deletion from a binary search tree, easy and difficult cases may be distinguished, and the deletion algorithm converts a difficult case to an easy one. Internal (nonleaf) items are deleted using essentially the same algorithm as for a binary search tree: Locate the in-order successor (or predecessor) item, overwrite the item to be deleted with a copy of the in-order successor (or predecessor) item, and then delete the original copy of the in-order successor (or predecessor);

- *Case 1 (easy):* The node containing the item to be deleted is a leaf containing two items.
- *Case 2 (difficult):* The node containing the item to be deleted is a leaf containing one item (i.e., the item to be deleted). This case is made even

more complex (as we shall see in Figure 10.7) if the parent of this node contains a single item.

- *Case 3 (easy):* The node containing the item to be deleted is internal, and the in-order successor (or predecessor) of the item to be deleted resides in a node with two items.
- *Case 4 (difficult):* The node containing the item to be deleted is internal and the in-order successor (or predecessor) of the item to be deleted resides in a node in which it is the *only* item.
- In addition, the node containing the item to be deleted may be the tree's root node.

Figure 10.7 illustrates several examples of cases 1 and 2, tracing the deletion of items within leaf nodes. Nodes where an action has just taken place or is currently taking place are indicated in boldface.

The algorithm for locating the in-order successor of an internal node in a 2-3 tree is either identical or similar to the algorithm used with a binary search tree:

1. If the item to be deleted is the only item in a node, follow the right edge to the right child (as with binary search trees).
   If the item to be deleted is one of two items within the same node and has the *lesser of the two key values,* follow the middle edge to the middle child; if it has the *greater of the two key values,* follow the item's right edge to the right child.
2. Follow every left edge until a leaf is encountered—this leaf node contains the item's in-order successor; if the leaf contains two items, the in-order successor is the item with the lesser key value.

Figure 10.8 provides several examples of deletion cases 3 and 4.

Pascal Representations of the ADT 2-3 Tree

Three important characteristics distinguish a 2-3 tree from a regular binary search tree:

1. In some cases of insertion, a node must be split into two nodes and an item sent up to the parent node. If no parent node exists, a new root node must be created.
2. In some cases of deletion, an item in a parent node must be sent down to a child node, an item must be moved from a sibling up to the parent, and two sibling nodes must be merged.
3. Any node may contain one or two items.

The first and second characteristics require quick access to a parent node. In fact, the insertion and deletion algorithms for a 2-3 tree also may need to access many ancestors of a particular node, unlike the algorithms for a binary search tree, so each node must store the address of its parent.

The third characteristic requires that our 2-3 nodes must somehow be "expandable" to accommodate up to two items; there are several ways to accomplish this. Each node could contain both a Boolean field called `OneItem`, indicating the number of items in the node, and two *arrays:* a

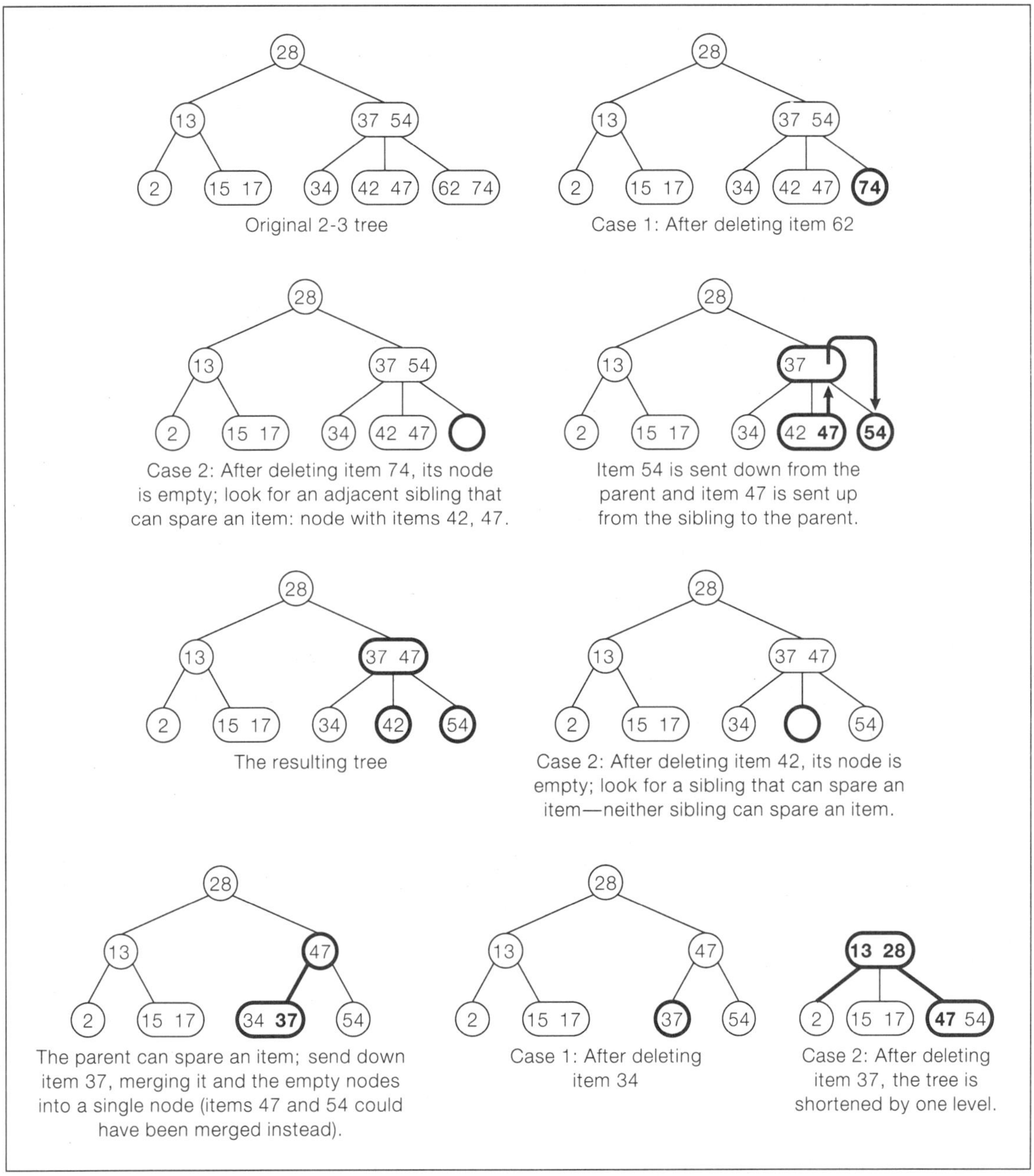

FIGURE 10.7 Deleting Items Within Leaves of a 2-3 Tree (Cases 1 and 2)

two-element array of item records and a three-element array of node pointers. Although this structure *will* work, it tends to waste heapspace memory: Enough memory for two items is allocated for every node in the tree, wasting memory for nodes that contain only one item. As with any ordered list, keeping each item array ordered by key value would save total search time in the average case of searching, but this will require shifting items within the arrays as items are inserted and deleted. An array of pointer values

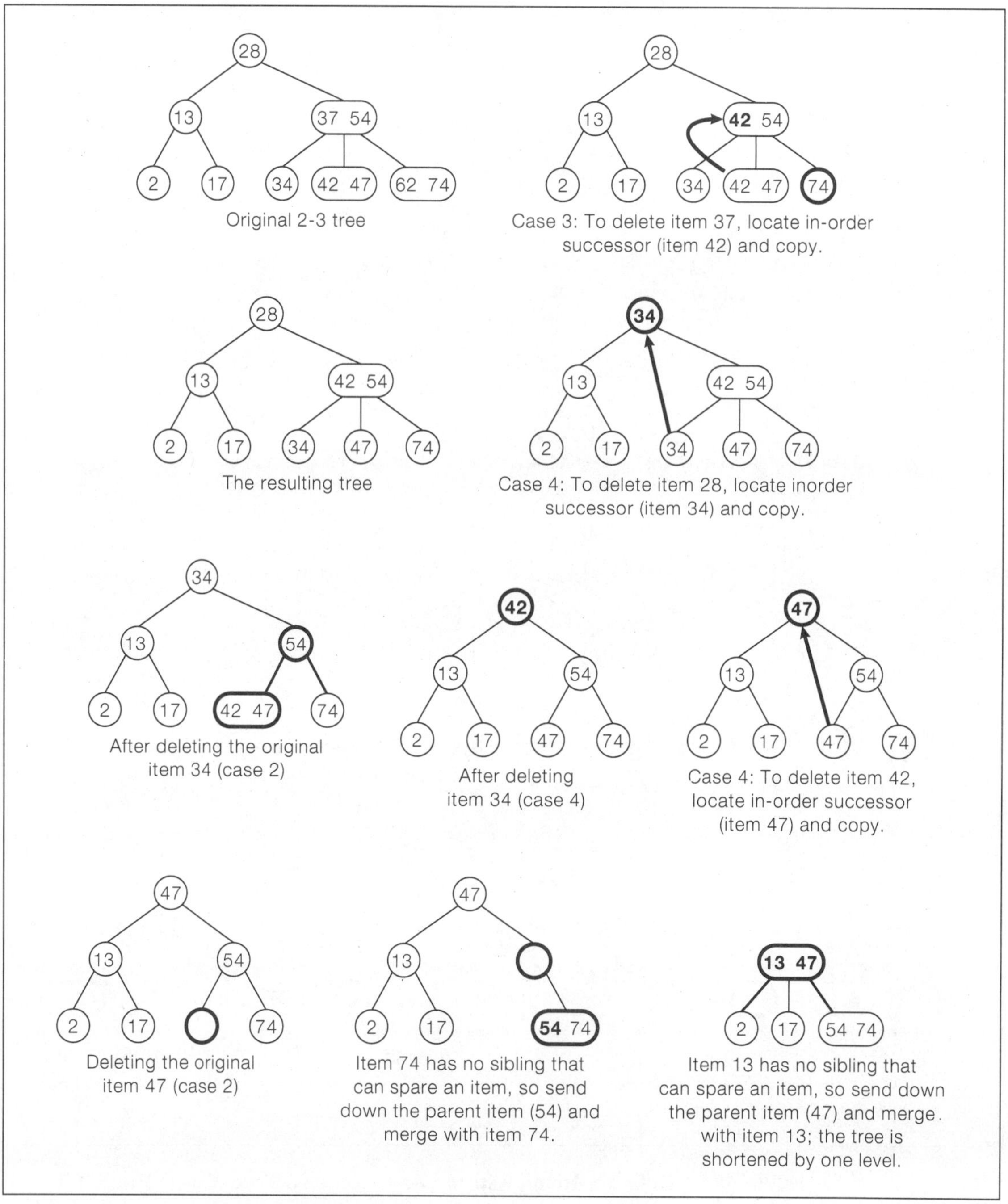

FIGURE 10.8 Deleting Items Within Internal Nodes of a 2-3 Tree (Cases 3 and 4)

could be used instead, however, the pointer values would need to be shifted frequently as well.

We can make the usual evolution from a simple array representation to a dynamically allocated linked list representation. Again, each node would contain a Boolean `OneItem` field and a pointer variable pointing into a linked list of one or two child nodes. This representation avoids wasting an item's worth of memory for nodes containing only one item but still requires keeping each two-item linked list ordered, to expedite searching. And, analogous to the shifting of elements with the simple array representation, nodes within each linked list may need to be shifted in the process of inserting or deleting an item.

Continuing the evolution of representations, we can replace the linear linked list with a small binary search tree of one node (if a single item) or two nodes (if two items). The declarations for this representation follow:

```
TYPE
  BTKeyType    =  ??;                     {Application dependent}
  BTInfoType   =  RECORD
                    Key    : BTKeyType;    {Key value}
                    {Other fields, as appropriate}
                  END;

  NodeStatus   =  ( OnlyItem, FirstOfTwoItems, SecondItemOfTwoItems );
  BTNodePtr    =  ^Node;                  {Pointer to one tree node}
  BTNode       =  RECORD
                    Status : NodeStatus;   {Occupancy status}
                    Data   : BTInfoType;   {The item itself}
                    Parent,                {Address of parent}
                    Left,                  {Left link field}
                    Right  : BTNodePtr     {Right link field}
                  END;

  BinTreeType  =  RECORD
                    Root   : BTNodePtr;    {Points to root node}
                    Count  : Integer       {Total count of all nodes in tree}
                  END;

VAR
  Tree23 : BinTreeType;
```

Figure 10.9 provides two diagrams of the same 2-3 tree: The top diagram depicts the tree as it has been presented thus far in our abstract level discussion; the bottom diagram depicts the same tree in a format more closely reflecting the actual representation of the tree. In the bottom diagram, items in the same 2-3 node are grouped by the shading. Actually, the bottom diagram depicts only one of many possible arrangements of the nodes. For example, it reflects the fact that item 16 was inserted *before* item 12. Had item 16 been inserted *after* item 12, item 16 would be the right child of item 12, which would then be the left child of item 19. Either way, items 12 and 16 are still considered as occupants of the same 2-3 node.

At the most abstract level, illustrated by the top diagram of Figure 10.9, a 2-3 tree is balanced and all leaves are always on the same level. Even when the tree is represented using a binary search tree, as illustrated by the bottom diagram, it remains balanced because the *subtrees of each node never differ in height by more than one level.* As a balanced tree, a 2-3 tree search is therefore rated as O (log N) in both the average and worst cases. This guarantee represents a tremendous improvement over a binary search tree, which may be anywhere from perfectly balanced—O (log N)—to perfectly *un*balanced (a degenerate tree)—O (N).

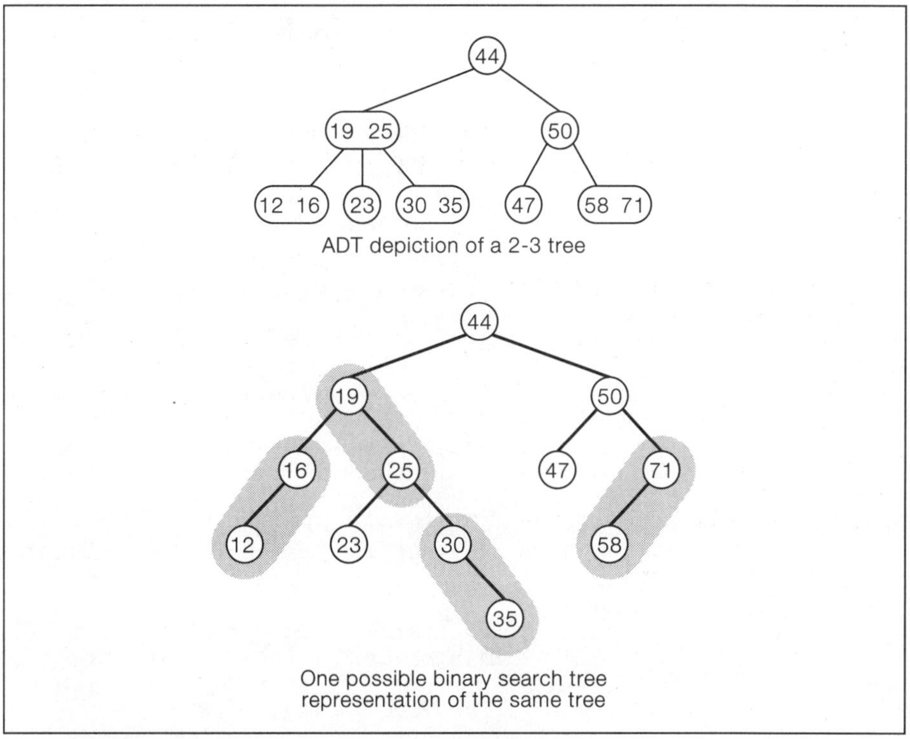

FIGURE 10.9 Diagrams of the Same 2-3 Tree

By choosing the binary search tree representation, most of the binary search tree algorithms developed in Chapter 8 and appearing in Appendix G may be used with 2-3 trees:

- Initializing the tree as empty: `InitBinTree`
- Testing the tree for emptiness: `BinTreeEmpty`
- Searching: `BinTreeSearch` (the `Parent` parameter may be ignored)
- All depth-first traversals: `PreOrdTraverse`, `PostOrdTraverse`, `InOrdTraverse`, and `ReverseOrdTraverse`

Only the insertion, deletion, and level-order traversal algorithms are distinct from their binary search tree counterparts.

10.2 SURPASSING THE O (LOG *N*) EFFICIENCY BARRIER

The ability to search a data base of information quickly is often crucial, either because the user needs an item of information immediately or because the application involves a great many searches, or both. For example, the real-time computer programs used aboard naval combat ships to identify an enemy ship or aircraft must provide split-second access to necessary data. Laser bar-code scanners in grocery stores must read a price quickly or else customers are apt to complain. Telephone directory programs can find a number faster and service more callers in a given time than could be done manually. In this section we examine several search techniques and their associated data structures that provide better average searching efficiency than the structures and techniques presented thus far. We also will examine techniques for searching internal memory structures; many of the concepts will carry over to our Section 10.3 discussions of techniques for searching external memory structures.

Overview of Searching Schemes

The *array* was the first data structure presented in this book (and no doubt in your first programming course) that supports **direct addressing**—i.e., immediate access to an element if its location (index value) within the array is already known. Typically, however, the location of the desired item is *not* known and the array must be searched by examining the key values of items. Although a binary search tends to be faster than the linear search, this advantage is counterbalanced somewhat by the relatively expensive task of keeping the array elements ordered by key value when an item is inserted or deleted, since this typically requires the shifting of items.

To improve upon the time cost of insertion and deletion operations, we evolved from arrays to *dynamically allocated linked lists* in Chapter 5. Inserting and deleting items in a linked list is simpler and faster than in an array-based list: Rather than physically shifting about groups of items in memory, we merely alter the values of a few link fields. A linked list offers the added benefit of flexible length, as opposed to the fixed length of an array. Unfortunately, these improvements may be offset by the fact that a linear linked list supports only a linear search. Linked lists do not support the faster binary search with any efficiency because the algorithm requires the direct accessing of the midpoint element of a list. And, although average search time *is* improved if the list is kept ordered by key value during the insertion and deletion process, even this requires a linear search to find the point of insertion for a new item.

To minimize average search time while retaining the efficiency of insertions and deletions and the advantage of flexible length, we then evolved from a linear list structure to a nonlinear linked list structure in Section 8.2—the *binary search tree*. The *shape* of the tree dramatically influences the efficiency of a tree search, however. If the search tree is balanced, a search operation enjoys the same efficiency as a binary array search operation. In the worst case, however, a degenerate binary search tree is effectively just an ordered linked list, and a tree search is therefore just a linear search.

The desire for guaranteed balance motivated our examination of *2-3 trees* in Section 10.1, which, by the design of its insertion and deletion operations, is guaranteed to remain balanced and therefore provides optimal searching efficiency. Unfortunately, the innate complexity of the insertion and deletion algorithms makes 2-3 trees efficient only for applications involving significantly more searching than inserting or deleting.

Can we improve upon the searching efficiency of O (log N) while avoiding the need to move data around during insertion and deletion operations? As always, *the efficiency of a search strategy is tied to the structure of the list being searched.* Two efficiency-limiting factors are apparent about the structures we have examined thus far:

1. *Array items are stored in a single structure.* For ordered linear lists in sequential storage (arrays), insertions and deletions require moving items about in memory.
2. *An item is sought in terms of other items within the list.* This is true of all four table structures examined thus far (the simple array, linked list, binary search tree, and 2-3 tree). For each, the search algorithm advances from item to item, examining key values. Search time therefore increases as the number of items in the list increases; i.e., search time is a function of problem size.

We now consider several data structures and their associated searching techniques that support searches with an average efficiency *better* than O(log N) by avoiding one or both of these limiting factors.

Indirect Addressing

To combat the first limiting factor, the **indirect addressing** scheme depicted in Figure 10.10 uses an array-based binary search algorithm to search a dynamically allocated set of items. The array is a **key table** of two-field records; one field contains a key value and the other contains the heapspace address of the dynamically allocated record associated with the key value. The key table is ordered by ascending key values, thereby supporting a binary search for a particular key value. If the search is successful, the search routine would return the heapspace address of the record sought; otherwise it would return a `NIL` value. You may recall from the Section 8.2 discussion about searching for items using different types of keys that this technique was followed with a key table represented by a binary search tree, rather

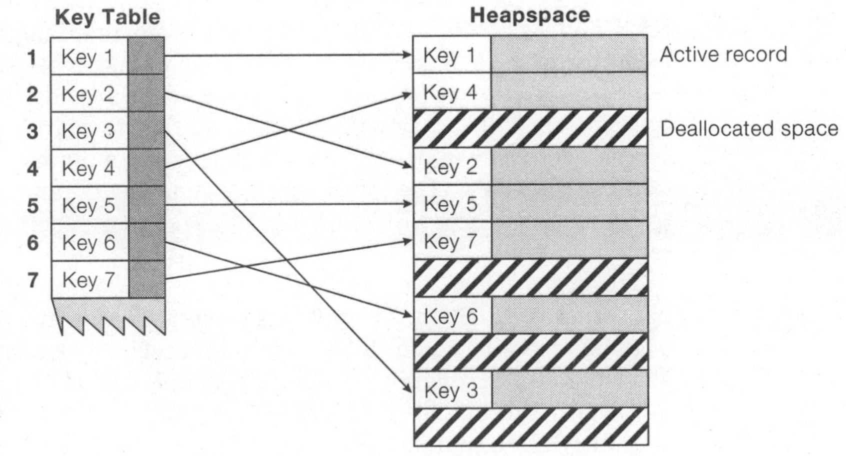

FIGURE 10.10 An Array-Based Key Table for Accessing Heapspace Record Items

than an array, for a data base of information about countries. (Briefly look back at Figure 8.24.)

Inserting a new data record into this array-based key table involves three steps, starting with the allocation of a record in the heapspace. Next, a binary search is performed to find the appropriate place in the key table for the new key-value heapspace address record. Finally, all records in the index table following this insertion point are shifted by one position toward the high end of the array, making room for this new key-value heapspace address record. Deleting a table record involves the converse of the third operation.

By storing in the array only the key value and address of each data record—instead of entire data records—the shifting of array elements during insertion and deletion may take significantly less time. This technique therefore minimizes the first limiting factor, although it does not alleviate the factor entirely.

Direct Addressing

As defined earlier in this section, direct addressing is the immediate accessing of an item within a structure rather than searching for items in terms of *other* items within the list. Direct addressing overcomes the second limiting factor and provides the perfect searching efficiency of O (1). Because an item's location may not be known beforehand, however, the item's key value itself must be used directly or manipulated in some way to render the address. This implies that there is a unique location for each item, eliminating the need to move items already in the list during insertions and deletions and thereby neutralizing the first and second limiting factors.

As an example of direct addressing, Figure 10.11 depicts two ends of an array to store records with key values in the range 1200 to 1300, inclusive. Since there will be, at most, only 101 different records, the array could be declared to contain 101 elements, indexed from 0 to 100. By subtracting an offset of 1200 from any key value, we can map an original key value to the index value of its associated record. In Figure 10.11, three original key values are mapped to their items' locations.

Unfortunately, for all its ease and speed in accessing items, direct addressing as described thus far is not viable for most applications. In addition to the limitation of a fixed array size, direct addressing poses two problems: First, if the key values of the actual items stored are not contiguous (i.e., adjacent in memory), then array space is wasted. For example, in the Fig-

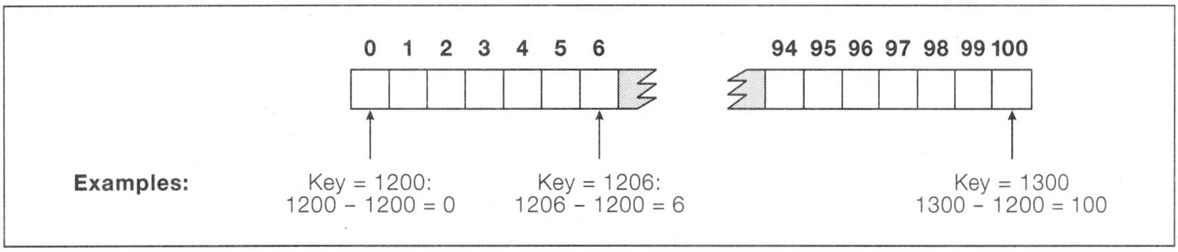

FIGURE 10.11 An Array to Store Items with Key Values 1200 to 1300, Inclusive

ure 10.11 structure, if there are no items with key values in the range 1225 through 1250, memory for the corresponding 26 array elements is allocated but never used. The wider the range of potential key values, the greater the potential for wasted memory. For instance, using a nine-digit social security number as a data base key might be appropriate for the Social Security Administration, since most numbers are valid. At a university of 20,000 students, however, only 0.002% of all possible nine-digit numbers are used, wasting 99.998% of the memory allocated for all possible numbers!

The second problem with direct addressing stems from the fact that keys are often alphanumeric character strings rather than numbers. Standard Pascal does permit the use of letters as array indices, but this is impractical because words are sparse. For example, the Department of Motor Vehicles may keep a data base of registration information ordered by a registration number (e.g., 2FABP19XXGB162114), whereas an automobile dealership may order its inventory of parts by a descriptive code (e.g., LAMP-TAURUS-882468). We can devise a strategy for converting a character string to a numeric array index value, but this process must be fast enough so that it does not counterbalance the efficiency of direct addressing.

The simplest technique is to call the standard Pascal `Ord` function repeatedly to convert each character in the alphanumeric key to its numeric memory representation, based on the character set in use, such as ASCII. All such numbers are summed to produce a single number. For example, the string `'HAT'` evaluates to 221 and the string `'Hello, I am Moe'` evaluates to 1208, based on the ASCII character set (you may refer to Appendix C to verify this). Examine function `TransformKey`, which follows:

```
{Necessary global declaration}

TYPE
  BuffType  =  String [ 80 ];

FUNCTION TransformKey ( VAR AlphaKey : BuffType ) : Integer;

VAR
  Sum, K : Integer;

BEGIN
Sum := 0;
FOR K := 1 TO Length ( AlphaKey ) DO
  Sum := Sum + Ord ( AlphaKey [ K ] );
TransformKey := Sum
END;
```

Another technique is to use a variant record to recast (i.e., reinterpret) a character string as a group of integer values, based on the memory representation of characters, an entire word at a time. Recall from Section 3.4 that a nonstandard String type variable is a packed array of char plus a preceding length byte. A character is represented in memory as a byte-long binary number, based on the character set in use, such as ASCII. For example, a 16-bit word can store two 8-bit character bytes. This algorithm recasts the String variable containing the alphanumeric key as an array of integer and then sums the element values. A real variable should be used to hold the sum if the sum is likely to exceed **MAXINT** for the compiler in use.

This transformation algorithm may prove faster than the previous algorithm because the character-to-number conversion process is nearly automatic; it is accomplished by simply interpreting groups of stored characters as numbers instead of characters rather than making many time-consuming calls to `Ord`. Also, it can convert two or more characters at a time to a single integer value before adding this value to the sum, as opposed to converting and summing characters one at a time. You are encouraged to design an algorithm for converting a character string to a number in this manner.

Unfortunately, either of the conversion algorithms just discussed may produce yet another problem: Many groups of unique character string keys will map to the same array element index. For example, the strings `'SPEAR'`, `'REAPS'`, `'PEARS'`, and `'SLASH'` all map to 379 using the `TransformKey` function. The consequence of two key values map to the same array index value is called a **collision.**

To surpass the O (log N) efficiency barrier, we must somehow devise a searching strategy and its associated data structure that does the following:

- *Involves direct addressing,* to provide an average search time less than O (log N)
- *Avoids having to move data items* about the structure in the course of performing insertions and deletions
- *Permits string type keys,* converting them to numeric key values quickly enough to not slow down the entire search process significantly
- *Handles collisions of numeric key values,* if they occur; this must be done fast enough to not delay the entire search process significantly.

We will now examine such a direct addressing searching scheme, called **hash addressing** (or simply **hashing**), and its associated data structure, the *hash table.*

Hash Addressing and Hash Tables

The *ADT hash table* is simply an array, with either of two basic strategies employed to handle collisions as they occur: *chaining* and *open addressing* (more will be said about these strategies later). Hashing employs a **hash function** to transform the original key value into an array index value (the hash table address), as depicted generically in Figure 10.12. Again, the data structure that supports hash addressing is called a hash table, and its ADT specifications follow.

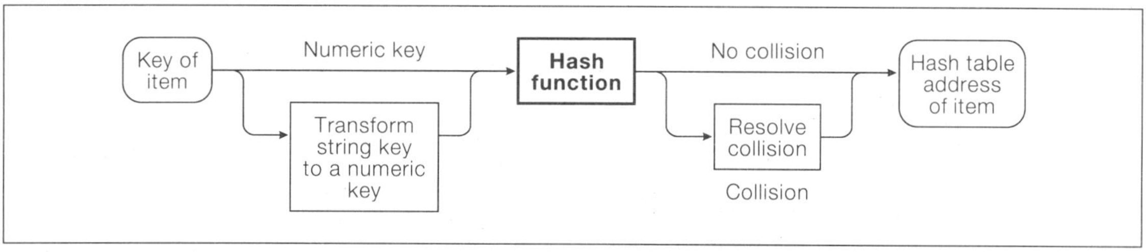

FIGURE 10.12 Hashing a Key to a Hash Table Index Value

Specifications for ADT Hash Table

The **ADT hash table** is a set-type structured data-type representation of ADT table. Its items belong to the same type, yet no ordering is imposed by the structure except that certain classes of key values will hash to the same hash table index value. Each stored item is completely independent of other stored items (as in any set-type structure), so the concept of linearity does not apply.

The structure and mechanics of searching for an item or inserting or deleting an item depend on the strategy implemented to resolve collisions—either *chaining* or *open addressing*.

Domain

The domain consists of items, typically of record data type.

Fundamental Operations

1. *Initialize:* Initialize the table as empty; i.e., a table containing no items.
2. *Test for emptiness:* Determine if the table is empty.
4. *Search for a particular item:* Search for an item already stored or for the location where a new item may be added.
5. *Add an item:* Add an item to the table.
6. *Remove an item:* Remove an item from the table.

As simple examples, look ahead briefly to Figure 10.13 to see a hash table based on an open addressing strategy and to Figure 10.14 to see a hash table based on a chaining strategy. In the open addressing strategy, all items reside (somewhere) within the hash table array. When the key value of an item about to be stored hashes to an array index that already contains an item (a collision), the new item is stored elsewhere in the array. In the chaining strategy, all items whose key values hash to the same array index are stored in the same **overflow list,** which emanates from that array element. More will be said about both strategies later in this section.

Although hashing may be quicker in the average case than linear or binary searching, it *does* present a significant drawback: Because items are distributed throughout the table when they are stored, *traversal is not a fundamental operation*. Therefore, a hash table is really a means of representing a *set structure* in which the items may all be of the same simple *or* structured type, unlike the standard Pascal set data type discussed in Section 3.1, in which all items must be of the same simple type.

In the design of algorithms we have frequently encountered the time-space trade-off, as described originally in Section 3.7:

- *Increasing memory space decreases execution time.* With no memory space limitations, we could locate any item immediately by allocating one array element per (possible) item and using direct addressing based on the key value.
- *Increasing execution time simplifies memory requirements.* With no execution time limitations, we could simply store all items in any linear structure and employ a linear search to locate any particular item.

Hashing provides a good compromise by providing the fastest average search time while using a reasonable amount of memory.

How large should the hash table array be? Clearly, the open addressing strategy requires at least as many elements as there are items, whereas the chaining strategy requires a far smaller array, since colliding items are stored in overflow lists. The general rules of thumb for any application involving up to N many possible items are as follows:

- *Open addressing*. The hash table should contain about $1.2N$ elements (20% of the array is unused).
- *Chaining*. The hash table should have $0.1N$ to $0.2N$ elements, so each overflow list contains an average of 10% to 20% of all items stored.

With either strategy, average search time decreases as the table size increases.

Hash Functions

A hash function is an example of a *many-to-one algorithm,* since many different key values may map to the same function value. A "good" hashing function should have the following characteristics:

- *Uniformity of index values produced.* Given a random assortment of key values, the function should produce an even distribution of hash table index values and should not be influenced abnormally by any group of key values. That is, the function should scatter items uniformly about the hash table during insertion of items, since this minimizes the probability of future collisions.
- *Simplicity.* The function should be simple enough so that the time necessary to execute it does not counterbalance the intended savings in search time. Accordingly, the algorithm used to convert string-type key values to numeric key values prior to hashing must be relatively simple and fast.

Of course, the hash function used to search for items must be the *same* function that had been used to store those items in the table. The same hash function must be used for all items stored in the same hash table.

Since handling collisions adds to the total search time for an item, elaborate hash functions have been developed to minimize the probability of collisions, although no hash function is perfect. Of course, as a routine becomes more elaborate, more time is required to execute it, thereby adding to the total search time. Thus, the programmer is faced with a paradox: A simple hashing function is fast but may not minimize collisions as well as an elaborate function, which takes longer to execute!

Since a hash function should produce a random distribution of index values, given a random distribution of key values, a **random-number generator** function seems a viable choice. A random-number generator function is intended to produce a random (i.e., unpredictable) sequence of values. Of course, any algorithm based on a mathematical formula, no matter how elaborate, is capable of producing only a series of ***pseudo*random numbers,** since the series is predictable (in fact, *pseudorandom-number gener-*

ator is the term used most commonly). The distribution of values by such an algorithm usually is erratic enough to give the appearance of randomness and is therefore useful in simulation and gaming applications. Pseudorandom-number generator functions require some type of numeric *seed value,* which is manipulated mathematically by the function to produce the next random number. The number produced then serves as the seed value the *next* time the function is invoked. (This is why the Pascal representation of random-number generator functions typically has a **VAR** Seed argument, as an exception to the rule of style that functions should not return modified argument values.)

A hash function is a pseudorandom number generator intended to produce a single pseudorandom number—a hash table array index. The seed value passed to it is the numeric key of a data item (perhaps a transformed character string key). We now examine three pseudorandom-number generator algorithms commonly used as hash functions: *division, extraction,* and *folding.*

Hashing by Division

Since the range of the hash table index values is typically much narrower than the range of possible key values, **division** seems to be the most natural method of mapping a key value to an index value. Simply using **DIV** to divide the key by some constant to produce an index value is a poor choice, however, because it may produce an index value beyond the array bounds. For example, if the table size is 13, the key value 269 hashes to 20 (269 **DIV** 13), which is beyond the upper array bound.

The **MOD** operator may be used instead to always bring the key value into the range of hash table indices. If the array size (here, 13) is used as the divisor, **MOD** always produces an integer remainder between zero and the array size minus 1, i.e., zero through 12. An even-numbered divisor should not be used, since even and odd key values would then be mapped to even and odd index values, respectively. It has been proven mathematically that a good distribution results when the table size is a prime number. Figure 10.13 shows a simple hash table of 13 elements, with 8 items already stored. The table uses open addressing, and the data type of item keys is integer. In the figure, only key values are shown, and a zero key indicates the absence of an item.

Hashing by Extraction

A second algorithm for deriving a hash table index uses **extraction**—that is, it extracts and uses a particular portion of the numeric key. For example, a social security number or a home telephone number is a common type of key for many data bases of information, including government and aca-

Hash (Key) = Key **MOD** 13

0	1	2	3	4	5	6	7	8	9	10	11	12
26	14	0	3	95	0	136	59	0	0	166	0	181

FIGURE 10.13 Items Stored in a Simple Hash Table, Using Open Addressing and MOD in the Hash Function

demic records, bank loan accounts, reservations, school and employment applications, and contests. For these applications, the *entire* key cannot be used directly as a hash table index because it is simply too large: A 9-digit social security number would require an array of 1 billion elements and a 10-digit telephone number would require a hash table of 10 billion elements, when only a fraction of the elements would ever likely be used.

If either of these large types of keys is represented as a real value, the `RealDivisionHash` function of Appendix K could be called to perform **`MOD`** like division and produce an integer result. Alternatively, we can use the N least significant digits of the mantissa to form the index for a hash table of up to 10^N elements. (Of course, division hashing will likely be necessary to bring the resulting N-digit result to a value within the array bounds.) For example, if N is 4, the social security number 313-49-0035 hashes to the value 35; the telephone number (617) 437-2462 hashes to the value 2462.

Deciding exactly *which* digits of the original key to extract can have a significant effect on distribution of the values generated. In many corporations, for example, an employee's identification number will contain several leading digits that indicate the division in which he or she works. In one particular company, Wilbur Workethic (#236138) and I. Emma Gogetter (#236029) both work in the Small Systems Customer Support division (as indicated by the leading 236 value), whereas Teddy Tenacious (#103446) works in the Personnel Office (as indicated by the leading 103 value). Extracting the four *least significant* digits for these values results in a much more diverse distribution of hash table index values than would be obtained by extracting the three *most significant* digits. Similar considerations must be made when using telephone numbers and social security numbers as keys, since the first three digits of either are determined geographically.

Greater variation is assured by squaring the key before extracting the middle digits, a technique known as **midsquare hashing.** Any numeric key of N digits, when squared, produces a product containing $2N - 1$ to $2N$ digits. If N is at least 3, the digits in positions N through $N + 2$ of the product (counting from right to left) can be extracted. The following example uses a four-digit key, so $N = 4$. Therefore, digits in positions 4 through 6 are extracted to produce a hash value of 880:

$$\begin{aligned} \text{Hash}(\ 4988\ ) &= 4988 \times 4988 = 24\underline{880}144 \\ &= 880 \end{aligned}$$

Hashing by Folding

Folding is an extension of the extraction technique in which portions of the key are extracted and then combined to produce a single hash table index value. In each of the following three examples, digit groups of differing size (1, 2, and 3) are extracted from a six-digit key. The group size and the number of digits in the key determine the range of index values produced:

Hash(435792) =	4 + 3 + 5 + 7 + 9 + 2 =	30	Range: 0–54
Hash(435792) =	43 + 57 + 92 =	192	Range: 0–297
Hash(435792) =	435 + 792 + =	1227	Range: 0–1998

As with the extraction hashing scheme, the value produced by folding is then fed to the division hashing algorithm to bring the resulting index value within the actual hash table bounds. Notice that the `TransformKey` function described earlier employs a folding algorithm.

Another common folding technique involves combining the individual bytes of a numeric key by performing bit-wise exclusive-OR operations (commonly referred to as **XOR**, although this is not a standard Pascal operator). In the following example, a four-digit key value is hashed using the representation of integers described in Section 2.2 for a 16-bit computer (two 8-bit bytes):

$$7591_{10} = 00011101\ 10100111_2 \qquad \begin{array}{rl} & 00011101 \\ \text{XOR} & \underline{10100111} \\ & 10111010_2 = 186_{10} \end{array}$$

Although standard Pascal does not provide an XOR operator, the standard **AND** and inclusive **OR** operators may be used to implement an exclusive-OR operation. The `FoldingHash` function, given in Appendix K, performs this 2-byte extraction operation on the 16-bit integer key, which is passed as a parameter.

Collision-Resolution Strategies and Hash Table Representations

A hash table collision may occur while searching for a place to store a new item or when searching for an existing item. Items whose keys hash to the same array element (i.e., a collision) are said to belong to the same **hash class.** *The choice of strategy for resolving collisions determines how the hash table is actually represented.* This choice also determines how the fundamental hash table operations are implemented. We examine the two simplest strategies:

1. **Chaining.** Each array element has an associated overflow list external to the hash table array. Each list is used to store a group of items whose keys hash to the same array index and is represented typically as a dynamically allocated linked list. A hash table search routine hashes the key of the item sought to produce an array index and then searches the overflow list emanating from this element.
2. **Open Addressing.** Each item stored occupies a single array element. When an item is being inserted and another item already occupies the hashed-to element, the new item must be stored in another, unoccupied element. (We will briefly examine several algorithms for locating another such element. If the hash table search routine is called to locate an existing item and does not find it immediately, it must employ the same type of relocation algorithm as is applied when searching for an unoccupied element prior to inserting a new item.)

With either chaining or open addressing, it must be noted that the search algorithm's performance deteriorates as the table fills up. We begin by examining the chaining strategy.

Chaining

Figure 10.14 depicts a simple hash table of 18 items, with each overflow list represented as a dynamically allocated linked list. In the figure, only key values are shown among the data items and a stripe-filled rectangle represents a **NIL** value.

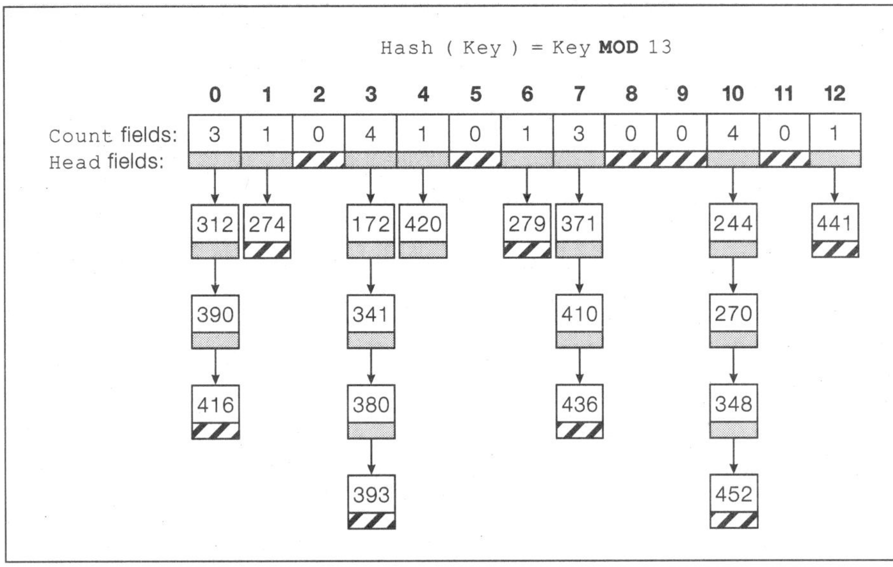

FIGURE 10.14 A Sample Hash Table of 18 Items, Using Chaining

A set of generic, global declarations for a hash table using this type of chaining follows:

```
CONST
  TableSize      = ??;  {Prime value ≈ 10% - 20% of possible number of items}
  TSizeLessOne   = ??;  {TableSize minus 1}
  MaxChars       = ??;  {Application dependent}

TYPE
  KeyType        = ??;                        {Integer or Real}
  AlphaKeyType   = String [ MaxChars ];       {Include if original key is a string}

  InfoType       = RECORD
                     Key       :  KeyType;      {Numeric value of key}
                     AlphaKey  :  AlphaKeyType; {Include if original key is a string}
                     {Other fields, as necessary}
                   END;

  NodePtr        = ^Node;
  Node           = RECORD
                     Data    :  InfoType;  {Data portion}
                     Next    :  NodePtr    {Address of next node in this overflow list}
                   END;

  LListType      = RECORD
                     Head    :  NodePtr;   {Points to 1st node in this overflow list}
                     Count   :  Integer    {Count of items in this overflow list}
                   END;

  HTableType   = RECORD
                   Buckets     :  ARRAY  [ 0..TSizeLessOne ] OF LListType;
                   ItemCount   :  Integer          {Count of all nodes in hash table}
                 END;

VAR
  HashTable : HTableType;
```

With the chaining technique, an array element is called a **bucket,** an array index value is called the **bucket value,** and a count of the number of data items stored in the overflow list emanating from a bucket is called the **bucket size.** All items stored in the same bucket are said to belong to the same hash class, since their keys all collided when hashed. For example, records with key values 371, 410, and 436 are all in the same hash class, in bucket 7 of the hash table of Figure 10.14.

Notice that each element is a `LListType` record, so we can use our linked list primitive routines of Chapter 5 and Appendix D. The hash table is initialized by assigning a **`NIL`** value to each `Head` field, a zero value to each `Count` field (the bucket size), and a zero to the `HashTable.ItemCount` field.

Variations on the chaining technique include the following:

- *Header nodes.* Each array element points to a header node, which contains a key value less than any legitimate key value. Header nodes eliminate the special case of inserting or deleting at the head of an overflow list (as described in the Application 5.2 telephone-address directory program.
- *Tail nodes.* Each overflow list ends with a tail node, which contains a key value greater than any legitimate key value. Tail nodes double the efficiency of linear searching, since the search algorithm has to compare only key values and no longer has to also test for a **`NIL`** `Next` field value as the end-of-list indicator.
- *Replacing each linear list with a nonlinear search tree.* Binary search trees or 2-3 trees may be used instead.

The second and third enhancements are intended to reduce search time, although overflow lists are typically short enough that the savings in time is probably negligible (especially when compared to the time-consuming operations of insertion and deletion with 2-3 trees).

With either chaining or open addressing, the use of character strings creates another type of collision problem. A computer can compare two numbers significantly faster than it can compare two character strings. When the source code includes instructions to compare two strings, the compiler actually generates instructions to perform a character-by-character comparison between the strings, based on their character set values. Since the goal of hashing is shortening search time and a search routine performs comparisons of key values, each overflow list node should therefore contain the numeric key to which its original character string key was transformed (via the `TransformKey` function) prior to hashing.

Recall, however, that many different character string keys may be transformed to the same numeric key value. Naturally, their identical numeric keys will hash to the same bucket, so these data items will be stored in the same overflow list. If the data items all have the same numeric key in the overflow list, how will the hash table search routine tell them apart?

The solution is to store *both* the numeric, transformed key (as the **primary key**) and the original, character string key (as the **secondary key**). This is why the declaration for an `InfoType` record contains the field `AlphaKey` when the original key is a character string. Upon a match on the numeric primary key, the search routine must then examine the `AlphaKey` field, and this approach is taken by any data base program that permits duplicate (primary) keys.

Analysis of Chaining

By convention, a hash table should have about $0.1N$ to $0.2N$ elements, so each overflow list contains an average of 10% to 20% of N, all items stored. Having M overflow lists reduces the number of key comparisons in the average searching case by a factor of M. A hash table's **load factor,** λ, (sometimes called the **density factor**) is the average length of an overflow list and is calculated as follows:

$$\lambda = \frac{\text{total number of items stored}}{\text{number of overflow lists}} = \frac{N}{M}$$

The load factor describes how well items are distributed throughout the table; the lower the value of λ, the better the distribution.

Average search time depends on λ and not on N, the total number of items stored. As N increases, λ improves as the predictor of average overflow list length and therefore of the average search time. In Section 3.7, we calculated average and worst cases of linear searching. We can now plug in λ as the (estimated) length of the overflow list to be searched (n):

$$\text{Average case (successful search)} \approx \frac{n + 1}{2} = \frac{\lambda + 1}{2} = O(\lambda)$$

$$\text{Worst case (unsuccessful search)} \approx n + 1 = \lambda + 1 = O(\lambda)$$

Keeping each overflow list ordered by primary key value and using header and tail nodes reduces average search time even further.

Open Addressing

Open addressing offers an advantage over chaining because linked overflow lists need not be maintained; however, it has the limitation that the table must be large enough to hold the maximum number of items to be stored plus at least 20% extra space, as a general rule. This technique therefore tends to waste computer memory, since the chaining technique allocates memory for a data item (in an overflow list) only when that item is actually stored. Because of the memory waste and other complications that arise with open addressing, chaining is typically the hashing technique of choice. We will, however, examine open addressing briefly.

A set of generic, global declarations for a hash table using open addressing follows:

```
CONST
  TableSize     =  ??;           {Positive prime number; application dependent}
  TSizeLessOne  =  ??;           {TableSize minus 1}

TYPE
  KeyType       =  ??;                       {Integer or Real}
  AlphaKeyType  =  String [ MaxChars ];      {Use if original key is a string}
```

```
  InfoType        = RECORD
                      Key        :  KeyType;       {Numeric value of key}
                      AlphaKey   :  AlphaKeyType; {Use if original key is a string}
                      {Other fields, as necessary}
                    END;

  HTableType      = RECORD
                      Items      :  ARRAY [ 0..TSizeLessOne ] OF InfoType;
                      Count      :  Integer         {Count of items in table}
                    END;

VAR
  HashTable  :  HTableType;
```

To illustrate how open addressing works, we will again use a simple 13-element array. For simplicity, we also will assume that `KeyType` is integer. Figure 10.15 depicts the table after seven items have been inserted without collision. In the figure, a key value of 0 indicates the absence of an item.

The simplest open addressing algorithm for resolving collisions is **linear probing:** When the search routine is called to locate an item and its key hashes to an array location that contains an item other than the item sought, a linear search (a linear probe) for the item is conducted. (If the search is performed prior to the insertion of a new item, the first unused element would be sought.) The linear search advances toward the high index end of the array and wraps around to the element 0 if necessary. The sequence of elements along the search path is the **probe sequence.** We briefly examine this algorithm, even though it performs poorly, because it was the first one developed and it illustrates that the simplest idea is sometimes inadequate in practice.

As an example of linear probing, when the search routine employs the division hash function to obtain the table index in which to store a new item with key value 33, a collision occurs at the hashed-to index value, 7, which is already occupied by item 59. The search routine must then perform a linear probe, starting with element 7. The probe continues to element 8, the first unoccupied element encountered, so the search routine returns 8 as the insertion point. Upon searching for the insertion point for a new item with key value 25, a collision occurs at the hashed-to index value, 12. A subsequent linear probe, wrapping around to the low index end of the array, reveals that element 1 is the first unoccupied location, so the value 1 is returned as the insertion point. Figure 10.16 depicts the sample hash table of Figure 10.15 *after* items with key values 33, 25, and 32 have been stored in the table of Figure 10.15.

Hash (Key) = Key **MOD** 13

0	1	2	3	4	5	6	7	8	9	10	11	12
26	0	15	3	0	0	19	59	0	0	23	0	51

FIGURE 10.15 The Open Addressing Hash Table after Seven Items Have Been Stored

Hash (Key) = Key **MOD** 13

0	1	2	3	4	5	6	7	8	9	10	11	12
26	**25**	15	**3**	0	0	19	59	**33**	**32**	23	0	51

FIGURE 10.16 The Hash Table of Figure 10.15 after Items with Keys 33, 25, and 32 Are Stored Using Linear Probing

If linear probing is used in the search of insertion points, it must also be used when searching for stored items later. For example, when the search routine is called to locate item 25, the hash function returns the index value 12. The ensuing collision during this search, caused by the fact that an item with key value 51 already occupies element 12, indicates that if the item sought is in the table it must have been stored elsewhere (since a similar collision would have occurred when the item was inserted). A linear probe starting with element 12 leads to the item sought in element 1; the probe sequence consists of elements 12, 0, and 1.

As another example, a search for an item with key value 21 follows the probe sequence 8, 9, 10, and 11, where the key value of 0 indicates that the item sought is not in the table. The collision at element 8 occurred because the occupant of 8—item 33—was stored there following its collision at element 7 earlier! The search for item 21 is therefore hampered by the aftermath of an unrelated *earlier* collision; this type of interference, called **clustering,** is one of the major problems with open addressing (more on this later). A failed search also would be indicated if the hash table were full and every element had been examined.

To delete an item from a hash table, we should not simply assign a zero value to that item's key field. For example, assigning a zero value to the key fields of the 51 and 32 items would indicate that these items are no longer in the table; however, this practice disrupts the probe sequence for other items in the table. If we subsequently search for an item with key value 25, for example, the hash function produces the index value 12. Since the item in this location now has a zero key value (with item 51 deleted), however, the search concludes *incorrectly* that item 25 is not in the table! The same is true of a search for item 32 if item 33 is deleted by zeroing its key value. Instead, three states of key value are necessary: *occupied* (positive key value), *unoccupied* (zero value), and *deleted* (−1 or negated key value).

Even if each element is a record, it is not necessary to "zero out," or "blank out," the other fields of the record when that item is deleted. Nor is it necessary to move to this location the next item along a probe sequence. For example, after deleting item 33, it is not necessary to move item 32 to element 8. If an item with the special "deleted" key value (such as −1) is encountered *while searching for a particular item,* the search routine would simply regard the element as occupied and continue probing. If an item with key value −1 is encountered *while searching for the next unoccupied element* as the insertion point for a new item, the new item can be stored in that very element, since doing so leaves the probe sequence intact.

Although marking a deleted item by assigning an unusual value, such as −1, to its key field will preserve existing probe sequences, frequent deletions can clutter up the hash table with many such key values. *Linear probing is just linear searching along an unordered list*—the slowest type of search in the average case—and therefore must be minimized if total search time is to be minimized. Assigning an unusual value to the key fields of deleted items preserves probe sequences but *it does not shorten them.* The process of **garbage collection** must also be performed from time to time, reclaiming discarded memory (garbage) within the array. With garbage collection, a second, temporary hash table is initialized by setting all key values to 0. Next, each element in the original hash table is visited linearly, starting with element 0. If the element is empty or contains a deleted item, nothing is done; otherwise, the hash function is applied to the item's key and the item is inserted in the second hash table (collisions are resolved in the normal way as they arise). Finally, all elements of the second table are copied back to the first table, so the second table becomes the current hash table. Since garbage collection is relatively time consuming, it should be performed only periodically, when the application that normally uses the hash table is not running. To signal the need for garbage collection, the program can maintain a count of deleted items and display a user message or simply perform the collection process automatically when this count reaches a particular value.

As if the inherent inefficiency of linear probing were not bad enough, **primary clustering** and **secondary clustering** are two additional side effects that increase average search time as more and more items are stored in a table. That is, they increase the average amount of linear probing necessary to find a particular item or an available element. All keys that collide at the same hash table element require the same probe sequence to resolve such collisions. With the linear probing technique, a colliding item is always stored in the first unoccupied location encountered, resulting in groups of items occupying contiguous locations (primary clusters).

The top and middle diagrams in Figure 10.17 illustrate this primary clustering phenomenon. Here, items with key values 4, 30, 43, and 56 are being inserted, creating a primary cluster that emanates from element 4. When items with key values 18, 44, and 57 are then stored, all three key values hash to the same table index value (5), therefore requiring the *same* probe

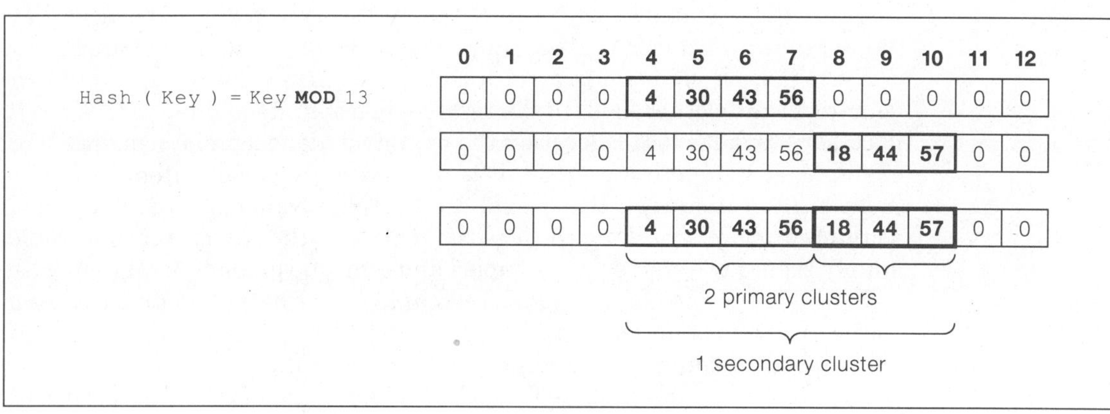

FIGURE 10.17 Example of Primary Clustering

sequence to resolve the collisions. This creates yet another primary cluster (elements 8, 9, and 10), as illustrated in the middle diagram of Figure 10.17. These two *primary clusters* occupy one contiguous group of locations, effectively resulting in one long *secondary cluster,* as indicated in the third diagram in the figure.

Two hash classes have now been merged, so our hashing scheme begins to lose all its direct-access advantage. Even this simple example illustrates the efficiency problems inherent with open addressing: When inserting an item, a collision creates or lengthens a primary cluster, since the item will be stored in the next available element via linear probing. Once a primary cluster has formed, it therefore tends to get longer and longer, making future collisions with *it* (i.e., with any element in the cluster) more likely. Each collision therefore raises the probability of future collisions.

To mitigate the clustering problems, the search routine must use a *nonlinear* approach to determine which element(s) to examine next following a collision. Two algorithms that are commonly used are quadratic probing and double hashing. Because of all these problems, chaining is generally preferred over open addressing.

10.3 SEARCHING FOR ITEMS IN EXTERNAL MEMORY

In Section 4.1, the ADT file was introduced as a way to preserve information when a program is not running as well as to provide a common area of memory that can be shared by many programs. Also pointed out was the fact that external memory is typically much larger than internal memory. In many applications, a collection of items may be simply too voluminous to fit in the internal memory of any one computer. Imagine, for example, the collection of all taxpayer records for the IRS, student records for a large university, or customer account records for a large bank. Such collections of items *must* be kept in external memory files, with individual records or groups of records read into internal memory only when needed for some type of processing. In this section we look at efficient ways of accessing records stored in external memory.

Magnetic Disks

We consider an item of information to be of Pascal record data type and focus on the magnetic disk as the medium used most commonly by programmers, whether the computer is a multiuser mainframe or a single-user microcomputer (a personal computer). Most microcomputers contain at least one diskette drive, for removable diskettes, and many contain an internal disk drive as well (our discussion in this section applies to files stored on either device).

A **magnetic disk** is a metal platter covered on both sides with a magnetic recording medium. When mounted within a **disk drive,** a disk rotates rapidly on a center spindle. Information in the form of magnetically charged bits is stored on one or both disk surfaces in concentric circles called **tracks.** A small recording or writing (*read/write*) head is attached to an *arm,* which may be moved across the tracks very close to the disk surface to read or

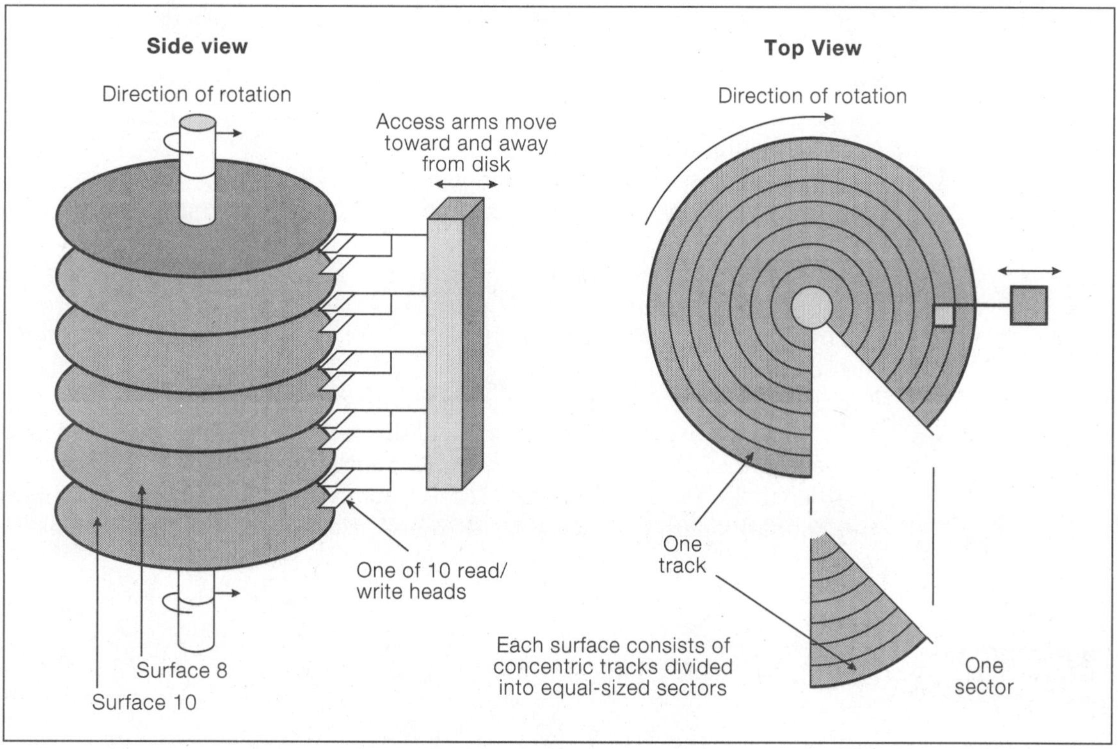

FIGURE 10.18 Magnetic Hard Disk System

write information. Many large multidisk drives are equipped with two read/ write heads per arm and one arm per disk surface. Most modern disk drives are Winchester type drives, in which both the disk(s) and the entire arm and read/write assemblies are enclosed in an airtight, dustproof box. Figure 10.18 depicts a simple, generic multidisk drive.

In a multidisk system, all arms move together. A **cylinder** is the collection of tracks that may be read or written based on the current position of the arms—i.e., those tracks, one per surface, in the same relative position on each disk. (If disks were made of glass and the current cylinder indicated by a fine etched line, a top view of the disks would reveal only the track on the top surface of the top disk; all other tracks in the cylinder would be directly beneath this track and equidistant from the spindle and, therefore, would not be visible.) Once the arms are moved to the desired cylinder, the read/write head of a particular arm may be turned on so that information from the current track of a particular disk surface may be read or written.

The smallest unit of information that an operating system program reads from or writes to a disk surface is called a **block,** or **page** (in this chapter, we use the term *block*). The size of a block varies among operating systems, but 512-, 1024-, and 4096-byte blocks are typical. Every track on each disk surface contains the same number of blocks. Because tracks increase in circumference the farther away they are from the center spindle, "empty" portions between blocks in a track must increase in length as well. This spacing is necessary because data on inner tracks rotate more rapidly under the heads than do data on outer tracks. To compensate for this faster rotational speed, the blocks of data are therefore spread out, allowing any one block of data to pass under the heads at the *same* rate. A **sector** is a pie-sliced portion of a disk surface containing a cross section of tracks. Each portion of track in a sector contains the same number of blocks.

Reading data from or writing data to a disk entails three operations, and the efficiency by which data may be read from or written to a disk is reflected in the time requirements of each:

- **Seek time** is the time expended to locate the correct track—i.e., to move the arm and its read/write heads toward or away from the spindle, to the correct cylinder, over the correct disk surface.
- Once a read/write head is positioned over the correct track, **rotational latency** is the time expended to locate the desired block; i.e., "waiting time" until the desired block of the track passes beneath the heads.
- Once the correct block in the correct track is located, **data-transfer time** is the time required for the read/write heads to pass over the block as data are being read or written.

In a **sequential file,** file data are stored by the operating system as a contiguous list of blocks. In a **nonsequential file,** file data are stored by the operating system as one linked list of blocks, distributed throughout external memory. All files stored on a magnetic tape must be sequential; either sequential or nonsequential files may be stored on a magnetic disk. Files on disk may be accessed in either a sequential or nonsequential ("direct") manner, regardless of how the file itself was stored. The physical layout of a file in external memory *does* affect the efficiency of certain operations, however. For example, sequential files provide the advantage of minimal seek time and rotational latency for such sequential operations as reading or writing the next blocks.

Because the operations of reading or writing a single block involve mechanical actions, a single block read or block write may take as much as 10,000 times longer to perform than the purely internal electronic operations performed by a computer's CPU, such as comparing two key values or assigning a value to a variable (i.e., to a memory location). *Programs should be designed to minimize disk accesses* (i.e., the reading or writing of blocks). In this section, we examine several techniques and data structures aimed at doing just that. Section 11.6 describes an algorithm for sorting data items in a file, with the aim of minimizing the total number of disk accesses.

Of course, the available computer hardware for accessing external memory, the physical arrangement of the files (as determined by the operating system), and the operating system itself all have a profound influence on actual file access time and, consequently, on the efficiency of file searching and sorting algorithms. For example, it generally takes less time to read a group of items from a file when they are stored contiguously along one track and in adjacent tracks rather than when they are stored randomly throughout the disk in a linked list fashion. The latter requires that the next group of file elements be located on the disk and the read/write disk head be positioned accordingly.

Most computers contain a special high-speed input/ output buffer called **cache memory,** which is used like a file buffer variable for all file accessing. File data are read into cache memory or written to a file from cache memory, one block at a time. When the compiler encounters a `Read`, `Readln`, or `Get` instruction in a user program, it generates machine-code instructions calling upon the operating system to read data into cache memory. The operating system might recognize that the desired file item *already* resides within the cache memory from the last disk read, thereby avoiding having to access the disk needlessly.

Preliminary Access Schemes

The fundamental operations performed on an external list of records are as follows:

- Test the list for emptiness or fullness.
- Search the list for a particular data item.
- Modify and replace a data item.
- Add a new data item to the list.
- Remove an existing data item from the list.
- Visit and process each data item in the list; i.e., traverse the list.

In the context of file handling, a data item is typically called a *record.*

There is one important difference between accessing internal and external memory, however, which will shape the ways we represent algorithms to perform these operations. When searching an internal list, we try to minimize the number of *key-value comparisons,* as was done during searching and sorting operations, and *assignments of whole data items,* such as exchanges of items during a sorting algorithm. As stated previously, with external lists, *accessing information from external memory takes substantially more time than does most internal program operations,* so we want to minimize the total number of such accesses when implementing an algorithm involving file handling.

Also stated previously, an operating system reads or writes information from a file in chunks called blocks, which may contain many records. (With internal lists, on the other hand, routines typically access individual records.) For example, a Pascal compiler might encounter an input operation, such as the standard `Get` routine. In the following call to `Get`, `InFile` is the file variable for a file of records open for reading:

```
Get ( InFile );
```

The compiler would then generate the machine instructions that direct the operating system to read an entire block of information from the file, starting with the current position, as indicated by the file pointer. If the length of an `InFile^` record is N bytes and is less than one block in length, the operating system will extract the first N bytes and return them to the Pascal program in the file buffer variable, `InFile^`. If N is greater than one block, the compiler will generate the machine instructions to read as many blocks as is necessary. A set of corollary operations is performed with an output operation, such as the standard `Put` routine. In the following call to `Put`, `OutFile` is a file variable for a file of records open for writing:

```
Put ( OutFile );
```

Some nonstandard Pascal compilers allow a user program itself to read or write an entire block of information, as suggested by the following call statements to two nonstandard procedures, **ReadBlock** and **WriteBlock**:

```
ReadBlock  ( {file variable}, {block number}, {List} );  {Read 1 block into List}
WriteBlock ( {file variable}, {block number}, {List} );  {Write block stored in List}
```

Here, List is the data structure into which data would be read (for ReadBlock) or from which data is written (for WriteBlock)—e.g., a single record, an array of records, an array of integer, and the like.

There are two techniques for accessing file data:

- **Sequential access.** File elements may be read or written only sequentially, starting with the first element. For example, to read (or write) the seventeenth element, the first through sixteenth elements must be read (or written) first.
- **Direct access.** Any element can be read or written next, without having to read (or write) other elements preceding it in the file.

Sequentially accessing file data is analogous to accessing nodes in a linear linked list. Sequentially accessing a file element by element via Get or Read (for binary files) or Read or Readln (for text files) or accessing a file block by block via a ReadBlock type procedure creates the illusion that all components of a file are stored contiguously, although they may actually be distributed throughout the disk(s). According to the tenets of standard Pascal, *all* file access is sequential; i.e., all files created using Rewrite are accessible only in a sequential manner, using the standard Get, Read, Readln, or Write routines.

By contrast, directly accessing file data is analogous to accessing any element of an array, in any order, using the combination of array name and element index value. Typically with files, a user program reference to a particular file record is made by using the combination of file name and file element number. At the operating system level, a file reference involves the file name, sector number, and block address. (The term **random access** means that each item in a collection of items may be accessed in the same length of time, regardless of its position within the collection. Arrays provide both direct and random access of their elements, since the computer needs the same amount of time to map each element reference to its actual memory location, regardless of the value of the index. Since the physical location of a block within a file determines the time required to access it due to seek time and rotational latency, files do not support true random access of data.)

A magnetic disk is a **direct access device** because any particular block of data may be read or written anywhere on the disk. A magnetic tape, on the other hand, is a **sequential access device** because blocks of data can be accessed only sequentially. For example, to access a particular block physically located halfway through a tape, the computer must prompt a human operator to locate and mount the correct tape in a tape drive and then must wait until the first half of that tape passes under the heads before the desired block is encountered. Although magnetic tape is cheaper than magnetic disk as a storage medium, it is so slow that its primary purpose in computing has become limited to simply **archiving** (preserving) large quantities of outdated, nonactive information. The latest technological innovations involve optical disks, which promise tremendous storage capacity, may be accessed directly with reasonable efficiency, and may be produced at a reasonable cost.

With files stored on magnetic disks, the accessing schemes available to the programmer depend on the capabilities of the operating system and the particular Pascal compiler in use and *not* on the physical layout of the file. For example, sequential accessing is possible on any Pascal file even if the blocks of the file are scattered across the disk or disks. Although standard Pascal compilers will generate machine instructions that support only sequential accessing, most nonstandard Pascal systems furnish some routine that facilitates the direct accessing of file elements stored on a direct access device.

Recall from Section 4.1 that files are divided logically into file elements (a file of records, a file of integers, etc.), each of which is associated with a file index (an integer value, starting with zero). Many nonstandard Pascal systems furnish a direct access routine typically named **Seek** (or something similar). A generic call to Seek follows:

```
Seek ( {file variable}, {file element index} );
```

The file element index parameter must be an integer value in the range zero to the number of file elements in the file minus 1. (Many nonstandard Pascal systems also offer a FileSize function that returns the number of file elements in a particular file.) Seek positions a file pointer to the file element specified by the index value passed as a parameter and is called prior to a Get or Put call to read or overwrite a particular file element. The imaginary ReadBlock and WriteBlock procedures would allow a user program to access whole blocks of data whereas the Get, Put, Read, Write, and nonstandard Seek procedures allow a user-program to access individual file elements.

For example, assume we (again) wish to have a program open a file and immediately read the seventeenth file element without having to read the first 16 elements. The following nonstandard code segment accomplishes this:

```
{Include statement to open file; this will position file window over 1st element}
Seek  ( InFile, 17 );  {Position file window over 17th file element}
Get   ( InFile );      {Read 17th file element into InFile^ file buffer variable
{Include statements here to process InFile^}
```

In this section's discussion of searching external memory, we will assume that the nonstandard Seek and FileSize routines are available to us.

Thus far, we have examined the accessing of external memory at two levels:

1. How the operating system actually arranges and retrieves an entire block of a file
2. How a Pascal program accesses a particular file element

The first level of operation is largely dependent upon the memory hardware and operating system software in use, although we discuss (in general terms) an external search tree data structure called a B-tree and an external hash table later in this section; further details are deferred to textbooks and courses specifically about file structures and operating systems.

We will begin by examining several data structures and techniques that a Pascal user program may employ to store and retrieve individual elements of a file.

External Indexing

Figures 8.24 and 10.10 depict an indexed addressing technique to access a record within a collection of records dynamically allocated in heapspace. The same principle can be applied to records that reside wholly within external memory as well, using an external key table. As a simple example, examine Figure 10.19. Here, the key table is a search tree residing entirely within internal memory, and each node contains both an integer key value and its file index number, indicating the file element that contains the associated data.

To access a particular data record, the search routine must search the key table first and then, if the desired key value is found, return its associated file index. The calling routine can use the file index number to position the file pointer correctly, via a call to `Seek`. The `Get` or `Put` procedures may then be called to read or overwrite the file element. The full **data file address** of a particular data item is therefore the combination of the file name plus the file index of the desired record, both of which are passed to the `Seek` procedure.

The insertion and deletion of data records (i.e., file elements) pose some interesting problems. We could begin with the simple rule that a new data record is always appended to the end of the file. The Pascal `Put` and `Write` procedures do this by default—if the file is manipulated in a purely sequential manner, without calls to `Seek`. Unfortunately, the practice of always appending new records results in wasted file space when records are deleted. For example, if the key table nodes for key values 321, 492, and 407 are deleted, their abandoned file space (**file garbage**) will never be reused if new records are always appended to the end of the file.

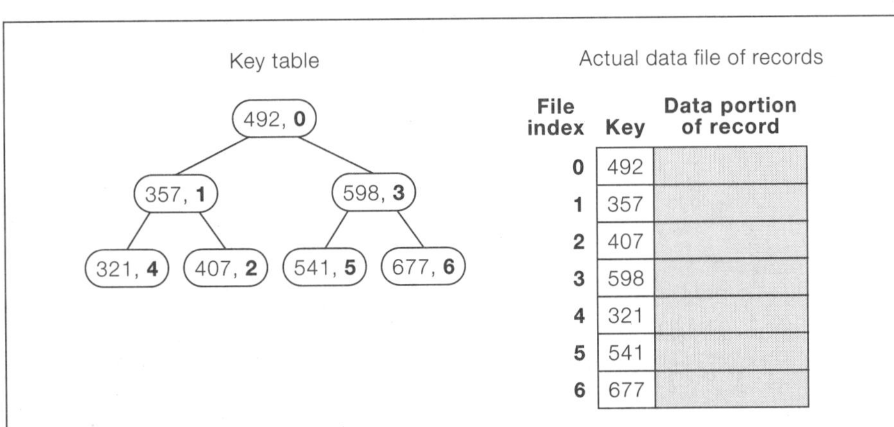

FIGURE 10.19 A Simple External Indexed Addressing Scheme

Instead, a program must manage the use and reuse of external memory more efficiently by using a *free list,* just as we did in the Section 5.3 array representation of a linked list. The program must maintain a list of index values for all file elements that are abandoned when records are deleted. When a new record is to be inserted and the free list is not empty, the file index for the new record is obtained from the list. The free list will be empty, on the other hand, when no abandoned file space is waiting to be reused; in this case, the new record is simply appended to the end of the data file and a new node added to the key table tree.

When the key table tree is saved in a file, the free list must be saved as well, and a single file of variant record can be used to store the nodes of both structures. (Most commercial data base programs store a key table in its own file, separate from the data file with which it is associated.) The program would begin by reading records from the key table file and reconstructing both the key table tree and the free list.

A single key table provides access to a data record via a single kind of key value—e.g., last and first names for an on-line telephone directory or student identification number for a university's data base of student records. As we saw in Section 8.2 on binary search trees, the ability to access the same data using N different types of key requires the maintenance of N additional key tables, each arranged according to a different key—e.g., street name for the online telephone directory or the combination of last and first names for the student data base.

Height-Balanced Index Search Trees: B-Trees

A height-balanced index search tree known as a *B-tree* is used most commonly to represent a key table for a large, external-memory data base of records. The B-tree was first documented in a paper by Bayer and McCreight in 1972, and several variations have been invented subsequently. Unlike the type of key table just presented, which resides within internal memory, a B-tree resides entirely in its own file. Nodes are read into internal memory during a B-tree search, record insertion, or record deletion operation.

Specifications for the ADT B-Tree

The **ADT B-tree** of order M is a height-balanced search tree with the following general characteristics:

- All leaf nodes are on the same level.
- Every node (excluding the root) must contain between M and $2M$ items.
- Every node containing K items has $K + 1$ children. The root has at least two children, unless it is a leaf node.
- In each internal node containing K items, each of the $K + 1$ link fields points to child node in the tree, as done in a 2-3 tree.

Domain

The domain is nodes of items, whose contents depend upon which of the three types of B-tree is being represented (in all three types, items are arranged within each node in order of ascending key value). The content also may vary if the node is an internal node or a leaf:

- **Primary index B-tree.** Data records are stored *only among the leaf nodes;* internal nodes contain key values whose only purpose is to guide a search to the appropriate leaf.
- **Secondary index B-tree.** A secondary index B-tree provides access to the data records stored in the leaves of a primary index B-tree based on a different key type than is used with the primary index; no data records are actually stored in this tree. For example, for a company's employee data base, if a primary index B-tree is structured using Social Security Number as the primary key, a secondary index B-tree might be built providing access to the *same* data using name as a secondary key. Each leaf node item contains a secondary key value along with the address of the primary index B-tree leaf which contains the associated data record. This concept of cross-referencing was introduced in Section 8.2 in the context of using *N* binary search trees to access the *same* set of data records *N* different ways—i.e., via *N* different types of keys.

Fundamental Operations

These include all search tree operations:

1. *Initialize as empty.*
2. *Test for emptiness.*
3. *Search for a particular data record.*
4. *Add a data record.*
5. *Remove a data record.*
6. *Traversal.*

Any B-tree that stores data only among the leaves is referred to as a **B$^+$-tree,** so the primary index B-tree just described is really a primary index B$^+$-tree, although the $^+$ is frequently dropped from the name. Some textbooks describe **B-trees with data spread throughout** the tree rather than stored only among the leaves, as with a 2-3 tree, however large, external memory data bases are almost never structured this way. A common enhancement to B-trees is to link all leaf nodes, forming a linked list. Whereas the tree structure itself provides nearly-direct access to a particular data record, linking the leaves provides sequential access of records as well. Figure 10.20 illustrates the generic layout of internal and leaf nodes of a primary index B$^+$-tree with linked leaves. Figure 10.21 depicts a simple primary index B$^+$-tree of order 2.

The binary search trees of Section 8.2 and the 2-3 trees of Section 10.1 reside entirely within internal memory. Each link field within a node of either tree is of Pascal pointer type and contains either the value of a heapspace memory address or else **NIL** (recall that binary search trees may also be represented using sequential storage and integer node "addresses" within the pseudoheapspace array). Our attempts to minimize search time focused on minimizing the average number of key comparisons during a search operation; for binary search trees, this is determined by the overall tree shape.

B-trees reside in external memory. Each link field within a node is the block address of another B-tree node. During the search of a B-tree, the root node is read into internal memory and searched. The next appropriate node block is read and searched, and so forth. The general searching algorithm is,

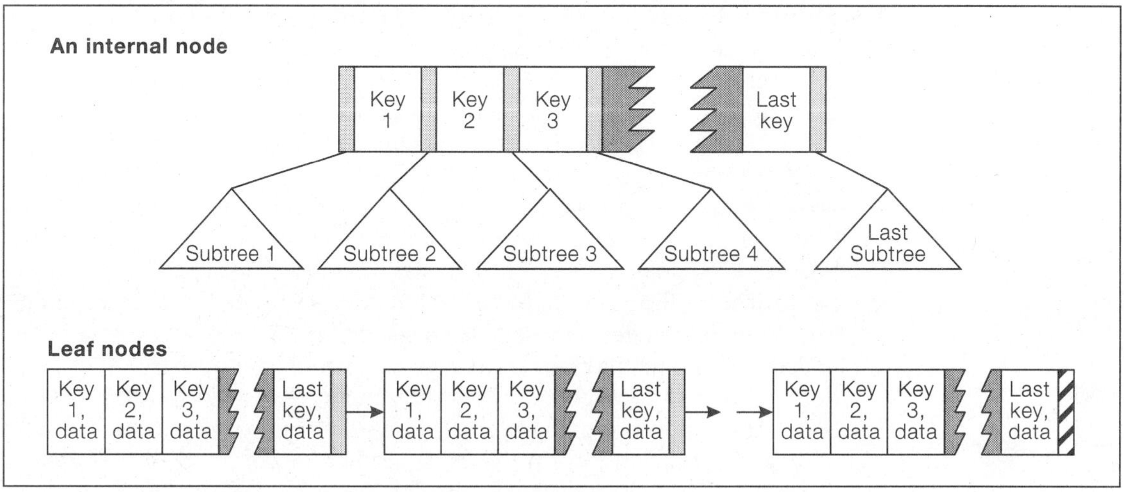

FIGURE 10.20 Internal and Leaf Nodes of a B$^+$-Tree

to a large extent, an extension of the operation of searching a 2-3 tree. Because items within a B-tree node are arranged by ascending key value, a modified binary search algorithm may be employed to search through the node once it has been read into internal memory. Since disk accesses take time, attempts to search for items in external memory focus on minimizing the number of disk accesses. *To minimize the total disk accesses during a search, as much of the B-tree (i.e., as large a subtree) as possible should be read in any one access.* As we shall see, this goal leads to the formula by which the order of the B-tree is determined. (A pseudocode algorithm for searching will be presented shortly.)

Why store key values among internal nodes and data records only among leaf nodes? Why not store data records throughout the tree, as has been done with most of the binary search trees presented in this textbook and with all of the 2-3 trees? Let us assume, for the moment, that our search tree in external memory is a binary search tree, with data spread throughout. Figure 10.22 depicts such a tree, divided into nine subtrees, and is based on a diagram in the classic textbook, *Algorithms + Data Structures = Programs* by Nicklaus Wirth. Further, let us assume that each of these nine subtrees has been stored in its own block of file memory. Since whole data records are typically much larger than a single key value, we will assume that seven data records are enough to fill or nearly fill a node.

Conceivably, a search routine could read block 1 via a nonstandard `ReadBlock` procedure and search it internally; if the data record were not found, it would read the next (child) block as appropriate—one of the blocks 2 through 9. This node would then be searched internally until the data record sought is either encountered or else the search terminates unsuccessfully.

In most applications, the key of an item requires far less physical space in its memory representation than do the data associated with that key. For example, a university's data base of student records may use a social security number for each record, which takes 9 bytes, compared to the hundreds of bytes required to represent all the associated data also stored in the record, such as name, address, courses taken, and so on. *By storing the data*

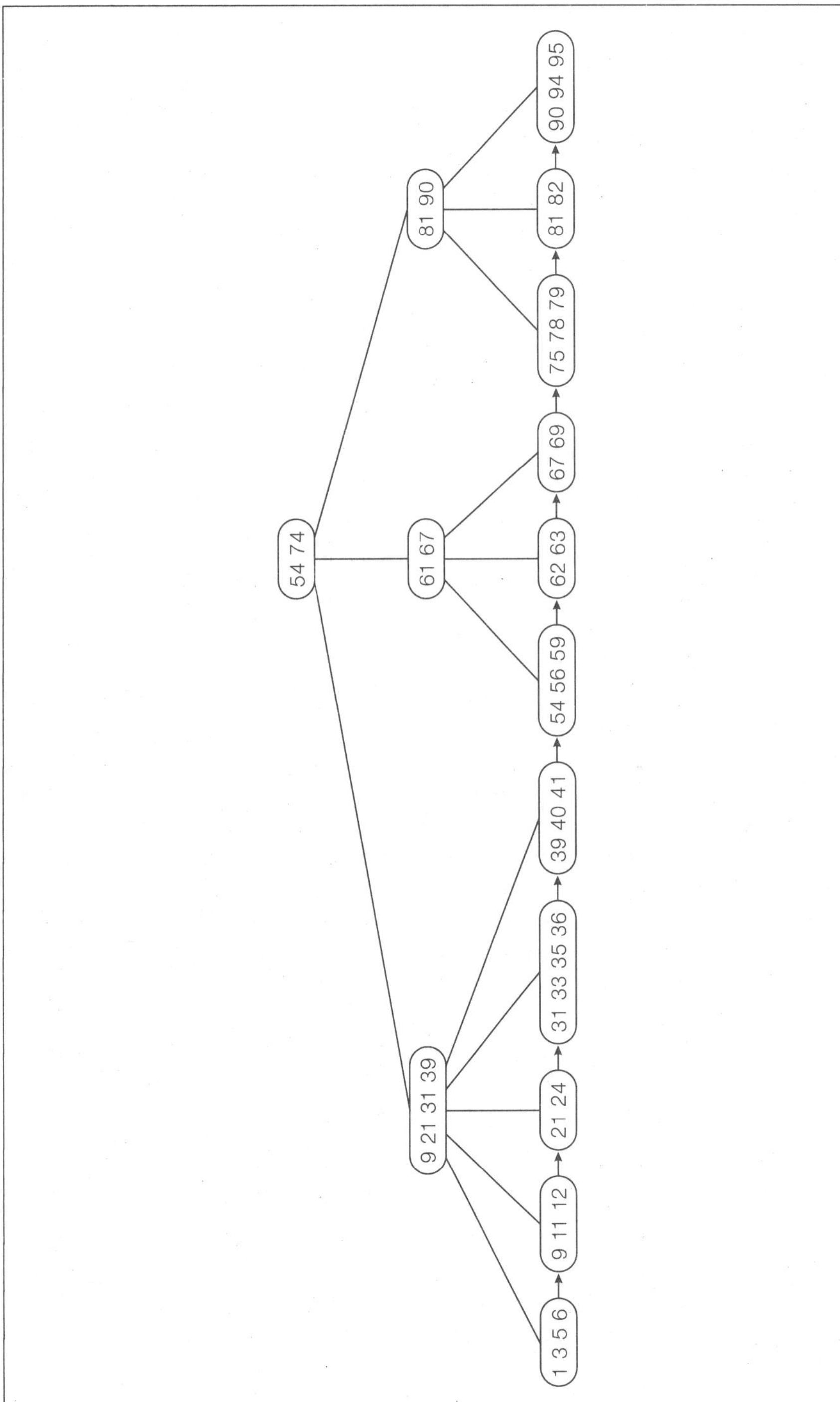

FIGURE 10.21 Sample B$^+$-Tree of Order 2

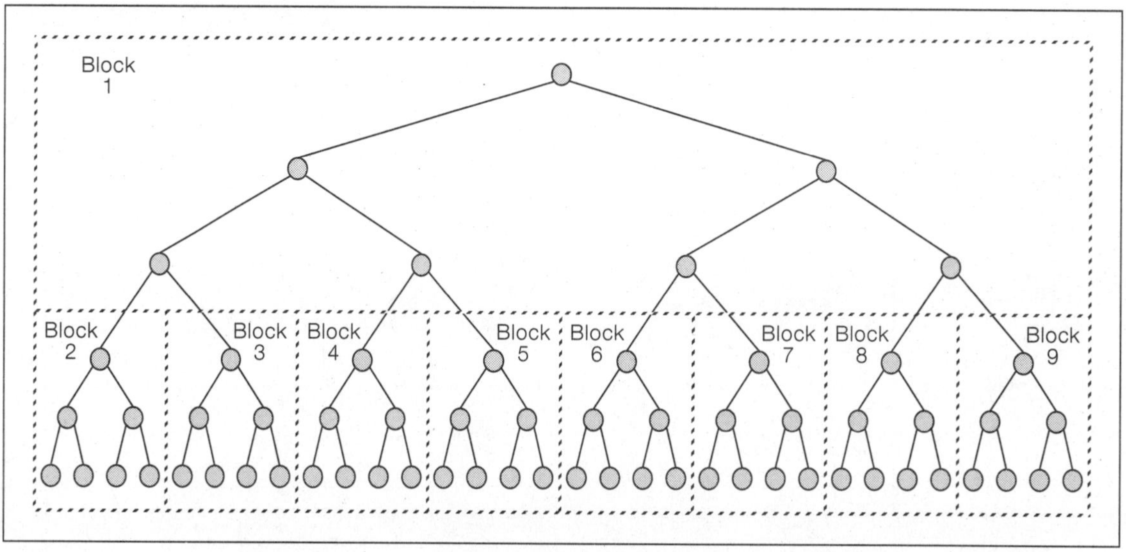

FIGURE 10.22 An External Binary Search Tree Divided into Nine Blocks (from Niklaus Wirth, *Algorithms + Data Structures = Programs*, Copyright © 1976, p. 245. Adapted by permission of Prentice Hall, Inc., Englewood Cliffs, New Jersey)

elsewhere (i.e., in leaf nodes), we can pack more keys into each B-tree node. And by storing more keys per block, each disk access becomes more "powerful," providing more information for searching purposes, so the total number of disk accesses (for any size tree) is reduced. This is why it is desirable to store as many keys as possible within every internal node block and to store the actual data records within leaf nodes. This also minimizes the total tree height, so a search routine gets to the appropriate leaf node with a minimum of disk accesses—i.e., as fast as possible.

How many keys may be stored in an internal tree node? If each node is one block in size, the maximum number of keys for a given block is then tied to the block size for the disk, computer, and operating system in use. And this brings us back to the concept of B-tree order value, *M*.

The **order of a B-tree,** *M,* is the minimum number of key values that must be stored in a one-block node. It is actually a function of the maximum number of key values that can physically fit within a one-block node. The following equations illustrate the relationship between the maximum number of keys per node and the resulting B-tree order:

$$\text{Maximum keys} \approx \frac{\text{block size}}{\text{maximum key size} + \text{link field size}} + (\text{link field size}) + (\text{key count})$$

$$\text{B-tree order} \approx \frac{\text{maximum keys}}{2}$$

These are only approximations because each node may contain other structure-related information as well, such as a Boolean value that is examined by a search routine to distinguish leaf nodes from internal nodes. B-trees tend to be short and wide, with each internal node having many children. The average number of children per internal node is called the **fan-out,** and fan-outs of 150 or more are not uncommon. The maximum number of data records in a leaf of a primary index B$^+$-tree (the **bucket factor**) or in any node of a B-tree with data spread throughout the tree may be less than $2M$ since data records tend to be larger than key and link field values.

It may seem that reducing the tree's height by storing more keys per node is offset by the fact that a search routine must now perform more comparisons per node. It is true that more key comparisons per node must be made; however, this is acceptable because shortening the tree's height results in fewer disk accesses, and *this* savings in time far outweighs any additional time spent searching a given node once it is read into internal memory. (Recall that the operation of reading or writing a single block may take as much as 10,000 times longer to perform than the time necessary to perform a single internal operation, such as comparing two key values.)

The operations of item insertion or deletion with a B-tree of order M are nearly identical to those operations for a 2-3 tree:

- *Insertion.* The new data record is inserted into the appropriate leaf, keeping the data records in the leaf ordered by ascending key value. If the leaf now contains no more than $2M$ data items, the insertion is complete; otherwise, the leaf node is split into two leaves and the key (only) of the middle data record is moved up to the parent internal node. If the parent node contains more than $2M$ data items, the insertion is complete; otherwise the parent node is split into two internal nodes and the middle key is sent "up" to its parent node, and so forth. As with a 2-3 tree, the root node itself may be split into two nodes and the middle key sent up to a new root node. Again, *only keys are moved up toward the tree root; all data records remain on the leaf level.*
- *Deletion.* After a data record is deleted from its leaf, if the leaf now contains at least M data records, the deletion is complete; otherwise, a data record must be transferred from a sibling leaf node or the leaf node must be merged with a sibling. Certain internal nodes may need to be modified as well, including bringing down parent keys and merging internal nodes, as with a 2-3 tree. Unlike a 2-3 tree, *keys are never deleted from internal nodes, even if their associated data records are deleted.* Leaving "old" keys behind avoids needless disk accesses and does not disrupt the search structure of the tree. This is why certain key values appearing in the internal nodes of the B-tree of Figure 10.21 have no corresponding data record in a leaf node.

Figure 10.23 traces the insertion of 22 data records into an empty B$^+$-tree of order 2.

Leaf nodes are linked to provide sequential accessing of data records by ascending key-value order, in addition to the direct accessing provided by the tree structure. If the leaves are *not* linked together, traversing the entire collection of data items in order of ascending key value would mean traversing the entire B-tree. Although this can be done, it involves reading and rereading the same internal node blocks just to access the leaf nodes to which they point. By linking the leaf nodes and remembering the block address of the first leaf (i.e., the leftmost leaf in conventional tree diagrams), a traversal routine can simply access the leaves, one after another. Linking the leaves also provides the ability to access the data records for keys within a particular range of key values—again, with a minimum number of disk accesses.

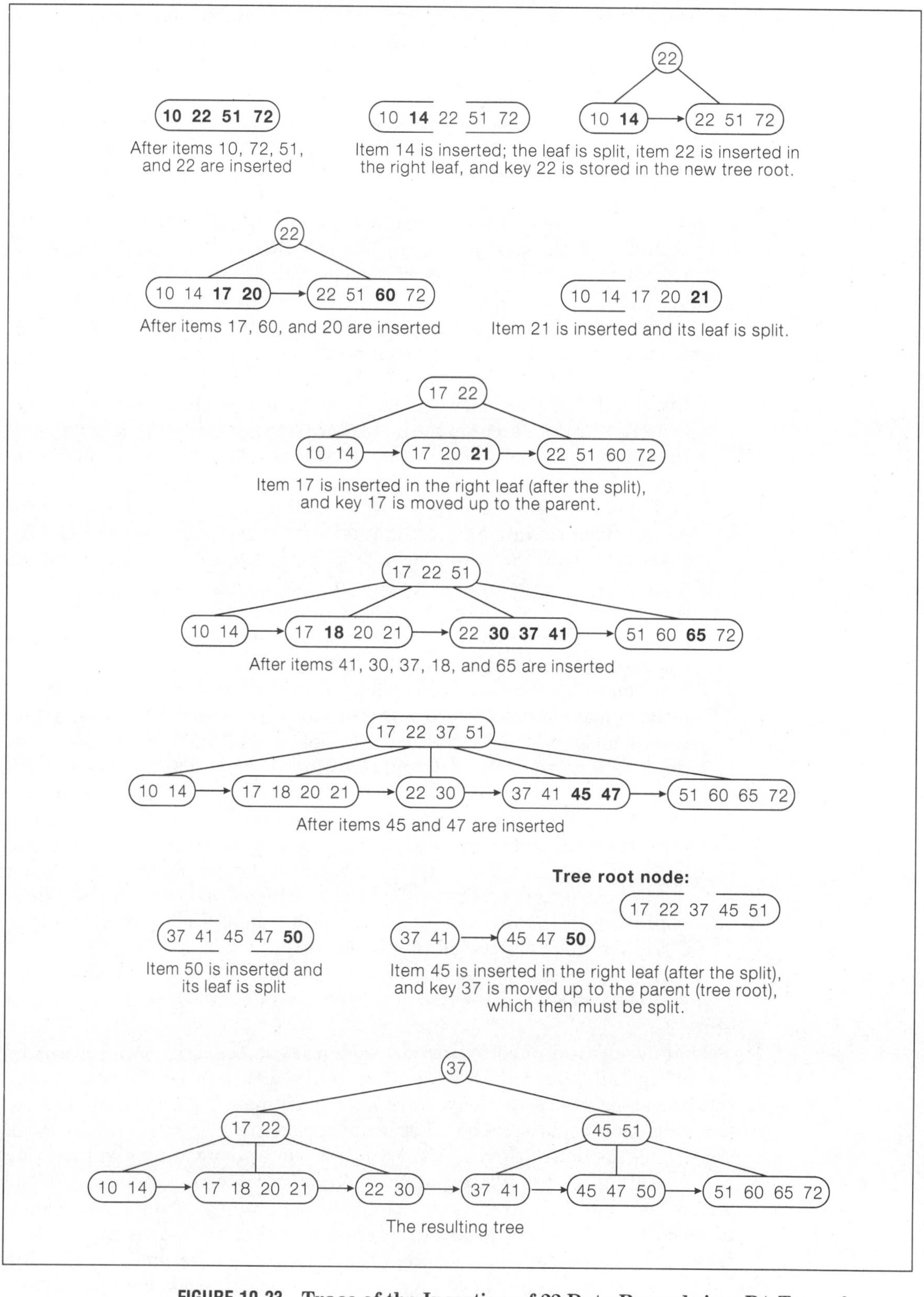

FIGURE 10.23 Trace of the Insertion of 22 Data Records in a B⁺-Tree of Order 2

The savings in total disk accesses gained by maximizing the number of keys per node would be undermined if the tree were greatly lopsided. In fact, our evolution from the binary search trees of Section 8.2 to the 2-3 trees of Section 10.1 was motivated by the desire for a search tree that remained height-balanced. This was done with 2-3 trees by having a tree grow upward if necessary during an insertion or shrink downward if necessary during a deletion. With B-trees, Bayer devised the rule that each node should contain between M and $2M$ keys, with M a constant based on the actual block size in use (as described previously). This provides the following advantages:

- The worst searching case requires $\log_M N$ disk accesses for a tree of N keys or items.
- Each block will be at least half full.

Pascal Representation of the ADT B-Tree

A given leaf node of a primary index B^+-tree may contain a single data record, but in most data base applications it will contain a number of data records. In Section 10.1, the entire 2-3 tree is represented using dynamic allocation. To expedite the search for items, each 2-3 node is represented as a binary search tree of either one or two single-item nodes. With B-trees, each block may be organized simply as an array of items (key value/block address pairs), *in ascending key value order.* Recall that this array representation of each 2-3 node was rejected for the 2-3 tree due to the time-expense of keeping the array ordered and the memory-expense of allocating array space that may go unused. Neither objection is of much concern with B-trees, however, for two reasons:

- *Domination of file access slowness.* It takes significantly more time to read a block than to insert or delete a key. Both operations require shifting other keys within the array to either create space for a new key or overwrite a deleted key.
- *Constant block size.* An entire block's worth of memory is always read or written, whether filled or not.

Data records can be stored in ascending key-value order within each array so that, once the desired leaf node is read into internal memory, a binary search may be performed to locate a particular data record. Because a given leaf may store more than one data record, the key value of its parent internal node need contain only the lowest (or highest) key among all keys in the leaf data records. The actual Pascal declarations are left as an exercise.

As described earlier, a secondary index is used to access data records stored in the leaves of a primary index tree but is structured based on some other type of key. Again, this concept of cross-referencing was actually introduced in Section 8.2 in the context of using N binary search trees to access the same set of data records N different ways—i.e., via N different types of keys. The internal nodes of primary and secondary indexes both contain key values and link fields (only); however, the structure of leaf nodes of the indexes differ:

- *Primary index B^+-tree leaves* contain *pairs of key values and associated data records,* plus a link field pointing to the next leaf if the leaves are linked.

- *Secondary index B-tree leaves* contain *pairs of key values and link fields*. The link field of a key points to the leaf in the associated primary index B-tree, which contains the data record associated with this key. Each secondary index B-tree leaf could also contain a link field pointing to the next leaf.

In most large data-base systems, several secondary indexes are maintained for the same primary index of data records. A university registrar may wish to access a particular student's records based not only on social security number (the primary key), but perhaps by full name as well, along with accessing records based on college, major, year of graduation, and cumulative grade point average. A secondary B-tree index is necessary for each of these alternative key types. Why not have a secondary index for *every* field? Although this might be useful, it would be prohibitive because secondary indexes incur an additional time expense: Any insertion of a data record into or deletion from a primary index requires the corresponding insertion or deletion of a leaf key-address pair in each of the secondary indexes.

External Hashing

In Section 10.2, we evolved from search trees to hash tables, motivated by the desire to devise an algorithm that provides the fastest search of an internal data structure. We can now make an analogous evolution from external key tables to **external hash tables.** Figure 10.24 depicts a portion of an external hash table in which the array is small enough to fit entirely within internal memory. (In many applications it will not fit and is, instead, divided into block-size portions, requiring that the block containing the hashed-to index value be read from the file as necessary.)

In the original presentation of hash tables using chaining in Section 10.2, each heapspace node contained a key, its associated data record, and a link field. In this external hash table, each overflow list block is filled with key-

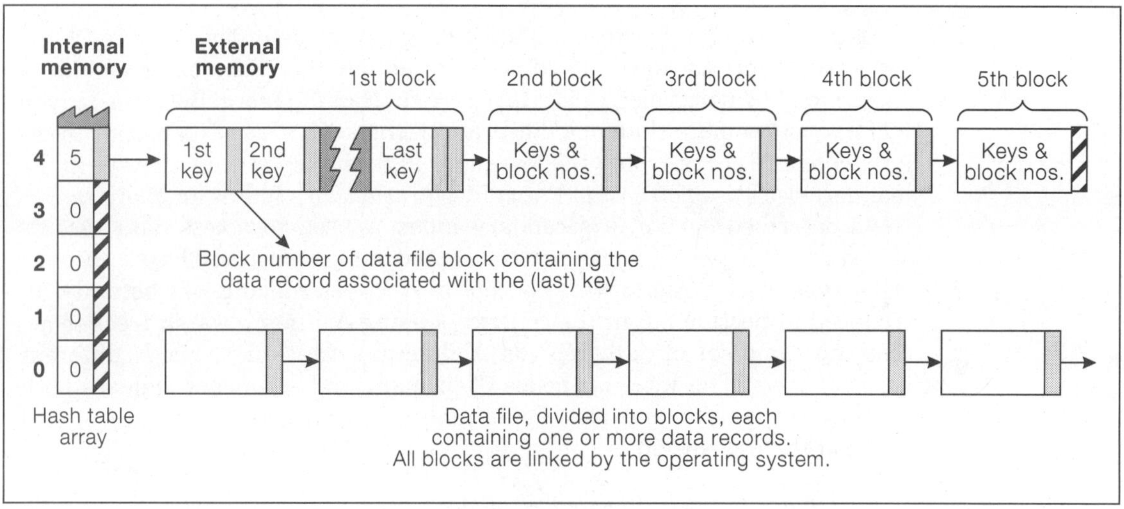

FIGURE 10.24 Portion of a Sample External Hash Table

block number pairs, with the associated data records stored in a separate file. Here, hash table overflow list blocks are functionally equivalent to B^+-tree internal nodes, and data file blocks are functionally equivalent to B^+-tree leaf nodes. As with B-trees, packing overflow list blocks only with keys allows more keys to be read per block read, speeding a search for a particular data record.

Each link field in the figure holds either a block number (indicated by a shaded rectangle) or a special number whose purpose is analogous to that of `NIL` (indicated by a stripe-filled rectangle). Each block in the overflow list contains numerous key-link field pairs; each link field in such a pair contains the number of the block in the data file that holds the actual data record associated with the key. In each overflow list block, key-link field pairs are arranged in ascending key order. Upon reading a block, the search routine can perform a modified binary search for the key of the desired data item.

SUMMARY

By its design, a height-balanced tree is always balanced and is used for applications requiring more searching than insertion and deletion. The ADT 2-3 tree is a height-balanced, oriented tree used to represent the ADT table. It is either empty or else any node may have one item and two subtrees (as in a binary search tree) or two items and three subtrees. Fundamental operations include initializing the tree as empty, testing for emptiness, searching for a node, adding or removing nodes, and traversal. The tree grows upward during an insertion operation or shrinks downward during a deletion operation, if necessary, to keep all leaves on the same level. The 2-3 tree search algorithm is rated at O (log N) in both the average and worst cases.

The efficiency of any search algorithm is tied to the structure of the list being searched. An indirect addressing scheme employs a key table to locate data stored elsewhere. With direct addressing, a key value is used as the address of the associated data item, and a character string type key must be converted to a numeric value; two key values mapping to the same array index is a collision. To surpass the O (log N) efficiency barrier, a master searching strategy and its associated data structure must (1) involve direct addressing to minimize searching for items in terms of other items, (2) avoid moving data items about the data structure, (3) permit character string-type keys, and (4) handle collisions of numeric key values if they occur. One such scheme is hashing and its associated data structure, the hash table.

The ADT hash table is a set-structured data type representation of the ADT table, implemented using an array. Fundamental operations include initializing the table as empty, testing for emptiness, searching for an item, and adding or removing an item. Because each item is completely independent of other stored items, as in any set, traversal is not a fundamental operation. A hash function transforms the original key value into an array index. A good hash function produces a uniform distribution of index values and is simple enough to execute quickly. Common hash functions include modulus division, extraction, and folding. The same function used to store an item must be used to search for that item subsequently.

The structure and mechanics of a hash table search for an item or the insertion point for a new item depend on the strategy implemented to resolve collisions. With chaining, each array element (bucket) points into an overflow list where the data items, whose key values hashed to that array location, are actually stored. An overflow list may be a linked list or a tree. Searching efficiency is O (λ) in the average case, where λ is (total number of items stored)/(number of overflow lists); with a good hash function and hash table, O (λ) $\approx$ O (1). With open addressing, all data items are stored within the array itself and collisions are resolved using probing. The problems of wasted array space and primary and secondary clustering with open addressing usually make chaining the method of choice.

Data are typically stored in external memory on magnetic disks, which an operating system writes to or reads from in chunks called blocks, or pages. Programs should be designed to minimize disk accesses, which slow execution time due to seek time, rotational latency, and data-transfer time. With sequential access, file elements are read or written only sequentially, starting with the first element, unlike direct access in which any file element can be read or written next. A magnetic disk is a direct-access device, whereas a magnetic tape is a sequential access device and so is used primarily to archive data. A nonstandard `Seek` procedure may be used in conjunction with an external key table for direct access of elements within one or more binary files.

The ADT B-tree of order *M* is a height-balanced search tree used to search for data items stored in external memory. Three forms of B-tree are (1) a B-tree with data spread throughout the tree, (2) a primary index B-tree (data are stored only in the leaves), and (3) a secondary index B-tree (leaves contain addresses of data stored in another primary index B-tree). A B^+-tree is a primary or secondary index B-tree whose leaf nodes are linked together to form a linked list. A B-tree resides entirely in its own file and only a single block of nodes (one subtree) is read into internal memory at a time during a search operation. Each node in a B-tree except the root contains between *M* and 2*M* items, such that 2*M* is the maximum number of items that can physically fit in one block. A 2-3 tree is really just a B-tree of order 1, with data spread throughout the tree.

External hashing is another method for accessing items stored in external memory. It uses chaining on a hash table in which each element points to an overflow list. Each overflow list consists of blocks of ordered key values and external addresses to their associated data items.

KEY TERMS

ADT 2-3 tree
ADT B-tree
ADT hash table
Archiving
B-tree with data spread throughout
B^+-tree
Block
Bucket
Bucket factor
Bucket size
Bucket value
Cache memory
Chaining
Clustering
Collision
Cylinder
Data file address
Data-transfer time
Density factor
Direct access
Direct access device
Direct addressing
Disk drive
Division hashing
External hash table
Extraction
Fan-out
File garbage
Folding
Garbage collection
Hash addressing
Hash class
Hash function
Hashing
Height-balanced tree
Indirect addressing
Key table
Linear probing
Load factor
Magnetic disk
Midsquare hashing

Nonsequential file
Open addressing
Order of a B-tree
Overflow list
Page
Primary clustering
Primary index B-tree
Primary key
Pseudorandom number
Probe sequence
Random access
Random-number generator
`ReadBlock`
Rotational latency
Secondary clustering
Secondary index B-tree
Secondary key
Sector
Seek
Seek time
Sequential access
Sequential access device
Sequential file
Track
`WriteBlock`
XOR

REVIEW QUESTIONS

1. Under what circumstances does a tree search of a binary search tree perform with the same efficiency as a binary array search? In everyday use, what problems may arise in using a binary search tree to store information, in terms of searching efficiency?
2. Describe the ADT 2-3 tree, including the domain, fundamental operations, and structure. For any node with two items in a 2-3 tree, what is the relationship between the keys of the two items, the keys in the left subtree, the keys in the middle subtree, and the keys in the right subtree? Is a 2-3 tree a type of graph?
3. Distinguish between 2-3 trees and binary search trees in terms of searching, insertion, and deletion operations. What are the two easy cases and the two difficult cases of item deletion for a 2-3 tree?
4. A binary search tree may be saved to a file while performing either a preorder or level-order traversal. What traversal(s) may be performed to save a 2-3 tree correctly to a file? In saving a 2-3 tree to a file, must the fact that a particular node has two items also be preserved in the file?
5. Describe several different implementation strategies for 2-3 trees, citing the advantages and disadvantages of each.
6. In Section 10.2, what is meant by the O (log N) barrier? Describe two factors common to the operations of linear searching, binary searching, and binary tree searching.
7. Distinguish between indirect addressing and direct addressing; describe everyday examples of both. Since direct addressing is the easiest and fastest technique for accessing an item, why is it not used exclusively?
8. Describe two algorithms for transforming a character string key into a number for addressing purposes. What problem(s) might such a transformation cause?
9. To surpass the O (log N) efficiency barrier, what four characteristics must be incorporated into a searching strategy/data structure? Describe how the hashing scheme, with its hash table data structure, attempts to accomplish these goals.
10. Describe the ADT hash table, including the domain, fundamental operations, and structure. Are any of the fundamental operations for search trees not supported by hashing?
11. What is the purpose of a hash function? Describe two characteristics of a "good" hash function and three commonly used algorithms. Why does the Pascal **MOD** operator perform better than the **DIV** operator for division hashing? Define random number, pseudorandom number, and pseudorandom number generator. What is the connection between pseudorandom numbers and hash functions?
12. What is a collision in hashing? Distinguish between the chaining and open addressing techniques for resolving collisions. How does the choice of a colli-

sion-resolution technique affect the Pascal declarations for the hash table itself? Distinguish among bucket, bucket size, bucket value, and hash class.

13. If item keys are of character string data type, each string must be transformed into a number before the hash function can be applied (either for simple searching or as a prelude to insertion or deletion). If chaining is used to resolve collisions, what should be stored in each node, the original character string, the number to which it was transformed prior to hashing, or both? Distinguish between primary and secondary keys.

14. What are the conventions for determining the size of a hash table?

15. To delete an item in a hash table (using open addressing), can the item's key merely be assigned some "unusual" value, such as zero, to mark the element as unoccupied? Describe the problems this may cause and suggest a better method.

16. What is garbage collection and why is it needed if the three-state item deletion scheme is used with hash tables that use open addressing?

17. Distinguish between primary and secondary clustering, and name two algorithms for resolving these problems.

18. What is a load factor and how is it used to gauge average searching efficiency of hash tables? Give three reasons for claiming that chaining is superior to open addressing. Can you think of scenarios in which open addressing is either sufficient or is superior to chaining? State the growth-rate functions and corresponding big O notation forms of the average and worst-case growth-rate functions and corresponding big O notation forms of the average and worst case searches of a hash table; for chaining and for open addressing.

19. Describe the physical and logical organization of magnetic disks and tapes. Distinguish among track, block, page, sector, and cylinder. Distinguish among seek time, rotational latency, and data-transfer time.

20. Distinguish among sequential, direct, and random accessing, and state which of these techniques (if any) is supported by the following: magnetic disks, magnetic tapes, Pascal files, sets, arrays, records, linked lists, search trees, hash tables.

21. What is the difference between a file element and a file block? Distinguish the `Read` procedure from a (nonstandard) `ReadBlock` procedure, regarding reading from a file; do the same for the `Write` and (nonstandard) `WriteBlock` procedures. Describe the purpose of a (nonstandard) `Seek` procedure, what parameters are passed to it, and how it is used in conjunction with `Get` and `Put`.

22. Describe how an external index table might be used to access a particular element of a binary file. If new items are always simply appended to the end of a file, describe the problem that arises when items are deleted. Also describe a solution to this problem.

23. Describe the ADT B-tree, including the domain, fundamental operations, and structure. For a B-tree of order *M*, every node (excluding the root) must contain how many items and how many children? Describe the operations of searching, insertion, and deletion. What is the fundamental difference between B-trees and other search trees presented in the textbook thus far?

24. Distinguish among the following types of B-tree: Primary index B-tree, secondary index B-tree, B-tree with data spread throughout the tree, B^+-tree. Can any of the first three types of B-tree also be a B^+-tree? For which of these trees is a 2-3 tree the simplest form? Distinguish between the structure of internal nodes and leaf nodes, if any difference exists, among the four types of B-trees. Should items in a B-tree node be ordered?

25. Describe how the order of a B-tree is determined. What is the relationship between the order of a B-tree and block size?
26. In what ways are the operations of insertion and deletion both similar and different when applied to 2-3 trees and B-trees?
27. What operation additional is supported by a B^+-tree with linked leaves but is not supported efficiently with unlinked leaves?
28. How efficient is the search of a B-tree in the best, average, and worst cases? What is guaranteed by the rule that a B-tree of order M must contain between M and $2M$ items?
29. Describe an external hash table. Compare it with the structure and usage of internal hash tables that use chaining.

EXERCISES

1. Draw the 2-3 tree that results from inserting items with the following key values into an empty tree. Insert in the order shown; e.g., 29, then 21, then 43, and so on.

   Key values: 29, 21, 43, 17, 10, 25, 30, 35, 45, 23

2. Parts (a) through (j) refer to the following 2-3 tree:

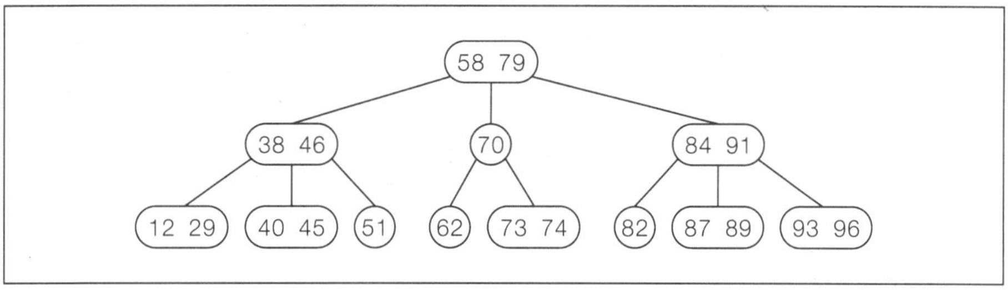

   a. What is the height of the subtree with item 84 as a root?
   b. What are the key values of the nodes visited during a search for item 45?
   c. What is (are) the descendant(s) of item 79?
   d. The node containing item 89 is at what level?
   e. What are the in-order successors of items 58, 79, and 84?
   f. State the key values of the sibling(s) of items 73, 51, and 70, if any.
   g. What tree traversal(s) might be used to save this tree to a file of records so that the original tree could be rebuilt later by reading each record and performing an insertion operation?
   h. What are the minimum and maximum number of items that may be stored maintaining the current tree height of 3? Derive general formulas to compute both amounts for *any* 2-3 tree of height H.
   i. Delete items with the following key values (delete in the order given here); then draw the resulting tree: 45, 40, 51, 38, 12, 29, 46, 58.
   j. Starting with the original tree as shown, again delete items with the following key values and draw the resulting tree: 91, 38, 46, 79, 70.

3. The following hash table was constructed using open addressing and the following function:

```
Hash ( Key ) = Key MOD 11
```

−22	0	46	−14	58	27	25	0	0	97	32
0	**1**	**2**	**3**	**4**	**5**	**6**	**7**	**8**	**9**	**10**

Collisions are resolved using linear probing, an empty location contains a 0 key value, and a location where an item has been deleted contains the negative value of that item's key.

a. How many items must be examined to find the entry with key value 25?
b. How many items must be examined to determine that no item in the table has key value 42?
c. Insert items with the following key values: 33, then 54, then 13; update the array diagram appropriately.

4. Using chaining, store items with the following key values in a hash table of 11 elements, in the order given, using the hash function of Exercise 4. Draw a diagram of the resulting structure. Key values: 46, 58, 27, 25, 97, 32, 33, 54, 13, 2, 86, 9, 3.

5. Draw the B-tree of order 2, with data spread throughout the tree, which results from inserting items with the following key values into an empty tree. Insert in the order shown; e.g., 29, then 21, then 43, and so on.

Key values: 29, 21, 43, 17, 10, 25, 30, 35, 45, 23, 8, 18, 2, 27, 28

6. What is the smallest number of items that will force the following:

a. A 2-3 tree to have height 2? Height 3?
b. A B-tree of order 2 to have height 2? Height 3?
c. A B-tree of order 3 to have height 2? Height 3?

7. A pseudorandom number function, `Random`, is given in Appendix K:

```
FUNCTION Random ( VAR Seed : Integer; High : Integer ) : Integer;
```

This function returns a pseudorandom number in the range 1 to `High`, inclusive. Modify this function so that it returns a pseudorandom number in the range `Low` to `High`, inclusive:

```
FUNCTION Random ( VAR Seed : Integer; Low, High : Integer ) : Integer;
```

8. Complete the following two hashing functions based on the discussion of folding and extraction in Section 10.2. Assume that integer key values are passed in. As the last operation in each function, use **MOD** (i.e., hashing by division) so that the integer hash table index value returned is between zero and `TableSizeLessOne`, a global constant (refer to the global hash table declarations given in Section 10.2).

```
FUNCTION ExtractionHash ( Key : Integer ) : Integer;

FUNCTION FoldingHash ( Key : Integer ) : Integer;
```

9. Write Pascal declarations for primary index and secondary index B^+-trees.

10. Write a pseudocode algorithm to perform an in-order traversal of the following (process each data item by passing its address to an imaginary procedure named `Process`):

a. A primary index B-tree and secondary index B-tree; leaves are not linked.
b. A primary index B^+-tree and secondary index B^+-tree.

11. The binary search algorithm was introduced in Application 7.5 with the example of looking for a name in a telephone book. If you were searching for the name "Snuffelopagous," for instance, rather than starting at the midpoint of the book you probably would start more toward the back of the book, where the names beginning with S would be found.

The binary search algorithm can therefore be improved by guessing more accurately where the key sought lies within the current sublist, rather than automatically examining the element that lies halfway between the `Low` and `High` elements. This variation, called *interpolation search,* involves calculating the percentage of the distance that the key being sought lies between the keys of the `Low` and `High` elements.

For example, in searching for the element with key value 46 in the following array, 49 is about 68% of the way between 11 (the key of the `Low` element, indicated by L) and 67 (the key of the `High` element, indicated by H); the search should therefore begin in element 0.68×10, or the seventh element, rather than the fifth element, which is the midpoint of 1 and 10.

L									H
11	23	25	31	34	35	46	49	58	67
1	**2**	**3**	**4**	**5**	**6**	**7**	**8**	**9**	**10**

Complete procedure `InterpolationSearch` (`ListType` is declared at the beginning of Appendix J and assume that `KeyType` is integer):

```
PROCEDURE Interpolation Search ( VAR List : ListType; Low, High : Integer;
                                  VAR Key : KeyType; VAR Found : Boolean );
```

12. In many applications, certain stored items are sought more often than are other stored items. Rather than keeping hash table overflow lists ordered by ascending key value, we can employ a strategy called *high-probability ordering:*

- Items are simply appended to the end of a particular overflow list.
- Any time a sought item is found by the hash table search routine, that item and the preceding item exchange places in the list. This way, the most frequently accessed items will drift toward the head of the list. As a variation, each time an item is accessed, it is moved to the head of the list.

a. What effect will high-probability ordering have on the best, average, and worst cases of linear searching?

b. Write search and insertion routines that support high-probability ordering.

13. a. Give a set of declarations to support the external hash table depicted in Figure 10.24.

b. Using your declarations of (a), write a hash table search routine. Assume that a `ReadBlock` procedure is available to you, as described in Section 10.3.

14. In a B-tree of order M, the rule that each node except the root must have between M and $2M$ items guarantees that every node is at least half full. Every node except the root in a *B*-tree* is at least two-thirds full. This is guaranteed during insertion by moving items about sibling nodes until two sibling nodes are completely full of items. These two nodes are then split into three nodes, each at least two-thirds full. This makes better use of memory by packing more items per node, but it makes the insertion algorithm a bit more complicated. On paper, try building a B*-tree of order 3, inserting a sequence of integer keys: 1, 2, 3, and so on.

CHAPTER ELEVEN

SORTING ALGORITHMS

Summary
Key Terms
Review Questions
Exercises

In this chapter you will learn a variety of popular algorithms designed to sort a collection of items; i.e., order the collection of items by key value. If necessary, at this time review Section 3.7, which introduces techniques for the mathematical analyses of algorithms.

11.1 PRELIMINARIES

Sorting a collection of items is often useful if you wish to process all items in different orders, based on particular key types. For example, a university registrar may wish to print student information in order of year of graduation and name, although the student record files are positioned within the data base by social security number; therefore, the data base must be sorted accordingly (in the absence of a secondary index B-tree, as described in Section 10.3).

The fundamental motivation for sorting a collection of items by a particular key value (and keeping the collection sorted) is to facilitate fast searches for items later. The operations of searching and sorting are therefore interdependent; searching is both the means by which a particular item within a sorted list is accessed and is a prerequisite to the operations of insertion and deletion so the list *remains* sorted. For example, imagine trying to locate a particular book within a large library if all library books were *not* stored in call number order! Figure 11.1 illustrates the interdependence of searching and sorting.

The notion of searching pertains only to *table* type data structures, whose constituent items are ordered by *key value*. By contrast, in such *time-of-arrival* structures as stacks, FIFO queues, and standard Pascal files, the way items are ordered expedites locating only the *next* item that may be accessed. There is no search operation for the access of *any other* item in the list, and selection of the next item that may be accessed is a simple consequence of *when* the items were stored. We will examine both linear structures (arrays, linked lists, and files) and nonlinear structures (trees and graphs). Although a file is a linear, time-of-arrival structure, this chapter includes algorithms for sorting a file based on the key values of items, so items can be accessed sequentially from the file in ascending key value order.

The efficiency of each sorting algorithm will be analyzed on the basis of the number of *key-comparison operations* and the number of *assignment operations* involving whole items. These two operations have been chosen because they are common to all sorting algorithms and tend to require significant amounts of CPU time relative to other operations. Sorting algorithms invariably repeat a set of operations within a loop, so their efficiency tends to be proportional to the number of times each loop is executed. (Recall that in our analysis of linear searching (Section 3.7), binary searching (Section 7.4) and binary search tree searching (Section 8.2), we only compared

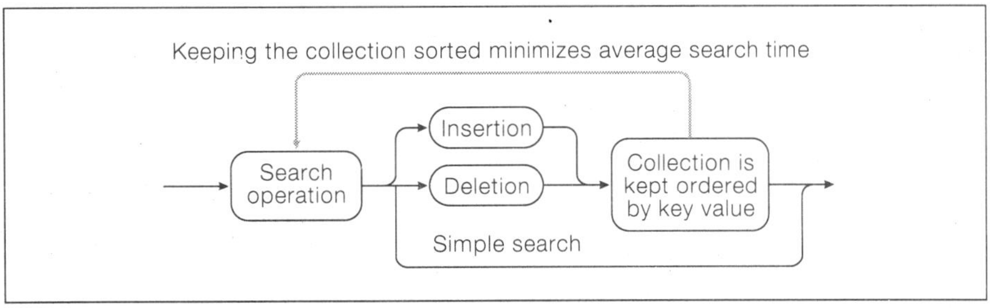

FIGURE 11.1 The Interdependence of Searching and Sorting

searching algorithms on the basis of the number of key comparisons, since searching does not involve the exchange of items.) We will also consider the amount of *additional memory* required for several of the algorithms.

The efficiencies of different algorithms will be analyzed in terms of their worst and average performances. These different levels of performance reflect the degree to which a list is already sorted before the sorting algorithm is applied. However, whether an already sorted list produces best or worst performance varies among the algorithms. For many of the sorting algorithms, we consider a simple version first and then modify that version to improve average searching efficiency.

Several array-sorting algorithms reference array element zero, whose key field is initialized to a value less than any legitimate key value (look ahead briefly to the array diagram of Figure 11.6 where this "negative infinity" value is represented by $-\infty$). This minimizes the number of comparisons performed in some algorithms since these algorithms compare only key values and do not need a separate test for end-of-array.

The following set of global declarations will be used by all array-based sorting algorithms. Procedure `Exchange`, which is referenced by several algorithms in this chapter to swap the contents of its two record parameters, is given as well:

```
{Global declarations for array-based sorting algorithms:

  Exchange sorts:    Bubble sort, straight selection sort, merge sort, quicksort
  Insertion sort:    Straight insertion sort
  Binary tree sort:  Heap sort  }

CONST
  MinKey     =  ??;          {-MAXINT or KeyType value less than any key value}
  MaxIndex   =  ??;          {Application dependent}

TYPE
  KeyType    =  ??;          {Application dependent; Integer in the examples}

  InfoType   =  RECORD
                  Key  :  KeyType;
                  {Possibly other fields, as required by the application}
                END;

  ListType   =  ARRAY [ 0..MaxIndex ] OF InfoType;

VAR
  List  :  ListType;
```

```
PROCEDURE  Exchange ( VAR  Item1, Item2 : InfoType );

VAR
  Temp : InfoType;

BEGIN
Temp  :=  Item1;
Item1 :=  Item2;              {Item1 now contains what Item2 contained originally}
Item2 :=  Temp                {Item2 now contains what Item1 contained originally}
END;
```

11.2 SORTING ARRAYS: SIMPLE EXCHANGE AND INSERTION SORTS

An exchange sort algorithm makes numerous passes through a list, comparing key values and swapping items to place them in their appropriate positions. Each of the two simple exchange sorting algorithms we will examine—bubble sort and straight exchange sort—require only one item of additional memory as a temporary variable for the purpose of swapping items in procedure `Exchange`. The advanced exchange sorting algorithms—merge sort and quicksort—are presented in Section 11.3. (When these algorithms are actually represented in Pascal, each may need several local loop index variables as well, but this expenditure is typically not considered when calculating and comparing relative efficiency.)

Bubble Sort (Straight Exchange Sort)

We begin our examination of sorting algorithms with the straight exchange sort, more commonly referred to as **bubble sort.** Although it is the least efficient of standard sorting algorithms, bubble sort is a useful first algorithm because it is easy to understand and to represent in Pascal. Bubble sort is also fairly easy to analyze and modify to improve its efficiency.

In a bubble sort, a number of passes are made through a list of N elements, *from the last (Nth) element down to the second element.* On each pass, `List [ K ].Key` is compared to its predecessor, `List [ K-1 ].Key`. If `List [ K ].Key < List [ K-1 ].Key`, then the `List [ K ]` and `List [ K-1 ]` items are in the wrong order within the list relative to each other and must be exchanged. We examine a basic version of bubble sort first and then devise a faster second version. A Pascal representation of the basic algorithm follows:

```
PROCEDURE BubbleSort ( VAR List : ListType;  Count : Integer );

VAR
  P, K : Integer;

BEGIN
FOR P := Count DOWNTO 2 DO
  FOR K := Count DOWNTO 2 DO
    IF List [ K ].Key < List [ K - 1 ].Key THEN
      Exchange ( List [ K ],  List [ K - 1 ] )
END;
```

Figure 11.2 traces all five passes in the bubble sorting of our sample array (the zeroth element is neither used nor shown). The state of the array is shown prior to executing the code segment shown to the right of it. In the array diagrams, only key values appear, with the two element key values currently being compared enclosed in a boldface rectangle. The number to the left of each diagram indicates the pass number, *P*. The initial call to `BubbleSort` for this example would be `BubbleSort ( List, 6 )`.

How may passes through a list of *N* items are necessary? Unless the array is completely sorted to begin with, one pass is not sufficient since only adjacent pairs of elements are compared. Upon completion of each pass, however, the item with the smallest key value not already in its proper location will *bubble* to the proper position within the list. That is, by the end of pass *P*, the *P*th smallest item will be placed in element *P* (on the first pass, the item with the smallest key is placed in the first list position, on the second pass, the item with the next smallest key is placed in the second position, etc.). Thus, for a list of *N* items, $N - 1$ passes must be made. An *N*th pass is not necessary: After $N - 1$ passes, $N - 1$ elements are correctly placed, leaving a single item, which *must* be in the correct place.

Analysis and Enhancement of Bubble Sort

The relative efficiency of this basic version of bubble sort is easy to compute. With $N - 1$ passes, each pass involving $N - 1$ key comparisons, the total number of key comparisons, $C(N)$, is calculated as follows:

$$C(N) = (N - 1)(N - 1) = N^2 - 2N + 1$$

N is 6 in our sample array, so 25 comparisons will be made. When *N* is very large, the N^2 term greatly overwhelms the other terms ($-2N - 1$), so this version of bubble sort requires time proportionate to N^2—i.e., O (N^2). Since we are measuring efficiency as a function of both the number of *key comparisons* and the number of *item exchanges,* we can decrease average sorting time by decreasing either.

Of course, calculating the *exact* time the computer's CPU will take to execute the routine requires knowing what machine-code instructions the compiler will generate when compiling the source code and how long each will take to execute. Recall from Section 3.7 that, in analyzing algorithms, we are not as concerned with the actual execution time as we are with how the execution time grows as a function of problem size; this rate is given by an algorithm's growth rate function and big O notation. The constant of proportionality in a growth rate function takes into account all implementation-dependent factors, such as coding style and instruction-execution speed for a given computer. Bubble sort is the first of the O (N^2) class of sorting routines we will examine.

The basic algorithm can be modified in two ways to decrease the total number of comparisons. First, once an item is correctly positioned, there is no reason to involve it in further key comparisons. For example, notice in Figure 11.2 that the item with key value 15 is positioned correctly in element 1 after the swap of Step 1(e), yet it participates in four more needless comparisons (Steps 2(e), 3(e), 4(e), and 5(e)). Since an item bubbles to its correct position of *N* items upon each pass, the sublist examined during each

Step	K	1	2	3	4	5	6	
		37	19	47	15	40	41	Original list
1. a.	6	37	19	47	15	40	41	41 > 40, so no swap
b.	5	37	19	47	15	40	41	40 > 15, so no swap
c.	4	37	19	47	15	40	41	15 < 47, so swap
d.	3	37	19	15	47	40	41	15 < 19, so swap
e.	2	37	15	19	47	40	41	15 < 37, so swap
2. a.	6	15	37	19	47	40	41	41 > 40, so no swap
b.	5	15	37	19	47	40	41	40 < 47, so swap
c.	4	15	37	19	40	47	41	40 > 19, so no swap
d.	3	15	37	19	40	47	41	19 < 37, so swap
e.	2	15	19	37	40	47	41	19 > 15, so no swap
3. a.	6	15	19	37	40	47	41	41 < 47, so swap
b.	5	15	19	37	40	41	47	41 > 40, so no swap
c.	4	15	19	37	40	41	47	40 > 37, so no swap
d.	3	15	19	37	40	41	47	37 > 19, so no swap
e.	2	15	19	37	40	41	47	19 > 15, so no swap
4. a.	6	15	19	37	40	41	47	47 > 41, so no swap
b.	5	15	19	37	40	41	47	41 > 40, so no swap
c.	4	15	19	37	40	41	47	40 > 37, so no swap

FIGURE 11.2 Performing a Basic Bubble Sort (Continues Next Page)

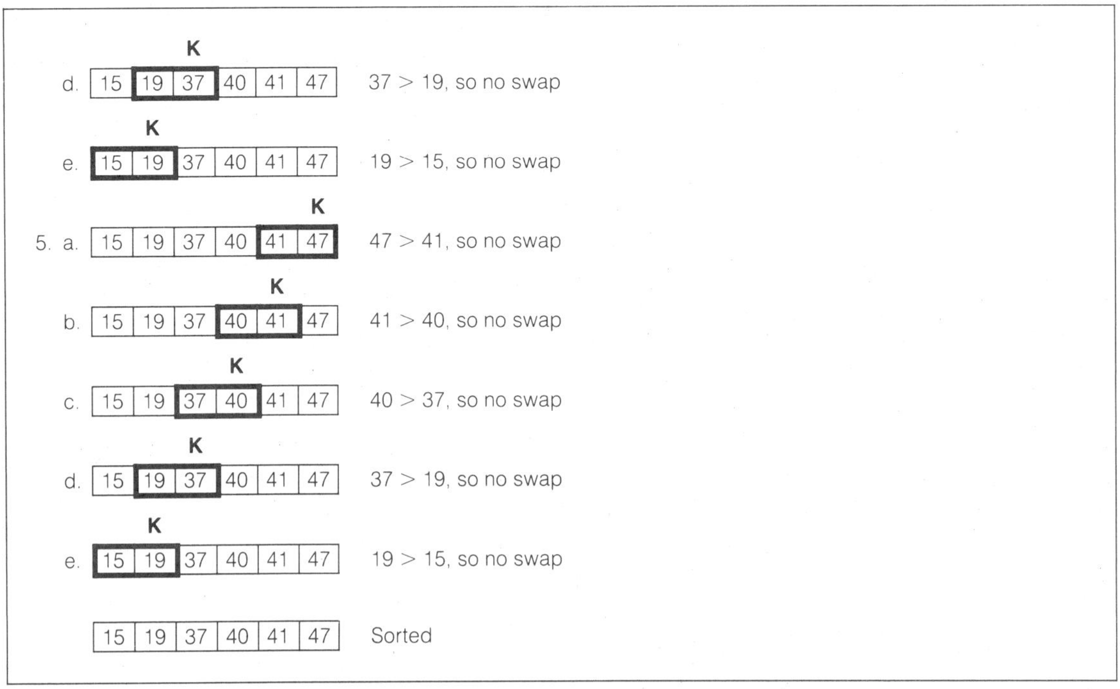

FIGURE 11.2 Performing a Basic Bubble Sort (Continued)

pass need include only items in position N down to (pass number + 1). No extra cost is incurred in this modification—we simply redesign the comparison loop so the Pth pass terminates on item P.

Our second modification to decrease the total number of comparisons is based on the fact that once the entire list is sorted, there is no reason to continue making passes through it. In our sample list, the final 14 comparisons, starting with Step 3(b), are unnecessary, since the list becomes sorted after the swap of Step 3(a). The algorithm can be written to recognize that the list is completely sorted when it is able to make an entire pass without exchanging any items. Of course, the algorithm must make one complete pass with no exchanges just to determine that this is the case. For example, although the sample list is sorted after the swap of Step 3(a), comparisons of 3(b) through 3(e) and the 5 comparisons of the fourth pass must still be made to determine that the list is sorted. Even so, terminating the algorithm as soon as the list is deemed sorted results in a savings of 5 comparisons in the example (the unnecessary fifth pass), or 20% of the original 25 comparisons. This way, the efficiency of bubble sort depends on how sorted the original list is, with the best case involving a list already sorted.

This modification does carry a significant cost, however. We need to introduce an additional Boolean flag which is initialized to a false value at the beginning of each pass, assigned a true value each time a swap is made, and tested before each pass is begun. Although the late passes are shorter than the first ones, this adds enough code to negate most or all of the savings gained by the modification unless the list was nearly sorted to begin with. In actual trials of 10, 100, 1000, and 10,000 randomly generated items, *no significant amount of time was saved.* This is a good example of the trickiness of introducing new mechanisms to solve efficiency problems.

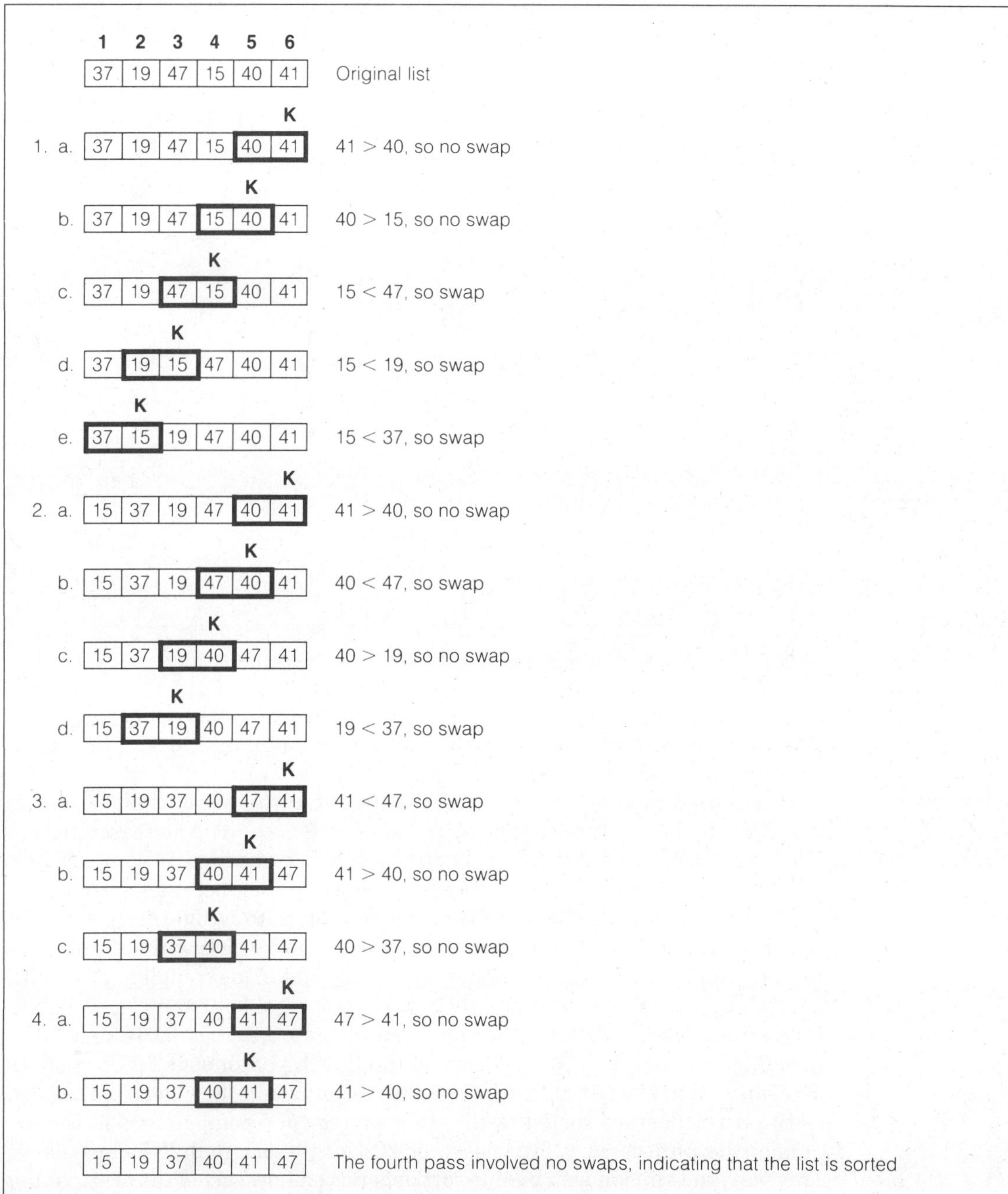

FIGURE 11.3 Performing an Enhanced Bubble Sort

While we have made modifications that minimize the number of key comparisons, no modifications can decrease the number of item exchanges. Figure 11.3 traces the operations of the enhanced bubble sort (again, the zeroth element is not shown).

Our basic bubble sort algorithm is always O (N^2). How well does our enhanced version perform? In the algorithm's *best performance,* the list is already sorted, as detected by a single pass of N comparisons with no exchanges. The best is therefore O (N). In the algorithm's *worst performance*, the list is completely unsorted—i.e., all items are positioned in decreasing key value order. This case requires all $N - 1$ passes, involving $N^2 - 2N + 1$ comparisons, or simply O (N^2). It has been proven that, in the average case, the number of comparisons is O (N^2) and the number of exchanges is O ($N - 1.25\sqrt{N}$).

At this time, examine the following routine in Appendix J.

```
PROCEDURE BubbleSort ( VAR List : ListType; Low, High : Integer );
```

Straight Selection Sort

In a **straight selection sort,** $N - 1$ passes are made through a list of N items. As with the bubble sort, by the end of pass P, the Pth smallest item is placed in position P within the list. A simple Pascal version of this algorithm follows:

```
PROCEDURE  SelectionSort ( VAR List : ListType;  Count : Integer );

VAR
  P, J : Integer;

BEGIN
FOR P := 1 TO Count DO
  FOR J := P + 1 TO Count DO
    IF List [ J ].Key < List [ P ].Key THEN
      Exchange ( List [ J ], List [ P ] )
END;
```

Figure 11.4 traces the execution of a straight selection sort on our sample list. The initial call for this example would be `SelectionSort ( List, 6 )`. Notice that, as P increases with each pass, a growing sorted sublist trails behind in positions 1 through P.

Analysis and Enhancement of Straight Selection Sort

A major inefficiency of the bubble sort just examined is that only *adjacent items* are compared and exchanged, a shortcoming unmitigated by the two improvements we made to the basic algorithm. Because the straight selection sort "reaches" across the list and compares items that may not be adjacent, it may intuitively *seem* more efficient, but this is only partially true. The number of passes and total comparisons is fixed, even if the list is sorted to begin with (the best performance), or is in descending key order (the worst performance). On the first pass through a list of N items, $N - 1$ comparisons are made. On the second pass, only $N - 2$ comparisons are made, since one of the items was correctly placed by the first pass and no longer

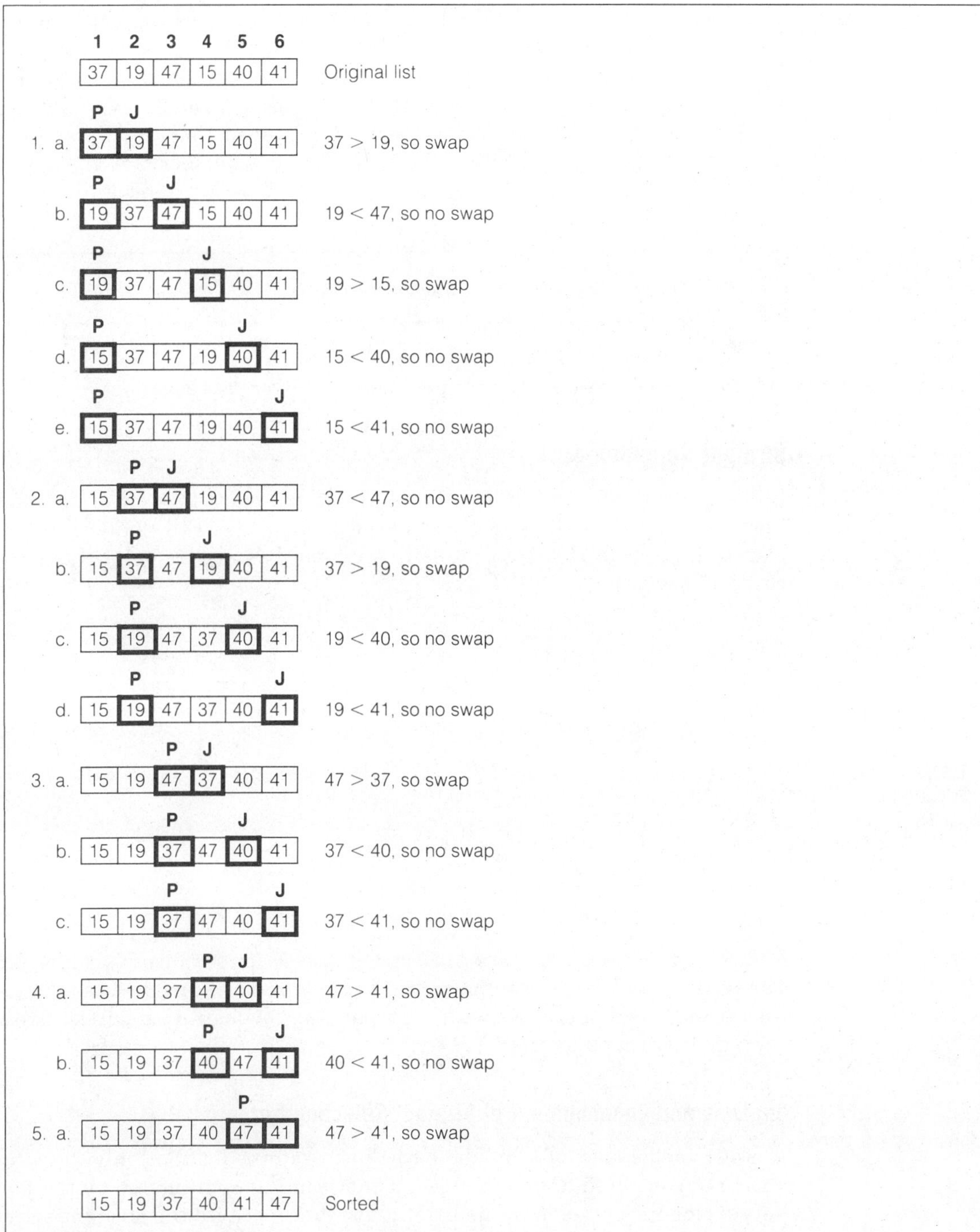

FIGURE 11.4 Performing a Basic Straight Selection Sort

participates in key comparisons. On the third pass, only $N - 3$ comparisons are made, and so forth. Therefore, each pass involves (N − pass number) comparisons, with the total number of comparisons, $C(N)$, calculated as follows:

$$C(N) = (N - 1) + (N - 2) + (N - 3) + \cdots + [N - (N - 1)]$$
$$= \frac{N(N - 1)}{2}$$
$$= \frac{N^2}{2} - \frac{N}{2}$$

Straight selection sort therefore requires O (N^2) comparisons in all performances, whereas bubble sort requires between O (N) and O (N^2) comparisons, depending on how sorted the list is to begin with (although the savings with bubble sort may be counterbalanced by the additional overhead involved in its enhanced version). Unlike bubble sort, selection sort offers no way to detect whether or not the list has already become sorted before $N - 1$ passes are made. Being able to make a complete pass without any exchanges does *not* necessarily mean that the list is sorted; it merely means on pass P that the item in list position P is already in *its* correct position, although items in positions $P + 1$ through N may not yet be in their correct positions.

Earlier in this section, we tried to improve the efficiency of the bubble sort algorithm by minimizing the number of key comparisons, but we were unable to minimize the number of item exchanges. With the straight selection sort, the opposite is true: While the number of key comparisons cannot be reduced for a given list, we *can* make a modification that will significantly reduce the number of item exchanges. During the Pth pass, the algorithm must find the Pth smallest key, but it need remember only the *value* and *where* it was found—there is no need to make a complete exchange each time a smaller key is found. The algorithm starts each pass by assuming that `List [ P ].Key` is smallest and assigns a false value to a Boolean flag. If a smaller key is found during the pass, the array index of that item is preserved in a separate variable, and the Boolean flag is assigned a true value. When the pass is completed, the algorithm can then perform a single exchange if the Boolean flag has a true value. This eliminates the item exchange of 1(a) in Figure 11.4.

If each item is a large record, it may take as much time to assign and test the Boolean flag repeatedly as it does to exchange the values. Also, finding a minimum key value requires either a separate variable to hold the minimum value or recomputing the address from the array index. (Given the general slowness in computing index values in Pascal, the separate variable method is preferable.) Even so, this strategy *does* reduce the average number of exchanges from O (N^2) in the worst and average performances to O (N) in the worst case. This way, less time is required to place an item in its proper position than with the bubble sort, which cannot postpone making exchanges.

Figure 11.5 summarizes the execution of our enhanced selection sort algorithm on the sample list.

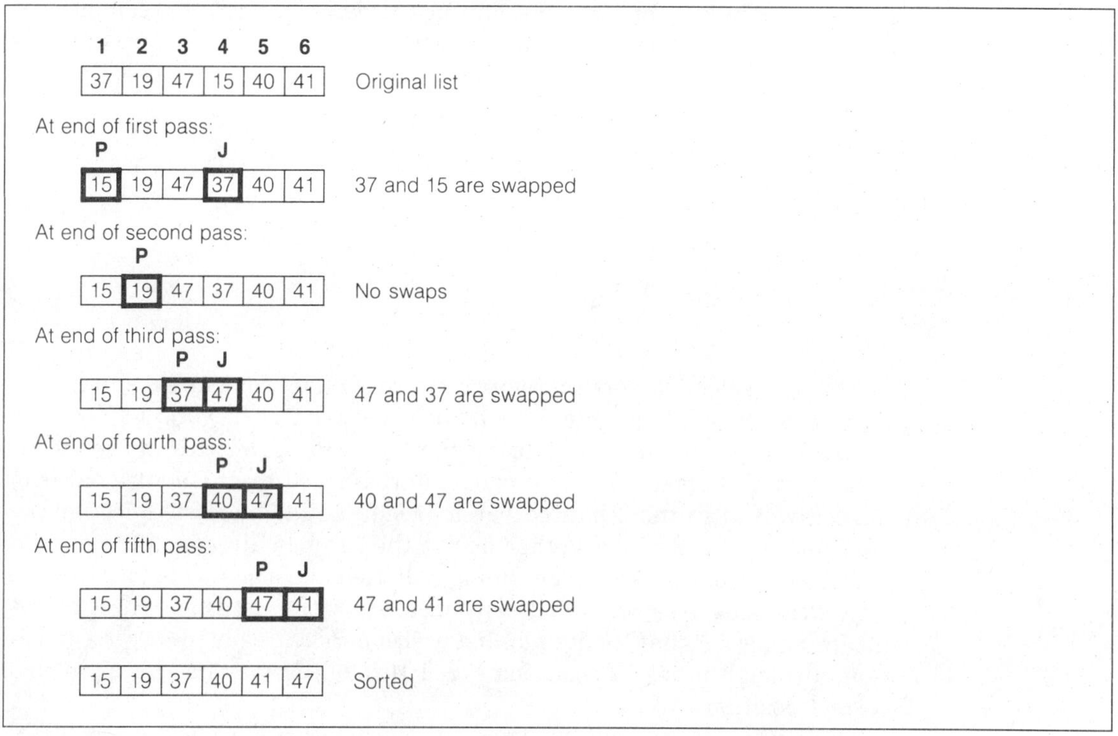

FIGURE 11.5 Performing an Enhanced Straight Selection Sort

At this time, examine the following routine in Appendix J.

```
PROCEDURE SelectionSort ( VAR List : ListType; Count : Integer );
```

Straight Insertion Sort

An insertion sort algorithm begins with a sorted list and an unsorted remainder of the list and inserts each of the items from the unsorted sublist into the appropriate place in the sorted list. As with the straight selection sort, the sorted list grows as the unsorted list shrinks.

A **straight insertion sort** begins with the sorted list containing a single item (a list of one item is already sorted). This algorithm does not require a separate array as a container for the sorted list as it grows; the total number of items included in the unsorted and sorted lists is fixed, so both lists can be contained in a single array—the array containing the original unsorted list. Only one more item-sized variable is needed, for the purpose of exchanging items.

The sorted list, initially of size 1, will grow from the low-index end of the array as items are added from the unsorted list in elements 2 through N. To sort a list of N elements, $N - 1$ passes are made to insert these items. As with the bubble and selection sorts, the Pth smallest item is placed in element P (its appropriate location) by the end of pass P. Unlike the bubble and straight selection sorting algorithms, straight insertion sort uses array element zero. A simple Pascal version of the algorithm follows:

```
PROCEDURE InsertionSort ( VAR List : ListType; Count : Integer );

VAR
  P, J  : Integer;

BEGIN
List [ 0 ].Key := MinKey;
FOR P := 2 TO Count DO
  BEGIN
  J  := P;                                        {Last item of unsorted sublist}
  WHILE List [ J ].Key < List [ J - 1 ].Key DO
    BEGIN
    Exchange ( List [ J ] , List [ J - 1 ] );     {Swap items to place correctly}
    J := J - 1
    END
  END
END;
```

Figure 11.6 traces the execution of a straight insertion sort on our sample list. In the figure, the items being compared are enclosed in a boldface rectangle. Also, the boldface line extending above each array diagram separates the sorted list and unsorted list. The initial call to `InsertionSort` for this example would be `InsertionSort ( List, 6 )`.

Analysis and Enhancement of Straight Insertion Sort

We can make the same improvement here that was made to the selection sort algorithm to avoid a complete exchange each time a smaller key is found. Instead, the algorithm will store the item being correctly placed only when its final location is determined. The worst performance of the algorithm occurs when the original list of N items is already sorted in reverse order, requiring the maximum number of item comparisons with each pass:

$$C(N) = 1 + 2 + 3 + \cdots + (N - 1) = \frac{N(N-1)}{2}$$

$$= \frac{N^2}{2} - \frac{N}{2}$$

Thus, straight insertion sort is O (N^2) in its worst performance.

During pass P, the Pth item is placed among the sorted list in elements 1 through $P - 1$. In the average case, the algorithm must perform approximately $(P - 1)/2$ comparisons to place this item correctly. The average number of comparisons may be computed as follows:

$$C(N) = \frac{1}{2} + \frac{2}{2} + \frac{3}{2} + \cdots + \frac{(N-1)}{2} = \frac{N(N-1)}{4}$$

$$= \frac{N^2}{4} - \frac{N}{4}$$

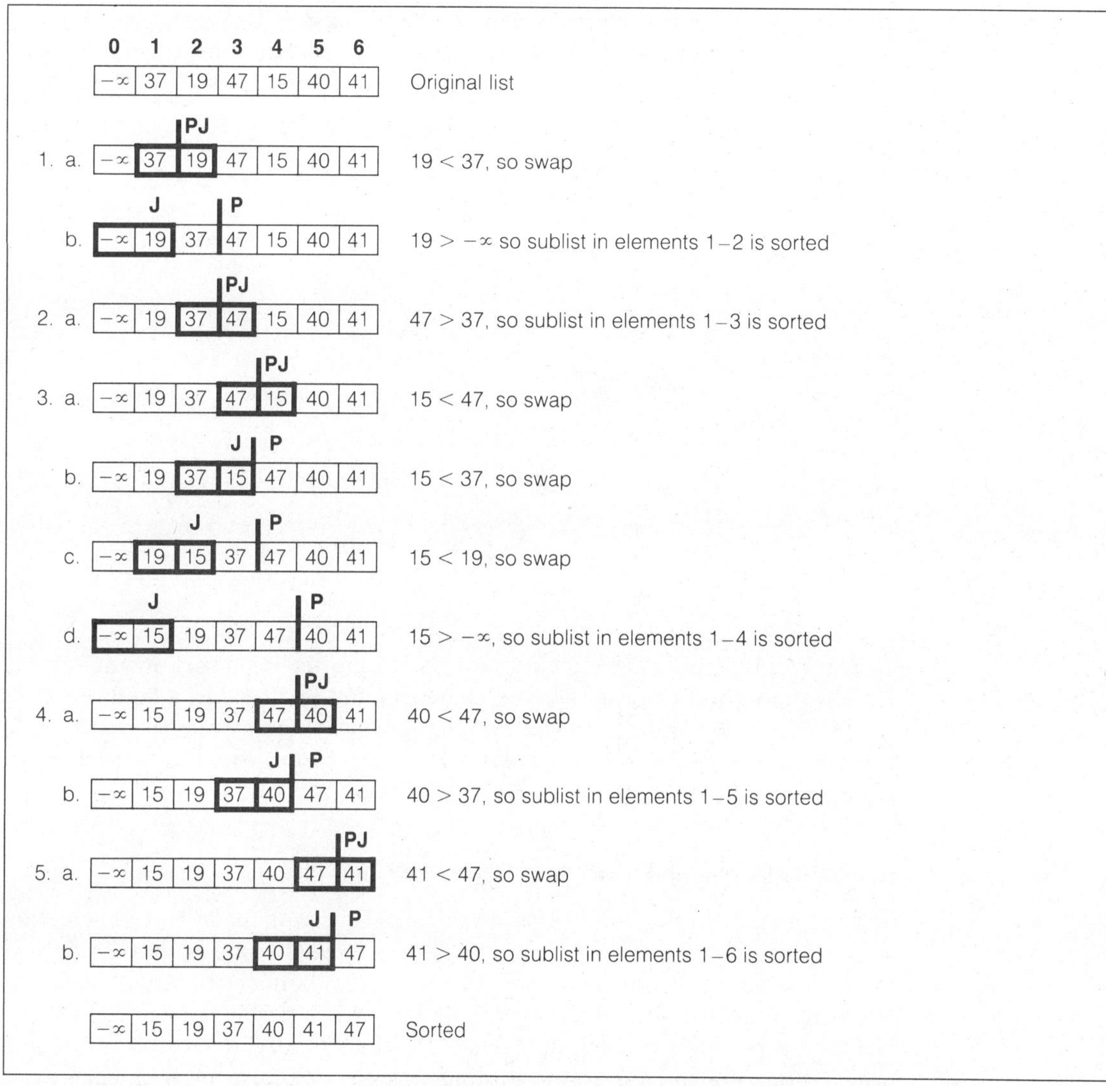

FIGURE 11.6 Performing a Basic Straight Insertion Sort

Straight insertion sort is therefore rated as O (N^2) in its average performance as well.

Intuitively, we needed an extra mechanism in the bubble sort algorithm to terminate early, but here every pass terminates early (if the data permit) without any extra effort. Although bubble sort, selection sort, and straight insertion sort are all rated at O (N^2), the straight insertion sort wins out every time because it is actually $N^2/4$, whereas the others are actually $N^2/2$.

At this time, examine the following routine in Appendix J.

```
PROCEDURE InsertionSort ( VAR List : ListType; Count : Integer );
```

11.3 SORTING ARRAYS: DIVIDE-AND-CONQUER SORTS

Since the total time required to sort a list is a function of N, the total number of items to be sorted, smaller lists can be sorted in less time than larger lists. The various sorts presented thus far are nonlinear—O (N^2)—so the rate of increase in time is significant. Suppose we begin by dividing an unsorted list in half, sort each half, and then merge the two halves to produce one sorted list. The growth rate for such a *divide-and-conquer* algorithm would be $N^2/2 + N^2/2 + N$, which is less than N^2 (the N is added to account for the operation of merging the two sorted halves). If we employ a more efficient algorithm to sort each half, the total time required is even less.

In this section, we examine two divide-and-conquer sorting algorithms, *quicksort* and *merge sort,* which are used here to sort arrays of records. A different version of merge sort, called *natural merge sort,* is presented in Section 11.5 to sort a linked list of records and again in Section 11.6 to sort a file of records. As with the binary search, the merge sort and quicksort algorithms are inherently recursive divide-and-conquer algorithms because they repeatedly perform the same *base operation* on smaller and smaller lists of the original list. (Of course, the algorithms could be modified to maintain their own stacks in lieu of recursion; this is one of the exercises at the end of this chapter.)

The quicksort and merge sort algorithms have nearly the same general structure, as given by the following pseudocode algorithms. In quicksort, most of the work is performed by the partitioning algorithm, which selects an item in the current list and moves it to its correct position within the list, relative to the other items. This creates an upper and lower list, either of which may be empty. In merge sort, the partitioning is implemented by merely dividing the current list length by 2, via **DIV**. Most of the work is performed instead by the merge algorithm, which must combine two sorted lists into a single sorted list (this may be the entire list).

```
ALGORITHM QuickSort ( VAR List );

BEGIN
IF List length > 1 THEN
  BEGIN
  Partition list into 2 lists by correctly
    placing a particular list (pivot) item;
  QuickSort ( Lower list );
  QuickSort ( Upper list )
  END
END;
```

```
ALGORITHM MergeSort ( VAR List );

BEGIN
IF List length > 1 THEN
  BEGIN
  Partition list into 2 lists of
    "equal" length;
  MergeSort ( Lower list );
  MergeSort ( Upper list );
  Merge ( Lower list, upper list )
  END
END;
```

Merge Sort for Arrays

In the basic **merge sort** algorithm, the list of items is successively halved, and the halves are sorted and merged. Recall from the binary search algorithm that a list is defined by its bounds, so two adjacent lists span the elements (`Low1..High1`) and (`High1 + 1..High2`). A list can be partitioned into two such lists by computing the midpoint of `Low1` and `High2`:

```
Mid := ( Low1 + High2 ) DIV 2;
```

The upper and lower (sub)lists are therefore delimited as (`Low1..Mid`) and (`Mid + 1..High2`), respectively. The terminal case of the recursive routine arises when a list of one item is passed. In this case, execution flow merely exits the routine, since a list of one item is already sorted. The Pascal representation of merge sort's main routine follows:

```
PROCEDURE MergeSort ( VAR List : ListType; Low, High : Integer );

VAR
  Mid : Integer;

  {Actual code for Merge appears on the next page}

  PROCEDURE Merge ( Low1, High1, High2 : Integer );

{***  Main routine for MergeSort  ***}

BEGIN
IF Low < High THEN              {IF current list contains 2 or more items THEN}
  BEGIN
  Mid := ( Low + High ) DIV 2;            { Partition list into two lists}
  MergeSort ( List, Low, Mid );           { Sort lower list}
  MergeSort ( List, Mid + 1, High );      { Sort upper list}
  Merge ( Low, Mid, High )                { Merge the lower and upper lists}
  END
END;
```

Clearly, most of the work of the merge sort algorithm is performed in the `Merge` algorithm, which merges two adjacent, sorted lists into a single sorted list. Merging requires an auxiliary array, into which the merged list is built from the two sorted lists. As an example, Figure 11.7 traces the

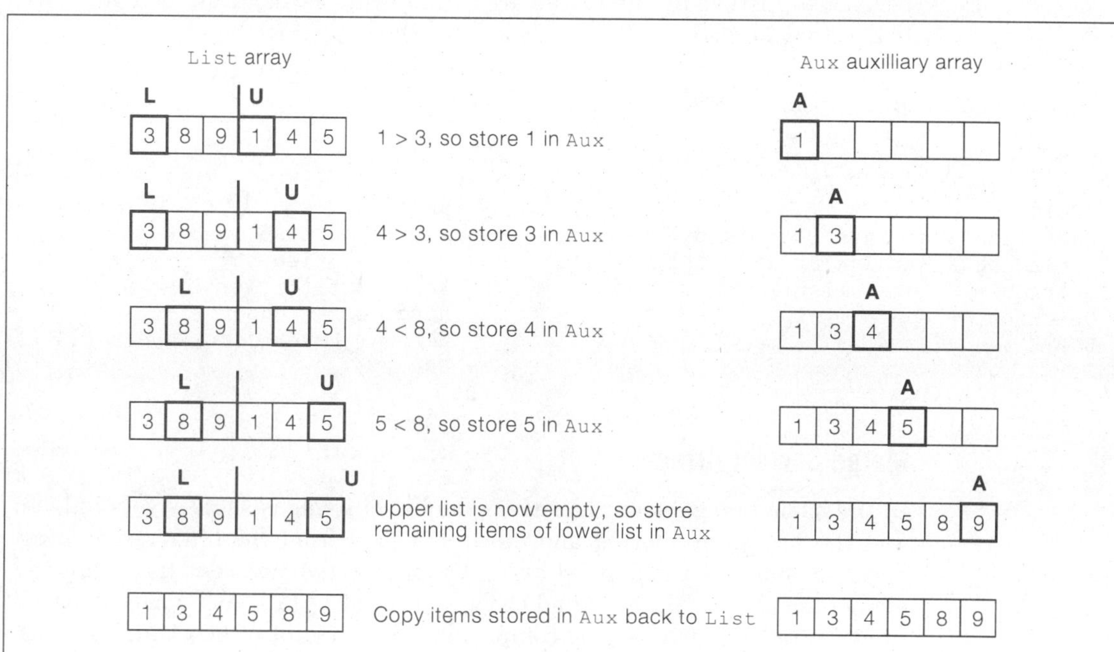

FIGURE 11.7 Merging Two Sorted Lists Using an Auxiliary Array

merging of two sorted lists, both contained in an array called `List` and separated in the figure with a boldface line. As usual, only integer key values are shown. The current item in the lower list is indicated by L, the current item in the upper list is indicated by U, and the current index into the auxiliary array is indicated by A.

A pseudocode algorithm for this operation follows. Again, the "lower list" and "upper list" are relative terms, with lower list occupying elements (`Low1..High1`) and the upper list occupying (`High1 + 1..High2`). The current-item variables are `Lower`, `Upper`, and `A`.

```
ALGORITHM Merge ( Low1, High1, High2 : Integer );

VAR
  Aux           : ListType;      {Auxiliary array, to hold merged lists temp.}
  A,                             {Index into Aux}
  Lower, Upper  : Integer;       {Current-item index into lower, upper lists}

BEGIN
Lower := Low1;                   {Initialize Lower to lowest index of lower list}
Upper := High1 + 1;              {Initialize Upper to lowest index of upper list}
A     := Low1;                   {Initialize Aux index to lowest index of lower list}

WHILE Items remaining in both lists DO
  BEGIN
  IF Lower item Key <= Upper item Key THEN    {IF Current lower key < current
    BEGIN                                     {   upper list key ...}
    Store Lower item in Aux;                  {  Store current lower list item}
    Lower := Lower + 1
    END
  ELSE
    BEGIN                                     {ELSE}
    Store Upper item in Aux;                  {  Store current upper list item}
    Upper := Upper + 1
    END;
  A := A + 1                                  {Always increment Aux index}
  END;

IF Remaining items in lower list THEN
  Copy remaining items in lower list to Aux
ELSE
  Copy remaining items in upper list to Aux;
Copy merged list back to List array
END;
```

Figure 11.8 traces the merge sorting of a generic six-item list, using code segments from `MergeSort`'s main routine. In the figure, the current (sub)-list being sorted is outlined with a boldface border, and the state of the array is pictured prior to executing the code segment shown to the right of it. Elements with the same shade represent a sorted list. Individual array diagrams and corresponding code segments are indented to reflect recursive nesting (vertical lines are also drawn as a guide). Also, the value of midpoint variable `Mid` is shown as a constant parameter to `MergeSort`. Refer back to the main routine of `MergeSort` as necessary.

Figure 11.9 traces the complete merge sorting of a sample six-item list. In the figure, both the `List` array and `Aux` auxiliary array are shown at each step (`List` is shown above `Aux`) and, as in Figure 11.7, the `Lower` variable

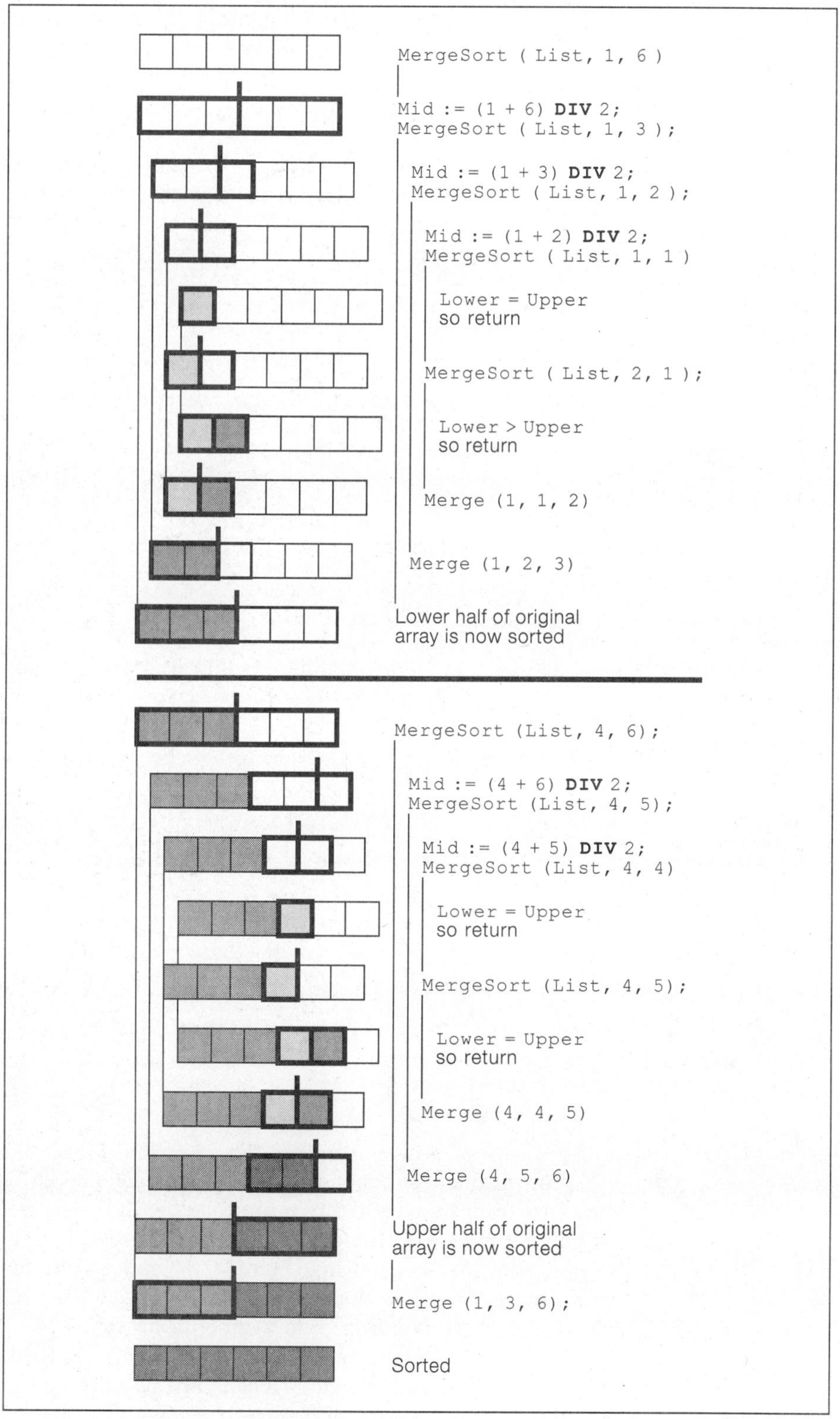

FIGURE 11.8 Generic Trace of the Lists Sorted and Merged by `MergeSort`

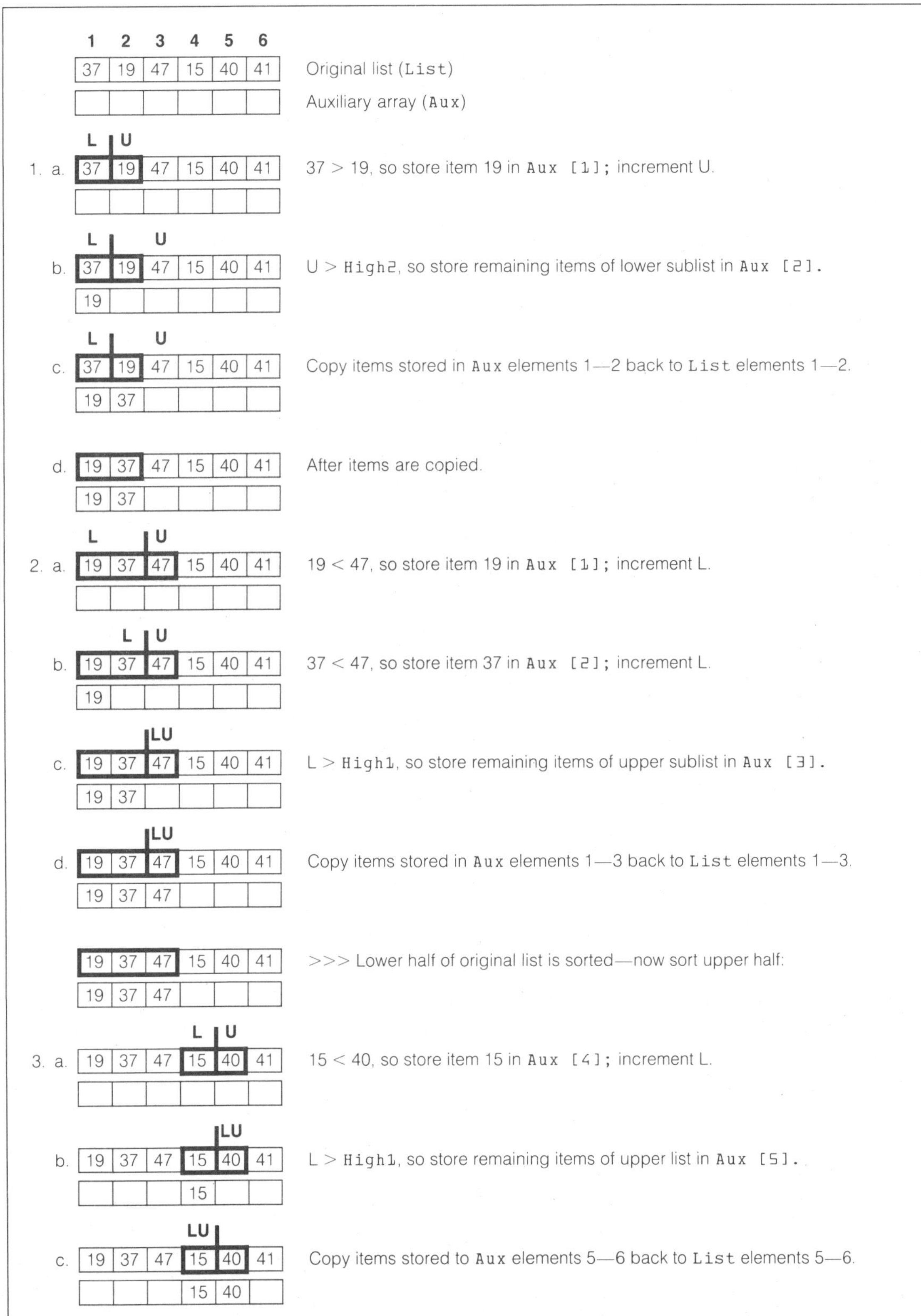

FIGURE 11.9 Performing a Merge Sort (Continues Next Page)

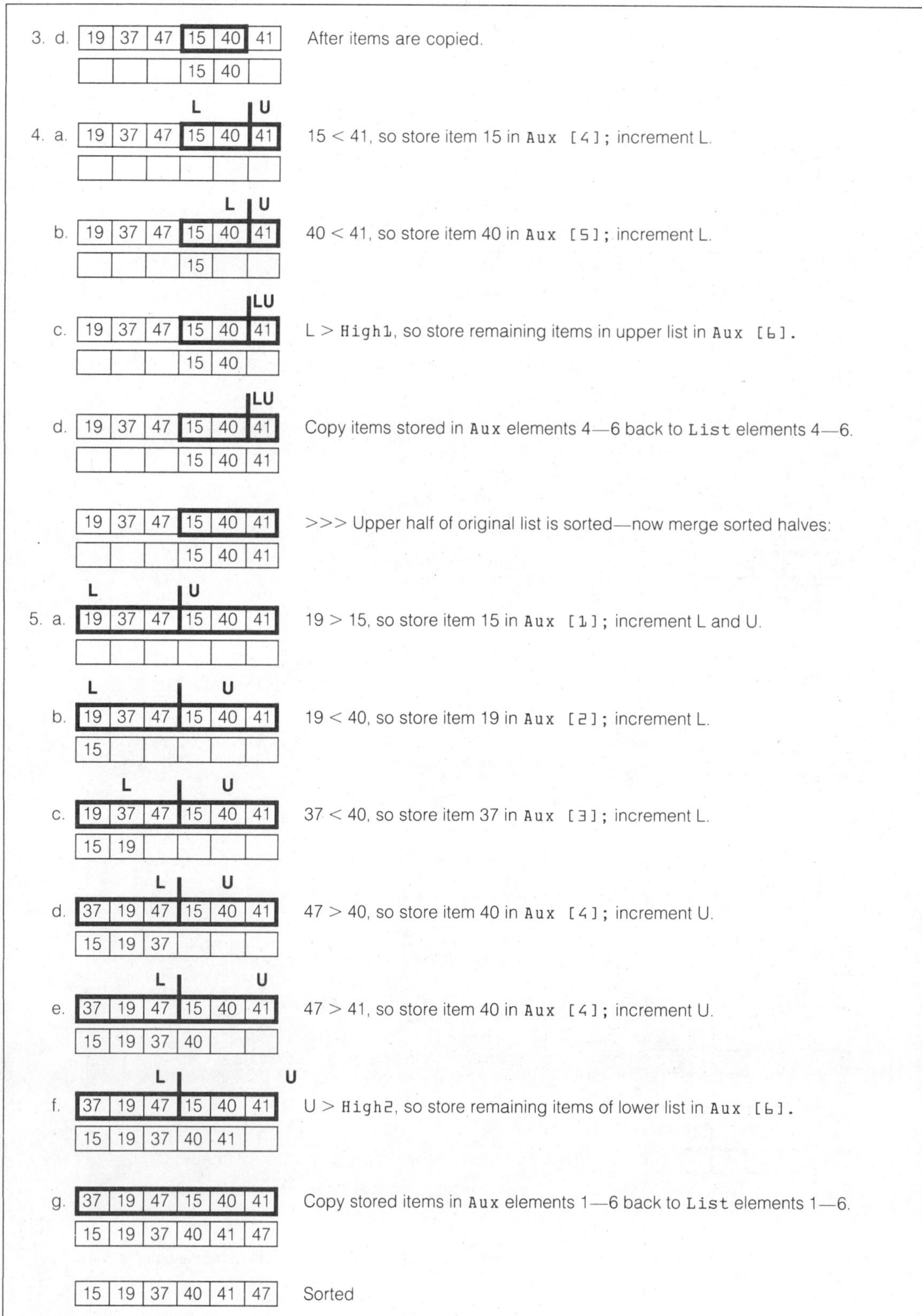

FIGURE 11.9 Performing a Merge Sort (Continued)

is indicated by L and the `Upper` variable is indicated by U. The initial call to `MergeSort` for this example would be `MergeSort ( List, 1, 6 )`.

> *At this time, examine the following routine in Appendix J.*

```
PROCEDURE MergeSort ( VAR List : ListType; Low, High : Integer );
```

Analysis of Merge Sort for Arrays

Let us consider the worst case performance of merge sort first. The merge sort algorithm compares key values at only one point—within the **WHILE** loop of the `Merge` procedure, which merges two adjacent sorted lists. As a result of each comparison and between the keys of two items, one of the items is copied to the auxiliary array. In the worst case of merging two lists, the comparing process continues until a single item remains in one of the two lists; this item is then copied to the auxiliary array. The maximum number of comparisons to merge two lists is (sum of list lengths) − 1. The 1 is subtracted because no comparison is performed if a single item remains; it is merely copied to the auxiliary array. The total number of comparisons made in the worst performance, $C(N)$, is therefore a function of the list lengths merged—i.e., the total length of all lists merged in the complete merge sorting process.

To simplify the calculations, let us assume that N, the number of items in the list to be merge sorted, is a power of 2. Because merge sort repeatedly divides lists in half, the number of list merges for a list of N items is calculated as follows:

$$\text{Number of merges} = \frac{N}{2} + \frac{N}{4} + \frac{N}{8} + \frac{N}{16} + \cdots + \frac{N}{N}$$
$$= N - 1$$

Notice that this also represents a sum of the lengths of the various lists merged. This means that, in the worst performance, the following holds:

$$C(N) \approx N \log N - N + 1$$

Merge sort is therefore $O(N \log N)$ in the worst case.

It is unlikely that all possible key comparisons will have to be made to merge every pair of lists, so the average number of key comparisons should be less. It has been proven that merge sort requires $N \log N - 1.158N + 1$ key comparisons in the average performance so the algorithm is still $O(N \log N)$.

The $O(N \log N)$ rate in both the worst and average performances is a substantial improvement over the $O(N^2)$ sorting routines presented thus far (bubble, straight selection, and straight insertion sorts). In fact, this growth-rate function estimates that this algorithm sorts a list of 1000 items between 9 and 10 times faster than will an N^2 algorithm! Unfortunately, merge sort requires an auxiliary array as large as the array being sorted, unlike the other algorithms, which require only a single additional item variable (for exchanging items); i.e., merge sort requires O (N) additional item-size variables, whereas the other sorting algorithms presented thus far require only O (1) additional item-size variables. Our natural merge sort for linked lists in Section 11.5 uses far less additional memory and dynamically allocates and disposes this memory as necessary.

Quicksort

The partition sort, more commonly known as **quicksort,** was invented in 1962 by mathematician C. A. R. Hoare. The superior efficiency of quicksort lies in the fact that item comparisons and exchanges occur over potentially great distances across the list being sorted, unlike such algorithms as the bubble sort, in which comparisons and exchanges take place only between adjacent items.

In general terms, quicksort may be summarized as follows:

> One of the items of a list is randomly chosen as the **pivot element.** Quicksort reconfigures the elements within a given list so the pivot element is moved to its proper place relative to all other elements in that list. This operation always partitions a list into two new lists (a lower list and an upper list), each of which is then sorted in the same manner.

For simplicity we will always select as the pivot item the *last* element in each list rather than calling a random-number generator function. The main routine of the Pascal representation of quicksort follows:

```
PROCEDURE QuickSort ( VAR List : ListType;  Low, High : Integer );

VAR
  PivotPosition : Integer;

  {Actual code for Partition appears on the next page}

  FUNCTION Partition ( Low, High : Integer ) : Integer;

{***  Main routine for QuickSort  ***}

BEGIN
IF High > Low THEN
  BEGIN
  PivotPosition := Partition ( Low, High );          {Reconfigure list, place pivot}
  QuickSort ( List,  Low,  PivotPosition - 1 );      {Sort lower list}
  QuickSort ( List,  PivotPosition + 1,  High )      {Sort upper list}
  END
END;
```

The start of the quicksort process is depicted in the generic example of Figure 11.10.

The partitioning operation is applied to the entire array first, dividing the list into upper and lower lists. Next, it is recursively applied to the lower list, creating two more lists. It is then recursively applied to the new lower list, and so forth until the new lower list is empty or else contains a single

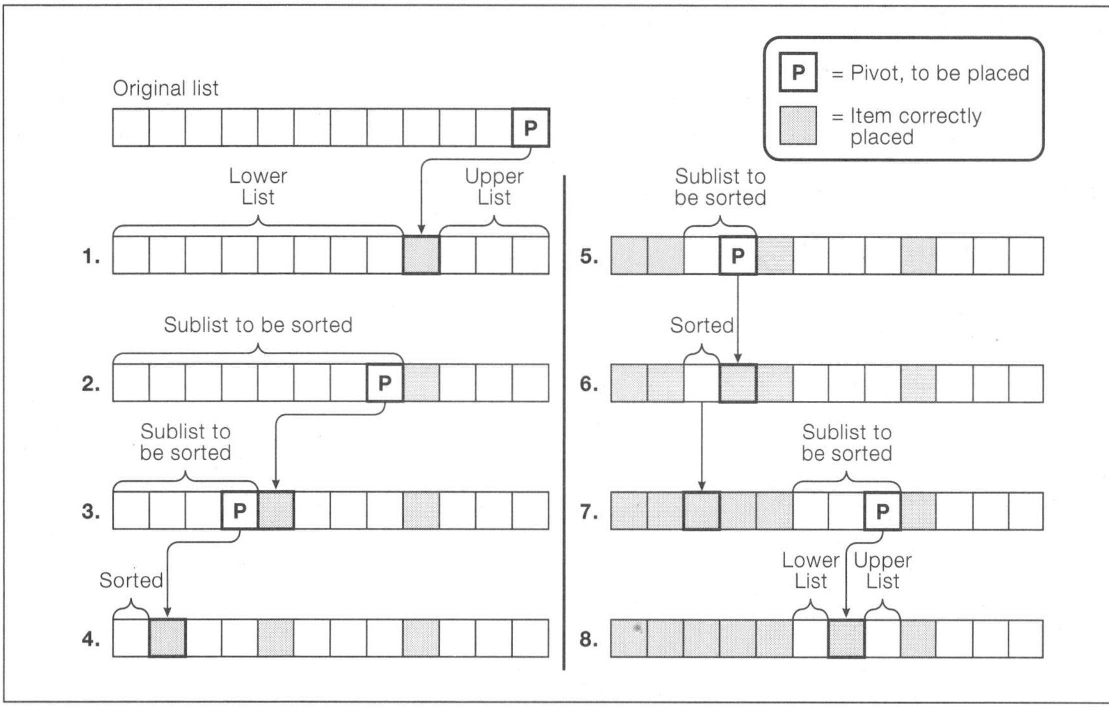

FIGURE 11.10 Generic Example of the Beginning of a Quicksort

element (which is considered a sorted list)—*these are the terminal conditions for the sorting of a given list.* Upon return from any recursive call made from the main routine to the `Partition` function to partition a lower list, the second recursive call statement is executed to partition the upper list resulting from the previous partitioning. Eventually, the entire lower list of the original list is sorted, and a recursive call is made to begin the process of sorting the original upper list. This continues until the entire original list is sorted *by correctly positioning all pivot elements of all lists.*

As you can see, most of the work in quicksort is being performed in the partitioning process, which places the current pivot element in its correct position relative to the other elements. A pseudocode version of this partitioning algorithm follows. (The Pascal representation in Appendix J is based on a version of quicksort furnished by Alice E. Fischer and Michael J. Fischer, University of Connecticut.)

```
ALGORITHM Partition ( Low, High : Integer ) : Integer;

VAR
  Lower, Upper : Integer;
  Pivot        : InfoType;

BEGIN
Pivot := last item in current list;     {Save Pivot's position within the array}
Upper := High;
Lower := Low - 1;
```

```
REPEAT

  {Increment Lower leaving elements <= Pivot to the left of it}
  REPEAT
    Lower := Lower + 1
  UNTIL item is found whose Key >= Pivot item;

  {Decrement Upper leaving elements >= Pivot to the left of it}
  REPEAT
    Upper := Upper - 1
  UNTIL item is found whose Key <= Pivot item;

  {If an element to the left of Pivot is > Pivot, swap this element with Pivot}
  IF Lower < Upper THEN
    Exchange ( Pivot item, Lower item )

UNTIL Lower >= Upper;                    {UNTIL Pivot item is in the correct place}

List [ High ] := List [ Upper + 1 ];
Store Pivot item in List [ Upper + 1 ] ; {Partition := final location of pivot item}
Partition := Upper + 1
END;
```

Figure 11.11 traces the execution of a quicksort algorithm on our sample six-item array. As with the straight insertion sort, quicksort uses the "negative infinity" value in element zero to minimize the number of comparisons performed. The pivot element is shown in boldface, and the list currently being sorted is shown within a boldface border. The array is redisplayed with each new list to partition after each comparison between the pivot and an element in position `Upper` (denoted by U) or an element in position `Lower` (denoted by L) and after any repositioning of the pivot item. The initial call to `QuickSort` for this example would be `QuickSort ( List, 1, 6 )`.

> *At this time, examine the following routine in Appendix J.*

```
PROCEDURE Quicksort ( VAR List : ListType; Low, High : Integer );
```

Analysis of Quicksort

To determine the efficiency of quicksort, we must analyze the `Partition` function, since it does the real work of quicksort. We will measure the total number of key comparisons, $C(N)$, made by `Partition` on a list of N items in the worst, best, and average performances of sorting.

For a given list of n items, `Partition` makes $n - 1$ comparisons, creating a lower list of m items and an upper list of $n - m - 1$ items. The number of key comparisons performed to create these lists is $C(n)$ and $C(n - m - 1)$. The number of comparisons to sort a given list of n items is therefore given by the following recurrence relation:

Step	L	U	0	1	2	3	4	5	6	
			−∞	37	19	47	15	40	41	Original list
1. a.	0	6	−∞	37	19	47	15	40	41	Sublist is elements 1—6; pivot is 41; increment L.
b.	1	6	−∞	37	19	47	15	40	41	37 < 41, so increment L.
c.	2	6	−∞	37	19	47	15	40	41	19 < 41, so increment L.
d.	3	6	−∞	37	19	47	15	40	41	47 > 41, so swap 47 and 41; decrement U.
e.	3	5	−∞	37	19	41	15	40	47	40 < 41, so swap 40 and 41; increment L.
f.	4	5	−∞	37	19	40	15	41	47	15 < 41, so increment L.
g.	5	5	−∞	37	19	40	15	41	47	L = U; `Partition` = 5; return from Partition.
2. a.	0	4	−∞	37	19	40	15	41	47	Lower sublist of pivot 41 is elements 1—4; new pivot is 15; increment L.
b.	1	4	−∞	37	19	40	15	41	47	37 > 15, so swap 37 and 15; decrement U.
c.	1	3	−∞	15	19	40	37	41	47	40 > 15, so decrement U.
d.	1	2	−∞	37	19	40	15	41	47	19 > 15, so decrement U.
e.	1	1	−∞	37	19	40	15	41	47	L = U; `Partition` = 1; return from Partition.
3.			−∞	15	19	40	37	41	47	No lower sublist for pivot 15.
4. a.	1	4	−∞	15	19	40	37	41	47	Upper sublist of pivot 15 is elements 2—4; new pivot is 37; increment L.
b.	2	4	−∞	15	19	40	37	41	47	19 < 37, so increment L.
c.	3	4	−∞	15	19	40	37	41	47	40 > 37, so swap 40 and 37; decrement U.
d.	3	3	−∞	15	19	37	40	41	47	40 > 37; L = U; `Partition` = 3; return from Partition.
5.			−∞	15	19	37	40	41	47	Lower sublist of pivot 37 is elements 2—2: sorted. No lower or upper sublist for pivot 19.

FIGURE 11.11 **Performing a Basic Quicksort (Continues Next Page)**

6.	$-\infty$	15	19	37	**[40]**	41	47	Upper sublist of 37 is elements 4—4: sorted. No lower or upper sublist for pivot 40.
7.	$-\infty$	15	19	37	40	41	**[47]**	Upper sublist of pivot 41 is elements 6—6: sorted. No lower or upper sublist for pivot 40.
	$-\infty$	15	19	37	40	41	47	Sorted

FIGURE 11.11 Performing a Basic Quicksort (Continued)

$$
\begin{aligned}
C(0) &= 0 \qquad \text{\{No comparisons in a list of 0 items\}}\\
C(1) &= 0 \qquad \text{\{No comparisons in a list of 1 item\}}\\
C(n) &= \text{(Number of comparisons to partition current list)} +\\
&\quad\ \text{(Number of comparisons to partition lower list)} +\\
&\quad\ \text{(Number of comparisons to partition upper list)}\\
&= n - 1 + C(n) + C(n - m - 1) \qquad \text{\{For lists} \geq 2 \text{ items\}}
\end{aligned}
$$

To compute the total number of comparisons for an unsorted list of N items, n is equal to N the first time $C(n)$ is solved, so we solve for $C(N)$. (As with any recurrence relation, our goal here is to obtain a closed form—i.e., an equation stating the total number of comparisons based on problem size (N) but not involving any recursive function calls to C.) Obviously, we must know the value of m for each list to solve for $C(N)$, and *this value will vary depending upon how sorted each list is prior to partitioning.*

The worst performance of quicksort arises when the original list of N items is already sorted, in which case `Partition` divides the current list of n items into one list of $n - 1$ items and the other into a list of zero items, producing the following simple equation:

$$C(n) = n - 1 + C(n - 1)$$

By plugging in increasing values of n, a pattern emerges:

$$
\begin{aligned}
C(1) &= 0\\
C(2) &= 1 + C(1) &&= 1\\
C(3) &= 2 + C(2) &&= 2 + 1\\
C(4) &= 3 + C(3) &&= 3 + 2 + 1\\
C(5) &= 4 + C(4) &&= 4 + 3 + 2 + 1\\
&\ \ \vdots\\
C(n) &= n - 1 + C(n - 1) = (n - 1) + (n - 2) + \cdots + (n - n)\\
&= \frac{n(n - 1)}{2}\\
&= \frac{n^2}{2} - \frac{n}{2}
\end{aligned}
$$

We now substitute N for n. quicksort is therefore $(N^2)/2 - N/2$, or $O(N^2)$ in its worst performance—as poor as the worst performance of bubble or selection sort.

Accordingly, the best performance of quicksort arises when items are distributed randomly about the list, in which case the `Partition` function always partitions each list into two more approximately equal-sized lists; i.e., it always places the pivot item as the middle element of a list. This is best because the function would always be called upon to partition a list approximately half the size of the previous list. In a list of N items, `Partition` function will partition the original list of N items, two lists of N **DIV** 2 items, four lists of N **DIV** 4 items, eight lists of N **DIV** 8 items, and so forth.

The following recurrence relation may be used to calculate the total number of comparisons, $C(N)$, in quicksort's best performance:

$$C(1) = 0$$

$$C(N) = 2C(N/2) + N \qquad \{\text{for } N \geq 2\}$$

$C(N/2)$ is the time necessary to partition one list, so this quantity is multiplied by 2 to obtain the total time to partition both lists created during the completion of a single call to `Partition`. The value N is added to account for the time expended for the operation of examining each item.

In *Algorithms* by Robert Sedgewick (Redding, Mass.: Addison-Wesley Publishing Co., Inc., 1983), the author provides the following simple solution to the recurrence by using the mathematical "trick" of replacing N with 2^n:

$$C(2^n) = 2C(2^{n-1}) + 2^n$$

$$\frac{C(2^n)}{2^n} = \frac{C(2^{n-1})}{2^{n-1}} + 1$$

$$\frac{C(2^n)}{2^n} = \frac{C(2^{n-2})}{2^{n-2}} + 1 + 1$$

$$\vdots$$

$$= n$$

Since $2^N = N$ (the initial substitution) and $n = \log N$, the following is also true:

$$C(2^n) = n2^n$$

$$C(N) = N \log_2 N$$

Thus, quicksort is $O(N \log N)$ in its best performance.

The analysis of the average performance of the quicksort algorithm is more complicated but has shown that the algorithm requires $1.39N \log N + N$ comparisons; quicksort is therefore rated at $O(N \log N)$ in its average performance.

Because quicksort involves a fair number of overhead operations, such as manipulating the `Lower` and `Upper` variables, its performance can be improved by calling one of the O (N^2) sorting algorithms when the list to partition next is very small; the O (N^2) routines perform faster with small lists that are nearly sorted. Since the worst performance rate of O (N^2) is unlikely to occur and requires only one item-size variable for item exchanges (unlike merge sort, which requires N item-size variables), quicksort is regarded as one of the fastest array-sorting algorithms.

Many algorithms take quicksort's divide-and-conquer approach, in which the original problem is divided into two parts. Solving these subproblems involves dividing each into two sub-subproblems, and so forth. The recurrence relation, $C(N) = 2C(N/2) + N$, describes this class of problems, which are all rated as O (log N). Interestingly enough, it has been proven mathematically that no sorting algorithm based on the comparison of key values can perform faster than O (N log N).

11.4 SORTING ARRAYS: BINARY TREE SORTS

The preorder, in-order, postorder, reverse-order, and level-order tree traversals were presented in Section 8.2. Although the algorithms for these traversals work for any binary tree structure, they have special significance when applied to binary search trees. Because all the items in a binary search tree are ordered by key value, an in-order traversal processes items in order of ascending key value, whereas a reverse-order traversal processes items in descending key-value order. Also presented was a description of how a compiler might build an expression tree to represent an arithmetic expression from a line of source code and then perform a preorder or postorder traversal to evaluate the expression as a preorder or postfix expression, respectively. And the discussion in Section 8.2 explained how a binary search tree may be preserved in a file by saving items during either a preorder or level-order traversal. In each of these examples, the traversal algorithms visit and process each item in a particular order, *as if they had restructured the entire tree* without physically moving a single node!

Binary Search Tree Sort

A simple sorting algorithm using a binary search tree may be performed as follows:

1. Initialize a binary search tree as empty.
2. Insert items repeatedly from an unsorted list, using the algorithm `BinTreeInsert` presented in Section 8.2 and Appendix G.
3. Perform an in-order traversal of the tree, processing each item by writing it back to the original list (or some application-dependent process task).

This algorithm is called the **binary search tree sort.**

Analysis of Binary Search Tree Sort

The algorithm performs worst if the original list is already sorted by ascending or descending key value order because the tree produced is completely degenerate—i.e., effectively a linear linked list. In this case, the algorithm becomes a straight insertion sort, which has already been analyzed as an O (N^2) algorithm.

In both the best and average performances, the average number of comparisons performed in the search of a balanced binary tree sort of N items is $\log N$ (as proven in Section 8.2). As more insertions are performed, any one search has an increasing number of items in the tree against which to (potentially) compare, so the total number of comparisons (for a list of N unsorted items) is calculated as follows:

$$\sum_{K=1}^{N} \lceil \log N \rceil \approx N \log N$$

To this estimation we must add N for the insertion of each item in the tree and another N for the time necessary to traverse the tree and copy each item back to the original structure. Therefore, binary tree sort has a growth-rate function of $N \log N + N$ and is rated at O $(N \log N)$. Although this algorithm is generally regarded as O $(N \log N)$, it actually varies between N^2 and $\log N$, depending on the shape of the tree. As with merge sort, this algorithm also requires enough internal memory to hold a binary tree sort of N items, including two link fields per tree node.

We will now examine the **heap sort** algorithm, which also requires building a binary tree of items. However, it provides two distinct advantages over the binary search tree sort:

1. If the original list is already contained within an array, no additional memory is required (other than an item-size variable used in the exchange of items).
2. The algorithm is guaranteed to be O $(N \log N)$, regardless of the order of the original list of items.

Heap Sort

In Section 8.3, the heap was introduced as a structure for representing a priority queue. Recall that a heap is a full or nearly full binary tree in which the key (priority) value of each parent is greater than or equal to the key values of either child (alternately, an application may require that the priority value of each parent be *less* than or equal to either child). The heap itself is represented using an array, so that the heap root item, which contains the greatest key value in the heap, is always stored in array element 1. Also recall that a heap remove operation involves the following four steps:

1. Return to the calling routine a copy of the item occupying element 1.
2. Move the last item in the heap to element 1.
3. Decrement the last-item index value.
4. Move the item in element 1, level by level down the heap, to the first node where its key is greater than or equal to the key of either child (if any).

By performing a heap removal operation repeatedly, items can be removed from the heap in descending key order to build a sorted list. Since the heap shrinks by one item and the sorted list grows by one item with each heap removal, the array containing the original heap can be used to store both lists. Each item removed is simply fed back into the array by swapping it with the last heap item, which is moved to element one anyway (Step 2 in the removal operation).

Of course, this sorting algorithm works only on lists structured as heaps. We must, therefore, perform a presort algorithm, which converts any array list of items into a heap. To do this, we will start with a one-item heap (whatever item is already in element 1) and perform a heap insertion operation repeatedly, inserting items from the remainder of the array. This is somewhat analogous to the straight insertion sort; here the heap portion of the original list grows as the unsorted portion shrinks.

The following code segment calls procedure `AdjustUp` (given in Appendix H) to place the *K*th item in array `Heap.List` in its appropriate place within the array:

```
FOR K := 2 TO Heap.Count DO
  AdjustUp ( Heap, K )
```

Figure 11.12 traces the heap conversion process for the sample six-item list. In the figure, P and C refer to parent and child items, respectively, and the small boldface line extending above each array diagram separates the growing heap (to the left of the line) and the shrinking list of nonheap items (to the right of the line). Figure 11.13 traces the execution of the `HeapSort` procedure on the heap.

The representation of the heap sort algorithm given in Appendix J—procedure `HeapSort`—requires that the unsorted list already be contained in array `Heap.List` (although it need not be a heap when `HeapSort` is called), with the item-count `Heap.Count` field properly assigned. This would allow `HeapSort` to use `AdjustUp`, `HeapDelete`, and `AdjustDown` as they were designed in Section 8.3 and given in Appendix H. Also notice that if the original list happens to be a heap, a true value is passed to the `NotAHeapYet` parameter, and the conversion code within `HeapSort` is bypassed.

At this time, examine the following routine in Appendix J.

```
PROCEDURE HeapSort ( VAR Heap : HeapType; NotAHeapYet : Boolean );
```

Analysis of Heap Sort

Heap sort is as fast as quicksort in its best performance, faster in its worst performance, but about twice as slow in its average performance. Even so,

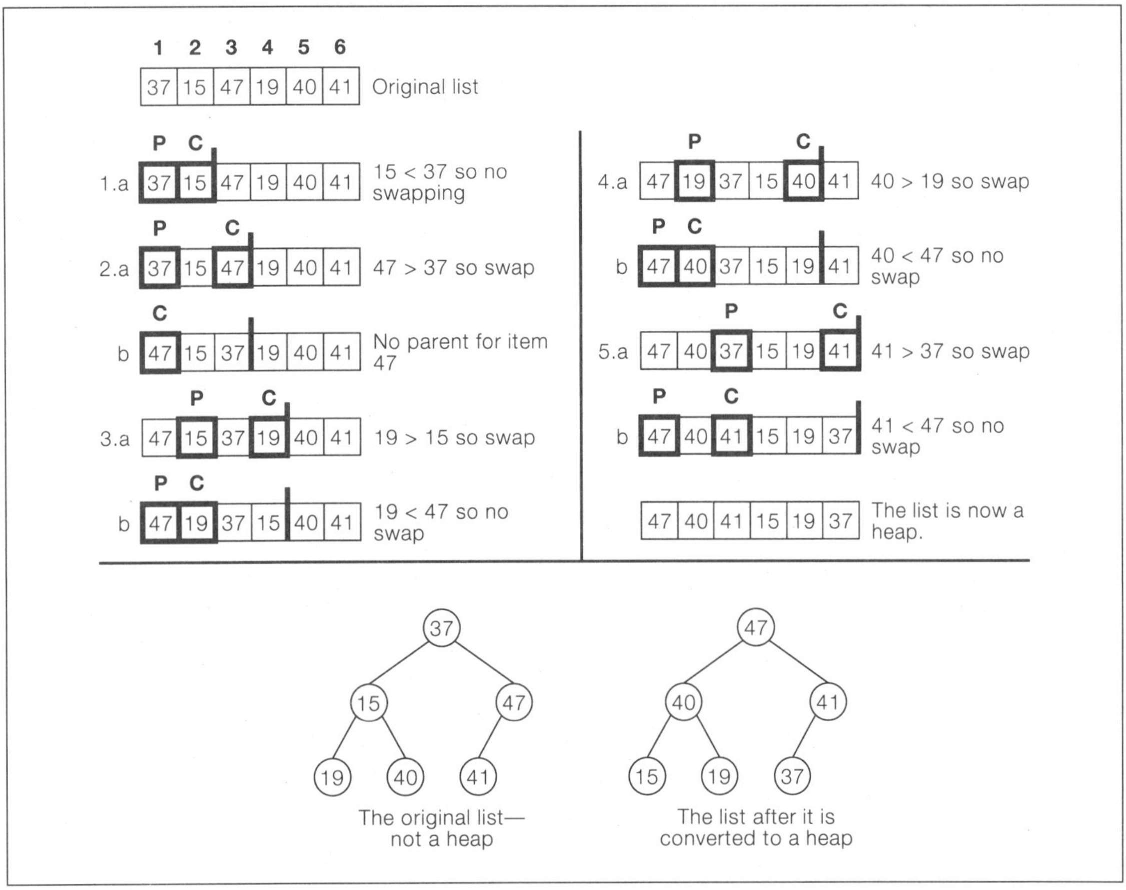

FIGURE 11.12 Converting the Sample List to a Heap

heap sort and quicksort are both rated at O (N log N). Since procedure `AdjustDown` does the real work of the heap sort algorithm when the original list is converted to a heap and `AdjustUp` does the real work as the list is adjusted back into a heap after each item is deleted, both algorithms must be analyzed to derive the efficiency of the entire sorting algorithm.

In its worst performance, `AdjustUp` must move each item inserted all the way from the leaf level to the root node of the heap. This occurs when the original list is already sorted in ascending key value order (recall that items with greater key values are placed nearer to the root of the heap as the heap is constructed). Recall from Section 8.2 that the height of a nearly full binary tree of N items is computed as follows:

$$\text{Height } (N) = \lceil \log_2(N + 1) \rceil$$

Placing a node at level L requires, at most, L key comparisons. The number of actual comparisons to place an item correctly in the heap grows as the total heap size (N) and, therefore, heap height grows:

FIGURE 11.13 Performing a Heap Sort

$$\left\lceil \log\left(\frac{N}{2}\right) \right\rceil, \left\lceil \log\left(\frac{N}{2}\right) - 1 \right\rceil, \left\lceil \log\left(\frac{N}{2}\right) - 2 \right\rceil, \ldots, \lceil \log(N-1) \rceil$$

This series sums to $N/2$. The total number of comparisons required to build a heap in the worst performance of `AdjustUp` is therefore $N/2 \times O(\log N)$, or $O(N \log N)$.

In the worst performance after the root item is removed to the head of the growing sorted list, `AdjustDown` must move the root item all the way down to the leaf level. Since a heap of N items is always balanced, this requires about $\log_2 N$ comparisons. `AdjustDown` is therefore rated as $O(\log N)$ in its worst performance for a single item; repeating this $N - 1$ times (for all N items) yields a rating of $O(N \log N)$ for all items. Combining this with the number of comparisons necessary to convert the original list to a heap, $O(N \log N)$, plus the number of comparisons necessary to perform successive heap deletions, also $O(N \log N)$, requires approximately $1.5N \log N$ total comparisons. Heap sort is therefore rated as $O(N \log N)$ in its worst performance.

As with quicksort, heap sort is not efficient for small lists, so the switch to an $O(N^2)$ algorithm could be made when the list of remaining unsorted items drops below a particular size.

11.5 SORTING LINKED LISTS

The items of a list in sequential storage may be accessed directly, using index values, whereas items of a linked list may be accessed linearly, so this rules out using quicksort algorithm to sort linked lists. (Of course, each item of a linked list could be assigned to an array element first; then the entire array could be sorted using quicksort, but the time cost of storing the items in the array would probably outweigh greatly the savings provided by the quicksorting.) Bubble sort or straight selection sort could be used if the list were doubly linked or binary tree sort could be used with any linked list, but we will consider two other sorting algorithms instead. We shall use as our sample linked list the unordered, nine-item list depicted at the top of Figure 11.14, which was built using the generic global declarations given at the start of Section 5.2 and in Appendix D. As usual, in the figure only key values are shown, and a stripe-filled link field represents a **`NIL`** pointer value.

Insertion Sort for Linked Lists

A preliminary approach to sorting the list is an insertion sort in which the list is traversed and each node is processed by placing it in a second list, which is kept ordered upon the insertion of each node. Early stages of this process for the sample list are depicted in Figure 11.14. The first node of the second list is pointed to by a pointer variable called `Temp`. Once the second, sorted list is built, `LList.Head` would be assigned the contents of `Temp` in order to point to this list. Notice that, as with the straight insertion sort of Section 11.3, the second, sorted list grows as the original, unsorted list shrinks.

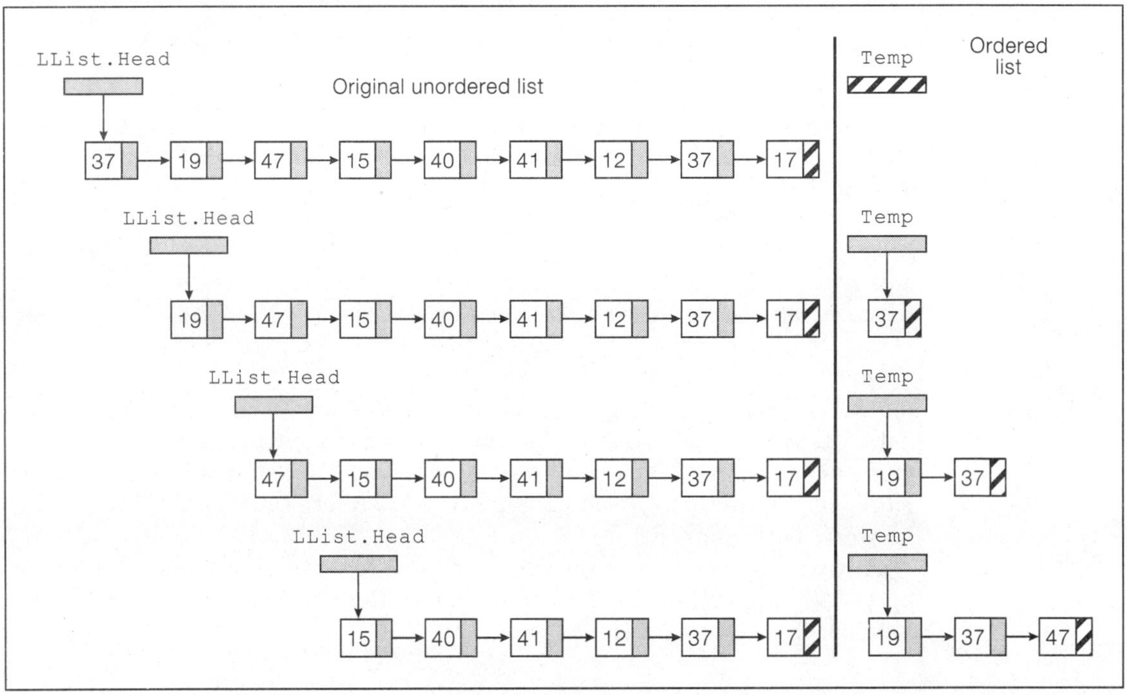

FIGURE 11.14 First Stages of an Insertion Sort

Although the use of linked lists rather than sequential storage precludes using quicksort, which relies on the direct access of items, linking does provide a unique advantage. Recall that the linked list insertion procedure, `LLInsert` of Section 5.2 and Appendix D, calls the standard `New` procedure to dynamically allocate heapspace for a new variable and then assigns an `InfoType` record to the data portion of the new node. Since each node of the linked list already exists and already contains data, we can save execution time and memory by merely modifying pointer values rather than allocating new heapspace and copying information. That is, *data items are not actually moved about,* as with all other sorting algorithms presented thus far, and this may save a substantial amount of execution time.

The `LLDelete` procedure of Section 5.2 and Appendix D must also be modified, however, since it calls the standard `Dispose` procedure to deallocate the heapspace containing the just-deleted item. Each item is deleted from the original list, only to be inserted into the ordered list, so its heapspace is not actually deallocated in the process.

Natural Merge Sort for Linked Lists

Let us consider an entirely different divide-and-conquer approach called a **natural merge sort.** As we see in Section 11.6, natural merge sorting is applicable to files of items as well. A pseudocode algorithm for a natural merge sort follows:

```
ALGORITHM NaturalMerge ( VAR List : ListType );

BEGIN
Divide the original list of N items into ⌈N/2⌉ lists;
Sort each list;
REPEAT
  Merge 2 lists of items into a single sorted list
UNTIL a single (sorted) list remains;
Return this sorted list
END;
```

The process of merging two sorted linked lists is similar to the merging of two sorted lists within an array, as was done in the array-based merge sort algorithm of Section 11.3. Figure 11.15 traces the beginning steps in the merging of two sorted linked lists (pointed to by pointer variables `Head1` and `Head2`) into a single sorted linked list (pointed to by `Head3`).

To manage all the lists created and merged, we will use a FIFO queue of pointers. Each queue item will point to the first node in a list, effectively serving the same function as `Head3` in Figure 11.15. Initially, the sorting algorithm divides the original list of N items into $\lceil N/2 \rceil$ lists of two items each (again, if N is odd, the last list contains a single node). Each pair of lists is then served from the front of the queue and merged using the insertion sort strategy just described, and the resulting list is then enqueued at the back of the queue. This process continues until the queue contains a single item: a pointer to the first node of the sorted list. The number of lists in the queue decreases with each merging of two lists.

A more detailed pseudocode algorithm for the merge sort process follows:

```
ALGORITHM  LLMergeSort ( VAR Head : NodePtr );

BEGIN
Divide the entire list into ⌈N/2⌉ 2-node lists, each ordered by key value,
  and enqueue pointers to every list (the last list enqueued may contain
  only 1 node);

WHILE there are 2 or more lists in the queue DO
  BEGIN
  Serve the next two queue lists;
  Merge these lists into 1 sorted list;
  Enqueue a new queue node, which should point to this just-merged list
  END;

Serve the remaining list and assign to Head the address of its 1st node
END;
```

Figure 11.16 traces these steps on the sample linked list, using a circular FIFO queue.

At this time, examine the following routine in Appendix J.

```
PROCEDURE LLMergeSort ( VAR LList : LListType );
```

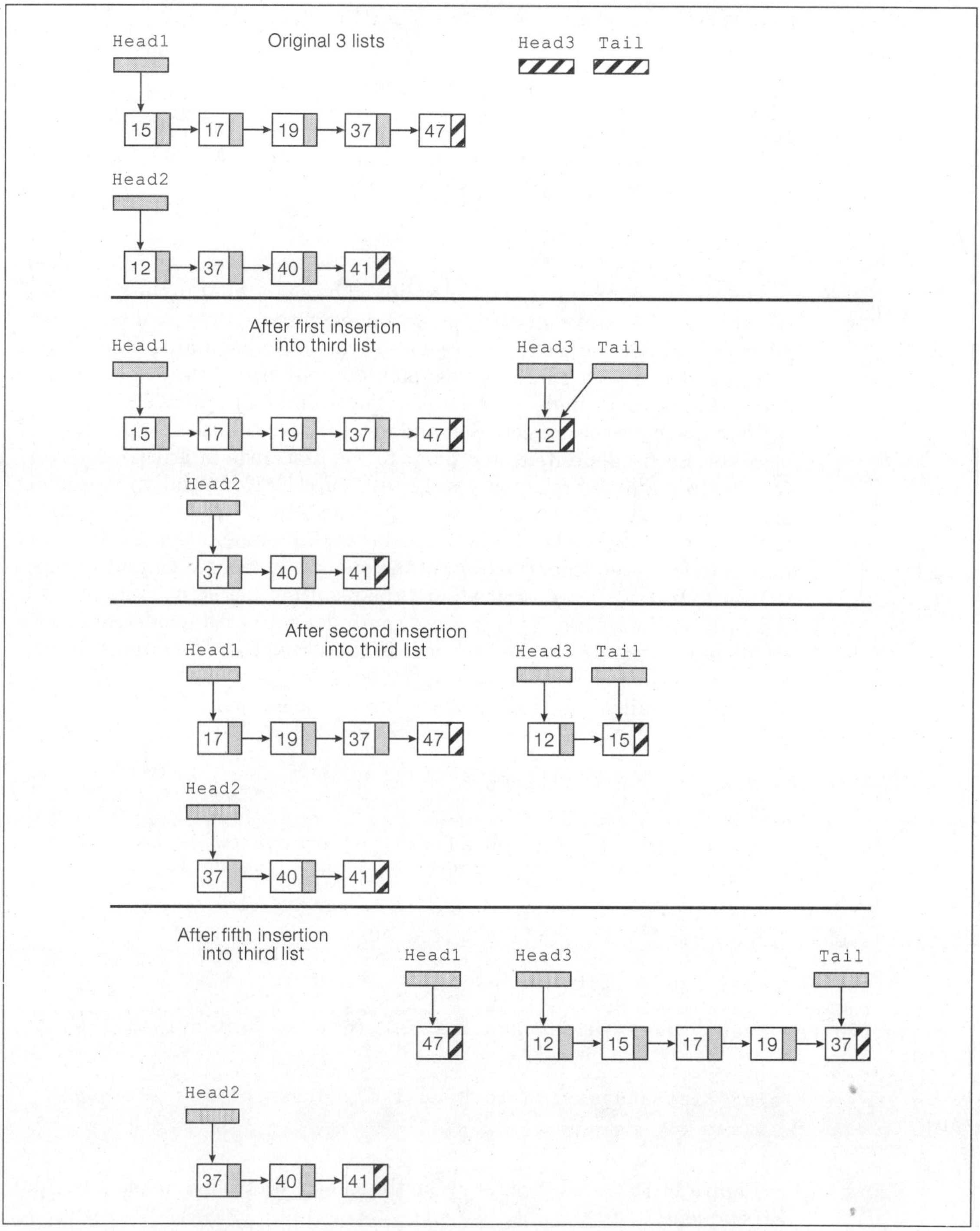

FIGURE 11.15 Beginning Steps in the Merging of Two Sorted Linked Lists

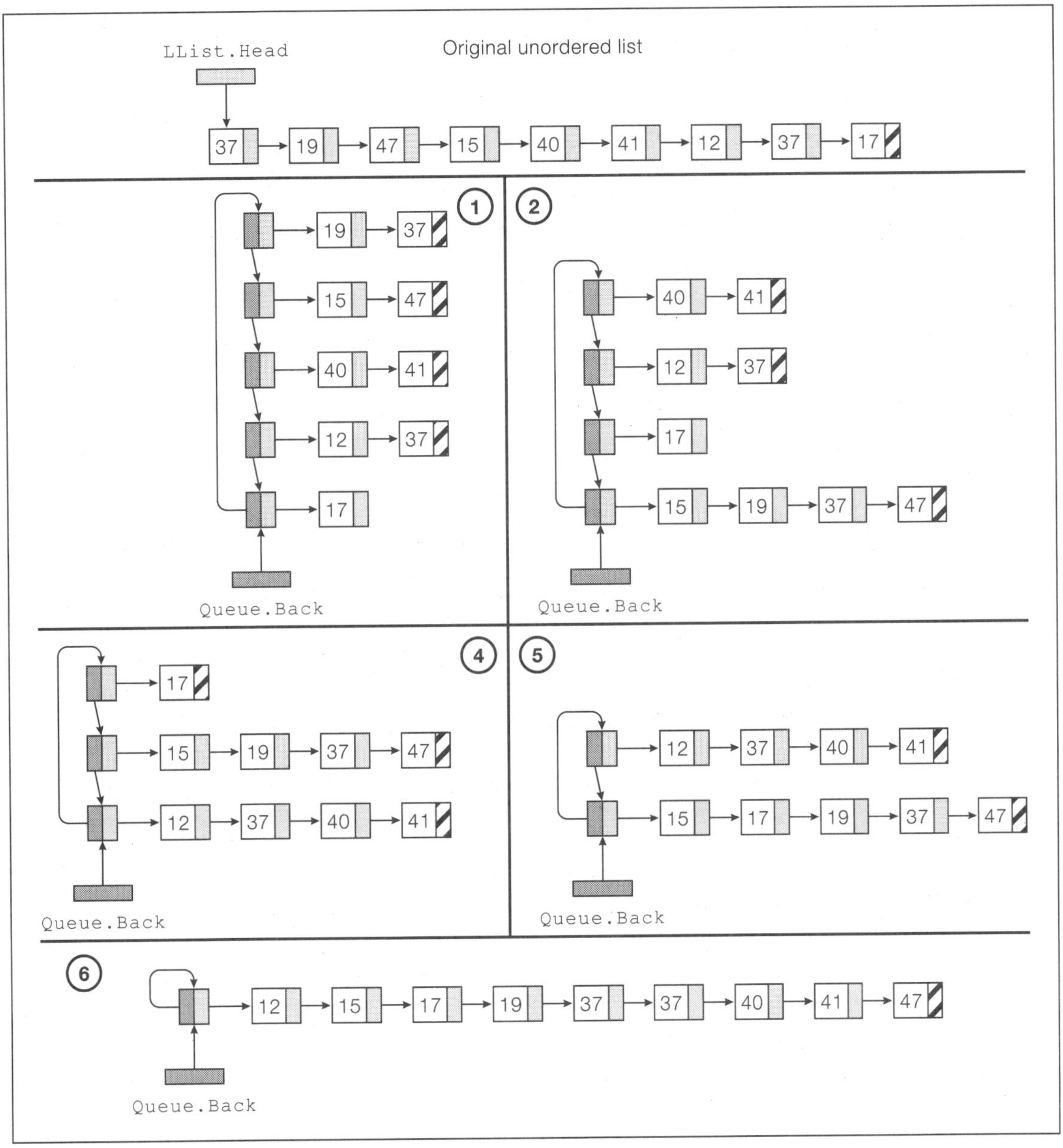

FIGURE 11.16 Performing a Natural Merge Sort

11.6 SORTING FILES

Merge Sort for Files

So far in this chapter we have examined algorithms for sorting a list of items contained entirely within *internal memory*. Many applications involve sorting a list of items stored in *external memory* instead (as opposed to building and accessing a secondary index B-tree, as described in Section

10.3). Although items in a file may already be sorted by key value, an application may require that the file items be ordered by some other key, so the file must be resorted (the time necessary to perform many searches on a large, unsorted file can be prohibitive compared to the time necessary to simply resort the file). If the file is small enough, it could be sorted by reading all its items into an internal structure and then applying one of the sorting algorithms presented in this chapter and rewriting the data items back to the file. In a great many applications, however, the list is simply too large to fit entirely within internal memory.

Recall that our natural merge sort algorithm for linked lists consisted of the following two stages (N is the number of data items):

1. *Presort.* Divide the list into $\lceil N/2 \rceil$ sorted segments.
2. *Merge.* Merge pairs of sorted segments repeatedly, until a single sorted list results.

With some modifications, we can adapt this approach to sort files.

Since a file of records is logically divided into blocks of records, our sort algorithm can begin by repeatedly reading in a block of records, sorting this list using quicksort or heap sort, and then writing the sorted block back to the file. As in Step 1 of the linked list merge sort, this Step 1 results in the file's containing a collection of blocks, each sorted by key value. Step 2 involves repeatedly comparing two file sections of K blocks each to produce a sorted section of $2K$ blocks each. Eventually a single sorted section results—the entire file of all blocks.

Our merge sorting algorithm requires three arrays and two temporary files, in addition to the original unsorted files. The two stages of standard merge sorting a file may be summarized as follows (M is the number of blocks available within internal memory for merging—i.e., excluding the `Array1` and `Array2` array buffers):

- *Presort.* Divide the file into $\lceil$(File size in blocks) / $M\rceil$ sorted segments, each M blocks long; use an array (`Array1`) and a temporary file (`Temp1`).
- *Merge.* Use the M blocks of memory to merge sorted file segments; use three arrays (`Array1`, `Array2`, `Array3`) and two temporary files (`Temp1` and `Temp2`).

Figure 11.17 provides a generic overview of these stages in the simple case of a four-block file, `InFile`, and two temporary files, `Temp1` and `Temp2`, which are also four blocks long.

In the presort stage, any efficient sorting algorithm, such as quicksort or heap sort, may be used to sort each of the file segments. In the merge stage, `Array1` and `Array2` serve as input buffers and `Array3` serves as an output buffer. The first step involves reading sorted segments of items into `Array1` and `Array2` and then merging these segments to form a sorted segment twice as long. This is done by comparing keys from each list and copying the record with the smaller (or equivalent) key to `Array3`. As soon as it fills up, the sorting routine writes the items to `File3`.

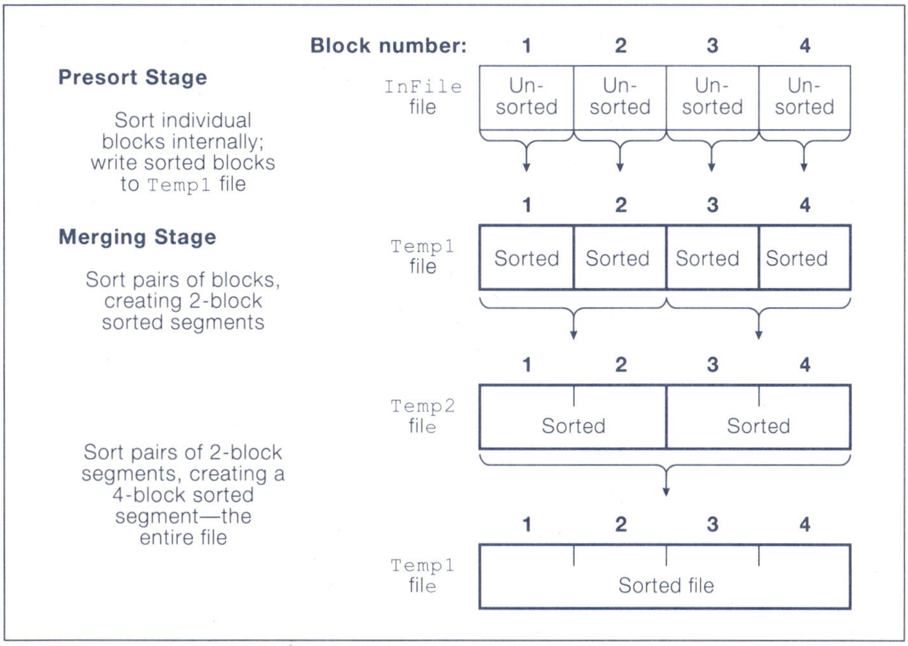

FIGURE 11.17 Merge Sorting a Four-Block Sample File

The remaining steps of the merge stage proceed in a similar manner, although, in the example of Figure 11.17, an entire sorted segment of two blocks will no longer fit in `Array1` or `Array2`. Instead, one-block portions of each segment must be read in and merged. In the second merge step, the first block of one segment—block 1—is read into `Array1` and the first block of the second segment—block 3—is read into `Array2`. These are merged, as before, by comparing keys and copying the record with the smaller (or equivalent) key to the next element in `Array3`. Whenever `Array3` fills up, its contents are written to `File1`. Another difference from Step 2(a) is that one of the arrays—`Array1` or `Array2`—may be copied entirely to `Array3` before the other. The sorting routine would then read into the emptied array the next block's worth of records from the corresponding file segment.

Figure 11.18 depicts a merge sort of a four-block sample file of 24 items. In this example, we assume the limit of three blocks of internal memory available to hold data temporarily in sorting process. This chunk of memory is divided among arrays named `Array1`, `Array2`, and `Array3`.

11.7 SORTING GRAPHS

It is often useful to access the nodes of a graph in order of ascending (or descending) key value, ignoring the directionality of edges. Examples of this might include displaying information about each city to which Chapter 9's Sky-High Airlines flies by alphabetical order of city name or displaying in-

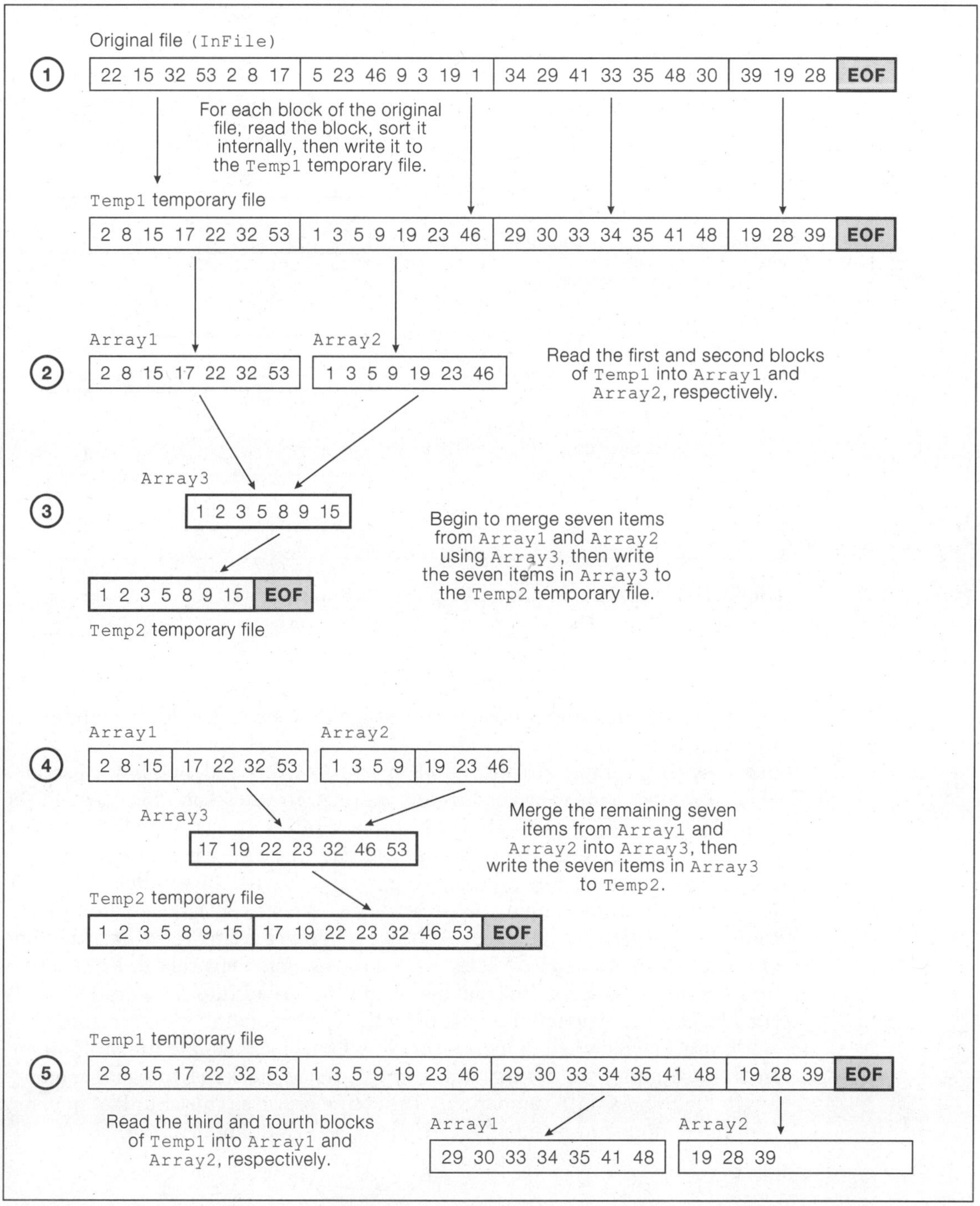

FIGURE 11.18 Performing a Merge Sort on a Four-Block File (Continues)

formation about each pumping station in the Lost Wages aqueduct system (Application 9.1) in alphabetical order of pumping station name. Whether a graph is represented as an adjacency matrix or as an adjacency list, there will likely be some kind of sorted lookup table containing node data, which can be traversed.

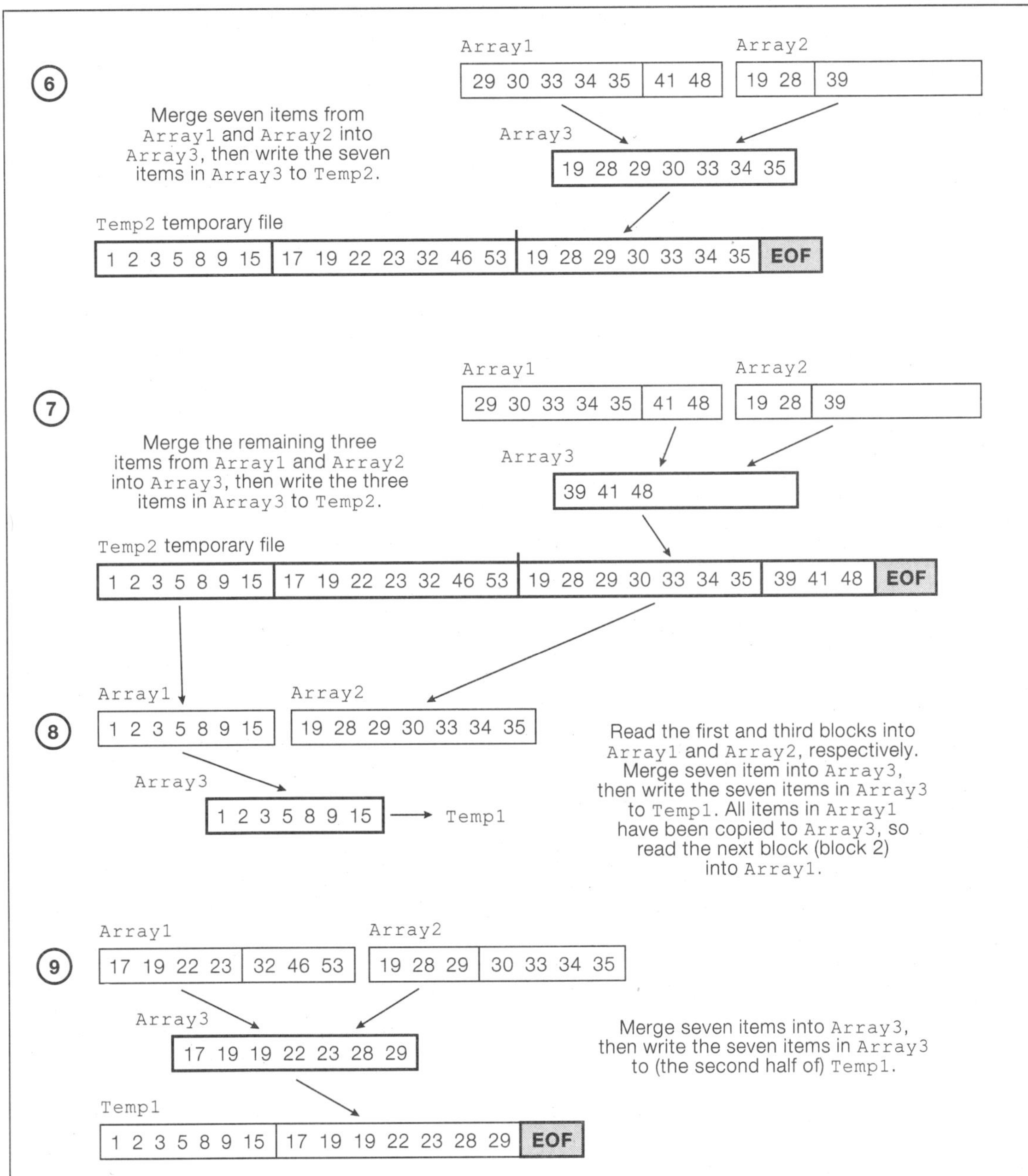

FIGURE 11.18 (Continues)

Topological Sort

A more interesting sorting problem arises with **PERT graphs.** A PERT graph is a directed acyclic graph (DAG) in which there are functional dependencies among groups of nodes:

- Each node represents the start of a task.
- Each edge represents the performance of a task.

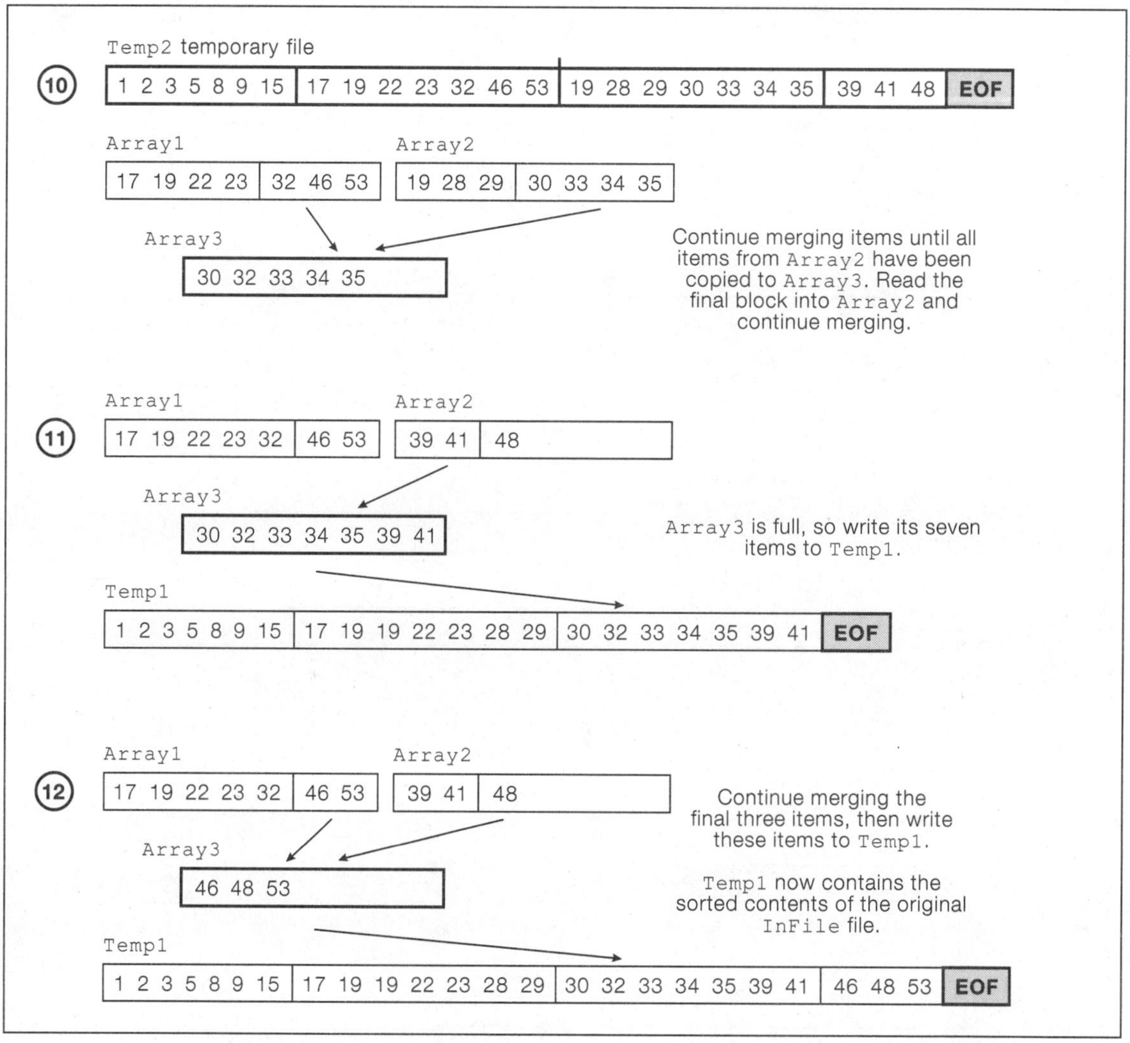

FIGURE 11.18 Performing a Merge Sort on a Four-Block File (Continued)

For example, in the sample PERT graph of Figure 11.19, the task represented by node G is functionally dependent upon the tasks represented by nodes C and F; task F is itself functionally dependent upon the task represented by nodes D and E.

For *any* project involving many interdependent tasks, it is often useful to perform a topological sort of the tasks, perhaps displaying a description of each task. As in the previous example, the appearance of a given task description in the list indicates that all prerequisite tasks have already appeared/been performed, so that task may be performed.

A **topological sort** produces a linear list from a PERT graph so each node appears after the node(s) upon which it is functionally dependent. The DAG of Figure 11.19 can be topologically sorted several different ways, including the following (differences among the sorted lists are underlined):

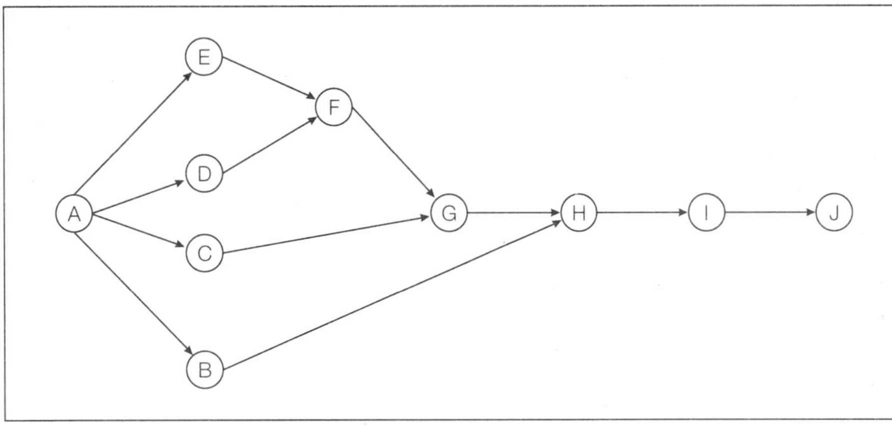

FIGURE 11.19 A Sample PERT Graph of 10 Tasks

```
ABCDEFGHIJ
ACDEFBGHIJ
ADEFBCGHIJ
AEDFCGBHIJ

ABCDEGFHIJ  {Not topologically sorted, since G is dependent upon F}
```

Other everyday examples of topological sorting include the following:

1. In any textbook words are defined in terms of other words; i.e., the topological sorting of the words involves arranging them in a list such that there are no forward references.
2. In a computer program, some procedures and functions contain calls to other procedures and functions. The topological sorting of all procedures and functions within the program involves arranging the procedures and functions such that there are no forward references. (A Pascal compiler *requires* such an arrangement, of course, unless the standard **FORWARD** declaration is used.)
3. In a university curriculum, certain courses (prerequisites) must be taken before other courses. The topological sorting of all course descriptions involves arranging the descriptions such that no course lists a later-appearing course as a prerequisite.

A topological sorting algorithm must involve a traversal of the graph, since every node is processed, e.g., inserted into a separate, topologically ordered list or, perhaps, simply displayed. Section 9.2 presented depth-first and breadth-first traversal algorithms and, accordingly, we can perform depth-first and breadth-first topological sorts (we will actually employ *depth-first* traversing here and in Application 11.1). Recall that in the depth-first traversal, a path is followed as far as possible into the graph, based on the directionality of edges; each time a node is visited, it is processed and "marked" as having been visited. At the end of a path, the traversal algorithm backtracks to the last visited node, from which an alternate path to unvisited nodes is then taken. The backtracking and following of new paths continues until all nodes have been visited and the traversal algorithm winds up back at the very first node visited. And, depending on the directionality of the edges and where in the graph the traversal begins, it may not be possible to visit all nodes.

As presented in Section 9.2, the depth-first and breadth-first traversal algorithms process a node as soon as it is visited, before advancing to another unvisited node. As a simple example, we will use the DAG of Figure 11.19 and assume that, whenever there is a choice of two or more adjacent nodes to visit next, the algorithm selects the unvisited child with the smallest key value. If a depth-first traversal is employed and the traversal starts with node A and "processing" means displaying the node's key value (here, a single letter), the following display would result:

```
A B H I J C G D F E
```

This list is not topologically sorted, however. H, I, and J are all functionally dependent upon G and should therefore follow G in the list. Also, G is dependent upon both C and F and should therefore follow C and F in the list.

As a variation, we could modify the traversal algorithm so it processes last node in the current path just prior to backtracking. This is accomplished by inserting the following statement as the last executable statement in the recursive `DFT` procedure, which is nested within procedure `DFVisit`, both given in Appendix I:

```
Writeln ( P^.VInfo.Key,' ' );
```

This modification produces the following display, which is *topologically sorted in reverse order.* This list can then be reversed to produce the final correctly sorted list:

```
J I H B G C F D E A  {Reverse topological order}
A E D F C G B H I J  {Topological order}
```

A DAG may therefore be topologically sorted by performing the following two operations, producing a linear list of node key values (the sorted list):

1. Perform a depth-first traversal in which each node is processed *after* its children are processed and just prior to backtracking (*processing* here means appending a copy of the node to the growing, topologically sorted list of nodes).
2. Reverse this list.

APPLICATION 11.1 Arranging College Course Numbers Based on Prerequisites

In the sample graph of Figure 11.19, the traversal began with node A because it has in-degree zero (i.e., it is not functionally dependent on any other node). The topological sorting problem is slightly more complex for DAGs that contain more than one node of in-degree zero. As an example, the DAG of Figure 11.20 represents the computer science courses and four mathematics courses offered at a prominent East Coast university. Course numbers, such as C1350, are the key values of the nodes. A directed edge from course C1201 to C1350, for example, means that C1201 and all courses prerequisite to C1201—C1100, C1101, and M1137—are all prerequisites for C1350. Our goal in this application is to display a linear list of course numbers so no course number is listed before the course numbers of its prerequisite courses.

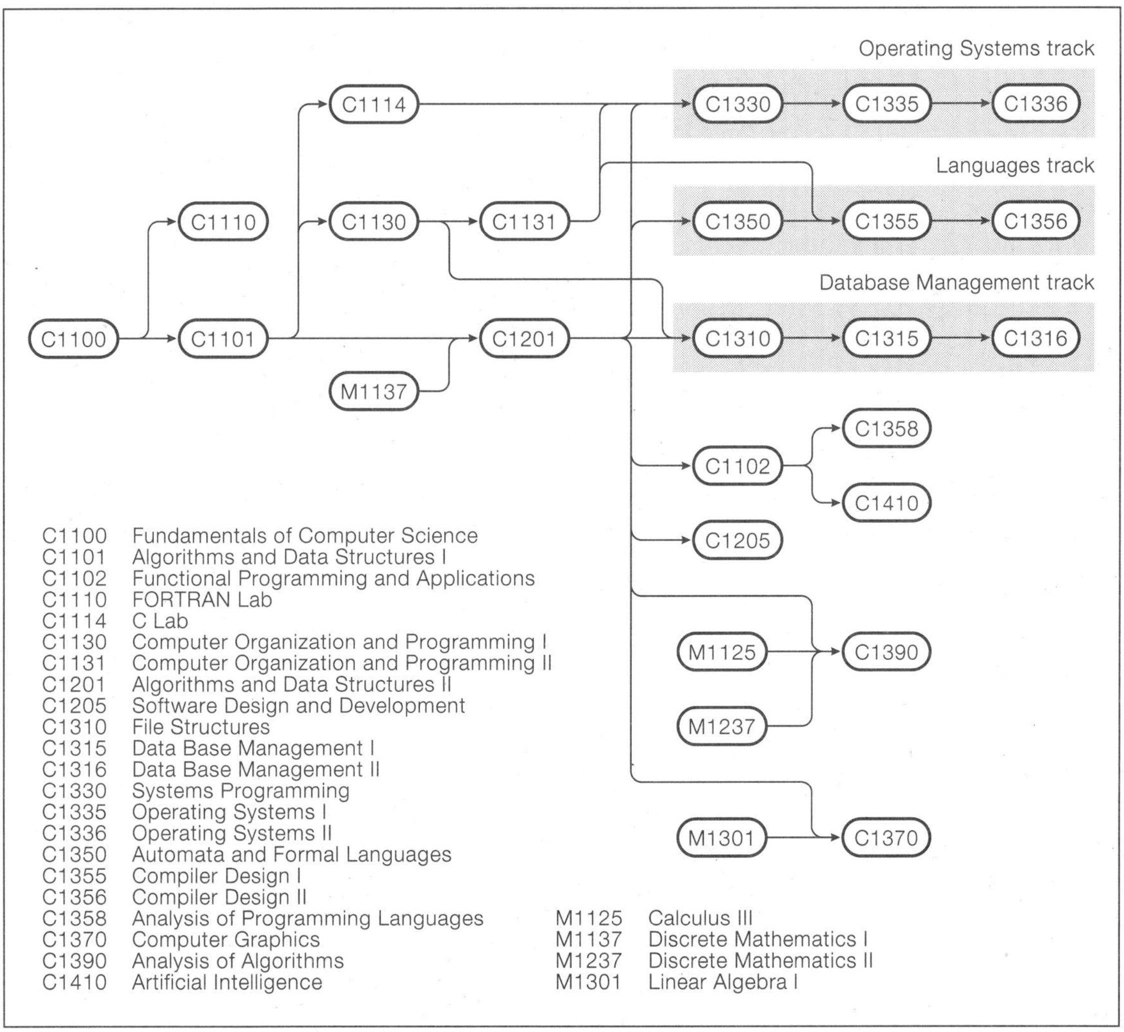

FIGURE 11.20 A DAG Representing Required Computer Science and Mathematics Courses

Since the nodes C1100, M1125, M1237, and M1301 each have in-degree zero, the traversal *could* begin with any of them. Commensurate with our general rule that, given a choice, the next node to visit is that node whose item has the smallest key value, the traversal will begin with the C1100 node. The C1100 node has two children: C1110 and C1101; C1101 is selected because it is the smallest key value. C1101 has three children: C1114, C1130, and C1201; C1114 is selected. From C1114 the algorithm advances to C1330, to C1335, and then to C1336. This is a dead end, so C1336 is displayed and the traversal algorithm backtracks to C1335. This is also a dead end now, so C1335 is displayed. The algorithm backtracks to C1330 (a dead end now, so C1330 is displayed), to C1114 (a dead end now, so C1114 is displayed), and then back to C1101. This time C1130 is selected. The algorithm then advances to C1131, C1355, and then C1356. C1356 is a dead end, so C1356 is displayed, followed by C1355 and C1131. From C1130, C1310 is selected next, and so forth. The complete display follows, read left to right on each line:

```
C1336,  C1335,  C1330,  C1114,  C1356,  C1355,  C1131,  C1316,
C1315,  C1310,  C1130,  C1358,  C1410,  C1102,  C1205,  C1350,
C1370,  C1390,  C1201,  C1101,  C1110,  C1100
```

Reversing this list produces the following list, again read left to right on each line:

```
C1100,  C1110,  C1101,  C1201,  C1390,  C1370,  C1350,  C1205,
C1102,  C1410,  C1358,  C1130,  C1310,  C1315,  C1316,  C1131,
C1355,  C1356,  C1114,  C1330,  C1335,  C1336
```

The reversed list would be correct except that the mathematics courses—M1125, M1137, M1237, and M1301—have been left out, a serious omission, since these three courses are prerequisites for many computer science courses.

As a simple solution to this dilemma, we can add one more operation to the algorithm. Each time the algorithm is finished processing all nodes accessible from a particular node of in-degree zero (such as the C1100 node), it should look for *another* node of in-degree zero and process all unvisited nodes accessible from it. This must be done for all nodes of in-degree zero. When this modification is employed, the first list ends with the following five course numbers:

```
... C1110,  C1100,  M1125,  M1137,  M1301
```

Reversing the entire list then produces a list that begins with the following five courses:

```
M1301,  M1137,  M1125,  C1100,  C1110 ...
```

To help the algorithm detect nodes with in-degree zero, Boolean field `InDegreeZero` must be added to the node declaration. All `InDegreeZero`

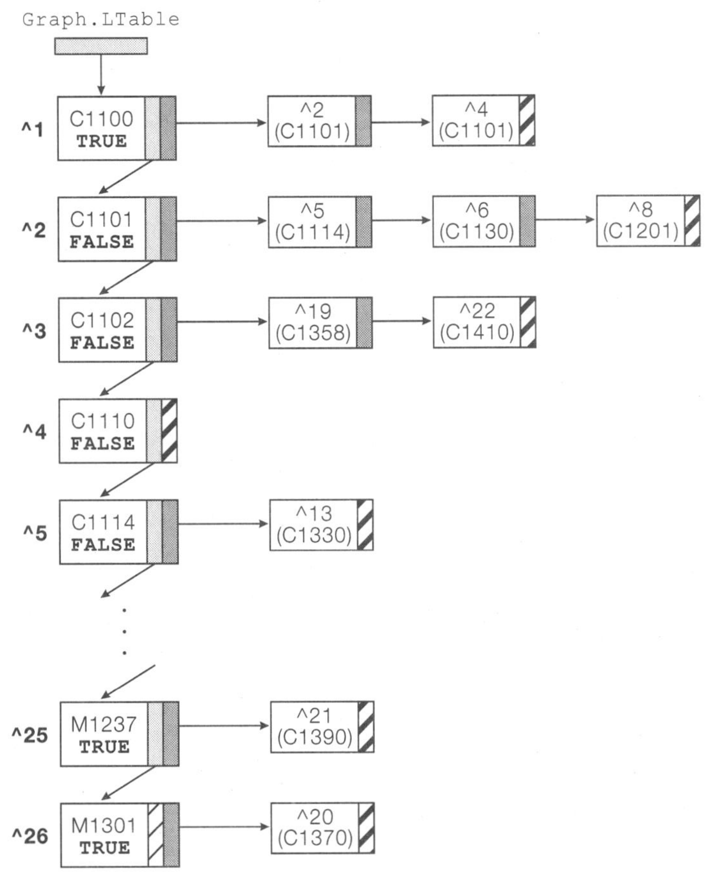

FIGURE 11.21 The (Abbreviated) Adjacency List for the DAG of Figure 11.20

fields are initialized to a true value prior to the sorting. As the adjacency list or matrix structure is being built or initialized, the `InDegreeZero` field for a particular node is assigned a false value if that node is adjacent to another node. `InDegreeZero` fields would have true values for the C1100, M1125, M1137, and M1301 nodes and false values for all other nodes.

We will represent our course prerequisites graph structure using an adjacency list, as depicted in Figure 11.21. The lookup table is a linked list of nodes, with `Graph.LTable` pointing to the first of these nodes (to simplify this figure, the lookup table nodes for courses C1201 through M1125 are not shown). As in many of the Chapter 9 adjacency list diagrams, a nonstandard caret (^) notation is used to indicate a heapspace address; e.g., course C1100 is a prerequisite for two courses—C1101, and C1110—whose lookup table addresses are ^2 and ^4, respectively. Also shown in each lookup table node record is that node's Boolean `InDegreeZero` field value.

A pseudocode algorithm for a topological sort follows. Algorithm `TopologicalSort` represents the topologically sorted list by correctly assigning pointer values to node `Child` fields. Each node's `Child` field is assigned the address of the next node in the sorted list. The algorithm returns the address of the node where the sorted list begins. Therefore, upon return, the sorted list can be traversed by starting with the node pointed to by parameter `Child` and following each node's `Child` field. `TopologicalSort` assumes that the `InDegreeZero` field of each node has been initialized to a true value if the node has no parent. This algorithm and its Appendix J implementation operate on graphs represented using an adjacency list.

```
ALGORITHM  TopologicalSort ( VAR Graph : GraphType;  VAR Child : NodePtr );

VAR
  Ptr : NodePtr;
      ________________________________________________________________
  ALGORITHM DFTopTraverse ( Parent : NodePtr );

  BEGIN
  Mark Parent node as having been visited;

  WHILE there is another unvisited Child, adjacent to Parent THEN
    DFTopTraverse ( next unvisited Child of Parent );

  Parent^.Child := Child; {This node points to the Child node}
  Child       := Parent    {This node becomes Child node next time}
  END;
      ________________________________________________________________
{***  Main routine for TopologicalSort  ***}

BEGIN
Mark all nodes as unvisited;
Ptr := address of 1st node in lookup table;

WHILE there is another unvisited lookup table node DO
  BEGIN
  IF ( Ptr node has not been visited ) AND ( Ptr node has no parents ) THEN
    DFTopTraverse ( Ptr );
  Ptr := Ptr^.Next
  END
END;
```

At this time, examine the following routines in Appendix J.

```
PROCEDURE TopologicalSort ( VAR Graph : GraphType;
                            VAR Child : NodePtr );
```

SUMMARY

The operations of searching and sorting are interdependent since a sorted list can be searched with greater efficiency than can an unsorted list. The operations of searching are applied only to data structures that are structured by a key value storage scheme, as opposed to a time-of-arrival scheme.

The relative efficiencies of sorting algorithms (worst and average performances) are usually analyzed on the basis of the number of key-comparison operations and the number of assignment operations involving whole items. The amount of additional memory required is frequently considered as well. The analyses in Chapter 11 focus on the number of comparisons of key values.

To sort an array, simple exchange sorting algorithms include the bubble sort and straight selection sort. Both have a best performance rating of O (N) and an average performance rating of O (N^2). Straight insertion sort is considered as the most efficient, however, since it actually performs at $N^2/4$ whereas the others are $N^2/2$.

An array may also be sorted using the divide-and-conquer strategies of merge sort and quicksort, both of which are inherently recursive. Merge sort is rated at O $(N \log N)$ in both its worst and average performances. Quicksort is rated at O $(N \log N)$ in its average performance but is only O (N^2) in its worst case. Even so, quicksort is generally preferable because merge sort requires N additional item-sized variables.

Finally, an array may be sorted using a binary tree sort (which requires a separate binary search tree of N items) or heap sort, which is generally more efficient. The worst and average performances of heap sort are rated as O $(N \log N)$.

A linked list may be sorted using a straight insertion sort approach (here, the linked list replaces the array) or a natural merge sort. A file may be sorted using form of merge sort and a graph may be sorted using topological sort.

KEY TERMS

Binary search tree sort	Merge sort for arrays	Pivot element
Bubble sort	Merge sort for files	Quicksort
Heap sort	Natural merge sort for linked lists	Straight insertion sort
Insertion sort for linked lists	PERT graph	Straight selection sort
		Topological sort

REVIEW QUESTIONS

1. Generally, when is sorting useful? Contrast the differences between a time-of-arrival structure and a table. On which might you apply a sorting algorithm?
2. What is measured when analyzing the efficiency of a sorting algorithm and why?
3. Without looking ahead to review question 4, name (a) seven algorithms presented for sorting an array, (b) two algorithms for sorting a linked list, (c) an algorithm for sorting a file, and (d) the algorithm for sorting a graph.
4. Do the following for each of the eleven algorithms listed below:
   a. Describe the operations in general terms.
   b. State the worst and average performance growth-rate functions and corresponding big O notation forms (based on total key comparisons and additional memory requirements). Describe the analysis steps in general terms.
   c. State whether the algorithm takes less time or more time if the original list is nearly sorted.

   - Bubble sort
   - Straight selection sort
   - Straight insertion sort (for arrays)
   - Insertion sort (for linked lists)
   - Natural merge sort (for linked lists)
   - Merge sort (for files)
   - Topological sort
   - Merge sort (for arrays)
   - Quicksort
   - Binary tree sort
   - Heap sort

   d. Which of these algorithms rely on the fact that $-\infty$ is stored in array element 0? How is this value used and why?

5. Describe the enhancements made to the basic bubble sort, straight selection sort, straight insertion sort, quicksort, and heap sort algorithms.

6. Although bubble sort, straight selection sort, and straight insertion sort are all rated at O (N^2), in practice some perform better than others on the average. Which algorithm would you expect to perform fastest, second fastest, and slowest when actually used on a list of random key values? Which would you expect to perform faster—merge sort (for arrays) or quicksort—in the average case (both are rated as O $(N \log N)$).

7. Describe the differences between the merge sort, as presented in Section 11.3 for arrays, and the merge sort presented in Section 11.5. Can a linked list be sorted using an array-based merge sort rather than a natural merge sort?

EXERCISES

1. Perform a bubble sort, straight selection sort, straight insertion sort, quicksort, and merge sort by hand on all three of the following array of records (only the integer keys are shown). Apply the fastest version of each algorithm. Redraw the array diagram each time it changes.

	1	2	3	4	5	6	7	8
Unsorted:	5	7	4	2	8	6	1	3
Sorted (ascending order):	1	2	3	4	5	6	7	8
Sorted (descending order):	8	7	6	5	4	3	2	1

2. Perform a binary tree sort and heap sort by hand on the three arrays of Exercise 1, but represent the lists as binary trees. Redraw the tree each time it changes.

3. Consider the three arrays of Exercise 1 to be three files of records. Perform a merge sort by hand on each of the files, and redraw your sorting structure each time it changes.

4. Perform a natural merge sort by hand on each of the following linked lists of records (assume that a list head variable points to each). Redraw your sorting structure each time it changes.

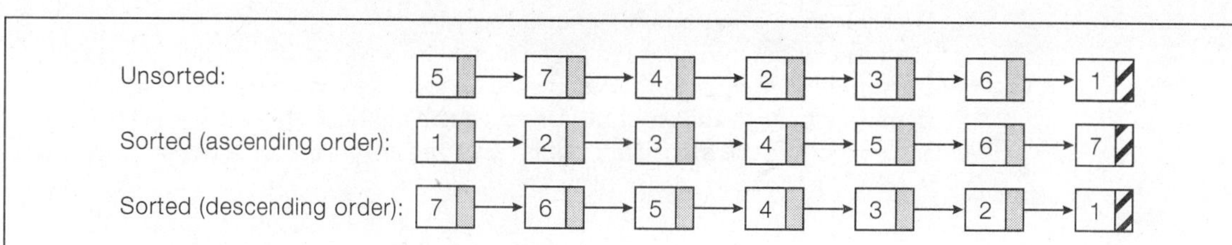

5. Perform a topological sort by hand on the PERT graph shown on the next page. The start of each task is designated by a single letter, which is unrelated to the

relative position of that task with a topologically sorted list of tasks. As you sort, if you have a choice of two or more nodes to visit, always visit the task whose letter designation is least alphabetically.

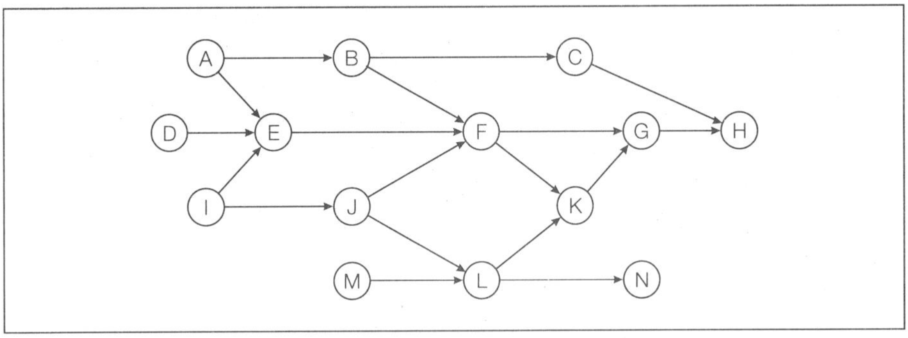

6. Derive the growth-rate functions and big O ratings for the topological sort algorithm presented in Section 11.7.

7. The City of Boston traffic department has a sorting problem. The police commissioner wants to find those drivers whose cars have five or more unpaid parking tickets. Unfortunately, the department keeps the stubs of unpaid parking tickets in a wooden box, in no particular order. The commissioner needs a list of the stubs for these cars, ordered by license plate number.

   The commissioner recommends that a clerk look through the box and pull out any two stubs bearing the same license plate number. These stubs are then sorted and groups of five or more stubs bearing the same license plate number are pulled. The commissioner says that this will take less time than sorting the entire box of stubs, since a smaller list is being sorted.

   The mayor recommends sorting the entire list first by license-plate number. This would make it easier to pinpoint drivers with five or more unpaid tickets, and the stubs pulled will already be ordered. Who is correct? Provide a big O analysis to support your choice.

8. Any of the array-based sorting algorithms can be used to sort a linked list by storing pointers to nodes in the elements rather than storing the data items themselves. Rewrite the `InsertionSort` and `QuickSort` procedures given in Appendix J to sort a linked list, adding whatever code is necessary to initialize the array.

9. Write nonrecursive `MergeSort` and `QuickSort` procedures.

10. A *tournament sort* is a binary tree sort that resembles a single elimination sports tournament (such as the basketball tournament depicted in Figure 8.2). All data items are stored only in the leaves. Starting at the leaf level, keys of sibling items are compared and the item with the smaller key value is moved up to the parent node; this repeats for all nodes up to the root node, so the root node will contain the item with the smallest key value. The data item in the root is then "removed" (e.g., copied to another array), and the key of this item is assigned a value lower than any legitimate key. The moving-up process is then repeated for all internal nodes that are ancestors of this leaf, all the way up to the root. The entire process is repeated for all data items stored at the leaf level. The following diagram depicts the tournament sorting of four items, with key values 5, 3, 4, and 7.

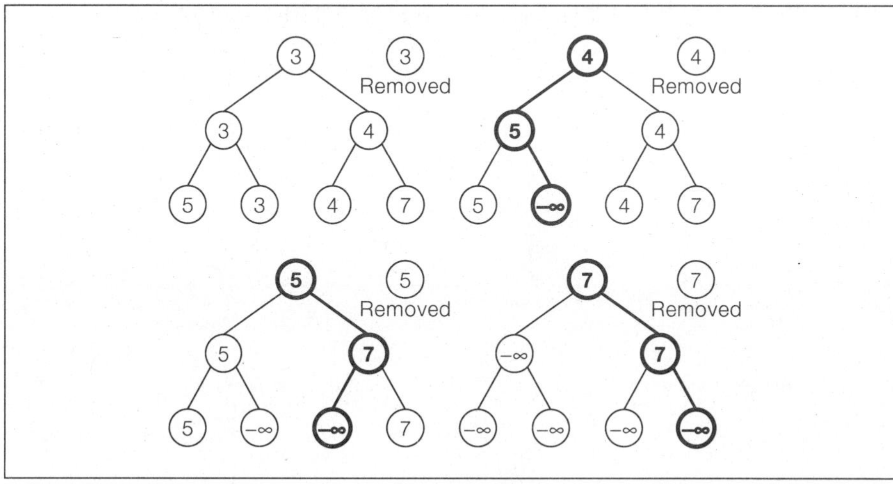

a. Complete procedure `TournamentSort` to implement this sorting algorithm. `ListType` is declared at the start of Section 11.1 and `Count` holds a count of records to be sorted.

```
PROCEDURE TournamentSort ( VAR List : ListType; Count : Integer );
```

Build the tree as a complete or nearly complete binary tree, using a local array variable. "Remove" a data item by copying it back to `List` in the next element (maintain a variable, initialized to 1, to hold the index of the next `List` element). Your procedure should work for any list of 1 to `MaxItems` items.

b. Analyze the time requirements (based on key comparisons) and memory requirements of this algorithm. How does it compare to the other binary tree sort algorithms, tree sort and heap sort? Is it necessary to move whole data items up the tree from the leaf level?

11. The *median value* of a sorted list is the value that is less than (or equal to) half of the remaining values and greater than (or equal to) the other half of the remaining values. For example, the median of the following list is 7: 1, 2, 2, 3, 5, 7, 8, 8, 10, 15, 16, 21. One method of finding a median value is to sort the list; the median value will occupy element `List [ (Low + High) DIV 2 ]`. A faster method is to use quicksort's partitioning operation repeatedly on lists until a pivot element is placed in this location; the pivot's key value will be the median value for the entire list.

The first three steps in a generic example follow. The lightly shaded region represents the list currently being partitioned, the dark element is where a pivot value has just been placed within a current list, and the striped element is the element the median value would occupy if the entire list were sorted. Notice how, by successive partitioning, the location of the placed pivot gets closer to the median element.

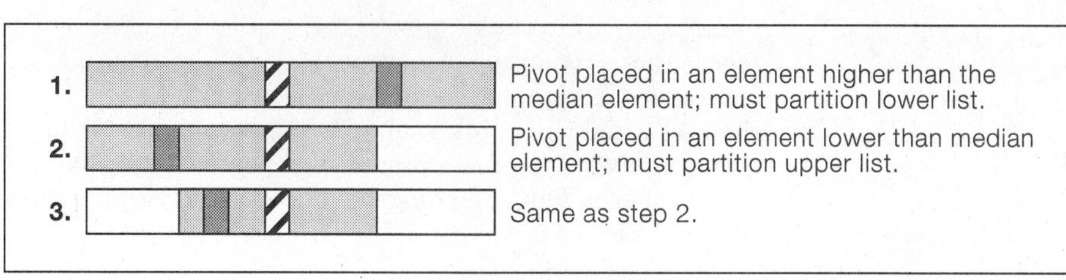

a. Complete function `MedianValue`, which should return the median value of `List`:

```
FUNCTION MedianValue ( VAR List : ListType, Low, High : Integer) : Integer;
```

b. Perform an analysis of the best, average, and worst cases of this algorithm.

c. Complete function `PercentileValue`, which should compute any percentile value of a list (a median is the 50th percentile value of a list):

```
FUNCTION PercentileValue ( VAR List : ListType; Low, High : Integer ) : Integer;
```

12. We can make yet another improvement to the enhanced bubble sort algorithm of Section 11.2. Both of the following lists have a single item out of place, but the first list will be sorted after one more pass, whereas the second list requires five more passes:

First list: 5 7 11 13 17 3

Second list: 17 3 5 7 11 13

That is, items with smaller keys "bubble" up to the front of the list faster than items with large keys "sink" to the end of the list. This occurs because each pass of key comparisons proceeds from the end of the list toward the front. The average number of comparisons may be reduced by *alternating the direction in which these passes are made.* This form of bubble sort is called a *shaker sort.*

a. Complete procedure `ShakerSort`:

```
PROCEDURE ShakerSort ( VAR List : ListType; Count : Integer );
```

b. Perform an analysis of a shaker sort in its best, average, and worst performances.

13. In the straight insertion sort of an array, a linear search of items in elements 1 through J is performed when inserting the item in element $J + 1$. Since these items are sorted by key value, a binary search could be used instead; this approach is called a *binary insertion sort.*

a. Rewrite procedure `InsertionSort` given in Appendix J, for arrays, to implement the binary insertion sort algorithm.

b. Although a binary search is typically faster than a linear search, would you expect a binary insertion sort to have a faster average performance? Why or why not?

APPENDIX A

STANDARD OPERATORS, IDENTIFIERS, FUNCTIONS, AND PROCEDURES

This appendix describes the operators, identifiers, functions and procedures of the ISO Pascal Standard language, based on the *Pascal User Manual And Report, Third Edition,* by Kathleen Jensen and Niklaus Wirth (New York, N.Y.: Springer-Verlag, 1985).

Constants

```
FALSE  MAXINT  NIL  TRUE
```

Data Type Identifiers

```
ARRAY    Char   Integer  RECORD  Text
Boolean  FILE   Real     SET
```

Variables

```
INPUT  OUTPUT
```

Compiler Directive

```
FORWARD
```

Operators

```
AND  DIV  IN  MOD  NOT  OR
```

Functions

```
Abs     Cos   Exp  Ord    Sin   Succ
ArcTan  Eof   Ln   Pred   Sqr   Trunc
Chr     Eoln  Odd  Round  Sqrt
```

Procedures

```
Dispose  New   Page  Read     Reset    Unpack  Writeln
Get      Pack  Put   Readln   Rewrite  Write
```

Program Structures

```
BEGIN  END       LABEL      PROGRAM  VAR
CONST  FUNCTION  PROCEDURE  TYPE
```

Miscellaneous Reserved Words

```
CASE    ELSE  IF      REPEAT  WHILE
DO      FOR   OF      THEN    WITH
DownTo  GoTo  PACKED  TO      UNTIL
```

Operator Symbols

```
+  *  :=  =   <  >=
-  /      <>  >  <=
```

Miscellaneous Symbols

```
.  :  ..  (  [  {  ↑  '
,  ;  ^   )  ]  }  @
```

Alternative Representations

```
(.     .)   for  [ ]
(*     *)   for  { }
 @  or  ↑   for  ^
```

All Reserved Words, Constants, Standard Procedures and Functions

Abs	Dispose	**FOR**	**MAXINT**	**PACKED**	Reset	**TRUE**
AND	**DIV**	**FORWARD**	**MOD**	Page	Rewrite	Trunc
ArcTan	**DO**	**FUNCTION**	New	Pred	Round	Unpack
Array	**DownTo**	Get	**NIL**	**PROCEDURE**	Set	**UNTIL**
BEGIN	**ELSE**	GoTo	**NOT**	**PROGRAM**	Sin	**VAR**
Boolean	**END**	**IF**	Odd	Put	Sqr	**WHILE**
CASE	Eof	**IN**	**OF**	Read	Sqrt	**WITH**
Char	Eoln	Input	**OR**	Readln	Succ	Write
Chr	Exp	Integer	Ord	Real	Text	Writeln
CONST	**FALSE**	**LABEL**	Output	**RECORD**	**THEN**	
Cos	**FILE**	Ln	**PACK**	**REPEAT**	**TO**	

Precedence of Operators

```
Highest: NOT
Second:  * / DIV MOD AND
Third:   + - OR
Lowest:  = <> < > <= >=
```

APPENDIX B

NUMBERING SYSTEMS

This appendix describes the four numbering systems commonly used in computer science, as shown in Figures B.1 and B.2. Refer to Section 2.3 for information regarding the representations of real numbers in computer memory. Appendix C also contains examples of binary, octal, decimal, and hexadecimal numbers.

CONVERSIONS

A decimal number can be converted to a binary number using Figures B.4 and B.5, while keeping track of the binary digits selected and subtracting each time.

For example, $26{,}847_{10}$ is converted to binary as follows:

$$
\begin{array}{rcr}
01000000\ 00000000_2 & = & 16{,}384_{10} \\
00100000\ 00000000_2 & = & 8{,}192_{10} \\
00001000\ 00000000_2 & = & 2{,}048_{10} \\
00000000\ 10000000_2 & = & 128_{10} \\
00000000\ 01000000_2 & = & 64_{10} \\
00000000\ 00010000_2 & = & 16_{10} \\
00000000\ 00001111_2 & = & 15_{10} \\
\hline
01101000\ 11011111_2 & = & 26{,}847_{10}
\end{array}
\qquad
\begin{array}{rcrcr}
26{,}847 & - & 16{,}384 & = & 10{,}463 \\
10{,}463 & - & 8{,}192 & = & 2{,}271 \\
2{,}271 & - & 2{,}048 & = & 233 \\
233 & - & 128 & = & 95 \\
95 & - & 64 & = & 31 \\
31 & - & 16 & = & 15 \\
15 & - & 15 & = & 0
\end{array}
$$

Numbering System	Base	Typical Use
Binary	Base 2	Bitwise representation used in computer memory
Octal	Base 8	Abbreviation of a binary number
Decimal	Base 10	Common, everyday numbering system
Hexidecimal	Base 16	Abbreviation of a binary number

FIGURE B.1 Four Bases Used in Computer Science

Decimal	Binary	Octal	Hexa-decimal
0	0	0	0
1	1	1	1
2	10	2	2
3	11	3	3
4	100	4	4
5	101	5	5
6	110	6	6
7	111	7	7
8	1000	10	8
9	1001	11	9
10	1010	12	A
11	1011	13	B
12	1100	14	C
13	1101	15	D
14	1110	16	E
15	1111	17	F

Decimal	Binary	Octal	Hexa-decimal
16	1 0000	20	10
50	11 0010	62	32
100	110 0100	144	64
128	1000 0000	200	80
256	1 0000 0000	400	100
512	10 0000 0000	1000	200
1000	11 1110 1000	1750	3E8
1024	100 0000 0000	2000	400
10,000	10 0111 0001 0000	23420	2710
16,384	100 0000 0000 0000	40000	4000
32,767	111 1111 1111 1111	77777	7FFF
32,768	1000 0000 0000 0000	100000	8000
43,690	1010 1010 1010 1010	125252	AAAA
100,000	1 1000 0110 1010 0000	303240	186A0

FIGURE B.2 Examples of the Four Bases

For example, $26{,}847_{10}$ = 0 1 1 0 1 0 0 0 1 1 0 1 1 1 1 1_2

Sequences of 3 bits for octal: 0 6 4 3 3 7 = 064337_8

0 1 1 0 1 0 0 0 1 1 0 1 1 1 1 1_2

Sequences of 4 bits for hexadecimal: 6 8 D F = $68DF_{16}$

FIGURE B.3 Converting from Binary to Octal or Hexadecimal

Converting a binary number back to decimal involves the opposite operations; i.e., the decimal value of each 1 bit is added.

A binary number can be converted to octal or hexadecimal by grouping sequences of bits, as shown in Figure B.3.

Converting octal or hexadecimal back to binary involves the opposite operations; i.e., sequences of bits are expanded to their binary equivalents (Figure B.4).

NEGATIVE INTEGERS

Negative integers may be represented using any of the following techniques, with 2's complement being the most commonly used with microcomputers:

Decimal

10^6	10^5	10^4	10^3	10^2	10^1	10^0 •	10^{-1}	10^{-2}	10^{-3}
1,000,000	100,000	10,000	1000	100	10	1	0.1	0.01	0.001

Binary

2^{15}	2^{14}	2^{13}	2^{12}	2^{11}	2^{10}	2^9	2^8	2^7	2^6	2^5	2^4	2^3	2^2	2^1	2^0 •	2^{-1}	2^{-2}	2^{-3}
32,768	16,384	8192	4096	2048	1024	512	256	128	64	32	16	8	4	2	1	0.5	0.25	0.125

n	2^n	*n*	2^n	*n*	2^n	*n*	2^n
0	1	**8**	256	**16**	65,536	**24**	16,777,216
1	2	**9**	512	**17**	131,072	**25**	33,554,432
2	4	**10**	1024	**18**	262,144	**26**	67,108,864
3	8	**11**	2048	**19**	524,288	**27**	134,217,728
4	16	**12**	4096	**20**	1,048,576	**28**	268,435,456
5	32	**13**	8192	**21**	2,097,152	**29**	536,870,912
6	64	**14**	16,384	**22**	4,194,304	**30**	1,073,741,824
7	128	**15**	32,768	**23**	8,388,608	**31**	2,147,483,648
						32	4,294,967,296

Octal

8^6	8^5	8^4	8^3	8^2	8^1	8^0 •	8^{-1}	8^{-2}	8^{-3}
262,144	32,768	4096	512	64	8	1	0.125	0.015625	0.0019531

Hexadecimal

16^6	16^5	16^4	16^3	16^2	16^1	16^0 •	16^{-1}	16^{-2}	16^{-3}
16,777,216	1,048,576	65,536	4096	256	16	1	0.0625	0.0039062	0.0002441

FIGURE B.4 Converting Octal or Hexadecimal Back to Binary

Decimal numbers

	10^0 •	10^{-1}	10^{-2}	10^{-3}	10^{-4}	10^{-5}	10^{-6}	10^{-7}
Decimal value	1	0.1	0.01	0.001	0.0001	0.00001	0.000001	0.0000001

Binary numbers

	2^0 •	2^{-1}	2^{-2}	2^{-3}	2^{-4}	2^{-5}	2^{-6}	2^{-7}
Decimal equivalent	1	0.5	0.25	0.125	0.0625	0.03125	0.015625	0.0078125

FIGURE B.5 Fractional Binary Numbers

Decimal	Binary: Signed Magnitude	Binary: 1's complement	Binary: 2's complement
−1	1000 0000 0000 0001	1111 1111 1111 1110	1111 1111 1111 1111
−2	1000 0000 0000 0010	1111 1111 1111 1101	1111 1111 1111 1110
−3	1000 0000 0000 0011	1111 1111 1111 1100	1111 1111 1111 1101
−4	1000 0000 0000 0100	1111 1111 1111 1011	1111 1111 1111 1100
−8	1000 0000 0000 1000	1111 1111 1111 0111	1111 1111 1111 1000
−10	1000 0000 0000 1010	1111 1111 1111 0101	1111 1111 1111 0110
−100	1000 0000 0110 0100	1111 1111 1001 1011	1111 1111 1001 1100
−500	1000 0001 1111 0100	1111 1110 0000 1011	1111 1110 0000 1100
−1000	1000 0011 1110 1000	1111 1100 0001 0111	1111 1100 0001 1000
−10,000	1010 0111 0001 0000	1101 1000 1110 1111	1101 1000 1111 0000
−32,767	1111 1111 1111 1111	1000 0000 0000 0000	1000 0000 0000 0001
−32,768	1000 0000 0000 0000	1111 1111 1111 1111	1000 0000 0000 0000

FIGURE B.6 Examples of Representations of Negative Numbers

- *Signed-magnitude.* The most significant (leftmost) bit of the word is the sign bit and the remaining bits contain the absolute magnitude of the number.
- *1's complement.* To negate a positive integer, each 1 is replaced by a 0, and each 0 is replaced by a 1. The most significant bit acts as a sign bit.
- *2's complement.* The most significant bit acts as a sign bit, each 1 is replaced by a 0, and each 0 is replaced by a 1. Next, 1 is added to the entire value; if there is a carry occurring from the most significant bit, it is disregarded. This is the most common technique used in small computers.

Figure B.6 compares the representations of twelve sample negative integers for a 16-bit computer.

APPENDIX C

THE ASCII CHARACTER SET

Char.	Dec.	Hex.	Binary
^@	0	00	00000000
^A	1	01	00000001
^B	2	02	00000010
^C	3	03	00000011
^D	4	04	00000100
^E	5	05	00000101
^F	6	06	00000110
^G	7	07	00000111
^H	8	08	00001000
^I	9	09	00001001
^J	10	0A	00001010
^K	11	0B	00001011
^L	12	0C	00001100
^M	13	0D	00001101
^N	14	0E	00001110
^O	15	0F	00001111
^P	16	10	00010000
^Q	17	11	00010001
^R	18	12	00010010
^S	19	13	00010011
^T	20	14	00010100
^U	21	15	00010101
^V	22	16	00010110
^W	23	17	00010111
^X	24	18	00011000
^Y	25	19	00011001
^Z	26	1A	00011010
^[	27	1B	00011011
^\	28	1C	00011100
^]	29	1D	00011101
^^	30	1E	00011110
^_	31	1F	00011111
SPACE	32	20	00100000
!	33	21	00100001
"	34	22	00100010
#	35	23	00100011
$	36	24	00100100
%	37	25	00100101
&	38	26	00100110
'	39	27	00100111
(	40	28	00101000
)	41	29	00101001
*	42	2A	00101010
+	43	2B	00101011
,	44	2C	00101100
-	45	2D	00101101
.	46	2E	00101110
/	47	2F	00101111

Char.	Dec.	Hex.	Binary
0	48	30	00110000
1	49	31	00110001
2	50	32	00110010
3	51	33	00110011
4	52	34	00110100
5	53	35	00110101
6	54	36	00110110
7	55	37	00110111
8	56	38	00111000
9	57	39	00111001
:	58	3A	00111010
;	59	3B	00111011
<	60	3C	00111100
=	61	3D	00111101
>	62	3E	00111110
?	63	3F	00111111
@	64	40	01000000
A	65	41	01000001
B	66	42	01000010
C	67	43	01000011
D	68	44	01000100
E	69	45	01000101
F	70	46	01000110
G	71	47	01000111
H	72	48	01001000
I	73	49	01001001
J	74	4A	01001010
K	75	4B	01001011
L	76	4C	01001100
M	77	4D	01001101
N	78	4E	01001110
O	79	4F	01001111
P	80	50	01010000
Q	81	51	01010001
R	82	52	01010010
S	83	53	01010011
T	84	54	01010100
U	85	55	01010101
V	86	56	01010110
W	87	57	01010111
X	88	58	01011000
Y	89	59	01011001
Z	90	5A	01011010

Char.	Dec.	Hex.	Binary
[	91	5B	01011011
\	92	5C	01011100
]	93	5D	01011101
^	94	5E	01011110
_	95	5F	01011111
`	96	60	01100000
a	97	61	01100001
b	98	62	01100010
c	99	63	01100011
d	100	64	01100100
e	101	65	01100101
f	102	66	01100110
g	103	67	01100111
h	104	68	01101000
i	105	69	01101001
j	106	6A	01101010
k	107	6B	01101011
l	108	6C	01101100
m	109	6D	01101101
n	110	6E	01101110
o	111	6F	01101111
p	112	70	01110000
q	113	71	01110001
r	114	72	01110010
s	115	73	01110011
t	116	74	01110100
u	117	75	01110101
v	118	76	01110110
w	119	77	01110111
x	120	78	01111000
y	121	79	01111001
z	122	7A	01111010
{	123	7B	01111011
|	124	7C	01111100
}	125	7D	01111101
~	126	7E	01111110
DEL	127	7F	01111111

APPENDIX D

LINEAR LINKED LIST ROUTINES

Dynamic Allocation Representation

```
TYPE
  KeyType    =  ??;                  {Application-dependent}
  InfoType   =  RECORD
                  Key    :  KeyType;    {Key value}
                  {Other fields, as necessary}
                END;

  NodePtr    =  ^Node;               {Pointer to linked list node}
  Node       =  RECORD
                  Data   :  InfoType;   {Data portion of node}
                  Next   :  NodePtr     {Link field; points to next node}
                END;

  LListType  =  RECORD
                  Head   :  NodePtr;    {Points to first node in list}
                  Count  :  Integer     {Count of nodes in list}
                END;
VAR
  LList  :  LListType;
```

```
{Initializes as empty a linked list without a header node}

PROCEDURE LLInit ( VAR LList : LListType );

BEGIN
WITH LList DO
  BEGIN
  Head   := NIL;            {Head pointer points to nothing}
  Count  := 0               {List is empty}
  END
END;
```

```
{Initializes as empty a linked list with a header node}

PROCEDURE LLInit ( VAR LList : LListType );

BEGIN
WITH LList DO
  BEGIN
  New ( Head );             {Allocate Node type record in heapspace}
  Head^.Data.Key  := ??;    {Header node gets lowest KeyType value}
  Head^.Next := NIL;        {Head pointer points to nothing}
  Count := 0                {List is empty}
  END
END;
```

```
{Tests a linked list for emptiness}

FUNCTION LLEmpty ( VAR LList : LListType ) : Boolean;

BEGIN
LLEmpty := LList.Count = 0
END;
```

```
{Searches a linked list, starting with node Start^, for a match on key value, Key}

PROCEDURE  LLSearch ( VAR Key : KeyType;  Start : NodePtr;
                      VAR Previous : NodePtr;  VAR Found : Boolean );
VAR
  Current  :  NodePtr;  {Holds address of node currently being examined}
  Done     :  Boolean;  {Abort-search flag}

BEGIN
Previous  := NIL;       {Initialized in case node sought is the first list node}
Current   := Start;     {Current now points to node where search begins}
Found     := FALSE;     {Item sought not yet found}
Done      := FALSE;     {Procedure is not yet done searching}
WHILE ( Current <> NIL ) AND NOT Done DO
  IF Current^.Data.Key > Key THEN     {Greater key value means that the}
    Done := TRUE                      { sought item is not in the list}
  ELSE
    IF Current^. Data.Key = Key THEN {IF sought node has been found...}
      BEGIN
      Done   := TRUE;
      Found  := TRUE
      END
    ELSE                              {ELSE continue searching...}
      BEGIN
      Previous  := Current;           { Previous "catches up" to Current}
      Current   := Current^.Next      { Current advances}
      END
END;
```

```
{Inserts a new node after Previous^ into a linked list with a header node}

PROCEDURE  LLInsert ( VAR LList: LListType;  Data : InfoType;
                      VAR Previous : NodePtr );
VAR
  P  :  NodePtr;                    {Holds address of new node}

BEGIN
WITH LList DO
  BEGIN
  New ( P );                        {Allocate new Node type record in heapspace}
  P^.Data  := Data;                 {Store Data record in data portion of new node}
  Count    := Count + 1;            {Increment total node count}
  P^.Next  := Previous^.Next;       {Link field now points to next node in the list}
  Previous^.Next := P               {Previous node now points to this new node}
  END;

Previous := P  {Facilitates appending of nodes upon subsequent calls to LLInsert }
END;
```

```
{Inserts a new node after Previous^ into a linked list without a header node}

PROCEDURE  LLInsert ( VAR LList: LListType;  VAR Data : InfoType;
                      VAR Previous : NodePtr );
VAR
  P  :  NodePtr;                      {Holds address of new node}

BEGIN
WITH LList DO
  BEGIN
  New ( P );                          {Allocate new Node type record in heapspace}
  P^.Data  := Data;                   {Store Data record in data portion of new node}
  Count    := Count + 1;              {Increment total node count}
  IF Previous <> NIL THEN             {IF node is not inserted at start of list}
    BEGIN
    P^.Next  := Previous^.Next;       { Link field now points to next node in the list}
    Previous^.Next := P               { Previous node now points to this new node}
    END
  ELSE                                {IF node is inserted at beginning of list}
    BEGIN
    P^.Next  := Head;                 { Link field now points to former 1st list node}
    Head     := P                     { List Head points to this new node,}
    END
  END;

Previous := P  {Facilitates appending of nodes upon subsequent calls to LLInsert }
END;
```

```
{Deletes node Previous^.Next or the first node from a linked list without a header node}

PROCEDURE  LLDelete ( VAR LList: LListType;  Previous : NodePtr );

VAR
  P  :  NodePtr;                      {Holds address of node to be deleted}

BEGIN
WITH LList DO
  BEGIN
  Count := Count - 1;                 {Increment total node count}
  IF Previous <> NIL THEN             {IF not a delete-first-node case...}
    BEGIN
    P := Previous^.Next;              { P points to node to be deleted}
    Previous^.Next := P^.Next         { Previous node points to next node}
    END
  ELSE                                {IF a delete-first-node case...}
    BEGIN
    P     := Head;                    { P points to the node to be deleted}
    Head  := Head^.Next               { List head points to 2nd node}
    END
  END;

Dispose ( P )                         {Deallocate node in heapspace}
END;
```

```
{Deletes node Previous^.Next or the first node from a linked list with a header node}

PROCEDURE  LLDelete ( VAR LList: LListType;  Previous : NodePtr );

VAR
  P  :  NodePtr;                      {Holds address of node to be deleted}

BEGIN
WITH LList DO
  BEGIN
  Count := Count - 1;                 {Increment total node count}
  P := Previous^.Next;                {P points to the node to be deleted}
  Previous^.Next := P^.Next;          {Previous node points to next node}
  Dispose ( P )                       {Deallocate node in heapspace}
  END
END;
```

```
{Traverses a noncircular linked list}

PROCEDURE  LLTraverse ( Current : NodePtr );

BEGIN
WHILE Current <> NIL DO
  BEGIN
  Process ( Current );                {Programmer-defined}
  Current := Current^.Next            {Advance to next node in the list}
  END
END;
```

```
{Deallocates all nodes from a linked list}

PROCEDURE DeallocateAll ( VAR LList : LListType );

VAR
  Current, Previous : NodePtr;

BEGIN
Current := LList.Head;          {Or  Current := LList.Head^.Next  if a header node}
WHILE Current <> NIL DO
  BEGIN
  Previous  := Current;         {Previous advances}
  Current   := Current^.Next;   {Current advances as well}
  Dispose ( Previous )          {Deallocate the node pointed-to by Previous}
  END;

LLInit ( LList )                {Assign NIL to Head pointer, 0 to Count}
END;
```

```
{Merges 2 ordered linked lists, pointed to by Head1 and Head2, into a single ordered
 linked list, pointed to by Head3}

PROCEDURE MergeLLists ( Head1, Head2 : NodePtr; VAR Head3 : NodePtr );

VAR
  Done  :  Boolean;
  Tail  :  NodePtr;                   {Points to last node in merged list}
```

```
{Initializes Tail and MergeLLists, avoiding testing for insert-first case each time}

PROCEDURE Prelude;

BEGIN
IF Head1 = NIL THEN
  Head3 := Head2                 {Merged list consists of Head2 list}
ELSE
  IF Head2 = NIL THEN
    Head3 := Head1               {Merged list consists of Head1 list}
  ELSE
    IF Head1^.Data.Key < Head2^.Data.Key THEN
      BEGIN
      Tail   := Head1;           {1st node of merged list is Head1's 1st node}
      Head1  := Head1^.Next;
      Head3  := Tail
      END
    ELSE
      BEGIN
      Tail   := Head2;           {1st node of merged list is Head2's 1st node}
      Head2  := Head2^.Next;
      Head3  := Tail
      END
END;
```

```
{***  Main routine for MergeLLists  ***}

BEGIN
Done := ( Head1 = NIL ) OR ( Head2 = NIL );
Prelude;                             {Initialize Tail and MergeLLists}

WHILE NOT Done DO
  IF Head1 = NIL THEN
    BEGIN
    Tail^.Next := Head2;             {Remainder of merged list is remainder of}
    Done := TRUE                     { Head2 list -- merging is complete}
    END
  ELSE
    IF Head2 = NIL THEN
      BEGIN
      Tail^.Next := Head1;           {Remainder of merged list is remainder of}
      Done := TRUE                   { Head1 list -- merging is complete}
      END
    ELSE
      IF Head1^.Data.Key <= Head2^.Data.Key THEN
        BEGIN
        Tail^.Next  := Head1;        {Next node in merged list is Head1's 1st node}
        Head1       := Head1^.Next;  {Head1 advances}
        Tail        := Tail^.Next    {Tail now points to last node in merged list}
        END
      ELSE
        BEGIN
        Tail^.Next  := Head2;        {Next node in merged list is Head2's 1st node}
        Head2       := Head2^.Next;  {Head2 advances}
        Tail        := Tail^.Next    {Tail now points to last node in merged list}
        END                          {WHILE NOT Done DO...}
END;
```

Sequential Storage (Array) Representation

```
CONST
  Null       =  0;  {Analagous to NIL, indicating "no more active nodes"}
  MaxNodes   = ??;  {Positive integer; maximum number of nodes allowable}

TYPE
  KeyType    = ??;                    {Application-dependent}
  InfoType   = RECORD
                 Key     : KeyType;
                 {Other fields as necesssary}
               END;

  NodePtr    = Null..MaxNodes;
  Node       = RECORD
                 Data    :  InfoType;  {Data portion of an active node}
                 Next    :  NodePtr    {Array index of next active node}
               END;

  PHeapType  = RECORD
                 Items   :  ARRAY [1..MaxNodes ] OF Node;  {Space for nodes}
                 Free,                 {Head type pointer into free node list}
                 FCount  :  NodePtr    {Count of available nodes}
               END;

  LListType  = RECORD
                 Head    :  NodePtr;   {Array index of first node in list}
                 Count   :  Integer    {Count of active nodes}
               END;

VAR
  PseudoHeap  :  PHeapType;            {Entire psuedoheapspace}
  LList       :  LListType;            {One active linked list}
```

```
{Initializes the pseudoheapspace as empty; i.e., as a linked list of free nodes}

PROCEDURE PHeapInit ( VAR PseudoHeap : PHeapType );

VAR
  K  :  Integer;

BEGIN
WITH PseudoHeap DO                    {Free list will span the pseudoheap array}
  BEGIN
  Free := 1;                          {Initialize list head variable for free list}
  FOR K := 1 TO MaxNodes - 1 DO       {Link all nodes in free list}
    Items [ K ].Next := K + 1;
  Items [ MaxNodes ].Next := Null;    {Mark the end of the free list}
  FCount := MaxNodes                  {All nodes belong to the free list}
  END
END;
```

```
{Initializes as empty a linked list without a header node}

PROCEDURE LLInit ( VAR LList : LListType );

BEGIN
WITH LList DO
  BEGIN
  Head   :=  Null;                    {Head pointer points to nothing}
  Count  :=  0                        {List is empty}
  END
END;
```

```
{Tests a linked list for emptiness}

FUNCTION LLEmpty ( VAR LList : LListType ) : Boolean;

BEGIN
LLEmpty := LList.Count = 0
END;
```

```
{Tests a linked list for fullness}

FUNCTION LLFull ( VAR LList : LListType ) : Boolean;

BEGIN
LLFull := LList.Count = MaxNodes
END;
```

```
{Returns the address of the next available node element in the free list and
 updates the free list accordingly (if the free list is empty, a null value is
 returned in P); this procedure is somewhat analogous to the standard New
 procedure}

PROCEDURE NewNode ( VAR PseudoHeap : PHeapType; VAR P : NodePtr );

BEGIN
WITH PseudoHeap DO
  BEGIN
  P := Free;                          {P holds address of node at head of free list}
  IF FCount <> 0 THEN                 {IF there are available nodes...}
    BEGIN
    FCount  := FCount - 1;            { Now one fewer free node}
    Free    := Items [ Free ].Next    { Free now points to next free list node}
    END
  END
END;
```

```
{Searches a linked list, starting with node Start^, for a match on key value, Key}

PROCEDURE  LLSearch ( VAR PseudoHeap : PHeapType;
                          Key : KeyType;  Start : NodePtr;
                      VAR Previous :  NodePtr;  VAR Found : Boolean );

VAR
  Done     :  Boolean; {Abort-search flag}
  Current  :  NodePtr; {Holds address of node currently being examined}

BEGIN
Previous  := Null;     {Initialized in case node sought is the first list node}
Current   := Start;    {Current now points to node where search begins}
Done      := FALSE;    {Item sought not yet found}
Found     := FALSE;    {Procedure is not yet done searching}
```

```
WHILE ( Current <> Null ) AND NOT Done DO
  WITH Pseudoheap.Items [ Current ] DO
    IF Data.Key > Key  THEN          {Greater key value means that the}
      Done := TRUE                   { sought item is not in the list}
    ELSE
      IF Key = Data.Key THEN         {IF sought node has been found...}
        BEGIN
        Done   := TRUE;
        Found  := TRUE
        END
      ELSE                           {ELSE continue searching...}
        BEGIN
        Previous  := Current;        { Previous "catches up" to Current}
        Current   := Next            { Current advances}
        END
END;
```

APPENDIX E

STACK ROUTINES

Sequential Storage (Array) Representation

```
CONST
  MaxSItems  =  ??;                  {Maximum number of items}

TYPE
  SInfoType  =  ??;                  {Application-dependent}
  StackType  =  RECORD
                  Items  :  ARRAY [ 1..MaxSItems ] OF SInfoType;
                  Top    :  Integer  {Top node index and item count}
                END;

VAR
  Stack  :  StackType;
```

```
{Initializes a stack as empty}

PROCEDURE StackInit ( VAR Stack : StackType );

BEGIN
Stack.Top := 0                      {Stack is empty}
END;
```

```
{Tests a stack for emptiness}

FUNCTION StackEmpty ( VAR Stack : StackType ) : Boolean;

BEGIN
StackEmpty := Stack.Top = 0
END;
```

```
{Tests a stack for fullness}

FUNCTION StackFull ( VAR Stack : StackType ) : Boolean;

BEGIN
StackFull := Stack.Top = MaxSItems
END;
```

```
{Pushes a new item on a stack}

PROCEDURE Push ( VAR Stack : StackType; VAR Data : SInfoType );

BEGIN
WITH Stack DO
  BEGIN
  Top   := Top + 1;                    {Advance stack top indicator}
  Items [ Top ] := Data                {Add the new item}
  END
END;
```

```
{Pops the top item from a stack}

PROCEDURE Pop ( VAR Stack : StackType;  VAR Data : SInfoType );

BEGIN
WITH Stack DO
  BEGIN
  Data  := Items [ Top ];              {Make copy of top stack item}
  Top   := Top - 1                     {Decrement stack top indicator}
  END
END;
```

```
{Returns a copy of the top stack item}

PROCEDURE InspectStack ( VAR Stack : StackType; VAR Data : SInfoType );

BEGIN
Data := Stack.Items [ Stack.Top ]   {Make copy of top stack item}
END;
```

Dynamically Allocated Linked List Representation

```
TYPE
  SInfoType   =  ??;                        {Application-dependent}

  StackPtr    =  ^StackNode;
  StackNode   =  RECORD
                   Data   :  SInfoType;   {Data portion of node}
                   Next   :  StackPtr     {Points to next node to be popped}
                 END;

  StackType   =  RECORD
                   Top    :  StackPtr;    {Top indicator}
                   Count  :  Integer      {Item count}
                 END;

VAR
  Stack   :  StackType;
```

```
{Initializes a stack as empty}

PROCEDURE StackInit ( VAR Stack : StackType );

BEGIN
WITH Stack DO
  BEGIN
  Top    := NIL;          {Stack is empty}
  Count  := 0
  END
END;
```

```
{Tests a stack for emptiness}

FUNCTION StackEmpty ( VAR Stack : StackType ) : Boolean;

BEGIN
StackEmpty := Stack.Top = NIL
END;
```

```
{Pushes an item onto a stack}

PROCEDURE Push ( VAR Stack : StackType; VAR Data : SInfoType );

VAR
  P  :  StackPtr;         {Holds address of new top node}

BEGIN
WITH Stack DO
  BEGIN
  New ( P );              {Allocate heapspace record for new top node}
  P^.Next    := Top;      {New top node now points to former top node}
  Top        := P;        {Stack top pointer now points to new top node}
  Top^.Data  := Data;     {Store data in new top node}
  Count      := Count + 1 {Increment total stack item count}
  END
END;
```

```
{Pops an item from a stack}

PROCEDURE Pop ( VAR Stack : StackType;  VAR Data : SInfoType );

VAR
  P  :  StackPtr;         {Holds address of former top node}

BEGIN
WITH Stack DO
  BEGIN
  Data   := Top^.Data;    {Make copy of top node}
  P      := Top;          {Save address of top node temporarily}
  Top    := P^.Next;      {Stack top pointer now points to new top node}
  Dispose ( P );          {Deallocate former top node in heapspace}
  Count  := Count - 1     {Decrement total stack item count}
  END
END;
```

```
{Returns a copy of the top stack item}

PROCEDURE InspectStack ( VAR Stack : StackType; VAR Data : SInfoType );

BEGIN
Data := Stack.Top^.Data  {Make copy of top stack item}
END;
```

APPENDIX F

FIFO QUEUE ROUTINES

Sequential Storage (Array) Representation

```
CONST
  MaxQItems  =  ??;                   {Maximum number of items}

TYPE
  QInfoType  =  ??;                   {Application-dependent}
  QPtr       =  Integer;              {Array index of queue item}

  QueueType  =  RECORD
                  Items  :  ARRAY [ 1..MaxQItems ] OF QInfoType;
                  Front,              {Array index of next item to be served}
                  Back   :  QPtr;     {Array index of item just enqueued}
                  Count  :  Integer   {Count of items in queue}
                END;

VAR
  Queue  :  QueueType;
```

```
{Initializes a FIFO queue as empty}

PROCEDURE QInit ( VAR Queue : QueueType );

BEGIN
WITH Queue DO
  BEGIN
  Back   := MaxQItems;  {Back initialized for first enque operation}
  Front  := 1;          {Front initialized for first enque operation
  Count  := 0           {Queue is empty}
  END
END;
```

```
{Tests a FIFO queue for emptiness}

FUNCTION QEmpty ( VAR Queue : QueueType ) : Boolean;

BEGIN
QEmpty := Queue.Count = 0
END;
```

```
{Tests a FIFO queue for fullness}

FUNCTION QFull ( VAR Queue : QueueType ) : Boolean;

BEGIN
QFull := Queue.Count = MaxQItems
END;
```

```
{Adds an item to the back of a FIFO queue}

PROCEDURE Enqueue ( VAR Queue : QueueType; VAR Data : QInfoType );

BEGIN
WITH Queue DO
  BEGIN
  Back   := ( Back + 1 ) MOD MaxQItems;    {Advance Back or wrap it around}
  Items [ Back ] := Data;                  {Store new data item}
  Count  := Count + 1                      {Increment total item count}
  END
END;
```

```
{Removes the front item from a FIFO queue}

PROCEDURE Serve ( VAR Queue : QueueType;  VAR Data : QInfoType );

BEGIN
WITH Queue DO
  BEGIN
  Data   := Items [ Front ];                {Make copy of oldest item in queue}
  Front  := ( Front + 1 ) MOD MaxQItems;    {Advance Front or wrap it around}
  Count  := Count - 1                       {Decrement total item count}
  END
END;
```

```
{Returns a copy of the front item of a FIFO queue}

PROCEDURE InspectQ ( VAR Queue : QueueType; VAR Item : QInfoType );

BEGIN
Item := Queue.Items [ Queue.Front ]        {Make copy of oldest item in queue}
END;
```

Dynamically Allocated Linked List Representation

```
TYPE
  QInfoType  =  ??;                        {Application-dependent}
  QPtr       =  ^QNode;                    {Pointer to an item node}
  QNode      =  RECORD
                  Data   :  QInfoType;     {Data portion of queue node}
                  Next   :  QPtr           {Points to next node}
                END;

  QueueType  =  RECORD                     {Back^ is back item just enqueued}
                  Back   :  QPtr;          {Back^.Next^ is front queue item stored}
                  Count  :  Integer        {Count of items in queue}
                END;

VAR
  Queue  :  QueueType;                     {Circular linked list queue structure}
```

```
{Initializes a FIFO queue as empty}

PROCEDURE QInit ( VAR Queue : QueueType );

BEGIN
WITH Queue DO
  BEGIN
  Back   := NIL;  {Queue is empty}
  Count  := 0
  END
END;
```

```
{Tests a FIFO queue for emptiness}

FUNCTION QEmpty ( VAR Queue : QueueType ) : Boolean;

BEGIN
QEmpty := Queue.Back = NIL
END;
```

```
{Adds an item to the back of a FIFO queue}

PROCEDURE Enqueue ( VAR Queue : QueueType; VAR Data : QInfoType );

VAR
  P : QPtr;

BEGIN
WITH Queue DO
  BEGIN
  New ( P );                     {Allocate heapspace record for new node}
  P^.Data := Data;               {Store data in this node}
  IF QEmpty ( Queue ) THEN       {IF this is the first node in the queue...}
    P^.Next := P                 { This first node points to itself}
  ELSE
    BEGIN                        {ELSE...}
    P^.Next    := Back^.Next;    { It now points to the oldest node in the queue}
    Back^.Next := P              { Former youngest node now points to new node}
    END;
  Back   := P;                   {Either way, Back now points to new node}
  Count  := Count + 1            {Increment total item count}
  END
END;
```

```
{Removes the front item from a FIFO queue}

PROCEDURE Serve ( VAR Queue : QueueType;  VAR Data : QInfoType );

VAR
  Front  :  QPtr;                  {Holds address of node to be served}

BEGIN
WITH Queue DO
  BEGIN
  Front  := Back^.Next;            {Front now points to node to be served}
  Data   := Front^.Data;           {Make copy of this (oldest node) item}
  IF Front = Back THEN             {IF this is the last node in the list...}
    Back := NIL                    { Indicate list emptiness}
  ELSE
      Back^.Next := Front^.Next;   {Back node now points to next oldest node}
  Dispose ( Front );               {Deallocate former-oldest node}
  Count := Count - 1               {Decrement total item count}
  END
END;
```

```
{Returns a copy of the front item of a FIFO queue}

PROCEDURE InspectQ ( VAR Queue : QueueType; VAR Data : QInfoType );

BEGIN
Data := Queue.Back^.Next^.Data    {Make copy of oldest queue item}
END;
```

APPENDIX G

BINARY SEARCH TREE ROUTINES

Dynamically Allocated Linked List Representation

```
TYPE
  BTKeyType    =  ??;                        {Application-dependent}
  BTInfoType   =  RECORD
                    Key    :  BTKeyType;     {Key value}
                    {Other fields, as necessary}
                  END;

  BTNodePtr    =  ^BTNode;                   {Pointer type for one tree node}
  BTNode       =  RECORD                     {Tree node type}
                    Data   :  BTInfoType;    {Data portion of node}
                    Left,                    {NIL or else points to left child}
                    Right  :  BTNodePtr      {NIL or else points to right child}
                  END;

  BinTreeType  =  RECORD
                    Root   :  BTNodePtr;     {Address of tree's root node}
                    Count  :  Integer        {Count of nodes in tree}
                  END;

VAR
  BinTree  :  BinTreeType;
```

```
{Initializes a binary search tree as empty}

PROCEDURE BinTreeInit ( VAR BinTree : BinTreeType );

BEGIN
WITH BinTree DO
  BEGIN
  Root   := NIL;  {Root pointer points to nothing}
  Count  := 0     {Tree is empty}
  END
END;
```

```
{Tests a binary search tree for emptiness}

FUNCTION BinTreeEmpty ( VAR BinTree : BinTreeType ) : Boolean;

BEGIN
BinTreeEmpty := BinTree.Root = NIL
END;
```

```
{Searches a binary search tree, for a match on key, Key, starting with Current^ node}

PROCEDURE  BinTreeSearch ( VAR Key : BTKeyType;  Current : BTNodePtr;
                           VAR LastNode, Parent : BTNodePtr;
                           VAR Found : Boolean );

BEGIN
IF Current = NIL THEN                    {Failure: Tree or subtree is empty}
  Found := FALSE
ELSE
  IF Key = Current^.Data.Key THEN        {Success: Item sought is found}
    BEGIN
    Found     := TRUE;
    LastNode  := Current                 { Save address of last node tested}
    END
  ELSE
    BEGIN                                {ELSE continue searching...}
    Parent    := Current;                { Current node is now the parent}
    LastNode  := Current;                { Save address of last node tested}
    IF Key < Current^.Data.Key THEN      { Branch to left or right subtree...}
      BinTreeSearch ( Key, Current^.Left, LastNode, Parent, Found )
    ELSE
      BinTreeSearch ( Key, Current^.Right, LastNode, Parent, Found )
    END
END;
```

```
{Inserts new node into a binary search tree (Parent^ is the parent node of the new node)}

PROCEDURE BinTreeInsert ( VAR BinTree : BinTreeType; VAR Data : BTInfoType;
                          Parent : BTNodePtr );

VAR
  NewNode : BTNodePtr;                     {Holds address of new tree node}

BEGIN
New ( NewNode );                           {Allocate new heapspace record}
NewNode^.Data := Data;                     {Store new data there}

WITH NewNode^, BinTree DO
  BEGIN
  Left   := NIL;                           {Initialize left link field}
  Right  := NIL;                           {Initialize right link field}
  Count  := Count + 1;                     {Increment total node count}

  IF BinTreeEmpty ( BinTree ) THEN         {IF this is the only tree node...}
    Root := NewNode                        { Root pointer now points to it}
  ELSE
    IF Data.Key < Parent^.Data.Key THEN    {ELSE Parent node points to it...}
      Parent^.Left := NewNode
    ELSE
      Parent^.Right := NewNode
  END
END;
```

```
{Deletes node Current^ from a binary search tree (Parent^ is the parent node of
Current^)}

PROCEDURE BinTreeDelete ( VAR BinTree : BinTreeType;
                          Current, Parent : BTNodePtr);

VAR
  Successor : BTNodePtr;  {Holds address of inorder successor node}

{Returns count of children of the Current^ node}

  FUNCTION NodeDegree ( Current : BTNodePtr ) : Integer;

  VAR
    Count : Integer;               {Count of children}

  BEGIN
  Count := 0;                      {Initially, assume no children}
  IF Current^.Left <> NIL THEN     {IF a left child...}
    Count := Count + 1;            { Increment child count}
  IF Current^.Right <> NIL THEN    {IF a right child...}
    Count := Count + 1;            { Increment child count}
  NodeDegree := Count              {Return child count as degree}
  END;

  PROCEDURE Degree0Case ( Current, Parent, Ptr : BTNodePtr );

  BEGIN
  IF Current^.Data.Key < Parent^.Data.Key THEN
    Parent^.Left := Ptr
  ELSE
    Parent^.Right := Ptr
  END;

  PROCEDURE Degree1Case ( Current, Parent : BTNodePtr );

  BEGIN
  IF Current^.Left = NIL THEN
    Degree0Case ( Current, Parent, Current^.Right )
  ELSE
    Degree0Case ( Current, Parent, Current^.Left )
  END;
```

```
{***  Main routine for BinTreeDelete  ***}

BEGIN
CASE NodeDegree ( Current ) OF                     {Determine number of children}
  0  :  IF Current = BinTree.Root THEN             {No children -- IF Current^ is the
                                                    root...}
          Bintree.Root := NIL                      { Tree Root pointer now points to
                                                    nothing}
        ELSE                                       {ELSE...}
          Degree0Case ( Current, Parent, NIL);     { Set Parent link field to NIL}

  1  :  IF Current = BinTree.Root THEN             {1 child -- IF Current^ is the
                                                    root...}
          IF Current^.Left <> NIL THEN             { Tree Root pointer now points to
                                                    left child}
            BinTree.Root := Current^.Left
          ELSE
            BinTree.Root := Current^.Right         { or to right child}
        ELSE
          Degree1Case ( Current, Parent );         {ELSE Parent points to child}

  2  :  BEGIN                                      {2 children}
        Successor  := Current^.Right;              {Find inorder successor node...}
        Parent     := Current;
        WHILE Successor^.Left <> NIL DO
          BEGIN
          Parent      :=  Successor;
          Successor   :=  Successor^.Left
          END;
        Current^.Data := Successor^.Data;          {Overwrite with successor's data}
        IF NodeDegree ( Successor ) = 0 THEN       {Successor node has no or 1 child}
          Degree0Case ( Successor, Parent, NIL )   {In either case, effectively}
        ELSE                                       { delete successor node}
          Degree1Case ( Successor, Parent );
        Current := Successor                       {Save address of successor node}
        END
END;

Dispose ( Current );                               {Deallocate heapspace}
BinTree.Count := BinTree.Count - 1                 {Decrement total node count}
END;
```

```
{Performs a preorder traversal on a binary tree}

PROCEDURE PreOrdTraverse ( Current : BTNodePtr );

BEGIN
IF Current <> NIL THEN
  BEGIN
  Process ( Current );                     {Programmer-defined}
  PreOrdTraverse ( Current^.Left );        {Traverse left subtree}
  PreOrdTraverse ( Current^.Right )        {Traverse right subtree}
  END
END;
```

```
{Performs an in-order traversal on a binary tree}

PROCEDURE InOrdTraverse ( Current : BTNodePtr );

BEGIN
IF Current <> NIL THEN
  BEGIN
  InOrdTraverse ( Current^.Left );         {Traverse left subtree}
  Process ( Current );                     {Programmer-defined}
  InOrdTraverse ( Current^.Right )         {Traverse right subtree}
  END
END;
```

```
{Performs a reverse-order traversal on a binary tree}

PROCEDURE ReverseOrdTraverse ( Current : BTNodePtr );

BEGIN
IF Current <> NIL THEN
  BEGIN
  ReverseOrdTraverse ( Current^.Right );  {Traverse right subtree}
  Process ( Current );                    {Programmer-defined}
  ReverseOrdTraverse ( Current^.Left )    {Traverse left subtree}
  END
END;
```

```
{Performs a postorder traversal on a binary tree}

PROCEDURE PostOrdTraverse ( Current : BTNodePtr );

BEGIN
IF Current <> NIL THEN
  BEGIN
  PostOrdTraverse ( Current^.Left );      {Traverse left subtree}
  PostOrdTraverse ( Current^.Right );     {Traverse right subtree}
  Process ( Current )                     {Programmer-defined}
  END
END;
```

```
{Performs a level-order traversal on a binary tree}

PROCEDURE LevelOrdTraverse ( Root : BTNodePtr );

TYPE
  QInfoType  =  BTNodePtr;               {Pointer type for tree node}

  {Insert standard binary tree declarations here}

  QPtr       =  ^QNode;                  {Pointer type for queue node}
  QNode      =  RECORD
                  Data   :  QInfoType;   {Queue item is address of tree node}
                  Next   :  QPtr         {Address of next queue node}
                END;

  QueueType  =  RECORD
                  Back   :  QPtr;        {Address of youngest queue item}
                  Count  :  Integer      {Total count of queue nodes}
                END;

VAR
  Current  :  BTNodePtr;
  Queue    :  QueueType;
```

```
  {The following routines (dynamic allocation) are defined in Appendix F}

  PROCEDURE QInit ( VAR Queue : QueueType );

  FUNCTION QEmpty ( VAR Queue : QueueType ) : Boolean;

  PROCEDURE Enqueue ( VAR Queue : QueueType; VAR Item : QInfoType );

  PROCEDURE Serve ( VAR Queue : QueueType;  VAR Item : QInfoType );
```

```
{***  Main routine for LevelOrdTraverse  ***}

BEGIN
QInit( Queue );                           {Initialize queue as empty}
Enqueue ( Queue, Root);                   {Enqueue address of tree root node}
WHILE NOT QEmpty ( Queue ) DO
  BEGIN
  Serve ( Queue, Current );               {Remove a tree-node address}
  Process ( Current );                    {Programmer-defined}
  IF Current^.Left <> NIL THEN            {IF this tree node has a left child...}
    Enqueue ( Queue, Current^.Left );     { Enqueue its address}
  IF Current^.Right <>  NIL THEN          {IF this tree node has a right child...}
    Enqueue ( Queue, Current^.Right )     { Enqueue its address}
  END
END;
```

```
{Recursive version of FindHeight—returns the height of a binary tree}

FUNCTION  FindHeight ( Root : BTNodePtr ) : Integer;

VAR
  H1, H2  :  Integer;

BEGIN
IF Root = NIL THEN
  FindHeight := 0                           {Initialize height}
ELSE
  BEGIN
  H1 := FindHeight ( Root^.Left ) + 1;      {Derive height of left subtree}
  H2 := FindHeight ( Root^.Right ) + 1;     {Derive height of right subtree}
  IF H1 > H2 THEN                           {FindHeight gets greater height value}
    FindHeight := H1
  ELSE
    FindHeight := H2
  END
END;
```

```
{In-order traversal-based version of FindHeight—returns the height of a binary tree}

FUNCTION  FindHeight ( Root : BTNodePtr ) : Integer;

VAR
  MaxLevel : Integer;

         ____________________________________________

  PROCEDURE  InOrderTraverse ( Current : BTNodePtr;  Level : Integer );

  BEGIN
  IF Current <> NIL THEN
    BEGIN
    IF Level > MaxLevel THEN  {IF a greater level encountered...}
      MaxLevel := Level;      { Assign MaxLevel this new value}
    InOrderTraverse ( Current^.Left, Level + 1 );   {Traverse left subtree}
    InOrderTraverse ( Current^.Right, Level + 1 )   {Traverse right subtree}
    END
  END;

         ____________________________________________
```

```
{***  Main routine for in-order traversal-based version of FindHeight  ***}

BEGIN
IF Root = NIL THEN                  {IF tree is empty...}
  FindHeight := 0                   { It's height is simply zero}
ELSE                                {ELSE ...}
  BEGIN
  MaxLevel    := 1;                 { Tree level is at least 1}
  InOrderTraverse ( Root, 1 );      { Traverse looking for greatest level}
  FindHeight  := MaxLevel           { Return greatest-level value}
  END
END;
```

Sequential Storage (Array) Representation

```
CONST
  Null          =  ??;          {Unusual BTKeyType value to indicate "no node"}
  MaxBTNodes    =  ??;          {Maximum number of nodes allowable}

TYPE
  BTNodePtr     =  Integer;     {Array index of a tree node}
  BTKeyType     =  ??;          {Application dependent}
  BTInfoType    =  RECORD
                     Key      :  BTKeyType;  {Key value}
                     {other fields, as necessary}
                   END;

  BinTreeType   =  RECORD
                     BTNodes  :  ARRAY [ 1..MaxBTNodes ] OF BTInfoType;
                     Count    :  Integer     {Count of all tree nodes}
                   END;

VAR
  BinTree  :  BinTreeType;
```

```
{Initializes a binary search tree as empty}

PROCEDURE InitBinTree ( VAR BinTree : BinTreeType );

VAR
  K : Integer;

BEGIN
WITH BinTree DO
  BEGIN
  Count := 0;                      {Tree is empty}
  FOR K := 1 TO MaxBTNodes DO
    BTNodes [ K ].Key := Null      {All node keys have Null value}
  END
END;
```

```
{Tests a binary search tree for emptiness}

FUNCTION BinTreeEmpty ( VAR BinTree : BinTreeType ) : Boolean;

BEGIN
BinTreeEmpty := BinTree.Count = 0
END;
```

```
{Searches a binary search tree for a match on key value, Key, starting with Current^ node}

PROCEDURE  BinTreeSearch ( VAR Key : BTKeyType;  Current : BTNodePtr;
                           VAR LastNode, Parent : BTNodePtr;
                           VAR Found : Boolean );

BEGIN
IF Current > MaxBTNodes THEN                            {Failure: Tree or subtree empty}
  Found := FALSE
ELSE
  IF Bintree.BTNodes[ Current ].Key = Null THEN         {Success: Item sought is found}
    Found := FALSE
  ELSE
    IF Key = Bintree.BTNodes [ Current ].Key THEN
      BEGIN
      Found     := TRUE;
      Lastnode  := Current                              { Save address of last node tested}
      END
    ELSE                                                {ELSE continue searching...}
      BEGIN
      Parent    := Current;                             { Current node now the parent}
      Lastnode  := Current;                             { Save address of last node tested}
      IF Key < Bintree.BTNodes [ Current ].Key THEN     {Branch to left or right}
        BinTreeSearch ( Key, ( Current * 2 ), Lastnode, Parent, Found )
      ELSE
        BintreeSearch ( Key, ( Current * 2 + 1 ), Lastnode, Parent, Found )
      END
END;
```

```
{Performs an inorder traversal on a binary tree}

PROCEDURE InOrdTraverse ( Current : BTNodePtr );

BEGIN
IF Current < MaxBTNodes THEN
  IF Bintree.BTNodes [ Current ].Key <> Null THEN
    BEGIN
    InOrdTraverse ( Current * 2 );                  {Traverse left subtree}
    Process ( Current );                            {Programmer-defined}
    InOrdTraverse ( Current * 2 + 1 )               {Traverse right subtree}
    END
END;
```

APPENDIX H

HEAP ROUTINES

```
CONST
  MaxHItems  =  ??;                          {Maximum number of items}

TYPE
  HKeyType   =  ??;                          {Application-dependent}
  HInfoType  =  RECORD
                  Key  :  HKeyType;          {Key value}
                  {Other fields, as necessary}
                END;

  HeapType   =  RECORD
                  Items  :  ARRAY [ 1..MaxHItems ] OF HInfoType;
                  Count  :  Integer          {Count of items in heap}
                END;

VAR
  Heap  :  HeapType;
```

```
{Initializes a heap as empty}

PROCEDURE HeapInit ( VAR Heap : HeapType );

BEGIN
Heap.Count := 0                 {Heap is empty}
END;
```

```
{Tests a heap for emptiness}

FUNCTION HeapEmpty ( VAR Heap : HeapType ) : Boolean;

BEGIN
HeapEmpty := Heap.Count = 0
END;
```

```
{Tests a heap for fullness}

FUNCTION HeapFull ( VAR Heap : HeapType ) : Boolean;

BEGIN
HeapFull := Heap.Count = MaxHItems
END;
```

```
{Returns a copy of the root node of a heap}

PROCEDURE InspectHeap ( VAR Heap : HeapType; VAR Item : HInfoType );

BEGIN
Item := Heap.Items [ 1 ]       {Make copy of next item to be deleted}
END;
```

```
{Moves just-straddled item upward in a heap, to its correct location}

PROCEDURE AdjustUp ( VAR Heap : HeapType; Hole : Integer );

VAR
  Parent  :  Integer;           {Holds address of parent node}
  Item    :  HInfoType;         {Holds item being adjusted upward}

BEGIN
WITH Heap DO
  BEGIN
  Item    := Items [ Hole ];    {Store new item temporarily}
  Parent  := Hole DIV 2;        {Parent holds address of its parent item}

  WHILE Parent >= 1 DO                          {WHILE not above the root...}
    BEGIN
    IF Item.Key > Items [ Parent ].Key THEN     { IF new item is in wrong place...}
      BEGIN
      Items [ Hole ] := Items [ Parent ];       {  Copy parent data over it}
      Hole := Parent                            {  Hole advances to parent location}
      END;
    Parent := Parent DIV 2                      {  Compute new Parent address}
    END;

  Items [ Hole ] := Item        {Copy item-item-to-be-adjusted to its final location}
  END
END;
```

```
{Inserts a new item on a heap}

PROCEDURE HeapInsert ( VAR Heap : HeapType; VAR Item : HInfoType  );

BEGIN
WITH Heap DO
  BEGIN
  Count   := Count + 1;          {Increment total item count}
  Items [ Count ] := Item;       {Store new item at bottom}
  AdjustUp ( Heap, Count )       {Move item up to appropriate location}
  END
END;
```

```
{Moves the item currently occupying the root node in a heap downward, to its correct
 location}

PROCEDURE AdjustDown ( VAR Heap : HeapType );

VAR
  Child,                          {Holds address of a child node}
  Parent  :  Integer;             {Holds address of a parent node}
  Item    :  HInfoType;           {Holds item being adjusted downward}

BEGIN
WITH Heap DO
  BEGIN
  Parent   := 1;                  {Root is the first parent}
  Item     := Items [ 1 ] ;       {Temporarily store item to be moved down}
  Child    := 2;                  {Left child will be examined first}

  WHILE Child <= Count DO         {WHILE more children to examine...}
    BEGIN
    IF Child + 1 <= Count THEN   { Find child with greater key value}
      IF Items [ Child + 1 ].Key > Items [ Child ].Key THEN
        Child := Child + 1;

    IF Item.Key < Items [ Child ].Key THEN  {IF item-to-be-adjusted is in the}
      BEGIN                                  {  wrong location...}
      Items [ Parent ] := Items [ Child ];   { Copy the larger child over it}
      Parent  := Child;                      { Compute new parent address}
      Child   := Parent * 2                  { Compute new left-child address}
      END
    ELSE                                     {ELSE item-to-be-adjusted is in the}
      Child := MAXINT                        { correct location (trick to exit loop)}
    END;

  Items [ Parent ] := Item        {Copy item-to-be-adjusted to final location}
  END
END;
```

```
{Deletes the item with the greatest priority from a heap}

PROCEDURE HeapDelete ( VAR Heap : HeapType; VAR Item : HInfoType );

BEGIN
WITH Heap DO
  BEGIN
  Item := Items [ 1 ] ;                   {Make copy of item to be removed}
  Items [ 1 ]  := Items [ Count ] ;       {Move last item into root position}
  Count := Count - 1;                     {Decrement total item count}
  AdjustDown ( Heap )                     {Move root item down to correct location}
  END
END;
```

APPENDIX I

GRAPH PRIMITIVE ROUTINES

Adjacency List (Linked List) Representation

```
CONST
  NullWeight      = ??;  {WeightType value < lowest weight that may arise}
  InfiniteWeight  = ??;  {WeightType value > highest weight that may arise}

TYPE
  {***  Edge-node declarations  ***}

  NodePtr     =  ^NodeType;                    {Pointer to lookup table node}
  WeightType  =  ??;                           {Application-dependent}
  EInfoType   =  RECORD
                   Child   :  NodePtr;         {Address of NodeType node}
                   Weight  :  WeightType       {Weight value of edge}
                 END;

  ENodePtr    =  ^ENodeType;                   {Pointer to edge node}
  ENodeType   =  RECORD                        {Edge/child node}
                   EInfo   :  EInfoType;       {Information about edge}
                   Next    :  ENodePtr         {Next edge/child node}
                 END;

  {***  Lookup table declarations  ***}

  KeyType     =  ??;
  InfoType    =  RECORD
                   Key  :  KeyType;            {Key value of node}
                   {Other fields, as necessary}
                 END;

  NodeType    =  RECORD                        {Information about one node}
                   Data       :  InfoType;     {Data portion of node}
                   InDegreeZero,               {Used in TopologicalSort}
                   Visited    :  Boolean;      {Used in path-finding and traversing}
                   Head       :  ENodePtr;     {Points to first edge node in list}
                   Parent,                     {Used in representing paths}
                   Child      :  NodePtr;      {Used in TopologicalSort}
                   HeapIndx   :  Integer;      {Used in FindMCPaths, BuildMCSTree}
                   MinCost    :  WeightType;   {Used in FindMCPaths, BuildMCSTree}
                   Next       :  NodePtr       {Points to next lookup table node}
                 END;

  {***  Main graph structure declarations  ***}

  GraphType   =  RECORD
                   LTable     :  NodePtr;      {Points to first lookup table node}
                   NodeCount,                  {Count of nodes in graph}
                   EdgeCount  :  Integer       {Count of edges in graph}
                 END;

VAR
  Graph  : GraphType;
```

```
{Initializes a graph as empty}

PROCEDURE GraphInit ( VAR Graph : GraphType );

BEGIN
WITH Graph DO
  BEGIN
  NodeCount  := 0;   {No nodes in graph}
  EdgeCount  := 0;   {No edges in graph}
  LTable     := NIL  {No items in lookup table}
  END
END;
```

```
{Tests a graph for emptiness}

FUNCTION GraphEmpty ( VAR Graph : GraphType ) : Boolean;

BEGIN
GraphEmpty := Graph.LTable = NIL
END;
```

```
{Initializes the Visited and Parent fields of a graph lookup table (pointed to by Ptr)}

PROCEDURE InitFields ( Ptr : NodePtr );  {Called by DFVisit and BFVisit}

BEGIN
WHILE Ptr <> NIL DO                       {For each lookup table node...}
  BEGIN
  Ptr^.Visited  := FALSE;                 { Mark node as unvisited}
  Ptr^.Parent   := NIL;                   { Initialize parent pointer}
  Ptr           := Ptr^.Next              { Advance to next table node}
  END
END;
```

```
{Provides a visual dump of a graph}

PROCEDURE DumpGraph ( VAR Graph : GraphType );

VAR
  NPtr  : NodePtr;       {Lookup table node pointer}
  EPtr  : ENodePtr;      {Edge-node pointer}

BEGIN
NPtr := Graph.LTable;    {Start with first lookup table node}
WHILE NPtr <> NIL DO     {For each table node...}
  BEGIN                  { Write its key value}
  Write ( 'Node Key: ', NPtr^.Data.Key, '; Children (edge weight):  ' );
  EPtr := NPtr^.Head;    { Next, starting with first edge node}
  WHILE EPtr <> NIL DO   {  write key value and weight of}
    BEGIN                {  each edge node}
    Write ( EPtr^.EInfo.Child^.Data.Key,' (', EPtr^.EInfo.Weight, ')   ' );
    EPtr := EPtr^.Next   {  Advance to next edge node}
    END;
  Writeln;
  NPtr := NPtr^.Next     { Advance to next lookup table node}
  END
END;
```

```
{Seeks a path from node Source^ to node Destination^ in a graph using a depth-first
 approach, if ATraversal is false, or else performs a depth-first traversal from
 Source^ if ATraversal is true}

PROCEDURE  DFVisit ( VAR Graph : GraphType; Source, Destination : NodePtr;
                     VAR Success : Boolean; ATraversal : Boolean );

VAR
  NCount : Integer;                       {Current count of nodes visited}
  ______________________________________________________________________
  PROCEDURE DFT ( Parent : NodePtr );

  VAR
    Edge  :  ENodePtr;                    {Edge-node pointer}

  BEGIN
  IF ATraversal THEN                      {IF this is a full traversal...}
    BEGIN
    Process ( Parent );                   { Application-dependent}
    NCount  := NCount + 1;                { Increment count of nodes visited}
    Success := NCount = Graph.NodeCount   { Determine if traversal is complete}
    END
  ELSE                                    {ELSE this is a depth-first search...}
    Success := Parent = Destination;      { Determine if sought node is found}

  IF NOT Success THEN                     {IF traversal or search not done...}
    BEGIN
    Parent^.Visited := TRUE;              { Mark current node as visited}
    Edge := Parent^.Head;                 { Start with its first edge node}
    WHILE NOT Success AND ( Edge <> NIL ) DO  {and visit edge nodes}
      WITH Edge^.EInfo DO
        BEGIN
        IF NOT Child^.Visited THEN        {IF current child not yet visited...}
          BEGIN
          Child^.Parent := Parent;        { Preserve parent-to-child path}
          DFT ( Child )                   { Recursive: continue from child}
          END;
        Edge := Edge^.Next                {Proceed to next child of parent}
        END
    END
  END;
  ______________________________________________________________________
{***  Main routine for DFVisit  ***}

BEGIN
InitFields ( Graph.LTable );              {Initialize Visited, Parent fields}
NCount := 0;                              {No nodes visited yet}
DFT ( Source )                            {Traverse or find path}
END;
```

```
{Insert global queue declarations, given in Appendix F, including the following:}
TYPE
  QInfoType  =  NodePtr;       {Each queue item holds a graph-node address}

{The following routines are defined in Appendix F}

PROCEDURE QInit ( VAR Queue : QueueType );

FUNCTION QEmpty ( VAR Queue : QueueType ) : Boolean;
```

```
PROCEDURE Enqueue ( VAR Queue : QueueType; VAR Data : QInfoType );

PROCEDURE Serve ( VAR Queue : QueueType;  VAR Data : QInfoType );
```

```
{Seeks a path from node Source^ to node Destination^ in a graph using a breadth-first
 approach, if ATraversal is false, or else performs a breadth-first traversal from
 Source^ if ATraversal is true}

PROCEDURE  BFVisit ( VAR Graph : GraphType;  Source, Destination : NodePtr;
                     VAR Success : Boolean;  ATraversal : Boolean );

VAR
  Queue    :  QueueType;                   {Queue to hold graph NodePtr addresses}
  Edge     :  ENodePtr;                    {Edge-node addresses}
  Parent   :  NodePtr;                     {Parent-node addresses}
  NCount   :  Integer;                     {Count of nodes visited}

BEGIN
InitFields ( Graph.LTable);                {Initialize visited, parent-pointer fields}
QInit ( Queue );                           {Initialize queue as empty}
NCount    := 0;                            {No nodes visited yet}
Success   := FALSE;                        {Traversal or breadth-first search not done}
Enqueue ( Queue, Source );                 {Enqueue address of Source graph node}
Source^.Visited := TRUE;                   {Mark this node as visited}
WHILE NOT QEmpty ( Queue ) AND NOT Success DO
  BEGIN
  Serve ( Queue, Parent );                 {Remove oldest item (node address) in queue}
  IF ATraversal THEN                       {IF this is a traversal and not a search...}
    BEGIN
    Process ( Parent );                    { Programmer-defined}
    NCount   := NCount + 1;                { Increment nodes-visited count}
    Success  := NCount = Graph.NodeCount   { Traversal complete if all nodes visited}
    END;

  Edge := Parent^.Head;                    {Start with first edge in parent's edge list}
  WHILE ( Edge <> NIL ) AND NOT Success DO  {WHILE more children to visit...}
    WITH Edge^.EInfo DO
      BEGIN
      IF NOT Child^.Visited THEN           {IF this child has not been visited...}
        BEGIN
        Child^.Visited  := TRUE;           { Mark node as visited}
        Child^.Parent   := Parent;         { Preserve parent-to-child path}
        Enqueue ( Queue, Child );          { Enqueue node address of child}
        Success := NOT ATraversal AND ( Child = Destination )
        END;
      Edge := Edge^.Next                   { Proceed to next child of parent}
      END
  END  {WHILE NOT QEmpty ( Queue ) AND NOT Success DO}
END;
```

```
{Upon return from DFVisit or BFVisit in which a path was found (not a traversal),
 FollowPath processes nodes along this path. The initial call to FollowPath is:
 FollowPath ( Destination ). }

PROCEDURE FollowPath ( Ptr : NodePtr );

BEGIN
IF Ptr <> NIL THEN
  BEGIN
  FollowPath ( Ptr^.Parent );
  Process ( Ptr );                         {Programmer-defined}
  END
END;
```

```
{Called by FindMCPaths and BuildMCSTree to initialize the MinCost, Parent, and
 HeapIndx fields of the graph lookup table}

PROCEDURE Init3Fields ( VAR Graph : GraphType );

VAR
  Ptr : NodePtr;

BEGIN
Ptr := Graph.LTable;                  {Start with first lookup table node}
WHILE Ptr <> NIL DO                   {For each lookup table node...}
  WITH Ptr^ DO
    BEGIN
    MinCost   := InfiniteWeight;      { Initialize MinCost field to a minimum}
    Parent    := NIL;                 { Initialize parent pointer}
    HeapIndx  := 0;                   { Initialize heap indicator}
    Ptr := Ptr^.Next                  { Advance to next lookup table node}
    END;
END;
```

```
{Additional heap-related global declarations for a single NodePQ priority queue
 item, for the FindMCPaths and BuildMCSTree procedures:}

CONST
  MaxItems   =  ??;                          {Maximum heap items}

TYPE
  HKeyType   =  WeightType;                  {Edge weight}
  HInfoType  =  RECORD
                  Key    :  HKeyType;        {Key value}
                  Node   :  NodePtr          {Lookup table node address}
                END;

  ItemsType  =  ARRAY [ 1..MaxItems ] OF HInfoType;  {Heap array}
  HeapType   =  RECORD
                  Items  :  ItemsType;       {Heap structure}
                  Count  :  Integer          {Count of all heap items}
                END;
```

```
{Finds minimal-cost paths from node Source^ to all other graph nodes}

PROCEDURE FindMCPaths ( VAR Graph : GraphType;   Source : NodePtr;
                        VAR FoundPathsToAllNodes : Boolean );

VAR
  NodePQ   :  HeapType;      {Priority queue (PQ) of (costs from Source and node
                              addresses)}
  Item     :  HInfoType;     {NodePQ item}
  Edge     :  ENodePtr;      {Address of edge node}
  Parent,                    {Address of parent node}
  Child    :  NodePtr;       {Address of child node}
  NewCost  :  WeightType;    {Cost from Source to node via node just served from PQ}
  NCount   :  Integer;       {Count of nodes reached from Source thus far}
```

```
{The following 6 heap primitives are defined in Appendix H.
 Notice the 3 modifications in AdjustUp and the 4 modifications in AdjustDown,
 all necessary for the FindMCPaths and BuildMCSTree procedures. All but HeapInit
 and HeapEmpty must be nested within the FindMCPaths and BuildMCSTree procedures. }

PROCEDURE HeapInit ( VAR Heap : HeapType );

FUNCTION HeapEmpty ( VAR Heap : HeapType ) : Boolean;
```

```
{Modified version of AdjustDown, from Appendix H}

PROCEDURE AdjustUp ( VAR Heap : HeapType; Hole : Integer );

VAR
  Parent  :  Integer;          {Address of parent item}
  Item    :  HInfoType;        {Item to be adjusted upward}

BEGIN
WITH Heap DO
  BEGIN
  Item    := Items [ Hole ];   {Store new item temporarily}
  Parent  := Hole DIV 2;       {Parent holds address of its parent item}

  WHILE Parent >= 1 DO
    BEGIN
    IF Item.Key < Items [ Parent ].Key THEN        {Change: > changed to < here}
      BEGIN
      Items [ Hole ] := Items [ Parent ];          { Copy parent data over it}
      Items [ Parent ].Node^.HeapIndx := Hole;     { Change}
      Hole := Parent                               { Hole advances to parent location}
      END;
    Parent := Parent DIV 2                         { Compute new Parent address}
    END;

    Items [ Hole ] := Item      {Copy item to its final location}
  END;

Child^.HeapIndx := Hole         {Change: store heap address}
END;
```

```
PROCEDURE HeapInsert ( VAR Heap : HeapType; VAR Item : HInfoType  );
```

```
{Modified version of AdjustDown, from Appendix H; changes are underlined}

PROCEDURE AdjustDown ( VAR Heap : HeapType );

VAR
  Child,                          {Address of child item}
  Parent  :  Integer;             {Address of parent item}
  Item    :  HInfoType;           {Item to be adjusted downward}

BEGIN
WITH Heap DO
  BEGIN
  Parent   := 1;                  {Parent is the root}
  Item     := Items [ 1 ] ;       {Temporarily store item to be moved down}
  Child    := 2;                  {Left child will be examined first}

  WHILE Child <= Count DO         {WHILE more children to examine...}
    BEGIN
    IF Child + 1 <= Count THEN  { Find child with greater key}
      IF Items [ Child + 1 ].Key < Items [ Child ].Key THEN  {> changed to < here}
        Child := Child + 1;
    IF Item.Key > Items [ Child ].Key THEN        {Change: < changed to > here}
      BEGIN
      Items [ Parent ] := Items [ Child ];        { Copy larger-child data over it}
      Items [ Child ].Node^.HeapIndx := Parent;   { Change}
      Parent   := Child;                          { Compute new parent address}
      Child    := Parent * 2                      { Compute new left-child address}
      END
    ELSE                                          {ELSE item-to-be-adjusted is in the}
      Child := MAXINT                             { correct location (trick to exit)}}
  END;

  Items [ Parent ] := Item;     {Copy item-to-be-adjusted to final location}
  Items [ Parent ].Node^.HeapIndx := Parent       {Change: Save heap address}
  END
END;
```

```
PROCEDURE HeapDelete ( VAR Heap : HeapType; VAR Item : HInfoType );
```

```
{*** Main routine for FindMCPaths  ***}

BEGIN
Init3Fields ( Graph );
HeapInit ( NodePQ );                {Initialize heap as empty}
Source^.MinCost  := 0;              {No cost from Source to Source}
Source^.Parent   := NIL;            {Source node has no parent}
Parent  := Source;                  {First parent node is the Source node}
NCount  := 1;                       {One node processed so far -- the Source}

REPEAT

  Edge := Parent^.Head;             {Start with parent's first child}

  WHILE Edge <> NIL DO              {Examine all children of parent}
    BEGIN
    Child    := Edge^.EInfo.Child;  {Child holds the node address of child node}
    NewCost  := Edge^.EInfo.Weight + Parent^.MinCost;  {Cost to Source via child}

    IF NewCost < Child^.MinCost THEN  {IF this represents a less costly path...}
      BEGIN
      Child^.Parent   := Parent;      { Preserve parent-to-child path}
      Child^.MinCost  := NewCost;     { Child's minimum cost from Source updated}

      IF Child^.HeapIndx <> 0 THEN    {IF child is already in heap...}
        BEGIN
        NodePQ.Items [ Child^.HeapIndx ].Key := NewCost;  {Update its cost value}
        AdjustUp ( NodePQ, Child^.HeapIndx )              {Move up if necessary}
        END
      ELSE                            {ELSE child is not yet in priority queue...}
        BEGIN
        Item.Node  := Child;          { Initialize Node to node address of child}
        Item.Key   := NewCost;        { Initialize Key to cost value}
        HeapInsert ( NodePQ, Item )   { Insert child}
        END;
      END;

    Edge := Edge^.Next                {Proceed to next child of parent}
    END;

  HeapDelete ( NodePQ, Item );        {Remove parent with next-lowest minimum}
  Parent  := Item.Node;               { cost from Source}
  NCount  := NCount + 1               {Increment nodes-visited count}

UNTIL HeapEmpty ( NodePQ );

FoundPathsToAllNodes := NCount = Graph.NodeCount
END;
```

```
{Builds a minimal-cost spanning tree, with node Source^ as the root}

PROCEDURE BuildMCSTree ( VAR Graph : GraphType; Source : NodePtr;
                         VAR AllNodesIncluded : Boolean );

VAR
  NodePQ   : HeapType;     {Priority Q of node address/costs-to-tree items}
  Item     : HInfoType;    {NodePQ item}
  Edge     : ENodePtr;     {Address of edge node}
  Parent,                  {Address of parent node}
  Child    : NodePtr;      {Address of child node}
  NewCost  : WeightType;   {New cost of connecting a node to the tree}
  NCount   : Integer;      {Count of nodes connected to MCS tree}
         ___________________________________________________________________
{The following 6 heap primitives are defined in Appendix H --
 The 3 modifications in AdjustUp and the 4 modifications in AdjustDown,
 described within the FindMCPaths procedure, must be made here as well. All but
 HeapInit and HeapEmpty must therefore be contained within the BuildMCSTree
 procedure. Necessary heap-related global declarations are given immediately
 before the FindMCPaths procedure. }

  PROCEDURE HeapInit ( VAR Heap : HeapType );

  FUNCTION HeapEmpty ( VAR Heap : HeapType ) : Boolean;

  {Insert the modified versions of the AdjustUp and AdjustDown procedures, as
   they are defined within the FindMCPaths procedure earlier in this Appendix}

  PROCEDURE AdjustUp ( VAR Heap : HeapType; Hole : Integer );

  PROCEDURE AdjustDown ( VAR Heap : HeapType );

  PROCEDURE HeapInsert ( VAR Heap : HeapType; VAR Item : HInfoType  );

  PROCEDURE HeapDelete ( VAR Heap : HeapType; VAR Item : HInfoType );
         ___________________________________________________________________
{***  Main Routine for BuildMCSTree  ***}

BEGIN
Init3Fields ( Graph );
HeapInit ( NodePQ );                {Initialize heap as empty}
Source^.MinCost  := 0;              {No cost from Source to Source}
Source^.Parent   := NIL;            {Source node has no parent}
Parent  := Source;                  {First parent node is the Source node}
NCount  := 1;                       {One node connected thus far -- the Source}
```

```
REPEAT
  Edge := Parent^.Head;                 {Start with parent's first child}
  WHILE Edge <> NIL DO                  {Examine all children of parent...}
    BEGIN
    Child    := Edge^.EInfo.Child;      {Child holds the node address of child node}
    NewCost  := Edge^.EInfo.Weight;     {Cost of connecting child to tree via parent}

    IF NewCost < Child^.MinCost THEN     {IF this is a less costly connection...}
      BEGIN
      Child^.Parent   := Parent;         { Preserve parent-to-child path}
      Child^.MinCost  := NewCost;        { Child's minimum cost to tree updated}

      IF Child^.HeapIndx <> 0 THEN       {IF child is already in heap...}
        BEGIN
        NodePQ.Items [ Child^.HeapIndx ].Key := NewCost;  {Update its cost value}
        AdjustUp ( NodePQ, Child^.HeapIndx )              {Move up if necessary}
        END
      ELSE                               {ELSE child is not yet in heap...}
        BEGIN
        Item.Node := Child;              { Initialize Node to node address of child}
        Item.Key  := NewCost;            { Initialize Key to cost value}
        HeapInsert ( NodePQ, Item )      { Insert child}
        END;

      END;

    Edge := Edge^.Next                   {Proceed to next child of parent}

    END;

  HeapDelete ( NodePQ, Item );           {Remove parent with next-lowest minimum}
  Parent  := Item.Node;                  { connection cost}
  Parent^.MinCost := 0;
  NCount  := NCount + 1                  {Increment nodes-connected count}

UNTIL HeapEmpty ( NodePQ );

AllNodesIncluded := NCount = Graph.NodeCount
END;
```

Adjacency Matrix Representation

```
CONST
  MaxNodes        =  ??;  {Maximum number of nodes}
  NullWeight      =  ??;  {WeightType value < lowest weight that may arise}
  InfiniteWeight  =  ??;  {WeightType value > highest weight that may arise}

TYPE
  KeyType     =  ??;                                {Application-dependent}
  InfoType    =  RECORD
                   Key  :  KeyType;                 {Key value of node}
                   {Other fields, as necessary}
                 END;

  NodePtr     =  Integer;                           {Address of graph node}
  NodeType    =  RECORD
                   Data     :  InfoType;            {Data portion of node}
                   Visited  :  Boolean;             {Used in traversing or path-finding}
                   Parent   :  NodePtr;             {Used in representing paths}
                 END;

  WeightType  =  ??;                                {Application-dependent}
  GraphType   =  RECORD
                   LTable   :  ARRAY [ 1..MaxNodes ] OF NodeType;
                   Matrix   :  ARRAY [ 1..MaxNodes, 1..MaxNodes ] OF WeightType;
                   NodeCount,                       {Count of nodes in graph}
                   EdgeCount  :  Integer            {Count of edges in graph}
                 END;

VAR
  Graph  :  GraphType;
```

```
{**  Global Declaration of WeightType for procedure MaximizeFlow  **}

WeightType  =  RECORD
                 Flow,                      {Actual current flow}
                 Capacity  :  Integer       {Maximum possible flow}
               END;
```

```
{Maximizes flow field values in the graph described in Application 9.1}

PROCEDURE MaximizeFlow ( VAR Graph : GraphType;
                         Source, Sink : NodePtr; VAR TotalFlow : Integer );

VAR
  Parent, Child,                   {Address of a parent or child node}
  FlowIncrease     :  Integer;  {Maximum flow increase in a path}
  PathFound        :  Boolean;  {Flag indicating path to sink found}
```

```
  {Actual code for this procedure appears on the next page.}

  PROCEDURE DFPathToSink ( Parent : NodePtr; FlowIncrSoFar : Integer );

  {NOTE: In this procedure, the code within the boxes is related to handling
   negative flows. If this code is omitted, MaximizeFlow performs only a
   preliminary maximization; if it is included, MaximizeFlow performs a complete
   maximization. }
```

```
{***  Main routine for MaximizeFlow  ***}

BEGIN
WITH Graph DO
  BEGIN
  FOR Parent := 1 TO NodeCount DO
    BEGIN
    LTable [ Parent ].Visited := FALSE;      {Initialize nodes as unvisited}
    FOR Child := 1 TO NodeCount DO           {Initialize all flows to zero}
      Matrix [ Parent, Child ].Flow := 0
    END;

  REPEAT
    DFPathToSink ( Source, InfiniteWeight )  {Configure flows}
  UNTIL NOT PathFound;

  TotalFlow := 0;                            {Initialize flow count}
  FOR Parent := 1 TO NodeCount DO            {Compute maximum flow to sink}
    TotalFlow := TotalFlow + Matrix [ Parent, Sink ].Flow
  END
END;
```

```
PROCEDURE DFPathToSink ( Parent : NodePtr; FlowIncrSoFar : Integer );

VAR
  Child, Difference  :  Integer;
  PositiveFlow       :  Boolean;

BEGIN
WITH Graph DO
  BEGIN
  PathFound := Parent = Sink;            {Test for completion of 1 path}
  IF PathFound THEN                      {IF source-to-sink path found...}
    FlowIncrease := FlowIncrSoFar        { Save maximum flow increase}
  ELSE                                   {ELSE still finding path to sink...}
    BEGIN
    LTable [ Parent].Visited := TRUE;    { Mark current node as visited}
    Child := 1;                          { Start with first child of parent}
    WHILE NOT PathFound AND ( Child <= NodeCount ) DO
      BEGIN
      IF NOT LTable [ Child ].Visited THEN
        BEGIN
        IF Matrix [ Parent, Child ].Capacity <> 0 THEN      {IF parent-to-child pipe}
          BEGIN
          Difference := Matrix [ Parent, Child ].Capacity -  { Calculate flow increase}
                        Matrix [ Parent, Child ].Flow;
          IF Difference > 0 THEN                             {IF flow can increase...}
            BEGIN
            PositiveFlow := TRUE;                            { Positive-flow situation}
            IF Difference < FlowIncrSoFar THEN               {IF new minimum flow}
              FlowIncrSoFar := Difference;                   { increase, save value}
            DFPathToSink ( Child, FlowIncrSoFar )            {Recursive: continue to}
            END                                              { search for path to sink}
          END                                                { from current child}
        ELSE
          IF Matrix [ Child, Parent ].Flow <> 0 THEN
            BEGIN
            IF  Matrix [ Child, Parent ].Flow < FlowIncrSoFar
                FlowIncrSoFar  := Matrix [ Child, Parent ].Flow;
            PositiveFlow  := FALSE;
            DFPathToSink ( Child, FlowIncrSoFar )
            END;
        IF PathFound THEN  {Adjust flows along path while unwinding}
          IF PositiveFlow THEN
            Matrix [ Parent, Child ].Flow :=  Matrix [ Parent, Child ].Flow +
                                              FlowIncrease
          ELSE
            Matrix [ Child, Parent ].Flow  := Matrix [ Child, Parent ].Flow -
                                              FlowIncrease;
        LTable [ Child ].Visited := FALSE
        END;                             {IF NOT LTable [ Child ].Visited THEN}
      Child := Child + 1                 {Next potential child of Parent}
      END                                {WHILE NOT PathFound AND ... }
    END                                  {ELSE BEGIN}
  END                                    {WITH Graph DO BEGIN}
END;
```

APPENDIX J

SEARCHING AND SORTING ROUTINES

The following declarations are used for all searching and sorting routines defined in this appendix:

```
{Global declarations for array-based sorting algorithms:

  Exchange sorts:     BubbleSort, SelectionSort, MergeSort, QuickSort
  Insertion sort:     InsertionSort
  Binary tree sort:   HeapSort  }

CONST
  MinKey    =  ??;  {-MAXINT or KeyType value less than any key value stored}
  MaxIndex  =  ??;  {Application-dependent}

TYPE
  KeyType   =  ??;  {Application-dependent}

  InfoType  =  RECORD
                 Key  :  KeyType;
                 {Possibly other fields, as required by the application}
               END;

  ListType  =  ARRAY [ 0..MaxIndex ] OF InfoType;

VAR
  List  :  ListType;
```

```
PROCEDURE Exchange ( VAR  Item1, Item2 : InfoType );

VAR
  Temp : InfoType;

BEGIN
Temp   :=  Item1;
Item1  :=  Item2;  {Item1 now contains what Item2 contained originally}
Item2  :=  Temp    {Item2 now contains what Item1 contained originally}
END;
```

SEARCHING ROUTINES

Note: This section contains the code for a linear search on an array and a binary search on an array; other search routines may be found in different appendices:

Linear search with a linked list search:	**Appendix D**	`(LLSearch)`
Binary tree search:	**Appendix G**	`(BinTreeSearch)`
Graph depth-first and breadth-first searches:	**Appendix I**	`(DFVisit, BFVisit)`

Linear Array Search

```
{Performs a search for a match on Key; no ordering of element values is assumed
 and the index of the found element is returned via parameter Index}

PROCEDURE LinearArraySearch ( VAR List : ListType; Low, High : Integer;
                              VAR Key : KeyType; VAR Index: integer;
                              VAR Found : Boolean );
BEGIN
Index  := Low;                              {Start with element Low}
Found  := FALSE;                            {Default value}
WHILE ( Index <= High ) AND NOT Found DO
  IF Key = List [ Index ].Key THEN          {IF a match on Key values...}
    Found :=  TRUE                          { Success: Set Found flag}
  ELSE                                      {ELSE continue searching}
    Index :=  Index + 1                     { Advance to next element}
END;
```

```
{The following version assumes a trailer record with a Key field containing a
 maximum KeyType value; the index of the found element is returned in Index}

PROCEDURE OrderedLinearArraySearch ( VAR List : ListType; Low, High : Integer;
                                     VAR Key : KeyType; VAR Index: Integer;
                                     VAR Found : Boolean);
VAR
  Done : Boolean;

BEGIN
Index  := Low;                              {Start with element Low}
Found  := FALSE;                            {Default value}
Done   := FALSE;                            {Not finished searching yet}
WHILE ( Index <= High ) NOT Done DO
  IF List [ Index ].Key > Key THEN          {IF greater Key value stored...}
    Done := TRUE                            { Sought item is not in List}
  ELSE                                      {ELSE...}
    IF Key = List [ Index ].Key THEN        { IF a match on Key values...}
      BEGIN                                 {  Success...}
      Done   := TRUE;
      Found  := TRUE
      END
    ELSE                                    { ELSE continue searching...}
      Index := Index + 1                    {  Advance to next element}
END;
```

Binary Search

```
{Performs a binary search for a match on Key; the index of the found
 element is returned via parameter Mid}

PROCEDURE BinarySearch ( VAR List : ListType;  Low, High : Integer;
                         VAR Key : KeyType; VAR Mid : Integer;
                         VAR Found : Boolean );

  PROCEDURE BSearch ( Low, High : Integer );

  BEGIN
  IF Low <= High THEN
    BEGIN
    Mid := ( Low + High ) DIV 2;         {Computer midpoint index}
    IF Key = List [ Mid ].Key THEN       {IF a match on Key values...}
      Found := TRUE                      { Success: set Found flag}
    ELSE                                 {ELSE continue searching...}
      IF Key < List [ Mid ].Key THEN
        BSearch ( Low, Mid - 1 )         { Search lower half}
      ELSE
        BSearch ( Mid + 1, High )        { or else search upper half}
    END
  END;

{***  Main routine for BinarySearch  ***}

BEGIN
Found := FALSE;                          {Default value}
IF ( Key >= List [ Low ].Key)  AND ( Key <= List [ High ].Key) THEN
  BSearch ( Low, High )
END;
```

SORTING ROUTINES

Bubble Sort (Straight Exchange Sort)

```
PROCEDURE BubbleSort ( VAR List : ListType;  Count : Integer );

VAR
  K, J        :  Integer;
  ListSorted  :  Boolean;

BEGIN
ListSorted := FALSE;                              {Default value}
J := 1;
WHILE NOT ListSorted AND ( J < Count ) DO         {All passes}
  BEGIN
  ListSorted := TRUE;
  FOR K := Count  DOWNTO  J + 1  DO               {One Pass}
    IF List [ K ].Key  <  List [ K - 1].Key THEN  {IF adjacent list items are in the}
      BEGIN                                       {  wrong relative locations...}
      ListSorted :=  FALSE;                       { List is not sorted yet}
      Exchange ( List [ K ], List [ K - 1 ] )     { and they must be swapped}
      END;
  J := J + 1
  END
END;
```

Straight Selection Sort

```
PROCEDURE  SelectionSort ( VAR List : ListType;  Count : Integer );

VAR
  K, J, SIndex      :  Integer;
  Smallest          :  KeyType;
  SmallerKeyFound   :  Boolean;

BEGIN
SmallerKeyFound := FALSE;
FOR K := 1 TO Count DO                    {FOR all elements except the last...}
  BEGIN
  Smallest := List [ K ].Key;             { Begin by assuming List [ K ] is smallest}
  SIndex := K;

  FOR J := K + 1 TO Count DO              {Compare current smallest value to others}
    IF List [ J ].Key <  Smallest  THEN   {IF smaller value is found...}
      BEGIN
      Smallest :=  List [ J ].Key;        { Save new smallest key}
      SIndex := J;                        { Save index of new smallest key}
      SmallerKeyFound := TRUE             { Set exchange flag}
      END;

  IF SmallerKeyFound THEN                 {IF a smaller key encountered...}
    BEGIN                                 { Exchange Kth and the SIndex'th item}
    Exchange ( List [ K ], List [ SIndex ] );
    SmallerKeyFound := FALSE              { Reset exchange flag}
    END
  END                                     {FOR K := 1 TO Count DO}
END;
```

Strait Insertion Sort (For Arrays)

```
PROCEDURE InsertionSort ( VAR List : ListType; Count : Integer );

VAR
  J, Pass        : Integer;
  ItemToInsert   : InfoType;                  {Next list item to be correctly placed}

BEGIN
List [ 0 ].Key := MinKey;                     {Store start-of-list marker}
FOR Pass := 2 TO Count DO                     {All passes}
  BEGIN
  ItemToInsert := List [ Pass ];              {Trying to insert List [ Pass ]}
  J := Pass - 1;                              {Last item of unsorted sublist}

  WHILE ItemToInsert.Key < List [ J ] .Key DO
    BEGIN
    List [ J + 1 ] := List [ J ];             {Shift larger-key item by 1 element}
    J := J - 1
    END;

  List [ J + 1 ] := ItemToInsert              {Store item in final location}
  END
END;
```

Merge Sort (For Arrays)

```
PROCEDURE MergeSort ( VAR List : ListType; Low, High : Integer );

VAR
  Mid  :  Integer;                     {Index of a list midpoint}

  {Merge merges lower list (Low1..High1) and upper list (High1+1..High2)}

  PROCEDURE Merge ( Low1, High1, High2 : Integer );

  VAR
    Aux           : ListType;          {Auxiliary array, to hold merged sublists}
    A,                                 {Index into auxilliary array, Aux}
    Lower, Upper  : Integer;           {Index into lower, upper list}

  BEGIN
  Lower  := Low1;                      {Initialize to lowest index of lower list}
  Upper  := High1 + 1;                 {Initialize to lowest index of upper list}
  A      := Low1;                      {Initialize to lowest index of lower list}

  WHILE ( Lower <= High1 ) AND ( Upper <= High2 ) DO  {WHILE both lists not}
    BEGIN                                             { copied totally to Aux ...}
    IF List [ Lower ].Key <= List [ Upper ].Key THEN  {IF current lower item key}
      BEGIN                                           { <= current upper item key}
      Aux [ A ] := List [ Lower ];    {THEN copy current lower list item to Aux}
      Lower     := Lower + 1
      END
    ELSE                              {ELSE}
      BEGIN
      Aux [ A ] := List [ Upper ];    { Copy current upper list item to Aux}
      Upper     := Upper + 1
      END;
    A := A + 1                        {Increment Aux index in either case}
    END;

  IF Lower <= High1 THEN
    WHILE Lower <= High1 DO           {Copy remaining items in lower list to Aux}
      BEGIN
      Aux [ A ] := List [ Lower ];
      Lower     := Lower + 1;
      A         := A + 1
      END
  ELSE
    WHILE Upper <= High2 DO           {Copy remaining items in upper list to Aux}
      BEGIN
      Aux [ A ] := List [ Upper ];
      Upper     := Upper + 1;
      A         := A + 1
      END;

  FOR A := Low1 TO High2 DO             {Copy merged list back to List array}
    List [ A ] := Aux [ A ]
  END;
```

```
{***  Main routine for MergeSort  ***}

BEGIN
IF Low < High THEN
  BEGIN
  Mid := ( Low + High ) DIV 2;            {Compute midpoint}
  MergeSort ( List, Low, Mid );           {Sort lower half}
  MergeSort ( List, Mid + 1, High );      {Sort upper half}
  Merge ( Low, Mid, High )                {Merge the two halves}
  END
END;
```

Quicksort

```
PROCEDURE QuickSort ( VAR  List : ListType;  First, Last : Integer );

VAR
  PivotPosition : Integer;

  FUNCTION Partition ( Low, High : Integer ) : Integer;

  VAR
    Lower, Upper  :  Integer;
    Pivot         :  InfoType;

  BEGIN
  Pivot  := List [ High ] ;                        {Store pivot item temporarily}
  Lower  := Low - 1;                               {Initialize Lower}
  Upper  := High;                                  {Initialize Upper}


  REPEAT
    REPEAT                                         {Increment Lower until it is the}
      Lower  := Lower + 1                          { index of an item that should be}
    UNTIL List [ Lower ].Key >= Pivot.Key;         { above the pivot in the array}

    REPEAT                                         {Decrement Upper until it is the}
      Upper  := Upper - 1                          { index of an item that should be}
    UNTIL List [ Upper ].Key <= Pivot.Key;         { below the pivot in the array}

    IF Lower < Upper THEN                          {Swap items if necessary}
      Exchange ( List [ Upper ], List [ Lower ] )
  UNTIL Lower >= Upper;

  List [ High ]        := List [ Upper + 1 ] ;
  List [ Upper + 1 ]   := Pivot;
  Partition            := Upper + 1
  END;

{***  Main routine for QuickSort  ***}

BEGIN
IF High > Low THEN
  BEGIN
  PivotPosition := Partition ( Low, High );        {Compute pivot item index}
  QuickSort ( List,  Low,  PivotPosition - 1 );    {Sort sublist below pivot location}
  QuickSort ( List,  PivotPosition + 1,  High )    {Sort sublist above pivot location}
  END
END;
```

Heap Sort

```
{Global declarations necessary for HeapSort}

CONST
  MaxHItems  =  ??;                   {Maximum number of heap items}

TYPE
  KeyType    =  ??;                   {Application-dependent}

  InfoType   =  RECORD
                  Key   :  KeyType;      {Key value}
                  {Possibly other fields, as required by the application}
                END;

  ListType   =  ARRAY [ 0..MaxHIndex ] OF InfoType;

  HeapType   =  RECORD
                  Items  :  ListType;   {List of heap items}
                  Count  :  Integer     {Count of heap items stored}
                END;

  HInfoType  =  InfoType;             {Necessary for HeapSort and HeapDelete}

VAR
  Heap : HeapType;
```

```
{The following routines are defined in Appendix H}

PROCEDURE AdjustDown ( VAR Heap : HeapType; Parent : Integer );

PROCEDURE HeapDelete ( VAR Heap : HeapType; VAR Item : HInfoType );

PROCEDURE AdjustUp ( VAR Heap : HeapType; Hole : Integer );
```

```
PROCEDURE HeapSort ( VAR Heap : HeapType; NotAHeapYet : Boolean );

VAR
  Item              : HInfoType;
  K, OriginalCount  : Integer;

BEGIN
WITH Heap DO
  BEGIN
  {Convert values contained in Heap.List to a heap structure if necessary:}

  IF NotAHeapYet THEN
    FOR K := 2 TO Count DO
      AdjustUp ( Heap, K );          {Place item in element K in appropriate place}

  {Heap.List is now a heap -- perform heap sort}

  OriginalCount := Count;            {Save item count -- HeapDelete decrements it}
  FOR K := 1 TO OriginalCount - 1 DO
    BEGIN
    HeapDelete ( Heap, Item );       {Delete root item and}
    Items [ Count + 1 ] := Item      { store it just beyond the end of the heap}
    END;
  Count := OriginalCount             {Restore original item count}
  END
END;
```

Natural Merge Sort (For Linked Lists)

```
{Necessary linked list declarations from Appendix D}

TYPE
  KeyType    =  ??;                         {Application-dependent}
  InfoType   =  RECORD
                  Key   :  KeyType;         {Key value}
                  {Other fields, as necessary}
                END;

  NodePtr    =  ^Node;                      {Pointer to linked list node}
  Node       =  RECORD
                  Data  :  InfoType;        {Data portion of node}
                  Next  :  NodePtr          {Link field; points to next node}
                END;

  LListType  =  RECORD
                  Head  :  NodePtr;         {Points to first node in list}
                  Count :  Integer          {Count of nodes in list}
                END;

{Necessary FIFO queue declarations from Appendix F}

  QInfoType  =  NodePtr;           {Queue item is a linked list node address}

  QPtr       =  ^QNode;            {Pointer to queue node}
  QNode      =  RECORD
                  Data  :  QInfoType;  {Data portion of queue node}
                  Next  :  QPtr        {Points to next node to be served}
                END;

  QueueType  =  RECORD             {Back^ is last item enqueued}
                  Back  :  QPtr;       {Back^.Next^ is oldest queue item stored}
                  Count :  Integer     {Total number of queue items}
                END;

VAR
  Queue  :  QueueType;             {Circular linked list queue structure}
  LList  :  LListType;             {Linked list to be sorted}
```

```
{The following FIFO queue primitives are defined in Appendix F}

PROCEDURE QInit ( VAR Queue : QueueType );

PROCEDURE Enqueue ( VAR Queue : QueueType; VAR Data : QInfoType );

PROCEDURE Serve ( VAR Queue : QueueType;  VAR Data : QInfoType );
```

```
{The following routine is defined in Appendix D}

PROCEDURE MergeLLists ( Head1, Head2 : NodePtr; VAR Head3 : NodePtr );
```

```
PROCEDURE  LLMergeSort ( VAR LList : LListType );

VAR
  Queue  :  QueueType;
  Head1, Head2, Head3  :  NodePtr;
```

```
PROCEDURE Store2ItemSublistsInQueue;

VAR
  Temp  :  NodePtr;

BEGIN
QInit ( Queue );                  {Initialize queue as empty}
WITH Queue, LList DO
  WHILE Head <> NIL DO            {WHILE more nodes in original list...}
    BEGIN
    Enqueue ( Queue, Head );      { New node will point to next sublist}
    Temp  := Head;                { Temp points to 1st node in original list}
    Head  := Head^.Next;          { LList.Head points to 2nd node in original list}

    IF Head = NIL THEN            {IF Temp points to last node in original list...}
      BEGIN                       { List is a sublist of 1 node }
      Back^.Data  := Temp;        { Queue.Back points to 1st node}
      Temp^.Next  := NIL          { This lone node points to nothing}
      END

    ELSE                          {ELSE a 2-node sublist is built...}
      IF Temp^.Data.Key <= Head^.Data.Key THEN  {IF Temp node key <= }
        BEGIN                                   { 2nd node key...}
        Head := Head^.Next;
        Temp^.Next^.Next := NIL    { 2nd node points to nothing}
        END

      ELSE                         {ELSE 2nd node key < Temp node key...}
        BEGIN
        Back^.Data := Head;        { 2nd original list node is 1st sublist node}
        Head := Head^.Next;        { Head points to next node in original list}
        Back^.Data^.Next := Temp;  { 1st sublist node points to Temp node}
        Temp^.Next := NIL          { Temp node points to nothing}
        END
    END                            {WHILE Head <> NIL DO}
END;

{***  Main routine for LLMergeSort  ***}

BEGIN
Store2ItemSublistsInQueue;

WHILE Queue.Back^.Next <> Queue.Back DO  {WHILE 2 or more sublists in queue ...}
  BEGIN
  Serve ( Queue, Head1 );
  Serve ( Queue, Head2 );
  MergeLLists ( Head1, Head2, Head3 );
  Enqueue ( Queue, Head3 )
  END;

Serve ( Queue, LList.Head )
END;
```

Topological Sort

Procedure `TopologicalSort` operates on a graph defined using the adjacency list declarations of Appendix I. Also, `TopologicalSort` assumes that all `InDegreeZero` fields have already been properly initialized: `Ptr^.InDegreeZero` has a true value if node `Ptr^` has no parent, and a false value otherwise. `TopologicalSort` returns the address of the `NodeType` lookup table node where the topologically sorted list begins; the `Child` field of each `NodeType` node links up all nodes in topological order. By traversing this list via `Child` fields, all graph nodes may be processed in topological order.

```
{The following routine is defined in Appendix I; it initializes each NodeType
 node Visited field to a false value}

PROCEDURE InitFields ( Parent : NodePtr );
```

```
PROCEDURE TopologicalSort ( VAR Graph : GraphType;  VAR Child : NodePtr );

VAR
  Parent  :  NodePtr;                            {Address of parent node}

  PROCEDURE DFTopTraverse ( Parent : NodePtr );

  VAR
    Edge  :  ENodePtr;                           {Address of edge node}

  BEGIN
  Parent^.Visited := TRUE;                       {Mark parent as visited}
  Edge := Parent^.Head;                          {Start with first child of parent}

  WHILE Edge <> NIL DO                           {Visit all children of parent}
    BEGIN
    IF NOT Edge^.EInfo.Child^.Visited THEN       {IF child has not been visited...}
      DFTopTraverse ( Edge^.EInfo.Child );       { Recursive: continue from child}
    Edge := Edge^.Next                           {Advance to next child}
    END;
  Parent^.Child  := Child;                       {Parent node points to Child node}
  Child := Parent                                {This node is Child node next time}
  END;

{***  Main routine for TopologicalSort  ***}

BEGIN
InitFields ( Graph.LTable );
Child  := NIL;
Parent := Graph.LTable;
WHILE Parent <> NIL DO
  BEGIN
  IF NOT Parent^.Visited AND Parent^.InDegreeZero THEN
    DFTopTraverse ( Parent );
  Parent := Parent^.Next
  END;

{To process each node included in the sorted list}

IF Child <> NIL THEN
  Process ( Child );                             {Programmer-defined}

WHILE Child <> NIL DO
  BEGIN
  Process ( Child );                             {Programmer-defined}
  Child := Child^.Next
  END;
END;
```

APPENDIX K

MISCELLANEOUS ROUTINES

```
{***  Necessary global declarations  ***}

CONST
  MaxBuff     =  ??;  {Maximum string length; application-dependent}
  TableSize   =  ??;  {Number of elements in hash table}

TYPE
  BuffType    =  String [ MaxBuff ] ;
  CharSet     =  SET OF Char;
```

```
FUNCTION LowerCase ( Ch : Char ) : Char;

BEGIN
LowerCase := Chr ( Ord ( Ch ) + 32 )  {Based on ASCII character set}
END;
```

```
FUNCTION UpperCase ( Ch : Char ) : Char;

BEGIN
UpperCase := Chr ( Ord ( Ch ) - 32 )  {Based on ASCII character set}
END;
```

```
FUNCTION PositiveResponse ( Ch : Char ) : Boolean;

BEGIN
PositiveResponse := Ch IN [ 'Y', 'y' ]
END;
```

```
FUNCTION CharToInteger ( Ch : Char ) : Integer;

BEGIN
CharToInteger := Ord ( Ch ) - 48      {Ord ('0') = 48 for ASCII set}
END;
```

```
{First version of Pause}

PROCEDURE Pause;

BEGIN
Writeln;  Write ( '>>>>>  Press [RETURN] to continue ...  <<<<<' );
Readln
END;
```

```
{Second version of Pause. This can be enhanced to skip leading spaces or to have
 additional user options other than just resuming or continuing the display}

PROCEDURE Pause ( VAR UserWantsToQuit : Boolean );

VAR
  Reply : Char;

BEGIN
Writeln ( '>>>>>  Press only [RETURN] to continue or Q then [RETURN] to quit  <<<<<' );
Readln ( Reply );
UserWantsToQuit := Reply IN [ 'Q', 'q' ]
END;
```

```
{Index is incremented until any character not in SkipSet is encountered in the Buffer
 string, or else Index exceeds the length of the string}

PROCEDURE SkipChars ( VAR Buffer : BuffType; VAR Index : Integer;
                      SkipSet : CharSet;  VAR Success : Boolean );
BEGIN
Success := FALSE;
WHILE ( Index <= Length ( Buffer ) ) AND NOT Success DO
  IF Buffer [ Index ] IN SkipSet THEN
    Index := Index + 1
  ELSE
    Success := TRUE
END;
```

```
{Index is incremented until a character in SeekSet is encountered in the Buffer
 string, or else Index exceeds the length of the string}

PROCEDURE SeekChars ( VAR Buffer : BuffType; VAR Index : Integer;
                      SeekSet : CharSet;  VAR Success : Boolean );
BEGIN
Success := FALSE;
WHILE ( Index <= Length ( Buffer ) ) AND NOT Success DO
  IF Buffer [ Index ] IN SeekSet THEN
    Success := TRUE
  ELSE
    Index := Index + 1
END;
```

```
{A simple random number generator function that returns an integer value in the range
 of 1 to High, inclusive}

FUNCTION Random ( VAR Seed : Integer; High : Integer ) : Integer;

CONST
  Prime1  = 2741;
  Prime2  = 5927;

BEGIN
Seed := ( Seed * Prime1 + Prime2 ) MOD MAXINT;
IF Seed < 0 THEN
  Seed := Seed + MAXINT;
Random := Trunc (( Seed / MAXINT ) * 1000 ) MOD ( High-1 ) + 1
END;
```

```
{Returns the value of Base raised to the power, Exponent}

FUNCTION Power ( Base : Real; Exponent : Integer ) : Real;

    FUNCTION CalcPower ( Exponent : Integer ) : Real;

    BEGIN
    IF Exponent = 0 THEN  {Terminal condition}
      CalcPower := 1
    ELSE
      IF Odd ( Exponent ) THEN
        CalcPower := Sqr ( CalcPower ( Exponent DIV 2 )) * Base
      ELSE
        CalcPower := Sqr ( CalcPower ( Exponent DIV 2 ))
    END;

{***  Main routine for Power  ***}

BEGIN
IF Base = 0 THEN
  Power := 0
ELSE
  IF Exponent >= 0 THEN
    Power := CalcPower ( Exponent )
  ELSE
    Power := 1 / CalcPower ( -Exponent )
END;
```

```
{Converts a string of digit characters in array Buffer to a single integer value, Value,
 starting at Buffer [Index]; the location of an illegal character is returned in Index}

PROCEDURE StringToInteger ( VAR Buffer : BuffType; VAR Index, Value : Integer;
                            VAR Success : Boolean );

VAR
  FirstIndex,                 {Index of first nonspace character in string}
  BuffLength  : Integer;      {Total length of string}
  Done        : Boolean;      {Abort-conversion flag}
  RValue      : Real;         {Real is used in case accumulated value > MAXINT}

BEGIN
BuffLength := Length ( Buffer );

{Preliminary error-testing regarding Buffer length and the value of Index:}

Success := ( BuffLength > 0 ) AND ( Index > 0 ) AND ( Index <= BuffLength );

IF Success THEN                                    {IF Buffer length and Index are valid ...}
  BEGIN
  SkipChars ( Buffer, Index, [ ' ' ] , Success );  {Skip leading blanks}
  IF Success THEN
    BEGIN
    FirstIndex := Index;                           {Save 1st Index value; check later for -}
    IF Buffer [ Index ] IN [ '-', '+' ] THEN       {Skip leading + or - sign characters}
      Index := Index + 1;

    RValue   := 0.0;                               {Initialize accumulated variable}
    Done     := FALSE;                             {Full conversion not complete yet}
    Success  := FALSE;                             {Reinitialization}
    WHILE ( Index <= BuffLength ) AND NOT Done DO
      IF Buffer [ Index ] IN [ '0'..'9' ] THEN
        BEGIN
        RValue   := RValue * 10 + CharToInteger ( Buffer [ Index ] );  {Convert}
        Index    := Index + 1;                                         { next digit}
        Success  := RValue <= MAXINT;              {Success = FALSE if value is too large}
        Done     := NOT Success                    {If so, abort loop}
        END
      ELSE
        Done := TRUE;                              {Nondigit encountered -- abort loop}

    IF Success THEN                                {IF no fatal syntax errors so far ...}
      BEGIN
      Value := Trunc ( RValue );                   { Convert accumulated real to integer}
      IF Buffer [ FirstIndex ] = '-'THEN           {IF a leading negative sign...}
        Value := -Value                            { then negate accumulated value}
      END
    END
  END
END;
```

```
{Converts a string contained in AlphaKey to a single integer value}

FUNCTION TransformKey ( VAR AlphaKey : BuffType ) : Integer;

VAR
  Sum, K : Integer;

BEGIN
Sum := 0;
FOR K := 1 TO Length ( AlphaKey ) DO
  Sum := Sum + Ord ( AlphaKey [ K ] );
TransformKey := Sum
END;
```

```
{Hashes an integer key value, Key, to a hash table index value}

FUNCTION DivisionHash ( Key : Integer ) : Integer;

BEGIN
DivisionHash := Key MOD TableSize
END;
```

```
{RealDivisionHash performs the same operation as DivisionHash does, but with a real
 key value, RKey}

FUNCTION RealDivisionHash ( RKey : Real ) : Integer;

BEGIN
RealDivisionHash := Trunc ( RKey - ( Trunc ( RKey / TableSize ) * TableSize ))
END;
```

```
{Hashes an integer key value, Key, to a hash table index using a folding hash
 algorithm, then a division hash algorithm; assumes a 16-bit word size}

FUNCTION FoldingHash ( Key : Integer ) : Integer;

VAR
  Temp, UpperByte, LowerByte : Integer;

BEGIN
UpperByte := Key DIV 256;                {Capture most significant 8-bit byte}
LowerByte := Key AND 255;                {Capture least significant 8-bit byte}

Temp := (( UpperByte OR LowerByte ) AND   {Exclusively-OR UpperByte}
       NOT ( UpperByte AND LowerByte ));  { with LowerByte}

FoldingHash := Temp MOD TableSize        {Bring within table indices}
END;
```

APPENDIX L

POPULAR PROGRAMMING CONVENTIONS

Parameter Passing

Generally, pass parameters rather than reference global variables directly within routines. Insert a **VAR** before formal parameters only if data are intended to be returned and/or if the formal parameter is a large record or array. Otherwise, do not use a **VAR** because (a) data unintentionally returned may cause side-effects in the calling routine upon return, and (b) it may be misleading for anyone reading the code (i.e., it looks as though the **VAR** was inserted to explicitly return data to the calling routine).

Functions versus Procedures

If a routine is designed to return a single, simple value, the routine is typically written as a function, with the new value returned as the value of the function identifier. If a routine is designed to return two or more values of any type, and/or one or more structured values (e.g., arrays, records), the routine is written as a procedure, with the new values returned via its parameters.

A common exception to the latter rule is with random number functions. These typically return two values, as does the `Random` function given in Appendix K:

```
FUNCTION Random ( VAR Seed : Integer, High : Integer ) : Integer;
```

Capitalization

Do not capitalize every character in the source program as this makes for tedious reading. A common practice, however, is to capitalize all characters of reserved identifiers, operators, and constants, as done in this text. Another common practice is to capitalize certain characters or to use the '_' character so the identifier reads like a phrase; e.g., `GetNewAverage` and `get_new_average`. Although the '_' character is nonstandard, most Pascal compilers allow it.

Meaningful Identifiers

Choose meaningful identifiers (i.e., names) for named constants, programmer-defined data types, variables, procedures, and functions. Meaningful identifiers for these items help to convey their purpose, and therefore help to document the code. When Boolean variables and functions have meaningful names, the expressions containing them often read like English prose—e.g., **REPEAT** ... **UNTIL** `EmptyList (List)` **OR** `Found`, or the test, **IF NOT** `Done` **THEN**, etc.

Blank Lines

Insert blank lines to delimit code segments. Always insert blank lines to separate procedures, functions, and declaration sections.

Spaces

Statements are easier to read if you use spaces to group your symbols into phrases before and after operators, parentheses, brackets, parameters, and colons. (Be careful—this can easily be overdone.) Another way to separate procedures and functions is with a combination of blank and dashed lines:

```
{ - - - - - - - - - - - - - - - - - - - - - - - - - - - - - - - - - - - - }
```

In the programs given in this text, procedures and functions are separated by solid lines for visual convenience.

Indentation

Indentation improves readability, but it must be done *consistently* and only where appropriate. Otherwise, the indentation creates confusion rather than clarity. Indent the following:

- Identifiers in a **CONST**, **TYPE**, and **VAR** declaration section
- Bodies of **FOR**, **WHILE**, and **REPEAT** loops
- **THEN** and **ELSE** sections of an **IF** statement
- Field declarations of a **RECORD** declaration
- Constants of a **CASE** statement
- **BEGIN/END** block of a **WITH** statement

Align the following:

- Constants in a **CASE** statement
- Field identifiers and their data type descriptors in a **RECORD** declaration
- Identifiers and their data type descriptors in **CONST**, **TYPE**, and **VAR** declaration sections
- Equal signs (=) in **CONST** and **TYPE** declaration sections
- Colons (:) in **VAR** and record declarations, and within a **CASE** statement

Indent no more than a few columns each time. Excessive indenting tends to make programs run off the right side of the screen or page and leaves no room for same-line comments.

Documentation is a general term that refers to any of the following:

- *Source code comments* inserted between lines of code or on the same line of code in a program. Source code comments explain the logic of statements that might not otherwise be clear to the reader.
- A *user manual,* which describes the features of a program and provides instructions related to its use. A common practice among software vendors is to provide a complete user manual in written form plus an abbreviated, online version of the same documentation, which the user can display while a program is running.
- A *programmer's guide,* which elaborates greatly upon the source code comments, describing in greater detail the logic flow of a program, the data structures used, the memory representation of data, and any other useful information about the internal workings of the program. Programmer's guides are especially useful to another programmer who must maintain, enhance, and/or debug the program.

Writing source code comments is an aspect of programming most novice programmers typically disdain but that veteran programmers know to be essential. *Source code comments save a programmer time and effort by explaining the logic and mechanics of obscure code segments.* Even in a high-level language like Pascal, where variables and routines can be given names so that a statement reads like English, the logic underlying a particular code segment may be complex enough to warrant a more in-depth explanation. It is not unusual for a programmer to forget the purpose and mechanics of a code segment written only a few hours or days earlier. Perhaps the worth of program comments is not fully appreciated by a novice programmer until he or she must read someone else's program that is replete with complicated routines and intricate data structures, yet has few or no source code comments or other helpful documentation!

The following types of source code comments should be included:

- *Header comments.* Comments should be included at the beginning of the program to furnish the following information (at least):
  - Program name, filename containing the source code
  - Program author(s') name(s)
  - Date created, date last modified
  - Brief summary of the purpose of the program
  - Description of other files or hardware needed to run the program, as needed.
  - Special instructions about how to run the program, as needed
- *Preprocedure* and *prefunction comments.* Comments should be included immediately before each procedure and function to furnish the following information:
  - Procedure or function name
  - Brief summary of the purpose of the procedure or function

  - Date created, date last modified
  - List of parameters, divided into a description of the data passed in from the calling routine and the data is returned to the calling routine

- *Inline comments.* Comments should also be included as follows:
  - On declaration section lines, to describe the purpose of each named constant, data type, record field, and variable
  - Before a code segment to explain the purpose and mechanics of the code segment if this information is not readily apparent
  - On the same line of any statement whose purpose needs clarification

In this text, header, prefunction, and preprocedure comments are sometimes omitted from code segments to conserve page space.

Write source code comments while you are typing in new source code or source code modifications. Do not wait until the entire program has been typed in, compiled, verified, and debugged before typing in comments. If you wait, the comments will not be as meaningful and complete as they would be if entered earlier, and they will not be available to you during the debugging process. Also, the overall task of documenting will seem more tedious this way.

APPENDIX M

DESIGN OF A BLACKJACK PROGRAM

In this appendix we design an interactive blackjack game from its abstract conception through the Pascal representation and its verification. The evolution of design, coding, and verification follows the seven stages depicted in Figure 1.11, which is shown in Figure M.1.

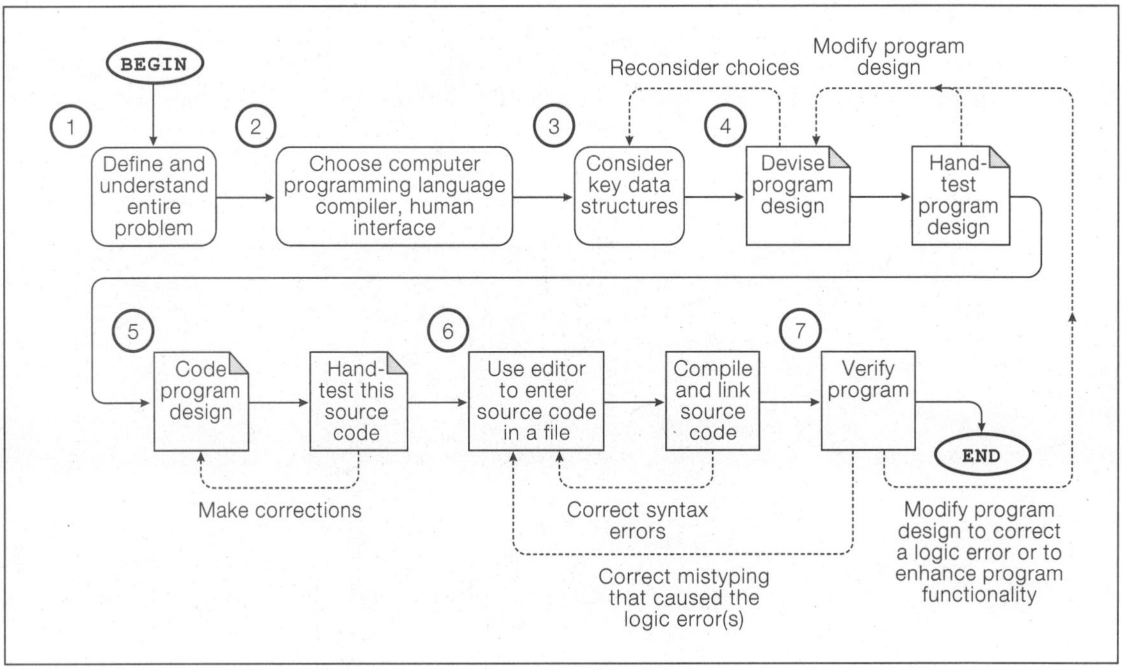

FIGURE M.1 **Stages of Program Development**

STAGE 1 DEFINE AND UNDERSTAND THE ENTIRE PROBLEM

Blackjack is a card game that may be played with two or more persons, one of whom is designated as the dealer. In our simple simulation, we will assume that only a single player—the human program user (player)—will be playing against the dealer—the program (dealer). At the start of a game, the dealer deals 2 cards to the player and 2 cards to himself, drawing from a 52-card deck; the dealer deals one card face down and the other card face up. The player and dealer may look at either face-up card but only at their own face-down cards.

The player and dealer play a series of games. During a game, both the player and dealer try to gather cards that total either 21 points or else fewer than 21 points but more than the points of the cards held in the other one's hand. Card point values are calculated as follows:

Ace	Worth 11 or 1 points
2, . . . , 10	Worth the face value of the card; e.g., a 7 card is worth 7 points
Jack, queen, king	Worth 10 points each

Suit values (clubs, spades, diamonds, hearts) are irrevelant in blackjack.

After the initial 4 cards are dealt, the non-dealing player plays first: If her 2 cards total 21 points (a "blackjack"), she automatically wins that game, regardless of the dealer's hand. Otherwise, she may elect to either stay with the cards dealt or else draw additional cards, one card at a time. If she accumulates more than 21 points, she loses that game. If her hand contains 5 cards with a point total equal to or less than 21 (a "5-card Charlie"), she automatically wins.

If the player has neither won nor lost yet in the current game and decides to stay with her current hand, it then becomes the dealer's turn. At this point, the dealer flips over his face-down card. The dealer is then required to draw cards until his hand has accumulated more than 16 points, at which time he may choose to stay or continue to draw cards. (The 5-card-Charlie rule applies only to the player's hand and not to the dealer's hand.) If the dealer accumulates more than 21 points, he automatically loses; otherwise, both of them flip over their face-down cards to reveal the winner: The hand with the greater point total wins, with the dealer winning in case of a tie. New games are played as long as the player wishes to play. Cards are drawn from the deck and not replaced until too few cards remain to play a single complete game. In this case, all cards are returned and the deck shuffled before the next game. Our program should simulate the game just described as closely as possible.

Note: The official rules of blackjack stipulate that the dealer cannot draw additional cards after his total points exceed 16. In our version, the dealer may draw additional cards if his point total is less than the point total of the player's face-up cards. This is done to further the exercise of having the program make intelligent decisions.

STAGE 2 CHOOSE THE COMPUTER, PROGRAMMING LANGUAGE, COMPILER, AND THE HUMAN INTERFACE

For the present application, we will not be concerned with the issues involved in selecting a particular computer. Virtually any machine that runs a Pascal compiler and supports a nonstandard String data type will suffice. The program will interact with the user via individual keyboard prompts and standard screen displays. The displays for five sample games follow; they are shown here just as they would appear on the screen. In the displays, a value within parentheses is the total point value for that hand. The first card value is that player's face-down card. (Again, the value of the player's face-down card is not considered by the program when determining if the dealer should draw a card.) The explanatory comments given within braces would not be displayed.

```
                ################# B l a c k j a c k ################

----------- Game #1 -----------

--> Player (15):  K 5
    Dealer (??):  ? 6

Want another card? (Y/N): y

    Player (24):  K 5 9
    Dealer (13):  7 6

*** I win! ***                 {Player exceeds 21 points and loses}

Play another game? (Y/N): y

----------- Game #2 -----------

--> Player (14):  A 3
    Dealer (??):  ? Q

Want another card? (Y/N): y

--> Player (15):  A 3 A
    Dealer (??):  ? Q

Want another card? (Y/N): y

--> Player (17):  A 3 A 2
    Dealer (??):  ? Q

Want another card? (Y/N): y

--> Player (19):  A 3 A 2 2
    Dealer (20):  T Q

*** You win! ***               {Player has 5-card Charlie and wins}

Play another game? (Y/N): y
```

```
----------- Game #3 -----------

    Player (21):  A K
    Dealer (20):  J T

*** You win! ***              {Player has blackjack and wins}

Play another game? (Y/N): y

--> Player (17):  T 7
    Dealer (??):  ? 6

Want another card? (Y/N): n

I will draw another card ...  {Dealer must draw with < 17 points}

    Player (17):  T 7
--> Dealer (??):  ? 6 2

I will stay with the cards in my hand ...

    Player (17):  T 7
    Dealer (18):  K 6 2

*** I win! ***                {Dealer has more points and wins}

Play another game? (Y/N): y

----------- Game #4 -----------

--> Player (18):  8 Q
    Dealer (??):  ? 4

Want another card? (Y/N): n

I will draw another card ...  {Dealer must draw with < 17 points}

    Player (18):  8 Q
--> Dealer (??):  ? 6 7

    Player (18):  8 Q
    Dealer (22):  9 6 7

*** You win! ***              {Dealer exceeds 21 points and loses}

Play another game? (Y/N): y

----------- Game #5 -----------

--> Player (12):  2 Q
    Dealer (??):  ? 7

Want another card? (Y/N): y

    Player (20):  2 Q 8
--> Dealer (??):  ? 7

Want another card? (Y/N): n
```

```
I will draw another card ...  {Dealer's total points ≤ Player's up-card points}

    Player (20):  2 Q 8
--> Dealer (??):  ? 7 3

    Player (20):  2 Q 8
    Dealer (20):  J 7 3

*** I win! ***                {Dealer wins}
```

STAGE 3 CONSIDER KEY DATA STRUCTURES

Since blackjack is a card game, a data structure to represent a deck of cards is needed. What information about a single card is necessary? The *card's integer value is necessary for the counting of points in a given hand.* Thinking ahead to the algorithm that will display card values for the player and dealer, the *card's character value is also necessary:* `A` for an ace, `2` for a 2 card, `3` for a 3 card, ... , `T` for a 10 card, `J` for a jack card, `Q` for a queen, and `K` for a king. Using single characters rather than words simplifies the display and allows the card values in both hands to be aligned vertically on the screen. The integer value and character values fields can be packaged in a single record, and the entire deck of cards may be represented as an array of 52 of these records. (Because a card's suit is irrelevant in blackjack, it need not be stored or displayed.)

Because the program will "deal" cards from the deck, an indication of which cards have and have not been picked is also needed. We can add to each card record a Boolean field named `Picked`, initialized to a false value and assigned a true value when that card is dealt. The program must also maintain a count of unpicked cards in order to determine when to return all picked cards to the deck between games. We can therefore declare the card deck structure as a record with two fields: the array of card records plus an integer field to hold the count of unpicked cards.

We must also choose a data structure to represent a given hand of cards, both for the player's hand and for the dealer's hand. The cards in each hand must be represented, and an array is a viable choice for this if the largest hand size can be determined (since array sizes are fixed at compile time). It is interesting to note that the 5-card-Charlie rule does not guarantee a maximum hand size of 5 cards, since the rule applies only to the player whereas the dealer's hand could contain as many as 11 cards:

Dealer (21 points): A A A A 2 3 3 2 2 2 3

Since we know the upper limit on hand size—11 cards—an array is indeed the appropriate structure. (Unlike standard blackjack, our version allows the dealer to draw additional cards beyond 16 points in his hand. This extreme situation of 11 cards might arise only in the dealer's hand, if the player's hand contains 20 points among the face-up cards and the player has not exceeded 21 points—indicating a face-down ace card—in which case the dealer needs 21 points to win.)

What should each array element contain? Thinking ahead, it may seem that the algorithm that deals a card to a particular hand should do so by copying a card record from the deck array to the hand array. In principle, however, this would be inefficient since duplicating data is one of the time- and memory-wasting practices to avoid. (This wastes memory because two copies of every picked card would be stored.) Instead, we will store in each element of the hand array only the *index number* of the associated card element in the deck array. This is an example of *indirect addressing,* since each hand record stores the address of a card record (i.e., its deck array index) rather than the card record itself. In contrast, accessing each deck array element directly to mark each card as unpicked at the start of the program is an example of *direct addressing* of the records.

Other information that must be stored in a hand record includes a sum of the total points in the hand and a count of the number of cards currently held in the hand (to test for the 5-card-Charlie rule). We will see later that a fourth field is also necessary.

Finally, a record to hold game-state information will be useful. One field will indicate the current state of the game: Player's turn, dealer's turn, player has just won, player has just lost, or player wishes to quit. An enumerated type is an appropriate data type for this field. The second record field will count the number of games played, for display purposes. (The usefulness of a game-state record reflects a level of detail that may not be apparent until the first draft of the program design is completed but is described at this time for your convenience.)

We have chosen the four key data structures for our blackjack program:

- A record data structure representing a single card (3 fields)
- A record data structure representing the entire deck of cards (2 fields)
- A record data structure representing a single hand of cards (4 fields)
- A record data structure holding game-state information (2 fields)

Look ahead briefly to the start of the program design on page 650 for a detailed description of each record. Now we will devise the algorithms that manipulate these data structures.

STAGE 4 DEVISE A PROGRAM DESIGN

Many of the operations in our blackjack application involve straightforward bookkeeping, such as initializing, storing, accessing, and displaying information. The program begins by displaying the program name. The fields in each card record in the deck array must be initialized; i.e., the deck must be "created." When too few unpicked cards remain for another game, all cards must be "returned to the deck." Each time a card is dealt, the program should redisplay information to which the player would have access if she were actually playing blackjack with another person. On two occasions, the program must prompt the player, asking her if she wants to draw another card during her turn and asking her at the end of the game if she wishes to play another game. These are all low-level, *primitive operations.*

An additional primitive operation involves choosing a card from the deck randomly. For this, the program will call the function `Random`, which is defined in Appendix K:

```
FUNCTION Random ( VAR Seed : Integer, High : Integer ) : Integer;
```

This function returns an integer in the range of 1 to `High`; by passing a `High` value of 52, the number returned can be used as an index value for the deck array. At the start of the program, an initial random number must be obtained and passed to argument `Seed` the first time `Random` is called (`Seed` is used in the computation of a random number). In `Random`, a computed random number is assigned to both the function identifier (`Random`) and to `Seed`; this way, `Seed` will have a new value the next time that `Random` is called. The program will need one more primitive routine to obtain the *initial* `Seed` value, perhaps by calling a native date/time function, if one is available, or from the user at the start of the program in some unobtrusive way.

The program must perform *high-level* operations as well, such as analyzing the point totals of the player's and dealer's hands to determine if either has won. The program must be able to deal a single card to either hand and adjust a hand's point total by counting a held ace as 1 point rather than 11 points. Of course, the determination of whether an operation is low-level or high-level is completely at the discretion of the programmer; the distinction merely aids the programmer in organizing her efforts. We now consider a variety of implementation details before writing the complete program design.

In Stage 3 we chose to represent the card deck as an array of records. This immediately presents two options: (1) A one-dimensional, 52-element array or (2) a two-dimensional array of 13 rows (1 per card value) and 4 columns (1 per suit). We will use a one-dimensional array for three reasons: First, suit values are irrelevant in blackjack so the division of rows and columns is meaningless. Second, referencing card record elements in a two-dimensional array would require two index values, thereby requiring twice as many calls to the random number function in the attempt to find and deal a single unpicked card. Third, using two array index values adds more syntax to the source and object code, thereby requiring slightly more execution time and memory.

Two High-Level Problems

As indicated in the second sample game given earlier in this appendix, an ace should be counted as 1 point rather than 11 points when a just-dealt card raises a hand's total point value beyond 21 points. Rather than changing the value field of the ace-card record itself, the program can adjust the total points field of the hand record immediately after such a card is dealt. This raises an interesting high-level problem, as illustrated in the following display of a sample game, when the second ace card is dealt (it is the player's turn here):

```
--> Player (17):  A 3 A 2
    Dealer (??):  ? Q
```

The problem is this: When a hand contains more than one ace, how can the program remember the intended value (11 points or only 1 point) of each ace?

This problem is reminiscent of the socks puzzle presented at the start of Chapter 1 because the solution is deceptively easy. We must simply recog-

Turn	Player card count	Dealer card count	Hand points so far this game	Game state
Initial deal	2	2	*	Player's turn
Player	3–4	*	Player points ≤ 21	Still player's turn—draw or stay
Player	2	*	Player points = 21	Game over: Player wins
Player	5	*	Player points ≤ 21	Game over: Player wins
Player	*	*	Player points > 21	Game over: Player loses
Player	2–4	*	Player points ≤ 21	Player stays—now dealer's turn
Dealer	*	*	Dealer points ≤ 16	Still dealer's turn—draw a card
Dealer	*	*	17 ≥ Dealer points ≤ Player's face-up cards	Still dealer's turn—draw a card
Dealer	*	*	17 ≥ Dealer points ≥ Player points	Game over: Player loses
Dealer	*	*	17 ≥ Dealer points < Player points	Game over: Player wins
Dealer	*	*	Dealer points > 21	Game over: Player wins

FIGURE M.2 Table to Determine Results of a Game of Our Version of Blackjack

nize that only one ace in a hand may ever be counted as 11 points, since doing so even twice results in a point value greater than 21 (2 times 11 is 22). To solve the problem, we will add to the hand record declaration a third Boolean field named `AceAs11` that must be initialized to a false value before each game. This Boolean flag can be used when the hand's point total is updated instead of counting the number of aces in a hand each time a new card is dealt. Whenever any card is drawn, its default value is added to the hand total (11 points, in the case of an ace). If an ace is drawn, `AceAs11` is assigned a true value. If the total hand points now exceed 21 (regardless of the card drawn) and `AceAs11` has a true value, the point total is simply reduced by 10 points and `AceAs11` is assigned a false value.

A second high-level problem is determining the current game state—i.e., determining if the player has just won or lost or, if neither, or simply determining whose turn is next. Just as the truth table of Figure 1.6 was used to derive the most concise form of the test for a leap year, a truth table may be constructed to derive the most concise form of the tests necessary to determine if the player has won or lost a game. Figure M.2 contains a table to determine the current game state and what actions should be taken next (based on our modified rules of blackjack). In the table, the * character means "doesn't care" (in fact, the dealer card count column could be removed entirely), and the terminal state in which the user wishes to stop altogether is not included. Again, the initial game state is "player's turn"; then, if the player has neither won nor lost and refuses any more cards, it becomes the dealer's turn.

In the first draft of the program design, the exact details of various algorithms may not yet be understood. Merely dividing the program into modules and stating the data needs and returns of each is a significant first step toward the finished program. Once this is done, the details of each algorithm can be spelled out. As more complete versions of the program design are drafted, other issues arise, a phenomenon that will occur periodically in the coding, verifying, and debugging stages. As illustrated in Figure M.1, one or more design flaws may be revealed that are so problematic that we must reevaluate our choice of data structures.

Try writing your own program design before examining the version that follows. Remember to describe what data each module *needs* from the calling module or input device to do its work and, as a result, what data it *returns* to the calling module or displays. Again, these needs and returns values will translate readily into formal parameters or input and output instructions once the program design is coded as a Pascal program. A module tree diagram for the program is given after the program design, in Figure M.3.

Program design for:	**BlackJack**
Author:	Your Name Here
Created:	5/3/1999
Last changed:	5/7/1999
Source code file:	`BlackJak.PAS`
Program function:	Simulates the card game, blackjack. One human user (the "player") plays against the computer program (the "dealer").

I. Key Structures

`OneCard` = Record describing a single card, with 3 fields:

- `Symbol` : Character value (`'A'`, `'2'`, .., `'9'`, `'T'`, `'J'`, `'Q'`, `'K'`);
- `Value` : Integer card value (`1..11`)
- `Picked` : Boolean value, indicating whether or not the card has been picked

`DeckType` = Record describing the deck of cards, with 2 fields:

- `DeckCards` : Array of 52 `OneCard` records
- `CardsLeft` : Integer count of unpicked cards in deck

`OneHand` = Record describing a single hand (Player's or Dealer's), with 4 fields:

- `Cards` : Array representing the current hand; each integer element holds the `DeckCards` array index for one card
- `Count` : Integer count of the cards currently in the hand
- `Points` : Integer sum of total points in hand
- `AceAs11` : Boolean indicator of whether or not the hand contains an ace card that is still counted as 11 points (false by default)

`GameInfo` = Record describing the state of the current game, with 2 fields:

- `GameState` : Enumerated type representing the game state: `Quit`, `PlayersTurn`, `DealersTurn`, `PlayerWins`, `PlayerLoses`
- `GameCount` : Integer indicating the number of the current game

II. Primitive Operations

`InitializeDeck`: Module that initializes all `OneCard` fields in the `DeckCards` array

Needs: Nothing
Returns: Completely initialized deck structure, with all cards available for picking

```
BEGIN
Display program name;
Within nested loops, initialize the fields of all card records in the deck as
  follows:

  Symbol fields:  'A','A','A','A', '2','2',..., 'T','T',..., 'J','J',...,
                  'Q','Q',..., 'K','K','K','K'
  Value fields:   1,1,1,1, 2,2,2,2,..., 10,10,10,10, 11,11,11,11, 12,12,12,12,
                  13,13,13,13
  Picked fields:  FALSE

Reassign 11 to the Value fields of ace cards;
Reassign 10 to Value fields of face cards (Jack, Queen, King);
Deck.CardsLeft := 52;       {A full deck}
GameData.GameCount := 0     {No games played yet}
END;
```

`ReturnAllCardsToDeck`: Module that "returns" all picked cards to the deck; called when the deck contains too few unpicked cards for another game.

Needs: Deck structure
Returns: Modified deck structure (all cards available for picking)

```
BEGIN
Display message to player;
Within a loop, assign a FALSE value to each OneCard Picked field;
Deck.CardsLeft := 52      {A full deck once again}
END;
```

`UpdateDisplay`: Module that updates the screen display after a card is dealt.

Needs: Player's and Dealer's hand structures, deck structure, indication of the turn
Returns: Nothing

```
BEGIN
Display indication of whose turn it is currently, if no winner yet;
Display total points and cards in player's hand, using char symbols;
Display total points and cards in dealer's hand, using char symbols (display ?? for
  total points and ? for the face-down card if it is still the player's turn);
IF player has won the current game THEN
  Sound a double beep and display a congratulatory message
ELSE
  Sound a single beep and display a consoling message
END;
```

`PromptPlayer:` Module that asks the player one of two questions.

Needs: Indication of which question to ask
Returns: Possibly modified game status

```
BEGIN
Ask player one of the following two questions:
  "Want another card?" -- If a negative response, set GameState to DealersTurn
  "Play another game?" -- If a negative response, set GameState to Quit
END;
```

`Random:` Module that returns a "random" integer value between 1 and the value of argument `High`.

Needs: Seed value (initial or previous random number), maximum random value
Returns: New random value, new seed value (these values are equal)

III. High-Level Operations

`Deal1Card:` Module that "deals" a single card to either the player or the dealer.

Needs: A hand structure, the deck structure
Returns: Modified hand structure (contains 1 more "card"), modified deck structure (contains 1 fewer available "cards")

```
BEGIN
REPEAT
  Call Random function to obtain a randomly chosen number between 1 and 52
UNTIL the DeckCards array index of an unpicked card is obtained;

Mark the card as picked;
Decrement the deck record CardsLeft field;
Increment the hand card count (Count);
Store the array index value (not the OneCard record itself) in the hand's
  Cards array;
Add the card's integer value to the hand's total point sum (Points);

IF card is an ace THEN
  AceAs11 for the hand := TRUE;  {Default value of an ace card is 11}

IF ( hand's total points > 21 ) AND AceAs11 THEN  {hand holds an 11-point ace}
  Count the ace as 1 rather than 11 points (i.e., subtract 10 from the hand's
    total);
END;
```

`AnalyzeGame:` Module that examines hand point sums to determine if the player or dealer has won; called each time the player has drawn a card and after the dealer is finished drawing cards.

Needs: Player's and Dealer's hand structures, indication of whose turn it is
Returns: An indication of who won, if a winner

```
BEGIN
IF it is the Player's turn THEN
  BEGIN
  IF ( a Blackjack ) OR ( a 5-Card Charlie ) THEN
    Player wins
  ELSE
    IF player total > 21 points THEN
      Player loses
  END

ELSE  {Dealer's turn -- AnalyzeGame called if Dealer's points >= 17}
  IF ( Dealer's points > 21 ) OR ( Player's points > Dealer's points ) THEN
    Player wins
  ELSE
    Player loses
END;
```

`InitialDeal:` Module that "deals" the initial 2 cards to both player and dealer.

Needs: Player's and Dealer's hand structures, deck structure
Returns: Modified Player's hand structure (2 cards) and Dealer's hand structure (2 cards), indication that it is the Player's turn (game status), incremented game count

```
BEGIN
In both Player's and Dealer's hand structures, initialize total points (Points) and
   card count (Count) to zero, AceAs11 to FALSE;
Call Deal1Card twice for the player and twice for the dealer (i.e., deal 2 cards to
  each);
Game status := Player's turn;
Game count  := current game count + 1
END;
```

`DealerShouldDrawAgain:` Module that analyzes the Dealer's cards and the Player's face up cards to determine whether or not the dealer should draw another card.

Needs: Player's and Dealer's hand structures, deck structure
Returns: A true value if dealer should draw another card and a false value otherwise

```
BEGIN
DealerShouldDrawAgain :=( Dealer's points <= 16 ) OR
                        ( Dealer's points <= Player's face-up card points );
Display a message indicating whether or not the dealer will draw another card
END;
```

`InitializeSeed:` Module that provides an initial (random) value to the Random function's seed argument.

Needs: Nothing
Returns: Seed value

```
BEGIN
Assign an integer value to seed by either reading the system clock, if the Pascal
  system in use provides a way to read the clock, or else from the user in some
  unobtrusive manner
END;
```

IV. Main Module Operations

```
BEGIN
Call InitializeDeck to display the program name and "create" the deck of cards;
REPEAT
  IF deck contains too few cards to play another game THEN
    Call ReturnAllCardsToDeck;

  Call InitialDeal to deal 2 cards to the player and 2 cards to the dealer;
  Call AnalyzeGame to determine if the player wins automatically via a blackjack;
  Call UpdateDisplay;

  WHILE it is Player's turn (i.e., no winner yet) DO
    BEGIN
    PromptPlayer ( player wants a card? )
    IF player wants another card THEN  {If not, it is the Dealer's turn}
      BEGIN
      Call Deal1Card to deal the player 1 card;
      Call AnalyzeGame to determine if the player wins, loses, or neither;
      Call UpdateDisplay
      END;

  WHILE it is Dealer's turn DO
    BEGIN
    IF ( Dealer's total points <= 16 ) OR
       ( Dealer's total points <= the total points of the Player's face-up cards )
      THEN
        Call Deal1Card to deal 1 card to the dealer;

    IF the Dealer's total > the minimimum necessary to stay THEN
      Call AnalyzeGame to determine if the dealer wins, loses, or neither;
    Call UpdateDisplay
    END;

  PromptPlayer ( player wishes to play again? );

UNTIL player wishes to quit
END.
```

Figure M.3 contains a module tree diagram for our blackjack program.

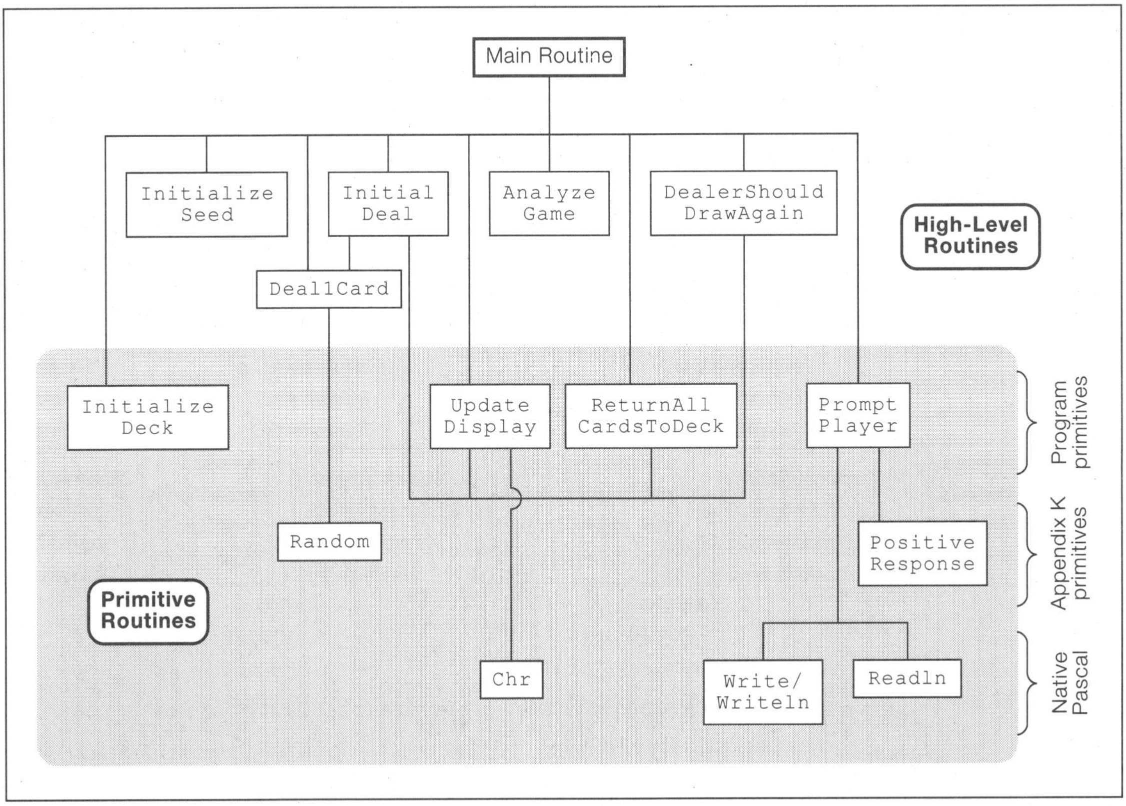

FIGURE M.3 Module Tree Diagram for the Blackjack Program

STAGE 5 CODE THE PROGRAM DESIGN

We can now represent the program design as a complete Pascal program. Since a coded program is even more specific than its program design, it is not surprising that a few additional primitive routines will be necessary.

```
{ Program:        Blackjack
  Author:         Your Name Here
  Source file:    Blackjak.PAS
  Created:        5/3/99
  Last changed:   5/7/99
  Objective:      Simulates the card game, blackjack. One human user (the "player")
                  plays against the computer program (the "dealer") }
```

```
PROGRAM  Blackjack ( INPUT, OUTPUT );

CONST
  MaxHandSize      =  11;  {Maximum cards (for dealer: A A A A 2 3 3 2 2 2 3)}
  MinCardsNeeded   =  10;  {Minimum cards for 1 game}
  MinDealerPoints  =  16;  {Minimum points that dealer may stay with}

TYPE
  OneCard       =  RECORD
                     Symbol     :  Char;         {Card character; e.g., A or 2}
                     Value      :  Integer;      {Actual card value}
                     Picked     :  Boolean       {TRUE if card has been picked}
                   END;

  DeckType      =  RECORD
                     DeckCards  :  ARRAY [ 1..52 ] OF OneCard;     {Deck of cards}
                     CardsLeft  :  Integer       {Count of unpicked cards left}
                   END;

  OneHand       =  RECORD
                     Cards      :  ARRAY [ 1..MaxHandSize ] OF Integer;
                     Count,                      {Count of cards in hand}
                     Points     :  Integer;      {Total points in hand}
                     AceAs11    :  Boolean       {TRUE if 11-point ace held}
                   END;

  StateType     =  ( Quit, PlayersTurn, DealersTurn, PlayerWins, PlayerLoses );

  GameInfo      =  RECORD
                     GameState  :  StateType;    {Current state of game}
                     GameCount  :  Integer       {Game number}
                   END;

  PromptType    =  ( AnotherCard, ToQuit );      {Two user-prompt types}

VAR
  Deck           :  DeckType;                    {Card deck structure}
  Player, Dealer :  OneHand;                     {Hand structures}
  Seed           :  Integer;                     {For random number function}
  GameData       :  GameInfo;                    {General data about current game}
```

```
{The following functions are defined in Appendix K}

FUNCTION PositiveResponse ( Ch : Char ) : Boolean;

FUNCTION Random ( VAR Seed : Integer; High : Integer ) : Integer;
```

```
{InitializeDeck displays the program name, then initializes each of the 3 fields in
 each OneCard record element of the Deck.DeckCards array:

  Symbol:  'A','A','A','A', '2','2',..., 'T','T',..., 'J','J',..., 'Q','Q',...,
           'K','K','K','K'
  Value:   1,1,1,1, 2,2,..., 11,11,11,11, 12,12,12,12, 13,13,13,13 then corrected to
           11,11,11,11, 2,2,..., 10,10,10,10, 10,10,10,10, 10,10,10,10
  Picked:  FALSE }

PROCEDURE  InitializeDeck ( VAR Deck : DeckType; VAR GameData : GameInfo );

VAR
  Symbols        :  String [ 13 ] ;       {String used to initialize deck}
  J, K, Offset   :  Integer;

BEGIN
Writeln ( '################### B l a c k j a c k  ###################' );
Writeln;
Symbols := 'A23456789TJQK';
Offset  := 0;
WITH Deck DO
  BEGIN
  FOR J := 1 TO 13 DO                     {FOR 13 groups of 4 cards...}
    BEGIN
    FOR K := 1 TO 4 DO                    { FOR 4 cards of the same suit...}
      WITH DeckCards [ Offset + K ] DO    {  Store same values 4 times...}
        BEGIN
        Symbol := Symbols [ J ] ;         {  Store card character (A..K)}
        Value  := J;                      {  Store card value (1..13)}
        Picked := FALSE                   {  Mark card as unpicked}
        END;
    Offset := Offset + 4                  { Move on to next group (suit)}
    END;

  FOR J := 1 TO 4 DO
    DeckCards [ J ].Value := 11;          {Initialize ace cards as 11 points}
  FOR J := 41 TO 52 DO
    DeckCards [ J ].Value := 10;          {Correct J, Q, K cards as 10 points}
  CardsLeft := 52                         {Initialize unpicked-card count}
  END;                                    {WITH Deck DO}
GameData.GameCount := 0;                  {Initialize game number}
END;
```

```
{ReturnAllCardsToDeck effectively returns to the deck all cards not in the deck;
 called when too few unpicked cards remain to play a single game}

PROCEDURE ReturnAllCardsToDeck ( VAR Deck : DeckType );

VAR
  K :  Integer;

BEGIN
WITH Deck DO
  BEGIN
  FOR K := 1 TO 52 DO                   {Mark all cards as unpicked}
    DeckCards [ K ].Picked := FALSE;
  CardsLeft := 52                       {Initialize unpicked card count}
  END
END;
```

```
{Deal1Card deals a single card to the hand structure passed in}

PROCEDURE Deal1Card ( VAR Hand : OneHand; VAR Deck : DeckType;
                      VAR Seed : Integer );
VAR
  Index  :  Integer;

BEGIN
WITH Deck DO
  BEGIN
  REPEAT                                  {Deal an unpicked card from the deck}
    Index := Random ( Seed, 52 )          {Obtain a random number, from 1 to 52}
  UNTIL NOT Deck.DeckCards [ Index ].Picked;

  WITH Hand, DeckCards [ Index ] DO
    BEGIN
    Picked      := TRUE;                  {Mark card as having been picked}
    CardsLeft   := CardsLeft - 1;         {Now, one less card in the deck}
    Count       := Count + 1;             { and one more card in the hand}
    Points      := Points + Value;        {Increment hand's total point value}
    Cards [ Count ] := Index;             {Store Deck.DeckCards index in hand array}

    IF Symbol = 'A' THEN                  {IF an ace card is dealt...}
      AceAs11 := TRUE;                    { Ace counts as 11 points; its default value}
    IF ( Points > 21 ) AND AceAs11 THEN   {But IF this raises hand total too high...}
      Points  := Points - 10;             { Count the last ace dealt as only 1 point}
    END
  END
END;
```

```
{AnalyzeGame examines GameState and hand point totals to determine if player or dealer
 has won or lost yet}

PROCEDURE AnalyzeGame ( VAR Player, Dealer : OneHand; VAR Deck : DeckType;
                        VAR GameData : GameInfo );

BEGIN
WITH GameData, Player DO
  BEGIN
  IF GameState = PlayersTurn THEN
    BEGIN
    IF (( Count = 2 ) AND ( Points = 21 )) OR      {IF player has a blackjack}
       (( Count = 5 ) AND ( Points <= 21 )) THEN   {  or a 5-card Charlie...}
      GameState := PlayerWins                      { Player wins}
    ELSE
      IF Points > 21 THEN                          {IF player exceeds 21 points...}
        GameState := PlayerLoses                   { Player loses}
    END

  ELSE    {Dealer's turn; AnalyzeGame called if Dealer's points >= MinDealerPts}
    IF (Dealer.Points > 21) THEN                   {IF dealer exceeds 21 points...}
      GameState := PlayerWins                      { Player wins}
    ELSE
      IF Dealer.Points >= Points THEN              {IF dealer ties player..}
        GameState := PlayerLoses                   { Player loses}
      ELSE                                         {ELSE dealer has fewer points...}
        GameState := PlayerWins                    { Player wins}
  END                                              {WITH GameData, Player DO}
END;
```

```
{UpdateDisplay displays game information}

PROCEDURE UpdateDisplay ( VAR Player, Dealer : OneHand;
                          VAR Deck : DeckType; GameData : GameInfo );
VAR
  K, Start : Integer;

BEGIN
Writeln;
WITH GameData, Player DO
  BEGIN
  IF GameState = PlayersTurn THEN          {Indicate that it is player's turn}
    Write ( '--> ' )
  ELSE
    Write ( '    ' );
  Write ( 'Player (', Points:2, '):  ' );  {Display player's points}

  FOR K := 1 TO Count DO                   {Display player's card characters}
    Write ( Deck.DeckCards [ Cards [ K ] ].Symbol, '   ' );

  Writeln;
  IF GameState = DealersTurn THEN          {Indicate that it is dealer's turn}
    Write ( '--> ' )
  ELSE
    Write ( '    ' );
  Write ( 'Dealer (' );
  IF GameState = PlayersTurn THEN          {IF it is still player's turn...}
    BEGIN
    Write ( '??):  ?   ' );                { Do not display dealer's points}
    Start := 2                             {  or face-down card}
    END
  ELSE                                     {ELSE it is now dealer's turn...}
    BEGIN
    Write ( Dealer. Points:2,'):  ' );     { Display Dealer's points and}
    Start := 1                             {  face-down card in next loop}
    END;

  FOR K := Start TO Dealer.Count DO
    Write ( Deck.DeckCards [ Dealer.Cards [ K ] ].Symbol, '   ' );

  Writeln; Writeln;
  IF GameState = PlayerWins THEN
    Writeln ( Chr ( 7 ), Chr ( 7 ), '***  You  win!  ***' )  {2 beeps sounded}
  ELSE
    IF GameState = PlayerLoses THEN
      Writeln ( Chr ( 7 ), '***  You  lose!  ***' )          {1 beep sounded}
  END                                                         {WITH GameData DO}
END;
```

```
{DealerShouldDrawAgain determines if the dealer should stay or draw another card}

FUNCTION DealerShouldDrawAgain ( VAR Dealer, Player : OneHand;
                                 VAR Deck : DeckType ) : Boolean;

VAR
  PlayersUpCardPts  :  Integer;
  DrawAgain         :  Boolean;

BEGIN
IF Dealer.Points <= MinDealerPoints THEN
  DrawAgain := TRUE                             {Dealer must draw}
ELSE
  WITH Player DO
    BEGIN
    {Only points from player's face-up cards may be considered}
    PlayersUpCardPts := Points - Deck.DeckCards [ Cards [ 1 ] ].Value;

    {Correct the face-up card point total, if necessary}
    IF ( Cards [ 1 ] <= 4 ) AND NOT AceAs11 THEN
      PlayersUpCardPts := PlayersUpCardPts + 10;

    IF Dealer.Points > PlayersUpCardPts THEN
      DrawAgain := FALSE
    END;

DealerShouldDrawAgain := DrawAgain;
Writeln;
IF DrawAgain THEN
  Writeln ( 'I will draw a card!' )
ELSE
  Writeln ( 'I will stay with the cards in my hand!' )
END;
```

```
{PromptPlayer prompts player for another card or another game}

PROCEDURE PromptPlayer ( WhichPrompt : PromptType;
                         VAR GameData : GameInfo );

VAR
  Reply  :  Char;

BEGIN
IF WhichPrompt = AnotherCard THEN
  BEGIN
  Write ( 'Want another card?  (Y/N):  ' );
  Readln ( Reply );
  IF NOT PositiveResponse ( Reply ) THEN
    GameData.GameState := DealersTurn
  END
ELSE
  BEGIN
  Writeln;  Write ( 'Play another game?  (Y/N):  ' );
  Readln ( Reply );
  IF NOT PositiveResponse ( Reply ) THEN
    GameData.GameState := Quit
  END
END;
```

```
{InitialDeal deals the first two cards to player and to dealer}

PROCEDURE InitialDeal ( VAR Player, Dealer : OneHand; VAR Deck : DeckType;
                        VAR GameData : GameInfo; VAR Seed : Integer );

VAR
  K : Integer;

BEGIN
WITH GameData DO
  BEGIN
  GameState  := PlayersTurn;         {Player goes first each game}
  GameCount  := GameCount + 1;       {New game}
  Writeln;  Writeln ( '-----------  Game #', GameCount, '  -----------' );  Writeln;
  END;

WITH Player DO
  BEGIN
  Points  := 0;                      {No points in hand yet}
  Count   := 0;                      {No cards in hand yet}
  AceAs11 := FALSE                   {No aces yet}
  END;

WITH Dealer DO
  BEGIN
  Points  := 0;                      {No points in hand yet}
  Count   := 0;                      {No cards in hand yet}
  AceAs11 := FALSE                   {No aces yet}
  END;

FOR K := 1 TO 2 DO
  BEGIN
  Deal1Card ( Player, Deck, Seed );  {Deal card to player}
  Deal1Card ( Dealer, Deck, Seed )   {Deal card to dealer}
  END
END;
```

```
{InitializeSeed procedure is left as an exercise. It should give Seed its initial
 value, for use by the Random function of Appendix K in picking cards from the deck.
 The Seed value may be obtained from the system clock, if a nonstandard function is
 available for reading the clock time, or unobtrusively from the user.}

PROCEDURE InitializeSeed ( VAR Seed : Integer );
```

```
{***  Main routine for program Blackjack  ***}

BEGIN
InitializeDeck( Deck, GameData );  {Store all card data in the Deck structure}
InitializeSeed ( Seed );           {Initialize Seed, for random numbers later}
WITH GameData DO
  REPEAT
    IF Deck.CardsLeft  <  MinCardsNeeded THEN                {IF too few cards to play..}
      ReturnAllCardsToDeck ( Deck );                         { Mark cards as unvisited}

    InitialDeal ( Player, Dealer, Deck, GameData, Seed );  {Deal 2 cards to each}
    AnalyzeGame ( Player, Dealer, Deck, GameData );        {Player got blackjack?}
    UpdateDisplay ( Player, Dealer, Deck, GameData );      {Display of initial deal}

    WHILE GameState = PlayersTurn DO
      BEGIN
      PromptPlayer ( AnotherCard, GameData );              {Another card for player?}
      IF GameState = PlayersTurn THEN                      {IF Player wants}
        BEGIN                                              { another card ...}
        Deal1Card ( Player, Deck, Seed );                  {Deal player a card}
        AnalyzeGame ( Player, Dealer, Deck, GameData );    {Analyze hand}
        UpdateDisplay ( Player, Dealer, Deck, GameData )   {Display hands}
        END
      END;

    WHILE GameState = DealersTurn DO
      BEGIN
      IF DealerShouldDrawAgain ( Dealer, Player, Deck ) THEN
        Deal1Card ( Dealer, Deck, Seed );
      IF Dealer.Points > MinDealerPoints THEN              {No point in analyzing since}
        AnalyzeGame ( Player, Dealer, Deck, GameData );    { dealer must draw}
      UpdateDisplay ( Player, Dealer, Deck, GameData );
      END;

    PromptPlayer ( ToQuit, GameData )                      {Ask for another game}
  UNTIL GameState = Quit
END.
```

Although the program employs the principles of structure, performance, and functionality described in Chapter 1 and Appendix L, the program's method for selecting unpicked cards is somewhat inefficient. `Deal1Card` calls the `Random` function for the deck array index of a card. If the indicated card has already been picked (i.e., its `Picked` field has a true value), `Deal1Card` must call `Random` again for another index value. The number of repeated calls to `Random` just to find a single, unpicked card increases as more games are played without returning cards to the deck. As an exercise, consider changes you might make to counteract this inefficiency.

STAGES 6 AND 7

COMPILE AND VERIFY THE PROGRAM

Section 1.3 discussed the importance of program stubs, i.e., temporary, abbreviated main routines designed to test individual routines. As an example, the following stub may be used to test the `InitializeDeck` procedure (integer variable `K` must be declared as global):

```
{***  Stub to test procedure Prelude  ***}                              {DEBUG}

BEGIN
Writeln ( 'Stub to test procedure InitializeDeck' );                     {DEBUG}
InitializeDeck ( Deck );                                                  {DEBUG}
WITH Deck DO                                                              {DEBUG}
  BEGIN                                                                   {DEBUG}
  Writeln  ( 'DEBUG:  Contents of Deck after initializing:' );            {DEBUG}
  Writeln ( '       Cards left = ', CardsLeft );  Writeln;                {DEBUG}
  FOR K := 1 TO 52 DO                                                     {DEBUG}
    BEGIN                                                                 {DEBUG}
    Write (  K:2, 'th Symbol = ', Symbol, '   Value = ', Value,           {DEBUG}
             '   Picked? ', Picked );                                     {DEBUG}
    IF K MOD 4 = 0 THEN                                                   {DEBUG}
      Writeln;     {Leave blank line between 4-card groups}               {DEBUG}
    IF K MOD 24 = 0 THEN                                                  {DEBUG}
      Readln;      {Pause after 1 screen's worth of output}               {DEBUG}
    END                                                                   {DEBUG}
  END;                                                                    {DEBUG}
Readln             {Pause after displaying final 4-card group}            {DEBUG}
END.
```

In many cases, particular parameter values must be passed to the routine being tested to determine if that routine works properly in a particular situation. For example, the following stub provides a versatile, interactive test of the `AnalyzeGame` procedure (character variable `Reply` must be declared as global):

```
{***  Stub to test procedure AnalyzeGame  ***}                           {DEBUG}

BEGIN                                                                     {DEBUG}
Writeln ( 'Stub to test procedure AnalyzeGame' );                         {DEBUG}
REPEAT                                                                    {DEBUG}
  Write ( 'Whose turn? (P/D):  ' );                                       {DEBUG}
  Readln ( Reply );                                                       {DEBUG}
  IF Reply IN [ 'P', 'p' ] THEN                                           {DEBUG}
    GameState := PlayersTurn                                              {DEBUG}
  ELSE                                                                    {DEBUG}
    GameState := DealersTurn;                                             {DEBUG}
  Write ( 'Player''s total points, Dealer''s total points:  ' );          {DEBUG}
  Readln ( Player.Points, Dealer.Points );                                {DEBUG}
  Write ( 'Player''s card count, Dealer''s card count:  ' );              {DEBUG}
  Readln ( Player.Count, Dealer.Count );                                  {DEBUG}

  AnalyzeGame ( Player, Dealer, Deck, GameState );                        {DEBUG}

  Write ( '>>> Result from AnalyzeGame:  ' );                             {DEBUG}
  CASE GameStatus OF                                                      {DEBUG}
    PlayersTurn  :  Write ( 'Player''s turn' );                           {DEBUG}
    DealersTurn  :  Write ( 'Dealer''s turn' );                           {DEBUG}
    PlayerWins   :  Write ( 'Player wins!' );                             {DEBUG}
    PlayerLoses  :  Write ( 'Player loses!' )                             {DEBUG}
  END;                                                                    {DEBUG}
  Writeln;  Write ( 'Try another combination?  (Y/N):  ' );               {DEBUG}
  Readln ( Reply )                                                        {DEBUG}
UNTIL Reply IN [ 'N', 'n' ]                                               {DEBUG}
END.                                                                      {DEBUG}
```

In these two stubs, the `{DEBUG}` comment serves as an important reminder that the statement is temporary, for verification/debugging purposes only, and must be removed later. Notice that great care has been taken to label any screen output, including prompts, and the usual elements of style (indentation, alignment, etc.) are employed. *Do not skimp on these practices simply because the code is temporary!* If you do not label values displayed for debugging purposes, you run the risk of misinterpreting those values when they are displayed, thereby wasting valuable time or even making inappropriate program modifications.

Be careful to verify that each routine deals with any special cases correctly; e.g., procedure `Deal1Card` should correctly adjust a hand's point total, if necessary, when an ace is dealt. Once all the routines have been verified individually, larger and larger portions of the main routine may be verified until you begin verifying the program in its entirety. Procedure `UpdateDisplay` should be verified early, since it can be used to display useful information upon return from other routines that you are testing explicitly.

The function call `Random ( Seed, 52 )` returns a *randomly* chosen integer value in the range 1 to 52 and is invoked in procedure `Deal1Card` to select a card from the deck. While verifying the program, it will be necessary to select particular cards from the deck rather than selecting them randomly, for two reasons:

- To verify that the program can manage a hand's particular combination of cards correctly—e.g., if the player is dealt an ace and a face card initially (a blackjack) or if the player's hand contains one ace already and she subsequently draws another ace.

Situation	Expected Result	Actual Result
1. Start of program	Display of program name	
2. Start of a game	It is player's turn	
3. Player dealt a blackjack hand	Player wins; end of game	
4. Player not dealt a blackjack hand	Prompt for another card	
5. Player dealt 2 or more aces	Player total adjusted	
6. Player draws cards, total $>$ 21 points	Player loses; end of game	
7. Player has total of 5 cards, $\leq$ 21 points	Player wins; end of game	
8. Player stays with initial 2 cards ($<$ 21 points)	It becomes dealer's turn	
9. Player stays after drawing card(s) ($\leq$ 21 points)	It becomes dealer's turn	
10. Dealer dealt a blackjack hand	Dealer wins; end of game	
11. Dealer not dealt a blackjack hand	Dealer draws until points $\geq$ 17	
12. Dealer dealt 2 or more aces	Dealer total adjusted	
13. Dealer has 5 cards, $\leq$ 21 points	Not necessarily a win	
14. Dealer total $>$ Player total	Player loses; end of game	
15. Dealer total = Player total	Player loses; end of game	
16. Dealer total $<$ Player total	Player wins; end of game	
17. 17 $\leq$ dealer points $<$ player's face-up cards	Dealer draws again	
18. End of game	Prompt for another game	
19. Too few cards in deck for next game	All card records marked as unpicked	

FIGURE M.4 Verification Checklist for the Blackjack Program

- To reproduce a previous combination of hand cards for reverification or to repeat a particular set of hand values that may be causing incorrect program processing.

Until the verification process is complete, in the `Deal1Card` procedure, card index values should be entered directly from the keyboard:

```
REPEAT

{
  Index := Random ( Seed, 52 )
}

  Write ( 'Enter card index:  ' );                              {DEBUG}
  Readln ( Index )                                              {DEBUG}
UNTIL NOT Deck.DeckCards [ Index ].Picked;
```

A *verification checklist,* such as the one shown in Figure M.4, can be devised and updated appropriately to monitor carefully the verification process of a program. As this process proceeds, additional situations that warrant testing may come to mind. Certainly, each display produced by procedure `UpdateDisplay` should be examined carefully to verify correct hand totals and card symbols as well as to verify that the program never deals the same card twice before all cards are returned to the deck.

Index